UNIVERSITY
OF LONDON

C000165474

This statute book is permitted material in the examination room for

Civil and criminal procedure [LA3004]

Annotations in statutes and other permitted materials

You may only <u>underline</u> and/or <mark>highlight</mark> passages with a coloured pen in this statute book and any other permitted materials. You may highlight different passages with different coloured pens. All other forms of personal annotation on statutes and other materials permitted to be taken into the examination room are strictly forbidden. You are forbidden to attach self-adhesive notelets or index tags or any other paper to the pages of statute books or other permitted materials.

The content of this statute book was correct at time of publication in June 2019. It does not take into account any developments in the law since the publication date, including any changes related to Brexit.

The *Macmillan Core Statutes* series

CORE STATUTES ON
CRIMINAL JUSTICE & SENTENCING
2019–20

Martin Wasik

macmillan
international
HIGHER EDUCATION

RED GLOBE
PRESS

This edition published 2019 by
RED GLOBE PRESS

Previous editions published under the imprint PALGRAVE

Red Globe Press in the UK is an imprint of Springer Nature Limited, registered in England, company number 785998, of 4 Crinan Street, London, N1 9XW.

Red Globe Press® is a registered trademark in the United States, the United Kingdom, Europe and other countries.

ISBN 978-1-352-00705-3

This book is printed on paper suitable for recycling and made from fully managed and sustained forest sources. Logging, pulping and manufacturing processes are expected to conform to the environmental regulations of the country of origin.

A catalogue record for this book is available from the British Library.

A catalog record for this book is available from the Library of Congress.

CONTENTS

Contents

ALPHABETICAL LIST OF CONTENTS

PREFACE

This volume provides coverage of the core statutory provisions in criminal justice and sentencing. Provisions relating to substantive criminal law and the rules of evidence have been excluded. In order to keep the collection compact, I have had to be selective in choosing, so far as possible, those matters which are most frequently covered in higher education courses in this area of study.

Statutory provisions in criminal justice undergo continual change, usually by inserting new sections into earlier statutes. There have been hundreds of amendments to the core statutes set out in this book since the first edition published in 2013. The book takes account of the most important amendments made by the Crime and Courts Act 2013, the Offender Rehabilitation Act 2014, the Anti-Social Behaviour, Crime and Policing Act 2014, the Criminal Justice and Courts Act 2015, the Serious Crime Act 2015, the Modern Slavery Act 2015, the Counter-Terrorism and Security Act 2015, the Immigration Act 2017, the Criminal Finances Act 2017, the Policing and Crime Act 2017, the Courts and Tribunals (Judiciary and Functions of Staff) Act 2018, the Assaults on Emergency Workers (Offences) Act 2018 and the Counter-Terrorism and Border Security Act 2019. In addition the Criminal Procedure Rules and the Codes of Practice to the Police and Criminal Evidence Act 1984 have been updated to include the 2018 amendments.

The book is up to date to June 2019.

Professor Martin Wasik
Keele University
June 2019

ANTI-SOCIAL BEHAVIOUR, CRIME AND POLICING ACT 2014

(2014, c. 12)

1. Power to grant injunctions

(1) A court may grant an injunction under this section against a person aged 10 or over ('the respondent') if two conditions are met.

(2) The first condition is that the court is satisfied, on the balance of probabilities, that the respondent has engaged or threatens to engage in anti-social behaviour.

(3) The second condition is that the court considers it just and convenient to grant the injunction for the purpose of preventing the respondent from engaging in anti-social behaviour.

(4) An injunction under this section may for the purpose of preventing the respondent from engaging in anti-social behaviour—

    (a) prohibit the respondent from doing anything described in the injunction;

    (b) require the respondent to do anything described in the injunction.

(5) Prohibitions and requirements in an injunction under this section must, so far as practicable, be such as to avoid—

    (a) any interference with the times, if any, at which the respondent normally works or attends school or any other educational establishment;

    (b) any conflict with the requirements of any other court order or injunction to which the respondent may be subject.

(6) An injunction under this section must—

    (a) specify the period for which it has effect, or

    (b) state that it has effect until further order.

In the case of an injunction granted before the respondent has reached the age of 18, a period must be specified and it must be no more than 12 months.

(7) An injunction under this section may specify periods for which particular prohibitions or requirements have effect.

(8) An application for an injunction under this section must be made to—

    (a) a youth court, in the case of a respondent aged under 18;

    (b) the High Court or the county court, in any other case.

Paragraph (b) is subject to any rules of court made under section 18(2).

2. Meaning of 'anti-social behaviour'

(1) In this Part 'anti-social behaviour' means—

    (a) conduct that has caused, or is likely to cause, harassment, alarm or distress to any person,

    (b) conduct capable of causing nuisance or annoyance to a person in relation to that person's occupation of residential premises, or

    (c) conduct capable of causing housing-related nuisance or annoyance to any person.

(2) Subsection (1)(b) applies only where the injunction under section 1 is applied for by—

    (a) a housing provider,

    (b) a local authority, or

    (c) a chief officer of police.

(3) In subsection (1)(c) 'housing-related' means directly or indirectly relating to the housing management functions of—

    (a) a housing provider, or

    (b) a local authority.

(4) For the purposes of subsection (3) the housing management functions of a housing provider or a local authority include—

    (a) functions conferred by or under an enactment;

    (b) the powers and duties of the housing provider or local authority as the holder of an estate or interest in housing accommodation.

22. Power to make orders

(1) This section applies where a person ('the offender') is convicted of an offence.

(2) The court may make a criminal behaviour order against the offender if two conditions are met.

(3) The first condition is that the court is satisfied, beyond reasonable doubt, that the offender has engaged in behaviour that caused or was likely to cause harassment, alarm or distress to any person.

(4) The second condition is that the court considers that making the order will help in preventing the offender from engaging in such behaviour.

(5) A criminal behaviour order is an order which, for the purpose of preventing the offender from engaging in such behaviour—

    (a) prohibits the offender from doing anything described in the order;

    (b) requires the offender to do anything described in the order.

(6) The court may make a criminal behaviour order against the offender only if it is made in addition to—

    (a) a sentence imposed in respect of the offence, or

    (b) an order discharging the offender conditionally.

(7) The court may make a criminal behaviour order against the offender only on the application of the prosecution.

(8) The prosecution must find out the views of the local youth offending team before applying for a criminal behaviour order to be made if the offender will be under the age of 18 when the application is made.

(9) Prohibitions and requirements in a criminal behaviour order must, so far as practicable, be such as to avoid—

    (a) any interference with the times, if any, at which the offender normally works or attends school or any other educational establishment;

    (b) any conflict with the requirements of any other court order or injunction to which the offender may be subject.

(10) In this section 'local youth offending team' means—

    (a) the youth offending team in whose area it appears to the prosecution that the offender lives, or

    (b) if it appears to the prosecution that the offender lives in more than one such area, whichever one or more of the relevant youth offending teams the prosecution thinks appropriate.

23. Proceedings on an application for an order

(1) For the purpose of deciding whether to make a criminal behaviour order the court may consider evidence led by the prosecution and evidence led by the offender.

(2) It does not matter whether the evidence would have been admissible in the proceedings in which the offender was convicted.

(3) The court may adjourn any proceedings on an application for a criminal behaviour order even after sentencing the offender.

(4) If the offender does not appear for any adjourned proceedings the court may—

    (a) further adjourn the proceedings,

    (b) issue a warrant for the offender's arrest, or

    (c) hear the proceedings in the offender's absence.

(5) The court may not act under paragraph (b) of subsection (4) unless it is satisfied that the offender has had adequate notice of the time and place of the adjourned proceedings.

(6) The court may not act under paragraph (c) of subsection (4) unless it is satisfied that the offender—

    (a) has had adequate notice of the time and place of the adjourned proceedings, and

    (b) has been informed that if the offender does not appear for those proceedings the court may hear the proceedings in his or her absence.

(7) Subsection (8) applies in relation to proceedings in which a criminal behaviour order is made against an offender who is under the age of 18.

(8) In so far as the proceedings relate to the making of the order—

    (a) section 49 of the Children and Young Persons Act 1933 (restrictions on reports of proceedings in which children and young persons are concerned) does not apply in respect of the offender;

    (b) section 39 of that Act (power to prohibit publication of certain matters) does so apply.

24.   Requirements included in orders

(1)   A criminal behaviour order that includes a requirement must specify the person who is to be responsible for supervising compliance with the requirement.

The person may be an individual or an organisation.

(2)   Before including a requirement, the court must receive evidence about its suitability and enforceability from—

   (a)   the individual to be specified under subsection (1), if an individual is to be specified;

   (b)   an individual representing the organisation to be specified under subsection (1), if an organisation is to be specified.

(3)   Before including two or more requirements, the court must consider their compatibility with each other.

(4)   It is the duty of a person specified under subsection (1)—

   (a)   to make any necessary arrangements in connection with the requirements for which the person has responsibility (the 'relevant requirements');

   (b)   to promote the offender's compliance with the relevant requirements;

   (c)   if the person considers that the offender—

      (i)   has complied with all the relevant requirements, or

      (ii)   has failed to comply with a relevant requirement,

      to inform the prosecution and the appropriate chief officer of police.

(5)   In subsection (4)(c) 'the appropriate chief officer of police' means—

   (a)   the chief officer of police for the police area in which it appears to the person specified under subsection (1) that the offender lives, or

   (b)   if it appears to that person that the offender lives in more than one police area, whichever of the relevant chief officers of police that person thinks it most appropriate to inform.

(6)   An offender subject to a requirement in a criminal behaviour order must—

   (a)   keep in touch with the person specified under subsection (1) in relation to that requirement, in accordance with any instructions given by that person from time to time;

   (b)   notify the person of any change of address.

These obligations have effect as requirements of the order.

25.   Duration of order etc

(1)   A criminal behaviour order takes effect on the day it is made, subject to subsection (2).

(2)   If on the day a criminal behaviour order ('the new order') is made the offender is subject to another criminal behaviour order ('the previous order'), the new order may be made so as to take effect on the day on which the previous order ceases to have effect.

(3)   A criminal behaviour order must specify the period ('the order period') for which it has effect.

(4)   In the case of a criminal behaviour order made before the offender has reached the age of 18, the order period must be a fixed period of—

   (a)   not less than 1 year, and

   (b)   not more than 3 years.

(5)   In the case of a criminal behaviour order made after the offender has reached the age of 18, the order period must be—

   (a)   a fixed period of not less than 2 years, or

   (b)   an indefinite period (so that the order has effect until further order).

(6)   A criminal behaviour order may specify periods for which particular prohibitions or requirements have effect.

26.   Interim orders

(1)   This section applies where a court adjourns the hearing of an application for a criminal behaviour order.

(2)   The court may make a criminal behaviour order that lasts until the final hearing of the application or until further order ('an interim order') if the court thinks it just to do so.

(3)   Section 22(6) to (8) and section 25(3) to (5) do not apply in relation to the making of an interim order.

(4)   Subject to that, the court has the same powers whether or not the criminal behaviour order is an interim order.

27.   Variation or discharge of orders

(1)   A criminal behaviour order may be varied or discharged by the court which made it on the application of—
       (a)   the offender, or
       (b)   the prosecution.

(2)   If an application by the offender under this section is dismissed, the offender may make no further application under this section without—
       (a)   the consent of the court which made the order, or
       (b)   the agreement of the prosecution.

(3)   If an application by the prosecution under this section is dismissed, the prosecution may make no further application under this section without—
       (a)   the consent of the court which made the order, or
       (b)   the agreement of the offender.

(4)   The power to vary an order includes power to include an additional prohibition or requirement in the order or to extend the period for which a prohibition or requirement has effect.

(5)   Section 24 applies to additional requirements included under subsection (4) as it applies to requirements included in a new order.

(6)   In the case of a criminal behaviour order made by a magistrates' court, the references in this section to the court which made the order include a reference to any magistrates' court acting in the same local justice area as that court.

28.   Review of orders

(1)   If—
       (a)   a person subject to a criminal behaviour order will be under the age of 18 at the end of a review period (see subsection (2)),
       (b)   the term of the order runs until the end of that period or beyond, and
       (c)   the order is not discharged before the end of that period,
       a review of the operation of the order must be carried out before the end of that period.

(2)   The 'review periods' are—
       (a)   the period of 12 months beginning with—
              (i)   the day on which the criminal behaviour order takes effect, or
              (ii)   if during that period the order is varied under section 27, the day on which it is varied (or most recently varied, if the order is varied more than once);
       (b)   a period of 12 months beginning with—
              (i)   the day after the end of the previous review period, or
              (ii)   if during that period of 12 months the order is varied under section 27, the day on which it is varied (or most recently varied, if the order is varied more than once).

(3)   A review under this section must include consideration of—
       (a)   the extent to which the offender has complied with the order;
       (b)   the adequacy of any support available to the offender to help him or her comply with it;
       (c)   any matters relevant to the question whether an application should be made for the order to be varied or discharged.

(4)   Those carrying out or participating in a review under this section must have regard to any relevant guidance issued by the Secretary of State under section 32 when considering—
       (a)   how the review should be carried out;
       (b)   what particular matters the review should deal with;
       (c)   what action (if any) it would be appropriate to take as a result of the findings of the review.

29.   Carrying out and participating in reviews

(1) A review under section 28 is to be carried out by the chief officer of police of the police force maintained for the police area in which the offender lives or appears to be living.

(2) The chief officer, in carrying out a review under section 28, must act in co-operation with the council for the local government area in which the offender lives or appears to be living; and the council must co-operate in the carrying out of the review.

(3) The chief officer may invite the participation in the review of any other person or body.

(4) In this section 'local government area' means—

    (a) in relation to England, a district or London borough, the City of London, the Isle of Wight and the Isles of Scilly;

    (b) in relation to Wales, a county or a county borough.

For the purposes of this section, the council for the Inner and Middle Temples is the Common Council of the City of London.

30.   Breach of order

(1) A person who without reasonable excuse—

    (a) does anything he or she is prohibited from doing by a criminal behaviour order, or

    (b) fails to do anything he or she is required to do by a criminal behaviour order, commits an offence.

(2) A person guilty of an offence under this section is liable—

    (a) on summary conviction, to imprisonment for a period not exceeding 6 months or to a fine, or to both;

    (b) on conviction on indictment, to imprisonment for a period not exceeding 5 years or to a fine, or to both.

(3) If a person is convicted of an offence under this section, it is not open to the court by or before which the person is convicted to make an order under subsection (1)(b) of section 12 of the Powers of Criminal Courts (Sentencing) Act 2000 (conditional discharge).

(4) In proceedings for an offence under this section, a copy of the original criminal behaviour order, certified by the proper officer of the court which made it, is admissible as evidence of its having been made and of its contents to the same extent that oral evidence of those things is admissible in those proceedings.

(5) In relation to any proceedings for an offence under this section that are brought against a person under the age of 18—

    (a) section 49 of the Children and Young Persons Act 1933 (restrictions on reports of proceedings in which children and young persons are concerned) does not apply in respect of the person;

    (b) section 45 of the Youth Justice and Criminal Evidence Act 1999 (power to restrict reporting of criminal proceedings involving persons under 18) does so apply.

(6) If, in relation to any proceedings mentioned in subsection (5), the court does exercise its power to give a direction under section 45 of the Youth Justice and Criminal Evidence Act 1999, it must give its reasons for doing so.

34.   Authorisations to use powers under section 35

(1) A police officer of at least the rank of inspector may authorise the use in a specified locality, during a specified period of not more than 48 hours, of the powers given by section 35.

'Specified' means specified in the authorisation.

(2) An officer may give such an authorisation only if satisfied on reasonable grounds that the use of those powers in the locality during that period may be necessary for the purpose of removing or reducing the likelihood of—

    (a) members of the public in the locality being harassed, alarmed or distressed, or

    (b) the occurrence in the locality of crime or disorder.

(3) In deciding whether to give such an authorisation an officer must have particular regard to the rights of freedom of expression and freedom of assembly set out in articles 10 and 11 of the Convention.

'Convention' has the meaning given by section 21(1) of the Human Rights Act 1998.

(4) An authorisation under this section—
    (a) must be in writing,
    (b) must be signed by the officer giving it, and
    (c) must specify the grounds on which it is given.

35. Directions excluding a person from an area

(1) If the conditions in subsections (2) and (3) are met and an authorisation is in force under section 34, a constable in uniform may direct a person who is in a public place in the locality specified in the authorisation—
    (a) to leave the locality (or part of the locality), and
    (b) not to return to the locality (or part of the locality) for the period specified in the direction ('the exclusion period').

(2) The first condition is that the constable has reasonable grounds to suspect that the behaviour of the person in the locality has contributed or is likely to contribute to—
    (a) members of the public in the locality being harassed, alarmed or distressed, or
    (b) the occurrence in the locality of crime or disorder.

(3) The second condition is that the constable considers that giving a direction to the person is necessary for the purpose of removing or reducing the likelihood of the events mentioned in subsection (2)(a) or (b).

(4) The exclusion period may not exceed 48 hours.
The period may expire after (as long as it begins during) the period specified in the authorisation under section 34.

(5) A direction under this section—
    (a) must be given in writing, unless that is not reasonably practicable;
    (b) must specify the area to which it relates;
    (c) may impose requirements as to the time by which the person must leave the area and the manner in which the person must do so (including the route).

(6) The constable must (unless it is not reasonably practicable) tell the person to whom the direction is given that failing without reasonable excuse to comply with the direction is an offence.

(7) If the constable reasonably believes that the person to whom the direction is given is under the age of 16, the constable may remove the person to a place where the person lives or a place of safety.

(8) Any constable may withdraw or vary a direction under this section; but a variation must not extend the duration of a direction beyond 48 hours from when it was first given.

(9) Notice of a withdrawal or variation of a direction—
    (a) must be given to the person to whom the direction was given, unless that is not reasonably practicable, and
    (b) if given, must be given in writing unless that is not reasonably practicable.

(10) In this section 'public place' means a place to which at the material time the public or a section of the public has access, on payment or otherwise, as of right or by virtue of express or implied permission.

(11) In this Part 'exclusion period' has the meaning given by subsection (1)(b).

ANTI-TERRORISM, CRIME AND SECURITY ACT 2001
(2001, c. 24)

47. Use etc of nuclear weapons

(1) A person who—
    (a) knowingly causes a nuclear weapon explosion;
    (b) develops or produces, or participates in the development or production of, a nuclear weapon;
    (c) has a nuclear weapon in his possession;
    (d) participates in the transfer of a nuclear weapon; or
    (e) engages in military preparations, or in preparations of a military nature, intending to use, or threaten to use, a nuclear weapon,
is guilty of an offence.

(2) Subsection (1) has effect subject to the exceptions and defences in sections 48 and 49.

(3) For the purposes of subsection (1)(b) a person participates in the development or production of a nuclear weapon if he does any act which—

    (a) facilitates the development by another of the capability to produce or use a nuclear weapon, or

    (b) facilitates the making by another of a nuclear weapon,

knowing or having reason to believe that his act has (or will have) that effect.

(4) For the purposes of subsection (1)(d) a person participates in the transfer of a nuclear weapon if—

    (a) he buys or otherwise acquires it or agrees with another to do so;

    (b) he sells or otherwise disposes of it or agrees with another to do so; or

    (c) he makes arrangements under which another person either acquires or disposes of it or agrees with a third person to do so.

(5) A person guilty of an offence under this section is liable on conviction on indictment to imprisonment for life.

(6) In this section 'nuclear weapon' includes a nuclear explosive device that is not intended for use as a weapon.

(7) This section applies to acts done outside the United Kingdom, but only if they are done by a United Kingdom person.

(8) Nothing in subsection (7) affects any criminal liability arising otherwise than under that subsection.

(9) Paragraph (a) of subsection (1) shall cease to have effect on the coming into force of the Nuclear Explosions (Prohibition and Inspections) Act 1998.

48. Exceptions

(1) Nothing in section 47 applies—

    (a) to an act which is authorised under subsection (2); or

    (b) to an act done in the course of an armed conflict.

(2) The Secretary of State may—

    (a) authorise any act which would otherwise contravene section 47 in such manner and on such terms as he thinks fit; and

    (b) withdraw or vary any authorisation given under this subsection.

(3) Any question arising in proceedings for an offence under section 47 as to whether anything was done in the course of an armed conflict shall be determined by the Secretary of State.

(4) A certificate purporting to set out any such determination and to be signed by the Secretary of State shall be received in evidence in any such proceedings and shall be presumed to be so signed unless the contrary is shown.

49. Defences

(1) In proceedings for an offence under section 47(1)(c) or (d) relating to an object it is a defence for the accused to show that he did not know and had no reason to believe that the object was a nuclear weapon.

(2) But he shall be taken to have shown that fact if—

    (a) sufficient evidence is adduced to raise an issue with respect to it; and

    (b) the contrary is not proved by the prosecution beyond reasonable doubt.

(3) In proceedings for such an offence it is also a defence for the accused to show that he knew or believed that the object was a nuclear weapon but, as soon as reasonably practicable after he first knew or believed that fact, he took all reasonable steps to inform the Secretary of State or a constable of his knowledge or belief.

50. Assisting or inducing certain weapons-related acts overseas

(1) A person who aids, abets, counsels or procures, or incites, a person who is not a United Kingdom person to do a relevant act outside the United Kingdom is guilty of an offence.

(2) For this purpose a relevant act is an act that, if done by a United Kingdom person, would contravene any of the following provisions—

    (a)   section 1 of the Biological Weapons Act 1974 (offences relating to biological agents and toxins);

    (b)   section 2 of the Chemical Weapons Act 1996 (offences relating to chemical weapons); or

    (c)   section 47 above (offences relating to nuclear weapons).

(3)   Nothing in this section applies to an act mentioned in subsection (1) which—

    (a)   relates to a relevant act which would contravene section 47; and

    (b)   is authorised by the Secretary of State;

     and section 48(2) applies for the purpose of authorising acts that would otherwise constitute an offence under this section.

(4)   A person accused of an offence under this section in relation to a relevant act which would contravene a provision mentioned in subsection (2) may raise any defence which would be open to a person accused of the corresponding offence ancillary to an offence under that provision.

(5)   A person convicted of an offence under this section is liable on conviction on indictment to imprisonment for life.

(6)   This section applies to acts done outside the United Kingdom, but only if they are done by a United Kingdom person.

(7)   Nothing in this section prejudices any criminal liability existing apart from this section.

51.   Extraterritorial application

(1)   Proceedings for an offence committed under section 47 or 50 outside the United Kingdom may be taken, and the offence may for incidental purposes be treated as having been committed, in any part of the United Kingdom.

(2)   Her Majesty may by Order in Council extend the application of section 47 or 50, so far as it applies to acts done outside the United Kingdom, to bodies incorporated under the law of any of the Channel Islands, the Isle of Man or any colony.

52.   Powers of entry

(1)   If—

    (a)   a justice of the peace is satisfied on information on oath that there are reasonable grounds for suspecting that evidence of the commission of an offence under section 47 or 50 is to be found on any premises; or

    (b)   in Scotland the sheriff is satisfied by evidence on oath as mentioned in paragraph (a),

     he may issue a warrant authorising an authorised officer to enter the premises, if necessary by force, at any time within one month from the time of the issue of the warrant and to search them.

(2)   The powers of a person who enters the premises under the authority of the warrant include power—

    (a)   to take with him such other persons and such equipment as appear to him to be necessary;

    (b)   to inspect, seize and retain any substance, equipment or document found on the premises;

    (c)   to require any document or other information which is held in electronic form and is accessible from the premises to be produced in a form—

        (i)   in which he can read and copy it; or

        (ii)   from which it can readily be produced in a form in which he can read and copy it;

    (d)   to copy any document which he has reasonable cause to believe may be required as evidence for the purposes of proceedings in respect of an offence under section 47 or 50.

(3)   A constable who enters premises under the authority of a warrant or by virtue of subsection (2)(a) may—

    (a)   give such assistance as an authorised officer may request for the purpose of facilitating the exercise of any power under this section; and

     (b)   search or cause to be searched any person on the premises who the constable has reasonable cause to believe may have in his possession any document or other thing which may be required as evidence for the purposes of proceedings in respect of an offence under section 47 or 50.

(4) No constable shall search a person of the opposite sex.

(5) The powers conferred by a warrant under this section shall only be exercisable, if the warrant so provides, in the presence of a constable.

(6) A person who—
     (a)   wilfully obstructs an authorised officer in the exercise of a power conferred by a warrant under this section; or
     (b)   fails without reasonable excuse to comply with a reasonable request made by an authorised officer or a constable for the purpose of facilitating the exercise of such a power,
is guilty of an offence.

(7) A person guilty of an offence under subsection (6) is liable—
     (a)   on summary conviction, to a fine not exceeding the statutory maximum; and
     (b)   on conviction on indictment, to imprisonment for a term not exceeding two years or a fine (or both).

(8) In this section 'authorised officer' means an authorised officer of the Secretary of State.

113. Use of noxious substances or things to cause harm and intimidate

(1) A person who takes any action which—
     (a)   involves the use of a noxious substance or other noxious thing;
     (b)   has or is likely to have an effect falling within subsection (2); and
     (c)   is designed to influence the government or an international governmental organisation or to intimidate the public or a section of the public,
is guilty of an offence.

(2) Action has an effect falling within this subsection if it—
     (a)   causes serious violence against a person anywhere in the world;
     (b)   causes serious damage to real or personal property anywhere in the world;
     (c)   endangers human life or creates a serious risk to the health or safety of the public or a section of the public; or
     (d)   induces in members of the public the fear that the action is likely to endanger their lives or create a serious risk to their health or safety;
but any effect on the person taking the action is to be disregarded.

(3) A person who—
     (a)   makes a threat that he or another will take any action which constitutes an offence under subsection (1); and
     (b)   intends thereby to induce in a person anywhere in the world the fear that the threat is likely to be carried out,
is guilty of an offence.

(4) A person guilty of an offence under this section is liable—
     (a)   on summary conviction, to imprisonment for a term not exceeding six months or a fine not exceeding the statutory maximum (or both); and
     (b)   on conviction on indictment, to imprisonment for a term not exceeding fourteen years or a fine (or both).

(5) In this section—
'the government' means the government of the United Kingdom, of a part of the United Kingdom or of a country other than the United Kingdom; and
'the public' includes the public of a country other than the United Kingdom.

113A. Application of section 113

(1) Section 113 applies to conduct done—
     (a)   in the United Kingdom; or
     (b)   outside the United Kingdom which satisfies the following two conditions.

(2) The first condition is that the conduct is done for the purpose of advancing a political, religious, racial or ideological cause.

(3) The second condition is that the conduct is—
    (a) by a United Kingdom national or a United Kingdom resident;
    (b) by any person done to, or in relation to, a United Kingdom national, a United Kingdom resident or a protected person; or
    (c) by any person done in circumstances which fall within section 63D(1)(b) and (c) or (3)(b) and (c) of the Terrorism Act 2000.

(4) The following expressions have the same meaning as they have for the purposes of sections 63C and 63D of that Act—
    (a) 'United Kingdom national';
    (b) 'United Kingdom resident';
    (c) 'protected person'.

(5) For the purposes of this section it is immaterial whether a person knows that another is a United Kingdom national, a United Kingdom resident or a protected person.

113B. Consent to prosecution for offence under section 113

(1) Proceedings for an offence committed under section 113 outside the United Kingdom are not to be started—
    (a) in England and Wales, except by or with the consent of the Attorney General;
    (b) in Northern Ireland, except by or with the consent of the Advocate General for Northern Ireland.

(2) Proceedings for an offence committed under section 113 outside the United Kingdom may be taken, and the offence may for incidental purposes be treated as having been committed, in any part of the United Kingdom.

(3) In relation to any time before the coming into force of section 27(1) of the Justice (Northern Ireland) Act 2002, the reference in subsection (1)(b) to the Advocate General for Northern Ireland is to be read as a reference to the Attorney General for Northern Ireland.

114. Hoaxes involving noxious substances or things

(1) A person is guilty of an offence if he—
    (a) places any substance or other thing in any place; or
    (b) sends any substance or other thing from one place to another (by post, rail or any other means whatever);
with the intention of inducing in a person anywhere in the world a belief that it is likely to be (or contain) a noxious substance or other noxious thing and thereby endanger human life or create a serious risk to human health.

(2) A person is guilty of an offence if he communicates any information which he knows or believes to be false with the intention of inducing in a person anywhere in the world a belief that a noxious substance or other noxious thing is likely to be present (whether at the time the information is communicated or later) in any place and thereby endanger human life or create a serious risk to human health.

(3) A person guilty of an offence under this section is liable—
    (a) on summary conviction, to imprisonment for a term not exceeding six months or a fine not exceeding the statutory maximum (or both); and
    (b) on conviction on indictment, to imprisonment for a term not exceeding seven years or a fine (or both).

115. Sections 113 and 114: supplementary

(1) For the purposes of sections 113 and 114 'substance' includes any biological agent and any other natural or artificial substance (whatever its form, origin or method of production).

(2) For a person to be guilty of an offence under section 113(3) or 114 it is not necessary for him to have any particular person in mind as the person in whom he intends to induce the belief in question.

ASSAULTS ON EMERGENCY WORKERS (OFFENCES) ACT 2018

(2018, c. 23)

1. Common assault and battery

(1) The section applies to an offence of common assault, or battery, that is committed against an emergency worker acting in the exercise of functions as such a worker.

(2) A person guilty of an offence to which this section applies is liable—

    (a) on summary conviction, to imprisonment for a term not exceeding 12 months, or to a fine, or to both;

    (b) on conviction on indictment, to imprisonment for a term not exceeding 12 months, or to a fine, or to both.

(3) For the purposes of subsection (1), the circumstances in which an offence is to be taken as committed against a person acting in the exercise of functions as an emergency worker include circumstances where the offence takes place at a time when the person is not at work but is carrying out functions which, if done in work time, would have been in the exercise of functions as an emergency worker.

(4) In relation to an offence committed before the coming into force of section 154(1) of the Criminal Justice Act 2003 (increase in maximum term that may be imposed on summary conviction of offence triable either way), the reference in subsection (2)(a) to 12 months is to be read as a reference to 6 months.

(5) In consequence of subsections (1) to (3), in section 39 of the Criminal Justice Act 1988 (which provides for common assault and battery to be summary offences punishable with imprisonment for a term not exceeding 6 months)—

    (a) the existing text becomes subsection (1);

    (b) after that subsection insert—

'(2) Subsection (1) is subject to section 1 of the Assaults on Emergency Workers (Offences) Act 2018 (which makes provision for increased sentencing powers for offences of common assault and battery committed against an emergency worker acting in the exercise of functions as such a worker).'

(6) This section applies only in relation to offences committed on or after the day it comes into force.

2. Aggravating factor

(1) This section applies where—

    (a) the court is considering for the purposes of sentencing the seriousness of an offence listed in subsection (3), and

    (b) the offence was committed against an emergency worker acting in the exercise of functions as such a worker.

(2) The court—

    (a) must treat the fact mentioned in subsection (1)(b) as an aggravating factor (that is to say, a factor that increases the seriousness of the offence), and

    (b) must state in open court that the offence is so aggravated.

(3) The offences referred to in subsection (1)(a) are—

    (a) an offence under any of the following provisions of the Offences against the Person Act 1861—

        (i) section 16 (threats to kill);

        (ii) section 18 (wounding with intent to cause grievous bodily harm);

        (iii) section 20 (malicious wounding);

        (iv) section 23 (administering poison etc);

        (v) section 28 (causing bodily injury by gunpowder etc);

        (vi) section 29 (using explosive substances etc with intent to cause grievous bodily harm);

        (vii) section 47 (assault occasioning actual bodily harm);

    (b) an offence under section 3 of the Sexual Offences Act 2003 (sexual assault);

    (c) manslaughter;

    (d) kidnapping;

    (e) an ancillary offence in relation to any of the preceding offences.

(4)   For the purposes of subsection (1)(b), the circumstances in which an offence is to be taken as committed against a person acting in the exercise of functions as an emergency worker include circumstances where the offence takes place at a time when the person is not at work but is carrying out functions which, if done in work time, would have been in the exercise of functions as an emergency worker.

(5)   In this section—

'ancillary offence', in relation to an offence, means any of the following—

(a)   aiding, abetting, counselling or procuring the commission of the offence;

(b)   an offence under Part 2 of the Serious Crime Act 2007 (encouraging or assisting crime) in relation to the offence;

(c)   attempting or conspiring to commit the offence;

'emergency worker' has the meaning given by section 3.

(6)   Nothing in this section prevents a court from treating the fact mentioned in subsection (1)(b) as an aggravating factor in relation to offences not listed in subsection (3).

(7)   This section applies only in relation to offences committed on or after the day it comes into force.

3.   Meaning of 'emergency worker'

(1)   In sections 1 and 2, 'emergency worker' means—

(a)   a constable;

(b)   a person (other than a constable) who has the powers of a constable or is otherwise employed for police purposes or is engaged to provide services for police purposes;

(c)   a National Crime Agency officer;

(d)   a prison officer;

(e)   a person (other than a prison officer) employed or engaged to carry out functions in a custodial institution of a corresponding kind to those carried out by a prison officer;

(f)   a prisoner custody officer, so far as relating to the exercise of escort functions;

(g)   a custody officer, so far as relating to the exercise of escort functions;

(h)   a person employed for the purposes of providing, or engaged to provide, fire services or fire and rescue services;

(i)   a person employed for the purposes of providing, or engaged to provide, search services or rescue services (or both);

(j)   a person employed for the purposes of providing, or engaged to provide—

(i)   NHS health services, or

(ii)   services in the support of the provision of NHS health services,

and whose general activities in doing so involve face to face interaction with individuals receiving the services or with other members of the public.

(2)   It is immaterial for the purposes of subsection (1) whether the employment or engagement is paid or unpaid.

(3)   In this section—

'custodial institution' means any of the following—

(a)   a prison;

(b)   a young offender institution, secure training centre, secure college or remand centre;

(c)   a removal centre, a short-term holding facility or pre-departure accommodation, as defined by section 147 of the Immigration and Asylum Act 1999;

(d)   services custody premises, as defined by section 300(7) of the Armed Forces Act 2006;

'custody officer' has the meaning given by section 12(3) of the Criminal Justice and Public Order Act 1994;

'escort functions'—

(a)   in the case of a prisoner custody officer, means the functions specified in section 80(1) of the Criminal Justice Act 1991;

(b)   in the case of a custody officer, means the functions specified in paragraph 1 of Schedule 1 to the Criminal Justice and Public Order Act 1994;

'NHS health services' means any kind of health services provided as part of the health service continued under section 1(1) of the National Health Service Act 2006 and under section 1(1) of the National Health Service (Wales) Act 2006;

'prisoner custody officer' has the meaning given by section 89(1) of the Criminal Justice Act 1991.

BAIL ACT 1976
(1976, c. 63)

3.   General provisions

(1)   A person granted bail in criminal proceedings shall be under a duty to surrender to custody, and that duty is enforceable in accordance with section 6 of this Act.

(2)   No recognizance for his surrender to custody shall be taken from him.

(3)   Except as provided by this section—

     (a)   no security for his surrender to custody shall be taken from him,

     (b)   he shall not be required to provide a surety or sureties for his surrender to custody, and

     (c)   no other requirement shall be imposed on him as a condition of bail.

(4)   He may be required, before release on bail, to provide a surety or sureties to secure his surrender to custody.

(5)   He may be required, before release on bail, to give security for his surrender to custody. The security may be given by him or on his behalf.

(6)   He may be required to comply, before release on bail or later, with such requirements as appear to the court to be necessary—

     (a)   to secure that he surrenders to custody,

     (b)   to secure that he does not commit an offence while on bail,

     (c)   to secure that he does not interfere with witnesses or otherwise obstruct the course of justice whether in relation to himself or any other person,

     (ca)   for his own protection or, if he is a child or young person, for his own welfare or in his own interests,

     (d)   to secure that he makes himself available for the purpose of enabling inquiries or a report to be made to assist the court in dealing with him for the offence.

     (e)   to secure that before the time appointed for him to surrender to custody, he attends an interview with a person who, for the purposes of the Legal Services Act 2007, is an authorised person in relation to an activity which constitutes the exercise of a right of audience or the conduct of litigation (within the meaning of that Act).

   and, in any Act, 'the normal powers to impose conditions of bail' means the powers to impose conditions under paragraph (a), (b), (c) or (ca) above.

(6ZAA) The requirements which may be imposed under subsection (6) include electronic monitoring requirements.

(6ZAB)–(7) ...

(8)   Where a court has granted bail in criminal proceedings that court or, where the court has sent a person on bail to the Crown Court for trial or committed him on bail to the Crown Court to be sentenced or otherwise dealt with, that court or the Crown Court may on application—

     (a)   by or on behalf of the person to whom the bail was granted, or

     (b)   by the prosecutor or a constable,

   vary the conditions of bail or impose conditions in respect of bail which has been granted unconditionally.

(9)   This section is subject to subsection (3) of section 11 of the Powers of Criminal Courts (Sentencing) Act 2000 (conditions of bail on remand for medical examination).

(10)   This section is subject, in its application to bail granted by a constable, to section 3A of this Act.

3A.   Conditions of bail in case of police bail

(1)   Section 3 of this Act applies, in relation to bail granted by a custody officer under Part IV of the Police and Criminal Evidence Act 1984 or Part 3 of the Criminal Justice Act 2003 in cases where the normal powers to impose conditions of bail are available to him, subject to the following modifications.

(2)   Subsection (6) does not authorise the imposition of a requirement to reside in a bail hostel or any requirement under paragraph (d) or (e).

(3)   Subsections (6ZAA) ... shall be omitted.

(4)   For subsection (8), substitute the following—

     '(8)   Where a custody officer has granted bail in criminal proceedings he or another custody officer serving at the same police station may, at the request of the person to whom it was granted, vary the conditions of bail; and in doing so he may impose conditions or more onerous conditions.'.

(5) Where a constable grants bail to a person no conditions shall be imposed under subsections (4), (5), (6) or (7) of section 3 of this Act unless it appears to the constable that it is necessary to do so—

   (a)   for the purpose of preventing that person from failing to surrender to custody, or

   (b)   for the purpose of preventing that person from committing an offence while on bail, or

   (c)   for the purpose of preventing that person from interfering with witnesses or otherwise obstructing the course of justice, whether in relation to himself or any other person, or

   (d)   for that person's own protection or, if he is a child or young person, for his own welfare or in his own interests.

(6) Subsection (5) above also applies on any request to a custody officer under subsection (8) of section 3 of this Act to vary the conditions of bail.

4. General right to bail of accused persons and others

(1) A person to whom this section applies shall be granted bail except as provided in Schedule 1 to this Act.

(2) This section applies to a person who is accused of an offence when—

   (a)   he appears or is brought before a magistrates' court or the Crown Court in the course of or in connection with proceedings for the offence, or

   (b)   he applies to a court for bail or for a variation of the conditions of bail in connection with the proceedings.

This subsection does not apply as respects proceedings on or after a person's conviction of the offence.

(2A) This section also applies to a person whose extradition is sought in respect of an offence, when—

   (a)   he appears or is brought before a court in the course of or in connection with extradition proceedings in respect of the offence, or

   (b)   he applies to a court for bail or for a variation of the conditions of bail in connection with the proceedings.

(2B) But subsection (2A) above does not apply if the person is alleged to have been convicted of the offence.

(3) This section also applies to a person who, having been convicted of an offence, appears or is brought before a magistrates' court or the Crown Court under—

   (za)   Schedule 1 to the Powers of Criminal Courts (Sentencing) Act 2000 (referral orders: referral back to appropriate court),

   (zb)   Schedule 8 to that Act (breach of reparation order),

   (a)   Schedule 2 to the Criminal Justice and Immigration Act 2008 (breach, revocation or amendment of youth rehabilitation orders),

   (b)   Part 2 of Schedule 8 to the Criminal Justice Act 2003 (breach of requirement of community order), or

   (c)   the Schedule to the Street Offences Act 1959 (breach of orders under section 1(2A) of that Act).

(4) This section also applies to a person who has been convicted of an offence and whose case is adjourned by the court for the purpose of enabling inquiries or a report to be made to assist the court in dealing with him for the offence.

(5) Schedule 1 to this Act also has effect as respects conditions of bail for a person to whom this section applies.

(6) In Schedule 1 to this Act 'the defendant' means a person to whom this section applies and any reference to a defendant whose case is adjourned for inquiries or a report is a reference to a person to whom this section applies by virtue of subsection (4) above.

(7) This section is subject to section 41 of the Magistrates' Courts Act 1980 (restriction of bail by magistrates' court in cases of treason) and section 115(1) of the Coroners and Justice Act 2009 (bail decisions in murder cases to be made by Crown Court judge).

(8) This section is subject to section 25 of the Criminal Justice and Public Order Act 1994 (exclusion of bail in cases of homicide and rape).

(9) In taking any decisions required by Part I or II of Schedule 1to this Act, the considerations to which the court is to have regard include, so far as relevant, any misuse of controlled drugs by the defendant ('controlled drugs' and 'misuse' having the same meanings as in the Misuse of Drugs Act 1971).

6. Offence of absconding by person released on bail

(1) If a person who has been released on bail in criminal proceedings fails without reasonable cause to surrender to custody he shall be guilty of an offence.

(2) If a person who—
   (a) has been released on bail in criminal proceedings, and
   (b) having reasonable cause therefor, has failed to surrender to custody,
   fails to surrender to custody at the appointed place as soon after the appointed time as is reasonably practicable he shall be guilty of an offence.

(3) It shall be for the accused to prove that he had reasonable cause for his failure to surrender to custody.

(4) A failure to give to a person granted bail in criminal proceedings a copy of the record of the decision shall not constitute a reasonable cause for that person's failure to surrender to custody.

(5) An offence under subsection (1) or (2) above shall be punishable either on summary conviction or as if it were a criminal contempt of court.

(6) Where a magistrates' court convicts a person of an offence under subsection (1) or (2) above the court may, if it thinks—
   (a) that the circumstances of the offence are such that greater punishment should be inflicted for that offence than the court has power to inflict, or
   (b) in a case where it sends that person for trial to the Crown Court for another offence, that it would be appropriate for him to be dealt with for the offence under subsection (1) or (2) above by the court before which he is tried for the other offence,
   commit him in custody or on bail to the Crown Court for sentence.

(7) A person who is convicted summarily of an offence under subsection (1) or (2) above and is not committed to the Crown Court for sentence shall be liable to imprisonment for a term not exceeding 3 months or to a fine not exceeding level 5 on the standard scale or to both and a person who is so committed for sentence or is dealt with as for such a contempt shall be liable to imprisonment for a term not exceeding 12 months or to a fine or to both.

7. Liability to arrest for absconding or breaking conditions of bail

(1) If a person who has been released on bail in criminal proceedings and is under a duty to surrender into the custody of a court fails to surrender at the time appointed for him to do so the court may issue a warrant for his arrest.

...

SCHEDULE 1
PERSONS ENTITLED TO BAIL: SUPPLEMENTARY PROVISIONS

PART I
DEFENDANTS ACCUSED OR CONVICTED OF IMPRISONABLE OFFENCES

...

Exceptions to right to bail

2. (1) The defendant need not be granted bail if the court is satisfied that there are substantial grounds for believing that the defendant, if released on bail (whether subject to conditions or not) would—
   (a) fail to surrender to custody, or
   (b) commit an offence while on bail, or
   (c) interfere with witnesses or otherwise obstruct the course of justice, whether in relation to himself or any other person.

3. The defendant need not be granted bail if the court is satisfied that the defendant should be kept in custody for his own protection or, if he is a child or young person, for his own welfare.

4. The defendant need not be granted bail if he is in custody in pursuance of a sentence of a court or a sentence imposed by an officer under the Armed Forces Act 2006.

5. The defendant need not be granted bail where the court is satisfied that it has not been practicable to obtain sufficient information for the purpose of taking the decisions required

by this Part of this Schedule for want of time since the institution of the proceedings against him.

6. The defendant need not be granted bail if, having previously been released on bail in, or in connection with, the proceedings, the defendant has been arrested in pursuance of section 7.

6ZA. If the defendant is charged with murder, the defendant may not be granted bail unless the court is of the opinion that there is no significant risk of the defendant committing, while on bail, an offence that would, or would be likely to, cause physical or mental injury to any person other than the defendant.

...

9. In taking the decisions required by paragraph 2(1) ... the court shall have regard to such of the following considerations as appear to it to be relevant, that is to say—
    (a) the nature and seriousness of the offence or default (and the probable method of dealing with the defendant for it),
    (b) the character, antecedents, associations and community ties of the defendant,
    (c) the defendant's record as respects the fulfilment of his obligations under previous grants of bail in criminal proceedings,
    (d) except in the case of a defendant whose case is adjourned for inquiries or a report, the strength of the evidence of his having committed the offence or having defaulted,
    (e) if the court is satisfied that there are substantial grounds for believing that the defendant, if released on bail (whether subject to conditions or not), would commit an offence while on bail, the risk that the defendant may do so by engaging in conduct that would, or would be likely to, cause physical or mental injury to any person other than the defendant,
    and to any others which appear to be relevant.
    ...

BAIL (AMENDMENT) ACT 1993
(1993, c. 26)

1. Prosecution right of appeal
(1) Where a magistrates' court grants bail to a person who is charged with, or convicted of, an offence punishable by imprisonment, the prosecution may appeal to a judge of the Crown Court against the granting of bail.

...

(3) An appeal under subsection (1) ... may be made only if—
    (a) the prosecution made representations that bail should not be granted; and
    (b) the representations were made before it was granted.

...

CHILDREN AND YOUNG PERSONS ACT 1933
(1933, c. 12)

44. General considerations
(1) Every court in dealing with a child or young person who is brought before it, either as an offender or otherwise, shall have regard to the welfare of the child or young person and shall in a proper case take steps for removing him from undesirable surroundings, and for securing that proper provision is made for his education and training.

(2) ...

45. Youth courts
(1) Magistrates' courts—
    (a) constituted in accordance with this section or section 66 of the Courts Act 2003 (judges having powers of District Judges (Magistrates' Courts)), and

   (b)   sitting for the purpose of—
       (i)   hearing any charge against a child or young person, or
       (ii) exercising any other jurisdiction conferred on youth courts by or under this
            or any other Act,
      are to be known as youth courts.
 (2) A justice of the peace is not qualified to sit as a member of a youth court for the
      purpose of dealing with any proceedings unless he has an authorisation extending to
      the proceedings.
 (3) He has an authorisation extending to the proceedings only if he has been authorised
      by the Lord Chief Justice, with the concurrence of the Lord Chancellor, to sit as a
      member of a youth court to deal with—
   (a)   proceedings of that description, or
   (b)   all proceedings dealt with by youth courts.

COMPANY DIRECTORS DISQUALIFICATION ACT 1986
(1986, c. 46)

1.   Disqualification orders: general

 (1) In the circumstances specified below in this Act a court may, and under sections 6 and
      9A shall, make against a person a disqualification order, that is to say an order that for
      a period specified in the order—
   (a)   he shall not be a director of a company, act as receiver of a company's property
        or in any way, whether directly or indirectly, be concerned or take part in the
        promotion, formation or management of a company unless (in each case) he has
        the leave of the court, and
   (b)   he shall not act as an insolvency practitioner.
 (2) In each section of this Act which gives to a court power or, as the case may be,
      imposes on it the duty to make a disqualification order there is specified the maximum
      (and, in sections 6 and 8ZA, the minimum) period of disqualification which may or
      (as the case may be) must be imposed by means of the order and, unless the court
      otherwise orders, the period of disqualification so imposed shall begin at the end of
      the period of 21 days beginning with the date of the order.
 (3) Where a disqualification order is made against a person who is already subject to such
      an order or to a disqualification undertaking, the periods specified in those orders or,
      as the case may be, in the order and the undertaking shall run concurrently.
 (4) A disqualification order may be made on grounds which are or include matters other
      than criminal convictions, notwithstanding that the person in respect of whom it is to
      be made may be criminally liable in respect of those matters.

2.   Disqualification on conviction of indictable offence

 (1) The court may make a disqualification order against a person where he is convicted
      of an indictable offence (whether on indictment or summarily) in connection with the
      promotion, formation, management liquidation or striking off of a company with the
      receivership of a company's property or with his being an administrative receiver of a
      company.
(1A) In subsection (1) 'company' includes overseas company.
 (2) 'The court' for this purpose means—
   (a)   any court having jurisdiction to wind up the company in relation to which the
        offence was committed, or
   (b)   the court by or before which the person is convicted of the offence, or
   (c)   in the case of a summary conviction in England and Wales, any other magistrates'
        court acting in the same local justice area;
      and for the purposes of this section the definition of 'indictable offence' in Schedule 1
      to the Interpretation Act 1978 applies for Scotland as it does for England and Wales.
 (3) The maximum period of disqualification under this section is—
   (a)   where the disqualification order is made by a court of summary jurisdiction,
        5 years, and
   (b)   in any other case, 15 years.

CONVENTION FOR THE PROTECTION OF HUMAN RIGHTS AND FUNDAMENTAL FREEDOMS
Rome, 4.XI.1950

Article 5   Right to liberty and security

1.   Everyone has the right to liberty and security of person. No one shall be deprived of his liberty save in the following cases and in accordance with a procedure prescribed by law:

   (a)   the lawful detention of a person after conviction by a competent court;

   (b)   the lawful arrest or detention of a person for noncompliance with the lawful order of a court or in order to secure the fulfilment of any obligation prescribed by law;

   (c)   the lawful arrest or detention of a person effected for the purpose of bringing him before the competent legal authority on reasonable suspicion of having committed an offence or when it is reasonably considered necessary to prevent his committing an offence or fleeing after having done so;

   (d)   the detention of a minor by lawful order for the purpose of educational supervision or his lawful detention for the purpose of bringing him before the competent legal authority;

   (e)   the lawful detention of persons for the prevention of the spreading of infectious diseases, of persons of unsound mind, alcoholics or drug addicts or vagrants;

   (f)   the lawful arrest or detention of a person to prevent his effecting an unauthorised entry into the country or of a person against whom action is being taken with a view to deportation or extradition.

2.   Everyone who is arrested shall be informed promptly, in a language which he understands, of the reasons for his arrest and of any charge against him.

3.   Everyone arrested or detained in accordance with the provisions of paragraph 1(c) of this Article shall be brought promptly before a judge or other officer authorised by law to exercise judicial power and shall be entitled to trial within a reasonable time or to release pending trial. Release may be conditioned by guarantees to appear for trial.

4.   Everyone who is deprived of his liberty by arrest or detention shall be entitled to take proceedings by which the lawfulness of his detention shall be decided speedily by a court and his release ordered if the detention is not lawful.

5.   Everyone who has been the victim of arrest or detention in contravention of the provisions of this Article shall have an enforceable right to compensation.

Article 6   Right to a fair trial

1.   In the determination of his civil rights and obligations or of any criminal charge against him, everyone is entitled to a fair and public hearing within a reasonable time by an independent and impartial tribunal established by law. Judgment shall be pronounced publicly but the press and public may be excluded from all or part of the trial in the interests of morals, public order or national security in a democratic society, where the interests of juveniles or the protection of the private life of the parties so require, or to the extent strictly necessary in the opinion of the court in special circumstances where publicity would prejudice the interests of justice.

2.   Everyone charged with a criminal offence shall be presumed innocent until proved guilty according to law.

3.   Everyone charged with a criminal offence has the following minimum rights:

   (a)   to be informed promptly, in a language which he understands and in detail, of the nature and cause of the accusation against him;

   (b)   to have adequate time and facilities for the preparation of his defence;

   (c)   to defend himself in person or through legal assistance of his own choosing or, if he has not sufficient means to pay for legal assistance, to be given it free when the interests of justice so require;

   (d)   to examine or have examined witnesses against him and to obtain the attendance and examination of witnesses on his behalf under the same conditions as witnesses against him;

   (e)   to have the free assistance of an interpreter if he cannot understand or speak the language used in court.

Article 7   No punishment without law

1.   No one shall be held guilty of any criminal offence on account of any act or omission which did not constitute a criminal offence under national or international law at the time when it was committed. Nor shall a heavier penalty be imposed than the one that was applicable at the time the criminal offence was committed.

2.   This Article shall not prejudice the trial and punishment of any person for any act or omission which, at the time when it was committed, was criminal according to the general principles of law recognised by civilised nations.

Article 8   Right to respect for private and family life

1.   Everyone has the right to respect for his private and family life, his home and his correspondence.

2.   There shall be no interference by a public authority with the exercise of this right except such as is in accordance with the law and is necessary in a democratic society in the interests of national security, public safety or the economic well-being of the country, for the prevention of disorder or crime, for the protection of health or morals, or for the protection of the rights and freedoms of others.

CORONERS AND JUSTICE ACT 2009
(2009, c. 25)

118.   Sentencing Council for England and Wales
(1)   There is to be a Sentencing Council for England and Wales.

(2)   Schedule 15 makes provision about the Council.

119.   Annual report
(1)   The Council must, as soon as practicable after the end of each financial year, make to the Lord Chancellor a report on the exercise of the Council's functions during the year.

(2)   The Lord Chancellor must lay a copy of the report before Parliament.

(3)   The Council must publish the report once a copy has been so laid.

120.   Sentencing guidelines
(1)   In this Chapter 'sentencing guidelines' means guidelines relating to the sentencing of offenders.

(2)   A sentencing guideline may be general in nature or limited to a particular offence, particular category of offence or particular category of offender.

(3)   The Council must prepare—
   (a)   sentencing guidelines about the discharge of a court's duty under section 144 of the Criminal Justice Act 2003 (reduction of sentences for guilty pleas), and
   (b)   sentencing guidelines about the application of any rule of law as to the totality of sentences.

(4)   The Council may prepare sentencing guidelines about any other matter.

(5)   Where the Council has prepared guidelines under subsection (3) or (4), it must publish them as draft guidelines.

(6)   The Council must consult the following persons about the draft guidelines—
   (a)   the Lord Chancellor;
   (b)   such persons as the Lord Chancellor may direct;
   (c)   the Justice Select Committee of the House of Commons (or, if there ceases to be a committee of that name, such committee of the House of Commons as the Lord Chancellor directs);
   (d)   such other persons as the Council considers appropriate.

(7)   In the case of guidelines within subsection (3), the Council must, after making any amendments of the guidelines which it considers appropriate, issue them as definitive guidelines.

(8)   In any other case, the Council may, after making such amendments, issue them as definitive guidelines.

(9) The Council may, from time to time, review the sentencing guidelines issued under this section, and may revise them.

(10) Subsections (5), (6) and (8) apply to a revision of the guidelines as they apply to their preparation (and subsection (8) applies even if the guidelines being revised are within subsection (3)).

(11) When exercising functions under this section, the Council must have regard to the following matters—

     (a) the sentences imposed by courts in England and Wales for offences;

     (b) the need to promote consistency in sentencing;

     (c) the impact of sentencing decisions on victims of offences;

     (d) the need to promote public confidence in the criminal justice system;

     (e) the cost of different sentences and their relative effectiveness in preventing re-offending;

     (f) the results of the monitoring carried out under section 128.

121. Sentencing ranges

(1) When exercising functions under section 120, the Council is to have regard to the desirability of sentencing guidelines which relate to a particular offence being structured in the way described in subsections (2) to (9).

(2) The guidelines should, if reasonably practicable given the nature of the offence, describe, by reference to one or more of the factors mentioned in subsection (3), different categories of case involving the commission of the offence which illustrate in general terms the varying degrees of seriousness with which the offence may be committed.

(3) Those factors are—

     (a) the offender's culpability in committing the offence;

     (b) the harm caused, or intended to be caused or which might foreseeably have been caused, by the offence;

     (c) such other factors as the Council considers to be particularly relevant to the seriousness of the offence in question.

(4) The guidelines should—

     (a) specify the range of sentences ('the offence range') which, in the opinion of the Council, it may be appropriate for a court to impose on an offender convicted of that offence, and

     (b) if the guidelines describe different categories of case in accordance with subsection (2), specify for each category the range of sentences ('the category range') within the offence range which, in the opinion of the Council, it may be appropriate for a court to impose on an offender in a case which falls within the category.

(5) The guidelines should also—

     (a) specify the sentencing starting point in the offence range, or

     (b) if the guidelines describe different categories of case in accordance with subsection (2), specify the sentencing starting point in the offence range for each of those categories.

(6) The guidelines should—

     (a) (to the extent not already taken into account by categories of case described in accordance with subsection (2)) list any aggravating or mitigating factors which, by virtue of any enactment or other rule of law, the court is required to take into account when considering the seriousness of the offence and any other aggravating or mitigating factors which the Council considers are relevant to such a consideration,

     (b) list any other mitigating factors which the Council considers are relevant in mitigation of sentence for the offence, and

     (c) include criteria, and provide guidance, for determining the weight to be given to previous convictions of the offender and such of the other factors within paragraph (a) or (b) as the Council considers to be of particular significance in relation to the offence or the offender.

(7) For the purposes of subsection (6)(b) the following are to be disregarded—

     (a) the requirements of section 144 of the Criminal Justice Act 2003 (reduction in sentences for guilty pleas);

(b)   sections 73 and 74 of the Serious Organised Crime and Police Act 2005 (assistance by defendants: reduction or review of sentence) and any other rule of law by virtue of which an offender may receive a discounted sentence in consequence of assistance given (or offered to be given) by the offender to the prosecutor or investigator of an offence;

(c)   any rule of law as to the totality of sentences.

(8)   The provision made in accordance with subsection (6)(c) should be framed in such manner as the Council considers most appropriate for the purpose of assisting the court, when sentencing an offender for the offence, to determine the appropriate sentence within the offence range.

(9)   The provision made in accordance with subsections (2) to (8) may be different for different circumstances or cases involving the offence.

(10) The sentencing starting point in the offence range—

(a)   for a category of case described in the guidelines in accordance with subsection (2), is the sentence within that range which the Council considers to be the appropriate starting point for cases within that category—

(i)   before taking account of the factors mentioned in subsection (6), and

(ii)   assuming the offender has pleaded not guilty, and

(b)   where the guidelines do not describe categories of case in accordance with subsection (2), is the sentence within that range which the Council considers to be the appropriate starting point for the offence—

(i)   before taking account of the factors mentioned in subsection (6), and

(ii)   assuming the offender has pleaded not guilty.

125. Sentencing guidelines: duty of court

(1)   Every court—

(a)   must, in sentencing an offender, follow any sentencing guidelines which are relevant to the offender's case, and

(b)   must, in exercising any other function relating to the sentencing of offenders, follow any sentencing guidelines which are relevant to the exercise of the function,

unless the court is satisfied that it would be contrary to the interests of justice to do so.

(2)   Subsections (3) and (4) apply where—

(a)   a court is deciding what sentence to impose on a person ('P') who is guilty of an offence, and

(b)   sentencing guidelines have been issued in relation to that offence which are structured in the way described in section 121(2) to (5) ('the offence specific guidelines').

(3)   The duty imposed on a court by subsection (1)(a) to follow any sentencing guidelines which are relevant to the offender's case includes—

(a)   in all cases, a duty to impose on P, in accordance with the offence specific guidelines, a sentence which is within the offence range, and

(b)   where the offence-specific guidelines describe categories of case in accordance with section 121(2), a duty to decide which of the categories most resembles P's case in order to identify the sentencing starting point in the offence range;

but nothing in this section imposes on the court a separate duty, in a case within paragraph (b), to impose a sentence which is within the category range.

(4)   Subsection (3)(b) does not apply if the court is of the opinion that, for the purpose of identifying the sentence within the offence range which is the appropriate starting point, none of the categories sufficiently resembles P's case.

(5)   Subsection (3)(a) is subject to—

(a)   section 144 of the Criminal Justice Act 2003 (reduction in sentences for guilty pleas),

(b)   sections 73 and 74 of the Serious Organised Crime and Police Act 2005 (assistance by defendants: reduction or review of sentence) and any other rule of law by virtue of which an offender may receive a discounted sentence in consequence of assistance given (or offered to be given) by the offender to the prosecutor or investigator of an offence, and

(c)   any rule of law as to the totality of sentences.

(6)   The duty imposed by subsection (1) is subject to the following provisions —

    (a)   section 148(1) and (2) of the Criminal Justice Act 2003 (restrictions on imposing community sentences);

    (b)   section 152 of that Act (restrictions on imposing discretionary custodial sentences);

    (c)   section 153 of that Act (custodial sentence must be for shortest term commensurate with seriousness of offence);

    (d)   section 164(2) of that Act (fine must reflect seriousness of offence);

    (da)   section 224A of that Act (life sentence for second listed offence for certain dangerous offenders);

    (e)   section 269 of and Schedule 21 to that Act (determination of minimum term in relation to mandatory life sentence);

    (ea)   sections 1(2B) and 1A(5) of the Prevention of Crime Act 1953 (minimum sentence for certain offences involving offensive weapons);

    (f)   section 51A of the Firearms Act 1968 (minimum sentence for certain offences under section 5 etc);

    (fa)   sections 139(6B), 139(5B) and 139AA(7) of the Criminal Justice Act 1988 (minimum sentence for certain offences involving article with blade or point or offensive weapon);

    (g)   sections 110(2) and 111(2) of the Powers of Criminal Courts (Sentencing) Act 2000 (minimum sentences for certain drug trafficking and burglary offences);

    (h)   section 29(4) and (6) of the Violent Crime Reduction Act 2006 (minimum sentences for certain offences involving firearms).

(7)   Nothing in this section or section 126 is to be taken as restricting any power (whether under the Mental Health Act 1983 or otherwise) which enables a court to deal with a mentally disordered offender in the manner it considers to be most appropriate in all the circumstances.

(8)   In this section —

    'mentally disordered', in relation to a person, means suffering from a mental disorder within the meaning of the Mental Health Act 1983;

    'sentencing guidelines' means definitive sentencing guidelines.

126.   Determination of tariffs etc

(1)   Section 125(3) (except as applied by virtue of subsection (3) below) is subject to any power a court has to impose —

    ...

    (c)   an extended sentence of imprisonment by virtue of section 226A of the Criminal Justice Act 2003;

    (d)   an extended sentence of detention by virtue of section 226B of that Act.

(2)   Subsection (3) applies where a court determines the notional determinate term for the purpose of determining in any case —

    (a)   the order to be made under section 82A of the Powers of Criminal Courts (Sentencing) Act 2000 (life sentence: determination of tariffs),

    ...

    (c)   the appropriate custodial term for the purposes of section 226A(6) of the Criminal Justice Act 2003 (extended sentence for certain violent, sexual or terrorism offences: persons 18 or over), or

    (d)   the appropriate term for the purposes of section 226B(4) of that Act (extended sentence for certain violent, sexual or terrorism offences: persons under 18).

(3)   Subsections (2) to (5) of section 125 apply for the purposes of determining the notional determinate term in relation to an offence as they apply for the purposes of determining the sentence for an offence.

(4)   In this section references to the notional determinate term are to the determinate sentence that would have been passed in the case if the need to protect the public and the potential danger of the offender had not required the court to impose a life sentence (in circumstances where the sentence is not fixed by law) or, as the case may be, an extended sentence of imprisonment or detention.

(5)   In subsection (4) 'life sentence' means a sentence mentioned in subsection (2) of section 34 of the Crime (Sentences) Act 1997 other than a sentence mentioned in paragraph (d) or (e) of that subsection.

COUNTER-TERRORISM ACT 2008

(2008, c. 28)

30. **Sentences for offences with a terrorist connection: England and Wales and Northern Ireland**

(1) This section applies where a court in England and Wales or Northern Ireland is considering for the purposes of sentence the seriousness of an offence specified in Schedule 2 (offences where terrorist connection to be considered).

(2) If having regard to the material before it for the purposes of sentencing it appears to the court that the offence has or may have a terrorist connection, the court must determine whether that is the case.

(3) For that purpose the court may hear evidence, and must take account of any representations made by the prosecution and the defence, as in the case of any other matter relevant for the purposes of sentence.

(4) If the court determines that the offence has a terrorist connection, the court—
   (a) must treat that fact as an aggravating factor, and
   (b) must state in open court that the offence was so aggravated.

(5) In this section 'sentence', in relation to an offence, includes any order made by a court when dealing with a person in respect of the offence.

COUNTER-TERRORISM AND SECURITY ACT 2015

(2015, c. 6)

2. **Temporary exclusion orders**

(1) A 'temporary exclusion order' is an order which requires an individual not to return to the United Kingdom unless—
   (a) the return is in accordance with a permit to return issued by the Secretary of State before the individual began the return, or
   (b) the return is the result of the individual's deportation to the United Kingdom.

(2) The Secretary of State may impose a temporary exclusion order on an individual if conditions A to E are met.

(3) Condition A is that the Secretary of State reasonably suspects that the individual is, or has been, involved in terrorism-related activity outside the United Kingdom.

(4) Condition B is that the Secretary of State reasonably considers that it is necessary, for purposes connected with protecting members of the public in the United Kingdom from a risk of terrorism, for a temporary exclusion order to be imposed on the individual.

(5) Condition C is that the Secretary of State reasonably considers that the individual is outside the United Kingdom.

(6) Condition D is that the individual has the right of abode in the United Kingdom.

(7) Condition E is that—
   (a) the court gives the Secretary of State permission under section 3, or
   (b) the Secretary of State reasonably considers that the urgency of the case requires a temporary exclusion order to be imposed without obtaining such permission.

(8) During the period that a temporary exclusion order is in force, the Secretary of State must keep under review whether condition B is met.

3. **Temporary exclusion orders: prior permission of the court**

(1) This section applies if the Secretary of State—
   (a) makes the relevant decisions in relation to an individual, and
   (b) makes an application to the court for permission to impose a temporary exclusion order on the individual.

(2) The function of the court on the application is to determine whether the relevant decisions of the Secretary of State are obviously flawed.

(3) The court may consider the application—
   (a) in the absence of the individual,
   (b) without the individual having been notified of the application, and
   (c) without the individual having been given an opportunity (if the individual was aware of the application) of making any representations to the court.

(4) But that does not limit the matters about which rules of court may be made.

(5) In determining the application, the court must apply the principles applicable on an application for judicial review.

(6) In a case where the court determines that any of the relevant decisions of the Secretary of State is obviously flawed, the court may not give permission under this section.

(7) In any other case, the court must give permission under this section.

COURTS ACT 2003
(2003, c. 39)

66. Judges having powers of District Judges (Magistrates' Courts)

(1) Every holder of a judicial office specified in subsection (2) has the powers of a justice of the peace who is a District Judge (Magistrates' Courts) in relation to—
  (a) criminal causes and matters, and
  (b) family proceedings ...

(2) The offices are—
  (a) judge of the High Court;
  (aa) Master of the Rolls;
  (ab) ordinary judge of the Court of Appeal;
  (ac) Senior President of Tribunals;
  (b) deputy judge of the High Court;
  (c) Circuit judge;
  (d) deputy Circuit judge;
  (e) recorder.

(3) For the purposes of section 45 of the 1933 Act, every holder of a judicial office specified in subsection (2) is qualified to sit as a member of a youth court.
  ...

(7) This section does not give a person any powers that a District Judge (Magistrates' Courts) may have to act in a court or tribunal that is not a magistrates' court.

69. Criminal Procedure Rules

(1) There are to be rules of court (to be called 'Criminal Procedure Rules') governing the practice and procedure to be followed in the criminal courts.

(2) Criminal Procedure Rules are to be made by a committee known as the Criminal Procedure Rule Committee.

(3) The power to make Criminal Procedure Rules includes power to make different provision for different cases or different areas, including different provision—
  (a) for a specified court or description of courts, or
  (b) for specified descriptions of proceedings or a specified jurisdiction.

(4) Any power to make Criminal Procedure Rules is to be exercised with a view to securing that—
  (a) the criminal justice system is accessible, fair and efficient, and
  (b) the rules are both simple and simply expressed.

CRIMINAL PROCEDURE RULES 2015
(SI 2015/1490)

1.1. The overriding objective

(1) The overriding objective of this new code is that criminal cases be dealt with justly.

(2) Dealing with a case justly includes—
  (a) acquitting the innocent and convicting the guilty;
  (b) dealing with the prosecution and defence fairly;
  (c) recognising the rights of a defendant, particularly those under Article 6 of the European Convention on Human Rights;
  (d) respecting the interests of witnesses, victims and jurors and keeping them informed of the progress of the case;
  (e) dealing with the case efficiently and expeditiously;

(f)   ensuring that appropriate information is available to the court when bail and sentence are considered; and

(g)   dealing with the case in ways that take into account—
   (i)   the gravity of the offence alleged,
   (ii)   the complexity of what is in issue,
   (iii)   the severity of consequences for the defendant and others affected, and
   (iv)   the needs of other cases.

1.2.   The duty of the participants in a criminal case

(1)   Each participant, in the conduct of each case, must—
   (a)   prepare and conduct the case in accordance with the overriding objective;
   (b)   comply with these Rules, practice directions and directions made by the court; and
   (c)   at once inform the court and all parties of any significant failure (whether or not that participant is responsible for that failure) to take any procedural step required by these Rules, any practice direction or any direction of the court. A failure is significant if it might hinder the court in furthering the overriding objective.

(2)   Anyone involved in any way with a criminal case is a participant in its conduct for the purposes of this rule.

1.3.   The application by the court of the overriding objective

The court must further the overriding objective in particular when—

(a)   exercising any power given to it by legislation (including these Rules);

(b)   applying any practice direction; or

(c)   interpreting any rule or practice direction.

3.2.   The duty of the court

(1)   The court must further the overriding objective by actively managing the case.

(2)   Active case management includes—
   (a)   the early identification of the real issues;
   (b)   the early identification of the needs of witnesses;
   (c)   achieving certainty as to what must be done, by whom, and when, in particular by the early setting of a timetable for the progress of the case;
   (d)   monitoring the progress of the case and compliance with directions;
   (e)   ensuring that evidence, whether disputed or not, is presented in the shortest and clearest way;
   (f)   discouraging delay, dealing with as many aspects of the case as possible on the same occasion, and avoiding unnecessary hearings;
   (g)   encouraging the participants to co-operate in the progression of the case; and
   (h)   making use of technology.

(3)   The court must actively manage the case by giving any directions appropriate to the needs of the case as early as possible.

(4)   Where appropriate live links are available, making use of technology for the purposes of this rule includes directing the use of such facilities, whether an application for such a direction is made or not—
   (a)   for the conduct of a pre-trial hearing, including a pre-trial case management hearing;
   (b)   for the defendant's attendance at such a hearing—
      (i)   where the defendant is in custody, or where the defendant is not in custody and wants to attend by live link, but
      (ii)   only if the court is satisfied that the defendant can participate effectively by such means, having regard to all the circumstances including whether the defendant is represented or not; and
   (c)   for receiving evidence under one of the powers to which the rules in Part 18 apply (Measures to assist a witness or defendant to give evidence).

(5)   Where appropriate telephone facilities are available, making use of technology for the purposes of this rule includes directing the use of such facilities, whether an application for such a direction is made or not, for the conduct of a pre-trial case management hearing—
   (a)   if telephone facilities are more convenient for that purpose than live links;
   (b)   unless at that hearing the court expects to take the defendant's plea; and

      (c)   only if—
         (i)   the defendant is represented, or
        (ii)   exceptionally, the court is satisfied that the defendant can participate effectively by such means without a representative.

3.3. The duty of the parties

(1)   Each party must—
     (a)   actively assist the court in fulfilling its duty under rule 3.2, without or of necessary with a direction; and
     (b)   apply for a direction if needed to further the overriding objective.
(2)   Active assistance for the purposes of this rule includes—
     (a)   at the beginning of the case, communication between the prosecutor and the defendant at the first available opportunity and in any event no later than the beginning of the day of the first hearing;
     (b)   after that, communication between the parties and with the court officer until the conclusion of the case;
     (c)   by such communication establishing among other things—
        (i)   whether the defendant is likely to plead guilty or not guilty,
        (ii)   what is agreed and what is likely to be disputed,
       (iii)   what information, or other material, is required by one party of another, and why, and
       (iv)   what is to be done, by whom, and when (without or if necessary with a direction);
     (d)   reporting on that first communication to the court—
        (i)   at the first hearing, and
        (ii)   after that, as directed by the court; and
     (e)   alerting the court to any reason why—
        (i)   a direction should not be made in any of the circumstances listed in rule 3.2(4) or (5) (The duty of the court: use of live link or telephone facilities), or
        (ii)   such a direction should be varied or revoked.

3.5. The court's case management powers

(1)   In fulfilling its duty under rule 3.2 the court may give any direction and take any step actively to manage a case unless that direction or step would be inconsistent with legislation, including these Rules.
(2)   In particular, the court may—
     (a)   nominate a judge, magistrate or justices' legal adviser to manage the case;
     (b)   give a direction on its own initiative or on application by a party;
     (c)   ask or allow a party to propose a direction;
     (d)   for the purpose of giving directions, receive applications and representations by letter, by telephone or by any other means of electronic communication, and conduct a hearing by such means;
     (e)   give a direction—
        (i)   at a hearing, in public or in private, or
        (ii)   without a hearing;
     (f)   fix, postpone, bring forward, extend, cancel or adjourn a hearing;
     (g)   shorten or extend (even after it has expired) a time limit fixed by a direction;
     (h)   require that issues in the case should be—
        (i)   identified in writing,
        (ii)   determined separately, and decide in what order they will be determined; and
     (i)   specify the consequences of failing to comply with a direction.
(3)   A magistrates' court may give a direction that will apply in the Crown Court if the case is to continue there.
(4)   The Crown Court may give a direction that will apply in a magistrates' court if the case is to continue there.
(5)   Any power to give a direction under this Part includes a power to vary or revoke that direction.
(6)   If a party fails to comply with a rule or a direction, the court may—
     (a)   fix, postpone, bring forward, extend, cancel or adjourn a hearing;

(b) exercise its powers to make a costs order; and

(c) impose such other sanction as may be appropriate.

3.9. Case preparation and progression

(1) At every hearing, if a case cannot be concluded there and then the court must give directions so that it can be concluded at the next hearing or as soon as possible after that.

(2) At every hearing the court must, where relevant—

    (a) if the defendant is absent, decide whether to proceed nonetheless;

    (b) take the defendant's plea (unless already done) or if no plea can be taken then find out whether the defendant is likely to plead guilty or not guilty;

    (c) set, follow or revise a timetable for the progress of the case, which may include a timetable for any hearing including the trial or (in the Crown Court) the appeal;

    (d) in giving directions, ensure continuity in relation to the court and to the parties' representatives where that is appropriate and practicable; and

    (e) where a direction has not been complied with, find out why, identify who was responsible, and take appropriate action.

(3) In order to prepare for the trial, the court must take every reasonable step—

    (a) to encourage and to facilitate the attendance of witnesses when they are needed; and

    (b) to facilitate the participation of any person, including the defendant.

(4) Facilitating the participation of the defendant includes finding out whether the defendant needs interpretation because—

    (a) the defendant dies not speak or understand English; or

    (b) the defendant has a hearing or speech impediment.

(5) Where the defendant needs interpretation –

    (a) the court officer must arrange for interpretation to be provided at every hearing which the defendant is due to attend;

    (b) interpretation may be by an intermediary where the defendant has a speech impediment, without the need for a defendant's evidence direction;

    (c) on application or on its own initiative, the court may require a written translation to be provided for the defendant of any document or part of a document, unless—

        (i) translation of that document, or part, is not needed to explain the case against the defendant, or

        (ii) the defendant agrees to do without and the court is satisfied that the agreement is clear and voluntary and that the defendant has had legal advice or otherwise understands the consequences

3.10. Readiness for trial or appeal

(1) This rule applies to a party's preparation for trial or appeal, and in this rule and rule 3.10 trial includes any hearing at which evidence will be introduced.

(2) In fulfilling his duty under rule 3.3, each party must—

    (a) comply with directions given by the court;

    (b) take every reasonable step to make sure his witnesses will attend when they are needed;

    (c) make appropriate arrangements to present any written or other material; and

    (d) promptly inform the court and the other parties of anything that may—

        (i) affect the date or duration of the trial or appeal, or

        (ii) significantly affect the progress of the case in any other way.

(3) The court may require a party to give a certificate of readiness.

3.11. Conduct of a trial or an appeal

In order to manage the trial or an appeal, the court—

(a) must establish, with the active assistance of the parties, what are the disputed issues;

(b) must consider setting a timetable that—

    (i) takes account of those issues and any timetable proposed by a party, and

    (ii) may limit the duration of any stage of the hearing;

(c) may require a party to identify—

    (i) which witnesses that party wants to give evidence in person,

    (ii) the order in which that party wants those witnesses to give their evidence,

     (iii)   whether that party requires an order compelling the attendance of a witness,

     (iv)   what arrangements are desirable to facilitate the giving of evidence by a witness

     (v)   what arrangements are desirable to facilitate the participation of any other person, including the defendant,

     (vi)   what written evidence that party intends to introduce,

     (vii)   what other material, if any, that person intends to make available to the court in the presentation of the case

     (viii)   whether that party intends to raise any point of law that could affect the conduct of the trial or appeal, and

  (d)   may limit—

     (i)   the examination, cross-examination or re-examination of witnesses, and

     (ii)   the direction of any stage of the hearing.

CRIME AND DISORDER ACT 1998
(1998, c. 37)

8.   Parenting orders

(1)   This section applies where, in any court proceedings—

  (a)   a child safety order is made in respect of a child or the court determines on an application under section 12(6) below that a child has failed to comply with any requirement included in such an order;

  (aa)   a parental compensation order is made in relation to a child's behaviour;

  (b)   an injunction is granted under section 1 of the Anti-social Behaviour Crime and Policing Act 2014, an order is made under section 22 of that Act or a sexual harm prevention order is made in respect of a child or young person;

  (c)   a child or young person is convicted of an offence; or

  (d)   a person is convicted of an offence under section 443 (failure to comply with school attendance order) or section 444 (failure to secure regular attendance at school of registered pupil) of the Education Act 1996.

(2)   Subject to subsection (3) and section 9(1) below, if in the proceedings the court is satisfied that the relevant condition is fulfilled, it may make a parenting order in respect of a person who is a parent or guardian of the child or young person or, as the case may be, the person convicted of the offence under section 443 or 444 ('the parent').

(3)   A court shall not make a parenting order unless it has been notified by the Secretary of State that arrangements for implementing such orders are available in the area in which it appears to the court that the parent resides or will reside and the notice has not been withdrawn.

(4)   A parenting order is an order which requires the parent—

  (a)   to comply, for a period not exceeding twelve months, with such requirements as are specified in the order; and

  (b)   subject to subsection (5) below, to attend, for a concurrent period not exceeding three months and not more than once in any week, such counselling or guidance sessions as may be specified in directions given by the responsible officer;

  and in this subsection 'week' means a period of seven days beginning with a Sunday.

(5)   A parenting order may, but need not, include such a requirement as is mentioned in subsection (4)(b) above in any case where such an order has been made in respect of the parent on a previous occasion.

(6)   The relevant condition is that the parenting order would be desirable in the interests of preventing—

  (a)   in a case falling within paragraph (a), (aa) or (b) of subsection (1) above, any repetition of the kind of behaviour which led to the order being made or the injunction granted;

  (b)   in a case falling within paragraph (c) of that subsection, the commission of any further offence by the child or young person;

  (c)   in a case falling within paragraph (d) of that subsection, the commission of any further offence under section 443 or 444 of the Education Act 1996.

(7) The requirements that may be specified under subsection (4)(a) above are those which the court considers desirable in the interests of preventing any such repetition or, as the case may be, the commission of any such further offence.

(7A) A counselling or guidance programme which a parent is required to attend by virtue of subsection (4)(b) above may be or include a residential course but only if the court is satisfied—

(a) that the attendance of the parent at a residential course is likely to be more effective than his attendance at a non-residential course in preventing any such repetition or, as the case may be, the commission of any such further offence, and

(b) that any interference with family life which is likely to result from the attendance of the parent at a residential course is proportionate in all the circumstances.

(8) In this section and section 9 below 'responsible officer', in relation to a parenting order, means one of the following who is specified in the order, namely—

(a) an officer of a local probation board or an officer of a provider of probation services;

(b) a social worker of a local authority social services department;

(bb) a person nominated by a person appointed as chief education officer under section 532 of the Education Act 1996;

(c) a member of a youth offending team.

(9) In this section 'sexual harm prevention order' means an order under section 103A of the Sexual Offences Act 2003 (sexual offences prevention orders).

9.   Parenting orders: supplemental

(1) Where a person under the age of 16 is convicted of an offence, the court by or before which he is so convicted—

(a) if it is satisfied that the relevant condition is fulfilled, shall make a parenting order; and

(b) if it is not so satisfied, shall state in open court that it is not and why it is not.

(1A) The requirements of subsection (1) do not apply where the court makes a referral order in respect of the offence.

(1B) If an injunction under section 1 of the Anti-social Behaviour, Crime and Policing Act 2014 is granted or an order made under section 22 of that Act is made in respect of a person under the age of 16 the court which grants the injunction or makes the order—

(a) must make a parenting order if it is satisfied that the relevant condition is fulfilled;

(b) if it is not so satisfied, must state in open court that it is not and why it is not.

(2) Before making a parenting order—

(a) in a case falling within paragraph (a) of subsection (1) of section 8 above;

(b) in a case falling within paragraph (b) or of that subsection, where the person concerned is under the age of 16; or

(c) in a case falling within paragraph (d) of that subsection, where the person to whom the offence related is under that age,

a court shall obtain and consider information about the person's family circumstances and the likely effect of the order on those circumstances.

(2A) In a case where a court proposes to make both a referral order in respect of a child or young person convicted of an offence and a parenting order, before making the parenting order the court shall obtain and consider a report by an appropriate officer—

(a) indicating the requirements proposed by that officer to be included in the parenting order;

(b) indicating the reasons why he considers those requirements would be desirable in the interests of preventing the commission of any further offence by the child or young person; and

(c) if the child or young person is aged under 16, containing the information required by subsection (2) above.

(2B) In subsection (2A) above 'an appropriate officer' means—

(a) an officer of a local probation board or an officer of a provider of probation services;

(b) a social worker of a local authority social services department; or

(c) a member of a youth offending team.

(3) Before making a parenting order, a court shall explain to the parent in ordinary language—

(a) the effect of the order and of the requirements proposed to be included in it;

(b) the consequences which may follow (under subsection (7) below) if he fails to comply with any of those requirements; and

(c)   that the court has power (under subsection (5) below) to review the order on the application either of the parent or of the responsible officer.

(4)   Requirements specified in, and directions given under, a parenting order shall, as far as practicable, be such as to avoid—

(a)   any conflict with the parent's religious beliefs; and

(b)   any interference with the times, if any, at which he normally works or attends an educational establishment.

(5)   If while a parenting order is in force it appears to the court which made it, on the application of the responsible officer or the parent, that it is appropriate to make an order under this subsection, the court may make an order discharging the parenting order or varying it—

(a)   by cancelling any provision included in it; or

(b)   by inserting in it (either in addition to or in substitution for any of its provisions) any provision that could have been included in the order if the court had then had power to make it and were exercising the power.

(6)   Where an application under subsection (5) above for the discharge of a parenting order is dismissed, no further application for its discharge shall be made under that subsection by any person except with the consent of the court which made the order.

(7)   If while a parenting order is in force the parent without reasonable excuse fails to comply with any requirement included in the order, or specified in directions given by the responsible officer, he shall be liable on summary conviction to a fine not exceeding level 3 on the standard scale.

(7A)   In this section 'referral order' means an order under section 16(2) or (3) of the Powers of Criminal Courts (Sentencing) Act 2000 (referral of offender to youth offender panel).

10.   Appeals against parenting orders

(1)   An appeal shall lie—

(a)   to a county court against the making of a parenting order by virtue of paragraph (a) of subsection (1) of section 8 above; and

(b)   to the Crown Court against the making of a parenting order by virtue of paragraph (b) of that subsection.

(2)   On an appeal under subsection (1) above a county court or the Crown Court—

(a)   may make such orders as may be necessary to give effect to its determination of the appeal; and

(b)   may also make such incidental or consequential orders as appear to it to be just.

(3)   Any order of a county court or the Crown Court made on an appeal under subsection (1) above (other than one directing that an application be re-heard by a magistrates' court) shall, for the purposes of subsections (5) to (7) of section 9 above, be treated as if it were an order of the court from which the appeal was brought and not an order of a county court or the Crown Court.

(4)   A person in respect of whom a parenting order is made by virtue of section 8(1)(c) above shall have the same right of appeal against the making of the order as if—

(a)   the offence that led to the making of the order were an offence committed by him; and

(b)   the order were a sentence passed on him for the offence.

(5)   A person in respect of whom a parenting order is made by virtue of section 8(1)(d) above shall have the same right of appeal against the making of the order as if the order were a sentence passed on him for the offence that led to the making of the order.

(6)   The Lord Chancellor, with the concurrence of the Lord Chief Justice, may by order make provision as to the circumstances in which appeals under subsection (1)(a) above may be made against decisions taken by courts on questions arising in connection with the transfer, or proposed transfer, of proceedings by virtue of any order under paragraph 2 of Schedule 11 (jurisdiction) to the Children Act 1989 ('the 1989 Act').

(7)   Except to the extent provided for in any order made under subsection (6) above, no appeal may be made against any decision of a kind mentioned in that subsection.

(8)   The Lord Chief Justice may nominate a judicial office holder (as defined in section 109(4) of the Constitutional Reform Act 2005) to exercise his functions under this section.

37. Aim of the youth justice system

(1) It shall be the principal aim of the youth justice system to prevent offending by children and young persons.

(2) In addition to any other duty to which they are subject, it shall be the duty of all persons and bodies carrying out functions in relation to the youth justice system to have regard to that aim.

57E. Use of live link in sentencing hearings

(1) This section applies where the accused is convicted of the offence.

(2) If it appears to the court by or before which the accused is convicted that it is likely that he will be held in custody during any sentencing hearing for the offence, the court may give a live link direction under this section in relation to that hearing.

(3) A live link direction under this section is a direction requiring the accused, if he is being held in custody during the hearing, to attend it through a live link from the place at which he is being held.

(4) Such a direction—

    (a) may be given by the court of its own motion or on an application by a party; and

    (b) may be given in relation to all subsequent sentencing hearings before the court or to such hearing or hearings as may be specified or described in the direction.

(5) The court may not give such a direction unless—

    ...

    (b) the court is satisfied that it is not contrary to the interests of justice to give the direction.

(6) The court may rescind such a direction at any time before or during a hearing to which it relates if it appears to the court to be in the interests of justice to do so (but this does not affect the court's power to give a further live link direction in relation to the offender). The court may exercise this power of its own motion or on an application by a party.

(7) The offender may not give oral evidence while attending a hearing through a live link by virtue of this section unless—

    ...

    (b) the court is satisfied that it is not contrary to the interests of justice for him to give it in that way.

(8) The court must—

    (a) state in open court its reasons for refusing an application for, or for the rescission of, a live link direction under this section; and

    (b) if it is a magistrates' court, cause those reasons to be entered in the register of its proceedings.

66ZA. Youth cautions

(1) A constable may give a child or young person ('Y') a caution under this section (a 'youth caution') if—

    (a) the constable decides that there is sufficient evidence to charge Y with an offence,

    (b) Y admits to the constable that Y committed the offence, and

    (c) the constable does not consider that Y should be prosecuted or given a youth conditional caution in respect of the offence.

(2) A youth caution must be given in the presence of an appropriate adult.

(3) If a constable gives a youth caution to a person, the constable must explain the matters referred to in subsection (4) in ordinary language to—

    (a) that person, and

    (b) the appropriate adult.

(4) Those matters are—

    (a) the effect of subsections (1) to (3) and (5) to (7) of section 66ZB, and

    (b) any guidance issued under subsection (4) of that section.

(5) The Secretary of State must publish, in such manner as the Secretary of State considers appropriate, guidance as to—

    (a) the circumstances in which it is appropriate to give youth cautions,

    (b) the places where youth cautions may be given,

    (c) the category of constable by whom youth cautions may be given, and

    (d) the form which youth cautions are to take and the manner in which they are to be given and recorded.

(6) No caution other than a youth caution or a youth conditional caution may be given to a child or young person.

(7) In this Chapter 'appropriate adult', in relation to a child or young person, means—

    (a) a parent or guardian of the child or young person,

    (b) if the child or young person is in the care of a local authority or voluntary organisation, a person representing that authority or organisation,

    (c) a social worker of a local authority, or

    (d) if no person falling within paragraph (a), (b) or (c) is available, any responsible person aged 18 or over who is not a police officer or a person employed for, or engaged on, police purposes.

66ZB. Effect of youth cautions

(1) If a constable gives a youth caution to a person, the constable must as soon as practicable refer the person to a youth offending team.

(2) Subject to subsection (3), on a referral of a person under subsection (1), the youth offending team—

    (a) must assess the person, and

    (b) unless they consider it inappropriate to do so, must arrange for the person to participate in a rehabilitation programme.

(3) If the person has not previously been referred under subsection (1) and has not previously been given a youth conditional caution, the youth offending team—

    (a) may assess the person, and

    (b) may arrange for the person to participate in a rehabilitation programme.

(4) The Secretary of State must publish, in such manner as the Secretary of State considers appropriate, guidance as to—

    (a) what should be included in a rehabilitation programme arranged for a person under subsection (2) or (3),

    (b) the manner in which any failure by a person to participate in a programme is to be recorded, and

    (c) the persons to whom any such failure must be notified.

(5) Subsection (6) applies if—

    (a) a person who has received two or more youth cautions is convicted of an offence committed within two years beginning with the date of the last of those cautions, or

    (b) a person who has received a youth conditional caution followed by a youth caution is convicted of an offence committed within two years beginning with the date of the youth caution.

(6) The court by or before which the person is convicted—

    (a) must not make an order under section 12(1)(b) of the Powers of Criminal Courts (Sentencing) Act 2000 (conditional discharge) in respect of the offence unless it is of the opinion that there are exceptional circumstances relating to the offence or the person that justify it doing so, and

    (b) where it does so, must state in open court that it is of that opinion and its reasons for that opinion.

(7) There may be cited in criminal proceedings—

    (a) a youth caution given to a person, and

    (b) a report on a failure by a person to participate in a rehabilitation programme arranged for the person under subsection (2) or (3),

in the same circumstances as a conviction of the person may be cited.

CRIMINAL APPEAL ACT 1968
(1968, c. 19)

1. Right of appeal

(1) Subject to subsection (3) below a person convicted of an offence on indictment may appeal to the Court of Appeal against his conviction.

(2) An appeal under this section lies only—

    (a) with the leave of the Court of Appeal; or

    (b) if, within 28 days from the date of the conviction, the judge of the court of trial grants a certificate that the case is fit for appeal.

(3) Where a person is convicted before the Crown Court of a scheduled offence it shall not be open to him to appeal to the Court of Appeal against the conviction on the ground that the decision of the court which sent him to the Crown Court for trial as to the value involved was mistaken.

(4) In subsection (3) above 'scheduled offence' and 'the value involved' have the same meanings as they have in section 22 of the Magistrates' Courts Act 1980 (certain offences against property to be tried summarily if value of property or damage is small).

2. Grounds for allowing appeal under s 1

(1) Subject to the provisions of this Act, the Court of Appeal—
   (a) shall allow an appeal against conviction if they think that the conviction is unsafe; and
   (b) shall dismiss such an appeal in any other case.

(2) In the case of an appeal against conviction the Court shall, if they allow the appeal, quash the conviction.

(3) An order of the Court of Appeal quashing a conviction shall, except when under section 7 below the appellant is ordered to be retried, operate as a direction to the court of trial to enter, instead of the record of conviction, a judgment and verdict of acquittal.

3. Power to substitute conviction of alternative offence

(1) This section applies on an appeal against conviction, where the appellant has been convicted of an offence to which he did not plead guilty and the jury could on the indictment have found him guilty of some other offence, and on the finding of the jury it appears to the Court of Appeal that the jury must have been satisfied of facts which proved him guilty of the other offence.

(2) The Court may, instead of allowing or dismissing the appeal, substitute for the verdict found by the jury a verdict of guilty of the other offence, and pass such sentence in substitution for the sentence passed at the trial as may be authorised by law for the other offence, not being a sentence of greater severity.

7. Power to order retrial

(1) Where the Court of Appeal allow an appeal against conviction and it appears to the Court that the interests of justice so require, they may order the appellant to be retried.

(2) A person shall not under this section be ordered to be retried for any offence other than—
   (a) the offence of which he was convicted at the original trial and in respect of which his appeal is allowed as mentioned in subsection (1) above;
   (b) an offence of which he could have been convicted at the original trial on an indictment for the first-mentioned offence; or
   (c) an offence charged in an alternative count of the indictment in respect of which no verdict was given in consequence of his being convicted of the first-mentioned offence.

8. Supplementary provisions as to retrial

(1) A person who is to be retried for an offence in pursuance of an order under section 7 of this Act shall be tried on a fresh indictment preferred by direction of the Court of Appeal, … but after the end of two months from the date of the order for his retrial he may not be arraigned on an indictment preferred in pursuance of such a direction unless the Court of Appeal give leave.

(1A) Where a person has been ordered to be retried but may not be arraigned without leave, he may apply to the Court of Appeal to set aside the order for retrial and to direct the court of trial to enter a judgment and verdict of acquittal of the offence for which he was ordered to be retried.

(1B) On an application under subsection (1) or (1A) above the Court of Appeal shall have power—
   (a) to grant leave to arraign; or
   (b) to set aside the order for retrial and direct the entry of a judgment and verdict of acquittal, but shall not give leave to arraign unless they are satisfied—
      (i) that the prosecution has acted with all due expedition; and
      (ii) that there is a good and sufficient cause for a retrial in spite of the lapse of time since the order under section 7 of this Act was made.

(2)   The Court of Appeal may, on ordering a retrial, make such orders as appear to them to be necessary or expedient—

(a)   for the custody or, subject to section 25 of the Criminal Justice and Public Order Act 1994, release on bail of the person ordered to be retried pending his retrial; or

(b)   for the retention pending the retrial of any property or money forfeited, restored or paid by virtue of the original conviction or any order made on that conviction.

...

(4)   Schedule 2 to this Act has effect with respect to the procedure in the case of a person ordered to be retried, the sentence which may be passed if the retrial results in his conviction and the order for costs which may be made if he is acquitted.

9.   Appeal against sentence following conviction on indictment

(1)   A person who has been convicted of an offence on indictment may appeal to the Court of Appeal against any sentence (not being a sentence fixed by law) passed on him for the offence, whether passed on his conviction or in subsequent proceedings.

(1A)   In subsection (1) of this section, the reference to a section fixed by law does not include a reference to an order made under subsection (2) or (4) of section 269 of the Criminal Justice Act 2003 in relation to a life sentence (as defined in section 227 of that Act) that is fixed by law.

...

11.   Supplementary provisions as to appeal against sentence

(1)   Subject to subsection (1A) below, an appeal against sentence, whether under section 9 or under section 10 of this Act, lies only with the leave of the Court of Appeal.

(1A)   If, within 28 days from the date on which sentence was passed, the judge who passed the sentence grants a certificate that the case is fit for appeal under section 9 or 10 of this Act, an appeal lies under this section without the leave of the Court of Appeal.

(2)   Where the Crown Court, in dealing with an offender either on his conviction on indictment or in a proceeding to which section 10(2) of this Act applies, has passed on him two or more sentences in the same proceeding (which expression has the same meaning in this subsection as it has for the purposes of section 10), being sentences against which an appeal lies under section 9 (1) or section 10, an appeal or application for leave to appeal against any one of those sentences shall be treated as an appeal or application in respect of both or all of them.

...

(3)   On an appeal against sentence the Court of Appeal, if they consider that the appellant should be sentenced differently for an offence for which he was dealt with by the court below may—

(a)   quash any sentence or order which is the subject of the appeal; an1

(b)   in place of it pass such sentence or make such order as they think appropriate for the case and as the court below had power to pass or make when dealing with him for the offence;

but the Court shall so exercise their powers under this subsection that, taking the case as a whole, the appellant is not more severely dealt with on appeal than he was dealt with by the court below.

...

18.   Initiating procedure

(1)   A person who wishes to appeal under this Part of this Act to the Court of Appeal, or to obtain the leave of that court to appeal, shall give notice of appeal or, as the case may be, notice of application for leave to appeal, in such manner as may be directed by rules of court.

(2)   Notice of appeal, or of application for leave to appeal, shall be given within twenty-eight days from the date of the conviction, verdict or finding appealed against, or in the case of appeal against sentence, from the date on which sentence was passed or, in the case of an order made or treated as made on conviction, from the date of the making of the order.

(3)   The time for giving notice under this section may be extended, either before or after it expires, by the Court of Appeal.

23.   Evidence

(1)   For the purposes of an appeal, or an application for leave to appeal, under this Part of this Act the Court of Appeal may, if they think it necessary or expedient in the interests of justice—

(a)   order the production of any document, exhibit or other thing connected with the proceedings, the production of which appears to them necessary for the determination of the case;

(b)   order any witness to attend for examination and be examined before the Court (whether or not he was called in the proceedings from which the appeal lies); and

(c)   receive any evidence which was not adduced in the proceedings from which the appeal lies.

(1A) ...

(2)   The Court of Appeal shall, in considering whether to receive any evidence, have regard in particular to—

(a)   whether the evidence appears to the Court to be capable of belief;

(b)   whether it appears to the Court that the evidence may afford any ground for allowing the appeal;

(c)   whether the evidence would have been admissible in the proceedings from which the appeal lies on an issue which is the subject of the appeal; and

(d)   whether there is a reasonable explanation for the failure to adduce the evidence in those proceedings.

(3)   Subsection (1)(c) above applies to any evidence of a witness (including the appellant) who is competent but not compellable ....

...

23A.   Power to order investigations

(1)   On an appeal against conviction or an application for leave to appeal the Court of Appeal may direct the Criminal Cases Review Commission to investigate and report to the Court on any matter if it appears to the Court that—

(a)   in the case of an appeal, the matter is relevant to the determination of the case and ought, if possible, to be resolved before the case is determined;

(aa)   in the case of an application for leave to appeal, the matter is relevant to the determination of the application and ought if possible to be resolved before the application is determined;

(b)   an investigation of the matter by the Commission is likely to result in the Court being able to resolve it; and

(c)   the matter cannot be resolved by the Court without an investigation by the Commission.

(1A) A direction under subsection (1) above may not be given by a single judge ...

...

(4)   Where the Commission have reported to the Court of Appeal on any matter which they have been directed under subsection (1) above to investigate, the Court—

(a)   shall notify the appellant and the respondent that the Commission have reported; and

(b)   may make available to the appellant and the respondent the report of the Commission and any statements, opinions and reports which accompanied it.

(5)   ...

33.   Right of appeal to Supreme Court

(1)   An appeal lies to the Supreme Court, at the instance of the defendant or the prosecutor, from any decision of the Court of Appeal on an appeal to that court under Part I of this Act or Part 9 of the Criminal Justice Act 2003 or section 9 (preparatory hearings) of the Criminal Justice Act 1987 or section 35 of the Criminal Procedure and Investigations Act 1996 or section 47 of the Criminal Justice Act 2003.

(1A) An appeal lies to the Supreme Court, at the instance of the acquitted person or the prosecutor, from any decision of the Court of Appeal on an application under section 76(1) or (2) of the Criminal Justice Act 2003 (retrial for serious offences).

(2) The appeal lies only with the leave of the Court of Appeal or the Supreme Court; and leave shall not be granted unless it is certified by the Court of Appeal that a point of law of general public importance is involved in the decision and it appears to the Court of Appeal or the Supreme Court (as the case may be) that the point is one which ought to be considered by the Supreme Court.

(3) Except as provided by this Part of this Act and section 13 of the Administration of Justice Act 1960 (appeal in cases of contempt of court), no appeal shall lie from any decision of the criminal division of the Court of Appeal.

34. Application for leave to appeal

(1) An application to the Court of Appeal for leave to appeal to the Supreme Court shall be made within the period of 28 days beginning with the relevant date; and an application to the Supreme Court for leave to appeal shall be made within the period of 28 days beginning with the date on which the application for leave is refused by the Court of Appeal.

(1A) In subsection (1) the 'relevant date' means—

(a) the date of the Court of Appeal's decision; or

(b) if later, the date on which the Court of Appeal gave reasons for its decision.

...

49. Saving for prerogative of mercy

Nothing in this Act is to be taken as affecting Her Majesty's prerogative of mercy.

50. Meaning of 'sentence'

(1) In this Act 'sentence', in relation to an offence, includes any order made by a court when dealing with an offender including, in particular—

(a) a hospital order under Part III of the Mental Health Act 1983, with or without a restriction order;

(b) an interim hospital order under that Part;

(bb) a hospital direction and a limitation direction under that Part;

(ca) a confiscation order under Part 2 of the Proceeds of Crime Act 2002;

(cb) an order which varies a confiscation order made under Part 2 of the Proceeds of Crime Act 2002 ...;

(c) a recommendation for deportation;

(d) a confiscation order under the Drug Trafficking Act 1994 other than one made by the High Court;

(e) a confiscation order under Part VI of the Criminal Justice Act 1988;

(f) an order varying a confiscation order of a kind which is included by virtue of paragraph (d) or (e) above;

(g) an order made by the Crown Court varying a confiscation order which was made by the High Court by virtue of section 19 of the Act of 1994;

(h) a declaration of relevance within the meaning of section 23 of the Football Spectators Act 1989; and

(i) an order under section 129(2) of the Licensing Act 203 (forfeiture or suspension of personal licence).

(1A) Section 14 of the Powers of Criminal Courts (Sentencing) Act (under which a conviction of an offence for which ... an order for a conditional or absolute discharge is made is deemed not to be a conviction except for certain purposes) shall not prevent an appeal under this Act, whether against conviction or otherwise.

(2) Any power of the criminal division of the Court of Appeal to pass a sentence includes a power to make a recommendation for deportation in cases where the court from which the appeal lies had power to make such a recommendation.

(3) An order relating to a requirement to make a payment under regulations under section 23 or 24 of the Legal Aid, Sentencing and Punishment of Offenders Act 2012 is not a sentence for the purposes of this Act.

CRIMINAL APPEAL ACT 1995
(1995, c. 35)

8. The Commission

(1) There shall be a body corporate to be known as the Criminal Cases Review Commission.

(2) The Commission shall not be regarded as the servant or agent of the Crown or as enjoying any status, immunity or privilege of the Crown; and the Commission's property shall not be regarded as property of, or held on behalf of, the Crown.

(3) The Commission shall consist of not fewer than eleven members.

(4) The members of the Commission shall be appointed by Her Majesty on the recommendation of the Prime Minister.

(5) At least one third of the members of the Commission shall be persons who are legally qualified; and for this purpose a person is legally qualified if—

    (a) he has a ten year general qualification, within the meaning of section 71 of the Courts and Legal Services Act 1990, or

    (b) he is a member of the Bar of Northern Ireland, or solicitor of the Supreme Court of Northern Ireland, of at least ten years' standing.

(6) At least two thirds of the members of the Commission shall be persons who appear to the Prime Minister to have knowledge or experience of any aspect of the criminal justice system and of them at least one shall be a person who appears to him to have knowledge or experience of any aspect of the criminal justice system in Northern Ireland; and for the purposes of this subsection the criminal justice system includes, in particular, the investigation of offences and the treatment of offenders.

(7) Schedule 1 (further provisions with respect to the Commission) shall have effect.

9. Cases dealt with on indictment in England and Wales

(1) Where a person has been convicted of an offence on indictment in England and Wales, the Commission—

    (a) may at any time refer the conviction to the Court of Appeal, and

    (b) (whether or not they refer the conviction) may at any time refer to the Court of Appeal any sentence (not being a sentence fixed by law) imposed on, or in subsequent proceedings relating to, the conviction.

(2) A reference under subsection (1) of a person's conviction shall be treated for all purposes as an appeal by the person under section1 of the 1968 Act against the conviction.

(3) A reference under subsection (1) of a sentence imposed on, or in subsequent proceedings relating to, a person's conviction on an indictment shall be treated for all purposes as an appeal by the person under section 9 of the 1968 Act against—

    (a) the sentence, and

    (b) any other sentence (not being a sentence fixed by law) imposed on, or in subsequent proceedings relating to, the conviction or any other conviction on the indictment.

(4) On a reference under subsection (1) of a person's conviction on an indictment the Commission may give notice to the Court of Appeal that any other conviction on the indictment which is specified in the notice is to be treated as referred to the Court of Appeal under subsection (1).

(5) Where a verdict of not guilty by reason of insanity has been returned in England and Wales in the case of a person, the Commission may at any time refer the verdict to the Court of Appeal; and a reference under this subsection shall be treated for all purposes as an appeal by the person under section 12 of the 1968 Act against the verdict.

(6) Where in England and Wales there have been findings that a person is under a disability and that he did the act or made the omission charged against him, the Commission may at any time refer either or both of those findings to the Court of Appeal; and a reference under this subsection shall be treated for all purposes as an appeal by the person under section 15 of the 1968 Act against the finding or findings referred.

13. Conditions for making of references

(1) A reference of a conviction, verdict, finding or sentence shall not be made under any of sections 9 to 12 unless—

> (a)   the Commission consider that there is a real possibility that the conviction, verdict, finding or sentence would not be upheld were the reference to be made,
> (b)   the Commission so consider—
>   (i)   in the case of a conviction, verdict or finding, because of an argument, or evidence, not raised in the proceedings which led to it or on any appeal or application for leave to appeal against it, or
>   (ii)   in the case of a sentence, because of an argument on a point of law, or information, not so raised, and
> (c)   an appeal against the conviction, verdict, finding or sentence has been determined or leave to appeal against it has been refused.
>
> (2)   Nothing in subsection (1)(b)(i) or (c) shall prevent the making of a reference if it appears to the Commission that there are exceptional circumstances which justify making it.

CRIMINAL JUSTICE ACT 1967
(1967, c. 80)

9.   Proof by written statement

(1)   In any criminal proceedings, a written statement by any person shall, if such of the conditions mentioned in the next following subsection as are applicable are satisfied, be admissible as evidence to the like extent as oral evidence to the like effect by that person.

(2)   The said conditions are—

(a)   the statement purports to be signed by the person who made it;

(b)   the statement contains a declaration by that person to the effect that it is true to the best of his knowledge and belief and that he made the statement knowing that, if it were tendered in evidence, he would be liable to prosecution if he wilfully stated in it anything which he knew to be false or did not believe to be true;

(c)   before the hearing at which the statement is tendered in evidence, a copy of the statement is served, by or on behalf of the party proposing to tender it, on each of the other parties to the proceedings; and

(d)   none of the other parties or their solicitors, within the relevant period, serves a notice on the party so proposing objecting to the statement being tendered in evidence under this section:

Provided that the conditions mentioned in paragraphs (c) and (d) of this subsection shall not apply if the parties agree before or during the hearing that the statement shall be so tendered.

(2A)   For the purposes of subsection (2)(d), 'the relevant period' is—

(a)   such number of days, which may not be less than seven, from the service of the copy of the statement as may be prescribed by Criminal Procedure Rules, or

(b)   if no such number is prescribed, seven days from the service of the copy of the statement.

10.   Proof by formal admission

(1)   Subject to the provisions of this section, any fact of which oral evidence may be given in any criminal proceedings may be admitted for the purpose of those proceedings by or on behalf of the prosecutor or defendant, and the admission by any party of any such fact under this section shall as against that party be conclusive evidence in those proceedings of the fact admitted.

(2)   An admission under this section—

(a)   may be made before or at the proceedings;

(b)   if made otherwise than in court, shall be in writing;

(c)   if made in writing by an individual, shall purport to be signed by the person making it and, if so made by a body corporate, shall purport to be signed by a director or manager, or the secretary or clerk, or some other similar officer of the body corporate;

(d)   if made on behalf of a defendant who is an individual, shall be made by his counsel or solicitor;

(e)   if made at any state before the trial by a defendant who is an individual, must be approved by his counsel or solicitor (whether at the time it was made or subsequently) before or at the proceedings in question.

(3)   An admission under this section for the purpose of proceedings relating to any matter shall be treated as an admission for the purpose of any subsequent criminal proceedings relating to that matter (including any appeal or retrial).

(4)   An admission under this section may with the leave of the court be withdrawn in the proceedings for the purpose of which it is made or any subsequent criminal proceedings relating to the same matter.

CRIMINAL JUSTICE ACT 1972
(1972, c. 71)

36.   Reference to Court of Appeal of point of law following acquittal on indictment

(1)   Where a person tried on indictment has been acquitted (whether in respect of the whole or part of the indictment) the Attorney General may, if he desires the opinion of the Court of Appeal on a point of law which has arisen in the case, refer that point to the court, and the court shall, in accordance with this section, consider the point and give their opinion on it.

(2)   For the purpose of their consideration of a point referred to them under this section the Court of Appeal shall hear argument—
    (a)   by, or by counsel on behalf of, the Attorney General; and
    (b)   if the acquitted person desires to present any argument to the court, by counsel on his behalf or, with the leave of the court, by the acquitted person himself.

(3)   Where the Court of Appeal have given their opinion on a point referred to them under this section, the court may, of their own motion or in pursuance of an application in that behalf, refer the point to the Supreme Court if it appears to the Court of Appeal that the point ought to be considered by the Supreme Court.

...

(7)   A reference under this section shall not affect the trial in relation to which the reference is made or any acquittal in that trial.

CRIMINAL JUSTICE ACT 1988
(1988, c. 33)

35.   Scope of Part IV

(1)   A case to which this Part of this Act applies may be referred to the Court of Appeal under section 36 below.

(2)   Subject to Rules of Court, the jurisdiction of the Court of Appeal under section 36 below shall be exercised by the criminal division of the Court, and references to the Court of Appeal in this Part of this Act shall be construed as references to that division.

(3)   This Part of this Act applies to any case—
    (a)   of a description specified in an order under this section; or
    (b)   in which sentence is passed on a person—
        (i)   for an offence triable only on indictment; or
        (ii)   for an offence of a description specified in an order under this section.

(4)   The Secretary of State may by order made by statutory instrument provide that this Part of this Act shall apply to any case of a description specified in the order or to any case in which sentence is passed on a person for an offence triable either way of a description specified in the order.

...

(6)   In this Part of this Act 'sentence' has the same meaning as in the Criminal Appeal Act 1968, except that it does not include an interim hospital order under Part III of the Mental Health Act 1983, and 'sentencing' shall be construed accordingly.

...

36.   Reviews of sentencing

(1)   If it appears to the Attorney General—
 (a) that the sentencing of a person in a proceeding in the Crown Court has been unduly lenient; and
 (b) that the case is one to which this Part of this Act applies,
he may, with the leave of the Court of Appeal, refer the case to them for them to review the sentencing of that person; and on such a reference the Court of Appeal may—
 (i) quash any sentence passed on him in the proceeding; and
 (ii) in place of it pass such sentence as they think appropriate for the case and as the court below had power to pass when dealing with him.

(2)   Without prejudice to the generality of subsection (1) above, the condition specified in paragraph (a) of that subsection may be satisfied if it appears to the Attorney General that the judge—
 (a) erred in law as to his powers of sentencing; or
 (b) failed to impose a sentence required by—
  (zi) section 1(2B) or 1A(5) of the Prevention of Crime Act 1953;
  (i) section 51A(2) of the Firearms Act 1968;
  (ia) section 139(6B), 139(5B) or 139AA(7) of this Act;
  (ii) section 110(2) or 111(2) of the Powers of Criminal Courts (Sentencing) Act 2000; ...
  (iii) section 224A, 225(2) or 226(2) of the Criminal Justice Act 2003.
  or
  (iv) under section 29(4) or (6) of the Violent Crime Reduction Act 2006.

(3)   For the purposes of this Part of this Act any two or more sentences are to be treated as passed in the same proceeding if they would be so treated for the purposes of section 11 of the Criminal Appeal Act 1968.

(3A) Where a reference under this section relates to an order under subsection (2) of section 269 of the Criminal Justice Act 2003 (determination of minimum term in relation to mandatory life sentence), the Court of Appeal shall not, in deciding what order under that section is appropriate for the case, make any allowance for the fact that the person to whom it relates is being sentenced for a second time.

(4)   No judge shall sit as a member of the Court of Appeal on the hearing of, or shall determine any application in proceedings incidental or preliminary to, a reference under this section of a sentence passed by himself.

(5)   Where the Court of Appeal have concluded their review of a case referred to them under this section the Attorney General or the person to whose sentencing the reference relates may refer a point of law involved in any sentence passed on that person in the proceeding to the Supreme Court for its opinion, and the Supreme Court shall consider the point and give its opinion on it accordingly, and either remit the case to the Court of Appeal to be dealt with or itself deal with the case.

(6)   A reference under subsection (5) above shall be made only with the leave of the Court of Appeal or the Supreme Court; and leave shall not be granted unless it is certified by the Court of Appeal that the point of law is of general public importance and it appears to the Court of Appeal or the Supreme Court (as the case may be) that the point is one which ought to be considered by the Supreme Court.

(7)   For the purpose of dealing with a case under this section the Supreme Court may exercise any powers of the Court of Appeal.

(8)   The supplementary provisions contained in Schedule 3 to this Act shall have effect.
 ...

139.   Offence of having article with blade or point in public place

(1)   Subject to subsections (4) and (5) below, any person who has an article to which this section applies with him in a public place shall be guilty of an offence.

(2)   Subject to subsection (3) below, this section applies to any article which has a blade or is sharply pointed except a folding pocketknife.

(3)   This section applies to a folding pocketknife if the cutting edge of its blade exceeds three inches.

(4)   It shall be a defence for a person charged with an offence under this section to prove that he had good reason or lawful authority for having the article with him in a public place.

(5)   Without prejudice to the generality of subsection (4) above, it shall be a defence for a person charged with an offence under this section to prove that he had the article with him—
   (a)   for use at work;
   (b)   for religious reasons; or
   (c)   as part of any national costume.

(6)   A person guilty of an offence under subsection (1) above shall be liable—
   (a)   on summary conviction, to imprisonment for a term not exceeding six months, or a fine, or both;
   (b)   on conviction on indictment, to imprisonment for a term not exceeding 4 years, or a fine, or both.

(6A) Subsection (6B) applies where—
   (a)   a person is convicted of an offence under subsection (1) by a court in England and Wales,
   (b)   the offence was committed after this subsection is commenced, and
   (c)   when the offence was committed, the person was aged 16 or over and had at least one relevant conviction (see section 139AZA).

(6B) Where this subsection applies, the court must impose an appropriate custodial sentence (with or without a fine) unless the court is of the opinion that there are particular circumstances which—
   (a)   relate to the offence, to the previous offence or to the offender, and
   (b)   would make it unjust to do so in all the circumstances.

(6C) In this section 'appropriate custodial sentence' means—
   (a)   in the case of a person who is aged 18 or over when convicted, a sentence of imprisonment for a term of at least 6 months;
   (b)   in the case of a person who is aged at least 16 but under 18 when convicted, a detention and training order of at least 4 months.

(6D) In considering whether it is of the opinion mentioned in subsection (6B) in the case of a person aged 16 or 17, the court must have regard to its duty under section 44 of the Children and Young Persons Act 1933 (general considerations).

(7)   In this section 'public place' means any place to which at the material time the public have or are permitted access, whether on payment or otherwise.
   …

139A. Offence of having article with blade or point (or offensive weapon) on school premises

(1)   Any person who has an article to which section 139 of this Act applies with him on school premises shall be guilty of an offence.

(2)   Any person who has an offensive weapon within the meaning of section 1 of the Prevention of Crime Act 1953 with him on school premises shall be guilty of an offence.

(3)   It shall be a defence for a person charged with an offence under subsection (1) or (2) above to prove that he had good reason or lawful authority for having the article with him on the premises in question.

(4)   Without prejudice to the generality of subsection (4) above, it shall be a defence for a person charged with an offence under this section to prove that he had the article with him—
   (a)   for use at work;
   (b)   for educational purposes;
   (c)   for religious reasons; or
   (d)   as part of any national costume.

(5)   A person guilty of an offence—
   (a)   under subsection (1) above shall be liable
      (i)   on summary conviction, to imprisonment for a term not exceeding six months, or a fine, or both;
      (ii)   on conviction on indictment, to imprisonment for a term not exceeding 4 years, or a fine, or both.
   (b)   under subsection (2) above shall be liable—
      (i)   on summary conviction, to imprisonment for a term not exceeding six

months, or a fine, or both;

    (ii) on conviction on indictment, to imprisonment for a term not exceeding 4 years, or a fine, or both.

(5A) Subsection (5B) applies where—

    (a) a person is convicted of an offence under subsection (1) or (2) by a court in England and Wales,

    (b) the offence was committed after this subsection is commenced, and

    (c) when the offence was committed, the person was aged 16 or over and had at least one relevant conviction (see section 139AZA).

(5B) Where this subsection applies, the court must impose an appropriate custodial sentence (with or without a fine) unless the court is of the opinion that there are particular circumstances which—

    (a) relate to the offence, to the previous offence or to the offender, and

    (b) would make it unjust to do so in all the circumstances.

(5C) In this section 'appropriate custodial sentence' means—

    (a) in the case of a person who is aged 18 or over when convicted, a sentence of imprisonment for a term of at least 6 months;

    (b) in the case of a person who is aged at least 16 but under 18 when convicted, a detention and training order of at least 4 months.

(5D) In considering whether it is of the opinion mentioned in subsection (5B) in the case of a person aged 16 or 17, the court must have regard to its duty under section 44 of the Children and Young Persons Act 1933 (general considerations).

(6) In this section and section 139B 'school premises' means land used for the purposes of school excluding land occupied solely as a dwelling by a person employed at the school; and 'school' has the meaning given by section 4(1) of the Education Act 1996.

...

139AA. Offence of threatening with article with blade or point or offensive weapon

(1) A person is guilty of an offence if that person—

    (a) has an article to which this section applies with him or her in a public place or on school premises,

    (b) unlawfully and intentionally threatens another person with the article, and

    (c) does so in such a way that there is an immediate risk of serious physical harm to that other person.

(2) In relation to a public place this section applies to an article to which section 139 applies.

(3) In relation to school premises the section applies to each of these—

    (a) an article to which section 139 applies;

    (b) an offensive weapon within the meaning of section 1 of the Prevention of Crime Act 1953.

(4) For the purposes of this section physical harm is serious if it amounts to grievous bodily harm for the purposes of the Offences against the Person Act 1981.

(5) In this section—

'public place' has the same meaning as in section 139;

'school premises' has the same meaning as in section 139A.

(6) A person guilty of an offence under this section is liable—

    (a) on summary conviction, to imprisonment for a term not exceeding 12 months or to a fine not exceeding the statutory maximum, or to both;

    (b) on conviction on indictment, to imprisonment for a term not exceeding 4 years or to a fine, or to both.

(7) Where a person is aged 16 or over is convicted of an offence under this section, the court must impose an appropriate custodial sentence (with or without a fine) unless the court is of the opinion that there are particular circumstances which—

    (a) relate to the offence or to the offender, and

    (b) would make it unjust to do so in all the circumstances.

(8) In this section 'appropriate custodial sentence' means—

    (a) in the case of a person who is aged 18 and over when convicted, a sentence of imprisonment for a term of at least 6 months;

    (b)   in the case of a person who is aged at least 16 but under 18 when convicted, a detention and training order of at least 4 months.

(9)   In considering whether it is of the opinion mentioned in subsection (5) in the case of a person aged under 18, the court must have regard to its duty under section 44 of the Children and Young Persons Act 1933.

…

139AZA. Offences under section 139 and 139A: previous relevant convictions

(1)   For the purposes of sections 139 and 139A, 'relevant conviction' means—
    (a)   a conviction for an offence under—
        (i)   section 1 or 1A of the Prevention of Crime Act 1953, or
        (ii)   section 139, 139A or 139AA of this Act,
    (a 'relevant offence'), whenever committed.

…

…

139B. Power of entry to search for articles with a blade or point and offensive weapons

(1)   A constable may enter school premises and search those premises and any person on those premises for—
    (a)   any article to which section 139 of this Act applies, or
    (b)   any offensive weapon within the meaning of section 1 of the Prevention of Crime Act 1953,
    if he has reasonable grounds for suspecting that an offence under section 139A or 139AA of this Act is being, or has been, committed.

(2)   If in the course of a search under this section a constable discovers an article or weapon which he has reasonable grounds for suspecting to be an article or weapon of a kind described in subsection (1) above, he may seize and retain it.

(3)   The constable may use reasonable force, if necessary, in the exercise of the power of entry conferred by this section.

…

CRIMINAL JUSTICE ACT 2003
(2003, c. 44)

22.   Conditional cautions

(1)   An authorised person may give a conditional caution to a person aged 18 or over ('the offender') if each of the five requirements in section 23 is satisfied.

(2)   In this Part 'conditional caution' means a caution which is given in respect of an offence committed by the offender and which has conditions attached to it with which the offender must comply.

(3)   The conditions which may be attached to such a caution are those which have one or more of the following objects—
    (a)   facilitating the rehabilitation of the offender;
    (b)   ensuring that the offender makes reparation for the offence;
    (c)   punishing the offender.

(3A)   The conditions which may be attached to a conditional caution include—
    (a)   (subject to section 23A) a condition that the offender pay a financial penalty;
    (b)   a condition that the offender attend at a specified place at specified times.
    'Specified' means specified in the condition.

(4)   In this Part 'authorised person' means—
    (a)   a constable,
    (b)   an investigating officer, or
    (c)   a person authorised by a relevant prosecutor for the purposes of this section.

23.   The five requirements

(1)   The first requirement is that the authorised person has evidence that the offender has committed an offence.

(2) The second requirement is that a relevant prosecutor or the authorised person decides—
   (a)   that there is sufficient evidence to charge the offender with the offence, and
   (b)   that a conditional caution should be given to the offender in respect of the offence.
(3) The third requirement is that the offender admits to the authorised person that he committed the offence.
(4) The fourth requirement is that the authorised person explains the effect of the conditional caution to the offender and warns him that failure to comply with any of the conditions attached to the caution may result in his being prosecuted for the offence.
(5) The fifth requirement is that the offender signs a document which contains—
   (a)   details of the offence,
   (b)   an admission by him that he committed the offence,
   (c)   his consent to being given the conditional caution, and
   (d)   the conditions attached to the caution.

23ZA. Duty to consult victims

(1) Before deciding what conditions to attach to a conditional caution, a relevant prosecutor or the authorised person must make reasonable efforts to obtain the views of the victim (if any) of the offence, and in particular the victim's views as to whether the offender should carry out any of the actions listed in the community remedy document.
(2) If the victim expresses the view that the offender should carry out a particular action listed in the community remedy document, the prosecutor or authorised person must attach that as a condition unless it seems to the prosecutor or authorised person that it would be inappropriate to do so.
(3) Where—
   (a)   there is more than one victim and they express different views, or
   (b)   for any other reason subsection (2) does not apply,
   the prosecutor or authorised person must nevertheless take account of any views expressed by the victim (or victims) in deciding what conditions to attach to the conditional caution.
(4) In this section—
   'community remedy document' means the community remedy document (as revised from time to time) published under section 101 of the Anti-social Behaviour, Crime and Policing Act 2014 for the police area in which the offence was committed;
   'victim' means the particular person who seems to the relevant prosecutor or authorised person to have been affected, or principally affected, by the offence.

23A. Financial penalties

(1) A condition that the offender pay a financial penalty (a 'financial penalty condition') may not be attached to a conditional caution given in respect of an offence unless the offence is one that is prescribed, or of a description prescribed, in an order made by the Secretary of State.
(2) An order under subsection (1) must prescribe, in respect of each offence or description of offence in the order, the maximum amount of the penalty that may be specified under subsection (5)(a).
(3) The amount that may be prescribed in respect of any offence (other than one to which subsection (4A) applies) must not exceed—
   (a)   one quarter of the amount of the maximum fine for which a person is liable on summary conviction of the offence, or
   (b)   £250,
   whichever is the lower.
(4) The Secretary of State may by order amend subsection (3) by—
   (a)   substituting a different fraction in paragraph (a);
   (b)   substituting a different figure in paragraph (b).
(4A) In the case of an offence for which the person is liable on summary conviction to a fine of an unlimited amount, the amount that may be prescribed must not exceed the amount for the time being specified in subsection (3)(b).
(5) Where a financial penalty condition is attached to a conditional caution, the condition must also specify—

(a)   the amount of the penalty,

(b)   the person to whom the financial penalty is to be paid and how it may be paid.

(6)   To comply with the condition, the offender must pay the penalty in accordance with the provision specified under subsection (5)(b).

(6A)   Where a financial penalty is (in accordance with the provision specified under subsection (5)(b)) paid to a person other than a designated officer for a local justice area, the person to whom it is paid must give the payment to such an officer.

23B. Variation of conditions

A relevant prosecutor or an authorised person may, with the consent of the offender, vary the conditions attached to a conditional caution by—

(a)   modifying or omitting any of the conditions;

(b)   adding a condition.

24. Failure to comply with conditions

(1)   If the offender fails, without reasonable excuse, to comply with any of the conditions attached to the conditional caution, criminal proceedings may be instituted against the person for the offence in question.

(2)   The document mentioned in section 23(5) is to be admissible in such proceedings.

(3)   Where such proceedings are instituted, the conditional caution is to cease to have effect.

44. Application by prosecution for trial to be conducted without a jury where danger of jury tampering

(1)   This section applies where one or more defendants are to be tried on indictment for one or more offences.

(2)   The prosecution may apply to a judge of the Crown Court for the trial to be conducted without a jury.

(3)   If an application under subsection (2) is made and the judge is satisfied that both of the following two conditions are fulfilled, he must make an order that the trial is to be conducted without a jury; but if he is not so satisfied he must refuse the application.

(4)   The first condition is that there is evidence of a real and present danger that jury tampering would take place.

(5)   The second condition is that, notwithstanding any steps (including the provision of police protection) which might reasonably be taken to prevent jury tampering, the likelihood that it would take place would be so substantial as to make it necessary in the interests of justice for the trial to be conducted without a jury.

(6)   The following are examples of cases where there may be evidence of a real and present danger that jury tampering would take place—

(a)   a case where the trial is a retrial and the jury in the previous trial was discharged because jury tampering had taken place,

(b)   a case where jury tampering has taken place in previous criminal proceedings involving the defendant or any of the defendants,

(c)   a case where there has been intimidation, or attempted intimidation, of any person who is likely to be a witness in the trial.

45. Procedure for applications under section 44

(1)   This section applies—

...

(b)   to an application under section 44.

(2)   An application to which this section applies must be determined at a preparatory hearing (within the meaning of the 1987 Act or Part 3 of the 1996 Act).

(3)   The parties to a preparatory hearing at which an application to which this section applies is to be determined must be given an opportunity to make representations with respect to the application.

(4)   ...

46. Discharge of jury because of jury tampering

(1)   This section applies where—

(a)   a judge is minded during a trial on indictment to discharge the jury, and

(b)   he is so minded because jury tampering appears to have taken place.

(2) Before taking any steps to discharge the jury, the judge must—
(a) inform the parties that he is minded to discharge the jury,
(b) inform the parties of the grounds on which he is so minded, and
(c) allow the parties an opportunity to make representations.
(3) Where the judge, after considering any such representations, discharges the jury, he may make an order that the trial is to continue without a jury if, but only if, he is satisfied—
(a) that jury tampering has taken place, and
(b) that to continue the trial without a jury would be fair to the defendant or defendants; but this is subject to subsection (4).
(4) If the judge considers that it is necessary in the interests of justice for the trial to be terminated, he must terminate the trial.
(5) Where the judge terminates the trial under subsection (4), he may make an order that any new trial which is to take place must be conducted without a jury if he is satisfied in respect of the new trial that both of the conditions set out in section 44 are likely to be fulfilled.
(6) Subsection (5) is without prejudice to any other power that the judge may have on terminating the trial.
(7) Subject to subsection (5), nothing in this section affects the application of section 44 in relation to any new trial which takes place following the termination of the trial.

75.   Cases that may be retried

(1) This Part applies where a person has been acquitted of a qualifying offence in proceedings—
(a) on indictment in England and Wales,
(b) on appeal against a conviction, verdict or finding in proceedings on indictment in England and Wales, or
(c) on appeal from a decision on such an appeal.
(2) A person acquitted of an offence in proceedings mentioned in subsection (1) is treated for the purposes of that subsection as also acquitted of any qualifying offence of which he could have been convicted in the proceedings because of the first-mentioned offence being charged in the indictment, except an offence—
(a) of which he has been convicted,
(b) of which he has been found not guilty by reason of insanity, or
(c) in respect of which, in proceedings where he has been found to be under a disability (as defined by section 4 of the Criminal Procedure (Insanity) Act 1964), a finding has been made that he did the act or made the omission charged against him.
(3) References in subsections (1) and (2) to a qualifying offence do not include references to an offence which, at the time of the acquittal, was the subject of an order under section 77(1) or (3).
(4) This Part also applies where a person has been acquitted, in proceedings elsewhere than in the United Kingdom, of an offence under the law of the place where the proceedings were held, if the commission of the offence as alleged would have amounted to or included the commission (in the United Kingdom or elsewhere) of a qualifying offence.
(5) Conduct punishable under the law in force elsewhere than in the United Kingdom is an offence under that law for the purposes of subsection (4), however it is described in that law.
(6) This Part applies whether the acquittal was before or after the passing of this Act.
(7) References in this Part to acquittal are to acquittal in circumstances within subsection (1) or (4).
(8) In this Part 'qualifying offence' means an offence listed in Part 1 of Schedule 5.

76.   Application to Court of Appeal

(1) A prosecutor may apply to the Court of Appeal for an order—
(a) quashing a person's acquittal in proceedings within section 75(1), and
(b) ordering him to be retried for the qualifying offence.
(2) A prosecutor may apply to the Court of Appeal, in the case of a person acquitted elsewhere than in the United Kingdom, for—

   (a)   a determination whether the acquittal is a bar to the person being tried in England and Wales for the qualifying offence, and

   (b)   if it is, an order that the acquittal is not to be a bar.

(3)   A prosecutor may make an application under subsection (1) or (2) only with the written consent of the Director of Public Prosecutions.

(4)   The Director of Public Prosecutions may give his consent only if satisfied that—

   (a)   there is evidence as respects which the requirements of section 78 appear to be met,

   (b)   it is in the public interest for the application to proceed, and

   (c)   any trial pursuant to an order on the application would not be inconsistent with obligations of the United Kingdom under Article 31 or 34 of the Treaty on European Union (as it had effect before 1 December 2009) or Article 82, 83 or 85 of the Treaty on the Functioning of the European Union relating to the principle of *ne bis in idem*.

(5)   Not more than one application may be made under subsection (1) or (2) in relation to an acquittal.

77.   Determination by Court of Appeal

(1)   On an application under section 76(1), the Court of Appeal—

   (a)   if satisfied that the requirements of sections 78 and 79 are met, must make the order applied for;

   (b)   otherwise, must dismiss the application.

(2)   Subsections (3) and (4) apply to an application under section 76(2).

(3)   Where the Court of Appeal determines that the acquittal is a bar to the person being tried for the qualifying offence, the court—

   (a)   if satisfied that the requirements of sections 78 and 79 are met, must make the order applied for;

   (b)   otherwise, must make a declaration to the effect that the acquittal is a bar to the person being tried for the offence.

(4)   Where the Court of Appeal determines that the acquittal is not a bar to the person being tried for the qualifying offence, it must make a declaration to that effect.

78.   New and compelling evidence

(1)   The requirements of this section are met if there is new and compelling evidence against the acquitted person in relation to the qualifying offence.

(2)   Evidence is new if it was not adduced in the proceedings in which the person was acquitted (nor, if those were appeal proceedings, in earlier proceedings to which the appeal related).

(3)   Evidence is compelling if—

   (a)   it is reliable,

   (b)   it is substantial, and

   (c)   in the context of the outstanding issues, it appears highly probative of the case against the acquitted person.

(4)   The outstanding issues are the issues in dispute in the proceedings in which the person was acquitted and, if those were appeal proceedings, any other issues remaining in dispute from earlier proceedings to which the appeal related.

(5)   For the purposes of this section, it is irrelevant whether any evidence would have been admissible in earlier proceedings against the acquitted person.

79.   Interests of justice

(1)   The requirements of this section are met if in all the circumstances it is in the interests of justice for the court to make the order under section 77.

(2)   That question is to be determined having regard in particular to—

   (a)   whether existing circumstances make a fair trial unlikely;

   (b)   for the purposes of that question and otherwise, the length of time since the qualifying offence was allegedly committed;

   (c)   whether it is likely that the new evidence would have been adduced in the earlier proceedings against the acquitted person but for a failure by an officer or by a prosecutor to act with due diligence or expedition;

   (d)   whether, since those proceedings or, if later, since the commencement of this Part, any officer or prosecutor has failed to act with due diligence or expedition.

(3)   In subsection (2) references to an officer or prosecutor include references to a person charged with corresponding duties under the law in force elsewhere than in England and Wales.

(4)   Where the earlier prosecution was conducted by a person other than a prosecutor, subsection (2)(c) applies in relation to that person as well as in relation to a prosecutor.

142.   Purposes of sentencing

(1)   Any court dealing with an offender in respect of his offence must have regard to the following purposes of sentencing—
   (a)   the punishment of offenders,
   (b)   he reduction of crime (including its reduction by deterrence),
   (c)   the reform and rehabilitation of offenders,
   (d)   the protection of the public, and
   (e)   the making of reparation by offenders to persons affected by their offences.

(2)   Subsection (1) does not apply—
   (a)   in relation to an offender who is aged under 18 at the time of conviction,
   (b)   to an offence the sentence for which is fixed by law,
   (c)   to an offence the sentence for which falls to be imposed under a provision mentioned in subsection (2A), or
   (d)   in relation to the making under Part 3 of the Mental Health Act 1983 of a hospital order (with or without a restriction order), an interim hospital order, a hospital direction or a limitation direction.

(2A) The provisions referred to in subsection (2)(c) are—
   (a)   section 1(2B) or 1A(5) of the Prevention of Crime Act 1953 (minimum sentence for certain offences involving offensive weapons);
   (b)   section 51A(2) of the Firearms Act 1968 (minimum sentence for certain firearms offences);
   (c)   section 139(6B), 139A(5B) or 139AA(7) of the Criminal Justice Act 1998 (minimum sentence for certain offences involving article with blade or point or offensive weapon);
   (d)   section 110(2) or 111(2) of the Sentencing Act (minimum sentence for certain drug trafficking and burglary offences);
   (e)   section 224A of this Act (life sentence for second listed offence for certain dangerous offenders);
   (f)   section 225(2) or 226(2) of this Act (imprisonment or detention for life for certain dangerous offenders);
   (g)   section 29(4) or (6) of the Violent Crime Reduction Act 2006 (minimum sentence in certain cases of using someone to mind a weapon).

(3)   In this Chapter 'sentence', in relation to an offence, includes any order made by a court when dealing with the offender in respect of his offence; and 'sentencing' is to be construed accordingly.

143.   Determining the seriousness of an offence

(1)   In considering the seriousness of any offence, the court must consider the offender's culpability in committing the offence and any harm which the offence caused, was intended to cause or might forseeably have caused.

(2)   In considering the seriousness of an offence ('the current offence') committed by an offender who has one or more previous convictions, the court must treat each previous conviction as an aggravating factor if (in the case of that conviction) the court considers that it can reasonably be so treated having regard, in particular, to—
   (a)   the nature of the offence to which the conviction relates and its relevance to the current offence, and
   (b)   the time that has elapsed since the conviction.

(3)   In considering the seriousness of any offence committed while the offender was on bail, the court must treat the fact that it was committed in those circumstances as an aggravating factor.

(4)   Any reference in subsection (2) to a previous conviction is to be read as a reference to—
   (a)   previous conviction by a court in the United Kingdom,

(aa)   previous conviction by a court in another member State of a relevant offence under the law of that State,

...

(5)   Subsections (2) and (4) do not prevent the court from treating—
   (a)   a previous conviction by a court outside both the United Kingdom and any other member State, or
   (b)   a previous conviction by a court in any member State (other than the United Kingdom) of an offence which is not a relevant offence,
   as an aggravating factor in any case where the court considers it appropriate to do so.
(6)   For the purposes of this section—
   (a)   an offence is 'relevant' if the offence would constitute an offence under the law of any part of the United Kingdom if it were done in that part at the time of the conviction of the defendant for the current offence,

...

144.   Reduction in sentences for guilty pleas

(1)   In determining what sentence to pass on an offender who has pleaded guilty to an offence in proceedings before that or another court, a court must take into account—
   (a)   the stage in the proceedings for the offence at which the offender indicated his intention to plead guilty, and
   (b)   the circumstances in which this indication was given.
(2)   In the case of an offender who—
   (a)   is convicted of an offence the sentence for which falls to be imposed under a provision mentioned in subsection (3), and
   (b)   is aged 18 or over when convicted,
   nothing in that provision prevents the court, after taking into account any matter referred to in subsection (1) of this section, from imposing any sentence which is not less than 80 per cent of that specified in that provision.
(3)   The provisions referred to in subsection (2) are—
   Section 1(2B) or 1A(5) of the Prevention of Crime Act 1953;
   section 110(2) of the Sentencing Act;
   section 111(2) of the Sentencing Act;
   section 139(6B), 139A(5B) or 139AA(7) of the Criminal Justice Act 1988.
(4)   In the case of an offender who—
   (a)   is convicted of an offence the sentence for which falls to be imposed under a provision mentioned in subsection (5), and
   (b)   is aged 16 or 17 when convicted,
   nothing in that provision prevents the court from imposing any sentence that it considers appropriate after taking into account any matter referred to in subsection (1) of this section.
(5)   The provisions referred to in subsection (4) are—
   section 1(2B) or 1A(5) of the Prevention of Crime Act 1953;
   section 139(6B), 139A(5B) or 139AA(7) of the Criminal Justice Act 1988.

145.   Increase in sentences for racial or religious aggravation

(1)   This section applies where a court is considering the seriousness of an offence other than one under sections 29 to 32 of the Crime and Disorder Act 1998 (racially or religiously aggravated assaults, criminal damage, public order offences and harassment etc).
(2)   If the offence was racially or religiously aggravated, the court—
   (a)   must treat that fact as an aggravating factor, and
   (b)   must state in open court that the offence was so aggravated.
(3)   Section 28 of the Crime and Disorder Act 1998 (meaning of 'racially or religiously aggravated') applies for the purposes of this section as it applies for the purposes of sections 29 to 32 of that Act.

146.   Increase in sentences for aggravation related to disability, sexual orientation or transgender identity

(1)   This section applies where the court is considering the seriousness of an offence committed in any of the circumstances mentioned in subsection (2).

(2)   Those circumstances are—
- (a)   that, at the time of committing the offence, or immediately before or after doing so, the offender demonstrated towards the victim of the offence hostility based on—
  - (i)   the sexual orientation (or presumed sexual orientation) of the victim,
  - (ii)   a disability (or presumed disability) of the victim, or
  - (iii)   the victim being (or being presumed to be) transgender, or
- (b)   that the offence is motivated (wholly or partly)—
  - (i)   by hostility towards persons who are of a particular sexual orientation,
  - (ii)   by hostility towards persons who have a disability or a particular disability, or
  - (iii)   by hostility towards persons who are transgender.

(3)   The court—
- (a)   must treat the fact that the offence was committed in any of those circumstances as an aggravating factor, and
- (b)   must state in open court that the offence was committed in such circumstances.

(4)   It is immaterial for the purposes of paragraph (a) or (b) of subsection (2) whether or not the offender's hostility is also based, to any extent, on any other factor not mentioned in that paragraph.

(5)   In this section 'disability' means any physical or mental impairment.

(6)   In this section references to being transgender include references to being transsexual, or undergoing, proposing to undergo or having undergone a process or part of a process of gender reassignment.

147. Meaning of 'community sentence' etc

(1)   In this Part 'community sentence' means a sentence which consists of or includes—
- (a)   a community order (as defined by section 177), or
- (b)   ...
- (c)   a youth rehabilitation order.

(2)   ...

148. Restrictions on imposing community sentences

(1)   A court must not pass a community sentence on an offender unless it is of the opinion that the offence, or the combination of the offence and one or more offences associated with it, was serious enough to warrant such a sentence.

(2)   Where a court passes a community sentence ... —
- (a)   the particular requirement or requirements forming part of the community order, or, as the case may be, youth rehabilitation order, comprised in the sentence must be such as, in the opinion of the court, is, or taken together are, the most suitable for the offender, and
- (b)   the restrictions on liberty imposed by the order must be such as in the opinion of the court are commensurate with the seriousness of the offence, or the combination of the offence and one or more offences associated with it.

(2A)   Subsection (2) is subject to section 177(2A) (community orders: punitive elements) and to paragraph 3(4) of Schedule 1 to the Criminal Justice and Immigration Act 2008 (youth rehabilitation order with intensive supervision and surveillance).

(3)   ...

(4)   Subsections (1) and (2)(b) have effect subject to section 151(2).

(5)   The fact that by virtue of any provision of this section—
- (a)   a community sentence may be passed in relation to an offence; or
- (b)   particular restrictions on liberty may be imposed by a community order or youth rehabilitation order,

does not require a court to pass such a sentence or to impose those restrictions.

149. Passing of community sentence on offender remanded in custody

(1)   In determining the restrictions on liberty to be imposed by a community order or youth rehabilitation order in respect of an offence, the court may have regard to any period for which the offender has been remanded in custody in connection with the offence or any other offence the charge for which was founded on the same facts or evidence.

(2)   In subsection (1) 'remanded in custody' has the meaning given by section 242(2).

150. Community sentence not available where sentence fixed by law etc

(1) The power to make a community order or youth rehabilitation order is not exercisable in respect of an offence for which the sentence—

    (a)   is fixed by law,

    (b)   falls to be imposed under section 51A(2) of the Firearms Act 1968 (required custodial sentence for certain firearms offences),

    (c)   falls to be imposed under section 110(2) or 111(2) of the Sentencing Act (requirement to impose custodial sentences for certain repeated offences committed by offenders aged 18 or over),

    (ca)   falls to be imposed under section 29(4) or (6) of the Violent Crime Reduction Act 2006 (required custodial sentence in certain cases of using someone to mind a weapon),

    (cb)   falls to be imposed under section 224A of this Act (life sentence for second listed offence for certain dangerous offenders), or

    (d)   falls to be imposed under section 225(2) or 226(2) of this Act (requirement to impose sentence of imprisonment for life or detention for life).

(2) The power to make a community order is not exercisable in respect of an offence for which the sentence—

    (a)   falls to be imposed under section 1(2B) or 1A(5) of the Prevention of Crime Act 1953 (minimum sentence for certain offences involving offensive weapons), or

    (b)   falls to be imposed under section 139(6B), 139A(5B) or 139AA(7) of the Criminal Justice Act 1988 (minimum sentence for certain offences involving article with blade or point or offensive weapon).

150A. Community order available only for offences punishable with imprisonment ...

(1) The power to make a community order is only exercisable in respect of an offence if—

    (a)   the offence is punishable with imprisonment; or

    ...

(2) For the purposes of this section ... an offence triable either way that was tried summarily is to be regarded as punishable with imprisonment only if it is so punishable by the sentencing court (and for this purpose section 148(1) is to be disregarded).

152. General restrictions on imposing discretionary custodial sentences

(1) This section applies where a person is convicted of an offence punishable with a custodial sentence other than one—

    (a)   fixed by law, or

    (b)   falling to be imposed under a provision mentioned in subsection (1A).

(1A) The provisions referred to in subsection (1)(b) are—

    (a)   section 1(2B) or 1A(5) of the Prevention of Crime Act 1953;

    (b)   section 51A(2) of the Firearms Act 1968;

    (c)   section 139(6B), 139A(5B) or 139AA(7) of the Criminal Justice Act 1988;

    (d)   section 110(2) or 111(2) of the Sentencing Act;

    (e)   section 224A, 225(2) or 226(2) of this Act;

    (f)   section 29(4) or (6) of the Violent Crime Reduction Act 2006.

(2) The court must not pass a custodial sentence unless it is of the opinion that the offence, or the combination of the offence and one or more offences associated with it, was so serious that neither a fine alone nor a community sentence can be justified for the offence.

(3) Nothing in subsection (2) prevents the court from passing a custodial sentence on the offender if—

    (a)   he fails to express his willingness to comply with a requirement which is proposed by the court to be included in a community order and which requires an expression of such willingness, or

    (b)   he fails to comply with an order under section 161(2) (pre-sentence drug testing).

153. Length of discretionary custodial sentences: general provision

(1) This section applies where a court passes a custodial sentence other than one fixed by law or ... imposed under section 224A, 225 or 226.

(2)   Subject to the provisions listed in subsection (3), the custodial sentence must be for the shortest term (not exceeding the permitted maximum) that in the opinion of the court is commensurate with the seriousness of the offence, or the combination of the offence and one or more offences associated with it.

(3)   The provisions referred to in subsection (2) are—

   (a)   sections 1(2B) and 1A(5) of the Prevention of Crime Act 1953;
   (b)   section 51A(2) of the Firearms Act 1968;
   (c)   sections 139(6B), 139A(5b) and 139AA(7) of the Criminal Justice Act 1988;
   (d)   sections 110(2) and 111(2) of the Sentencing Act;
   (e)   sections 226A(4) and 226B(2) of this Act;
   (f)   section 29(4) or (6) of the Violent Crime Reduction Act 2016.

156. Pre-sentence reports and other requirements

(1)   In forming any such opinion as is mentioned in section 148(1) or (2)(b), section 152(2) or section 153(2), or in section 1(4)(b) or (c) of the Criminal Justice and Immigration Act 2008 (youth rehabilitation orders with intensive supervision and surveillance or fostering), a court must take into account all such information as is available to it about the circumstances of the offence or (as the case may be) of the offence and the offence or offences associated with it, including any aggravating or mitigating factors.

(2)   In forming any such opinion as is mentioned in section 148(2)(a) … the court may take into account any information about the offender which is before it.

(3)   Subject to subsection (4), a court must obtain and consider a pre-sentence report before—

   (a)   in the case of a custodial sentence, forming any such opinion as is mentioned in section 152(2), section 153(2), section 225(1)(b), section 226(1)(b), section 226A(1)(b) or section 226B(1)(b), or
   (b)   in the case of a community sentence, forming any such opinion as is mentioned in section 148(1) or (2)(b), or in section 1(4)(b) or (c) of the Criminal Justice and Immigration Act 2008, or any opinion as to the suitability for the offender of the particular requirement or requirements to be imposed by the community order or youth rehabilitation order.

(4)   Subsection (3) does not apply if, in the circumstances of the case, the court is of the opinion that it is unnecessary to obtain a pre-sentence report.

(5)   In a case where the offender is aged under 18, the court must not form the opinion mentioned in subsection (4) unless—

   (a)   there exists a previous pre-sentence report obtained in respect of the offender, and
   (b)   the court has had regard to the information contained in that report, or, if there is more than one such report, the most recent report.

(6)   No custodial sentence or community sentence is invalidated by the failure of a court to obtain and consider a pre-sentence report before forming an opinion referred to in subsection (3), but any court on an appeal against such a sentence—

   (a)   must, subject to subsection (7), obtain a pre-sentence report if none was obtained by the court below, and
   (b)   must consider any such report obtained by it or by that court.

(7)   Subsection (6)(a) does not apply if the court is of the opinion—

   (a)   that the court below was justified in forming an opinion that it was unnecessary to obtain a pre-sentence report, or
   (b)   that, although the court below was not justified in forming that opinion, in the circumstances of the case at the time it is before the court, it is unnecessary to obtain a pre-sentence report.

(8)   In a case where the offender is aged under 18, the court must not form the opinion mentioned in subsection (7) unless—

   (a)   there exists a previous pre-sentence report obtained in respect of the offender, and
   (b)   the court has had regard to the information contained in that report, or, if there is more than one such report, the most recent report.

157. Additional requirements in case of mentally disordered offender

(1)   Subject to subsection (2), in any case where the offender is or appears to be mentally disordered, the court must obtain and consider a medical report before passing a custodial sentence other than one fixed by law.

(2) Subsection (1) does not apply if, in the circumstances of the case, the court is of the opinion that it is unnecessary to obtain a medical report.

(3) Before passing a custodial sentence other than one fixed by law on an offender who is or appears to be mentally disordered, a court must consider—

   (a) any information before it which relates to his mental condition (whether given in a medical report, a pre-sentence report or otherwise), and

   (b) the likely effect of such a sentence on that condition and on any treatment which may be available for it.

(4) No custodial sentence which is passed in a case to which subsection (1) applies is invalidated by the failure of a court to comply with that subsection, but any court on an appeal against such a sentence—

   (a) must obtain a medical report if none was obtained by the court below, and

   (b) must consider any such report obtained by it or by that court.

(5) In this section 'mentally disordered', in relation to any person, means suffering from a mental disorder within the meaning of the Mental Health Act 1983.

(6) In this section 'medical report' means a report as to an offender's mental condition made or submitted orally or in writing by a registered medical practitioner who is approved for the purposes of section 12 of the Mental Health Act 1983 by the Secretary of State or another person by virtue of section 12ZA or 12ZB of that Act as having special experience in the diagnosis or treatment of mental disorder.

(7) Nothing in this section is to be taken to limit the generality of section 156.

158. Meaning of 'pre-sentence report'

(1) In this Part 'pre-sentence report' means a report which—

   (a) with a view to assisting the court in determining the most suitable method of dealing with an offender, is made or submitted by an appropriate officer, and

   (b) contains information as to such matters, presented in such manner, as may be prescribed by rules made by the Secretary of State.

(1A) Subject to any rules made under subsection (1)(b) and to subsection (1B), the court may accept a pre-sentence report given orally in open court.

(1B) But a pre-sentence report that—

   (a) relates to an offender aged under 18, and

   (b) is required to be obtained and considered before the court forms an opinion mentioned in section 156(3)(a),

   must be in writing.

(2) In subsection (1) 'an appropriate officer' means—

   (a) where the offender is aged 18 or over, an officer of a local probation board or an officer of a provider of probation services, and

   (b) where the offender is aged under 18, an officer of a local probation board, an officer of a provider of probation services, a social worker of a local authority … or a member of a youth offending team.

161A. Court's duty to order payment of surcharge

(1) A court when dealing with a person for one or more offences must also (subject to subsections (2) and (3)) order him to pay a surcharge.

(2) Subsection (1) does not apply in such cases as may be prescribed by an order made by the Secretary of State.

(3) Where a court dealing with an offender considers—

   (a) that it would be appropriate to make one or more of a compensation order, an unlawful profit order and a slavery and trafficking reparation order, but

   (b) that he has insufficient means to pay both the surcharge and appropriate amounts under such of those orders as it would be appropriate to make,

   the court must reduce the surcharge accordingly (if necessary to nil).

(4) For the purposes of this section a court does not 'deal with' a person if it—

   (a) discharges him absolutely, or

   (b) makes an order under the Mental Health Act 1983 in respect of him.

(5) In this section 'slavery and trafficking reparation order' means an order under section 8 of the Modern Slavery Act 2015, and 'unlawful profit order' means an unlawful profit order under section 4 of the Prevention of Social Housing Fraud Act 2013.

161B. Amount of surcharge

(1) The surcharge payable under section 161A is such amount as the Secretary of State may specify by order.

(2) An order under this section may provide for the amount to depend on—
   (a) the offence or offences committed,
   (b) how the offender is otherwise dealt with (including, where the offender is fined, the amount of the fine),
   (c) the age of the offender.
   This is not to be read as limiting section 330(3) (power to make different provision for different purposes etc).

(3)–(5) …

162. Powers to order statement as to offender's financial circumstances

(1) Where an individual has been convicted of an offence, the court may, before sentencing him, make a financial circumstances order with respect to him.

(2) Where a magistrates' court has been notified in accordance with section 12(4) of the Magistrates' Courts Act 1980 that an individual desires to plead guilty without appearing before the court, the court may make a financial circumstances order with respect to him.

(3) In this section 'a financial circumstances order' means, in relation to any individual, an order requiring him to give to the court, within such period as may be specified in the order, such a statement of his assets and other financial circumstances as the court may require.

(4) An individual who without reasonable excuse fails to comply with a financial circumstances order is liable on summary conviction to a fine not exceeding level 3 on the standard scale.

(5) If an individual, in furnishing any statement in pursuance of a financial circumstances order—
   (a) makes a statement which he knows to be false in a material particular,
   (b) recklessly furnishes a statement which is false in a material particular, or
   (c) knowingly fails to disclose any material fact,
   he is liable on summary conviction to a fine not exceeding level 4 on the standard scale.

   …

163. General power of Crown Court to fine offender convicted on indictment

Where a person is convicted on indictment of any offence, other than an offence for which the sentence is fixed by law or falls to be imposed under section 110(2) or 111(2) of the Sentencing Act or under section 224A, 225(2) or 226(2) of this Act, the court, if not precluded from sentencing an offender by its exercise of some other power, may impose a fine instead of or in addition to dealing with him in any other way in which the court has power to deal with him, subject however to any enactment requiring the offender to be dealt with in a particular way.

164. Fixing of fines

(1) Before fixing the amount of any fine to be imposed on an offender who is an individual, a court must inquire into his financial circumstances.

(2) The amount of any fine fixed by a court must be such as, in the opinion of the court, reflects the seriousness of the offence.

(3) In fixing the amount of any fine to be imposed on an offender (whether an individual or other person), a court must take into account the circumstances of the case including, among other things, the financial circumstances of the offender so far as they are known, or appear, to the court.

(4) Subsection (3) applies whether taking into account the financial circumstances of the offender has the effect of increasing or reducing the amount of the fine.

(4A) In applying subsection (3), a court must not reduce the amount of a fine on account of any surcharge it orders the offender to pay under section 161A, except to the extent that he has insufficient means to pay both.

(5) Where—
   (a) an offender has been convicted in his absence in pursuance of section 11 or 12 of the Magistrates' Courts Act 1980 (non-appearance of accused), or

(aa) an offender has been convicted in the offender's absence in proceedings conducted in accordance with section 16A of the Magistrates' Courts Act 1980 (trial by single justice on the papers),

(b) an offender—

(i) has failed to furnish a statement of his financial circumstances in response to a request which is an official request for the purposes of section 20A of the Criminal Justice Act 1991 (offence of making false statement as to financial circumstances),

(ii) has failed to comply with an order under section 162(1) above, or

(iii) has otherwise failed to co-operate with the court in its inquiry into his financial circumstances,

and the court considers that it has insufficient information to make a proper determination of the financial circumstances of the offender, it may make such determination as it thinks fit.

165. Remission of fines

(1) This section applies where a court has, in fixing the amount of a fine, determined the offender's financial circumstances under section 164(5).

(2) If, on subsequently inquiring into the offender's financial circumstances, the court is satisfied that had it had the results of that inquiry when sentencing the offender it would—

(a) have fixed a smaller amount, or

(b) not have fined him,

it may remit the whole or part of the fine.

(3) Where under this section the court remits the whole or part of a fine after a term of imprisonment has been fixed under section 139 of the Sentencing Act (powers of Crown Court in relation to fines) or section 82(5) of the Magistrates' Courts Act 1980 (magistrates' powers in relation to default) it must reduce the term by the corresponding proportion.

...

166. Savings for powers to mitigate sentences and deal appropriately with mentally disordered offenders

(1) Nothing in—

(a) section 148 (imposing community sentences),

(b) section 152, 153 or 157 (imposing custodial sentences),

(c) section 156 (pre-sentence reports and other requirements),

(d) section 164 (fixing of fines),

(e) paragraph 3 of Schedule 1 to the Criminal Justice and Immigration Act 2008 (youth rehabilitation order with intensive supervision and surveillance), or

(f) paragraph 4 of Schedule 1 to that Act (youth rehabilitation order with fostering),

prevents a court from mitigating an offender's sentence by taking into account any such matters as, in the opinion of the court, are relevant in mitigation of sentence.

(2) Section 152(2) does not prevent a court, after taking into account such matters, from passing a community sentence even though it is of the opinion that the offence, or the combination of the offence and one or more offences associated with it, was so serious that a community sentence could not normally be justified for the offence.

(3) Nothing in the sections mentioned in subsection (1)(a) to (f) prevents a court—

(a) from mitigating any penalty included in an offender's sentence by taking into account any other penalty included in that sentence, and

(b) in the case of an offender who is convicted of one or more other offences, from mitigating his sentence by applying any rule of law as to the totality of sentences.

(4) Subsections (2) and (3) are without prejudice to the generality of subsection (1).

(5) Nothing in the sections mentioned in subsection (1)(a) to (f) is to be taken—

(a) as requiring a court to pass a custodial sentence, or any particular custodial sentence, on a mentally disordered offender, or

(b) as restricting any power (whether under the Mental Health Act 1983 or otherwise) which enables a court to deal with such an offender in the manner it considers to be most appropriate in all the circumstances.

(6) In subsection (5) 'mentally disordered', in relation to a person, means suffering from a mental disorder within the meaning of the Mental Health Act 1983.

174. Duty to give reasons for and to explain effect of sentence

(1)　A court passing sentence on an offender has the duties in subsections (2) and (3).

(2)　The court must state in open court, in ordinary language and in general terms, the court's reasons for deciding on the sentence.

(3)　The court must explain to the offender in ordinary language—

　(a)　the effect of the sentence,

　(b)　the effects of non-compliance with any order that the offender is required to comply with and that forms part of the sentence,

　(c)　any power of the court to vary or review any order that forms part of the sentence, and

　(d)　the effects of failure to pay a fine, if the sentence consists of or includes a fine.

(4)　Criminal Procedure Rules may—

　(a)　prescribe cases in which either duty does not apply, and

　(b)　make provision about how an explanation under subsection (3) is to be given.

(5)　Subsections (6) to (8) are particular duties of the court in complying with the duty in subsection (2).

(6)　The court must identify any definitive sentencing guidelines relevant to the offender's case and—

　(a)　explain how the court discharged any duty imposed on it by section 125 of the Coroners and Justice Act 2009 (duty to follow guidelines unless satisfied it would be contrary to the interests of justice to do so);

　(b)　where the court was satisfied it would be contrary to the interests of justice to follow the guidelines, state why.

(7)　Where, as a result of taking into account any matter referred to in section 144(1) (guilty pleas), the court imposes a punishment on the offender which is less severe than the punishment it would otherwise have imposed, the court must state that fact.

(8)　Where the offender is under 18 and the court imposes a sentence that may only be imposed in the offender's case if the court is of the opinion mentioned in—

　(a)　section 1(4)(a) to (c) of the Criminal Justice and Immigration Act 2008 and section 148(1) of this Act (youth rehabilitation order with intensive supervision and surveillance or with fostering), or

　(b)　section 152(2) of this Act (discretionary custodial sentence),

the court must state why it is of that opinion.

(9)　In this section 'definitive sentencing guidelines' means sentencing guidelines issued by the Sentencing Council for England and Wales under section 120 of the Coroners and Justice Act 2009 as definitive guidelines, as revised by any subsequent guidelines so issued.

177. Community orders

(1)　Where a person aged 18 or over is convicted of an offence, the court by or before which he is convicted may make an order (in this Part referred to as a 'community order') imposing on him any one or more of the following requirements—

　(a)　an unpaid work requirement (as defined by section 199),

　(aa)　a rehabilitation activity requirement (as defined by section 200A),

　(c)　a programme requirement (as defined by section 202),

　(d)　a prohibited activity requirement (as defined by section 203),

　(e)　a curfew requirement (as defined by section 204),

　(f)　an exclusion requirement (as defined by section 205),

　(g)　a residence requirement (as defined by section 206),

　(ga)　a foreign travel prohibition requirement (as defined by section 206A),

　(h)　a mental health treatment requirement (as defined by section 207),

　(i)　a drug rehabilitation requirement (as defined by section 209),

　(j)　an alcohol treatment requirement (as defined by section 212),

　(ja)　an alcohol abstinence and monitoring requirement (as defined by section 212A),

　(l)　in a case where the offender is aged under 25, an attendance centre requirement (as defined by section 214), and

　(m)　an electronic monitoring requirement (as defined by section 215).

(2) Subsection (1) has effect subject to sections 150 and 218 and to the following provisions of Chapter 4 relating to particular requirements—
   (a)   section 199(3) (unpaid work requirement),
   (d)   section 203(2) (prohibited activity requirement),
   (e)   section 207(3) (mental health treatment requirement),
   (f)   section 209(2) (drug rehabilitation requirement),
   (g)   section 212(2) and (3) (alcohol treatment requirement),
   (h)   section 212A(8) to (12) (alcohol abstinence and monitoring requirement), and
   (i)   section 215(2) (electronic monitoring requirement).

(2A) Where the court makes a community order, the court must—
   (a)   include in the order at least one requirement imposed for the purpose of punishment, or
   (b)   impose a fine for the offence in respect of which the community order is made, or
   (c)   comply with both of paragraphs (a) and (b).

(2B) Subsection (2A) does not apply where there are exceptional circumstances which—
   (a)   relate to the offence or to the offender,
   (b)   would make it unjust in all the circumstances for the court to comply with subsection (2A)(a) in the particular case, and
   (c)   would make it unjust in all the circumstances for the court to impose a fine for the offence concerned.

(3) Where the court makes a community order imposing a curfew requirement or an exclusion requirement, the court must also impose an electronic monitoring requirement (as defined by section 215) unless—
   (a)   it is prevented from doing so by section 215(2) or 218(4), or
   (b)   in the particular circumstances of the case, it considers it inappropriate to do so.

(4) Where the court makes a community order imposing an unpaid work requirement, a programme requirement, a prohibited activity requirement, a residence requirement, a mental health treatment requirement, a drug rehabilitation requirement, an alcohol treatment requirement, or an attendance centre requirement, the court may also impose an electronic monitoring requirement unless prevented from doing so by section 215(2) or 218(4).

(5) A community order must specify a date ('the end date'), not more than three years after the date of the order, by which all the requirements in it must have been complied with.

(5A) If a community order imposes two or more different requirements falling within subsection (1), the order may also specify a date by which each of those requirements must have been complied with, and the last of those dates must be the same as the end date.

(5B) Subject to section 200(3) (duration of community order imposing unpaid work requirement), a community order ceases to be in force on the end date.

(6) Before making a community order imposing two or more different requirements falling within subsection (1), the court must consider whether, in the circumstances of the case, the requirements are compatible with each other.

179.　Breach, revocation or amendment of community order

Schedule 8 (which relates to failures to comply with the requirements of community orders and to the revocation or amendment of such orders) shall have effect.

189.　Suspended sentences of imprisonment

(1) If a court passes a sentence of imprisonment or, in the case of a person aged at least 18 but under 21, a sentence of detention in a young offender institution for a term of least 14 days but not more than 2 years, it may make an order providing that the sentence of imprisonment or detention in a young offender institution is not to take effect unless—
   (a)   during a period specified in the order for the purposes of this paragraph ('the operational period') the offender commits another offence in the United Kingdom (whether or not punishable with imprisonment), and
   (b)   a court having power to do so subsequently orders under paragraph 8 of Schedule 12 that the original sentence is to take effect.

(1A) An order under subsection (1) may also provide that the offender must comply during a period specified in the order for the purposes of this subsection ('the supervision period') with one or more requirements falling within section 190(1) and specified in the order.

(1B) Where an order under subsection (1) contains provision under subsection (1A), it must provide that the sentence of imprisonment or detention in a young offender institution will also take effect if—

    (a)   during the supervision period the offender fails to comply with a requirement imposed under subsection (1A), and

    (b)   a court having power to do so subsequently orders under paragraph 8 of Schedule 12 that the original sentence is to take effect.

(2)   Where two or more sentences imposed on the same occasion are to be served consecutively, the power conferred by subsection (1) is not exercisable in relation to any of them unless the aggregate of the terms of the sentences does not exceed 2 years.

(3)   The supervision period (if any) and the operational period must each be a period of not less than six months and not more than two years beginning with the date of the order.

(4)   Where an order under subsection (1) imposes one or more community requirements, the supervision period must not end later than the operational period.

(5)   A court which passes a suspended sentence on any person for an offence may not impose a community sentence in his case in respect of that offence or any other offence of which he is convicted by or before the court or for which he is dealt with by the court.

(6)   Subject to any provision to the contrary contained in the Criminal Justice Act 1967, the Sentencing Act or any other enactment passed or instrument made under any enactment after 31st December 1967, a suspended sentence which has not taken effect under paragraph 8 of Schedule 12 is to be treated as a sentence of imprisonment or in the case of a person aged at least 18 but under 21, a sentence of detention in a young offender institution for the purposes of all enactments and instruments made under enactments.

(7)   In this Part—

    (a)   'suspended sentence order' means an order under subsection (1),

    (b)   'suspended sentence' means a sentence to which a suspended sentence order relates, and

    (c)   'community requirement', in relation to a suspended sentence order, means a requirement imposed under subsection (1A).

190.   Imposition of requirements by suspended sentence order

(1)   The requirements falling within this subsection are—

    (a)   an unpaid work requirement (as defined by section 199),

    (aa)   a rehabilitation activity requirement (as defined by section 200A),

    (c)   a programme requirement (as defined by section 202),

    (d)   a prohibited activity requirement (as defined by section 203),

    (e)   a curfew requirement (as defined by section 204),

    (f)   an exclusion requirement (as defined by section 205),

    (g)   a residence requirement (as defined by section 206),

    (ga)   a foreign travel prohibition requirement (as defined by section 206A),

    (h)   a mental health treatment requirement (as defined by section 207),

    (i)   a drug rehabilitation requirement (as defined by section 209),

    (j)   an alcohol treatment requirement (as defined by section 212),

    (ja)   an alcohol abstinence and monitoring requirement (as defined by section 212A),

    (l)   in a case where the offender is aged under 25, an attendance centre requirement (as defined by section 214), and

    (m)   an electronic monitoring requirement (as defined by section 215).

(2)   Section 189(1)(a) has effect subject to section 218 and to the following provisions of Chapter 4 relating to particular requirements—

    (a)   section 199(3) (unpaid work requirement),

    (d)   section 203(2) (prohibited activity requirement),

    (e)   section 207(3) (mental health treatment requirement),

    (f)   section 209(2) (drug rehabilitation requirement),

    (g)   section 212(2) and (3) (alcohol treatment requirement),

    (h)   section 212A(8) to (12) (alcohol abstinence and monitoring requirement), and

    (i)   section 215(2) (electronic monitoring requirement).

(3)   Where the court makes a suspended sentence order imposing a curfew requirement or an exclusion requirement, it must also impose an electronic monitoring requirement (as defined by section 215) unless—

(a)   the court is prevented from doing so by section 215(2) or 218(4), or

(b)   in the particular circumstances of the case, it considers it inappropriate to do so.

(4)   Where the court makes a suspended sentence order imposing an unpaid work requirement, a rehabilitation activity requirement, a programme requirement, a prohibited activity requirement, a residence requirement, a mental health treatment requirement, a drug rehabilitation requirement, an alcohol treatment requirement, a foreign travel prohibition requirement, or an attendance centre requirement, the court may also impose an electronic monitoring requirement unless the court is prevented from doing so by section 215(2) or 218(4).

(5)   Before making a suspended sentence order imposing two or more different requirements falling within subsection (1), the court must consider whether, in the circumstances of the case, the requirements are compatible with each other.

191.   Power to provide for review of suspended sentence order

(1)   A suspended sentence order that imposes one or more community requirements may—

(a)   provide for the order to be reviewed periodically at specified intervals,

(b)   provide for each review to be made, subject to section 192(4), at a hearing held for the purpose by the court responsible for the order (a 'review hearing'),

(c)   require the offender to attend each review hearing, and

(d)   provide for an officer of a provider of probation services to make to the court responsible for the order, before each review, a report on the offender's progress in complying with the community requirements of the order.

(2)   Subsection (1) does not apply in the case of an order imposing a drug rehabilitation requirement (provision for such a requirement to be subject to review being made by section 210).

(3)   In this section references to the court responsible for a suspended sentence order are references—

(a)   where a court is specified in the order in accordance with subsection (4), to that court;

(b)   in any other case, to the court by which the order is made.

(4)   Where the area specified in a suspended sentence order made by a magistrates' court is not the area for which the court acts, the court may, if it thinks fit, include in the order provision specifying for the purpose of subsection (3) a magistrates' court which acts for the area specified in the order.

(5)   Where a suspended sentence order has been made on an appeal brought from the Crown Court or from the criminal division of the Court of Appeal, it is to be taken for the purposes of subsection (3)(b) to have been made by the Crown Court.

192.   Periodic reviews of suspended sentence order

(1)   At a review hearing (within the meaning of subsection (1) of section 191) the court may, after considering the officer's report referred to in that subsection ('the review officer's report'), amend the community requirements of the suspended sentence order, or any provision of the order which relates to those requirements.

(2)   The court—

(a)   may not amend the community requirements of the order so as to impose a requirement of a different kind unless the offender expresses his willingness to comply with that requirement,

(b)   may not amend a mental health treatment requirement, a drug rehabilitation requirement or an alcohol treatment requirement unless the offender expresses his willingness to comply with the requirement as amended,

(c)   may amend the supervision period only if the period as amended complies with section 189(3) and (4),

(d)   may not amend the operational period of the suspended sentence, and

(e)   except with the consent of the offender, may not amend the order while an appeal against the order is pending.

(3)   For the purposes of subsection (2)(a)—

    (a)   a community requirement falling within any paragraph of section 190(1) is of the same kind as any other community requirement falling within that paragraph, and

    (b)   an electronic monitoring requirement is a community requirement of the same kind as any requirement falling within section 190(1) to which it relates.

(4)   If before a review hearing is held at any review the court, after considering the review officer's report, is of the opinion that the offender's progress in complying with the community requirements of the order is satisfactory, it may order that no review hearing is to be held at that review; and if before a review hearing is held at any review, or at a review hearing, the court, after considering that report, is of that opinion, it may amend the suspended sentence order so as to provide for each subsequent review to be held without a hearing.

(5)   If at a review held without a hearing the court, after considering the review officer's report, is of the opinion that the offender's progress under the order is no longer satisfactory, the court may require the offender to attend a hearing of the court at a specified time and place.

(6)   If at a review hearing the court is of the opinion that the offender has without reasonable excuse failed to comply with any of the community requirements of the order, the court may adjourn the hearing for the purpose of dealing with the case under paragraph 8 of Schedule 12.

(7)   At a review hearing the court may amend the suspended sentence order so as to vary the intervals specified under section 191(1).

(8)   In this section any reference to the court, in relation to a review without a hearing, is to be read—

    (a)   in the case of the Crown Court, as a reference to a judge of the court, and

    (b)   in the case of a magistrates' court, as a reference to a justice of the peace

193. Breach, revocation or amendment of suspended sentence order, and effect of further conviction

Schedule 12 (which relates to the breach, revocation or amendment of the community requirements of suspended sentence orders, and to the effect of any further conviction) shall have effect.

199. Unpaid work requirement

(1)   In this Part 'unpaid work requirement', in relation to a relevant order, means a requirement that the offender must perform unpaid work in accordance with section 200.

(2)   The number of hours which a person may be required to work under an unpaid work requirement must be specified in the relevant order and must be in the aggregate—

    (a)   not less than 40, and

    (b)   not more than 300.

(3)   A court may not impose an unpaid work requirement in respect of an offender unless after hearing (if the courts thinks necessary) an officer of a local probation board or an officer of a provider of probation services, the court is satisfied that the offender is a suitable person to perform work under such a requirement.

(4)   …

(5)   Where the court makes relevant orders in respect of two or more offences of which the offender has been convicted on the same occasion and includes unpaid work requirements in each of them, the court may direct that the hours of work specified in any of those requirements is to be concurrent with or additional to those specified in any other of those orders, but so that the total number of hours which are not concurrent does not exceed the maximum specified in subsection (2)(b).

200. Obligations of person subject to unpaid work requirement

(1)   An offender in respect of whom an unpaid work requirement of a relevant order is in force must perform for the number of hours specified in the order such work at such times as he may be instructed by the responsible officer.

(2)   Subject to paragraph 20 of Schedule 8 and paragraph 18 of Schedule 12 (power to extend order), the work required to be performed under an unpaid work requirement of a community order or a suspended sentence order must be performed during a period of twelve months.

(3)   Unless revoked, a community order imposing an unpaid work requirement remains in force until the offender has worked under it for the number of hours specified in it.

(4)   Where an unpaid work requirement is imposed by a suspended sentence order, the supervision period as defined by section 189(1A) continues until the offender has worked under the order for the number of hours specified in the order, but does not continue beyond the end of the operational period as defined by section 189(1)(a).

200A. Rehabilitation activity requirement

(1)   In this Part 'rehabilitation activity requirement', in relation to a relevant order, means a requirement that, during the relevant period, the offender must comply with any instructions given by the responsible officer to attend appointments or participate in activities or both.

(2)   A relevant order imposing a rehabilitation activity requirement must specify the maximum number of days for which the offender may be instructed to participate in activities.

(3)   Any instructions given by the responsible officer must be given with a view to promoting the offender's rehabilitation; but this does not prevent the responsible officer giving instructions with a view to other purposes in addition to rehabilitation.

(4)   The responsible officer may instruct the offender to attend appointments with the responsible officer or with someone else.

(5)   The responsible officer, when instructing the offender to participate in activities, may require the offender to—

    (a)   participate in specified activities and, while doing so, comply with instructions given by the person in charge of the activities, or

    (b)   go to a specified place and, while there, comply with any instructions given by the person in charge of the place.

(6)   The references in subsection (5)(a) and (b) to instructions given by a person include instructions given by anyone acting under the person's authority.

(7)   The activities that responsible officers may instruct offenders to participate in include—

    (a)   activities forming an accredited programme (see section 202(2);

    (b)   activities whose purpose is reparative, such as restorative justice activities.

(8)   For the purposes of subsection (7)(b) an activity is a restorative justice activity if—

    (a)   the participants consist of, or include, the offender and one or more of the victims,

    (b)   the aim of the activity is to maximise the offender's awareness of the impact of the offending concerned on the victims, and

    (c)   the activity gives a victim or victims an opportunity to talk about, or by other means express experience of, the offending and its impact.

(9)   In subsection (8) 'victim' means a victim of, or other person affected by, the offending concerned.

(10) Where compliance with an instruction would require the co-operation of a person other than the offender, the responsible officer may give the instruction only if that person agrees.

(11) In this section 'the relevant period' means—

    (a)   in relation to a community order, the period for which the community order remains in force, and

    (b)   in relation to a suspended sentence order, the supervision period as defined by section 189(1A).

202. Programme requirement

(1)   In this Part 'programme requirement' in relation to a relevant order, means a requirement that the offender must participate in accordance with this subsection in an accredited programme on the number of days specified in the order.

(2)   In this Part 'accredited programme' means a programme that is for the time being accredited by the Secretary of State for the purposes of this section.

(3)   In this section—

    (a)   'programme' means a systematic set of activities, and

    (b)   ...

(4), (5) ...

(6) A programme requirement operates to require the offender—

    (a) in accordance with instructions given by the responsible officer, to participate in the accredited programme that is from time to time specified by the responsible officer at the place that is so specified on the number if days specified in the order, and

    (b) while at that place, to comply with instructions given by, or under the authority of, the person in charge of the programme.

203. Prohibited activity requirement

(1) In this Part 'prohibited activity requirement', in relation to a relevant order, means a requirement that the offender must refrain from participating in activities specified in the order—

    (a) on a day or days so specified, or

    (b) during a period so specified.

(2) A court may not include a prohibited activity requirement in a relevant order unless it has consulted an officer of a local probation board or an officer of a provider of probation services.

(3) The requirements that may by virtue of this section be included in a relevant order include a requirement that the offender does not possess, use or carry a firearm within the meaning of the Firearms Act 1968.

204. Curfew requirement

(1) In this Part 'curfew requirement', in relation to a relevant order, means a requirement that the offender must remain, for periods specified in the relevant order, at a place so specified.

(2) A relevant order imposing a curfew requirement may specify different places or different periods for different days, but may not specify periods which amount to less than two hours or more than sixteen hours in any day.

(3) A community order or suspended sentence order which imposes a curfew requirement may not specify periods which fall outside the period of twelve months beginning with the day on which it is made.

(4), (5) ...

(6) Before making a relevant order imposing a curfew requirement, the court must obtain and consider information about the place proposed to be specified in the order (including information as to the attitude of persons likely to be affected by the enforced presence there of the offender).

205. Exclusion requirement

(1) In this Part 'exclusion requirement', in relation to a relevant order, means a provision prohibiting the offender from entering a place specified in the order for a period so specified.

(2) Where the relevant order is a community order, the period specified must not be more than two years.

(3) An exclusion requirement—

    (a) may provide for the prohibition to operate only during the periods specified in the order, and

    (b) may specify different places for different periods or days.

(4) In this section 'place' includes an area.

206. Residence requirement

(1) In this Part, 'residence requirement', in relation to a community order or a suspended sentence order, means a requirement that, during a period specified in the relevant order, the offender must reside at a place specified in the order.

(2) If the order so provides, a residence requirement does not prohibit the offender from residing, with the prior approval of the responsible officer, at a place other than that specified in the order.

(3) Before making a community order or suspended sentence order containing a residence requirement, the court must consider the home surroundings of the offender.

(4)   A court may not specify a hostel or other institution as the place where an offender must reside, except on the recommendation of an officer of a local probation board or an officer of a provider of probation services.

206A. Foreign travel prohibition requirement

(1)   In this Part 'foreign travel prohibition requirement', in relation to a relevant order, means a requirement prohibiting the offender from travelling, on a day or days specified in the order, or for a period so specified—

    (a)   to any country or territory outside the British Islands specified or described in the order,

    (b)   to any country or territory outside the British Islands other than a country or territory specified or described in the order, or

    (c)   to any country or territory outside the British Islands.

(2)   A day specified under subsection (1) may not fall outside the period of 12 months beginning with the day on which the order is made.

(3)   A period specified under that subsection may not exceed 12 months beginning with the day on which the relevant order is made.

207. Mental health treatment requirement

(1)   In this Part, 'mental health treatment requirement', in relation to a community order or suspended sentence order, means a requirement that the offender must submit, during a period or periods specified in the order, to treatment by or under the direction of a registered medical practitioner or a registered psychologist (or both, for different periods) with a view to the improvement of the offender's mental condition.

(2)   The treatment required must be such one of the following kinds of treatment as may be specified in the relevant order—

    (a)   treatment as a resident patient in a care home within the meaning of the Care Standards Act 2000, an independent hospital or a hospital within the meaning of the Mental Health Act 1983, but not in hospital premises where high security psychiatric services within the meaning of that Act are provided;

    (b)   treatment as a non-resident patient at such institution or place as may be specified in the order;

    (c)   treatment by or under the direction of such registered medical practitioner or registered psychologist (or both) as may be so specified;

but the nature of the treatment is not to be specified in the order except as mentioned in paragraph (a), (b) or (c).

(3)   A court may not by virtue of this section include a mental health treatment requirement in a relevant order unless—

    (a)   the court is satisfied ... that the mental condition of the offender—

        (i)   is such as requires and may be susceptible to treatment, but

        (ii)   is not such as to warrant the making of a hospital order or guardianship order within the meaning of the Mental Health Act 1983;

    (b)   the court is also satisfied that arrangements have been or can be made for the treatment intended to be specified in the order (including arrangements for the reception of the offender where he is to be required to submit to treatment as a resident patient); and

    (c)   the offender has expressed his willingness to comply with such a requirement.

(4)   While the offender is under treatment as a resident patient in pursuance of a mental health requirement of a relevant order, his responsible officer shall carry out the supervision of the offender to such extent only as may be necessary for the purpose of the revocation or amendment of the order.

(4A) In subsection (2) 'independent hospital'—

    (a)   in relation to England, means a hospital as defined by section 275 of the National Health Service Act 2006 that is not a health service hospital as defined by that section; and

    (b)   in relation to Wales, has the same meaning as in the Care Standards Act 2000.

(5)   ...

(6)   In this section and section 208, 'registered psychologist' means a person registered in the part of the register maintained under the Health and Social Work Professions Order 2001 which relates to practitioner psychologists.

208.   Mental health treatment at place other than that specified in order

(1)   Where the medical practitioner or registered psychologist by whom or under whose direction an offender is being treated for his mental condition in pursuance of a mental health treatment requirement is of the opinion that part of the treatment can be better or more conveniently given in or at an institution or place which—

(a)   is not specified in the relevant order, and

(b)   is one in or at which the treatment of the offender will be given by or under the direction of a registered medical practitioner or registered psychologist,

he may, with the consent of the offender, make arrangements for him to be treated accordingly.

(2)   Such arrangements as are mentioned in subsection (1) may provide for the offender to receive part of his treatment as a resident patient in an institution or place notwithstanding that the institution or place is not one which could have been specified for that purpose in the relevant order.

(3)   Where any such arrangements as are mentioned in subsection (1) are made for the treatment of an offender—

(a)   the medical practitioner or registered psychologist by whom the arrangements are made shall give notice in writing to the offender's responsible officer, specifying the institution or place in or at which the treatment is to be carried out; and

(b)   the treatment provided for by the arrangements shall be deemed to be treatment to which he is required to submit in pursuance of the relevant order.

209.   Drug rehabilitation requirement

(1)   In this Part 'drug rehabilitation requirement', in relation to a community order or suspended sentence order, means a requirement that during a period specified in the order ('the treatment and testing period') the offender—

(a)   must submit to treatment by or under the direction of a specified person having the necessary qualifications or experience with a view to the reduction or elimination of the offender's dependency on or propensity to misuse drugs, and

(b)   for the purpose of ascertaining whether he has any drug in his body during that period, must provide samples of such description as may be so determined, at such times or in such circumstances as may (subject to the provisions of the order) be determined by the responsible officer or by the person specified as the person by or under whose direction the treatment is to be provided.

(2)   A court may not impose a drug rehabilitation requirement unless—

(a)   it is satisfied—

(i)   that the offender is dependent on, or has a propensity to misuse, drugs, and

(ii)   that his dependency or propensity is such as requires and may be susceptible to treatment,

(b)   it is also satisfied that arrangements have been or can be made for the treatment intended to be specified in the order (including arrangements for the reception of the offender where he is to be required to submit to treatment as a resident),

(c)   the requirement has been recommended to the court as being suitable for the offender by an officer of a local probation board or an officer of a provider of probation services, and

(d)   the offender expresses his willingness to comply with the requirement.

(3)   ...

(4)   The required treatment for any particular period must be—

(a)   treatment as a resident in such institution or place as may be specified in the order, or

(b)   treatment as a non-resident in or at such institution or place, and at such intervals, as may be so specified;

but the nature of the treatment is not to be specified in the order except as mentioned in paragraph (a) or (b) above.

(5) The function of making a determination as to the provision of samples under provision included in the community order or suspended sentence order by virtue of subsection (1)(b) is to be exercised in accordance with guidance given from time to time by the Secretary of State.

(6) A community order or suspended sentence order imposing a drug rehabilitation requirement must provide that the results of tests carried out on any samples provided by the offender in pursuance of the requirement to a person other than the responsible officer are to be communicated to the responsible officer.

(7) In this section 'drug' means a controlled drug as defined by section 2 of the Misuse of Drugs Act 1971.

210. Drug rehabilitation requirement: provision for review by court

(1) A community order or suspended sentence order imposing a drug rehabilitation requirement may (and must if the treatment and testing period is more than 12 months)—
  (a) provide for the requirement to be reviewed periodically at intervals of not less than one month,
  (b) provide for each review of the requirement to be made, subject to section 211(6), at a hearing held for the purpose by the court responsible for the order (a 'review hearing'),
  (c) require the offender to attend each review hearing,
  (d) provide for an officer of a provider of probation services to make to the court responsible for the order, before each review, a report in writing on the offender's progress under the requirement, and
  (e) provide for each such report to include the test results communicated to the responsible officer under section 209(6) or otherwise and the views of the treatment provider as to the treatment and testing of the offender.

(2) In this section references to the court responsible for a community order or suspended sentence order imposing a drug rehabilitation requirement are references—
  (a) where a court is specified in the order in accordance with subsection (3), to that court;
  (b) in any other case, to the court by which the order is made.

(3) Where the area specified in a community order or suspended sentence order which is made by a magistrates' court and imposes a drug rehabilitation requirement is not the area for which the court acts, the court may, if it thinks fit, include in the order provision specifying for the purposes of subsection (2) a magistrates' court which acts for the area specified in the order.

(4) Where a community order or suspended sentence order imposing a drug rehabilitation requirement has been made on an appeal brought from the Crown Court or from the criminal division of the Court of Appeal, for the purposes of subsection (2)(b) it shall be taken to have been made by the Crown Court.

211. Periodic review of drug rehabilitation requirement

(1) At a review hearing (within the meaning given by subsection (1) of section 210) the court may, after considering the officer's report referred to in that subsection ('the review officer's report'), amend the community order or suspended sentence order, so far as it relates to the drug rehabilitation requirement.

(2) The court—
  (a) may not amend the drug rehabilitation requirement unless the offender expresses his willingness to comply with the requirement as amended, and
  (b) ...
  (c) except with the consent of the offender, may not amend any requirement or provision of the order while an appeal against the order is pending.

(3) If the offender fails to express his willingness to comply with the drug rehabilitation requirement as proposed to be amended by the court, the court may—
  (a) revoke the community order, or the suspended sentence order and the suspended sentence to which it relates, and
  (b) deal with him, for the offence in respect of which the order was made, in any way in which he could have been dealt with for that offence by the court which made the order if the order had not been made.

(4)　In dealing with the offender under subsection (3)(b), the court—

    (a)　shall take into account the extent to which the offender has complied with the requirements of the order, and

    (b)　may impose a custodial sentence (where the order was made in respect of an offence punishable with such a sentence) notwithstanding anything in section 152(2).

(5)　...

(6)　If at a review hearing (as defined by section 210(1)(b)) the court, after considering the review officer's report, is of the opinion that the offender's progress under the requirement is satisfactory, the court may so amend the order as to provide for each subsequent review to be made by the court without a hearing.

(7)　If at a review without a hearing the court, after considering the review officer's report, is of the opinion that the offender's progress under the requirement is no longer satisfactory, the court may require the offender to attend a hearing of the court at a specified time and place.

(8)　At that hearing the court, after considering that report, may—

    (a)　exercise the powers conferred by this section as if the hearing were a review hearing, and

    (b)　so amend the order as to provide for each subsequent review to be made at a review hearing.

(9)　In this section any reference to the court, in relation to a review without a hearing, is to be read—

    (a)　in the case of the Crown Court, as a reference to a judge of the court;

    (b)　in the case of a magistrates' court, as a reference to a justice of the peace.

212. Alcohol treatment requirement

(1)　In this Part 'alcohol treatment requirement', in relation to a community order or suspended sentence order, means a requirement that the offender must submit during a period specified in the order to treatment by or under the direction of a specified person having the necessary qualifications or experience with a view to the reduction or elimination of the offender's dependency on alcohol.

(2)　A court may not impose an alcohol treatment requirement in respect of an offender unless it is satisfied—

    (a)　that he is dependent on alcohol,

    (b)　that his dependency is such as requires and may be susceptible to treatment, and

    (c)　that arrangements have been or can be made for the treatment intended to be specified in the order (including arrangements for the reception of the offender where he is to be required to submit to treatment as a resident).

(3)　A court may not impose an alcohol treatment requirement unless the offender expresses his willingness to comply with its requirements.

(4)　...

(5)　The treatment required by an alcohol treatment requirement for any particular period must be—

    (a)　treatment as a resident in such institution or place as may be specified in the order,

    (b)　treatment as a non-resident in or at such institution or place, and at such intervals, as may be so specified, or

    (c)　treatment by or under the direction of such person having the necessary qualification or experience as may be so specified;

but the nature of the treatment shall not be specified in the order except as mentioned in paragraph (a), (b) or (c) above.

212A. Alcohol abstinence and monitoring requirement

(1)　In this Part 'alcohol abstinence and monitoring requirement' in relation to a relevant order, means a requirement—

    (a)　that, subject to such exceptions (if any) as are specified—

        (i)　the offender must abstain from consuming alcohol throughout a specified period, or

       (ii)   the offender must not consume alcohol so that at any time during a specified period there is more than a specified level of alcohol in the offender's body, and

   (b)   that the offender must, for the purpose of ascertaining whether the offender is complying with provision under paragraph (a), submit during the specified period to monitoring in accordance with specified arrangements.

(2)   A period specified under subsection (1)(a) must not exceed 120 days.

(3)   If the Secretary of State by order specifies a minimum period for the purposes of subsection (1)(a), a period specified under that provision must be at least as long as the period prescribed.

(4)   The level of alcohol specified under subsection (1)(a)(ii) must be that prescribed by the Secretary of State by order for the purposes of that provision (and a requirement under that provision may not be imposed unless such an order is in force).

(5)   An order under subsection (4) may prescribed a level—

   (a)   by reference to the proportion of alcohol in any one or more of an offender's breath, blood, urine or sweat, or

   (b)   by some other means.

(6)   The arrangements for monitoring specified under subsection (1)(b) must be consistent with those prescribed by the Secretary of State (and an alcohol abstinence and monitoring requirement may not be imposed unless such an order is in force).

(7)   An order under subsection (6) may in particular prescribe—

   (a)   arrangements for monitoring by electronic means;

   (b)   arrangements for monitoring by other means of testing.

(8)   A court may not include an alcohol abstinence and monitoring requirement in a relevant order unless the following conditions are met.

(9)   The first condition is that—

   (a)   the consumption of alcohol by the offender is an element of the offence for which the order is to be imposed or an associated offence, or

   (b)   the court is satisfied that the consumption of alcohol by the offender was a factor that contributed to the commission of that offence or an associated offence.

(10)   The second condition is that the court is satisfied that the offender is not dependent on alcohol.

(11)   The third condition is that the court does not include an alcohol treatment requirement in the order.

(12)   The fourth condition is that the court has been notified by the Secretary of State that arrangements for monitoring of the kind to be specified are available in the local justice area to be specified.

(13)   In this section—

   'alcohol' includes anything containing alcohol;

   'specified', in relation to a relevant order, means specified in the order.

214. Attendance centre requirement

(1)   In this Part 'attendance centre requirement', in relation to a relevant order, means a requirement that the offender must attend at an attendance centre for such number of hours as may be specified in the relevant order.

(2)   The aggregate number of hours for which the offender may be required to attend at an attendance centre must not be less than 12 or more than 36.

(3)   The court may not impose an attendance centre requirement unless the court is satisfied that an attendance centre which is available for persons of the offender's description is reasonably accessible to the offender concerned, having regard to the means of access available to him and any other circumstances.

(3A)   The attendance centre at which the offender is required to attend is to be notified to the offender by the responsible officer from time to time.

(3B)   When choosing an attendance centre, the responsible officer must consider—

   (a)   the accessibility of the attendance centre to the offender, having regard to the means of access available to the offender and any other circumstances, and

   (b)   the description of persons for whom it is available.

(4)   The first time at which the offender is required to attend at the attendance centre is a time notified to the offender by the responsible officer.

(5)   The subsequent hours are to be fixed by the officer in charge of the centre, having regard to the offender's circumstances.

(6)   An offender may not be required under this section to attend at an attendance centre on more than one occasion on any day, or for more than three hours on any occasion.

(7)   A requirement to attend at an attendance centre for any period on any occasion operates as a requirement, during that period, to engage in occupation, or receive instruction, under the supervision of and in accordance with instructions given by, or under the authority of, the officer in charge of the centre, whether at the centre or elsewhere.

215.   Electronic monitoring requirement

(1)   In this Part 'electronic monitoring requirement', in relation to a relevant order, means a requirement for securing the electronic monitoring of the offender's compliance with other requirements imposed by the order during a period specified in the order, or determined by the responsible officer in accordance with the relevant order.

(2)   Where—
   (a)   it is proposed to include in a relevant order a requirement for securing electronic monitoring in accordance with this section, but
   (b)   there is a person (other than the offender) without whose co-operation it will not be practicable to secure the monitoring,
   the requirement may not be included in the order without that person's consent.

(3)   A relevant order which includes an electronic monitoring requirement must include provision for making a person responsible for the monitoring; and a person who is made so responsible must be of a description specified in an order made by the Secretary of State.

(4)   Where an electronic monitoring requirement is required to take effect during a period determined by the responsible officer in accordance with the relevant order, the responsible officer must, before the beginning of that period, notify—
   (a)   the offender,
   (b)   the person responsible for the monitoring, and
   (c)   any person falling within subsection (2)(b),
   of the time when the period is to begin.

217.   Requirement to avoid conflict with religious beliefs, etc

(1)   The court must ensure, as far as practicable, that any requirement imposed by a relevant order is such as to avoid—
   (a)   any conflict with the offender's religious beliefs or with the requirements of any other relevant order to which he may be subject; and
   (b)   any interference with the times, if any, at which he normally works or attends any educational establishment.

(2)   The responsible officer in relation to an offender to whom a relevant order relates must ensure, as far as practicable, that any instruction given or requirement imposed by him in pursuance of the order is such as to avoid the conflict or interference mentioned in subsection (1).

(3)   The Secretary of State may by order provide that subsection (1) or (2) is to have effect with such additional restrictions as may be specified in the order.

218.   Availability of arrangements in local area

(1)   A court may not include an unpaid work requirement in a relevant order unless the court is satisfied that provision for the offender to work under such a requirement can be made under the arrangements for persons to perform work under such a requirement which exist in the local justice area in which he resides or will reside.

(2)   ...

(3)   A court may not include an attendance centre requirement in a relevant order in respect of an offender unless the court has been notified by the Secretary of State that an attendance centre is available for persons of his description.

(4)   A court may not include an electronic monitoring requirement in a relevant order in respect of an offender unless the court—

    (a)   has been notified by the Secretary of State that electronic monitoring arrangements are available in the relevant areas mentioned in subsections (5) to (7), and

    (b)   is satisfied that the necessary provision can be made under those arrangements.

(5)   In the case of a relevant order containing a curfew requirement or an exclusion requirement, the relevant area for the purposes of subsection (4) is the area in which the place proposed to be specified in the order is situated.

(6)   In the case of a relevant order containing an attendance centre requirement, the relevant area for the purposes of subsection (4) an area in which there is an attendance centre which is available for persons of the offender's description and which the court is satisfied is reasonably accessible to the offender.

(7)   In the case of any other relevant order, the relevant area for the purposes of subsection (4) is the local justice area proposed to be specified in the order.

(8)   In subsection (5) 'place', in relation to an exclusion requirement, has the same meaning as in section 205.

220. Duty of offender to keep in touch with responsible officer

(1)   An offender in respect of whom a community order or a suspended sentence order is in force—

    (a)   must keep in touch with the responsible officer in accordance with such instructions as he may from time to time be given by that officer.

    ...

(2)   The obligation imposed by subsection (1) is enforceable as if it were a requirement imposed by the order.

220A. Duty to obtain permission before changing residence

(1)   An offender in respect of whom a relevant order is in force must not change residence without permission given in accordance with this section by—

    (a)   the responsible officer, or

    (b)   a court.

(2)   The appropriate court may, on an application by the offender, give permission in a case in which the responsible officer has refused.

(3)   A court may also give permission in any proceedings before it under Schedule 8 or 12 (breach or amendment of orders etc).

    ...

224. Meaning of 'specified offence' etc

(1)   An offence is a 'specified offence' for the purposes of this Chapter if it is a specified violent offence, a specified sexual offence or a specified terrorism offence.

(2)   An offence is a 'serious offence' for the purposes of this Chapter if and only if—

    (a)   it is a specified offence, and

    (b)   it is, apart from section 224A, punishable in the case of a person aged 18 or over by—

        (i)   imprisonment for life or, in the case of a person aged at least 18 but under 21, custody for life, or

        (ii)   imprisonment or, in the case of a person aged at least 18 but under 21, detention in a young offender institution, for a determinate period of ten years or more.

(3)   In this Chapter—

    'serious harm' means death or serious personal injury, whether physical or psychological;

    'specified violent offence' means an offence specified in Part 1 of Schedule 15;

    'specified sexual offence' means an offence specified in Part 2 of that Schedule.

    'specified terrorism offence' means an offence specified in Part 3 of that Schedule.

224A. Life sentence for second listed offence

(1)   This section applies where—

    (a)   a person aged 18 or over is convicted of an offence listed in Part 1 of Schedule 15B,

    (b)   the offence was committed after this section comes into force, and

    (c)   the sentence condition and the previous offence condition are met.

(2)   The court must impose a sentence of imprisonment for life or, in the case of a person aged at least 18 but under 21, custody for life under section 94 of the Sentencing Act unless the court is of the opinion that there are particular circumstances which—
     (a)   relate to the offence, to the previous offence referred to in subsection (4) or to the offender, and
     (b)   would make it unjust to do so in all the circumstances.

(3)   The sentence condition is that, but for this section, the court would, in compliance with sections 152(2) and 153(2), impose a sentence of imprisonment for 10 years or more or, if the person is aged at least 18 but under 21, a sentence of detention in a young offender institution for such a period, disregarding any extension period imposed under section 226A.

(4)   The previous offence condition is that—
     (a)   at the time the offence was committed, the offender had been convicted of an offence listed in Schedule 15B ('the previous offence'), and
     (b)   a relevant life sentence or a relevant sentence of imprisonment or detention for a determinate period was imposed on the offender for the previous offence.

(5)   A life sentence is relevant for the purposes of subsection (4)(b) if—
     (a)   the offender was not eligible for release during the first 5 years of the sentence, or
     (b)   the offender would not have been eligible for release during that period but for the reduction of the period of ineligibility to take account of a relevant pre-sentence period.

(6)   An extended sentence imposed under this Act ... is relevant for the purposes of subsection (4)(b) if the appropriate custodial term imposed was 10 years or more.

(7)   Any other extended sentence is relevant for the purposes of subsection (4)(b) if the custodial term imposed was 10 years or more.

(8)   Any other sentence of imprisonment or detention for a determinate period is relevant for the purposes of subsection (4)(b) if it was for a period of 10 years or more.

(9)   An extended sentence or other sentence of imprisonment or detention is also relevant if it would have been relevant under subsection (7) or (8) but for the reduction of the sentence, or any part of the sentence, to take account of a relevant pre-sentence period.

(10) For the purposes of subsections (4) to (9)—
     'extended sentence' means—
     (a)   a sentence imposed under section 85 of the Sentencing Act or under section 226A, 226B, 227 or 228 of this Act ... or
     (b)   an equivalent sentence imposed under the law of Scotland, Northern Ireland or member State (other than the United Kingdom);
     'life sentence' means—
     (a)   a life sentence as defined in section 34 of the Crime (Sentences) Act 1997, or
     (b)   an equivalent sentence imposed under the law of Scotland, Northern Ireland or a member State (other than the United Kingdom);
     'relevant pre-sentence period' in relation to the previous offence referred to in subsection (4) means any period which the offender spent in custody or on bail before the sentence for that offence was imposed;
     'sentence of imprisonment or detention' includes any sentence of a period in custody (however expressed).

(11) An offence the sentence for which is imposed under this section is not to be regarded as an offence the sentence for which is fixed by law.

225.   Life sentence for serious offences

(1)   This section applies where—
     (a)   a person aged 18 or over is convicted of a serious offence committed after the commencement of this section, and
     (b)   the court is of the opinion that there is a significant risk to members of the public of serious harm occasioned by the commission by him of further specified offences.

(2)   If—
     (a)   the offence is one in respect of which the offender would apart from this section be liable to imprisonment for life, and

(b)   the court considers that the seriousness of the offence, or of the offence and one or more offences associated with it, is such as to justify the imposition of a sentence of imprisonment for life,

the court must impose a sentence of imprisonment for life.

(3)–(4) ...

(5)   An offence the sentence for which is imposed under this section is not to be regarded as an offence the sentence for which is fixed by law.

226.   Detention for life for serious offences committed by those under 18

(1)   This section applies where—

(a)   a person aged under 18 is convicted of a serious offence committed after the commencement of this section, and

(b)   the court is of the opinion that there is a significant risk to members of the public of serious harm occasioned by the commission by him of further specified offences.

(2)   If—

(a)   the offence is one in respect of which the offender would apart from this section be liable to a sentence of detention for life under section 91 of the Sentencing Act, and

(b)   the court considers that the seriousness of the offence, or of the offence and one or more offences associated with it, is such as to justify the imposition of a sentence of detention for life,

the court must impose a sentence of detention for life under that section.

(3)–(4) ...

(5)   An offence the sentence for which is imposed under this section is not to be regarded as an offence the sentence for which is fixed by law.

226A. Extended sentence for certain violent, sexual or terrorism offences: persons 18 or over

(1)   This section applies where—

(a)   a person aged 18 or over is convicted of a specified offence (whether the offence was committed before or after this section comes into force),

(b)   the court considers that there is a significant risk to members of the public of serious harm occasioned by the commission by the offender of further specified offences,

(c)   the court is not required by section 224A or 225(2) to impose a sentence of imprisonment for life, and

(d)   condition A or B is met.

(2)   Condition A is that, at the time the offence was committed, the offender had been convicted of an offence listed in Schedule 15B.

(3)   Condition B is that, if the court were to impose an extended sentence of imprisonment, the term that it would specify as the appropriate custodial term would be at least 4 years.

(4)   The court may impose an extended sentence of imprisonment on the offender.

(5)   An extended sentence of imprisonment is a sentence of imprisonment the term of which is equal to the aggregate of—

(a)   the appropriate custodial term, and

(b)   a further period (the 'extension period') for which the offender is to be subject to a licence.

(6)   The appropriate custodial term is the term of imprisonment that would (apart from this section) be imposed in compliance with section 153(2).

(7)   The extension period must be a period of such length as the court considers necessary for the purpose of protecting members of the public from serious harm occasioned by the commission by the offender of further specified offences, subject to subsections (8) and (9).

(7A)   The extension period must be at least 1 year.

(8)   The extension period must not exceed—

(a)   5 years in the case of a specified violent offence, and

(b)   8 years in the case of a specified sexual offence or a specified terrorism offence.

(9)   The term of an extended sentence of imprisonment imposed under this section in respect of an offence must not exceed the term that, at the time the offence was committed, was the maximum term permitted for the offence.

(10)   In subsections (1)(a) and (8), references to a specified offence, a specified violent offence and a specified sexual offence include an offence that—

    (a)   was abolished before 4 April 2005, and

    (b)   would have constituted such an offence if committed on the day on which the offender was convicted of the offence.

226B. Extended sentence for certain violent, sexual or terrorism offences: persons under 18

(1)   This section applies where—

    (a)   a person aged under 18 is convicted of a specified offence (whether the offence was committed before or after this section comes into force),

    (b)   the court considers that there is a significant risk to members of the public of serious harm occasioned by the commission by the offender of further specified offences,

    (c)   the court is not required by section 226(2) to impose a sentence of detention for life under section 91 of the Sentencing Act, and

    (d)   if the court were to impose an extended sentence of detention, the term that it would specify as the appropriate custodial term would be at least 4 years.

(2)   The court may impose an extended sentence of detention on the offender.

(3)   An extended sentence of detention is a sentence of detention the term of which is equal to the aggregate of—

    (a)   the appropriate custodial term, and

    (b)   a further period (the 'extension period') for which the offender is to be subject to a licence.

(4)   The appropriate custodial term is the term of detention that would (apart from this section) be imposed in compliance with section 153(2).

(5)   The extension period must be a period of such length as the court considers necessary for the purpose of protecting members of the public from serious harm occasioned by the commission by the offender of further specified offences, subject to subsections (6) and (7).

(5A)   The extension period must be at least 1 year.

(6)   The extension period must not exceed—

    (a)   5 years in the case of a specified violent offence, and

    (b)   8 years in the case of a specified sexual offence or a specified terrorism offence.

(7)   The term of an extended sentence of detention imposed under this section in respect of an offence may not exceed the term that, at the time the offence was committed, was the maximum term of imprisonment permitted for the offence in the case of a person aged 18 or over.

(8)   In subsections (1)(a) and (6), references to a specified offence, a specified violent offence and a specified sexual offence include an offence that—

    (a)   was abolished before 4 April 2005, and

    (b)   would have constituted such an offence if committed on the day on which the offender was convicted of the offence.

229. The assessment of dangerousness

(1)   This section applies where—

    (a)   a person has been convicted of a specified offence, and

    (b)   it falls to a court to assess under any of sections 225 to 228 whether there is a significant risk to members of the public of serious harm occasioned by the commission by him of further such offences.

(2)   ..., the court in making the assessment referred to in subsection (1)(b)—

    (a)   must take into account all such information as is available to it about the nature and circumstances of the offence,

    (aa)   may take into account all such information as is available to it about the nature and circumstances of any other offences of which the offender has been convicted by a court anywhere in the world,

(b)   may take into account any information which is before it about any pattern of behaviour of which any of the offences mentioned in paragraph (a) or (aa) forms part, and

(c)   may take into account any information about the offender which is before it.

236A. Special custodial sentence for certain offenders of particular concern

(1)   Subsection (2) applies where—

    (a)   a person is convicted of an offence listed in Schedule 18A (whether the offence was committed before or after this section comes into force),

    (b)   the person was aged 18 or over when the offence was committed, and

    (c)   the court does not impose one of the following for the offence—

        (i)   a sentence of imprisonment for life, or

        (ii)   an extended sentence under section 226A.

(2)   If the court imposes a sentence of imprisonment for the offence, the term of the sentence must be equal to the aggregate of—

    (a)   the appropriate custodial term, and

    (b)   a further period of 1 year for which the offender is to be subject to a licence.

(3)   The 'appropriate custodial term' is the term that, in the opinion of the court, ensures that the sentence is appropriate.

(4)   The term of a sentence of imprisonment imposed under this section for an offence must not exceed the term that, at the time the offence was committed, was the maximum term permitted for the offence.

(5)   The references in subsections (1)(c) and (2) to a sentence imposed for the offence include a sentence imposed for the offence and one or more offences associated with it.

(6)   The Secretary of State may by order amend Schedule 18A by—

    (a)   adding offences, or

    (b)   varying or omitting offences listed in the Schedule.

(7)   An order under subsection (6) may, in particular, make provision that applies in relation to the sentencing of a person for an offence committed before the provision comes into force.

(8)   In the case of a person aged under 21, this section applies as if the references to imprisonment were to detention in a young offender institution.

237.   Meaning of 'fixed-term prisoner'

(1)   In this Chapter 'fixed-term prisoner' means—

    (a)   a person serving a sentence of imprisonment for a determinate term, or

...

    (b)   a person serving a determinate sentence of detention under section 91 or 96 of the Sentencing Act or under section 226A, 226B, 227, 228 or 236A of this Act.

(1B) In this Chapter—

    (a)   references to a sentence of imprisonment include such a sentence passed by a service court;

    (b)   references to a sentence of detention under section 91 of the Sentencing Act include a sentence of detention under section 209 of the Armed Forces Act 2006;

    (c)   references to a sentence under section 227 of this Act include a sentence under that section passed as a result of section 220 of the Armed Forces Act 2006 or section 240A; and

    (d)   references to a sentence under section 228 of this Act include a sentence under that section passed as a result of section 222 of that Act.

(1C) Nothing in subsection (1B) has the effect that section 241ZA or 265 (provision equivalent to which is made by the Armed Forces Act 2006) applies to a service court.

(2)   In this Chapter, unless the context otherwise requires, 'prisoner' includes a person serving a sentence falling within subsection (1)(b); and 'prison' includes any place where a person serving such a sentence is liable to be detained.

(3)   In this chapter references to a sentence of detention under section 96 of the Sentencing Act or section 226A or 227 of this Act are references to a sentence of detention in a young offender institution.

238. Power of court to recommend licence conditions for certain prisoners

(1) A court which sentences an offender to a term of imprisonment or detention in a young offender institution of twelve months or more in respect of any offence may, when passing sentence, recommend to the Secretary of State particular conditions which in its view should be included in any licence granted to the offender under this Chapter on his release from prison.

(2) In exercising his powers under section 250(4)(b) in respect of an offender, the Secretary of State must have regard to any recommendation under subsection (1).

(3) A recommendation under subsection (1) is not to be treated for any purpose as part of the sentence passed on the offender.

(4) This section does not apply in relation to a sentence of detention under section 91 of the Sentencing Act or section 226B of this Act.

240ZA. Time remanded in custody to count as time served: terms of imprisonment and detention

(1) This section applies where—
    (a) an offender is serving a term of imprisonment in respect of an offence, and
    (b) the offender has been remanded in custody (within the meaning given by section 242) in connection with the offence or a related offence.

(2) It is immaterial for that purpose whether, for all or part of the period during which the offender was remanded in custody, the offender was also remanded in custody in connection with other offences (but see subsection (5)).

(3) The number of days for which the offender was remanded in custody in connection with the offence or a related offence is to count as time served by the offender as part of the sentence.
But this is subject to subsections (4) to (6).

(4) If, on any day on which the offender was remanded in custody, the offender was also detained in connection with any other matter, that day is not to count as time served.

(5) A day counts as time served—
    (a) in relation to only one sentence, and
    (b) only once in relation to that sentence.

(6) A day is not to count as time served as part of any automatic release period served by the offender (see section 255B(1)).

(7) For the purposes of this section a suspended sentence—
    (a) is to be treated as a sentence of imprisonment when it takes effect under paragraph 8(2)(a) or (b) of Schedule 12, and
    (b) is to be treated as being imposed by the order under which it takes effect.
    ...

240A. Time remanded on bail to count towards time served: terms of imprisonment and detention

(1) This section applies where—
    (a) a court sentences an offender to imprisonment for a term in respect of an offence,
    (b) the offender was remanded on bail by a court in course of or in connection with proceedings for the offence, or any related offence, after the coming into force of section 21 of the Criminal Justice and Immigration Act 2008, and
    (c) the offender's bail was subject to a qualifying curfew condition and an electronic monitoring condition ('the relevant conditions').

(2) Subject to subsections (3A) and (3B), the court must direct that the credit period is to count as time served by the offender as part of the sentence.

(3) The credit period is calculated by taking the following steps.
    Step 1
    Add—
    (a) the day on which the offender's bail was first subject to the relevant conditions (and for this purpose a condition is not prevented from being a relevant condition by the fact that it does not apply for the whole of the day in question), and
    (b) the number of other days on which the offender's bail was subject to those conditions (but exclude the last of those days if the offender spends the last part of it in custody).

Step 2

Deduct the number of days on which the offender, whilst on bail subject to the relevant conditions, was also—

(a)   subject to any requirement imposed for the purpose of securing the electronic monitoring of the offender's compliance with a curfew requirement, or

(b)   on temporary release under rules made under section 47 of the Prison Act 1952.

Step 3

From the remainder, deduct the number of days during that remainder on which the offender has broken either or both of the relevant conditions.

Step 4

Divide the result by 2.

Step 5

If necessary, round up to the nearest whole number.

(3A) A day of the credit period counts as time served—

(a)   in relation to only one sentence, and

(b)   only once in relation to that sentence.

(3B) A day of the credit period is not to count as time served as part of any automatic release period served by the offender (see section 255B(1)).

(4)–(7) ...

(8)   Where the court gives a direction under subsection (2) it shall state in open court—

(a)   the number of days on which the offender was subject to the relevant conditions, and

(b)   the number of days which it deducted under each of steps 2 and 3.

(9), (10) ...

(11) Subsections (7) to (9) and (11) of section 240ZA apply for the purposes of this section as they apply for the purposes of that section but as if—

(a)   in subsection (7)—

(i)   the reference to a suspended sentence is to be read as including a reference to a sentence to which an order under section 118(1) of the Sentencing Act relates;

(ii)   in paragraph (a) after 'Schedule 12' there were inserted 'or section 119(1)(a) or (b) of the Sentencing Act'; and

(b)   in subsection (9) the references to subsections (3) and (5) of section 240ZA are to be read as a reference to subsection (2) of this section and, in paragraph (b), after 'Chapter' there were inserted 'or Part 2 of the Criminal Justice Act 1991'.

(12) In this section—

'curfew requirement' means a requirement (however described) to remain at one or more specified places for a specified number of hours in any given day, provided that the requirement is imposed by a court or the Secretary of State and arises as a result of a conviction;

'electronic monitoring condition' means any electronic monitoring requirements imposed under section 3(6ZAA) of the Bail Act 1976 for the purpose of securing the electronic monitoring of a person's compliance with a qualifying curfew condition;

'qualifying curfew condition' means a condition of bail which requires the person granted bail to remain at one or more specified places for a total of not less than 9 hours in any given day.

241.   Effect of section 240ZA or direction under section 240A on release on licence

(1)   In determining for the purposes of this Chapter whether a person to whom section 240ZA applies or a direction under section 240A relates—

(a)   has served, or would (but for his release) have served, a particular proportion of his sentence, or

(b)   has served a particular period,

the number of days specified in section 240ZA or in the direction under section 240A are to be treated as having been served by him as part of that sentence or period.

242. Interpretation of sections 240ZA, 240A and 241

(1) For the purposes of sections 240ZA, 240A and 241, the definition of 'sentence of imprisonment' in section 305 applies as if for the words from the beginning of the definition to the end of paragraph (a) there were substituted—

'sentence of imprisonment' does not include a committal—

    (a)   in default of payment of any sum of money, other than one adjudged to be paid on a conviction';

and references in those sections to sentencing an offender to imprisonment, and to an offender's sentence, are to be read accordingly.

(2) References in sections 240ZA and 241 to an offender's being remanded in custody are references to his being—

    (a)   remanded in or committed to custody by order of a court,

    (b)   remanded to youth detention accommodation under section 91(4) of the Legal Aid, Sentencing and Punishment of Offenders Act 2012, or

    (c)   remanded, admitted or removed to hospital under section 35, 36, 38 or 48 of the Mental Health Act 1983.

244A. Release on licence of prisoners serving sentence under section 236A

(1) This section applies to a prisoner ('P') who is serving a sentence imposed under section 236A.

(2) The Secretary of State must refer P's case to the Board—

    (a)   as soon as P has served the requisite custodial period, and

    (b)   where there has been a previous reference of P's case to the Board under this subsection and the Board did not direct P's release, not later than the second anniversary of the disposal of that reference.

(3) It is the duty of the Secretary of State to release P on licence under this section as soon as—

    (a)   P has served the requisite custodial period, and

    (b)   the Board has directed P's release under this section.

(4) The Board must not give a direction under subsection (3) unless—

    (a)   the Secretary of State has referred P's case to the Board, and

    (b)   the Board is satisfied that it is not necessary for the protection of the public that P should be confined.

(5) It is the duty of the Secretary of State to release P on licence under this section as soon as P has served the appropriate custodial term, unless P has previously been released on licence under this section and recalled under section 254 (provision for the release of such persons being made by sections 255A to 255C).

(6) For the purposes of this section—

'the appropriate custodial term' means the term determined as such by the court under section 236A;

'the requisite custodial period' means—

    (a)   in relation to a person serving one sentence, one-half of the appropriate custodial term, and

    (b)   in relation to a person serving two or more concurrent or consecutive sentences, the period determined under sections 263(2) and 264(2).

246A. Release of prisoners serving extended sentence under section 226A or 226B

(1) This section applies to a prisoner ('P') who is serving an extended sentence imposed under sections 226A or 226B.

(2) It is the duty of the Secretary of State to release P on licence under this section as soon as P has served the requisite custodial period for the purposes of this section if—

    (a)   the sentence was imposed before the coming into force of section 4 of the Criminal Justice and Courts Act 2015,

    (b)   the appropriate custodial term is less than 10 years, and

    (c)   the sentence was not imposed in respect of an offence listed in Parts 1 to 3 of Schedule 15B or in respect of offences that include one or more offences listed in those Parts of that Schedule.

(3) In any other case, it is the duty of the Secretary of State to release P on licence in accordance with subsections (4) to (7).

(4)   The Secretary of State must refer P's case to the Board—
    (a)   as soon as P has served the requisite custodial period, and
    (b)   where there has been a previous reference of P's case to the Board under this subsection and the Board did not direct P's release, not later than the second anniversary of the disposal of that reference.

(5)   It is the duty of the Secretary of State to release P on licence under this section as soon as—
    (a)   P has served the requisite custodial period, and
    (b)   the Board has directed P's release under this section.

(6)   The Board must not give a direction under subsection (5) unless—
    (a)   the Secretary of State has referred P's case to the Board, and
    (b)   the Board is satisfied that it is no longer necessary for the protection of the public that P should be confined.

(7)   It is the duty of the Secretary of State to release P on licence under this section as soon as P has served the appropriate custodial term unless P has previously been released on licence under this section and recalled under section 254 (provision for the release of such persons being made by section 255C).

(8)   For the purposes of this section—
    'appropriate custodial term' means the term determined as such by the court under section 226A or 226B (as appropriate);
    'the requisite custodial period' means—
    (a)   in relation to a person serving one sentence, two-thirds of the appropriate custodial term, and
    (b)   in relation to a person serving two or more concurrent or consecutive sentences, the period determined under sections 263(2) and 264(2).

248. Power to release prisoners on compassionate grounds

(1)   The Secretary of State may at any time release a fixed-term prisoner on licence if he is satisfied that exceptional circumstances exist which justify the prisoner's release on compassionate grounds.

249. Duration of licence

(1)   Subject to subsection (3), where a fixed-term prisoner other than one to whom section 243A applies is released on licence, the licence shall, subject to any revocation under section 254 or 255, remain in force for the remainder of his sentence.

(1A) Where a prisoner to whom section 243A applies is released on licence, he licence shall, subject to any revocation under section 254 or 255, remain in force until the date on which, but for the release, the prisoner would have served one-half of the sentence. This is subject to subsection (3).

(2)   ...

(3)   Subsections (1) and (1A) have effect subject to sections 263(2) (concurrent terms) and 264(3) (consecutive terms).

(4)   ...

256AA. Supervision after end of sentence of prisoners serving less than 2 years

(1)   This section applies where a person ('the offender') has served a fixed term sentence which was for a term of more than 1 day but less than 2 years, except where—
    (a)   the offender was aged under 18 on the last day of the requisite custodial period (as defined in section 243A(3)),
    (b)   the sentence was an extended sentence imposed under section 226A or 226B, or
    (ba) the sentence was imposed under section 236A, or
    (c)   the sentence was imposed in respect of an offence committed before the day on which section 2(2) of the Offender Rehabilitation Act 2014 came into force.

(2)   The offender must comply with the supervision requirements during the supervision period, except at any time when the offender is—
    (a)   in legal custody,
    (b)   subject to a licence under this Chapter or Chapter 2 of Part 2 of the 1997 Act, or
    (c)   subject to DTO supervision.

(3)   The supervision requirements are the requirements for the time being specified in a notice given to the offender by the Secretary of State (but see the restrictions in section 256AB).

(4)   'The supervision period' is the period which—

(a)   begins on the expiry of the sentence, and

(b)   ends on the expiry of the period of 12 months beginning immediately after the offender has served the requisite custodial period (as defined in section 244(3)).

(5)   The purpose of the supervision period is the rehabilitation of the offender.

269.   Determination of minimum term in relation to mandatory life sentence

(1)   This section applies where after the commencement of this section a court passes a life sentence in circumstances where the sentence is fixed by law.

(2)   The court must, unless it makes an order under subsection (4), order that the provisions of section 28(5) to (8) of the Crime (Sentences) Act 1997 (referred to in this Chapter as 'the early release provisions') are to apply to the offender as soon as he has served the part of his sentence which is specified in the order.

(3)   The part of his sentence is to be such as the court considers appropriate taking into account—

(a)   the seriousness of the offence, or of the combination of the offence and any one or more offences associated with it, and

(b)   the effect of section 240ZA (crediting periods of remand in custody) or of any direction which it would have given under section 240A (crediting periods of remand on certain types of bail) … if it had sentenced him to a term of imprisonment.

(4)   If the offender was 21 or over when he committed the offence and the court is of the opinion that, because of the seriousness of the offence, or of the combination of the offence and one or more offences associated with it, no order should be made under subsection (2), the court must order that the early release provisions are not to apply to the offender.

(5)   In considering under subsection (3) or (4) the seriousness of an offence (or of the combination of an offence and one or more offences associated with it), the court must have regard to—

(a)   the general principles set out in Schedule 21, and

(b)   any guidelines relating to offences in general which are relevant to the case and are not incompatible with the provisions of Schedule 21.

(6)   The Lord Chancellor may by order amend Schedule 21.

(7)   Before making an order under subsection (6), the Lord Chancellor must consult the Sentencing Council for England and Wales.

270.   Duty to give reasons

(1)   Subsection (2) applies where a court makes an order under section 269(2) or (4).

(2)   In complying with the duty under section 174(2) to state its reasons for deciding on the order made, the court must, in particular—

(a)   state which of the starting points in Schedule 21 it has chosen and its reasons for doing so, and

(b)   state its reasons for any departure from that starting point.

SCHEDULE 21
DETERMINATION OF MINIMUM TERM IN RELATION TO MANDATORY LIFE SENTENCE

Interpretation

1.   In this Schedule—

'child' means a person under 18 years;

'mandatory life sentence' means a life sentence passed in circumstances where the sentence is fixed by law;

'minimum term', in relation to a mandatory life sentence, means the part of the sentence to be specified in an order under section 269(2);

'whole life order' means an order under subsection (4) of section 269.

2.   Section 28 of the Crime and Disorder Act 1998 (meaning of 'racially or religiously aggravated') applies for the purposes of this Schedule as it applies for the purposes of sections 29 to 32 of that Act.

3.   For the purposes of this Schedule—

(a)   an offence is aggravated by sexual orientation if it is committed in circumstances mentioned in section 146(2)(a)(i) or (b)(i);

(b)   an offence is aggravated by disability if it is committed in circumstances mentioned in section 146(2)(a)(ii) or (b)(ii);

(c)   an offence is aggravated by transgender identity if it is committed in circumstances mentioned in section 146(2)(a)(iii) or (b)(iii).

Starting points

4.   (1)   If—

(a)   the court considers that the seriousness of the offence (or the combination of the offence and one or more offences associated with it) is exceptionally high, and

(b)   the offender was aged 21 or over when he committed the offence, the appropriate starting point is a whole life order.

(2)   Cases that would normally fall within sub-paragraph (1)(a) include—

(a)   the murder of two or more persons, where each murder involves any of the following—

(i)   a substantial degree of premeditation or planning,

(ii)   the abduction of the victim, or

(iii)   sexual or sadistic conduct,

(b)   the murder of a child if involving the abduction of the child or sexual or sadistic motivation,

(ba)   the murder of a police officer or prison officer in the course of his or her duty,

(c)   a murder done for the purpose of advancing a political, religious, racial or ideological cause, or

(d)   a murder by an offender previously convicted of murder.

5.   (1)   If—

(a)   he case does not fall within paragraph 4(1) but the court considers that the seriousness of the offence (or the combination of the offence and one or more offences associated with it) is particularly high, and

(b)   the offender was aged 18 or over when he committed the offence,

the appropriate starting point, in determining the minimum term, is 30 years.

(2)   Cases that (if not falling within paragraph 4(1)) would normally fall within sub-paragraph (1)(a) include—

(b)   a murder involving the use of a firearm or explosive,

(c)   a murder done for gain (such as a murder done in the course or furtherance of robbery or burglary, done for payment or done in the expectation of gain as a result of the death),

(d)   a murder intended to obstruct or interfere with the course of justice, .

(e)   a murder involving sexual or sadistic conduct,

(f)   the murder of two or more persons,

(g)   a murder that is racially or religiously aggravated or aggravated by sexual orientation, disability or transgender identity, or

(h)   a murder falling within paragraph 4(2) committed by an offender who was aged under 21 when he committed the offence.

5A.   (1)   If—

(a)   the case does not fall within paragraph 4(1) or 5(1),

(b)   the offence falls within sub-paragraph (2), and

(c)   the offender was aged 18 or over when the offender committed the offence,

the offence is normally to be regarded as sufficiently serious for the appropriate starting point, in determining the minimum term, to be 25 years.

(2)   The offence falls within this sub-paragraph if the offender took a knife or other weapon to the scene intending to—

(a)   commit any offence, or

(b)   have it available to use as a weapon,

and used that knife or other weapon in committing the murder.

6.   If the offender was aged 18 or over when he committed the offence and the case does not fall within paragraph 4(1), 5(1) or 5A(1), the appropriate starting point, in determining the minimum term, is 15 years.

7.   If the offender was aged under 18 when he committed the offence, the appropriate starting point, in determining the minimum term, is 12 years.

Aggravating and mitigating factors

8.   Having chosen a starting point, the court should take into account any aggravating or mitigating factors, to the extent that it has not allowed for them in its choice of starting point.

9.   Detailed consideration of aggravating or mitigating factors may result in a minimum term of any length (whatever the starting point), or in the making of a whole life order.

10.   Aggravating factors (additional to those mentioned in paragraph 4(2), 5(2) and 5A(2)) that may be relevant to the offence of murder include—
   (a)   significant degree of planning or premeditation,
   (b)   the fact that the victim was particularly vulnerable because of age or disability,
   (c)   mental or physical suffering inflicted on the victim before death,
   (d)   the abuse of a position of trust,
   (e)   the use of duress or threats against another person to facilitate the commission of the offence,
   (f)   the fact that the victim was providing a public service or performing a public duty, and
   (g)   concealment, destruction or dismemberment of the body.

11.   Mitigating factors that may be relevant to the offence of murder include—
   (a)   an intention to cause serious bodily harm rather than to kill,
   (b)   lack of premeditation,
   (c)   the fact that the offender suffered from any mental disorder or mental disability which (although not falling within section 2(1) of the Homicide Act 1957), lowered his degree of culpability,
   (d)   the fact that the offender was provoked (for example, by prolonged stress)
   (e)   the fact that the offender acted to any extent in self-defence or in fear of violence,
   (f)   a belief by the offender that the murder was an act of mercy, and
   (g)   the age of the offender.

12.   Nothing in this Schedule restricts the application of—
   (a)   section 143(2) (previous convictions),
   (b)   section 143(3) (bail), or
   (c)   section 144 (guilty plea).
   or of section 238(1)(b) or (c) or 239 of the Armed Forces Act 2006.

CRIMINAL JUSTICE AND COURTS ACT 2015

17.   Restrictions on use of cautions
   (1)   This section applies where, in England and Wales, a person aged 18 or over admits that he or she has committed an offence.
   (2)   If the offence is an indictable-only offence, a constable may not give the person a caution except—
       (a)   in exceptional circumstances relating to the person or the offence, and
       (b)   with the consent of the Director of Public Prosecutions.
   (3)   If the offence is an either-way offence specified by order made by the Secretary of State, a constable may not give the person a caution except in exceptional circumstances relating to the person or the offence.
   (4)   If—
       (a)   the offence is a summary offence or an either-way offence not specified under subsection (3), and
       (b)   in the two years before the commission of the offence the person has been convicted of, or cautioned for, a similar offence,
       a constable may not give the person a caution except in exceptional circumstances relating to the person, the offence admitted or the previous offence.

(5) It is for a police officer not below a rank specified by order made by the Secretary of State to determine—

    (a) whether there are exceptional circumstances for the purposes of subsection (2), (3) or (4), and

    (b) whether a previous offence is similar to the offence admitted for the purposes of subsection (4)(b).

(6) A determination under subsection (5) must be made in accordance with guidance issued by the Secretary of State.

(7) The Secretary of State may by order amend this section so as to provide for a different period for the purposes of subsection (4)(b).

(8) For the purposes of this section—

    (a) 'caution' does not include a conditional caution under Part 3 of the Criminal Justice Act 2003, but

    (b) a person has been 'cautioned for' an offence if he or she has been given a caution, a conditional caution or a youth caution or youth conditional caution under Chapter 1 of Part 4 of the Crime and Disorder Act 1998.

(9) In this section—

'either-way offence' means an offence triable either way;

'indictable-only offence' means an offence which, if committed by an adult, is triable only on indictment.

(10) This section applies whether the offence admitted was committed before or after the time when this section comes into force.

CRIMINAL JUSTICE AND IMMIGRATION ACT 2008
(2008, c. 4)

1.   **Youth rehabilitation orders**

(1) Where a person aged under 18 is convicted of an offence, the court by or before which the person is convicted may in accordance with Schedule 1 make an order (in this Part referred to as a 'youth rehabilitation order') imposing on the person any one or more of the following requirements—

    (a) an activity requirement (see paragraphs 6 to 8 of Schedule 1),

    (b) a supervision requirement (see paragraph 9 of that Schedule),

    (c) in a case where the offender is aged 16 or 17 at the time of the conviction, an unpaid work requirement (see paragraph 10 of that Schedule),

    (d) a programme requirement (see paragraph 11 of that Schedule),

    (e) an attendance centre requirement (see paragraph 12 of that Schedule),

    (f) a prohibited activity requirement (see paragraph 13 of that Schedule),

    (g) a curfew requirement (see paragraph 14 of that Schedule),

    (h) an exclusion requirement (see paragraph 15 of that Schedule),

    (i) a residence requirement (see paragraph 16 of that Schedule),

    (j) a local authority residence requirement (see paragraph 17 of that Schedule),

    (k) a mental health treatment requirement (see paragraph 20 of that Schedule),

    (l) a drug treatment requirement (see paragraph 22 of that Schedule),

    (m) a drug testing requirement (see paragraph 23 of that Schedule),

    (n) an intoxicating substance treatment requirement (see paragraph 24 of that Schedule), and

    (o) an education requirement (see paragraph 25 of that Schedule).

(2) A youth rehabilitation order—

    (a) may also impose an electronic monitoring requirement (see paragraph 26 of Schedule 1), and

    (b) must do so if paragraph 2 of that Schedule so requires.

(3) A youth rehabilitation order may be—

    (a) a youth rehabilitation order with intensive supervision and surveillance (see paragraph 3 of Schedule 1), or

    (b) a youth rehabilitation order with fostering (see paragraph 4 of that Schedule).

(4)   But a court may only make an order mentioned in subsection (3)(a) or (b) if—
    (a)   the court is dealing with the offender for an offence which is punishable with imprisonment,
    (b)   the court is of the opinion that the offence, or the combination of the offence and one or more offences associated with it, was so serious that, but for paragraph 3 or 4 of Schedule 1, a custodial sentence would be appropriate (or, if the offender was aged under 12 at the time of conviction, would be appropriate if the offender had been aged 12), and
    (c)   if the offender was aged under 15 at the time of conviction, the court is of the opinion that the offender is a persistent offender.
(5)   Schedule 1 makes further provision about youth rehabilitation orders.
(6)   This section is subject to—
    (a)   sections 148 and 150 of the Criminal Justice Act 2003 (restrictions on community sentences etc), and
    (b)   the provisions of Parts 1 and 3 of Schedule 1.

2.   Breach, revocation or amendment of youth rehabilitation orders

Schedule 2 makes provision about failures to comply with the requirements of youth rehabilitation orders and about the revocation or amendment of such orders.

CRIMINAL JUSTICE AND PUBLIC ORDER ACT 1994
(1994, c. 33)

25.   No bail for defendants charged with or convicted of homicide or rape after previous conviction of such offences

(1)   A person who in any proceedings has been charged with or convicted of an offence to which this section applies in circumstances to which it applies shall be granted bail in those proceedings only if the court or, as the case may be, the constable considering the grant of bail is of the opinion that there are exceptional circumstances which justify it.
(2)   This section applies, subject to subsection (3) below, to the following offences, that is to say—
    (a)   murder;
    (b)   attempted murder;
    (c)   manslaughter;
    (d)   rape under the law of Scotland ...;
    (e)   an offence under section 1 of the Sexual Offences Act 1956 (rape);
    (f)   an offence under section 1 of the Sexual Offences Act 2003 (rape);
    (g)   an offence under section 2 of that Act (assault by penetration);
    (h)   an offence under section 4 of that Act (causing a person to engage in sexual activity without consent), where the activity caused involved penetration within subsection (4)(a) to (d) of that section;
    (i)   an offence under section 5 of that Act (rape of a child under 13);
    (j)   an offence under section 6 of that Act (assault of a child under 13 by penetration);
    (k)   an offence under section 8 of that Act (causing or inciting a child under 13 to engage in sexual activity), where an activity involving penetration within subsection (3)(a) to (d) of that section was caused;
    (l)   an offence under section 30 of that Act (sexual activity with a person with a mental disorder impeding choice), where the touching involved penetration within subsection (3)(a) to (d) of that section;
    (m)   an offence under section 31 of that Act (causing or inciting a person, with a mental disorder impeding choice, to engage in sexual activity), where an activity involving penetration within subsection (3)(a) to (d) of that section was caused;
    (n)   an attempt to commit an offence within any of paragraphs (d) to (m).
(3)   This section applies in the circumstances described in subsection (3A) or (3B) only.

(3A) This section applies where—

    (a) the person has been previously convicted by or before a court in any part of the United Kingdom of any offence within subsection (2) or of culpable homicide, and

    (b) if that previous conviction is one of manslaughter or culpable homicide—

        (i) the person was then a child or young person and was sentenced to long-term detention under any of the relevant enactments, or

        (ii) the person was not then a child or young person, and was sentenced to imprisonment or detention.

(3B) This section applies where—

    (a) the person has been previously convicted by or before a court in another member State of any relevant foreign offence corresponding to an offence within subsection (2) or to culpable homicide, and

    (b) if the previous conviction is of a relevant foreign offence corresponding to the offence of manslaughter or culpable homicide—

        (i) the person was then a child or young person, and was sentenced to detention for a period in excess of 2 years, or

        (ii) the person was not then a child or young person, and was sentenced to detention.

(4) This section applies whether or not an appeal is pending against conviction or sentence.

(5) In this section—

    'conviction' includes—

    (a) a finding that a person is not guilty by reason of insanity;

    (b) a finding under section 4A(3) of the Criminal Procedure (Insanity) Act 1964 (cases of unfitness to plead) that a person did the act or made the omission charged against him; and

    (c) a conviction of an offence for which an order is made ... discharging the offender absolutely or conditionally;

    and 'convicted' shall be construed accordingly; and

    'the relevant enactments' means—

    (a) as respects England and Wales, section 91 of the Powers of Criminal Courts (Sentencing) Act 2000;

    ...

...

60. Powers to stop and search in anticipation of, or after, violence

(1) If a police officer of or above the rank of inspector reasonably believes—

    (a) that incidents involving serious violence may take place in any locality in his police area, and that it is expedient to give an authorisation under this section to prevent their occurrence, or

    (aa) that—

        (i) an incident involving serious violence has taken place in England and Wales in his police area;

        (ii) a dangerous instrument or offensive weapon used in the incident is being carried in any locality in his police area by a person; and

        (iii) it is expedient to give an authorisation under this section to find the instrument or weapon; or

    (b) that persons are carrying dangerous instruments or offensive weapons in any locality in his police area without good reason,

he may give an authorisation that the powers conferred by this section are to be exercisable at any place within that locality for a specified period not exceeding 24 hours.

(2) ...

(3) If it appears to an officer of or above the rank of superintendent that it is expedient to do so, having regard to offences which have, or are reasonably suspected to have, been committed in connection with any activity falling within the authorisation, he may direct that the authorisation shall continue in being for a further 24 hours.

(3A) If an inspector gives an authorisation under subsection (1) he must, as soon as it is practicable to do so, cause an officer of or above the rank of superintendent to be informed.

(4) This section confers on any constable in uniform power—

    (a) to stop any pedestrian and search him or anything carried by him for offensive weapons or dangerous instruments;

    (b) to stop any vehicle and search the vehicle, its driver and any passenger for offensive weapons or dangerous instruments.

(4A) ...

(5) A constable may, in the exercise of the powers conferred by subsection (4) above, stop any person or vehicle and make any search he thinks fit whether or not he has any grounds for suspecting that the person or vehicle is carrying weapons or articles of that kind.

(6) If in the course of a search under this section a constable discovers a dangerous instrument or an article which he has reasonable grounds for suspecting to be an offensive weapon, he may seize it.

...

(8) A person who fails ... to stop, or to stop a vehicle when required to do so by a constable in the exercise of his powers under this section shall be liable on summary conviction to imprisonment for a term not exceeding one month or to a fine not exceeding level 3 on the standard scale or both.

(9) Subject to subsection (9ZA), any authorisation under this section shall be in writing signed by the officer giving it and shall specify the grounds on which it is given and]the locality in which and the period during which the powers conferred by this section are exercisable and a direction under subsection (3) above shall also be given in writing or, where that is not practicable, recorded in writing as soon as it is practicable to do so.

(9ZA)An authorisation under subsection (1)(aa) need not be given in writing where it is not practicable to do so but any oral authorisation must state the matters which would otherwise have to be specified under subsection (9) and must be recorded in writing as soon as it is practicable to do so.

(9A) ...

(10) Where a vehicle is stopped by a constable under this section, the driver shall be entitled to obtain a written statement that the vehicle was stopped under the powers conferred by this section if he applies for such a statement not later than the end of the period of twelve months from the day on which the vehicle was stopped..

(10A) A person who is searched by a constable under this section shall be entitled to obtain a written statement that he was searched under the powers conferred by this section if he applies for such a statement not later than the end of the period of twelve months from the day on which he was searched.

...

(12) The powers conferred by this section are in addition to and not in derogation of, any power otherwise conferred.

60AA. Powers to require removal of disguises

(1) Where—

    (a) an authorisation under section 60 is for the time being in force in relation to any locality for any period, or

    (b) an authorisation under subsection (3) that the powers conferred by subsection (2) shall be exercisable at any place in a locality is in force for any period,

those powers shall be exercisable at any place in that locality at any time in that period.

(2) This subsection confers power on any constable in uniform—

    (a) to require any person to remove any item which the constable reasonably believes that person is wearing wholly or mainly for the purpose of concealing his identity;

    (b) to seize any item which the constable reasonably believes any person intends to wear wholly or mainly for that purpose.

(3) If a police officer of or above the rank of inspector reasonably believes—

    (a) that activities may take place in any locality in his police area that are likely (if they take place) to involve the commission of offences, and

(b)   that it is expedient, in order to prevent or control the activities, to give an authorisation under this subsection,

he may give an authorisation that the powers conferred by this section shall be exercisable at any place within that locality for a specified period not exceeding twenty-four hours.

(4)   If it appears to an officer of or above the rank of superintendent that it is expedient to do so, having regard to offences which—

(a)   have been committed in connection with the activities in respect of which the authorisation was given, or

(b)   are reasonably suspected to have been so committed,

he may direct that the authorisation shall continue in force for a further twenty-four hours.

(5)   If an inspector gives an authorisation under subsection, he must, as soon as it is practicable to do so, cause an officer of or above the rank of superintendent to be informed.

(6)   Subject to subsection (6A), an authorisation under subsection (3)—

(a)   shall be in writing and signed by the officer giving it; and

(b)   shall specify—

(i)   the grounds on which it is given;

(ii)   the locality in which the powers conferred by this section are exercisable; and

(iii)   the period during which those powers are exercisable.

(6A) An authorisation under subsection (3) need not be given in writing where it is not practicable to do so but any oral authorisation—

(a)   must state the matters which would otherwise have to be specified under subsection (6); and

(b)   must be recorded in writing as soon as it is practicable to do so.

(6B) A direction under subsection (4) shall be given in writing or, where that is not practicable, recorded in writing as soon as it is practicable to do so.

(7)   A person who fails to remove an item worn by him when required to do so by a constable in the exercise of his power under this section shall be liable, on summary conviction, to imprisonment for a term not exceeding one month or to a fine not exceeding level 3 on the standard scale or both.

...

(10) The powers conferred by this section are in addition to, and not in derogation of, any power otherwise conferred.

...

CRIMINAL LAW ACT 1826
(1826, c. 64)

28.   Courts may order compensation to those who have been active in the apprehension of certain offenders

Where any person shall appear to the Crown Court, to have been active in or towards the apprehension of any person charged with an indictable offence, the Crown Court is hereby authorized and empowered, in any of the cases aforesaid, to order the high sheriff of the county in which the offence shall have been committed to pay to the person or persons who shall appear to the court to have been active in or towards the apprehension of any person charged with that offence such sum or sums of money as to the court shall seem reasonable and sufficient to compensate such person or persons for his, her, or their expenses, exertions, and loss of time in or towards such apprehension; ...

29.   Such orders to be paid by the sheriff, who may obtain immediate repayment on application to the Treasury

Every order for payment to any person in respect of such apprehension as aforesaid shall be forthwith made out and delivered by the proper officer of the court unto such person; and the high sheriff of the county for the time being is hereby authorised and required, upon sight of such order, forthwith to pay to such person, or to any one duly authorized on his or her behalf, the money in such order mentioned; and every such high sheriff may immediately apply for repayment of the same to the Treasury, who, upon inspecting such order, together with the acquittance of the person entitled to receive the money thereon, shall forthwith order repayment to the high sheriff of the money so by him paid, without any fee or reward whatsoever.

CRIMINAL LAW ACT 1967
(1967, c. 58)

6.   Trial of offences

(1)   Where a person is arraigned on an indictment—
  (a)   he shall in all cases be entitled to make a plea of not guilty in addition to any demurrer or special plea;
  (b)   he may plead not guilty of the offence specifically charged in the indictment but guilty of another offence of which he might be found guilty on that indictment;
  (c)   if he stands mute of malice or will not answer directly to the indictment, the court may order a plea of not guilty to be entered on his behalf, and he shall then be treated as having pleaded not guilty.

(2)   On an indictment for murder a person found not guilty of murder may be found guilty—
  (a)   of manslaughter, or of causing grievous bodily harm with intent to do so; or
  (b)   of any offence of which he may be found guilty under an enactment specifically so providing, or under section 4(2) of this Act; or
  (c)   of an attempt to commit murder, or of an attempt to commit any other offence of which he might be found guilty;
  but may not be found guilty of any offence not included above.

(3)   Where, on a person's trial on indictment for any offence except treason or murder, the jury find him not guilty of the offence specifically charged in the indictment, but the allegations in the indictment amount to or include (expressly or by implication) an allegation of another offence falling within the jurisdiction of the court of trial, the jury may find him guilty of that other offence or of an offence of which he could be found guilty on an indictment specifically charging that other offence.

(3A)   For the purposes of subsection (3) above an offence falls within the jurisdiction of the court of trial if it is an offence to which section 40 of the Criminal Justice Act 1988 applies (power to join in indictment count for common assault etc), even if a count charging the offence is not included in the indictment.

(3B)   A person convicted of an offence by virtue of subsection (3A) may only be dealt with for it in a manner in which a magistrates' court could have dealt with him.

(4)   For purposes of subsection (3) above any allegation of an offence shall be taken as including an allegation of attempting to commit that offence; and where a person is charged on indictment with attempting to commit an offence or with any assault or other act preliminary to an offence, but not with the completed offence, then (subject to the discretion of the court to discharge the jury or otherwise act with a view to the preferment of an indictment for the completed offence) he may be convicted of the offence charged notwithstanding that he is shown to be guilty of the completed offence.

CRIMINAL PROCEDURE (ATTENDANCE OF WITNESSES) ACT 1965
(1965, c. 69)

2.   Issue of witness summons on application to Crown Court

(1)   This section applies where the Crown Court is satisfied that—
  (a)   a person is likely to be able to give evidence likely to be material evidence, or produce any document or thing likely to be material evidence, for the purpose of any criminal proceedings before the Crown Court, and
  (b)   it is in the interests of justice to issue a summons under this section to secure the attendance of that person to give evidence or to produce the document or thing.

(2) In such a case the Crown Court shall, subject to the following provisions of this section, issue a summons (a witness summons) directed to the person concerned and requiring him to—
   (a) attend before the Crown Court at the time and place stated in the summons, and
   (b) give the evidence or produce the document or thing.
(3) A witness summons may only be issued under this section on an application; and the Crown Court may refuse to issue the summons if any requirement relating to the application is not fulfilled.
(4) Where a person has been sent for trial for any offence to which the proceedings concerned relate, an application must be made as soon as is reasonably practicable after service on that person, in pursuance of regulations made under paragraph 1 of Schedule 3 to the Crime and Disorder Act 1998, of the documents relevant to that offence.

CRIMINAL PROCEDURE (INSANITY) ACT 1964
(1964, c. 84)

1. Acquittal on grounds of insanity

The special verdict required by section 2 of the Trial of Lunatics Act 1883 (hereinafter referred to as a 'special verdict') shall be that the accused is not guilty by reason of insanity; and accordingly in subsection (1) of that section for the words from 'a special verdict' to the end there shall be substituted the words 'a special verdict that the accused is not guilty by reason of insanity'.

4. Finding of unfitness to plead

(1) This section applies where on the trial of a person the question arises (at the instance of the defence or otherwise) whether the accused is under a disability, that is to say, under any disability such that apart from this Act it would constitute a bar to his being tried.
(2) If, having regard to the nature of the supposed disability, the court are of opinion that it is expedient to do so and in the interests of the accused, they may postpone consideration of the question of fitness to be tried until any time up to the opening of the case for the defence.
(3) If, before the question of fitness to be tried falls to be determined, the jury return a verdict of acquittal on the count or each of the counts on which the accused is being tried, that question shall not be determined.
(4) Subject to subsections (2) and (3) above, the question of fitness to be tried shall be determined as soon as it arises.
(5) The question of fitness to be tried shall be determined by the court without a jury
(6) The court shall not make a determination under subsection (5) above except on the written or oral evidence of two or more registered medical practitioners at least one of whom is duly approved.

4A. Finding that the accused did the act or made the omission charged against him

(1) This section applies where in accordance with section 4(5) above it is determined by a court that the accused is under a disability.
(2) The trial shall not proceed or further proceed but it shall be determined by a jury—
   (a) on the evidence (if any) already given in the trial; and
   (b) on such evidence as may be adduced or further adduced by the prosecution, or adduced by a person appointed by the court under this section to put the case for the defence,
   whether they are satisfied, as respects the count or each of the counts on which the accused was to be or was being tried, that he did the act or made the omission charged against him as the offence.
(3) If as respects that count or any of those counts the jury are satisfied as mentioned in subsection (2) above, they shall make a finding that the accused did the act or made the omission charged against him.

(4)   If as respects that count or any of those counts the jury are not so satisfied, they shall return a verdict of acquittal as if on the count in question the trial had proceeded to a conclusion.

(5)   Where the question of disability was determined on the arraignment of the accused, the determination under subsection (2) is to be made by the jury by whom he was being tried.

5.   Powers to deal with persons not guilty by reason of insanity or unfit to plead etc

(1)   This section applies where—

    (a)   a special verdict is returned that the accused is not guilty by reason of insanity; or

    (b)   findings are recorded that the accused is under a disability and that he did the act or made the omission charged against him.

(2)   The court shall make in respect of the accused—

    (a)   a hospital order (with or without a restriction order);

    (b)   a supervision order; or

    (c)   an order for his absolute discharge.

(3)   Where—

    (a)   the offence to which the special verdict or the findings relate is an offence the sentence for which is fixed by law, and

    (b)   the court has power to make a hospital order,

the court shall make a hospital order with a restriction order (whether or not they would have power to make a restriction order apart from this subsection).

CRIMINAL PROCEDURE AND INVESTIGATIONS ACT 1996
(1996, c. 25)

1.   Application of this Part

(1)   This Part applies where—

    (a)   a person is charged with a summary offence in respect of which a court proceeds to summary trial and in respect of which he pleads not guilty,

    (b)   a person who has attained the age of 18 is charged with an offence which is triable either way, in respect of which a court proceeds to summary trial and in respect of which he pleads not guilty, or

    (c)   a person under the age of 18 is charged with an indictable offence in respect of which a court proceeds to summary trial and in respect of which he pleads not guilty.

(2)   This Part also applies where—

    (cc)   a person is charged with an offence for which he is sent for trial.

    (d)   a count charging a person with a summary offence is included in an indictment under the authority of section 40 of the Criminal Justice Act 1988 (common assault etc), or

    (e)   a bill of indictment charging a person with an indictable offence is preferred under the authority of section 2(2)(b) of the Administration of Justice (Miscellaneous Provisions) Act 1933 (bill preferred by direction of Court of Appeal, or by direction or with consent of a judge), or

    (f)   a bill of indictment charging a person with an indictable offence is preferred under section 22B(3)(a) of the Prosecution of Offences Act 1985, or

    (g)   following the preferment of a bill of indictment charging a person with an indictable offence under the authority of section 2(2)(ba) of the Administration of Justice (Miscellaneous Provisions) Act 1933 (bill of indictment preferred with consent of Crown Court judge following approval of deferred prosecution agreement), the suspension of the proceedings against the person under paragraph 2(2) of Schedule 17 to the Crime and Courts Act 2013 is lifted under paragraph 2(3) of that Schedule.

(3)   This Part applies in relation to alleged offences into which no criminal investigation has begun before the appointed day.

(4) For the purposes of this section a criminal investigation is an investigation which police officers or other persons have a duty to conduct with a view to it being ascertained—
    (a) whether a person should be charged with an offence, or
    (b) whether a person charged with an offence is guilty of it.

(5) The reference in subsection (3) to the appointed day is to such day as is appointed for the purposes of this Part by the Secretary of State by order.

2. General interpretation

(1) References to the accused are to the person mentioned in section 1(1) or (2).

(2) Where there is more than one accused in any proceedings this Part applies separately in relation to each of the accused.

(3) References to the prosecutor are to any person acting as prosecutor, whether an individual or a body.

(4) References to material are to material of all kinds, and in particular include references to—
    (a) information, and
    (b) objects of all descriptions.

(5) References to recording information are to putting it in a durable or retrievable form (such as writing or tape).

(6) This section applies for the purposes of this Part.

3. Initial duty of prosecutor to disclose

(1) The prosecutor must—
    (a) disclose to the accused any prosecution material which has not previously been disclosed to the accused and which might reasonably be considered capable of undermining the case for the prosecution against the accused or of assisting the case for the accused, or
    (b) give to the accused a written statement that there is no material of a description mentioned in paragraph (a).

(2) For the purposes of this section prosecution material is material—
    (a) which is in the prosecutor's possession, and came into his possession in connection with the case for the prosecution against the accused, or
    (b) which, in pursuance of a code operative under Part II, he has inspected in connection with the case for the prosecution against the accused.

(3) Where material consists of information which has been recorded in any form the prosecutor discloses it for the purposes of this section—
    (a) by securing that a copy is made of it and that the copy is given to the accused, or
    (b) if in the prosecutor's opinion that is not practicable or not desirable, by allowing the accused to inspect it at a reasonable time and a reasonable place or by taking steps to secure that he is allowed to do so;
    and a copy may be in such form as the prosecutor thinks fit and need not be in the same form as that in which the information has already been recorded.

(4) Where material consists of information which has not been recorded the prosecutor discloses it for the purposes of this section by securing that it is recorded in such form as he thinks fit and—
    (a) by securing that a copy is made of it and that the copy is given to the accused, or
    (b) if in the prosecutor's opinion that is not practicable or not desirable, by allowing the accused to inspect it at a reasonable time and a reasonable place or by taking steps to secure that he is allowed to do so.

(5) Where material does not consist of information the prosecutor discloses it for the purposes of this section by allowing the accused to inspect it at a reasonable time and a reasonable place or by taking steps to secure that he is allowed to do so.

(6) Material must not be disclosed under this section to the extent that the court, on an application by the prosecutor, concludes it is not in the public interest to disclose it and orders accordingly.

(7) Material must not be disclosed under this section to the extent that it is material the disclosure of which is prohibited by section 17 of the Regulation of Investigatory Powers Act 2000.

(8) The prosecutor must act under this section during the period which, by virtue of section 12, is the relevant period for this section.

4.   Initial duty to disclose: further provisions

(1)   This section applies where—

 (a)   the prosecutor acts under section 3, and

 (b)   before doing so he was given a document in pursuance of provision included, by virtue of section 24(3), in a code operative under Part II.

(2)   In such a case the prosecutor must give the document to the accused at the same time as the prosecutor acts under section 3.

5.   Compulsory disclosure by accused

(1)   Subject to subsections (3A) and (4), this section applies where—

 (a)   this Part applies by virtue of section 1(2), and

 (b)   the prosecutor complies with section 3 or purports to comply with it.

(2), (3) …

(3A) Where this Part applies by virtue of section 1(2)(cc), this section does not apply unless—

 (a)   copies of the documents containing the evidence have been served on the accused under regulations made under paragraph 1 of Schedule 3 to the Crime and Disorder Act 1998; and

 (b)   a copy of the notice under subsection (1) of section 51D of that Act has been served on him under that subsection.

(4)   Where this Part applies by virtue of section 1(2)(e), this section does not apply unless the prosecutor has served on the accused a copy of the indictment and a copy of the set of documents containing the evidence which is the basis of the charge.

(5)   Where this section applies, the accused must give a defence statement to the court and the prosecutor.

(5A) Where there are other accused in the proceedings and the court so orders, the accused must also give a defence statement to each other accused specified by the court.

(5B) The court may make an order under subsection (5A) either of its own motion or on the application of any party.

(5C) A defence statement that has to be given to the court and the prosecutor (under subsection (5)) must be given during the period which, by virtue of section 12, is the relevant period for this section.

(5D) A defence statement that has to be given to a co-accused (under subsection (5A)) must be given within such period as the court may specify.

6.   Voluntary disclosure by accused

(1)   This section applies where—

 (a)   this Part applies by virtue of section 1(1), and

 (b)   the prosecutor complies with section 3 or purports to comply with it.

(2)   The accused—

 (a)   may give a defence statement to the prosecutor, and

 (b)   if he does so, must also give such a statement to the court.

(3)   …

(4)   If the accused gives a defence statement under this section he must give it during the period which, by virtue of section 12, is the relevant period for this section.

6A.   Contents of defence statement

(1)   For the purposes of this Part a defence statement is a written statement—

 (a)   setting out the nature of the accused's defence, including any particular defences on which he intends to rely,

 (b)   indicating the matters of fact on which he takes issue with the prosecution,

 (c)   setting out, in the case of each such matter, why he takes issue with the prosecution,

 (ca) setting out particulars of the matter of fact on which he intends to rely for the purposes of his defence, and

 (d)   indicating any point of law (including any point as to the admissibility of evidence or an abuse of process) which he wishes to take, and any authority on which he intends to rely for that purpose.

(2)   A defence statement that discloses an alibi must give particulars of it, including—

 (a)   the name, address and date of birth of any witness the accused believes is able to give evidence in support of the alibi, or as many of those details as are known to the accused when the statement is given;

    (b)   any information in the accused's possession which might be of material assistance in identifying or finding any such witness in whose case any of the details mentioned in paragraph (a) are not known to the accused when the statement is given.

(3)   For the purposes of this section evidence in support of an alibi is evidence tending to show that by reason of the presence of the accused at a particular place or in a particular area at a particular time he was not, or was unlikely to have been, at the place where the offence is alleged to have been committed at the time of its alleged commission.

(4)   The Secretary of State may by regulations make provision as to the details of the matters that, by virtue of subsection (1), are to be included in defence statements.

6C.   Notification of intention to call defence witnesses

(1)   The accused must give to the court and the prosecutor a notice indicating whether he intends to call any persons (other than himself) as witnesses at his trial and, if so—

    (a)   giving the name, address and date of birth of each such proposed witness, or as many of those details as are known to the accused when the notice is given;

    (b)   providing any information in the accused's possession which might be of material assistance in identifying or finding any such proposed witness in whose case any of the details mentioned in paragraph (a) are not known to the accused when the notice is given.

(2)   Details do not have to be given under this section to the extent that they have already been given under section 6A(2).

(3)   The accused must give a notice under this section during the period which, by virtue of section 12, is the relevant period for this section.

(4)   If, following the giving of a notice under this section, the accused—

    (a)   decides to call a person (other than himself) who is not included in the notice as a proposed witness, or decides not to call a person who is so included, or

    (b)   discovers any information which, under subsection (1), he would have had to include in the notice if he had been aware of it when giving the notice,

he must give an appropriately amended notice to the court and the prosecutor.

6E.   Disclosure by accused: further provisions

(1)   Where an accused's solicitor purports to give on behalf of the accused—

    (a)   a defence statement under section 5, 6 or 6B, or

    (b)   a statement of the kind mentioned in section 6B(4),

the statement shall, unless the contrary is proved, be deemed to be given with the authority of the accused.

(2)   If it appears to the judge at a pre-trial hearing that an accused has failed to comply fully with section 5, 6B or 6C, so that there is a possibility of comment being made or inferences drawn under section 11(5), he shall warn the accused accordingly.

(3)   In subsection (2) 'pre-trial hearing' has the same meaning as in Part 4 (see section 39).

(4)   The judge in a trial before a judge and jury—

    (a)   may direct that the jury be given a copy of any defence statement, and

    (b)   if he does so, may direct that it be edited so as not to include references to matters evidence of which would be inadmissible.

(5)   A direction under subsection (4)—

    (a)   may be made either of the judge's own motion or on the application of any party

    (b)   may be made only if the judge is of the opinion that seeing a copy of the defence statement would help the jury to understand the case or to resolve any issue in the case.

(6)   The reference in subsection (4) to a defence statement is a reference—

    (a)   where the accused has given only an initial defence statement (that is, a defence statement given under section 5 or 6), to that statement;

    (b)   where he has given both an initial defence statement and an updated defence statement (that is, a defence statement given under section 6B), to the updated defence statement;

    (c)   where he has given both an initial defence statement and a statement of the kind mentioned in section 6B(4), to the initial defence statement.

7A. Continuing duty of prosecutor to disclose

(1) This section applies at all times—

    (a) after the prosecutor has complied with section 3 or purported to comply with it, and

    (b) before the accused is acquitted or convicted or the prosecutor decides not to proceed with the case concerned.

(2) The prosecutor must keep under review the question whether at any given time (and, in particular, following the giving of a defence statement) there is prosecution material which—

    (a) might reasonably be considered capable of undermining the case for the prosecution against the accused or of assisting the case for the accused, and

    (b) has not been disclosed to the accused.

(3) If at any time there is any such material as is mentioned in subsection (2) the prosecutor must disclose it to the accused as soon as is reasonably practicable (or within the period mentioned in subsection (5)(a), where that applies).

(4) In applying subsection (2) by reference to any given time the state of affairs at that time (including the case for the prosecution as it stands at that time) must be taken into account.

(5) Where the accused gives a defence statement under section 5, 6 or 6B—

    (a) if as a result of that statement the prosecutor is required by this section to make any disclosure, or further disclosure, he must do so during the period which, by virtue of section 12, is the relevant period for this section;

    (b) if the prosecutor considers that he is not so required, he must during that period give to the accused a written statement to that effect.

(6) For the purposes of this section prosecution material is material—

    (a) which is in the prosecutor's possession and came into his possession in connection with the case for the prosecution against the accused, or

    (b) which, in pursuance of a code operative under Part 2, he has inspected in connection with the case for the prosecution against the accused.

(7) Subsections (3) to (5) of section 3 (method by which prosecutor discloses) apply for the purposes of this section as they apply for the purposes of that.

(8) Material must not be disclosed under this section to the extent that the court, on an application by the prosecutor, concludes it is not in the public interest to disclose it and orders accordingly.

(9) Material must not be disclosed under this section to the extent that it is material the disclosure of which is prohibited by section 17 of the Regulation of Investigatory Powers Act 2000.

8. Application by accused for disclosure

(1) This section applies where the accused has given a defence statement under section 5, 6 or 6B and the prosecutor has complied with section 7A(5) or has purported to comply with it or has failed to comply with it.

(2) If the accused has at any time reasonable cause to believe that there is prosecution material which is required by section 7A to be disclosed to him and has not been, he may apply to the court for an order requiring the prosecutor to disclose it to him.

(3) For the purposes of this section prosecution material is material—

    (a) which is in the prosecutor's possession and came into his possession in connection with the case for the prosecution against the accused,

    (b) which, in pursuance of a code operative under Part II, he has inspected in connection with the case for the prosecution against the accused, or

    (c) which falls within subsection (4).

(4) Material falls within this subsection if in pursuance of a code operative under Part II the prosecutor must, if he asks for the material, be given a copy of it or be allowed to inspect it in connection with the case for the prosecution against the accused.

(5) Material must not be disclosed under this section to the extent that the court, on an application by the prosecutor, concludes it is not in the public interest to disclose it and orders accordingly.

(6)   Material must not be disclosed under this section to the extent that it is material the disclosure of which is prohibited by section 17 of the Regulation of Investigatory Powers Act 2000.

10.   Prosecutor's failure to observe time limits

(1)   This section applies if the prosecutor—
   (a)   purports to act under section 3 after the end of the period which, by virtue of section 12, is the relevant period for section 3, or
   (b)   purports to act under section 7A(5) after the end of the period which, by virtue of section 12, is the relevant period for section 7A.
(2)   Subject to subsection (3), the failure to act during the period concerned does not on its own constitute grounds for staying the proceedings for abuse of process.
(3)   Subsection (2) does not prevent the failure constituting such grounds if it involves such delay by the prosecutor that the accused is denied a fair trial.

11.   Faults in disclosure by accused

(1)   This section applies in the three cases set out in subsections (2), (3) and (4).
(2)   The first case is where section 5 applies and the accused—
   (a)   fails to give an initial defence statement,
   (b)   gives an initial defence statement but does so after the end of the period which, by virtue of section 12, is the relevant period for section 5,
   (c)   is required by section 6B to give either an updated defence statement or a statement of the kind mentioned in subsection (4) of that section but fails to do so,
   (d)   gives an updated defence statement or a statement of the kind mentioned in section 6B(4) but does so after the end of the period which, by virtue of section 12, is the relevant period for section 6B,
   (e)   sets out inconsistent defences in his defence statement, or
   (f)   at his trial—
      (i)   puts forward a defence which was not mentioned in his defence statement or is different from any defence set out in that statement,
      (ii)   relies on a matter which, in breach of the requirements imposed by or under section 6A, was not mentioned in his defence statement,
      (iii)   adduces evidence in support of an alibi without having given particulars of the alibi in his defence statement, or
      (iv)   calls a witness to give evidence in support of an alibi without having complied with section 6A(2)(a) or (b) as regards the witness in his defence statement.
(3)   The second case is where section 6 applies, the accused gives an initial defence statement, and the accused—
   (a)   gives the initial defence statement after the end of the period which, by virtue of section 12, is the relevant period for section 6, or
   (b)   does any of the things mentioned in paragraphs (c) to (f) of subsection (2).
(4)   The third case is where the accused—
   (a)   gives a witness notice but does so after the end of the period which, by virtue of section 12, is the relevant period for section 6C, or
   (b)   at his trial calls a witness (other than himself) not included, or not adequately identified, in a witness notice.
(5)   Where this section applies—
   (a)   the court or any other party may make such comment as appears appropriate;
   (b)   the court or jury may draw such inferences as appear proper in deciding whether the accused is guilty of the offence concerned.
(6)   Where—
   (a)   this section applies by virtue of subsection (2)(f)(ii)(including that provision as it applies by virtue of subsection (3)(b)), and
   (b)   the matter which was not mentioned is a point of law (including any point as to the admissibility of evidence or an abuse of process) or an authority,
   comment by another party under subsection (5)(a) may be made only with the leave of the court.

(7)   Where this section applies by virtue of subsection (4), comment by another party under subsection (5)(a) may be made only with the leave of the court.

(8)   Where the accused puts forward a defence which is different from any defence set out in his defence statement, in doing anything under subsection (5) or in deciding whether to do anything under it the court shall have regard—

     (a)   to the extent of the differences in the defences, and

     (b)   to whether there is any justification for it.

(9)   Where the accused calls a witness whom he has failed to include, or to identify adequately, in a witness notice, in doing anything under subsection (5) or in deciding whether to do anything under it the court shall have regard to whether there is any justification for the failure.

(10)   A person shall not be convicted of an offence solely on an inference drawn under subsection (5).

(11)   Where the accused has given a statement of the kind mentioned in section 6B(4), then, for the purposes of subsections (2)(f)(ii) and (iv), the question as to whether there has been a breach of the requirements imposed by or under section 6A or a failure to comply with section 6A(2)(a) or (b) shall be determined—

     (a)   by reference to the state of affairs at the time when that statement was given, and

     (b)   as if the defence statement was given at the same time as that statement.

(12)   In this section—

     (a)   'initial defence statement' means a defence statement given under section 5 or 6;

     (b)   'updated defence statement' means a defence statement given under section 6B;

     (c)   a reference simply to an accused's 'defence statement' is a reference—

         (i)   where he has given only an initial defence statement, to that statement;

         (ii)   where he has given both an initial and an updated defence statement, to the updated defence statement;

         (iii)   where he has given both an initial defence statement and a statement of the kind mentioned in section 6B(4), to the initial defence statement;

     (d)   a reference to evidence in support of an alibi shall be construed in accordance with section 6A(3);

     (e)   'witness notice' means a notice given under section 6C.

29.   Power to order preparatory hearing

(1)   Where it appears to a judge of the Crown Court that an indictment reveals a case of such complexity, a case of such seriousness, or a case whose trial is likely to be of such length, that substantial benefits are likely to accrue from a hearing—

     (a)   before the time when the jury are sworn, and

     (b)   for any of the purposes mentioned in subsection (2),

     he may order that such a hearing (in this Part referred to as a preparatory hearing) shall be held.

(1A)   A judge of the Crown Court may also order that a preparatory hearing shall be held if an application to which section 45 of the Criminal Justice Act 2003 applies (application for trial without jury) is made.

(1B)   An order that a preparatory hearing shall be held must be made by a judge of the Crown Court in every case which (whether or not it falls within subsection (1) or (1A)) is a case in which at least one of the offences charged by the indictment against at least one of the persons charged is a terrorism offence.

(1C)   An order that a preparatory hearing shall be held must also be made by a judge of the Crown court in every case which (whether or not it falls within subsection (1) or (1A)) is a case in which—

     (a)   at least one of the offences charged by the indictment against at least one of the persons charged is an offence carrying a maximum of at least 10 years' imprisonment; and

     (b)   it appears to the judge that evidence on the indictment reveals that conduct in respect of which that offence is charged had a terrorist connection.

(2) The purposes are those of—
- (a) identifying issues which are likely to be material to the determinations and findings which are likely to be required during the trial,
- (b) if there is to be a jury, assisting their comprehension of those issues and expediting the proceedings before them,
- (c) determining an application to which section 45 of the Criminal Justice Act 2003 applies,
- (d) assisting the judge's management of the trial;
- (e) considering questions as to the severance or joinder of charges.

39. Meaning of pre-trial hearing

(1) For the purposes of this Part a hearing is a pre-trial hearing if it relates to a trial on indictment and it takes place—
- (a) after the accused has been sent for trial for the offence, and
- (b) before the start of the trial.

(2) For the purposes of this Part a hearing is also a pre-trial hearing if—
- (a) it relates to a trial on indictment to be held in pursuance of a bill of indictment preferred under the authority of section 2(2)(b) of the Administration of Justice (Miscellaneous Provisions) Act 1933 (bill preferred by direction of Court of Appeal, or by direction or with consent of a judge), and
- (b) it takes place after the bill of indictment has been preferred and before the start of the trial.

(3) For the purposes of this section the start of a trial on indictment occurs at the time when a jury is sworn to consider the issue of guilt or fitness to plead or, if the court accepts a plea of guilty before the time when a jury is sworn, when that plea is accepted; but this is subject to section 8 of the Criminal Justice Act 1987 and section 30 of this Act (preparatory hearings).

(4) The references in subsection (3) to the time when a jury is sworn include the time when that jury would be sworn but for the making of an order under Part 7 of the Criminal Justice Act 2003.

40. Power to make rulings

(1) A judge may make at a pre-trial hearing a ruling as to—
- (a) any question as to the admissibility of evidence;
- (b) any other question of law relating to the case concerned.

(2) A ruling may be made under this section—
- (a) on an application by a party to the case, or
- (b) of the judge's own motion.

(3) Subject to subsection (4), a ruling made under this section has binding effect from the time it is made until the case against the accused or, if there is more than one, against each of them is disposed of; and the case against an accused is disposed of if—
- (a) he is acquitted or convicted, or
- (b) the prosecutor decides not to proceed with the case against him.

(4) A judge may discharge or vary (or further vary) a ruling made under this section if it appears to him that it is in the interests of justice to do so; and a judge may act under this subsection—
- (a) on an application by a party to the case, or
- (b) of the judge's own motion.

(5) No application may be made under subsection (4)(a) unless there has been a material change of circumstances since the ruling was made or, if a previous application has been made, since the application (or last application) was made.

(6) The judge referred to in subsection (4) need not be the judge who made the ruling or, if it has been varied, the judge (or any of the judges) who varied it.

(7) For the purposes of this section the prosecutor is any person acting as prosecutor, whether an individual or a body.

54. Acquittals tainted by intimidation etc

(1) This section applies where—
- (a) a person has been acquitted of an offence, and

(b)   a person has been convicted of an administration of justice offence involving interference with or intimidation of a juror or a witness (or potential witness) in any proceedings which led to the acquittal.

(2)   Where it appears to the court before which the person was convicted that—

(a)   there is a real possibility that, but for the interference or intimidation, the acquitted person would not have been acquitted, and

(b)   subsection (5) does not apply,

the court shall certify that it so appears.

(3)   Where a court certifies under subsection (2) an application may be made to the High Court for an order quashing the acquittal, and the Court shall make the order if (but shall not do so unless) the four conditions in section 55 are satisfied.

(4)   Where an order is made under subsection (3) proceedings may be taken against the acquitted person for the offence of which he was acquitted.

(5)   This subsection applies if, because of lapse of time or for any other reason, it would be contrary to the interests of justice to take proceedings against the acquitted person for the offence of which he was acquitted.

(6)   For the purposes of this section the following offences are administration of justice offences—

(a)   the offence of perverting the course of justice;

(b)   the offence under section 51(1) of the Criminal Justice and Public Order Act 1994 (intimidation etc of witnesses, jurors and others);

(c)   an offence of aiding, abetting, counselling, procuring, suborning or inciting another person to commit an offence under section 1 of the Perjury Act 1911.

(7)   This section applies in relation to acquittals in respect of offences alleged to be committed on or after the appointed day.

(8)   The reference in subsection (7) to the appointed day is to such day as is appointed for the purposes of this section by the Secretary of State by order.

55.   Conditions for making order

(1)   The first condition is that it appears to the High Court likely that, but for the interference or intimidation, the acquitted person would not have been acquitted.

(2)   The second condition is that it does not appear to the Court that, because of lapse of time or for any other reason, it would be contrary to the interests of justice to take proceedings against the acquitted person for the offence of which he was acquitted.

(3)   The third condition is that it appears to the Court that the acquitted person has been given a reasonable opportunity to make written representations to the Court.

(4)   The fourth condition is that it appears to the Court that the conviction for the administration of justice offence will stand.

(5)   In applying subsection (4) the Court shall—

(a)   take into account all the information before it, but

(b)   ignore the possibility of new factors coming to light.

(6)   Accordingly, the fourth condition has the effect that the Court shall not make an order under section 54(3) if (for instance) it appears to the Court that any time allowed for giving notice of appeal has not expired or that an appeal is pending.

FIREARMS ACT 1968
(1968, c. 27)

5.   Weapons subject to general prohibition

(1)   A person commits an offence if, without authority he has in his possession, or purchases or acquires—

(a)   any firearm which is so designed or adapted that two or more missiles can be successively discharged without repeated pressure on the trigger;

(ab)   any self-loading or pump-action rifled gun other than one which is chambered for .22 rim-fire cartridges;

(aba) any firearm which either has a barrel less than 30 centimetres in length or is less than 60 centimetres in length overall, other than an air weapon, a muzzle-loading gun or a firearm designed as signalling apparatus;

(ac) any self-loading or pump-action smooth-bore gun which is not an air weapon or chambered for .22 rim-fire cartridges and either has a barrel less than 24 inches in length or is less than 40 inches in length overall;

(ad) any smooth-bore revolver gun other than one which is chambered for 9mm. rim-fire cartridges or a muzzle-loading gun;

(ae) any rocket launcher, or any mortar, for projecting a stabilised missile, other than a launcher or mortar designed for line-throwing or pyrotechnic purposes or as signalling apparatus;

(af) any air rifle, air gun or air pistol which uses, or is designed or adapted for use with, a self-contained gas cartridge system;

(b) any weapon of whatever description designed or adapted for the discharge of any noxious liquid, gas or other thing; and

(c) any cartridge with a bullet designed to explode on or immediately before impact, any ammunition containing or designed or adapted to contain any such noxious thing as is mentioned in paragraph (b) above and, if capable of being used with a firearm of any description, any grenade, bomb (or other like missile), or rocket or shell designed to explode as aforesaid.

(1A) Subject to section 5A of this Act, a person commits an offence if, without authority he has in his possession or purchases or acquires—

(a) any firearm which is disguised as another object;

(b) any rocket or ammunition not falling within paragraph (c) of subsection (1) of this section which consists in or incorporates a missile designed to explode on or immediately before impact and is for military use;

(c) any launcher or other projecting apparatus not falling within paragraph (ae) of that subsection which is designed to be used with any rocket or ammunition falling within paragraph (b) above or with ammunition which would fall within that paragraph but for its being ammunition falling within paragraph (c) of that subsection;

(d) any ammunition for military use which consists in or incorporates a missile designed so that a substance contained in the missile will ignite on or immediately before impact;

(e) any ammunition for military use which consists in or incorporates a missile designed, on account of its having a jacket and hard-core, to penetrate armour plating, armour screening or body armour;

(f) any ammunition which incorporates a missile designed or adapted to expand on impact;

(g) anything which is designed to be projected as a missile from any weapon and is designed to be, or has been, incorporated in—

(i) any ammunition falling within any of the preceding paragraphs; or

(ii) any ammunition which would fall within any of those paragraphs but for its being specified in subsection (1) of this section.

(2) The weapons and ammunition specified in subsections (1) and (1A) of this section (including, in the case of ammunition, any missiles falling within subsection (1A)(g) of this section) are referred to in this Act as 'prohibited weapons' and 'prohibited ammunition' respectively.

(2A) A person commits an offence if without authority—

(a) he manufactures any weapon or ammunition specified in subsection (1) of this section,

(b) he sells or transfers any prohibited weapon or prohibited ammunition,

(c) he has in his possession for sale or transfer any prohibited weapon or prohibited ammunition, or

(d) he purchases or acquires for sale or transfer any prohibited weapon or prohibited ammunition.

(3) In this section 'authority' means an authority given in writing by—

(a) the Secretary of State (in or as regards England and Wales), or

(b) the Scottish Ministers (in or as regards Scotland).

...

(8) For the purposes of subsection (1)(aba) and (ac) above, any detachable, folding, retractable or other movable butt-stock shall be disregarded in measuring the length of any firearm.

(9) Any reference in this section to a muzzle-loading gun is a reference to a gun which is designed to be loaded at the muzzle end of the barrel or chamber with a loose charge and a separate ball (or other missile).

47. Powers of constables to stop and search

(1) A constable may require any person whom he has reasonable cause to suspect—

    (a)   of having a firearm, with or without ammunition, with him in a public place; or

    (b)   to be committing or about to commit, elsewhere than in a public place, an offence relevant for the purposes of this section,

to hand over the firearm or any ammunition for examination by the constable.

(2) It is an offence for a person having a firearm or ammunition with him to fail to hand it over when required to do so by a constable under subsection (1) of this section.

(3) If a constable has reasonable cause to suspect a person of having a firearm with him in a public place, or to be committing or about to commit, elsewhere than in a public place, an offence relevant for the purposes of this section, the constable may search that person and may detain him for the purpose of doing so.

(4) If a constable has reasonable cause to suspect that there is a firearm in a vehicle in a public place, or that a vehicle is being or is about to be used in connection with the commission of an offence relevant for the purposes of this section elsewhere than in a public place, he may search the vehicle and for that purpose require the person driving or in control of it to stop it.

(5) For the purpose of exercising the powers conferred by this section a constable may enter any place.

(6) The offences relevant for the purpose of this section are those under sections 18(1) and (2) and 20 of this Act.

51A. Minimum sentence for certain offences under section 5

(1) This section applies where—

    (a)   an individual is convicted of—

        (i)   an offence under section 5(1)(a), (ab), (aba), (ac), (ad), (ae), (af) or (c) of this Act,

        (ii)   an offence under section 5(1A)(a) of this Act, or

        (iii)   an offence under any of the provisions of this Act listed in subsection (1A) in respect of a firearm or ammunition specified in section 5(1)(a), (ab), (aba), (ac), (ad), (ae),(af) or (c) or section 5(1A)(a) of this Act, and .

    (b)   the offence was committed after the commencement of this section and at a time when he was aged 16 or over.

(1A) The provisions are—

    (za)   section 5(2A) (manufacture, sale or transfer of firearm, or possession etc for sale or transfer);

    (a)   section 16 (possession of firearm with intent to injure);

    (b)   section 16A (possession of firearm with intent to cause fear of violence);

    (c)   section 17 (use of firearm to resist arrest);

    (d)   section 18 (carrying firearm with criminal intent);

    (e)   section 19 (carrying a firearm in a public place);

    (f)   section 20(1) (trespassing in a building with firearm).

(2) The court shall impose an appropriate custodial sentence (or order for detention) for a term of at least the required minimum term (with or without a fine) unless the court is of the opinion that there are exceptional circumstances relating to the offence or to the offender which justify its not doing so.

(3) Where an offence is found to have been committed over a period of two or more days, or at some time during a period of two or more days, it shall be taken for the purposes of this section to have been committed on the last of those days.

(4) In this section 'appropriate custodial sentence (or order for detention)' means—

    (a)   in relation to England and Wales—

        (i)   in the case of an offender who is aged 18 or over when convicted, a sentence of imprisonment, and

        (ii)   in the case of an offender who is aged under 18 at that time, a sentence of detention under section 91 of the Powers of Criminal Courts (Sentencing) Act 2000;

      ...

(5)   In this section 'the required minimum term' means—

    (a)   in relation to England and Wales—

        (i)   in the case of an offender who was aged 18 or over when he committed the offence, five years, and

        (ii)   in the case of an offender who was under 18 at that time, three years; and

      ...

    ...

FOOTBALL SPECTATORS ACT 1989
(1989, c. 37)

14.   Main definitions

(1)   This section applies for the purposes of this Part.

(2)   'Regulated football match' means an association football match (whether in the United Kingdom or elsewhere) which is a prescribed match or a match of a prescribed description.

(3)   'External tournament' means a football competition which includes regulated football matches outside the United Kingdom.

(4)   'Banning order' means an order made by the court under this Part which—

    (a)   in relation to regulated football matches in the United Kingdom, prohibits the person who is subject to the order from entering any premises for the purpose of attending such matches, and

    (b)   in relation to regulated football matches outside the United Kingdom, requires that person to report at a police station in accordance with this Part.

(5)   'Control period', in relation to a regulated football match outside the United Kingdom, means the period—

    (a)   beginning five days before the day of the match, and

    (b)   ending when the match is finished or cancelled.

(6)   'Control period', in relation to an external tournament, means any period described in an order made by the Secretary of State—

    (a)   beginning five days before the day of the first football match outside the United Kingdom which is included in the tournament, and

    (b)   ending when the last football match outside the United Kingdom which is included in the tournament is finished or cancelled,

but, for the purposes of paragraph (a), any football match included in the qualifying or pre-qualifying stages of the tournament is to be left out of account.

(7)   References to football matches are to football matches played or intended to be played.

(8)   'Relevant offence' means an offence to which Schedule 1 to this Act applies.

14A.   Banning orders made on conviction of an offence

(1)   This section applies where a person (the 'offender') is convicted of a relevant offence.

(2)   If the court is satisfied that there are reasonable grounds to believe that making a banning order would help to prevent violence or disorder at or in connection with any regulated football matches, it must make such an order in respect of the offender.

(3)   If the court is not so satisfied, it must in open court state that fact and give its reasons.

(3A) For the purpose of deciding whether to make an order under this section the court may consider evidence led by the prosecution and the defence.

(3B) It is immaterial whether evidence led in pursuance of subsection (3A) would have been admissible in the proceedings in which the offender was convicted.

(4)   A banning order may only be made under this section—

    (a)   in addition to a sentence imposed in respect of the relevant offence, or

    (b)   in addition to an order discharging him conditionally.

(4A) The court may adjourn any proceedings in relation to an order under this section even after sentencing the offender.

(4B) If the offender does not appear for any adjourned proceedings, the court may further adjourn the proceedings or may issue a warrant for his arrest.

(4BA) If the court adjourns or further adjourns any proceedings under subsection (4A) or (4B), the court may remand the offender.

(4BB) A person who, by virtue of subsection (4BA), is remanded on bail may be required by the conditions of his bail—

    (a)   not to leave England and Wales before his appearance before the court, and

    (b)   if the control period relates to a regulated football match outside the United Kingdom or to an external tournament which includes such matches, to surrender his passport to a police constable, if he has not already done so.

(4C) The court may not issue a warrant under subsection (4B) above for the offender's arrest unless it is satisfied that he has had adequate notice of the time and place of the adjourned proceedings.

(5) A banning order may be made as mentioned in subsection (4)(b) above in spite of anything in sections 12 and 14 of the Powers of the Criminal Courts (Sentencing) Act 2000 (which relate to orders discharging a person absolutely or conditionally and their effect).

(5A) The prosecution has a right of appeal against a failure by the court to make a banning order under this section—

    (a)   where the failure is by a magistrates' court, to the Crown Court; and

    (b)   where it is by the Crown Court, to the Court of Appeal.

(5B) An appeal under subsection (5A)(b) may be brought only if the Court of Appeal gives permission or the judge who decided not to make an order grants a certificate that his decision is fit for appeal.

(5C) An order made on appeal under this section (other than one directing that an application be re-heard by the court from which the appeal was brought) is to be treated for the purposes of this Part as if it were an order of the court from which the appeal was brought.

(6) In this section, 'the court' in relation to an offender means—

    (a)   the court by or before which he is convicted of the relevant offence, or

    (b)   if he is committed to the Crown Court to be dealt with for that offence, the Crown Court.

14C. Banning orders: supplementary

(1) In this Part, 'violence' means violence against persons or property and includes threatening violence and doing anything which endangers the life of any person.

(2) In this Part, 'disorder' includes—

    (a)   stirring up hatred against a group of persons defined by reference to colour, race, nationality (including citizenship) or ethnic or national origins, or against an individual as a member of such a group,

    (b)   using threatening, abusive or insulting words or behaviour or disorderly behaviour,

    (c)   displaying any writing or other thing which is threatening, abusive or insulting.

(3) In this Part, 'violence' and 'disorder' are not limited to violence or disorder in connection with football.

(4) The magistrates' court may take into account the following matters (among others), so far as they consider it appropriate to do so, in determining whether to make an order under section 14B above—

    (a)   any decision of a court or tribunal outside the United Kingdom,

    (b)   deportation or exclusion from a country outside the United Kingdom,

    (c)   removal or exclusion from premises used for playing football matches, whether in the United Kingdom or elsewhere,

    (d)   conduct recorded on video or by any other means.

(5) In determining whether to make such an order—

    (a)   the magistrates' court may not take into account anything done by the respondent before the beginning of the period of ten years ending with the application under section 14B(1) above, except circumstances ancillary to a conviction,

(b)   before taking into account any conviction for a relevant offence, where a court made a statement under section 14A(3) above (or section 15(2A) below or section 30(3) of the Public Order Act 1986), the magistrates' court must consider the reasons given in the statement,

and in this subsection 'circumstances ancillary to a conviction' has the same meaning as it has for the purposes of section 4 of the Rehabilitation of Offenders Act 1974 (effect of rehabilitation).

(6)   Subsection (5) does not prejudice anything in the Rehabilitation of Offenders Act 1974.

14E. Banning orders: general

(1)   On making a banning order, a court must in ordinary language explain its effect to the person subject to the order.

(2)   A banning order must require the person subject to the order to report initially at a police station specified in the order within the period of five days beginning with the day on which the order is made.

(2A)   A banning order must require the person subject to the order to give notification of the events mentioned in subsection (2B) to the enforcing authority.

(2B)   The events are—
(a)   a change of any of his names;
(b)   the first use by him after the making of the order of a name for himself that was not disclosed by him at the time of the making of the order;
(c)   a change of his home address;
(d)   his acquisition of a temporary address;
(e)   a change of his temporary address or his ceasing to have one;
(f)   his becoming aware of the loss of his passport;
(g)   receipt by him of a new passport;
(h)   an appeal made by him in relation to the order;
(i)   an application made by him under section 14H(2) for termination of the order;
(j)   an appeal made by him under section 23(3) against the making of a declaration of relevance in respect of an offence of which he has been convicted.

(2C)   A notification required by a banning order by virtue of subsection (2A) must be given before the end of the period of seven days beginning with the day on which the event in question occurs and—
(a)   in the case of a change of a name or address or the acquisition of a temporary address, must specify the new name or address;
(b)   in the case of a first use of a previously undisclosed name, must specify that name; and
(c)   in the case of a receipt of a new passport, must give details of that passport.

(3)   A banning order must impose a requirement as to the surrender in accordance with this Part, in connection with regulated football matches outside the United Kingdom, of the passport of the person subject to the order.

(4)   ...

(5)   In the case of a person detained in legal custody—
(a)   the requirement under this section to report at a police station, and
(b)   any requirement imposed under section 19 below,
is suspended until his release from custody.

(6)   If—
(a)   he is released from custody more than five days before the expiry of the period for which the order has effect, and
(b)   he was precluded by his being in custody from reporting initially,
the order is to have effect as if it required him to report initially at the police station specified in the order within the period of five days beginning with the date of his release.

(7)   ...

(8)   In this section—
'declaration of relevance' has the same meaning as in section 23;
'home address', in relation to any person, means the address of his sole or main residence; 'loss' includes theft or destruction;
'new' includes replacement;

'temporary address', in relation to any person, means the address (other than his home address) of a place at which he intends to reside, or has resided, for a period of at least four weeks.

14F. Period of banning orders

(1) Subject to the following provisions of this Part, a banning order has effect for a period beginning with the day on which the order is made.

(2) The period must not be longer than the maximum or shorter than the minimum.

(3) Where the order is made under section 14A above in addition to a sentence of imprisonment taking immediate effect, the maximum is ten years and the minimum is six years; and in this subsection 'imprisonment' includes any form of detention.

(4) In any other case where the order is made under section 14A above, the maximum is five years and the minimum is three years.

(5) Where the order is made under section 14B above, the maximum is five years and the minimum is three years.

14G. Additional requirements of orders

(1) A banning order may, if the court making the order thinks fit, impose additional requirements on the person subject to the order in relation to any regulated football matches.

(2) The court by which a banning order was made may, on an application made by—
   (a) the person subject to the order, or
   (b) the person who applied for the order or who was the prosecutor in relation to the order,
   vary the order so as to impose, replace or omit any such requirements.

(3) In the case of a banning order made by a magistrates' court, the reference in subsection (2) above to the court by which it was made includes a reference to any magistrates' court acting in the same local justice area as that court.

14H. Termination of orders

(1) If a banning order has had effect for at least two-thirds of the period determined under section 14F above, the person subject to the order may apply to the court by which it was made to terminate it.

(2) On the application, the court may by order terminate the banning order as from a specified date or refuse the application.

(3) In exercising its powers under subsection (2) above, the court must have regard to the person's character, his conduct since the banning order was made, the nature of the offence or conduct which led to it and any other circumstances which appear to it to be relevant.

(4) Where an application under subsection (1) above in respect of a banning order is refused, no further application in respect of the order may be made within the period of six months beginning with the day of the refusal.

(5) The court may order the applicant to pay all or any part of the costs of an application under this section.

(6) In the case of a banning order made by a magistrates' court, the reference in subsection (1) above to the court by which it was made includes a reference to any magistrates' court acting in the same local justice area as that court.

14J. Offences

(1) A person subject to a banning order who fails to comply with—
   (a) any requirement imposed by the order, or
   (b) any requirement imposed under section 19(2B) or (2C) below,
   is guilty of an offence.

(2) A person guilty of an offence under this section is liable on summary conviction to imprisonment for a term not exceeding six months, or a fine not exceeding level 5 on the standard scale, or both.

HUMAN RIGHTS ACT 1998
(1998, c. 42)

1.   The Convention Rights

(1) In this Act 'the Convention rights' means the rights and fundamental freedoms set out in—

   (a) Articles 2 to 12 and 14 of the Convention,

   (b) Articles 1 to 3 of the First Protocol, and

   (c) Article 1 of the Thirteenth Protocol,

as read with Articles 16 to 18 of the Convention.

(2) Those Articles are to have effect for the purposes of this Act subject to any designated derogation or reservation (as to which see sections 14 and 15).

(3) The Articles are set out in Schedule 1.

(4) The Secretary of State may by order make such amendments to this Act as he considers appropriate to reflect the effect, in relation to the United Kingdom, of a protocol.

(5) In subsection (4) 'protocol' means a protocol to the Convention—

   (a) which the United Kingdom has ratified; or

   (b) which the United Kingdom has signed with a view to ratification.

(6) No amendment may be made by an order under subsection (4) so as to come into force before the protocol concerned is in force in relation to the United Kingdom.

2.   Interpretation of Convention rights

(1) A court or tribunal determining a question which has arisen in connection with a Convention right must take into account any—

   (a) judgment, decision, declaration or advisory opinion of the European Court of Human Rights,

   (b) opinion of the Commission given in a report adopted under Article 31 of the Convention,

   (c) decision of the Commission in connection with Article 26 or 27(2) of the Convention, or

   (d) decision of the Committee of Ministers taken under Article 46 of the Convention,

whenever made or given, so far as, in the opinion of the court or tribunal, it is relevant to the proceedings in which that question has arisen.

(2) Evidence of any judgment, decision, declaration or opinion of which account may have to be taken under this section is to be given in proceedings before any court or tribunal in such manner as may be provided by rules.

(3) In this section 'rules' means rules of court or, in the case of proceedings before a tribunal, rules made for the purposes of this section—

   (a) by the Lord Chancellor or the Secretary of State, in relation to any proceedings outside Scotland;

   (b) by the Secretary of State, in relation to proceedings in Scotland; or

   (c) by a Northern Ireland department, in relation to proceedings before a tribunal in Northern Ireland—

      (i) which deals with transferred matters; and

      (ii) for which no rules made under paragraph (a) are in force.

3.   Interpretation of legislation

(1) So far as it is possible to do so, primary legislation and subordinate legislation must be read and given effect in a way which is compatible with the Convention rights.

(2) This section—

   (a) applies to primary legislation and subordinate legislation whenever enacted;

   (b) does not affect the validity, continuing operation or enforcement of any incompatible primary legislation; and

   (c) does not affect the validity, continuing operation or enforcement of any incompatible subordinate legislation if (disregarding any possibility of revocation) primary legislation prevents removal of the incompatibility.

4.   Declaration of incompatibility

(1)   Subsection (2) applies in any proceedings in which a court determines whether a provision of primary legislation is compatible with a Convention right.

(2)   If the court is satisfied that the provision is incompatible with a Convention right, it may make a declaration of that incompatibility.

(3)   Subsection (4) applies in any proceedings in which a court determines whether a provision of subordinate legislation, made in the exercise of a power conferred by primary legislation, is compatible with a Convention right.

(4)   If the court is satisfied—

    (a)   that the provision is incompatible with a Convention right, and

    (b)   that (disregarding any possibility of revocation) the primary legislation concerned prevents removal of the incompatibility,

  it may make a declaration of that incompatibility.

(5)   In this section 'court' means—

    (a)   the Supreme Court;

    (b)   the Judicial Committee of the Privy Council;

    (c)   the Court Martial Appeal Court;

    (d)   in Scotland, the High Court of Justiciary sitting otherwise than as a trial court or the Court of Session;

    (e)   in England and Wales or Northern Ireland, the High Court or the Court of Appeal.

    (f)   the Court of Protection, in any matter being dealt with by the President of the Family Division, the Vice-Chancellor or a puisne judge of the High Court.

(6)   A declaration under this section ('a declaration of incompatibility')—

    (a)   does not affect the validity, continuing operation or enforcement of the provision in respect of which it is given; and

    (b)   is not binding on the parties to the proceedings in which it is made.

6.   Acts of public authorities

(1)   It is unlawful for a public authority to act in a way which is incompatible with a Convention right.

(2)   Subsection (1) does not apply to an act if—

    (a)   as the result of one or more provisions of primary legislation, the authority could not have acted differently; or

    (b)   in the case of one or more provisions of, or made under, primary legislation which cannot be read or given effect in a way which is compatible with the Convention rights, the authority was acting so as to give effect to or enforce those provisions.

(3)   In this section 'public authority' includes—

    (a)   a court or tribunal, and

    (b)   any person certain of whose functions are functions of a public nature,

  but does not include either House of Parliament or a person exercising functions in connection with proceedings in Parliament.

(4)   ...

(5)   In relation to a particular act, a person is not a public authority by virtue only of subsection (3)(b) if the nature of the act is private.

(6)   'An act' includes a failure to act but does not include a failure to—

    (a)   introduce in, or lay before, Parliament a proposal for legislation; or

    (b)   make any primary legislation or remedial order.

IMMIGRATION ACT 1971
(1971, c. 77)

3.   General provisions for regulation and control

    ...

(5)   A person who is not a British citizen is liable to deportation from the United Kingdom if—

    (a)   the Secretary of State deems his deportation to be conducive to the public good; or

(b)   another person to whose family he belongs is or has been ordered to be deported.

(6)   Without prejudice to the operation of subsection (5) above, a person who is not a British citizen shall also be liable to deportation from the United Kingdom if, after he has attained the age of seventeen, he is convicted of an offence for which he is punishable with imprisonment and on his conviction is recommended for deportation by a court empowered by this Act to do so.

...

(8)   When any question arises under this Act whether or not a person is a British citizen, or is entitled to any exemption under this Act, it shall lie on the person asserting it to prove that he is.

...

6.   Recommendations by court for deportation

(1)   Where under section 3(6) above a person convicted of an offence is liable to deportation on the recommendation of a court, he may be recommended for deportation by any court having power to sentence him for the offence unless the court commits him to be sentenced or further dealt with for that offence by another court.

...

(2)   A court shall not recommend a person for deportation unless he has been given not less than seven days' notice in writing stating that a person is not liable to deportation if he is a British citizen describing the persons who are British citizens and stating (so far as material) the effect of section 3(8) above and section 7 below; but the powers of adjournment conferred by section 10(3) of the Magistrates' Courts Act 1980, ... shall include power to adjourn, after convicting an offender, for the purpose of enabling a notice to be given to him under this subsection or, if a notice was so given to him less than seven days previously, for the purpose of enabling the necessary seven days to elapse.

...

(4)   Notwithstanding any rule of practice restricting the matters which ought to be taken into account in dealing with an offender who is sentenced to imprisonment, a recommendation for deportation may be made in respect of an offender who is sentenced to imprisonment for life.

(5)   Where a court recommends or purports to recommend a person for deportation, the validity of the recommendation shall not be called in question except on an appeal against the recommendation or against the conviction on which it is made; but—

(a)   the recommendation shall be treated as a sentence for the purpose of any enactment providing an appeal against sentence ...

(b)   ...

...

IMMIGRATION ACT 2016
(2016, c. 19)

14.   Power to request Labour Market Enforcement undertaking

(4)   'Trigger offence' means—

(a)   an offence under the Employment Agencies Act 1973 other than one under section 9(4)(b) of that Act;

(b)   an offence under the National Minimum Wage Act 1988;

(c)   an offence under the Gangmaster (Licensing) Act 2004;

(d)   any other offence prescribed by regulations made by the Secretary of State;

(e)   an offence of attempting or conspiring to commit an offence mentioned in paragraphs (a) to (d);

(f)   an offence under Part 2 of the Serious Crime Act 2007 in relation to an offence so mentioned;

(g)   an offence of inciting a person to commit an offence so mentioned;

(h)   an offence of aiding, abetting, counselling or procuring the commission of an offence so mentioned.

20. Power to make Labour Market Enforcement order on conviction

(1) This section applies where a court deals with a person in respect of a conviction for a trigger offence.

(2) The court may make an LME order against the person if the court considers it is just and reasonable to do so.

(3) An LME order must not be made under this section except—

    (a) in addition to a sentence imposed in respect of the offence concerned, or

    (b) in addition to an order discharging the person conditionally or, in Scotland, discharging the person absolutely.

INTERPRETATION ACT 1978
(1978, c. 30)

SCHEDULE 1
WORDS AND EXPRESSIONS DEFINED

Construction of certain expressions relating to offences

In relation to England and Wales—

(a) 'indictable offence' means an offence which, if committed by an adult, is triable on indictment, whether it is exclusively so triable or triable either way;

(b) 'summary offence' means an offence which, if committed by an adult, is triable only summarily;

(c) 'offence triable either way' means an offence, other than an offence triable on indictment only by virtue of Part V of the Criminal Justice Act 1988 which, if committed by an adult, is triable either on indictment or summarily;

and the terms 'indictable', 'summary' and 'triable either way', in their application to offences, are to be construed accordingly.

In the above definitions references to the way or ways in which an offence is triable are to be construed without regard to the effect, if any, of section 22 of the Magistrates' Courts Act 1980 on the mode of trial in a particular case.

JURIES ACT 1974
(1974, c. 23)

1. Qualification for jury service

(1) Subject to the provisions of this Act, every person shall be qualified to serve as a juror in the Crown Court, the High Court and county courts and be liable accordingly to attend for jury service when summoned under this Act, if—

    (a) he is for the time being registered as a parliamentary or local government elector and aged eighteen or over but under seventy six;

    (b) he has been ordinarily resident in the United Kingdom, the Channel Islands or the Isle of Man for any period of at least five years since attaining the age of thirteen, and

    (c) ...

    (d) he is not disqualified for jury service.

(2) ...

(3) The persons who are disqualified for jury service are those listed in Part 1 of Schedule 1 to this Act.

2. Summoning

(1) Subject to the provisions of this Act, the Lord Chancellor shall be responsible for the summoning of jurors to attend for service in the Crown Court, the High Court and county courts and for determining the occasions on which they are to attend when so summoned, and the number to be summoned.

(2) In making arrangements to discharge his duty under subsection (1) above the Lord Chancellor shall have regard to the convenience of the persons summoned and to their respective places of residence, and in particular to the desirability of selecting jurors within reasonable daily travelling distance of the place where they are to attend.

(3) Subject to subsection (2) above, there shall be no restriction on the places in England and Wales at which a person may be required to attend or serve on a jury under this Act.

(4) Subject to the provisions of this Act, jurors shall be so summoned by notice in writing sent by post, or delivered by hand.

...

5. Panels

(1) The arrangements to be made by the Lord Chancellor under this Act shall include the preparation of lists (called panels) of persons summoned as jurors, and the information to be included in panels, the court sittings for which they are prepared, their division into parts or sets (whether according to the day of first attendance or otherwise), their enlargement or amendment, and all other matters relating to the contents and form of the panels shall be such as the Lord Chancellor may from time to time direct.

(2) A party to proceedings in which jurors are or may be called on to try an issue, and any person acting on behalf of a party to such proceedings, shall be entitled to reasonable facilities for inspecting the panel from which the jurors are or will be drawn.

(3) The right conferred by subsection (2) above shall not be exercisable after the close of the trial by jury (or after the time when it is no longer possible for there to be a trial by jury).

(4) ...

6. Summoning in exceptional circumstances

(1) If it appears to the court that a jury to try any issue before the court will be, or probably will be, incomplete, the court may, if the court thinks fit, require any persons who are in, or in the vicinity of, the court, to be summoned (without any written notice) for jury service up to the number needed (after allowing for any who may not be qualified under section 1 of this Act, and for excusals and challenges) to make up a full jury.

(2) The names of the persons so summoned shall be added to the panel and the court shall proceed as if those so summoned had been included in the panel in the first instance.

8. Excusal for previous jury service

(1) If a person summoned under this Act shows to the satisfaction of the appropriate officer, or of the court (or any of the courts) to which he is summoned—

    (a) that he has served on a jury, or duly attended to serve on a jury, in the prescribed period ending with the service of the summons on him, or

    (b) that the Crown Court or any other court has excused him from jury service for a period which has not terminated,

the officer or court shall excuse him from attending, or further attending, in pursuance of the summons.

(2) In subsection (1) above 'the prescribed period' means two years or such longer period as the Lord Chancellor may prescribe by order ....

...

(5) In subsection (1) above the words 'served on a jury' refer to service on a jury in any court, including any court of assize or other court abolished by the Courts Act 1971, but excluding service on a jury in a coroner's court.

9. Excusal for certain persons and discretionary excusal

...

(2) If any person summoned under this Act shows to the satisfaction of the appropriate officer that there is good reason why he should be excused from attending in pursuance of the summons, the appropriate officer may, subject to section 9A(1A) of this Act, excuse him from so attending.

...

9A.   Discretionary deferral

(1)   If any person summoned under this Act shows to the satisfaction of the appropriate officer that there is good reason why his attendance in pursuance of the summons should be deferred, the appropriate officer may defer his attendance, and, if he does so, he shall vary the days on which that person is summoned to attend and the summons shall have effect accordingly.

...

9B.   Discharge of summonses to disabled persons only if incapable of acting effectively as a juror

(1)   Where it appears to the appropriate officer, in the case of a person attending in pursuance of a summons under this Act, that on account of physical disability there is doubt as to his capacity to act effectively as a juror, the person may be brought before the judge.

(2)   The judge shall determine whether or not the person should act as a juror; but he shall affirm the summons unless he is of the opinion that the person will not, on account of his disability, be capable of acting effectively as a juror, in which case he shall discharge the summons.

10.   Discharge of summonses in case of doubt as to capacity to act effectively as a juror

Where it appears to the appropriate officer, in the case of a person attending in pursuance of a summons under this Act, that on account of insufficient understanding of English there is doubt as to his capacity to act effectively as a juror, the person may be brought before the judge, who shall determine whether or not he should act as a juror and, if not, shall discharge the summons.

13.   Separation

If, on the trial of any person for an offence on indictment, the court thinks fit, it may at any time (whether before or after the jury have been directed to consider their verdict) permit the jury to separate.

15A.   Surrender of electronic communications devices

(1)   A judge dealing with an issue may order the members of a jury trying the issue to surrender any electronic communications devices for a period.

(2)   An order may be made only if the judge considers that—

(a)   the order is necessary or expedient in the interests of justice, and

(b)   the terms of the order are a proportionate means of safeguarding those interests.

(3)   An order may only specify a period during which the members of the jury are—

(a)   in the building in which the trial is being heard,

(b)   in other accommodation provided at the judge's request,

(c)   visiting a place in accordance with arrangements made by the court, or

(d)   travelling to or from a place mentioned in paragraph (b) or (c).

(4)   An order may be made subject to exceptions.

(5)   It is a contempt of court for a member of a jury to fail to surrender an electronic communications device in accordance with an order under this section.

17.   Majority verdicts

(1)   Subject to subsections (3) and (4) below, the verdict of a jury in proceedings in the Crown Court or the High Court need not be unanimous if—

(a)   in a case where there are not less than eleven jurors, ten of them agree on the verdict; and

(b)   in a case where there are ten jurors, nine of them agree on the verdict.

(2)   Subject to subsection (4) below, the verdict of a jury (that is to say a complete jury of eight) in proceedings in a county court need not be unanimous if seven of them agree on the verdict.

(3)   The Crown Court shall not accept a verdict of guilty by virtue of subsection (1) or (2) above unless the foreman of the jury has stated in open court the number of jurors who respectively agreed to and dissented from the verdict.

(4) No court shall accept a verdict by virtue of subsection (1) or (2) above unless it appears to the court that the jury have had such period of time for deliberation as the court thinks reasonable having regard to the nature and complexity of the case; and the Crown Court shall in any event not accept such a verdict unless it appears to the court that the jury have had at least two hours for deliberation.

(5) ...

20A. Offence: research by jurors

(1) It is an offence for a member of a jury that tries an issue in a case before a court to research the case during the trial period, subject to the exceptions in subsections (6) and (7).

(2) A person researches a case if (and only if) the person —
  (a) intentionally seeks information, and
  (b) when doing so, knows or ought reasonably to know that the information is or may be relevant to the case.

(3) The ways in which a person may seek information include —
  (a) asking a question,
  (b) searching an electronic database, including by means of the internet,
  (c) visiting or inspecting a place or object,
  (d) conducting an experiment, and
  (e) asking another person to seek the information.

(4) Information relevant to the case includes information about —
  (a) a person involved in events relevant to the case,
  (b) the judge dealing with the issue,
  (c) any other person involved in the trial, whether as a lawyer, a witness or otherwise,
  (d) the law relating to the case,
  (e) the law of evidence, and
  (f) court procedure.

(5) 'The trial period', in relation to a member of a jury that tries an issue, is the period —
  (a) beginning when the person is sworn to try the issue, and
  (b) ending when the judge discharges the jury or, if earlier, when the judge discharges the person.

(6) It is not an offence under this section for a person to seek information if the person needs the information for a reason which is not connected with the case.

(7) It is not an offence under this section for a person —
  (a) to attend proceedings before the court on the issue;
  (b) to seek information from the judge dealing with the issue;
  (c) to do anything which the judge dealing with the issue directs or authorises the person to do;
  (d) to seek information from another member of the jury, unless the person knows or ought reasonably to know that the other member of the jury contravened this section in the process of obtaining the information;
  (e) to do anything else which is reasonably necessary in order for the jury to try the issue.

(8) A person guilty of an offence under this section is liable, on conviction on indictment, to imprisonment for a term not exceeding 2 years or a fine (or both).

(9) Proceedings for an offence under this section may only be instituted by or with the consent of the Attorney General.

20B. Offence: sharing research with other jurors

(1) It is an offence for a member of a jury that tries an issue in a case before a court intentionally to disclose information to another member of the jury during the trial period if —
  (a) the member contravened section 20A in the process of obtaining the information, and
  (b) the information has not been provided by the court.

(2)   Information has been provided by the court if (and only if) it has been provided as part of—
    (a)   evidence presented in the proceedings on the issue, or
    (b)   other information provided to the jury or a juror during the trial period by, or with the permission of, the judge dealing with the issue.

(3)   A person guilty of an offence under this section is liable, on conviction on indictment, to imprisonment for a term not exceeding 2 years or a fine (or both).

(4)   Proceedings for an offence under this section may not be instituted except by or with the consent of the Attorney General.

(5)   In this section, 'the trial period' has the same meaning as in section 20A.

20C. Offence: jurors engaging in other prohibited conduct

(1)   It is an offence for a member of a jury that tries an issue in a case before a court intentionally to engage in prohibited conduct during the trial period, subject to the exceptions in subsections (4) and (5).

(2)   'Prohibited conduct' means conduct from which it may reasonably be concluded that the person intends to try the issue otherwise than on the basis of the evidence presented in the proceedings on the issue.

(3)   An offence under this section is committed whether or not the person knows that the conduct is prohibited conduct.

(4)   It is not an offence under this section for a member of the jury to research the case (as defined in section 20A(2) to (4)).

(5)   It is not an offence under this section for a member of the jury to disclose information to another member of the jury.

(6)   A person guilty of an offence under this section is liable, on conviction on indictment, to imprisonment for a term not exceeding 2 years or a fine (or both).

(7)   Proceedings for an offence under this section may not be instituted except by or with the consent of the Attorney General.

(8)   In this section, 'the trial period' has the same meaning as in section 20A.

20D. Offence: disclosing jury's deliberations

(1)   It is an offence for a person intentionally—
    (a)   to disclose information about statements made, opinions expressed, arguments advanced or votes cast by members of a jury in the course of their deliberations in proceedings before a court, or
    (b)   to solicit or obtain such information,
    subject to the exceptions in sections 20E to 20G.

(2)   A person guilty of an offence under this section is liable, on conviction on indictment, to imprisonment for a term not exceeding 2 years or a fine (or both).

(3)   Proceedings for an offence under this section may not be instituted except by or with the consent of the Attorney General.

20E. Offence of disclosing jury's deliberations: initial exceptions

(1)   It is not an offence under section 20D for a person to disclose information in the proceedings mentioned in section 20D(1) for the purposes of enabling the jury to arrive at their verdict or in connection with the delivery of that verdict.

(2)   It is not an offence under section 20D for the judge dealing with those proceedings to disclose information—
    (a)   for the purposes of dealing with the case, or
    (b)   for the purposes of an investigation by a relevant investigator into whether an offence or contempt of court has been committed by or in relation to a juror in the proceedings mentioned in section 20D(1).

(3)   It is not an offence under section 20D for a person who reasonably believes that a disclosure described in subsection (2)(b) has been made to disclose information for the purposes of the investigation.

(4)   It is not an offence under section 20D to publish information disclosed as described in subsection (1) or (2)(a) in the proceedings mentioned in section 20D(1).

(5) In this section—

'publish' means make available to the public or a section of the public;

'relevant investigator' means—

    (a)   a police force;

    (b)   the Attorney General;

    (c)   any other person or class of person specified by the Lord Chancellor for the purposes of this section by regulations made by statutory instrument.

(6) The Lord Chancellor must obtain the consent of the Lord Chief Justice before making regulations under this section.

(7) A statutory instrument containing regulations under this section is subject to annulment in pursuance of a resolution of either House of Parliament.

20F. Offence of disclosing jury's deliberations: further exceptions

(1) It is not an offence under section 20D for a person to disclose information to a person listed in subsection (2) if—

    (a)   the disclosure is made after the jury in the proceedings mentioned in section 20D(1) has been discharged, and

    (b)   the person making the disclosure reasonably believes that—

        (i)   an offence or contempt of court has been, or may have been, committed by or in relation to a juror in connection with those proceedings, or

        (ii)   conduct of a juror in connection with those proceedings may provide grounds for an appeal against conviction or sentence.

(2) Those persons are—

    (a)   a member of a police force;

    (b)   a judge of the Court of Appeal;

    (c)   the registrar of criminal appeals;

    (d)   a judge of the court where the proceedings mentioned in section 20D(1) took place;

    (e)   a member of staff of that court who would reasonably be expected to disclose the information only to a person mentioned in paragraphs (b) to (d).

(3) It is not an offence under section 20D for a member of a police force to disclose information for the purposes of obtaining assistance in deciding whether to submit the information to a judge of the Court of Appeal or the registrar of criminal appeals, provided that the disclosure does not involve publishing the information.

(4) It is not an offence under section 20D for a judge of the Court of Appeal or the registrar of criminal appeals to disclose information for the purposes of an investigation by a relevant investigator into—

    (a)   whether an offence or contempt of court has been committed by or in relation to a juror in connection with the proceedings mentioned in section 20D(1), or

    (b)   whether conduct of a juror in connection with those proceedings may provide grounds for an appeal against conviction or sentence.

(5) It is not an offence under section 20D for a judge of the Court of Appeal or the registrar of criminal appeals to disclose information for the purposes of enabling or assisting—

    (a)   a person who was the defendant in the proceedings mentioned in section 20D(1), or

    (b)   a legal representative of such a person,

to consider whether conduct of a juror in connection with those proceedings may provide grounds for an appeal against conviction or sentence.

(6) It is not an offence under section 20D for a person who reasonably believes that a disclosure described in subsection (4) or (5) has been made to disclose information for the purposes of the investigation or consideration in question.

(7) It is not an offence under section 20D for a person to disclose information in evidence in—

    (a)   proceedings for an offence or contempt of court alleged to have been committed by or in relation to a juror in connection with the proceedings mentioned in section 20D(1),

(b) proceedings on an appeal, or an application for leave to appeal, against a decision in the proceedings mentioned in section 20D(1) where an allegation relating to conduct of or in relation to a juror forms part of the grounds of appeal, or

(c) proceedings on any further appeal or reference arising out of proceedings mentioned in paragraph (a) or (b).

(8) It is not an offence under section 20D for a person to disclose information in the course of taking reasonable steps to prepare for proceedings described in subsection (7)(a) to (c).

(9) It is not an offence under section 20D to publish information disclosed as described in subsection (7).

(10) In this section—

'publish' means make available to the public or a section of the public;

'relevant investigator' means—

(a) a police force;

(b) the Attorney General;

(c) the Criminal Cases Review Commission;

(d) the Crown Prosecution Service;

(e) any other person or class of person specified by the Lord Chancellor for the purposes of this section by regulations made by statutory instrument.

(11) The Lord Chancellor must obtain the consent of the Lord Chief Justice before making regulations under this section.

(12) A statutory instrument containing regulations under this section is subject to annulment in pursuance of a resolution of either House of Parliament.

20G. Offence of disclosing jury's deliberations: exceptions for soliciting disclosures or obtaining information

(1) It is not an offence under section 20D to solicit a disclosure described in section 20E(1) to (4) or section 20F(1) to (9).

(2) It is not an offence under section 20D to obtain information—

(a) by means of a disclosure described in section 20E(1) to (4) or section 20F(1) to (9), or

(b) from a document that is available to the public or a section of the public.

SCHEDULE 1

MENTALLY DISORDERED PERSONS AND PERSONS DISQUALIFIED FOR JURY SERVICE

PART 1

MENTALLY DISORDERED PERSONS

1.   A person for the time being liable to be detained under the Mental Health Act 1983.

1A.   A person for the time being resident in a hospital on account of mental disorder as defined by the Mental Health Act 1983.

2.   A person for the time being under guardianship under section 7 of the Mental Health Act 1983 or subject to a community treatment order under section 17A of that Act.

3.   A person who lacks capacity, within the meaning of the Mental Capacity Act 2005, to serve as a juror.

4.   ...

PART 2

PERSONS DISQUALIFIED

5.   A person who is on bail in criminal proceedings (within the meaning of the Bail Act 1976)

6.   A person who has at any time been sentenced in the United Kingdom, the Channel Islands or the Isle of Man—

(a) to imprisonment for life, detention for life or custody for life,

(b) to detention during her Majesty's pleasure or during the pleasure of the Secretary of State,

(c) to imprisonment for public protection or detention for public protection,

(d) to an extended sentence under section 226A, 226B, 227 or 228 of the Criminal Justice Act 2003 or section 210A of the Criminal Procedure (Scotland) Act 1995, or

(e) to a term of imprisonment of five years or more or a term of detention of five years or more.

6A. A person who at any time in the last ten years has been convicted of—

(a) an offence under section 20A, 20B, 20C,or 20D of this Act,

(b) an offence under paragraph 5A, 5B, 5C or 5D of Schedule 6 to the Coroners and Justice Act 2009 (equivalent offences relating to jurors at inquests), or

(c) an offence under paragraph 2, 3, 4 or 5 of Schedule 2A to the Armed Forces Act 2006 (equivalent offences relating to members of the Court Martial).

7. A person who at any time in the last ten years has—

(a) in the United Kingdom, the Channel Islands or the Isle of Man—

(i) served any part of a sentence of imprisonment or a sentence of detention, or

(ii) had passed on him a suspended sentence of imprisonment or had made in respect of him a suspended order for detention,

(b) in England and Wales, had made in respect of him a community order under section 177 of the Criminal Justice Act 2003, a community rehabilitation order, a community punishment order, a community punishment and rehabilitation order, a drug treatment and testing order or a drug abstinence order, or

(c) had made in respect of him any corresponding order under the law of Scotland, Northern Ireland, the Isle of Man or any of the Channel Islands or a service community order or overseas community order under the Armed Forces Act 2006.

JUSTICES OF THE PEACE ACT 1968
(1968, c. 69)

1. Appointment of justices, oaths of office, etc

(1)–(6) ...

(7) It is hereby declared that any court of record having a criminal jurisdiction has, as ancillary to that jurisdiction, the power to bind over to keep the peace, and power to bind over to be of good behaviour, a person who or whose case is before the court, by requiring him to enter into his own recognisances or to find sureties or both, and committing him to prison if he does not comply ...

LEGAL AID, SENTENCING AND PUNISHMENT OF OFFENDERS ACT 2012
(2012, c. 10)

1. Lord Chancellor's functions

(1) The Lord Chancellor must secure that legal aid is made available in accordance with this Part.

(2) In this Part 'legal aid' means—

(a) civil legal services required to be made available under section 9 or 10 or paragraph 3 of Schedule 3 (civil legal aid), and

(b) services consisting of advice, assistance and representation required to be made available under section 13, 15 or 16 or paragraph 4 or 5 of Schedule 3 (criminal legal aid).

4. Director of Legal Aid Casework

(1) The Lord Chancellor must designate a civil servant as the Director of Legal Aid Casework ('the Director').

13.   Advice and assistance for individuals in custody

(1)   Initial advice and initial assistance are to be available under this Part to an individual who is arrested and held in custody at a police station or other premises if the Director has determined that the individual qualifies for such advice and assistance in accordance with this Part (and has not withdrawn the determination).

(2)   The Director must make a determination under this section having regard, in particular, to the interests of justice.

(3)   A determination under this section must specify the type of advice or assistance (or both) to be available under this Part.

(4)   Regulations may make provision about the making and withdrawal of determinations under this section.

...

14.   Criminal proceedings

In this Part 'criminal proceedings' means—

(a)   proceedings before a court for dealing with an individual accused of an offence,

(b)   proceedings before a court for dealing with an individual convicted of an offence, including proceedings in respect of a sentence or order,

(c)   proceedings for dealing with an individual under the Extradition Act 2003,

(d)   proceedings for binding an individual over to keep the peace or to be of good behaviour under section 115 of the Magistrates' Courts Act 1980 and for dealing with an individual who fails to comply with an order under that section,

(e)   proceedings on an appeal brought by an individual under section 44A of the Criminal Appeal Act 1968 (appeal in case of death of appellant),

(f)   proceedings on a reference under section 36 of the Criminal Justice Act 1972 on a point of law following the acquittal of an individual on indictment,

(g)   proceedings for contempt committed, or alleged to have been committed, by an individual in the face of a court, and

(h)   such other proceedings, before any court, tribunal or other person, as may be prescribed.

15.   Advice and assistance for criminal proceedings

(1)   Regulations may provide that prescribed advice and assistance is to be available under this Part to an individual described in subsection (2) if—

(a)   prescribed conditions are met, and

(b)   the Director has determined that the individual qualifies for such advice and assistance in accordance with the regulations (and has not withdrawn the determination).

(2)   Those individuals are—

(a)   individuals who are involved in investigations which may lead to criminal proceedings (other than individuals arrested and held in custody at a police station or other premises),

(b)   individuals who are before a court, tribunal or other person in criminal proceedings, and

(c)   individuals who have been the subject of criminal proceedings.

(3)   When making the regulations, the Lord Chancellor must have regard, in particular, to the interests of justice.

(4)   The regulations must require the Director to make determinations under the regulations having regard, in particular, to the interests of justice.

(5)   The regulations may require the Director to make such determinations in accordance with—

(a)   section 21 (financial resources) and regulations under that section, and

(b)   criteria set out in the regulations.

(6)   The regulations may make provision about the making and withdrawal of determinations under the regulations.

...

(10)   In this section 'assistance' includes, in particular, assistance in the form of advocacy.

16.   Representation for criminal proceedings

(1)   Representation for the purposes of criminal proceedings is to be available under this Part to an individual if—

(a)   the individual is a specified individual in relation to the proceedings, and

(b)   the relevant authority has determined (provisionally or otherwise) that the individual qualifies for such representation in accordance with this Part (and has not withdrawn the determination).

(2)   Representation for the purposes of criminal proceedings is to be available under this Part to an individual if—

(a)   the proceedings involve the individual resisting an appeal to the Crown Court otherwise than in an official capacity, and

(b)   the relevant authority has determined (provisionally or otherwise) that the individual qualifies for such representation in accordance with this Part (and has not withdrawn the determination).

(3)   Where an individual qualifies under this Part for representation for the purposes of criminal proceedings ('the principal proceedings'), representation is also to be available to the individual for the purposes of—

(a)   any related bail proceedings, and

(b)   any preliminary or incidental proceedings.

...

17.   Qualifying for representation

(1)   The relevant authority must determine whether an individual qualifies under this Part for representation for the purposes of criminal proceedings (whether provisionally or otherwise) in accordance with—

(a)   section 21 (financial resources) and regulations under that section, and

(b)   the interests of justice.

(2)   In deciding what the interests of justice consist of for the purposes of such a determination, the following factors must be taken into account—

(a)   whether, if any matter arising in the proceedings is decided against the individual, the individual would be likely to lose his or her liberty or livelihood or to suffer serious damage to his or her reputation,

(b)   whether the determination of any matter arising in the proceedings may involve consideration of a substantial question of law,

(c)   whether the individual may be unable to understand the proceedings or to state his or her own case,

(d)   whether the proceedings may involve the tracing, interviewing or expert cross-examination of witnesses on behalf of the individual, and

(e)   whether it is in the interests of another person that the individual be represented.

...

18.   Determinations by Director

(1)   The Director is authorised to determine whether an individual qualifies under this Part for representation for the purposes of criminal proceedings, except in circumstances in which a court is authorised to make the determination under regulations under section 19.

...

19.   Determinations by court

(1)   Regulations may—

(a)   provide that a court before which criminal proceedings take place, or are to take place, is authorised to determine whether an individual qualifies under this Part for representation for the purposes of criminal proceedings of a prescribed description, and

(b)   make provision about the making and withdrawal of such determinations by a court.

...

85. Removal of limit on certain fines on conviction by magistrates' court

(1) Where, on the commencement day, a relevant offence would, apart from this subsection, be punishable on summary conviction by a fine or maximum fine of £5,000 or more (however expressed), the offence is punishable on summary conviction on or after that day by a fine of any amount.

(2) Where, on the commencement day, a relevant power could, apart from this subsection, be exercised to create an offence punishable on summary conviction by a fine or maximum fine of £5,000 or more (however expressed), the power may be exercised on or after that day to create an offence punishable on summary conviction by a fine of any amount.

...

86. Power to increase certain other fines on conviction by magistrates' court

(1) Subsection (2) applies in relation to a relevant offence which, immediately before the commencement day, is punishable on summary conviction by a fine or maximum fine of a fixed amount of less than £5,000.

(2) The Secretary of State may by regulations make provision for the offence to be punishable on summary conviction by a fine or maximum fine of an amount specified or described in the regulations.

LICENSED PREMISES (EXCLUSION OF CERTAIN PERSONS) ACT 1980
(1980, c. 32)

1. Exclusion orders

(1) Where a court by or before which a person is convicted of an offence committed on licensed premises is satisfied that in committing that offence he resorted to violence or offered or threatened to resort to violence, the court may, subject to subsection (2) below, make an order (in this Act referred to as an 'exclusion order') prohibiting him from entering those premises or any other specified premises, without the express consent of the licensee of the premises or his servant or agent.

(2) An exclusion order may be made either—

    (a) in addition to any sentence which is imposed in respect of the offence of which the person is convicted; or

    (b) where the offence was committed in England and Wales, notwithstanding the provisions of sections 12 and 14 of the Powers of Criminal Courts (Sentencing) Act 2000 (cases in which absolute and conditional discharges may be made, and their effect), in addition to an order discharging him absolutely or conditionally;

    (c) where the offence was committed in Scotland, notwithstanding the provisions of sections 228, 246(2) and (3) and 247 of the Criminal Procedure (Scotland) Act 1995 (cases in which probation orders and absolute discharges may be made, and their effect), in addition to a probation order or an order discharging him absolutely;

but not otherwise.

(3) An exclusion order shall have effect for such period, not less than three months or more than two years, as is specified in the order, unless it is terminated under section 2(2) below.

MAGISTRATES' COURTS ACT 1980
(1980, c. 43)

2. Trial of summary offences

(1) A magistrates' court has jurisdiction to try any summary offence.

(2) A magistrates' court has jurisdiction under sections 51 and 51A of the Crime and Disorder Act 1998 in respect of any offence committed by a person who appears or is brought before the court.

(3) Subject to—
    (a) sections 18 to 22A, and
    (b) any other enactment (wherever contained) relating to the mode of trial of offences triable either way,
    a magistrates' court has jurisdiction to try summarily any offence which is triable either way.

(4) A magistrates' court has jurisdiction, in the exercise of its powers under section 24, to try summarily an indictable offence.

(5) This section does not affect any jurisdiction over offences conferred on a magistrates' court by any enactment not contained in this Act.

9. Procedure on trial

(1) On the summary trial of an information, the court shall, if the accused appears, state to him the substance of the information and ask him whether he pleads guilty or not guilty.

(2) The court, after hearing the evidence and the parties, shall convict the accused or dismiss the information.

(3) If the accused pleads guilty, the court may convict him without hearing evidence.

11. Non-appearance of accused: general provisions

(1) Subject to the provisions of this Act, where at the time and place appointed for the trial or adjourned trial of an information the prosecutor appears but the accused does not —
    (a) if the accused is under 18 years of age, the court may proceed in his absence; and
    (b) if the accused has attained the age of 18 years, the court shall proceed in his absence unless it appears to the court to be contrary to the interests of justice to do so.
    This is subject to subsections (2), (2A), (3), (4) and (8).

(2) Where a summons has been issued, the court shall not begin to try the information in the absence of the accused unless either it is proved to the satisfaction of the court, on oath or in such other manner as may be prescribed, that the summons was served on the accused within what appears to the court to be a reasonable time before the trial or adjourned trial or the accused has appeared on a previous occasion to answer to the information.

(2A) The court shall not proceed in the absence of the accused if it considers that there is an acceptable reason for his failure to appear.

(3) In proceedings to which this subsection applies, the court shall not in a person's absence sentence him to imprisonment or detention in a young offender institution or make a detention and training order or an order under paragraph 8(2)(a) or (b) of Schedule 12 to the Criminal Justice Act 2003 that a suspended sentence passed on him shall take effect.

(3A) But where a sentence or order of a kind mentioned in subsection (3) is imposed or given in the absence of the offender, the offender must be brought before the court before being taken to a prison or other institution to begin serving his sentence (and the sentence or order is not to be regarded as taking effect until he is brought before the court).

(4) In proceedings to which this subsection applies, the court shall not in a person's absence impose any disqualification on him, except on resumption of the hearing after an adjournment under section 10(3) above; and where a trial is adjourned in pursuance of this subsection the notice required by section 10(2) above shall include notice of the reason for the adjournment.

(5) Subsections (3) and (4) apply to—
    (a) proceedings instituted by an information, where a summons has been issued; and
    (b) proceedings instituted by a written charge.

(6) Nothing in this section requires the court to enquire into the reasons for the accused's failure to appear before deciding whether to proceed in his absence.

(7)   The court shall state in open court its reasons for not proceeding under this section in the absence of an accused who has attained the age of 18 years; and the court shall cause those reasons to be entered in its register of proceedings.

(8)   This section and sections 12 to 16 do not apply if and for so long as a written charge is to be tried by a magistrates' court in accordance with section 16A.

17.   Certain offences triable either way

(1)   The offences listed in Schedule 1 to this Act shall be triable either way.

(2)   Subsection (1) above is without prejudice to any other enactment by virtue of which any offence is triable either way.

17A.   Initial procedure: accused to indicate intention as to plea

(1)   This section shall have effect where a person who has attained the age of 18 years appears or is brought before a magistrates' court on an information charging him with an offence triable either way.

(2)   Everything that the court is required to do under the following provisions of this section must be done with the accused present in court.

(3)   The court shall cause the charge to be written down, if this has not already been done, and to be read to the accused.

(4)   The court shall then explain to the accused in ordinary language that he may indicate whether (if the offence were to proceed to trial) he would plead guilty or not guilty, and that if he indicates that he would plead guilty—

(a)   the court must proceed as mentioned in subsection (6) below; and

(b)   he may (unless section 17D(2) below were to apply) be committed for sentence to the Crown Court under section 3 or (if applicable) 3A of the Powers of Criminal Courts (Sentencing) Act 2000 if the court is of such opinion as is mentioned in subsection (2) of the applicable section.

(5)   The court shall then ask the accused whether (if the offence were to proceed to trial) he would plead guilty or not guilty.

(6)   If the accused indicates that he would plead guilty the court shall proceed as if—

(a)   the proceedings constituted from the beginning the summary trial of the information; and

(b)   section 9(1) above was complied with and he pleaded guilty under it.

(7)   If the accused indicates that he would plead not guilty section 18(1) below shall apply.

(8)   If the accused in fact fails to indicate how he would plead, for the purposes of this section and section 18(1) below he shall be taken to indicate that he would plead not guilty.

(9)   Subject to subsection (6) above, the following shall not for any purpose be taken to constitute the taking of a plea—

(a)   asking the accused under this section whether (if the offence were to proceed to trial) he would plead guilty or not guilty;

(b)   an indication by the accused under this section of how he would plead.

(10)   ...

17B.   Intention as to plea: absence of accused

(1)   This section shall have effect where—

(a)   a person who has attained the age of 18 years appears or is brought before a magistrates' court on an information charging him with an offence triable either way,

(b)   the accused is represented by a legal representative,

(c)   the court considers that by reason of the accused's disorderly conduct before the court it is not practicable for proceedings under section 17A above to be conducted in his presence, and

(d)   the court considers that it should proceed in the absence of the accused.

(2)   In such a case—

(a)   the court shall cause the charge to be written down, if this has not already been done, and to be read to the representative;

(b)   the court shall ask the representative whether (if the offence were to proceed to trial) the accused would plead guilty or not guilty;

(c)   if the representative indicates that the accused would plead guilty the court shall proceed as if the proceedings constituted from the beginning the summary trial of the information, and as if section 9(1) above was complied with and the accused pleaded guilty under it;

(d)   if the representative indicates that the accused would plead not guilty section 18(1) below shall apply.

(3)   If the representative in fact fails to indicate how the accused would plead, for the purposes of this section and section 18(1) below he shall be taken to indicate that the accused would plead not guilty.

(4)   Subject to subsection (2)(c) above, the following shall not for any purpose be taken to constitute the taking of a plea—

(a)   asking the representative under this section whether (if the offence were to proceed to trial) the accused would plead guilty or not guilty;

(b)   an indication by the representative under this section of how the accused would plead.

17C.   Intention as to plea: adjournment

A magistrates' court proceeding under section 17A or 17B above may adjourn the proceedings at any time, and on doing so on any occasion when the accused is present may remand the accused, and shall remand him if—

(a)   on the occasion on which he first appeared, or was brought, before the court to answer to the information he was in custody or, having been released on bail, surrendered to the custody of the court; or

(b)   he has been remanded at any time in the course of proceedings on the information; and where the court remands the accused, the time fixed for the resumption of proceedings shall be that at which he is required to appear or be brought before the court in pursuance of the remand or would be required to be brought before the court but for section 128(3A) below.

17D.   Maximum penalty under section 17A(6) or 17B(2)(c) for certain offences

(1)   If—

(a)   the offence is a scheduled offence (as defined in section 22(1) below);

(b)   the courts proceeds in relation to the offence in accordance with section 17A(6) or 17B(2)(c) above; and

(c)   the court convicts the accused of the offence,

the court shall consider whether, having regard to any representations made by him or by the prosecutor, the value involved (as defined in section 22(10) below) appears to the court to exceed the relevant sum (as specified for the purposes of section 22 below).

(2)   If it appears to the court clear that the value involved does not exceed the relevant sum, or it appears to the court for any reason not clear whether the value involved does or does not exceed the relevant sum—

(a)   subject to subsection (4) below, the court shall not power to impose on the accused in respect of the offence a sentence in excess of the limits mentioned in section 33(1)(a) below, and

(b)   sections 3 and 4 of the Powers of Criminal Courts (Sentencing) Act 2000 shall not apply as regards that offence.

(3)   ...

(4)   Subsection (2)(a) above does not apply to an offence under section 12A of the Theft Act 1968 (aggravated vehicle-taking).

18.   Initial procedure on information against adult for offence triable either way

(1)   Sections 19 to 23 below shall have effect where a person who has attained the age of 18 years appears or is brought before a magistrates' court on an information charging him with an offence triable either way and—

(a)   he indicates under section 17A above that (if the offence were to proceed to trial) he would plead not guilty, or

(b)   his representative indicates under section 17B above that (if the offence were to proceed to trial) he would plead not guilty.

(2)   Without prejudice to section 11(1) above, everything that the court is required to do under sections 19 to 22 below must be done before any evidence is called and, subject to subsection (3) below and section 23 below, with the accused present in court.

(3)   The court may proceed in the absence of the accused in accordance with such of the provisions of sections 19 to 22 below as are applicable in the circumstances if

the court considers that by reason of his disorderly conduct before the court it is not practicable for the proceedings to be conducted in his presence; and the subsections (3) to (5) of section 23 below, so far as applicable, shall have effect in relation to proceedings conducted in the absence of the accused by virtue of this subsection (references in those subsections to the person representing the accused being for this purpose read as references to the person, if any, representing him).

(4) A magistrates' court proceeding under sections 19 to 23 below may adjourn the proceedings at any time, and on doing so on any occasion when the accused is present may remand the accused, and shall remand him if—

    (a) on the occasion on which he first appeared, or was brought, before the court to answer to the information he was in custody or, having been released on bail, surrendered to the custody of the court; or

    (b) he has been remanded at any time in the course of proceedings on the information; and where the court remands the accused, the time fixed for the resumption of the proceedings shall be that at which he is required to appear or be brought before the court in pursuance of the remand or would be required to be brought before the court but for section 128(3A) below.

(5) The functions of a magistrates' court under sections 19 to 23 below may be discharged by a single justice, but this subsection shall not be taken as authorising—

    (a) the summary trial of an information (otherwise than in accordance with section 20(7) below); or

    (b) the imposition of a sentence,

by a magistrates' courts composed of fewer than two justices.

19. Decision as to allocation

(1) The court shall decide whether the offence appears to it more suitable for summary trial or for trial on indictment.

(2) Before making a decision under this section, the court—

    (a) shall give the prosecution an opportunity to inform the court of the accused's previous convictions (if any); and

    (b) shall give the prosecution and the accused an opportunity to make representations as to whether summary trial or trial on indictment would be more suitable.

(3) In making a decision under this section, the court shall consider—

    (a) whether the sentence which a magistrates' court would have power to impose for the offence would be adequate; and

    (b) any representations made by the prosecution or the accused under subsection (2)(b) above, and shall have regard to any allocation guidelines (or revised allocation guidelines) issued as definitive guidelines under section 122 of the Coroners and Justice Act 2009.

(4) Where—

    (a) the accused is charged with two or more offences; and

    (b) it appears to the court that the charges for the offences could be joined in the same indictment or that the offences arise out of the same or connected circumstances,

subsection (3)(a) above shall have effect as if references to a sentence which a magistrates' court would have power to impose for the offence were a reference to the maximum aggregate sentence which a magistrates' court would have power to impose for all of the offences taken together.

...

20. Procedure where summary trial appears more suitable

(1) If the court decides under section 19 above that the offence appears to it more suitable for summary trial, the following provisions of this section shall apply (unless they are excluded by section 23 below).

(2) The court shall explain to the accused in ordinary language—

    (a) that it appears to the court more suitable for him to be tried summarily for the offence;

    (b) that he can either consent to be so tried or, if he wishes, be tried on indictment; and

     (c)   that if he is tried summarily and is convicted by the court, he may be committed for sentence to the Crown Court under section 3 of (if applicable) section 3A of the Powers of Criminal Courts (Sentencing) Act 2000 if the court is of such opinion as is mentioned in subsection (2) of the applicable section.

(3)   The accused may then request an indication (an indication of sentence) of whether a custodial sentence or non-custodial sentence would be more likely to be imposed if he were to be tried summarily for the offence and to plead guilty.

(4)   If the accused requests an indication of sentence, the court may, but need not, give such an indication.

(5)   If the accused requests an indication of sentence, the court shall ask the accused whether he wishes, on the basis of the indication, to reconsider the indication of plea which was given, or is taken to have been given, under section 17A or 17B above.

(6)   If the accused indicates that he wishes to reconsider the indication under section 17A or 17B above, the court shall ask the accused whether (if the offence were to proceed to trial) he would plead guilty or not guilty.

(7)   If the accused indicates that he would plead guilty the court shall proceed as if—

     (a)   the proceedings constituted from that time the summary trial of the of information; and

     (b)   section 9(1) above were complied with and he pleaded guilty under it.

(8)   Subsection (9) below applies where—

     (a)   the court does not give an indication of sentence (whether because the accused does not request one or because the court does not agree to give one);

     (b)   the accused either—

        (i)   does not indicate, in accordance with subsection (5) above, that he wishes, or

        (ii)   indicates, in accordance with subsection (5) above, that he does not wish, to reconsider the indication of plea under section 17A or 17B above; or

     (c)   the accused does not indicate, in accordance with subsection (6) above, that he would plead guilty.

(9)   The court shall ask the accused whether he consents to be tried summarily or wishes to be tried on indictment and—

     (a)   if he consents to be tried summarily, shall proceed to the summary trial of the information; and

     (b)   if he does not so consent, shall proceed in relation to the offence in accordance with section 51(1) of the Crime and Disorder Act 1998.

20A. Procedure where summary trial appears more suitable: supplementary

(1)   Where the case is dealt with in accordance with section 20(7) above, no court (whether a magistrates' court or not) may impose a custodial sentence for the offence unless such a sentence was indicated in the indication of sentence referred to in section 20 above.

(2)   Subsection (1) above is subject to sections 3A(4), 4(8) and 5(3) of the Powers of Criminal Courts (Sentencing) Act 2000.

(3)   Except as provided in subsection (1) above—

     (a)   an indication of sentence shall not binding on any court (whether a magistrates' court or not); and

     (b)   no sentence may be challenged or be the subject of appeal in any court on the ground that it is not consistent with an indication of sentence.

(4)   Subject to section 20(7) above, the following shall not for any purpose be taken to constitute the taking of a plea—

     (a)   asking the accused under section 20 above whether (if the offence were to proceed to trial) he would plead guilty or not guilty; or

     (b)   an indication by the accused under that section of how he would plead.

(5)   Where a court gives an indication of sentence under section 20 above, it shall cause each such indication to be entered in the register.

...

21.   Procedure where trial on indictment appears more suitable

(1)   If the court decides under section 19 above that the offence appears to it more suitable for trial on indictment, the court shall tell the accused that the court has decided that it is more suitable for him to be tried on indictment, and shall proceed in relation to the offence in accordance with section 51(1) of the Crime and Disorder Act 1998.

...

22.   Certain offences triable either way to be tried summarily if value involved is small

(1)   If the offence charged by the information is one of those mentioned in the first column of Schedule 2 to this Act (in this section referred to as 'scheduled offences') then, ... the court shall, before proceeding in accordance with section 19 above, consider whether, having regard to any representations made by the prosecutor or the accused, the value involved (as defined in subsection (10) below) appears to the court to exceed the relevant sum.

For the purposes of this section the relevant sum is £5,000.

(2)   If, where subsection (1) above applies, it appears to the court clear that, for the offence charged, the value involved does not exceed the relevant sum, the court shall proceed as if the offence were triable only summarily, and sections 19 to 21 above shall not apply.

(3)   If, where subsection (1) above applies, it appears to the court clear that, for the offence charged, the value involved exceeds that relevant sum, the court shall thereupon proceed in accordance with section 19 above in the ordinary way without further regard to the provisions of this section.

(4)   If, where subsection (1) above applies, it appears to the court for any reason not clear whether, for the offence charged, the value involved does or does not exceed the relevant sum, the provisions of subsections (5) and (6) below shall apply.

(5)   The court shall cause the charge to be written down, if this has not already been done, and read to the accused, and shall explain to him in ordinary language—

     (a)   that he can, if he wishes, consent to be tried summarily for the offence and that if he consents to be so tried, he will definitely be tried in that way; and

     (b)   that if he is tried summarily and is convicted by the court, his liability to imprisonment or a fine will be limited as provided in section 33 below.

(6)   After explaining to the accused as provided by subsection (5) above the court shall ask him whether he consents to be tried summarily and—

     (a)   if he so consents, shall proceed in accordance with subsection (2) above as if that subsection applied;

     (b)   if he does not so consent, shall proceed in accordance with subsection (3) above as if that subsection applied.

(7)   ...

...

22A.   Low-value shoplifting to be a summary offence

(1)   Low-value shoplifting is triable only summarily.

(2)   But where a person accused of low-value shoplifting is aged 18 or over, and appears or is brought before the court before the summary trial of the offence begins, the court must give the person the opportunity of electing to be tried by the Crown Court for the offence and, if the person elects to be so tried—

     (a)   subsection (1) does not apply, and

     (b)   the court must proceed in relation to the offence in accordance with section 51(1) of the Crime and Disorder Act 1998.

(3)   'Low-value shoplifting' means an offence under section 1 of the Theft Act 1968 in circumstances where—

     (a)   the value of the stolen goods does not exceed £200,

     (b)   the goods were being offered for sale in a shop or any other premises, stall, vehicle or place from which there is carried on a trade or business, and

     (c)   at the time of the offence, the person accused of low-value shoplifting was, or was purporting to be, a customer or potential customer of the person offering the goods for sale.

(4)　For the purposes of subsection (3)(a)—
　　(a)　the value of the stolen goods is the price at which they were being offered for sale at the time of the offence, and
　　(b)　where the accused is charged on the same occasion with two or more offences of low-value shoplifting, the reference to the value involved has effect as if it were a reference to the aggregate of the values involved.

(5)　A person guilty of low-value shoplifting is liable on summary conviction to—
　　(a)　imprisonment for a period not exceeding 51 weeks (or 6 months, if the offence was committed before the commencement of section 281(4) and (5) of the Criminal Justice Act 2003),
　　(b)　a fine, or
　　(c)　both.

23. Power of court, with consent of legally represented accused, to proceed in his absence

(1)　Where—
　　(a)　the accused is represented by a legal representative who in his absence signifies to the court the accused's consent to the proceedings for determining how he is to be tried for the offence being conducted in his absence; and
　　(b)　the court is satisfied that there is good reason for proceeding in the absence of the accused,
　　the following provisions of this section shall apply.

(2)　Subject to the following provisions of this section, the court may proceed in the absence of the accused in accordance with such of the provisions of sections 19 to 22 above as are applicable in the circumstances.

…

25. Power to change from summary trial to committal proceedings and vice versa

(1)　Subsections (2) to (2D) below shall have effect where a person who has attained the age of 18 years appears or is brought before a magistrates' court on an information charging him with an offence triable either way.

(2)　Where the court is required under section 20(9) above to proceed to the summary trial of the information, the prosecution may apply to the court for the offence to be tried on indictment instead.

(2A)　An application under subsection (2) above—
　　(a)　must be made before the summary trial begins; and
　　(b)　must be dealt with by the court before any other application in relation to the summary trial is dealt with.

(2B)　The court may grant an application under subsection (2) above but only if it is satisfied that the sentence which a magistrates' court would have had power to impose for the offence would be inadequate.

(2C)　Where—
　　(a)　the accused is charged on the sane occasion with two or more offences; and
　　(b)　it appears to the court that they constitute or form part of a series of two or more offences of the same or similar character,
　　subsection (2B) shall have effect as if references to the sentence which a magistrates' court would have power to impose for the offence were a reference to the maximum aggregate sentence which a magistrates' court would have power to impose for all of the offences taken together.

(2D)　Where the court grants an application under subsection (2) above it shall proceed in relation to the offence in accordance with section 51(1) of the Crime and Disorder Act 1998.

…

26. Power to issue summons to accused in certain circumstances

(1)　Where, in the circumstances mentioned in section 23(1)(a) above, the court is not satisfied that there is good reason for proceeding in the absence of the accused, the justice or any of the justices of which the court is composed may issue a summons directed to the accused requiring his presence before the court.

(2)   In a case within subsection (1) above, if the accused is not present at the time and place appointed for the proceedings under section 19 or section 22(1) above, the court may issue a warrant for his arrest.

32.   Penalties on summary conviction for offences triable either way

(1)   On summary conviction of any of the offences triable either way listed in Schedule 1 to this Act a person shall be liable to imprisonment for a term not exceeding 6 months or to a fine not exceeding the prescribed sum or both, except that—

(a)   a magistrates' court shall not have power to impose imprisonment for an offence so listed if the Crown Court would not have that power in the case of an adult convicted of it on indictment;

(b), (c) ...

(2)   For any offence triable either way which is not listed in Schedule 1 to this Act, being an offence under a relevant enactment, the maximum fine which may be imposed on summary conviction shall by virtue of this subsection be the prescribed sum unless the offence is one for which by virtue of an enactment other than this subsection a larger fine may be imposed on summary conviction.

...

108.   Right of appeal to the Crown Court

(1)   A person convicted by a magistrates' court may appeal to the Crown Court—

(a)   if he pleaded guilty, against his sentence;

(b)   if he did not, against the conviction or sentence.

(1A) Section 14 of the Powers of Criminal Courts(Sentencing) Act 2000 (under which a conviction of an offence for which ... an order for conditional or absolute discharge is made is deemed not to be a conviction except for certain purposes) shall not prevent an appeal under this Act, whether against conviction or otherwise.

(2)   A person sentenced by a magistrates' court for an offence in respect of which . . . an order for conditional discharge has been previously made may appeal to the Crown Court against the sentence.

(3)   In this section 'sentence' includes any order made on conviction by a magistrates' court, not being—

(a)   ...

(b)   an order for the payment of costs;

(c)   an order under section 37(1) of the Animal Welfare Act 2006 (which enables a court to order the destruction of an animal); or

(d)   an order made in pursuance of any enactment under which the court has no discretion as to the making of the order or its terms

and also includes a declaration of relevance, within the meaning of section 23 of the Football Spectators Act 1989.

(4)   Subsection (3)(d) above does not prevent an appeal against a surcharge imposed under section 161A of the Criminal Justice Act 2003.

111.   Statement of case by magistrates' court

(1)   Any person who was a party to any proceeding before a magistrates' court or is aggrieved by the conviction, order, determination or other proceeding of the court may question the proceeding on the ground that it is wrong in law or is in excess of jurisdiction by applying to the justices composing the court to state a case for the opinion of the High Court on the question of law or jurisdiction involved; but a person shall not make an application under this section in respect of a decision against which he has a right of appeal to the High Court or which by virtue of any enactment passed after 31st December 1879 is final.

(2)   An application under subsection (1) above shall be made within 21 days after the day on which the decision of the magistrates' court was given.

(3)   For the purpose of subsection (2) above, the day on which the decision of the magistrates' court is given shall, where the court has adjourned the trial of an information after conviction, be the day on which the court sentences or otherwise deals with the offender.

(4)   On the making of an application under this section in respect of a decision any right of the applicant to appeal against the decision to the Crown Court shall cease.

...

115.   Binding over to keep the peace or be of good behaviour

(1)   The power of a magistrates' court on the complaint of any person to adjudge any other person to enter into a recognizance, with or without sureties, to keep the peace or to be of good behaviour towards the complainant shall be exercised by order on complaint.

(2)   Where a complaint is made under this section, the power of the court to remand the defendant under subsection (5) of section 55 above shall not be subject to the restrictions imposed by subsection (6) of that section.

(3)   If any person ordered by a magistrates' court under subsection (1) above to enter into a recognizance, with or without sureties, to keep the peace or to be of good behaviour fails to comply with the order, the court may commit him to custody for a period not exceeding 6 months or until he sooner complies with the order.

121.   Constitution and place of sitting of court

(1)   A magistrates' court shall not try an information summarily or hear a complaint except when composed of at least 2 justices unless the trial or hearing is one that by virtue of any enactment may take place before a single justice.

(2)   A magistrates' court shall not hold an inquiry into the means of an offender for the purposes of section 82 above or determine under that section at a hearing at which the offender is not present whether to issue a warrant of commitment except when composed of at least 2 justices.

...

(4)   Subject to the provisions of any enactment to the contrary, a magistrates' court must sit in open court if it is—
   (a)   trying summarily an information for an indictable offence,
   (b)   trying an information for a summary offence,
   (c)   imposing imprisonment,
   (d)   hearing a complaint, or
   (e)   holding an inquiry into the means of an offender for the purposes of section 82.

(5)   A magistrates' court composed of a single justice shall not impose imprisonment for a period exceeding 14 days or order a person to pay more than £1.

(8)   ...

127.   Limitation of time

(1)   Except as otherwise expressly provided by any enactment and subject to subsection (2) below, a magistrates' court shall not try an information or hear a complaint unless the information was laid, or the complaint made, within 6 months from the time when the offence was committed, or the matter of complaint arose.

(2)   Nothing in—
   (a)   subsection (1) above; or
   (b)   subject to subsection (4) below, any other enactment (however framed or worded) which, as regards any offence to which it applies, would but for this section impose a time-limit on the power of a magistrates' court to try an information summarily or impose a limitation on the time for taking summary proceedings,
   shall apply in relation to any indictable offence.

(3)   ...

132.   Minimum term

A magistrates' court shall not impose imprisonment for less than 5 days.

133.   Consecutive terms of imprisonment

(1)   Subject to section 265 of the Criminal Justice Act 2003, a magistrates' court imposing imprisonment or detention in a young offender institution on any person may order that the term of imprisonment or detention in a young offender institution shall commence on the expiration of any other term of imprisonment or detention in a young offender

institution imposed by that or any other court; but where a magistrates' court imposes two or more terms of imprisonment or detention in a young offender institution to run consecutively the aggregate of such terms shall not, subject to the provisions of this section, exceed 65 weeks.

(2) If two or more of the terms imposed by the court are imposed in respect of an offence triable either way which was tried summarily otherwise than in pursuance of section 22(2) above, the aggregate of the terms so imposed and any other terms imposed by the court may exceed 6 months but shall not, subject to the following provisions of this section, exceed 12 months.

...

142. Power of magistrates' court to re-open cases to rectify mistakes etc

(1) A magistrates' court may vary or rescind a sentence or other order imposed or made by it when dealing with an offender if it appears to the court to be in the interests of justice to do so, and it is hereby declared that this power extends to replacing a sentence or order which for any reason appears to be invalid by another which the court has power to impose or make.

(1A)–(3) ...

(5) Where a sentence or order is varied under subsection (1) above, the sentence or other order, as so varied, shall take effect from the beginning of the day on which it was originally imposed or made, unless the court otherwise directs.

MENTAL HEALTH ACT 1983
(1983, c. 20)

1. Application of Act: 'mental disorder'

(1) The provisions of this Act shall have effect with respect to the reception, care and treatment of mentally disordered patients, the management of their property and other related matters.

(2) In this Act—
'mental disorder' means any disorder or disability of the mind; and
'mentally disordered' shall be construed accordingly;
and other expressions shall have the meanings assigned to them in section 145 below.

(2A) But a person with learning disability shall not be considered by reason of that disability to be—

    (a) suffering from mental disorder for the purposes of the provisions mentioned in subsection (2B) below; or

    (b) requiring treatment in hospital for mental disorder for the purposes of sections 17E and 50 to 53 below,

unless that disability is associated with abnormally aggressive or seriously irresponsible conduct on his part.

(2B) The provisions are—

    (a) sections 3, 7, 17A, 20 and 20A below;

    (b) sections 35 to 38, 45A, 47, 48 and 51 below; and

    (c) section 72(1)(b) and (c) and (4) below.

(3) Dependence on alcohol or drugs is not considered to be a disorder or disability of the mind for the purposes of subsection (2) above.

(4) In subsection (2A) above, 'learning disability' means a state of arrested or incomplete development of the mind which includes significant impairment of intelligence and social functioning.

37. Powers of courts to order hospital admission or guardianship

(1) Where a person is convicted before the Crown Court of an offence punishable with imprisonment other than an offence the sentence for which is fixed by law, or is convicted by a magistrates' court of an offence punishable on summary conviction with imprisonment, and the conditions mentioned in subsection (2) below are satisfied, the court may by order authorise his admission to and detention in such hospital as

may be specified in the order or, as the case may be, place him under the guardianship of a local social services authority or of such other person approved by a local social services authority as may be so specified.

(1A) In the case of an offence the sentence for which would otherwise fall to be imposed—

    (za)   under section 1(2B) or 1A(5) of the Prevention of Crime Act 1953,

    (a)   under section 51A(2) of the Firearms Act 1968,

    (aa)   under section 139(6B), 139A(5B) or 139AA(7) of the Criminal Justice Act 1988,

    (b)   under section 110(2) or 111(2) of the Powers of Criminal Courts (Sentencing) Act 2000, ...

    (ba)   under section 224A of the Criminal Justice Act 2003,

    (c)   under section 225(2) or 226(2) of the Criminal Justice Act 2003,

    or

    (d)   under section 29(4) or (6) of the Violent Crime Reduction Act 2006 (minimum sentences in certain cases of using someone to mind a weapon),

nothing in those provisions shall prevent a court from making an order under subsection (1) above for the admission of the offender to a hospital.

(1B) References in subsection (1A) above to a sentence falling to be imposed under any of the provisions mentioned in that subsection are to be read in accordance with section 305(4) of the Criminal Justice Act 2003.

(2)   The conditions referred to in subsection (1) above are that—

    (a)   the court is satisfied, on the written or oral evidence of two registered medical practitioners, that the offender is suffering from mental disorder and that either—

        (i)   the mental disorder from which the offender is suffering is of a nature or degree which makes it appropriate for him to be detained in a hospital for medical treatment and appropriate medical treatment is available for him; or

        (ii)   in the case of an offender who has attained the age of 16 years, the mental disorder is of a nature or degree which warrants his reception into guardianship under this Act; and

    (b)   the court is of the opinion, having regard to all the circumstances including the nature of the offence and the character and antecedents of the offender, and to the other available methods of dealing with him, that the most suitable method of disposing of the case is by means of an order under this section.

(3)   Where a person is charged before a magistrates' court with any act or omission as an offence and the court would have power, on convicting him of that offence, to make an order under subsection (1) above in his case, then, if the court is satisfied that the accused did the act or made the omission charged, the court may, if it thinks fit, make such an order without convicting him.

(4)   An order for the admission of an offender to a hospital (in this Act referred to as 'a hospital order') shall not be made under this section unless the court is satisfied on the written or oral evidence of the approved clinician who would have overall responsibility for his case or of some other person representing the managers of the hospital that arrangements have been made for his admission to that hospital ..., and for his admission to it within the period of 28 days beginning with the date of the making of such an order; and the court may, pending his admission within that period, give such directions as it thinks fit for his conveyance to and detention in a place of safety.

(5)   If within the said period of 28 days it appears to the Secretary of State that by reason of an emergency or other special circumstances it is not practicable for the patient to be received into the hospital specified in the order, he may give directions for the admission of the patient to such other hospital as appears to be appropriate instead of the hospital so specified; and where such directions are given—

    (a)   the Secretary of State shall cause the person having the custody of the patient to be informed, and

    (b)   the hospital order shall have effect as if the hospital specified in the directions were substituted for the hospital specified in the order.

(6)   An order placing an offender under the guardianship of a local social services authority or of any other person (in this Act referred to as 'a guardianship order') shall not be made under this section unless the court is satisfied that that authority or person is willing to receive the offender into guardianship.

(7)　...

(8)　Where an order is made under this section, the court shall not—

　　(a)　pass sentence of imprisonment or impose a fine or make a community order (within the meaning of Part 12 of the Criminal Justice Act 2003) or a youth rehabilitation order (within the meaning of Part 1 of the Criminal Justice and Immigration Act 2008) in respect of the offence,

　　(b)　if the order under this section is a hospital order, make a referral order (within the meaning of the Powers of Criminal Courts (Sentencing) Act 2000) in respect of the offence, or

　　(c)　make in respect of the offender ... an order under section 150 of that Act (binding over of parent or guardian),

but the court may make any other order which it has power to make apart from this section; and for the purposes of this subsection 'sentence of imprisonment' includes any sentence or order for detention.

38.　Interim hospital orders

(1)　Where a person is convicted before the Crown Court of an offence punishable with imprisonment (other than an offence the sentence for which is fixed by law) or is convicted by a magistrates' court of an offence punishable on summary conviction with imprisonment and the court before or by which he is convicted is satisfied, on the written or oral evidence of two registered medical practitioners—

　　(a)　that the offender is suffering from mental disorder; and

　　(b)　that there is reason to suppose that the mental disorder from which the offender is suffering is such that it may be appropriate for a hospital order to be made in his case,

the court may, before making a hospital order or dealing with him in some other way, make an order (in this Act referred to as 'an interim hospital order') authorising his admission to such hospital as may be specified in the order and his detention there in accordance with this section.

(2)　In the case of an offender who is subject to an interim hospital order the court may make a hospital order without his being brought before the court if he is represented by an authorised person who is given an opportunity of being heard.

(3)　At least one of the registered medical practitioners whose evidence is taken into account under subsection (1) above shall be employed at the hospital which is to be specified in the order.

(4)　An interim hospital order shall not be made for the admission of an offender to a hospital unless the court is satisfied, on the written or oral evidence of the approved clinician who would have overall responsibility for his case or of some other person representing the managers of the hospital, that arrangements have been made for his admission to that hospital and for his admission to it within the period of 28 days beginning with the date of the order; and if the court is so satisfied the court may, pending his admission, give directions for his conveyance to and detention in a place of safety.

(5)　An interim hospital order—

　　(a)　shall be in force for such period, not exceeding 12 weeks, as the court may specify when making the order; but

　　(b)　may be renewed for further periods of not more than 28 days at a time if it appears to the court, on the written or oral evidence of the responsible clinician, that the continuation of the order is warranted;

but no such order shall continue in force for more than twelve months in all and the court shall terminate the order if it makes a hospital order in respect of the offender or decides after considering the written or oral evidence of the responsible clinician to deal with the offender in some other way.

(6)　The power of renewing an interim hospital order may be exercised without the offender being brought before the court if he is represented by counsel or a solicitor and his counsel or solicitor is given an opportunity of being heard.

(7)　If an offender absconds from a hospital in which he is detained in pursuance of an interim hospital order, or while being conveyed to or from such a hospital, he may be arrested without warrant by a constable and shall, after being arrested, be brought as soon as practicable before the court that made the order; and the court may thereupon terminate the order and deal with him in any way in which it could have dealt with him if no such order had been made.

40.   Effect of hospital orders, guardianship orders and interim hospital orders

(1)   A hospital order shall be sufficient authority—

(a)   for a constable, an approved mental health professional or any other person directed to do so by the court to convey the patient to the hospital specified in the order within a period of 28 days; and

(b)   for the managers of the hospital to admit him at any time within that period and thereafter detain him in accordance with the provisions of this Act.

(2)   A guardianship order shall confer on the authority or person named in the order as guardian the same powers as a guardianship application made and accepted under Part II of this Act.

(3)   Where an interim hospital order is made in respect of an offender—

(a)   a constable or any other person directed to do so by the court shall convey the offender to the hospital specified in the order within the period mentioned in section 38(4) above; and

(b)   the managers of the hospital shall admit him within that period and thereafter detain him in accordance with the provisions of section 38 above.

(4)   A patient who is admitted to a hospital in pursuance of a hospital order, or placed under guardianship by a guardianship order, shall, subject to the provisions of this subsection, be treated for the purposes of the provisions of this Act mentioned in Part I of Schedule 1 to this Act as if he had been so admitted or placed on the date of the order in pursuance of an application for admission for treatment or a guardianship application, as the case may be, duly made under Part II of this Act, but subject to any modifications of those provisions specified in that Part of that Schedule.

(5)   Where a patient is admitted to a hospital in pursuance of a hospital order, or placed under guardianship by a guardianship order, any previous application, hospital order or guardianship order by virtue of which he was liable to be detained in a hospital or subject to guardianship shall cease to have effect; but if the first-mentioned order, or the conviction on which it was made, is quashed on appeal, this subsection shall not apply and section 22 above shall have effect as if during any period for which the patient was liable to be detained or subject to guardianship under the order, he had been detained in custody as mentioned in that section.

(6)   Where—

(a)   a patient admitted to a hospital in pursuance of a hospital order is absent without leave;

(b)   a warrant to arrest him has been issued under section 72 of the Criminal Justice Act 1967; and

(c)   he is held pursuant to the warrant in any country or territory other than the United Kingdom, any of the Channel Islands and the Isle of Man,

he shall be treated as having been taken into custody under section 18 above on first being so held.

41.   Power of higher courts to restrict discharge from hospital

(1)   Where a hospital order is made in respect of an offender by the Crown Court, and it appears to the court, having regard to the nature of the offence, the antecedents of the offender and the risk of his committing further offences if set at large, that it is necessary for the protection of the public from serious harm so to do, the court may, subject to the provisions of this section, further order that the offender shall be subject to the special restrictions set out in this section; and an order under this section shall be known as 'a restriction order'.

(2)   A restriction order shall not be made in the case of any person unless at least one of the registered medical practitioners whose evidence is taken into account by the court under section 37(2)(a) above has given evidence orally before the court.

(3)   The special restrictions applicable to a patient in respect of whom a restriction order is in force are as follows—

(a)   none of the provisions of Part II of this Act relating to the duration, renewal and expiration of authority for the detention of patients shall apply, and the patient shall continue to be liable to be detained by virtue of the relevant hospital order until he is duly discharged under the said Part II or absolutely discharged under section 42, 73, 74 or 75 below;

(aa)   none of the provisions of Part II of this Act relating to community treatment orders and community patients shall apply;

(b)   no application shall be made to the appropriate tribunal in respect of a patient under section 66 or 69(1) below;

(c)   the following powers shall be exercisable only with the consent of the Secretary of State, namely—

(i)   power to grant leave of absence to the patient under section 17 above;

(ii)   power to transfer the patient in pursuance of regulations under section 19 above or in pursuance of subsection 3 of that section; and

(iii)   power to order the discharge of the patient under section 23 above;

and if leave of absence is granted under the said section 17 power to recall the patient under that section shall vest in the Secretary of State as well as the responsible clinician; and

(d)   the power of the Secretary of State to recall the patient under the said section 17 and power to take the patient into custody and return him under section 18 above may be exercised at any time;

and in relation to any such patient section 40(4) above shall have effect as if it referred to Part II of Schedule 1 to this Act instead of Part I of that Schedule.

(4)   A hospital order shall not cease to have effect under section 40(5) above if a restriction order in respect of the patient is in force at the material time.

(5)   Where a restriction order in respect of a patient ceases to have effect while the relevant hospital order continues in force, the provisions of section 40 above and Part I of Schedule 1 to this Act shall apply to the patient as if he had been admitted to the hospital in pursuance of a hospital order (without a restriction order) made on the date on which the restriction order ceased to have effect.

(6)   While a person is subject to a restriction order the responsible clinician shall at such intervals (not exceeding one year) as the Secretary of State may direct examine and report to the Secretary of State on that person; and every report shall contain such particulars as the Secretary of State may require.

42.   Powers of Secretary of State in respect of patients subject to restriction orders

(1)   If the Secretary of State is satisfied that in the case of any patient a restriction order is no longer required for the protection of the public from serious harm, he may direct that the patient shall cease to be subject to the special restrictions set out in section 41(3) above; and where the Secretary of State so directs, the restriction order shall cease to have effect, and section 41(5) above shall apply accordingly.

(2)   At any time while a restriction order is in force in respect of a patient, the Secretary of State may, if he thinks fit, by warrant discharge the patient from hospital, either absolutely or subject to conditions; and where a person is absolutely discharged under this subsection, he shall thereupon cease to be liable to be detained by virtue of the relevant hospital order, and the restriction order shall cease to have effect accordingly.

(3)   The Secretary of State may at any time during the continuance in force of a restriction order in respect of a patient who has been conditionally discharged under subsection (2) above by warrant recall the patient to such hospital as may be specified in the warrant.

...

45.   Appeals from magistrates' courts

(1)   Where on the trial of an information charging a person with an offence a magistrates' court makes a hospital order or guardianship order in respect of him without convicting him, he shall have the same right of appeal against the order as if it had been made on his conviction; and on any such appeal the Crown Court shall have the same powers as if the appeal had been against both conviction and sentence.

(2)   An appeal by a child or young person with respect to whom any such order has been made, whether the appeal is against the order or against the finding upon which the order was made, may be brought by him or by his parent or guardian on his behalf.

45A.   Power of higher courts to direct hospital admission

(1)   This section applies where, in the case of a person convicted before the Crown Court of an offence the sentence for which is not fixed by law—

(a)   the conditions mentioned in subsection (2) below are fulfilled; and

(b)   the court considers making a hospital order in respect of him before deciding to impose a sentence of imprisonment ('the relevant sentence') in respect of the offence.

(2)   The conditions referred to in subsection (1) above are that the court is satisfied, on the written or oral evidence of two registered medical practitioners—

(a)   that the offender is suffering from mental disorder;

(b)   that the mental disorder from which the offender is suffering is of a nature or degree which makes it appropriate for him to be detained in a hospital for medical treatment; and

(c)   that appropriate medical treatment is available for him.

(3)   The court may give both of the following directions, namely—

(a)   a direction that, instead of being removed to and detained in a prison, the offender be removed to and detained in such hospital as may be specified in the direction (in this Act referred to as a 'hospital direction'); and

(b)   a direction that the offender be subject to the special restrictions set out in section 41 above (in this Act referred to as a 'limitation direction').

(4)   A hospital direction and a limitation direction shall not be given in relation to an offender unless at least one of the medical practitioners whose evidence is taken into account by the court under subsection (2) above has given evidence orally before the court.

(5)   A hospital direction and a limitation direction shall not be given in relation to an offender unless the court is satisfied on the written or oral evidence of the approved clinician who would have overall responsibility for his case, or of some other person representing the managers of the hospital that arrangements have been made—

(a)   for his admission to that hospital; and

(b)   for his admission to it within the period of 28 days beginning with the day of the giving of such directions;

and the court may, pending his admission within that period, give such directions as it thinks fit for his conveyance to and detention in a place of safety.

...

45B.   Effect of hospital and limitation directions

(1)   A hospital direction and a limitation direction shall be sufficient authority—

(a)   for a constable or any other person directed to do so by the court to convey the patient to the hospital specified in the hospital direction within a period of 28 days; and

(b)   for the managers of the hospital to admit him at any time within that period and thereafter detain him in accordance with the provisions of this Act.

(2)   With respect to any person—

(a)   a hospital direction shall have effect as a transfer direction; and

(b)   a limitation direction shall have effect as a restriction direction.

(3)   While a person is subject to a hospital direction and a limitation direction the responsible clinician shall at such intervals (not exceeding one year) as the Secretary of State may direct examine and report to the Secretary of State on that person; and every report shall contain such particulars as the Secretary of State may require.

54.   Requirements as to medical evidence

(1)   The registered medical practitioner whose evidence is taken into account under section 35(3)(a) above and at least one of the registered medical practitioners whose evidence is taken into account under sections 36(1), 37(2)(a), 38(1), 45A(2) and 51(6)(a) above and whose reports are taken into account under sections 47(1) and 48(1) above shall be a practitioner approved for the purposes of section 12 above by the Secretary

of State or another person by virtue of section 12ZA or 12ZB above as having special experience in the diagnosis or treatment of mental disorder.

(2) For the purposes of any provision of this Part of this Act under which a court may act on the written evidence of any person, a report in writing purporting to be signed by that person may, subject to the provisions of this section, be received in evidence without proof of the following—
   (a) the signature of the person; or
   (b) his having the requisite qualifications or approval or authority or being of the requisite description to give the report.

(2A) But the court may require the signatory of any such report to be called to give oral evidence.

(3) Where, in pursuance of a direction of the court, any such report is tendered in evidence otherwise than by or on behalf of the person who is the subject of the report, then—
   (a) if that person is represented by an authorised person, a copy of the report shall be given to that authorised person;
   (b) if that person is not so represented, the substance of the report shall be disclosed to him or, where he is a child or young person, to his parent or guardian if present in court; and
   (c) except where the report relates only to arrangements for his admission to a hospital, that person may require the signatory of the report to be called to give oral evidence, and evidence to rebut the evidence contained in the report may be called by or on behalf of that person.

MISUSE OF DRUGS ACT 1971
(1971, c. 38)

23. Powers to search and obtain evidence

(1) A constable or other person authorised in that behalf by a general or special order of the Secretary of State (or in Northern Ireland either of the Secretary of State or the Ministry of Home Affairs for Northern Ireland) shall, for the purposes of the execution of this Act, have power to enter the premises of a person carrying on business as a producer or supplier of any controlled drugs and to demand the production of, and to inspect, any books or documents relating to dealings in any such drugs and to inspect any stocks of any such drugs.

(2) If a constable has reasonable grounds to suspect that any person is in possession of a controlled drug in contravention of this Act or of any regulations or orders made thereunder, the constable may—
   (a) search that person, and detain him for the purpose of searching him;
   (b) search any vehicle or vessel in which the constable suspects that the drug may be found, and for that purpose require the person in control of the vehicle or vessel to stop it;
   (c) seize and detain, for the purposes of proceedings under this Act, anything found in the course of the search which appears to the constable to be evidence of an offence under this Act.

(3) If a justice of the peace ... is satisfied by information on oath that there is reasonable ground for suspecting—
   (a) that any controlled drugs are, in contravention of this Act or of any regulations or orders made thereunder, in the possession of a person on any premises; or
   (b) that a document directly or indirectly relating to, or connected with, a transaction or dealing which was, or an intended transaction or dealing which would if carried out be, an offence under this Act, or in the case of a transaction or dealing carried out or intended to be carried out in a place outside the United Kingdom, an offence against the provisions of a corresponding law in force in that place, is in the possession of a person on any premises,

he may grant a warrant authorising any constable at any time or times within one month from the date of the warrant, to enter, if need be by force, the premises named in the warrant, and to search the premises and any persons found therein and, if there is reasonable ground for suspecting that an offence under this Act has been committed in relation to any controlled drugs found on the premises or in the possession of any such persons, or that a document so found is such a document as is mentioned in paragraph (b) above, to seize and detain those drugs or that document, as the case may be.

...

(4) A person commits an offence if he—

    (a) intentionally obstructs a person in the exercise of his powers under this section; or

    (b) conceals from a person acting in the exercise of his powers under subsection (1) above any such books, documents, stocks or drugs as are mentioned in that subsection; or

    (c) without reasonable excuse (proof of which shall lie on him) fails to produce any such books or documents as are so mentioned where their production is demanded by a person in the exercise of his power under that subsection.

...

27. Forfeiture

(1) Subject to subsection (2) below, the court by or before which a person is convicted of an offence under this Act or an offence falling within subsection (3) below ... may order anything shown to the satisfaction of the court to relate to the offence, to be forfeited and either destroyed or dealt with in such other manner as the court may order.

(2) The court shall not order anything to be forfeited under this section, where a person claiming to be the owner of or otherwise interested in it applies to be heard by the court, unless an opportunity has been given to him to show cause why the order should not be made.

(3) An offence falls within this subsection if it is an offence which is specified in—

    (a) paragraph 1 of Schedule 2 to the Proceeds of Crime Act 2002 (drug trafficking offences), or

    (b) so far as it relates to that paragraph, paragraph 10 of that Schedule.

MODERN SLAVERY ACT 2015

(2015, c. 30)

14. Slavery and trafficking prevention orders on sentencing

(1) A court may make a slavery and trafficking prevention order against a person ('the defendant') where it deals with the defendant in respect of—

    (a) a conviction for a slavery or human trafficking offence,

    (b) a finding that the defendant is not guilty of a slavery or human trafficking offence by reason of insanity, or

    (c) a finding that the defendant is under a disability and has done the act charged against the defendant in respect of a slavery or human trafficking offence.

(2) The court may make the order only if it is satisfied that—

    (a) there is a risk that the defendant may commit a slavery or human trafficking offence, and

    (b) it is necessary to make the order for the purpose of protecting persons generally, or particular persons, from the physical or psychological harm which would be likely to occur if the defendant committed such an offence.

(3) A 'slavery or human trafficking offence' means an offence listed in Schedule 1.

(4) The Secretary of State may by regulations amend Schedule 1.

(5) For the purposes of this section, convictions and findings include those taking place before this section comes into force.

15. Slavery and trafficking prevention orders on application

(1) A magistrates' court may make a slavery and trafficking prevention order against a person ('the defendant') on an application by—

    (a) a chief officer of police,

    (b) an immigration officer,

        (c)   the Director General of the National Crime Agency ('the Director General'), or

        (d)   the Gangmasters and Labour Abuse Authority.

(2)   The court may make the order only if it is satisfied that—

        (a)   the defendant is a relevant offender (see section 16), and

        (b)   since the defendant first became a relevant offender, the defendant has acted in a way which means that the condition in subsection (3) is met.

(3)   The condition is that—

        (a)   there is a risk that the defendant may commit a slavery or human trafficking offence, and

        (b)   it is necessary to make the order for the purpose of protecting persons generally, or particular persons, from the physical or psychological harm which would be likely to occur if the defendant committed such an offence.

16.   Meaning of 'relevant offender'

(1)   A person is a 'relevant offender' for the purposes of section 15 if subsection (2) or (3) applies to the person.

(2)   This subsection applies to a person if—

        (a)   the person has been convicted of a slavery or human trafficking offence,

        (b)   a court has made a finding that the person is not guilty of a slavery or human trafficking offence by reason of insanity,

        (c)   a court has made a finding that the person is under a disability and has done the act charged against the person in respect of a slavery or human trafficking offence, or

        (d)   the person has been cautioned in respect of a slavery or human trafficking offence.

(3)   This subsection applies to a person if, under the law of a country outside the United Kingdom—

        (a)   the person has been convicted of an equivalent offence (whether or not the person has been punished for it),

        (b)   a court has made, in relation to an equivalent offence, a finding equivalent to a finding that the person is not guilty by reason of insanity,

        (c)   a court has made, in relation to an equivalent offence, a finding equivalent to a finding that the person is under a disability and has done the act charged against the person, or

        (d)   the person has been cautioned in respect of an equivalent offence.

17.   Effect of slavery and trafficking prevention orders

(1)   A slavery and trafficking prevention order is an order prohibiting the defendant from doing anything described in the order.

(2)   The only prohibitions that may be included in the order are those which the court is satisfied are necessary for the purpose of protecting persons generally, or particular persons, from the physical or psychological harm which would be likely to occur if the defendant committed a slavery or human trafficking offence.

(3)   The order may prohibit the defendant from doing things in any part of the United Kingdom, and anywhere outside the United Kingdom.

(4)   Subject to section 18(1), a prohibition contained in a slavery and trafficking prevention order has effect—

        (a)   for a fixed period, specified in the order, of at least 5 years, or

        (b)   until further order.

(5)   A slavery and trafficking prevention order—

        (a)   may specify that some of its prohibitions have effect until further order and some for a fixed period;

        (b)   may specify different periods for different prohibitions.

(6)   If a court makes a slavery and trafficking prevention order in relation to a person who is already subject to such an order (whether made by that court or another), the earlier order ceases to have effect.

22. Appeals

(1) A defendant may appeal against the making of a slavery and trafficking prevention order—

    (a) where the order was made under section 14(1)(a), as if the order were a sentence passed on the defendant for the offence;

    (b) where the order was made under section 14(1)(b) or (c), as if the defendant had been convicted of the offence and the order were a sentence passed on the defendant for the offence;

    (c) where the order was made on an application under section 15, to the Crown Court.

(2) A defendant may appeal to the Crown Court against the making of an interim slavery and trafficking prevention order.

(3) A defendant may appeal against the making of an order under section 20, or the refusal to make such an order—

    (a) where the application for such an order was made to the Crown Court, to the Court of Appeal;

    (b) in any other case, to the Crown Court.

(4) On an appeal under subsection (1)(c), (2) or (3)(b), the Crown Court may make such orders as may be necessary to give effect to its determination of the appeal, and may also make such incidental or consequential orders as appear to it to be just.

(5) Any order made by the Crown Court on an appeal under subsection (1)(c) or (2) is for the purposes of section 20(10) or 21(8) (respectively) to be treated as if it were an order of the court from which the appeal was brought.

(6) Subsection (5) does not apply to an order directing that an application be reheard by a magistrates' court.

MURDER (ABOLITION OF DEATH PENALTY) ACT 1965
(1965, c. 71)

1. Abolition of death penalty for murder

(1) No person shall suffer death for murder, and a person convicted of murder shall ... be sentenced to imprisonment for life.

...

POLICE AND CRIMINAL EVIDENCE ACT 1984
(1984, c. 60)

1. Power of constable to stop and search persons, vehicles etc

(1) A constable may exercise any power conferred by this section—

    (a) in any place to which at the time when he proposes to exercise the power the public or any section of the public has access, on payment or otherwise, as of right or by virtue of express or implied permission; or

    (b) in any other place to which people have ready access at the time when he proposes to exercise the power but which is not a dwelling.

(2) Subject to subsection (3) to (5) below, a constable—

    (a) may search—

        (i) any person or vehicle;

        (ii) anything which is in or on a vehicle,

    for stolen or prohibited articles, any article to which subsection (8A) below applies or any firework to which subsection (8B) below applies, and

    (b) may detain a person or vehicle for the purpose of such a search.

(3) This section does not give a constable power to search a person or vehicle or anything in or on a vehicle unless he has reasonable grounds for suspecting that he will find stolen or prohibited articles, any article to which subsection (8A) below applies or any firework to which subsection (8B) below applies .

(4)   If a person is in a garden or yard occupied with and used for the purposes of a dwelling or on other land so occupied and used, a constable may not search him in the exercise of the power conferred by this section unless the constable has reasonable grounds for believing—

      (a)   that he does not reside in the dwelling; and

      (b)   that he is not in the place in question with the express or implied permission of a person who resides in the dwelling.

(5)   If a vehicle is in a garden or yard occupied with and used for the purposes of a dwelling or on other land so occupied and used, a constable may not search the vehicle or anything in or on it in the exercise of the power conferred by this section unless he has reasonable grounds for believing—

      (a)   that the person in charge of the vehicle does not reside in the dwelling; and

      (b)   that the vehicle is not in the place in question with the express or implied permission of a person who resides in the dwelling.

(6)   If in the course of such a search a constable discovers an article which he has reasonable grounds for suspecting to be a stolen or prohibited article, an article to which subsection (8A) below applies or a firework to which subsection (8B) below applies, he may seize it.

(7)   An article is prohibited for the purposes of this Part of this Act if it is—

      (a)   an offensive weapon; or

      (b)   an article—

           (i)   made or adapted for use in the course of or in connection with an offence to which this sub-paragraph applies; or

           (ii)   intended by the person having it with him for such use by him or by some other person.

(8)   The offences to which subsection (7)(b)(i) above applies are—

      (a)   burglary;

      (b)   theft;

      (c)   offences under section 12 of the Theft Act 1968 (taking motor vehicle or other conveyance without authority); ....

      (d)   fraud (contrary to section 1 of the Fraud Act 2006); and

      (e)   offences under section 1 of the Criminal Damage Act 1971 (destroying or damaging property).

(8A)   This subsection applies to any article in relation to which a person has committed, or is committing or is going to commit an offence under section 139 or 139AA of the Criminal Justice Act 1988.

(8B)   This subsection applies to any firework which a person possesses in contravention of a prohibition imposed by fireworks regulations.

(8C)   In this section—

      (a)   'firework' shall be construed in accordance with the definition of 'fireworks' in section 1(1) of the Fireworks Act 2003; and

      (b)   'fireworks regulations' has the same meaning as in that Act.

(9)   In this Part of this Act 'offensive weapon' means any article—

      (a)   made or adapted for use for causing injury to persons; or

      (b)   intended by the person having it with him for such use by him or by some other person.

2.   Provisions relating to search under section 1 and other powers

(1)   A constable who detains a person or vehicle in the exercise—

      (a)   of the power conferred by section 1 above; or

      (b)   of any other power—

           (i)   to search a person without first arresting him; or

           (ii)   to search a vehicle without making an arrest,

      need not conduct a search if it appears to him subsequently—

           (i)   that no search is required; or

           (ii)   that a search is impracticable.

(2)   If a constable contemplates a search, other than a search of an unattended vehicle, in the exercise—

      (a)   of the power conferred by section 1 above; or

(b)   of any other power, except the power conferred by section 6 below and the power conferred by section 27(2) of the Aviation Security Act 1982—
    (i)   to search a person without first arresting him; or
    (ii)   to search a vehicle without making an arrest,
it shall be his duty, subject to subsection (4) below, to take reasonable steps before he commences the search to bring to the attention of the appropriate person—
    (i)   if the constable is not in uniform, documentary evidence that he is a constable; and
    (ii)   whether he is in uniform or not, the matters specified in subsection (3) below;
and the constable shall not commence the search until he has performed that duty.

(3)   The matters referred to in subsection (2)(ii) above are—
    (a)   the constable's name and the name of the police station to which he is attached;
    (b)   the object of the proposed search;
    (c)   the constable's grounds for proposing to make it; and
    (d)   the effect of section 3(7) or (8) below, as may be appropriate.

(4)   The constable need not bring the effect of section 3(7) or (8) below to the attention of the appropriate person if it appears to the constable that it will not be practicable to make the record in section 3(1) below.

(5)   In this section 'the appropriate person' means—
    (a)   if the constable proposes to search a person, that person; and
    (b)   if he proposes to search a vehicle, or anything in or on a vehicle, the person in charge of the vehicle.

(6)   On completing a search of an unattended vehicle or anything in or on such a vehicle in the exercise of any such power as is mentioned in subsection (2) above a constable shall leave a notice—
    (a)   stating that he has searched it;
    (b)   giving the name of the police station to which he is attached;
    (c)   stating that an application for compensation for any damage caused by the search may be made to that police station; and
    (d)   stating the effect of section 3(8) below.

(7)   The constable shall leave the notice inside the vehicle unless it is not reasonably practicable to do so without damaging the vehicle.

(8)   The time for which a person or vehicle may be detained for the purposes of such a search is such time as is reasonably required to permit a search to be carried out either at the place where the person or vehicle was first detained or nearby.

(9)   Neither the power conferred by section 1 above nor any other power to detain and search a person without first arresting him or to detain and search a vehicle without making an arrest is to be construed—
    (a)   as authorising a constable to require a person to remove any of his clothing in public other than an outer coat, jacket or gloves; or
    (b)   as authorising a constable not in uniform to stop a vehicle.

(10)   This section and section 1 above apply to vessels, aircraft and hovercraft as they apply to vehicles.

3.   Duty to make records concerning searches

(1)   Where a constable has carried out a search in the exercise of any such power as is mentioned in section 2(1) above, other than a search—
    (a)   under section 6 below; or
    (b)   under section 27(2) of the Aviation Security Act 1982,
a record of the search shall be made in writing unless it is not practicable to do so.

(2)   If a record of a search is required to be made by subsection (1) above—
    (a)   in a case where the search results in a person being arrested and taken to a police station, the constable shall secure that the record is made as part of the person's custody record;
    (b)   in any other case, the constable shall make the record on the spot, or, if that is not practicable, as soon as practicable after the completion of the search.

...

(6)   The record of a search of a person or a vehicle—
    (a)   shall state—
        (i)   the object of the search;
        (ii)   the grounds for making it;
        (iii)   the date and time when it was made;
        (iv)   the place where it was made;
        (v)   except in the case of a search of an unattended vehicle, the ethnic origins of the person searched or the person in charge of the vehicle searched (as the case may be); and
    (b)   shall identify the constable who carried out the search.
(6A) The requirements in subsection (6)(a)(v) above for a record to state a person's ethnic origins is a requirement to state—
    (a)   the ethnic origin of the person as described by the person; and
    (b)   if different, the ethnic origin of the person as perceived by the constable.
(7)   If a constable who conducted a search of a person made a record of it, the person who was searched shall be entitled to a copy of the record if he asks for one before the end of the period specified in subsection (9) below.
(8)   If—
    (a)   the owner of a vehicle which has been searched or the person who was in charge of the vehicle at the time when it was searched asked for a copy of the record of the search before the end of the period specified in subsection (9) below; and
    (b)   a record of the search of the vehicle has been made under this section, the person who made the request shall be entitled to a copy.
(9)   The period mentioned in subsections (7) and (8) above is the period of 3 months beginning with the date on which the search was made.
...

8.   Power of justice of the peace to authorise entry and search of premises

(1)   If on an application made by a constable a justice of the peace is satisfied that there are reasonable grounds for believing—
    (a)   that an indictable offence has been committed; and
    (b)   that there is material on premises mentioned in subsection (1A) below which is likely to be of substantial value (whether by itself or together with other material) to the investigation of the offence; and
    (c)   that the material is likely to be relevant evidence; and
    (d)   that it does not consist of or include items subject to legal privilege, excluded material or special procedure material; and
    (e)   that any of the conditions specified in subsection (3) below applies in relation to each set of premises specified in the application,
he may issue a warrant authorising a constable to enter and search the premises.
(1A) The premises referred to in subsection (1)(b) above are—
    (a)   one or more sets of premises specified in the application (in which case the application is for a 'specific premises warrant'); or
    (b)   any premises occupied or controlled by a person specified in the application, including such sets of premises as are so specified (in which case the application is for an 'all premises warrant').
(1B) If the application is for an all premises warrant, the justice of the peace must also be satisfied—
    (a)   that because of the particulars of the offence referred to in paragraph (a) of subsection (1) above, there are reasonable grounds for believing that it is necessary to search premises occupied or controlled by the person in question which are not specified in the application in order to find the material referred to in paragraph (b) of that subsection; and
    (b)   that it is not reasonably practicable to specify in the application all the premises which he occupies or controls and which might need to be searched.
(1C) The warrant may authorise entry to and search of premises on more than one occasion if, on the application, the justice of the peace is satisfied that it is necessary to authorise multiple entries in order to achieve the purpose for which he issues the warrant.

(1D) If it authorises multiple entries, the number of entries authorised may be unlimited, or limited to a maximum.

(2) A constable may seize and retain anything for which a search has been authorised under subsection (1) above.

(3) The conditions mentioned in subsection (1)(e) above are—

(a) that it is not practicable to communicate with any person entitled to grant entry to the premises;

(b) that it is practicable to communicate with a person entitled to grant entry to the premises but it is not practicable to communicate with any person entitled to grant access to the evidence;

(c) that entry to the premises will not be granted unless a warrant is produced;

(d) that the purpose of a search may be frustrated or seriously prejudiced unless a constable arriving at the premises can secure immediate entry to them.

(4) In this Act '*relevant evidence*', in relation to an offence, means anything that would be admissible in evidence at a trial for the offence.

(5) The power to issue a warrant conferred by this section is in addition to any such power otherwise conferred.

15. Search warrants—safeguards

(1) This section and section 16 below have effect in relation to the issue to constables under any enactment, including an enactment contained in an Act passed after this Act, of warrants to enter and search premises; and an entry on or search of premises under a warrant is unlawful unless it complies with this section and section 16 below.

(2) Where a constable applies for any such warrant, it shall be his duty—

(a) to state—

(i) the ground on which he makes the application;

(ii) the enactment under which the warrant would be issued; and

(iii) if the application is for a warrant authorising entry and search on more than one occasion, the ground on which he applies for such a warrant, and whether he seeks a warrant authorising an unlimited number of entries, or (if not) the maximum number of entries desired;

(b) to specify the matters set out in subsection (2A) below; and

(c) to identify, so far as is practicable, the articles or persons to be sought.

(2A) The matters which must be specified pursuant to subsection (2)(b) above are—

(a) if the application relates to one or more sets of premises specified in the application, each set of premises which it is desired to enter and search;

(b) if the application relates to any premises occupied or controlled by a person specified in the application—

(i) as many sets of premises which it is desired to enter and search as it is reasonably practicable to specify;

(ii) the person who is in occupation or control of those premises and any others which it is desired to enter and search;

(iii) why it is necessary to search more premises than those specified under sub-paragraph (i); and

(iv) why it is not reasonably practicable to specify all the premises which it is desired to enter and search.

(3) An application for such a warrant shall be made ex parte and supported by an information in writing.

(4) The constable shall answer on oath any question that the justice of the peace or judge hearing the application asks him.

(5) A warrant shall authorise an entry on one occasion only unless it specifies that it authorises multiple entries.

(5A) If it specifies that it authorises multiple entries, it must also specify whether the number of entries authorised is unlimited, or limited to a specified maximum.

(6) A warrant—

(a) shall specify—

(i) the name of the person who applies for it;

(ii) the date on which it is issued;

(iii) the enactment under which it is issued; and

(iv)   each set of premises to be searched, or (in the case of an all premises warrant) the person who is in occupation or control of premises to be searched, together with any premises under his occupation or control which can be specified and which are to be searched; and

(b)   shall identify, so far as is practicable, the articles or persons to be sought.

(7)   Two copies shall be made of a warrant which specifies only one set of premises and does not authorise multiple entries; and as many copies as are reasonably required may be made of any other kind of warrant.

(8)   The copies shall be clearly certified as copies.

16.   Execution of warrants

(1)   A warrant to enter and search premises may be executed by any constable.

(2)   Such a warrant may authorise persons to accompany any constable who is executing it.

(2A)   A person so authorised has the same powers as the constable whom he accompanies in respect of—

(a)   the execution of the warrant, and

(b)   the seizure of anything to which the warrant relates.

(2B)   But he may exercise those powers only in the company, and under the supervision, of a constable.

(3)   Entry and search under a warrant must be within three months from the date of its issue.

(3A)   If the warrant is an all premises warrant, no premises which are not specified in it may be entered or searched unless a police officer of at least the rank of inspector has in writing authorised them to be entered.

(3B)   No premises may be entered or searched for the second or any subsequent time under a warrant which authorises multiple entries unless a police officer of at least the rank of inspector has in writing authorised that entry to those premises.

(4)   Entry and search under a warrant must be at a reasonable hour unless it appears to the constable executing it that the purpose of a search may be frustrated on an entry at a reasonable hour.

(5)   Where the occupier of premises which are to be entered and searched is present at the time when a constable seeks to execute a warrant to enter and search them, the constable—

(a)   shall identify himself to the occupier and, if not in uniform, shall produce to him documentary evidence that he is a constable;

(b)   shall produce the warrant to him; and

(c)   shall supply him with a copy of it.

(6)   Where—

(a)   the occupier of such premises is not present at the time when a constable seeks to execute such a warrant; but

(b)   some other person who appears to the constable to be in charge of the premises is present,

subsection (5) above shall have effect as if any reference to the occupier were a reference to that other person.

(7)   If there is no person present who appears to the constable to be in charge of the premises, he shall leave a copy of the warrant in a prominent place on the premises.

(8)   A search under a warrant may only be a search to the extent required for the purpose for which the warrant was issued.

(9)   A constable executing a warrant shall make an endorsement on it stating—

(a)   whether the articles or persons sought were found; and

(b)   whether any articles were seized, other than articles which were sought,

and, unless the warrant is a warrant specifying one set of premises only, he shall do so separately in respect of each set of premises entered and searched, which he shall in each case state in the endorsement.

(10)   A warrant shall be returned to the appropriate person mentioned in subsection (10A) below—

(a)   when it has been executed; or

(b)   in the case of a specific premises warrant which has not been executed, or an all premises warrant, or any warrant authorising multiple entries, upon the expiry of the period of three months referred to in subsection (3) above or sooner.

(10A)The appropriate person is —
- (a) if the warrant was issued by a justice of the peace, the designated officer for the local justice area in which the justice was acting when he issued the warrant;
- (b) if it was issued by a judge, the appropriate officer of the court from which he issued it.

(11) A warrant which is returned under subsection (10) above shall be retained for 12 months from its return —
- (a) by the designated officer for the local justice area, if it was returned under paragraph (i) of that subsection; and
- (b) by the appropriate officer, if it was returned under paragraph (ii).

(12) If during the period for which a warrant is to be retained the occupier of premises to which it relates asks to inspect it, he shall be allowed to do so.

17. Entry for purpose of arrest etc

(1) Subject to the following provisions of this section, and without prejudice to any other enactment, a constable may enter and search any premises for the purpose —
- (a) of executing —
  - (i) a warrant of arrest issued in connection with or arising out of criminal proceedings; or
  - (ii) a warrant of commitment issued under section 76 of the Magistrates' Courts Act 1980;
- (b) of arresting a person for an indictable offence;
- (c) of arresting a person for an offence under —
  - (i) section 1 (prohibition of uniforms in connection with political objects) of the Public Order Act 1936;
  - (ii) any enactment contained in sections 6 to 8 or 10 of the Criminal Law Act 1977 (offences relating to entering and remaining on property);
  - (iii) section 4 of the Public Order Act 1986 (fear or provocation of violence);
  - (iiia) section 4 (driving etc when under influence of drink or drugs) or 163 (failure to stop when required to do so by constable in uniform) of the Road Traffic Act 1988;
  - (iiib) section 27 of the Transport and Works Act 1992 (which relates to offences involving drink or drugs);
  - (iv) section 76 of the Criminal Justice and Public Order Act 1994 (failure to comply with interim possession order);
  - (v) any of sections 4, 5, 6(1) and (2), 7 and 8(1) and (2) of the Animal Welfare Act 2006 (offences relating to the prevention of harm to animals);
  - (vi) section 144 of the Legal Aid, Sentencing and Punishment of Offenders Act 2012 (squatting in a residential building);
- (ca) of arresting, in pursuance of section 32(1A) of the Children and Young Persons Act 1969, any child or young person who has been remanded to local authority accommodation or youth detention accommodation under section 91 of the Legal aid, Sentencing and Punishment of Offenders Act 2012;
- (caa) of arresting a person for an offence to which section 61 of the Animal Health Act 1981 applies;
- (cab) of arresting a person under any of the following provisions —
  - (i) section 30D(1) or (2A);
  - (ii) section 46A(1) or (1A);
  - (iii) section 5B(7) of the Bail Act 1976 (arrest where a person fails to surrender to custody in accordance with a court order);
  - (iv) section 7(3) of the Bail Act 1976 (arrest where a person is not likely to surrender to custody etc);
  - (v) section 97(1) of the Legal Aid, Sentencing and Punishment of Offenders Act 2012 (arrest where a child is suspected of breaking conditions of remand);
- (cb) of recapturing any person who is, or is deemed for any purpose to be, unlawfully at large while liable to be detained —
  - (i) in a prison, young offender institution, secure training centre or secure college, or

        (ii)   in pursuance of section 92 of the Powers of Criminal Courts (Sentencing) Act 2000 (dealing with children and young persons guilty of grave crimes), in any other place;

   (d)   of recapturing any person whatever who is unlawfully at large and whom he is pursuing; or

   (e)   of saving life or limb or preventing serious damage to property.

(2)   Except for the purpose specified in paragraph (e) of subsection (1) above, the powers of entry and search conferred by this section—

   (a)   are only exercisable if the constable has reasonable grounds for believing that the person whom he is seeking is on the premises; and

   (b)   are limited, in relation to premises consisting of two or more separate dwellings, to powers to enter and search—

        (i)   any parts of the premises which the occupiers of any dwelling comprised in the premises use in common with the occupiers of any other such dwelling; and

        (ii)   any such dwelling in which the constable has reasonable grounds for believing that the person whom he is seeking may be.

(3)   The powers of entry and search conferred by this section are only exercisable for the purposes specified in subsection (1)(c)(ii), (iv) or (vi) above by a constable in uniform.

(4)   The power of search conferred by this section is only a power to search to the extent that is reasonably required for the purpose for which the power of entry is exercised.

(5)   Subject to subsection (6) below, all the rules of common law under which a constable has power to enter premises without a warrant are hereby abolished.

(6)   Nothing in subsection (5) above affects any power of entry to deal with or prevent a breach of the peace.

18.   Entry and search after arrest

(1)   Subject to the following provisions of this section, a constable may enter and search any premises occupied or controlled by a person who is under arrest for an indictable offence, if he has reasonable grounds for suspecting that there is on the premises evidence, other than items subject to legal privilege, that relates—

   (a)   to that offence; or

   (b)   to some other indictable offence which is connected with or similar to that offence.

(2)   A constable may seize and retain anything for which he may search under subsection (1) above.

(3)   The power to search conferred by subsection (1) above is only a power to search to the extent that is reasonably required for the purpose of discovering such evidence.

(4)   Subject to subsection (5) below, the powers conferred by this section may not be exercised unless an officer of the rank of inspector or above has authorised them in writing.

(5)   A constable may conduct a search under subsection (1)—

   (a)   before the person is taken to a police station or released under section 30A, and

   (b)   without obtaining an authorisation under subsection (4),

if the condition in subsection (5A) is satisfied.

(5A) The condition is that the presence of the person at a place (other than a police station) is necessary for the effective investigation of the offence.

(6)   If a constable conducts a search by virtue of subsection (5) above, he shall inform an officer of the rank of inspector or above that he has made the search as soon as practicable after he has made it.

(7)   An officer who—

   (a)   authorises a search; or

   (b)   is informed of a search under subsection (6) above, shall make a record in writing—

        (i)   of the grounds for the search; and

        (ii)   of the nature of the evidence that was sought.

(8)   If the person who was in occupation or control of the premises at the time of the search is in police detention at the time the record is to be made, the officer shall make the record as part of his custody record.

24.   Arrest without warrant: constables

(1)   A constable may arrest without a warrant—
   (a)   anyone who is about to commit an offence;
   (b)   anyone who is in the act of committing an offence;
   (c)   anyone whom he has reasonable grounds for suspecting to be about to commit an offence;
   (d)   anyone whom he has reasonable grounds for suspecting to be committing an offence.

(2)   If a constable has reasonable grounds for suspecting that an offence has been committed, he may arrest without a warrant anyone whom he has reasonable grounds to suspect of being guilty of it.

(3)   If an offence has been committed, a constable may arrest without a warrant—
   (a)   anyone who is guilty of the offence;
   (b)   anyone whom he has reasonable grounds for suspecting to be guilty of it.

(4)   But the power of summary arrest conferred by subsection (1), (2) or (3) is exercisable only if the constable has reasonable grounds for believing that for any of the reasons mentioned in subsection (5) it is necessary to arrest the person in question.

(5)   The reasons are—
   (a)   to enable the name of the person in question to be ascertained (in the case where the constable does not know, and cannot readily ascertain, the person's name, or has reasonable grounds for doubting whether a name given by the person as his name is his real name);
   (b)   correspondingly as regards the person's address;
   (c)   to prevent the person in question—
      (i)   causing physical injury to himself or any other person;
      (ii)   suffering physical injury;
      (iii)   causing loss of or damage to property;
      (iv)   committing an offence against public decency (subject to subsection (6)); or
      (v)   causing an unlawful obstruction of the highway;
   (d)   to protect a child or other vulnerable person from the person in question;
   (e)   to allow the prompt and effective investigation of the offence or of the conduct of the person in question;
   (f)   to prevent any prosecution for the offence from being hindered by the disappearance of the person in question.

(6)   Subsection (5)(c)(iv) applies only where members of the public going about their normal business cannot reasonably be expected to avoid the person in question.

24A.   Arrest without warrant: other persons

(1)   A person other than a constable may arrest without a warrant—
   (a)   anyone who is in the act of committing an indictable offence;
   (b)   anyone whom he has reasonable grounds for suspecting to be committing an indictable offence.

(2)   Where an indictable offence has been committed, a person other than a constable may arrest without a warrant—
   (a)   anyone who is guilty of the offence;
   (b)   anyone whom he has reasonable grounds for suspecting to be guilty of it.

(3)   But the power of summary arrest conferred by subsection (1) or (2) is exercisable only if—
   (a)   the person making the arrest has reasonable grounds for believing that for any of the reasons mentioned in subsection (4) it is necessary to arrest the person in question; and
   (b)   it appears to the person making the arrest that it is not reasonably practicable for a constable to make it instead.

(4)   The reasons are to prevent the person in question—
   (a)   causing physical injury to himself or any other person;
   (b)   suffering physical injury;
   (c)   causing loss of or damage to property; or
   (d)   making off before a constable can assume responsibility for him.

(5)   This section does not apply in relation to an offence under Part 3 or 3A of the Public Order Act 1986.

27. Fingerprinting of certain offenders

...

(4) The Secretary of State may by regulations make provision for recording in national police records convictions for such offences as are specified in the regulations.

(4A) In subsection (4) 'conviction' includes—

(a) a caution within the meaning of Part 5 of the Police Act 1997; and

(b) a reprimand or warning given under Section 65 of the Crime and Disorder Act 1998.

(5) Regulations under this section shall be made by statutory instrument and shall be subject to annulment in pursuance of a resolution of either House of Parliament.

28. Information to be given on arrest

(1) Subject to subsection (5) below, where a person is arrested, otherwise than by being informed that he is under arrest, the arrest is not lawful unless the person arrested is informed that he is under arrest as soon as is practicable after his arrest.

(2) Where a person is arrested by a constable, subsection (1) above applies regardless of whether the fact of the arrest is obvious.

(3) Subject to subsection (5) below, no arrest is lawful unless the person arrested is informed of the ground for the arrest at the time of, or as soon as is practicable after, the arrest.

(4) Where a person is arrested by a constable, subsection (3) above applies regardless of whether the ground for the arrest is obvious.

(5) Nothing in this section is to be taken to require a person to be informed—

(a) that he is under arrest; or

(b) of the ground for the arrest,

if it was not reasonably practicable for him to be so informed by reason of his having escaped from arrest before the information could be given.

29. Voluntary attendance at police station etc

Where for the purpose of assisting with an investigation a person attends voluntarily at a police station or at any other place where a constable is present or accompanies a constable to a police station or any such other place without having been arrested—

(a) he shall be entitled to leave at will unless he is placed under arrest;

(b) he shall be informed at once that he is under arrest if a decision is taken by a constable to prevent him from leaving at will.

30. Arrest elsewhere than at police station

(1) Subsection (1A) applies where a person is, at any place other than a police station—

(a) arrested by a constable for an offence, or

(b) taken into custody by a constable after being arrested for an offence by a person other than a constable.

(1A) The person must be taken by a constable to a police station as soon as practicable after the arrest.

(1B) Subsection (1A) has effect subject to section 30A (release of a person arrested elsewhere than at police station) and subsection (7) (release without bail).

(2) Subject to subsections (3) and (5) below, the police station to which an arrested person is taken under subsection (1A) above shall be a designated police station.

(3) A constable to whom this subsection applies may take an arrested person to any police station unless it appears to the constable that it may be necessary to keep the arrested person in police detention for more than six hours.

(4) Subsection (3) above applies—

(a) to a constable who is working in a locality covered by a police station which is not a designated police station; and

(b) to a constable belonging to a body of constables maintained by an authority other than a local policing body.

(5) Any constable may take an arrested person to any police station if—

(a) either of the following conditions is satisfied—

(i) the constable has arrested him without the assistance of any other constable and no other constable is available to assist him;

(ii) the constable has taken him into custody from a person other than a constable without the assistance of any other constable and no other constable is available to assist him; and

(b)   it appears to the constable that he will be unable to take the arrested person to a designated police station without the arrested person injuring himself, the constable or some other person.

(6)   If the first police station to which an arrested person is taken after his arrest is not a designated police station, he shall be taken to a designated police station not more than six hours after his arrival at the first police station unless he is released previously.

(7)   A person arrested by a constable at any place other than a police station must be released without bail if the condition in subsection (7A) is satisfied.

(7A) The condition is that, at any time before the person arrested reaches a police station, a constable is satisfied that there are no grounds for keeping him under arrest.

(8)   A constable who releases a person under subsection (7) above shall record the fact that he has done so.

(9)   The constable shall made the record as soon as is practicable after the release.

(10)   Nothing in subsection (1A) or in section 30A prevents a constable delaying taking a person to a police station or releasing him under section 30A if the condition in subsection (10A) is satisfied.

(10A) The condition is that the presence of the person at a place (other than a police station) is necessary in order to carry out such investigations as it is reasonable to carry out immediately.

(11)   Where there is any such delay the reasons for the delay must be recorded when the person first arrives at the police station or (as the case may be) is released on bail.

...

30A. Release of a person arrested elsewhere than at police station

(1)   A constable may release a person who is arrested or taken into custody in the circumstances mentioned in section 30(1)—
   (a)   without bail unless subsection (1A) applies, or
   (b)   on bail if subsection (1A) applies.

(1A) This subsection applies if—
   (a)   the constable is satisfied that releasing the person on bail is necessary and proportionate in all the circumstances (having regard, in particular, to any conditions of bail which would be imposed), and
   (b)   a police officer of the rank of inspector or above authorises the release on bail (having considered any representations made by the person).

(2)   A person may be released under subsection (1) at any time before he arrives at a police station.

(3)   A person released on bail under subsection (1) must be required to attend a police station.

(3A) Where a constable releases a person on bail under subsection (1)–
   (a)   no recognizance for the person's surrender to custody shall be taken from the person,
   (b)   no security for the person's surrender to custody shall be taken from the person or from anyone else on the person's behalf,
   (c)   the person shall not be required to provide a surety or sureties for his surrender to custody, and
   (d)   no requirement to reside in a bail hostel may be imposed as a condition of bail.

(3B) Subject to subsection (3A), where a constable releases a person on bail under subsection (1) the constable may impose, as conditions of the bail, such requirements as appear to the constable to be necessary–
   (a)   to secure that the person surrenders to custody,
   (b)   to secure that the person does not commit an offence while on bail,
   (c)   to secure that the person does not interfere with witnesses or otherwise obstruct the course of justice, whether in relation to himself or any other person, or
   (d)   for the person's own protection or, if the person is under the age of 18, for the person's own welfare or in the person's own interests.

(4)   Where a person is released on bail under subsection (1), a requirement may be imposed on the person as a condition of bail only under the preceding provisions of this section.

(5)   The police station which the person is required to attend may be any police station.

32. Search upon arrest

(1) A constable may search an arrested person, in any case where the person to be searched has been arrested at a place other than a police station, if the constable has reasonable grounds for believing that the arrested person may present a danger to himself or others.

(2) Subject to subsections (3) to (5) below, a constable shall also have power in any such case—
   (a) to search the arrested person for anything—
      (i)   which he might use to assist him to escape from lawful custody; or
      (ii)   which might be evidence relating to an offence; and
   (b) if the offence for which he has been arrested is an indictable offence, to enter and search any premises in which he was when arrested or immediately before he was arrested for evidence relating to the offence.

(3) The power to search conferred by subsection (2) above is only a power to search to the extent that is reasonably required for the purpose of discovering any such thing or any such evidence.

(4) The powers conferred by this section to search a person are not to be construed as authorising a constable to require a person to remove any of his clothing in public other than an outer coat, jacket or gloves but they do authorise a search of a person's mouth.

(5) A constable may not search a person in the exercise of the power conferred by subsection (2)(a) above unless he has reasonable grounds for believing that the person to be searched may have concealed on him anything for which a search is permitted under that paragraph.

(6) A constable may not search premises in the exercise of the power conferred by subsection (2)(b) above unless he has reasonable grounds for believing that there is evidence for which a search is permitted under that paragraph on the premises.

(7) In so far as the power of search conferred by subsection (2)(b) above relates to premises consisting of two or more separate dwellings, it is limited to a power to search—
   (a) any dwelling in which the arrest took place or in which the person arrested was immediately before his arrest; and
   (b) any parts of the premises which the occupier of any such dwelling uses in common with the occupiers of any other dwellings comprised in the premises.

(8) A constable searching a person in the exercise of the power conferred by subsection (1) above may seize and retain anything he finds, if he has reasonable grounds for believing that the person searched might use it to cause physical injury to himself or to any other person.

(9) A constable searching a person in the exercise of the power conferred by subsection (2)(a) above may seize and retain anything he finds, other than an item subject to legal privilege, if he has reasonable grounds for believing—
   (a) that he might use it to assist him to escape from lawful custody; or
   (b) that it is evidence of an offence or has been obtained in consequence of the commission of an offence.

(10) Nothing in this section shall be taken to affect the power conferred by section 43 of the Terrorism Act 2000.

37. Duties of custody officer before charge

(1) Where—
   (a) a person is arrested for an offence—
      (i)   without a warrant; or
      (ii)   under a warrant not endorsed for bail,
   the custody officer at each police station where he is detained after his arrest shall determine whether he has before him sufficient evidence to charge that person with the offence for which he was arrested and may detain him at the police station for such period as is necessary to enable him to do so.

(2) If the custody officer determines that he does not have such evidence before him, the person arrested shall be released—

- (a) without bail unless the pre-conditions for bail are satisfied, or
- (b) on bail if those pre-conditions are satisfied,

(subject to subsection (3)).

(3) If the custody officer has reasonable grounds for believing that the person's detention without being charged is necessary to secure or preserve evidence relating to an offence for which the person is under arrest or to obtain such evidence by questioning the person, he may authorise the person arrested to be kept in police detention.

(4) Where a custody officer authorises a person who has not been charged to be kept in police detention, he shall, as soon as is practicable, make a written record of the grounds for the detention.

(5) Subject to subsection (6) below, the written record shall be made in the presence of the person arrested who shall at that time be informed by the custody officer of the grounds for his detention.

(6) Subsection (5) above shall not apply where the person arrested is, at the time when the written record is made—
- (a) incapable of understanding what is said to him;
- (b) violent or likely to become violent; or
- (c) in urgent need of medical attention.

(6A) Subsection (6B) applies where—
- (a) a person is released under subsection (2), and
- (b) the custody officer determines that—
  - (i) there is not sufficient evidence to charge the person with an offence, or
  - (ii) there is sufficient evidence to charge the person with an offence but the person should not be charged with an offence or given a caution in respect of an offence.

(6B) The custody officer must give the person notice in writing that the person is not to be prosecuted.

(6C) Subsection (6B) does not prevent the prosecution of the person for an offence if new evidence comes to light after the notice was given.

(7) Subject to section 41(7) below, if the custody officer determines that he has before him sufficient evidence to charge the person arrested with the offence for which he was arrested—
- (a) shall be—
  - (i) released without charge and on bail, or
  - (ii) kept in police detention,
  for the purpose of enabling the Director of Public Prosecutions to make a decision under section 37B below,
- (b) shall be released without charge and without bail unless the pre-conditions for bail are satisfied,
- (c) shall be released without charge and on bail if those pre-conditions are satisfied but not for the purpose mentioned in paragraph (a), or
- (d) shall be charged.

(7A) The decision as to how a person is to be dealt with under subsection (7) above shall be that of the custody officer.

(7B) Where a person is dealt with under subsection (7)(a) above, it shall be the duty of the custody officer to inform him that he is being released or (as the case may be) detained, to enable the Director of Public Prosecutions to make a decision under section 37B below.

(8) Where—
- (a) a person is released under subsection (7)(b) or (c) above; and
- (b) at the time of his release a decision whether he should be prosecuted for the offence for which he was arrested has not been taken,

it shall be the duty of the custody officer so to inform him.

(8ZA) Where—
- (a) a person is released under subsection (7)(b) or (c), and
- (b) the custody officer makes a determination as mentioned in subsection (6A)(b),

subsections (6B) and (6C) apply.

(8A) Subsection (8B) applies if the offence for which the person is arrested is one in relation to which a sample could be taken under section 63B below and the custody officer–

    (a)   is required in pursuance of subsection (2) above to release the person arrested and decides to release him on bail, or

    (b)   decides in pursuance of subsection (7)(a) or (c) above to release the person without charge and on bail.

(8B) The detention of the person may be continued to enable a sample to be taken under section 63B, but this subsection does not permit a person to be detained for a period of more than 24 hours after the relevant time.

(9)   If the person arrested is not in a fit state to be dealt with under subsection (7) above, he may be kept in police detention until he is.

(10)   The duty imposed on the custody officer under subsection (1) above shall be carried out by him as soon as practicable after the person arrested arrives at the police station or, in the case of a person arrested at the police station, as soon as practicable after the arrest.

38.　Duties of custody officer after charge

(1)   Where a person arrested for an offence otherwise than under a warrant endorsed for bail is charged with an offence, the custody officer shall, subject to section 25 of the Criminal Justice and Public Order Act 1994, order his release from police detention, either on bail or without bail, unless—

    (a)   if the person arrested is not an arrested juvenile—

        (i)   his name or address cannot be ascertained or the custody officer has reasonable grounds for doubting whether a name or address furnished by him as his name or address is his real name or address;

        (ii)   the custody officer has reasonable grounds for believing that the person arrested will fail to appear in court to answer to bail;

        (iii)   in the case of a person arrested for an imprisonable offence, the custody officer has reasonable grounds for believing that the detention of the person arrested is necessary to prevent him from committing an offence;

        (iiia)   in a case where a sample may be taken from the person under section 63B below, the custody officer has reasonable grounds for believing that the detention of the person is necessary to enable the sample to be taken from him;

        (iv)   in the case of a person arrested for an offence which is not an imprisonable offence, the custody officer has reasonable grounds for believing that the detention of the person arrested is necessary to prevent him from causing physical injury to any other person or from causing loss of or damage to property;

        (v)   he custody officer has reasonable grounds for believing that the detention of the person arrested is necessary to prevent him from interfering with the administration of justice or with the investigation of offences or of a particular offence; or

        (vi)   the custody officer has reasonable grounds for believing that the detention of the person arrested is necessary for his own protection;

    (b)   if he is an arrested juvenile—

        (i)   any of the requirements of paragraph (a) above is satisfied (but, in the case of paragraph (a)(iiia) above, only if the arrested juvenile has attained the minimum age); or

        (ii)   the custody officer has reasonable grounds for believing that he ought to be detained in his own interests.

    (c)   the offence with which the person is charged is murder.

(2)   If the release of a person arrested is not required by subsection (1) above, the custody officer may authorise him to be kept in police detention but may not authorise a person to be kept in police detention by virtue of subsection (1)(a)(iiia) after the end of the period of six hours beginning when he was charged with the offence.

(2A) The custody officer, in taking the decisions required by subsection (1)(a) and (b) above (except (a)(i) and (vi) and (b)(ii)), shall have regard to the same considerations as those which a court is required to have regard to in taking the corresponding decisions under paragraph 2(1) of Part I of Schedule 1 to the Bail Act 1976 disregarding paragraph 2(2) of that Part).

(3) Where a custody officer authorises a person who has been charged to be kept in police detention, he shall, as soon as practicable, make a written record of the grounds for the detention.

(4) Subject to subsection (5) below, the written record shall be made in the presence of the person charged who shall at that time be informed by the custody officer of the grounds for his detention.

(5) Subsection (4) above shall not apply where the person charged is, at the time when the written record is made—

    (a) incapable of understanding what is said to him;

    (b) violent or likely to become violent; or

    (c) in urgent need of medical attention.

(6) Where a custody officer authorises an arrested juvenile to be kept in police detention under subsection (1) above, the custody officer shall, unless he certifies—

    (a) that, by reason of such circumstances as are specified in the certificate, it is impracticable for him to do so; or

    (b) in the case of an arrested juvenile who has attained the age of 12 years, that no secure accommodation is available and that keeping him in other local authority accommodation would not be adequate to protect the public from serious harm from him,

secure that the arrested juvenile is moved to local authority accommodation.

(6A)–(8) ...

39. Responsibilities in relation to persons detained

(1) Subject to subsections (2) and (4) below, it shall be the duty of the custody officer at a police station to ensure—

    (a) that all persons in police detention at that station are treated in accordance with this Act and any code of practice issued under it and relating to the treatment of persons in police detention; and

    (b) that all matters relating to such persons which are required by this Act or by such codes of practice to be recorded are recorded in the custody records relating to such persons.

(2) If the custody officer, in accordance with any code of practice issued under this Act, transfers or permits the transfer of a person in police detention—

    (a) to the custody of another police officer at the police station where the person is in police detention, for the purpose of an interview that is part of the investigation of an offence for which the person is in police detention or otherwise in connection with the investigation of such an offence; or

    (b) to the custody of an officer who has charge of that person outside the police station,

the custody officer shall cease in relation to that person to be subject to the duty imposed on him by subsection (1)(a) above; and it shall be the duty of the officer to whom the transfer is made to ensure that he is treated in accordance with the provisions of this Act and of any such codes of practice as are mentioned in subsection (1) above.

(3) If the person detained is subsequently returned to the custody of the custody officer, it shall be the duty of the officer investigating the offence to report to the custody officer as to the manner in which this section and the codes of practice have been complied with while that person was in his custody.

(3A) Subsections (3B) and (3C) apply if the custody officer, in accordance with any code of practice issued under this Act, transfers or permits the transfer of a person in police detention to an officer mentioned in subsection (2)(a) for the purpose of an interview that is to be conducted to any extent by means of a live link by another police officer who is investigating the offence but is not at the police station where the person in police detention is held at the time of the interview.

(3B) The officer who is not at the police station has the same duty as the officer mentioned in subsection (2)(a) to ensure that the person is treated in accordance with the provisions of this Act and of any such codes of practice as are mentioned in subsection (1).

(3C) If the person detained is subsequently returned to the custody of the custody officer, the officer who is not at the police station also has the same duty under subsection (3) as the officer mentioned in subsection (2)(a).

40. Review of police detention

(1) Reviews of the detention of each person in police detention in connection with the investigation of an offence shall be carried out periodically in accordance with the following provisions of this section—

    (a) in the case of a person who has been arrested and charged, by the custody officer; and

    (b) in the case of a person who has been arrested but not charged, by an officer of at least the rank of inspector who has not been directly involved in the investigation.

(2) The officer to whom it falls to carry out a review is referred to in this section as a 'review officer'.

(3) Subject to subsection (4) below—

    (a) the first review shall be not later than six hours after the detention was first authorised;

    (b) the second review shall be not later than nine hours after the first;

    (c) subsequent reviews shall be at intervals of not more than nine hours.

(4) A review may be postponed—

    (a) if, having regard to all the circumstances prevailing at the latest time for it specified in subsection (3) above, it is not practicable to carry out the review at that time;

    (b) without prejudice to the generality of paragraph (a) above—

        (i) if at that time the person in detention is being questioned by a police officer and the review officer is satisfied that an interruption of the questioning for the purpose of carrying out the review would prejudice the investigation in connection with which he is being questioned; or

        (ii) if at that time no review officer is readily available.

(5) If a review is postponed under subsection (4) above it shall be carried out as soon as practicable after the latest time specified for it in subsection (3) above.

(6) If a review is carried out after postponement under subsection (4) above, the fact that it was so carried out shall not affect any requirement of this section as to the time at which any subsequent review is to be carried out.

(7) The review officer shall record the reasons for any postponement of a review in the custody record.

(8) ...

40A. Use of telephone for review under s. 40

(1) A review under section 40(1)(b) may be carried out by means of a discussion, conducted by telephone, with one or more persons at the police station where the arrested person is held.

(2) But subsection (1) does not apply if—

    (a) the review is of a kind authorised by regulations under section 45A to be carried out using a live link; and

    (b) it is reasonably practicable to carry it out in accordance with those regulations.

(3) Where any review is carried out under this section by an officer who is not present at the station where the arrested person is held—

    (a) any obligation of that officer to make a record in connection with the carrying out of the review shall have effect as an obligation to cause another officer to make the record;

    (b) any requirement for the record to be made in the presence of the arrested person shall apply to the making of that record by that other officer; and

    (c) the requirements under section 40(12) and (13) above for—

        (i) the arrested person, or

        (ii) a solicitor representing him,

    to be given any opportunity to make representations (whether in writing or orally) to that officer shall have effect as a requirement for that person, or such a solicitor, to be given an opportunity to make representations in a manner authorised by subsection (4) below.

(4) Representations are made in a manner authorised by this subsection—

    (a) in a case where facilities exist for the immediate transmission of written representations to the officer carrying out the review, if they are made either—

        (i) orally by telephone to that officer; or

        (ii) in writing to that officer by means of those facilities;

        and

    (b) in any other case, if they are made orally by telephone to that officer.

(5) In this section 'live link' has the same meaning as in section 45A below.

41. Limits on period of detention without charge

(1) Subject to the following provisions of this section and to sections 42 and 43 below, a person shall not be kept in police detention for more than 24 hours without being charged.

(2) The time from which the period of detention of a person is to be calculated (in this Act referred to as 'the relevant time')—

    (a) in the case of a person to whom this paragraph applies, shall be—

        (i) the time at which that person arrives at the relevant police station; or

        (ii) the time 24 hours after the time of that person's arrest,

        whichever is the earlier;

    (b) in the case of a person arrested outside England and Wales, shall be—

        (i) the time at which that person arrives at the first police station to which he is taken in the police area in England or Wales in which the offence for which he was arrested is being investigated; or

        (ii) the time 24 hours after the time of that person's entry into England and Wales,

        whichever is the earlier;

    (c) in the case of a person who—

        (i) attends voluntarily at a police station; or

        (ii) accompanies a constable to a police station without having been arrested,

        and is arrested at the police station, the time of his arrest;

    (ca) in the case of a person who attends a police station to answer to bail granted under section 30A, the time when he arrives at the police station;

    (d) in any other case, except where subsection (5) below applies, shall be the time at which the person arrested arrives at the first police station to which he is taken after his arrest.

(3) Subsection (2)(a) above applies to a person if—

    (a) his arrest is sought in one police area in England and Wales;

    (b) he is arrested in another police area; and

    (c) he is not questioned in the area in which he is arrested in order to obtain evidence in relation to an offence for which he is arrested;

and in sub-paragraph (i) of that paragraph 'the relevant police station' means the first police station to which he is taken in the police area in which his arrest was sought.

(4) Subsection (2) above shall have effect in relation to a person arrested under section 31 above as if every reference in it to his arrest or his being arrested were a reference to his arrest or his being arrested for the offence for which he was originally arrested.

…

42. Authorisation of continued detention

(1) Where a police officer of the rank of superintendent or above who is responsible for the police station at which a person is detained has reasonable grounds for believing that—

    (a) the detention of that person without charge is necessary to secure or preserve evidence relating to an offence for which he is under arrest or to obtain such evidence by questioning him;

    (b) an offence for which he is under arrest is an indictable offence; and

    (c) the investigation is being conducted diligently and expeditiously,

he may authorise the keeping of that person in police detention for a period expiring at or before 36 hours after the relevant time.

(2) Where an officer such as is mentioned in subsection (1) above has authorised the keeping of a person in police detention for a period expiring less than 36 hours after the relevant

time, such an officer may authorise the keeping of that person in police detention for a further period expiring not more than 36 hours after that time if the conditions specified in subsection (1) above are still satisfied when he gives the authorisation.

...

(4) No authorisation under subsection (1) above shall be given in respect of any person—
    (a)   more than 24 hours after the relevant time; or
    (b)   before the second review of his detention under section 40 above has been carried out.

(5) Where an officer authorises the keeping of a person in police detention under subsection (1) above, it shall be his duty—
    (a)   to inform that person of the grounds for his continued detention; and
    (b)   to record the grounds in that person's custody record.

(6) Before determining whether to authorise the keeping of a person in detention under subsection (1) or (2) above, an officer shall give—
    (a)   that person; or
    (b)   any solicitor representing him who is available at the time when it falls to the officer to determine whether to give the authorisation,
    an opportunity to make representations to him about the detention.

(7) Subject to subsection (8) below, the person in detention or his solicitor may make representations under subsection (6) above either orally or in writing.

(8) The officer to whom it falls to determine whether to give the authorisation may refuse to hear oral representations from the person in detention if he considers that he is unfit to make such representations by reason of his condition or behaviour.

(9) Where—
    (a)   an officer authorises the keeping of a person in detention under subsection (1) above; and .
    (b)   at the time of the authorisation he has not yet exercised a right conferred on him by section 56 or 58 below,
    the officer—
        (i)   shall inform him of that right;
        (ii)   shall decide whether he should be permitted to exercise it;
        (iii)   shall record the decision in his custody record; and
        (iv)   if the decision is to refuse to permit the exercise of the right, shall also record the grounds for the decision in that record.

(10) Where an officer has authorised the keeping of a person who has not been charged in detention under subsection (1) or (2) above, he shall be released from detention, not later than 36 hours after the relevant time
    (a)   without bail unless the pre-conditions for bail are satisfied, or
    (b)   on bail if those pre-conditions are satisfied,
    (subject to subsection (10A)).

(10A) Subsection (10) does not apply if—
    (a)   the person has been charged with an offence, or
    (b)   the person's continued detention is authorised or otherwise permitted in accordance with section 43.

(11) A person released under subsection (10) above shall not be re-arrested without a warrant for the offence for which he was previously arrested unless new evidence justifying a further arrest has come to light since his release; but this subsection does not prevent an arrest under section 46A below.

43.   Warrants of further detention

(1) Where, on an application on oath made by a constable and supported by an information, a magistrates' court is satisfied that there are reasonable grounds for believing that the further detention of the person to whom the application relates is justified, it may issue a warrant of further detention authorising the keeping of that person in police detention.

(2) A court may not hear an application for a warrant of further detention unless the person to whom the application relates—
    (a)   has been furnished with a copy of the information; and
    (b)   has been brought before the court for the hearing.

(3) The person to whom the application relates shall be entitled to be legally represented at the hearing and, if he is not so represented but wishes to be so represented—
 (a) the court shall adjourn the hearing to enable him to obtain representation; and
 (b) he may be kept in police detention during the adjournment.

(4) A person's further detention is only justified for the purposes of this section or section 44 below if—
 (a) his detention without charge is necessary to secure or preserve evidence relating to an offence for which he is under arrest or to obtain such evidence by questioning him;
 (b) an offence for which he is under arrest is an indictable offence; and
 (c) the investigation is being conducted diligently and expeditiously.

(5) Subject to subsection (7) below, an application for a warrant of further detention may be made—
 (a) at any time before the expiry of 36 hours after the relevant time; or
 (b) in a case where—
  (i) it is not practicable for the magistrates' court to which the application will be made to sit at the expiry of 36 hours after the relevant time; but
  (ii) the court will sit during the 6 hours following the end of that period,
 at any time before the expiry of the said 6 hours.

(6) In a case to which subsection (5)(b) above applies—
 (a) the person to whom the application relates may be kept in police detention until the application is heard; and
 (b) the custody officer shall make a note in that person's custody record—
  (i) of the fact that he was kept in police detention for more than 36 hours after the relevant time; and
  (ii) of the reason why he was so kept.

(7) If—
 (a) an application for a warrant of further detention is made after the expiry of 36 hours after the relevant time; and
 (b) it appears to the magistrates' court that it would have been reasonable for the police to make it before the expiry of that period,
 the court shall dismiss the application.

(8) Where on an application such as is mentioned in subsection (1) above a magistrates' court is not satisfied that there are reasonable grounds for believing that the further detention of the person to whom the application relates is justified, it shall be its duty—
 (a) to refuse the application; or
 (b) to adjourn the hearing of it until a time not later than 36 hours after the relevant time.

(9) The person to whom the application relates may be kept in police detention during the adjournment.

(10) A warrant of further detention shall—
 (a) state the time at which it is issued;
 (b) authorise the keeping in police detention of the person to whom it relates for the period stated in it.

(11) Subject to subsection (12) below, the period stated in a warrant of further detention shall be such period as the magistrates' court thinks fit, having regard to the evidence before it.

(12) The period shall not be longer than 36 hours.

(13) If it is proposed to transfer a person in police detention to a police area other than that in which he is detained when the application for a warrant of further detention is made, the court hearing the application shall have regard to the distance and the time the journey would take.

(14) Any information submitted in support of an application under this section shall state—
 (a) the nature of the offence for which the person to whom the application relates has been arrested;
 (b) the general nature of the evidence on which that person was arrested;
 (c) what inquiries relating to the offence have been made by the police and what further inquiries are proposed by them;
 (d) the reasons for believing the continued detention of that person to be necessary for the purposes of such further inquiries.

(15) Where an application under this section is refused, the person to whom the application relates shall forthwith be charged or, subject to subsection (16) below, released—
  (a)   without bail unless the pre-conditions for bail are satisfied, or
  (b)   on bail if those pre-conditions are satisfied.

(16) A person need not be released under subsection (15) above—
  (a)   before the expiry of 24 hours after the relevant time; or
  (b)   before the expiry of any longer period for which his continued detention is or has been authorised under section 42 above.

(17) Where an application under this section is refused, no further application shall be made under this section in respect of the person to whom the refusal relates, unless supported by evidence which has come to light since the refusal.

(18) Where a warrant of further detention is issued, the person to whom it relates shall be released from police detention, either on bail or without bail, upon or before the expiry of the warrant—
  (a)   without bail unless the pre-conditions for bail are satisfied, or
  (b)   on bail if those pre-conditions are satisfied.

(19) A person released under subsection (18) above shall not be re-arrested without a warrant for the offence for which he was previously arrested unless new evidence justifying a further arrest has come to light since his release; but this subsection does not prevent an arrest under section 46A below.

44.   Extension of warrants of further detention

(1)   On an application on oath made by a constable and supported by an information a magistrates' court may extend a warrant of further detention issued under section 43 above if it is satisfied that there are reasonable grounds for believing that the further detention of the person to whom the application relates is justified.

(2)   Subject to subsection (3) below, the period for which a warrant of further detention may be extended shall be such period as the court thinks fit, having regard to the evidence before it.

(3)   The period shall not—
  (a)   be longer than 36 hours; or
  (b)   end later than 96 hours after the relevant time.

(4)   Where a warrant of further detention has been extended under subsection (1) above, or further extended under this subsection, for a period ending before 96 hours after the relevant time, on an application such as is mentioned in that subsection a magistrates' court may further extend the warrant if it is satisfied as there mentioned; and subsections (2) and (3) above apply to such further extensions as they apply to extensions under subsection (1) above.

(5)   A warrant of further detention shall, if extended or further extended under this section, be endorsed with a note of the period of the extension.

(6)   Subsections (2), (3) and (14) of section 43 above shall apply to an application made under this section as they apply to an application made under that section.

(7)   Where an application under this section is refused, the person to whom the application relates shall forthwith be charged or, subject to subsection (8) below, released
  (a)   without bail unless the pre-conditions for bail are satisfied, or
  (b)   on bail if those pre-conditions are satisfied.

(8)   A person need not be released under subsection (7) above before the expiry of any period for which a warrant of further detention issued in relation to him has been extended or further extended on an earlier application made under this section.

(9)   Subsection (10) applies where—
  (a)   a person is released under subsection (7), and
  (b)   a custody officer determines that—
    (i)   there is not sufficient evidence to charge the person with an offence, or
    (ii)   there is sufficient evidence to charge the person with an offence but the person should not be charged with an offence or given a caution in respect of an offence.

(10) The custody officer must give the person notice in writing that the person is not to be prosecuted.

(11) Subsection (10) does not prevent the prosecution of the person for an offence if new evidence comes to light after the notice was given.

45.   Detention before charge—supplementary

(1)   In sections 43, 44 and 45ZB of this Act 'magistrates' court' means a court consisting of two or more justices of the peace sitting otherwise than in open court.

(2)   Any reference in this Part of this Act to a period of time or a time of day is to be treated as approximate only.

45ZA. Functions of extending detention: use of live links

(1)   The functions of a police officer under section 42(1) or (2) may be performed, in relation to an arrested person who is held at a police station, by an officer who is not present at the police station but has access to the use of a live link if—

(a)   a custody officer considers that the use of the live link is appropriate,

(b)   the arrested person has had advice from a solicitor on the use of the live link, and

(c)   the appropriate consent to the use of the live link has been given.

(2)   In subsection (1)(c), 'the appropriate consent' means—

(a)   in relation to a person who has attained the age of 18, the consent of that person;

(b)   in relation to a person who has not attained that age but has attained the age of 14, the consent of that person and of his or her parent or guardian;

(c)   in relation to a person who has not attained the age of 14, the consent of his or her parent or guardian.

(3)   The consent of a person who has not attained the age of 18 (but has attained the age of 14), or who is a vulnerable adult, may only be given in the presence of an appropriate adult.

(4)   Section 42 applies with the modifications set out in subsections (5) to (7) below in any case where the functions of a police officer under that section are, by virtue of subsection (1), performed by an officer who is not at the police station where the arrested person is held.

(5)   Subsections (5)(b) and (9)(iii) and (iv) of that section are each to be read as if, instead of requiring the officer to make a record, they required the officer to cause another police officer to make a record.

(6)   Subsection (6) of that section is to be read as if it required the officer to give the persons mentioned in that subsection an opportunity to make representations—

(a)   if facilities exist for the immediate transmission of written representations to the officer, either in writing by means of those facilities or orally by means of the live link, or

(b)   in any other case, orally by means of the live link.

(7)   Subsection (9) of that section is to be read as if the reference in paragraph (b) to the right conferred by section 58 were omitted.

(8) and (9) ...

45ZB. Warrants for further detention: use of live links

(1)   A magistrates' court may give a live link direction for the purpose of the hearing of an application under section 43 for a warrant authorising further detention of a person, or the hearing of an application under section 44 for an extension of such a warrant, if—

(a)   a custody officer considers that the use of a live link for that purpose is appropriate,

(b)   the person to whom the application relates has had legal advice on the use of the live link,

(c)   the appropriate consent to the use of the live link has been given, and

(d)   it is not contrary to the interests of justice to give the direction.

(2)   ...

45A. Use of live links for other decisions about detention

(1)   Subject to the following provisions of this section, the Secretary of State may by regulations provide that, in the case of an arrested person who is held in a police station, some or all of the functions mentioned in subsection (2) may be performed (notwithstanding anything in the preceding provisions of this Part) by an officer who—

(a)   is not present in that police station; but

(b)   has access to the use of a live link.

(2)   Those functions are—
    (a)   the functions in relation to an arrested person taken to, or answering to bail at, a police station that is not a designated police station which, in the case of an arrested person taken to a station that is a designated police station, are functions of a custody officer under section 37, 38 or 40 above; and
    (b)   the function of carrying out a review under section 40(1)(b) above (review, by an officer of at least the rank of inspector, of the detention of person arrested but not charged).
(3)   Regulations under this section shall specify the use to be made in the performance of the functions mentioned in subsection (2) above of a live link.
(4)   Regulations under this section shall not authorise the performance of any of the functions mentioned in subsection (2)(a) above by such an officer as is mentioned in subsection (1) above unless he is a custody officer for a designated police station.
(5)   ...

46.   Detention after charge

(1)   Where a person—
    (a)   is charged with an offence; and
    (b)   after being charged—
        (i)   is kept in police detention; or
        (ii)   is detained by a local authority in pursuance of arrangements made under section 38(6) above,
he shall be brought before a magistrates' court in accordance with the provisions of this section.
(2)   If he is to be brought before a magistrates' court in the local justice area in which the police station at which he was charged is situated, he shall be brought before such a court as soon as is practicable and in any event not later than the first sitting after he is charged with the offence.
    ...
(9)   Nothing in this section requires a person who is in hospital to be brought before a court if he is not well enough.

46A.   Power of arrest for failure to answer to police bail

(1)   A constable may arrest without a warrant any person who, having been released on bail under this Part of this Act subject to a duty to attend at a police station, fails to attend at that police station at the time appointed for him to do so.
    ...

47.   Bail after arrest

(1)   Subject to the following provisions of this section, a release on bail of a person under this Part of this Act shall be a release on bail granted in accordance with sections 3, 3A, 5 and 5A of the Bail Act 1976 as they apply to bail granted by a constable.
(1A) The normal powers to impose conditions of bail shall be available to him where a custody officer releases a person on bail under this Part (except sections 37C(2)(b) and 37CA(2)(b)). In this subsection 'the normal powers to impose conditions of bail' has the meaning given in section 3(6) of the Bail Act 1976.
    ...
(1E) A magistrates' court may, on an application by or on behalf of the person, vary the conditions of bail; and in this subsection 'vary' has the same meaning as in the Bail Act 1976.
(1F) Where a magistrates' court varies the conditions of bail under subsection (1E) above, that bail shall not lapse but shall continue subject to the conditions as so varied.
(2)   Nothing in the Bail Act 1976 shall prevent the re-arrest without warrant of a person released on bail subject to a duty to attend at a police station if, since the person's release, new evidence has come to light or an examination or analysis of existing evidence has been made which could not reasonably have been made before the person's release.
    ...

55. Intimate searches

(1) Subject to the following provisions of this section, if an officer of at least the rank of inspector has reasonable grounds for believing—

    (a) that a person who has been arrested and is in police detention may have concealed on him anything which—

        (i) he could use to cause physical injury to himself or others; and

        (ii) he might so use while he is in police detention or in the custody of a court; or

    (b) that such a person—

        (i) may have a Class A drug concealed on him; and

        (ii) was in possession of it with the appropriate criminal intent before his arrest,

he may authorise an intimate search of that person.

(2) An officer may not authorise an intimate search of a person for anything unless he has reasonable grounds for believing that it cannot be found without his being intimately searched.

(3) An officer may give an authorisation under subsection (1) above orally or in writing but, if he gives it orally, he shall confirm it in writing as soon as is practicable.

(3A) A drug offence search shall not be carried out unless the appropriate consent has been given in writing.

(3B) Where it is proposed that a drug offence search be carried out, an appropriate officer shall inform the person who is to be subject to it—

    (a) of the giving of the authorisation for it; and

    (b) of the grounds for giving the authorisation.

(4) An intimate search which is only a drug offence search shall be by way of examination by a suitably qualified person.

(5) Except as provided by subsection (4) above, an intimate search shall be by way of examination by a suitably qualified person unless an officer of at least the rank of inspector considers that this is not practicable.

(6) An intimate search which is not carried out as mentioned in subsection (5) above shall be carried out by a constable.

(7) A constable may not carry out an intimate search of a person of the opposite sex.

(8) No intimate search may be carried out except—

    (a) at a police station;

    (b) at a hospital;

    (c) at a registered medical practitioner's surgery; or

    (d) at some other place used for medical purposes.

(9) An intimate search which is only a drug offence search may not be carried out at a police station.

(10) If an intimate search of a person is carried out, the custody record relating to him shall state—

    (a) which parts of his body were searched; and

    (b) why they were searched.

(10A) If the intimate search is a drug offence search, the custody record relating to that person shall also state—

    (a) the authorisation by virtue of which the search was carried out;

    (b) the grounds for giving the authorisation; and

    (c) the fact that the appropriate consent was given.

(11) The information required to be recorded by subsections (10) and (10A) above shall be recorded as soon as practicable after the completion of the search.

(12) The custody officer at a police station may seize and retain anything which is found on an intimate search of a person, or cause any such thing to be seized and retained—

    (a) if he believes that the person from whom it is seized may use it—

        (i) to cause physical injury to himself or any other person;

        (ii) to damage property;

        (iii) to interfere with evidence; or

        (iv) to assist him to escape; or

(b)   if he has reasonable grounds for believing that it may be evidence relating to an offence.

(13) Where anything is seized under this section, the person from whom it is seized shall be told the reason for the seizure unless he is—

(a)   violent or likely to become violent; or

(b)   incapable of understanding what is said to him

...

55A.   X-rays and ultrasound scans

(1)   If an officer of at least the rank of inspector has reasonable grounds for believing that a person who has been arrested for an offence and is in police detention—

(a)   may have swallowed a Class A drug, and

(b)   was in possession of it with the appropriate criminal intent before his arrest,

the officer may authorise that an x-ray is taken of the person or an ultrasound scan is carried out on the person (or both).

(2)   An x-ray must not be taken of a person and an ultrasound scan must not be carried out on him unless the appropriate consent has been given in writing.

(3)   If it is proposed that an x-ray is taken or an ultrasound scan is carried out, an appropriate officer must inform the person who is to be subject to it—

(a)   of the giving of the authorisation for it, and

(b)   of the grounds for giving the authorisation.

(4)   An x-ray may be taken or an ultrasound scan carried out only by a suitably qualified person and only at—

(a)   a hospital,

(b)   a registered medical practitioner's surgery, or

(c)   some other place used for medical purposes.

...

56.   Right to have someone informed when arrested

(1)   Where a person has been arrested and is being held in custody in a police station or other premises, he shall be entitled, if he so requests, to have one friend or relative or other person who is known to him or who is likely to take an interest in his welfare told, as soon as is practicable except to the extent that delay is permitted by this section, that he has been arrested and is being detained there.

(2)   Delay is only permitted—

(a)   in the case of a person who is in police detention for an indictable offence; and

(b)   if an officer of at least the rank of inspector authorises it.

(3)   In any case the person in custody must be permitted to exercise the right conferred by subsection (1) above within 36 hours from the relevant time, as defined in section 41(2) above.

(4)   An officer may give an authorisation under subsection (2) above orally or in writing but, if he gives it orally, he shall confirm it in writing as soon as is practicable.

(5)   Subject to sub-section (5A) below an officer may only authorise delay where he has reasonable grounds for believing that telling the named person of the arrest—

(a)   will lead to interference with or harm to evidence connected with an indictable offence or interference with or physical injury to other persons; or

(b)   will lead to the alerting of other persons suspected of having committed such an offence but not yet arrested for it; or

(c)   will hinder the recovery of any property obtained as a result of such an offence.

...

(6)   If a delay is authorised—

(a)   the detained person shall be told the reason for it; and

(b)   the reason shall be noted on his custody record.

(7)   The duties imposed by subsection (6) above shall be performed as soon as is practicable.

...

(9)   There may be no further delay in permitting the exercise of the right conferred by subsection (1) above once the reason for authorising delay ceases to subsist.

(10)   Nothing in this section applies to a person arrested or detained under the terrorism provisions or detained under Part I of Schedule 3 to the Counter-Terrorism and Border Security Act 2019.

58.   Access to legal advice

(1)   A person arrested and held in custody in a police station or other premises shall be entitled, if he so requests, to consult a solicitor privately at any time.

(2)   Subject to subsection (3) below, a request under subsection (1) above and the time at which it was made shall be recorded in the custody record.

(3)   Such a request need not be recorded in the custody record of a person who makes it at a time while he is at a court after being charged with an offence.

(4)   If a person makes such a request, he must be permitted to consult a solicitor as soon as is practicable except to the extent that delay is permitted by this section.

(5)   In any case he must be permitted to consult a solicitor within 36 hours from the relevant time, as defined in section 41(2) above.

(6)   Delay in compliance with a request is only permitted—
       (a)   in the case of a person who is in police detention for an indictable offence; and
       (b)   if an officer of at least the rank of superintendent authorises it.

(7)   An officer may give an authorisation under subsection (6) above orally or in writing but, if he gives it orally, he shall confirm it in writing as soon as is practicable.

(8)   Subject to sub-section (8A) below an officer may only authorise delay where he has reasonable grounds for believing that the exercise of the right conferred by subsection (1) above at the time when the person detained desires to exercise it—
       (a)   will lead to interference with or harm to evidence connected with an indictable offence or interference with or physical injury to other persons; or
       (b)   will lead to the alerting of other persons suspected of having committed such an offence but not yet arrested for it; or
       (c)   will hinder the recovery of any property obtained as a result of such an offence.
       ...

60.   Audio recording of interviews

(1)   It shall be the duty of the Secretary of State—
       (a)   to issue a code of practice in connection with the audio recording of interviews of persons suspected of the commission of criminal offences which are held by police officers at police stations; and
       (b)   to make an order requiring the audio recording of interviews of persons suspected of the commission of criminal offences, or of such descriptions of criminal offences as may be specified in the order, which are so held, in accordance with the code as it has effect for the time being.

(2)   An order under subsection (1) above shall be made by statutory instrument and shall be subject to annulment in pursuance of a resolution of either House of Parliament.

60A.   Visual recording of interviews

(1)   The Secretary of State shall have power—
       (a)   to issue a code of practice for the visual recording of interviews held by police officers at police stations; and
       (b)   to make an order requiring the visual recording of interviews so held, and requiring the visual recording to be in accordance with the code for the time being in force under this section.

(2)   A requirement imposed by an order under this section may be imposed in relation to such cases or police stations in such areas, or both, as may be specified or described in the order.

(3)   An order under subsection (1) above shall be made by statutory instrument and shall be subject to annulment in pursuance of a resolution of either House of Parliament.

(4) In this section—
- (a) references to any interview are references to an interview of a person suspected of a criminal offence; and
- (b) references to a visual recording include references to a visual recording in which an audio recording is comprised.

61. Finger-printing

(1) Except as provided by this section no person's fingerprints may be taken without the appropriate consent.

(2) Consent to the taking of a person's fingerprints must be in writing if it is given at a time when he is at a police station.

(3) The fingerprints of a person detained at a police station may be taken without the appropriate consent if—
- (a) he is detained in consequence of his arrest for a recordable offence; and
- (b) he has not had his fingerprints taken in the course of the investigation of the offence by the police.

(3A) Where a person mentioned in paragraph (a) of subsection (3) or (4) has already had his fingerprints taken in the course of the investigation of the offence by the police, that fact shall be disregarded for the purposes of that subsection if—
- (a) the fingerprints taken on the previous occasion do not constitute a complete set of his fingerprints; or
- (b) some or all of the fingerprints taken on the previous occasion are not of sufficient quality to allow satisfactory analysis, comparison or matching (whether in the case in question or generally).

(4) The fingerprints of a person detained at a police station may be taken without the appropriate consent if—
- (a) he has been charged with a recordable offence or informed that he will be reported for such an offence; and
- (b) he has not had his fingerprints taken in the course of the investigation of the offence by the police.

(4A) The fingerprints of a person who has answered to bail at a court or police station may be taken without the appropriate consent at the court or station if—
- (a) the court, or
- (b) an officer of at least the rank of inspector,

authorises them to be taken.

(4B) A court or officer may only give an authorisation under subsection (4A) if—
- (a) the person who has answered to bail has answered to it for a person whose fingerprints were taken on a previous occasion and there are reasonable grounds for believing that he is not the same person; or
- (b) the person who has answered to bail claims to be a different person from a person whose fingerprints were taken on a previous occasion.

(5) An officer may give an authorisation under subsection (4A) above orally or in writing but, if he gives it orally, he shall confirm it in writing as soon as is practicable.

(5A) The fingerprints of a person may be taken without the appropriate consent if ... he has been arrested for a recordable offence and released and—
- (a) he has not had his fingerprints taken in the course of the investigation of the offence by the police; or
- (b) he has had his fingerprints taken in the course of that investigation but subsection (3A)(a) or (b) above applies.

(5B) The fingerprints of a person not detained at a police station may be taken without the appropriate consent if ... he has been charged with a recordable offence or informed that he will be reported for such an offence, and—
- (a) he has not had his fingerprints taken in the course of the investigation of the offence by the police; or
- (b) he has had his fingerprints taken in the course of that investigation but subsection (3A)(a) or (b) applies.

(6) Any person's fingerprints may be taken without the appropriate consent if—
- (a) he has been convicted of a recordable offence; or

(b)   he has been given a caution in respect of a recordable offence which, at the time of the caution, he has admitted;

(c)   ...

(6ZA)–(6ZC) ...

(6A) A constable may take a person's fingerprints without the appropriate consent if —

(a)   the constable reasonably suspects that the person is committing or attempting to commit an offence, or has committed or attempted to commit an offence; and

(b)   either of the two conditions mentioned in subsection (6B) is met.

(6B) The conditions are that:

(a)   the name of the person is unknown to, and cannot be readily ascertained by, the constable;

(b)   the constable has reasonable grounds for doubting whether a name furnished by the person as his name is his real name.

...

61A. Impressions of footwear

(1)   Except as provided by this section, no impression of a person's footwear may be taken without the appropriate consent.

(2)   Consent to the taking of an impression of a person's footwear must be in writing if it is given at a time when he is at a police station.

(3)   Where a person is detained at a police station, an impression of his footwear may be taken without the appropriate consent if—

(a)   he is detained in consequence of his arrest for a recordable offence, or has been charged with a recordable offence, or informed that he will be reported for a recordable offence; and

(b)   he has not had an impression taken of his footwear in the course of the investigation of the offence by the police.

(4)   Where a person mentioned in paragraph (a) of subsection (3) above has already had an impression taken of his footwear in the course of the investigation of the offence by the police, that fact shall be disregarded for the purposes of that subsection if the impression of his footwear taken previously is—

(a)   incomplete; or

(b)   is not of sufficient quality to allow satisfactory analysis, comparison or matching (whether in the case in question or generally).

(5)   If an impression of a person's footwear is taken at a police station, whether with or without the appropriate consent—

(a)   before it is taken, an officer shall inform him that it may be the subject of a speculative search; and

(b)   the fact that the person has been informed of this possibility shall be recorded as soon as is practicable after the impression has been taken, and if he is detained at a police station, the record shall be made on his custody record.

(6)   In a case where, by virtue of subsection (3) above, an impression of a person's footwear is taken without the appropriate consent—

(a)   he shall be told the reason before it is taken; and

(b)   the reason shall be recorded on his custody record as soon as is practicable after the impression is taken.

(7)   The power to take an impression of the footwear of a person detained at a police station without the appropriate consent shall be exercisable by any constable.

(8)   Nothing in this section applies to any person—

(a)   arrested or detained under the terrorism provisions or detained under Part I of Schedule 3 to the Counter-Terrorism and Border Security Act 2019;

(b)   arrested under an extradition arrest power.

62. Intimate samples

(1)   Subject to section 63B below an intimate sample may be taken from a person in police detention only—

(a)   if a police officer of at least the rank of inspector authorises it to be taken; and

(b)   if the appropriate consent is given.

(1A) An intimate sample may be taken from a person who is not in police detention but from whom, in the course of the investigation of an offence, two or more non-intimate samples suitable for the same means of analysis have been taken which have proved insufficient—

    (a)   if a police officer of at least the rank of inspector authorises it to be taken; and

    (b)   if the appropriate consent is given.

(2)   An officer may only give an authorisation under subsection (1) or (1A) above if he has reasonable grounds—

    (a)   for suspecting the involvement of the person from whom the sample is to be taken in a recordable offence; and

    (b)   for believing that the sample will tend to confirm or disprove his involvement.

(2A), (2B) …

(3)   An officer may give an authorisation under subsection (1) or (1A) above orally or in writing but, if he gives it orally, he shall confirm it in writing as soon as is practicable.

(4)   The appropriate consent must be given in writing.

(5)   Where—

    (a)   an authorisation has been given; and

    (b)   it is proposed that an intimate sample shall be taken in pursuance of the authorisation,

an officer shall inform the person from whom the sample is to be taken—

        (i)   of the giving of the authorisation; and

        (ii)   of the grounds for giving it.

(6)   The duty imposed by subsection (5)(ii) above includes a duty to state the nature of the offence in which it is suspected that the person from whom the sample is to be taken has been involved.

…

63.   Other samples

(1)   Except as provided by this section, a non-intimate sample may not be taken from a person without the appropriate consent.

(2)   Consent to the taking of a non-intimate sample must be given in writing.

(2A) A non-intimate sample may be taken from a person without the appropriate consent if two conditions are satisfied.

(2B) The first is that the person is in police detention in consequence of his arrest for a recordable offence.

(2C) The second is that—

    (a)   he has not had a non-intimate sample of the same type and from the same part of the body taken in the course of the investigation of the offence by the police, or

    (b)   he has had such a sample taken but it proved insufficient.

(3)   A non-intimate sample may be taken from a person without the appropriate consent if—

    (a)   he … is being held in custody by the police on the authority of a court; and

    (b)   an officer of at least the rank of inspector authorises it to be taken without the appropriate consent.

(3ZA) A non-intimate sample may be taken from a person without the appropriate consent if … he has been arrested for a recordable offence and released and—

    (a)   he has not had a non-intimate sample of the same type and from the same part of the body taken from him in the course of the investigation of the offence by the police; or

    (b)   he has had a non-intimate sample taken from him in the course of that investigation but—

        (i)   it was not suitable for the same means of analysis, or

        (ii)   it proved insufficient, or

        (iii)   subsection (3AA) below applies.

(3A) A non-intimate sample may be taken from a person (whether or not he is in police detention or held in custody by the police on the authority of a court) without the appropriate consent if he has been charged with a recordable offence or informed that he will be reported for such an offence; and

> (a)   he has not had a non-intimate sample taken from him in the course of the investigation of the offence by the police, or
> (b)   he has had a non-intimate sample taken from him but—
>> (i)   it was not suitable for the same means of analysis, or
>> (ii)   it proved insufficient, or
>> (iii) subsection (3AA) below applies.
> (c)   he has had a non-intimate sample taken from him in the course of the investigation and—
>> (i)   the sample has been destroyed pursuant to section 63R below or any other enactment, and
>> (ii)   it is disputed, in relation to any proceedings relating to the offence, whether a DNA profile relevant to the proceedings is derived from the sample.

(3AA) This subsection applies where the investigation was discontinued but subsequently resumed, and before the resumption of the investigation—
> (a)   any DNA profile derived from the sample was destroyed pursuant to section 63D(3) below, and
> (b)   the sample itself was destroyed pursuant to section 63R(4), (5) or (12) below.

(3B)–(3H) ...

(4)   An officer may only give an authorisation under subsection (3) above if he has reasonable grounds—
> (a)   for suspecting the involvement of the person from whom the sample is to be taken in a recordable offence; and
> (b)   for believing that the sample will tend to confirm or disprove his involvement.

(5)   An officer may give an authorisation under subsection (3) above orally or in writing but, if he gives it orally, he shall confirm it in writing as soon as is practicable.

(5A) An officer shall not give an authorisation under subsection (3) above for the taking from any person of a non-intimate sample consisting of a skin impression if—
> (a)   a skin impression of the same part of the body has already been taken from that person in the course of the investigation of the offence; and
> (b)   the impression previously taken is not one that has proved insufficient. ...

63A. Fingerprints and samples: supplementary provisions

(1)   Where a person has been arrested on suspicion of being involved in a recordable offence or has been charged with such an offence or has been informed that he will be reported for such an offence, fingerprints, impressions of footwear or samples or the information derived from samples taken under any power conferred by this Part of this Act from the person may be checked against—
> (a)   other fingerprints, impressions of footwear or samples to which the person seeking to check has access and which are held by or on behalf of any one or more relevant law-enforcement authorities or which are held in connection with or as a result of an investigation of an offence;
> (b)   information derived from other samples if the information is contained in records to which the person seeking to check has access and which are held as mentioned in paragraph (a) above.

...

63B. Testing for presence of Class A drugs

(1)   A sample of urine or a non-intimate sample may be taken from a person in police detention for the purpose of ascertaining whether he has any specified Class A drug in his body if—
> (a)   either the arrest condition or the charge condition is met;
> (b)   both the age condition and the request condition are met; and
> (c)   the notification condition is met in relation to the arrest condition, the charge condition or the age condition (as the case may be).

(1A) The arrest condition is that the person concerned has been arrested for an offence but has not been charged with that offence and either—
> (a)   the offence is a trigger offence; or
> (b)   a police officer of at least the rank of inspector has reasonable grounds for suspecting that the misuse by that person of a specified Class A drug caused or contributed to the offence and has authorised the sample to be taken.

(2)   The charge condition is either—
    (a)   that the person concerned has been charged with a trigger offence; or
    (b)   that the person concerned has been charged with an offence and a police officer of at least the rank of inspector, who has reasonable grounds for suspecting that the misuse by that person of any specified Class A drug caused or contributed to the offence, has authorised the sample to be taken.

(3)   The age condition is—
    (a)   if the arrest condition is met, that the person concerned has attained the age of 18;
    (b)   if the charge condition is met, that he has attained the age of 14.

(4)   The request condition is that a police officer has requested the person concerned to give the sample.

(4A) The notification condition is that—
    (a)   the relevant chief officer has been notified by the Secretary of State that appropriate arrangements have been made for the police area as a whole, or for the particular police station, in which the person is in police detention, and
    (b)   the notice has not been withdrawn.

(4B) For the purposes of subsection (4A) above, appropriate arrangements are arrangements for the taking of samples under this section from whichever of the following is specified in the notification—
    (a)   persons in respect of whom the arrest condition is met;
    (b)   persons in respect of whom the charge condition is met;
    (c)   persons who have not attained the age of 18.
    ...

63C.   Testing for presence of Class A drugs: supplementary

(1)   A person guilty of an offence under section 63B above shall be liable on summary conviction to imprisonment for a term not exceeding three months, or to a fine not exceeding level 4 on the standard scale, or to both.

(2)   A police officer may give an authorisation under section 63B above orally or in writing but, if he gives it orally, he shall confirm it in writing as soon as is practicable.

(3)   If a sample is taken under section 63B above by virtue of an authorisation, the authorisation and the grounds for the suspicion shall be recorded as soon as is practicable after the sample is taken.

(4)   If the sample is taken from a person detained at a police station, the matters required to be recorded by subsection (3) above shall be recorded in his custody record.

(5)   Subsections (11) and (12) of section 62 above apply for the purposes of section 63B above as they do for the purposes of that section; and section 63B above does not prejudice the generality of sections 62 and 63 above.
    ...

63D.   Destruction of fingerprints and DNA profiles

(1)   This section applies to—
    (a)   fingerprints—
        (i)   taken from a person under any power conferred by this Part of this Act, or
        (ii)   taken by the police, with the consent of the person from whom they were taken, in connection with the investigation of an offence by the police, and
    (b)   a DNA profile derived from a DNA sample taken as mentioned in paragraph (a)(i) or (ii).

(2)   Fingerprints and DNA profiles to which this section applies ('section 63D material') must be destroyed if it appears to the responsible chief officer of police that—
    (a)   the taking of the fingerprint or, in the case of a DNA profile, the taking of the sample from which the DNA profile was derived, was unlawful, or
    (b)   the fingerprint was taken, or, in the case of a DNA profile, was derived from a sample taken, from a person in connection with that person's arrest and the arrest was unlawful or based on mistaken identity.

(3)   In any other case, section 63D material must be destroyed unless it is retained under any power conferred by sections 63E to 63O (including those sections as applied by section 63P).

(4) Section 63D material which ceases to be retained under a power mentioned in subsection (3) may continue to be retained under any other such power which applies to it.

(5) Nothing in this section prevents a speculative search, in relation to section 63D material, from being carried out within such time as may reasonably be required for the search if the responsible chief officer of police considers the search to be desirable.

64A. Photographing of suspects etc

(1) A person who is detained at a police station may be photographed—
  (a) with the appropriate consent; or
  (b) if the appropriate consent is withheld or it is not practicable to obtain it, without it.

(1A) A person falling within subsection (1B) below may, on the occasion of the relevant event referred to in subsection (1B), be photographed elsewhere than at a police station—
  (a) with the appropriate consent; or
  (b) if the appropriate consent is withheld or it is not practicable to obtain it, without it.

(1B) A person falls within this subsection if he has been—
  (a) arrested by a constable for an offence;
  (b) taken into custody by a constable after being arrested for an offence by a person other than a constable;
  ...

(2) A person proposing to take a photograph of any person under this section—
  (a) may, for the purpose of doing so, require the removal of any item or substance worn on or over the whole or any part of the head or face of the person to be photographed; and
  (b) if the requirement is not complied with, may remove the item or substance himself.

(3) Where a photograph may be taken under this section, the only persons entitled to take the photograph are constables.

(4) A photograph taken under this section—
  (a) may be used by, or disclosed to, any person for any purpose related to the prevention or detection of crime, the investigation of an offence or the conduct of a prosecution or to the enforcement of a sentence; and
  (b) after being so used or disclosed, may be retained but may not be used or disclosed except for a purpose so related.
  ...

(6) References in this section to taking a photograph include references to using any process by means of which a visual image may be produced; and references to photographing a person shall be construed accordingly.

(7) Nothing in this section applies to a person arrested under an extradition arrest power.

65. Part V—supplementary

(1) In this Part of this Act—
  'analysis', in relation to a skin impression, includes comparison and matching;
  'appropriate consent' means—
  (a) in relation to a person who has attained the age of 18 years, the consent of that person;
  (b) in relation to a person who has not attained that age but has attained the age of 14 years, the consent of that person and his parent or guardian; and
  (c) in relation to a person who has not attained the age of 14 years, the consent of his parent or guardian;
  'DNA profile' means any information derived from a DNA sample; 'DNA sample' means any material that has come from a human body and consists of or includes human cells;
  'fingerprints', in relation to any person, means a record (in any form and produced by any method) of the skin pattern and other physical characteristics or features of—
  (a) any of that person's fingers; or
  (b) either of his palms;

'intimate sample' means—

(a)   a sample of blood, semen or any other tissue fluid, urine or pubic hair;

(b)   a dental impression;

(c)   a swab taken from any part of a person's genitals (including pubic hair) or from a person's body orifice other than the mouth;

'intimate search' means a search which consists of the physical examination of a person's body orifices other than the mouth;

'non-intimate sample' means—

(a)   a sample of hair other than pubic hair;

(b)   a sample taken from a nail on from under a nail;

(c)   a swab taken from any part of a person's body other than a part from which a swab taken would be an intimate sample;

(d)   saliva;

(e)   a skin impression;

'registered health care professional' means a person (other than a medical practitioner) who is—

(a)   a registered nurse; or

(b)   a registered member of a health care profession which is designated for the purposes of this paragraph by an order made by the Secretary of State;

(2)   References in this Part of this Act to a sample's proving insufficient include references to where, as a consequence of–

(a)   the loss, destruction or contamination of the whole or any part of the sample,

(b)   any damage to the whole or a part of the sample, or

(c)   the use of the whole or a part of the sample for an analysis which produced no results or which produced results some or all of which must be regarded, in the circumstances, as unreliable,

the sample has become unavailable or insufficient for the purpose of enabling information, or information of a particular description, to be obtained by means of analysis of the sample.

76.   Confessions

(1)   In any proceedings a confession made by an accused person may be given in evidence against him in so far as it is relevant to any matter in issue in the proceedings and is not excluded by the court in pursuance of this section.

(2)   If, in any proceedings where the prosecution proposes to give in evidence a confession made by an accused person, it is represented to the court that the confession was or may have been obtained—

(a)   by oppression of the person who made it; or

(b)   in consequence of anything said or done which was likely, in the circumstances existing at the time, to render unreliable any confession which might be made by him in consequence thereof,

the court shall not allow the confession to be given in evidence against him except in so far as the prosecution proves to the court beyond reasonable doubt that the confession (notwithstanding that it may be true) was not obtained as aforesaid.

(3)   In any proceedings where the prosecution proposes to give in evidence a confession made by an accused person, the court may of its own motion require the prosecution, as a condition of allowing it to do so, to prove that the confession was not obtained as mentioned in subsection (2) above.

(4)   The fact that a confession is wholly or partly excluded in pursuance of this section shall not affect the admissibility in evidence—

(a)   of any facts discovered as a result of the confession; or

(b)   where the confession is relevant as showing that the accused speaks, writes or expresses himself in a particular way, of so much of the confession as is necessary to show that he does so.

(5)   Evidence that a fact to which this subsection applies was discovered as a result of a statement made by an accused person shall not be admissible unless evidence of how it was discovered is given by him or on his behalf.

(6)   Subsection (5) above applies—

(a)   to any fact discovered as a result of a confession which is wholly excluded in pursuance of this section; and

(b) to any fact discovered as a result of a confession which is partly so excluded, if the fact is discovered as a result of the excluded part of the confession.

(7) Nothing in Part VII of this Act shall prejudice the admissibility of a confession made by an accused person.

(8) In this section 'oppression' includes torture, inhuman or degrading treatment, and the use or threat of violence (whether or not amounting to torture).

76A. Confessions may be given in evidence for co-accused

(1) In any proceedings a confession made by an accused person may be given in evidence for another person charged in the same proceedings (a co-accused) in so far as it is relevant to any matter in issue in the proceedings and is not excluded by the court in pursuance of this section.

(2) If, in any proceedings where a co-accused proposes to give in evidence a confession made by an accused person, it is represented to the court that the confession was or may have been obtained—

(a) by oppression of the person who made it; or

(b) in consequence of anything said or done which was likely, in the circumstances existing at the time, to render unreliable any confession which might be made by him in consequence thereof,

the court shall not allow the confession to be given in evidence for the co-accused except in so far as it is proved to the court on the balance of probabilities that the confession (notwithstanding that it may be true) was not so obtained.

(3) Before allowing a confession made by an accused person to be given in evidence for a co-accused in any proceedings, the court may of its own motion require the fact that the confession was not obtained as mentioned in subsection (2) above to be proved in the proceedings on the balance of probabilities.

(4) The fact that a confession is wholly or partly excluded in pursuance of this section shall not affect the admissibility in evidence—

(a) of any facts discovered as a result of the confession; or

(b) where the confession is relevant as showing that the accused speaks, writes or expresses himself in a particular way, of so much of the confession as is necessary to show that he does so.

(5) Evidence that a fact to which this subsection applies was discovered as a result of a statement made by an accused person shall not be admissible unless evidence of how it was discovered is given by him or on his behalf.

(6) Subsection (5) above applies—

(a) to any fact discovered as a result of a confession which is wholly excluded in pursuance of this section; and

(b) to any fact discovered as a result of a confession which is partly so excluded, if the fact is discovered as a result of the excluded part of the confession.

(7) In this section 'oppression' includes torture, inhuman or degrading treatment, and the use or threat of violence (whether or not amounting to torture).

78. Exclusion of unfair evidence

(1) In any proceedings the court may refuse to allow evidence on which the prosecution proposes to rely to be given if it appears to the court that, having regard to all the circumstances, including the circumstances in which the evidence was obtained, the admission of the evidence would have such an adverse effect on the fairness of the proceedings that the court ought not to admit it.

(2) Nothing in this section shall prejudice any rule of law requiring a court to exclude evidence.

79. Time for taking accused's evidence

If at the trial of any person for an offence—

(a) the defence intends to call two or more witnesses to the facts of the case; and

(b) those witnesses include the accused,

the accused shall be called before the other witness or witnesses unless the court in its discretion otherwise directs.

80. Competence and compellability of accused's spouse or civil partner

(1) ...

(2) In any proceedings the spouse or civil partner of a person charged in the proceedings shall, subject to subsection (4) below, be compellable to give evidence on behalf of that person.

(2A) In any proceedings the spouse or civil partner of a person charged in the proceedings shall, subject to subsection (4) below, be compellable—

(a) to give evidence on behalf of any other person charged in the proceedings but only in respect of any specified offence with which that other person is charged; or

(b) to give evidence for the prosecution but only in respect of any specified offence with which any person is charged in the proceedings.

(3) In relation to the spouse or civil partner of a person charged in any proceedings, an offence is a specified offence for the purposes of subsection (2A) above if—

(a) it involves an assault on, or injury or a threat of injury to, the spouse or civil partner or a person who was at the material time under the age of 16;

(b) it is a sexual offence alleged to have been committed in respect of a person who was at the material time under that age; or

(c) it consists of attempting or conspiring to commit, or of aiding, abetting, counselling, procuring or inciting the commission of, an offence falling within paragraph (a) or (b) above.

(4) No person who is charged in any proceedings shall be compellable by virtue of subsection (2) or (2A) above to give evidence in the proceedings.

(4A) References in this section to a person charged in any proceedings do not include a person who is not, or is no longer, liable to be convicted of any offence in the proceedings (whether as a result of pleading guilty or for any other reason).

(5) In any proceedings a person who has been but is no longer married to the accused shall be compellable to give evidence as if that person and the accused had never been married.

(5A) In any proceedings a person who has been but is no longer the civil partner of the accused shall be compellable to give evidence as if that person and the accused had never been civil partners.

(6) Where in any proceedings the age of any person at any time is material for the purposes of subsection (3) above, his age at the material time shall for the purposes of that provision be deemed to be or to have been that which appears to the court to be or to have been his age at that time.

(7) In subsection (3)(b) above 'sexual offence' means an offence under the Protection of Children Act 1978 or Part 1 of the Sexual Offences Act 2003, or an offence under section 2 of the Modern Slavery Act 2015 (human trafficking) committed with a view to exploitation that consists of or includes behaviour within section 3(3) of that Act (sexual exploitation).

(8) ...

(9) ...

80A. Rule where accused's spouse or civil partner not compellable

The failure of the spouse or civil partner of a person charged in any proceedings to give evidence in the proceedings shall not be made the subject of any comment by the prosecution.

82. Part VIII—interpretation

(1) In this Part of this Act—

'confession', includes any statement wholly or partly adverse to the person who made it, whether made to a person in authority or not and whether made in words or otherwise;

'proceedings' means criminal proceedings, including service proceedings; and

'Service court' means the Court Martial or the Service Civilian Court.

(1A) In subsection (1) 'service proceedings' means proceedings before a court (other than a civilian court) in respect of a service offence; and 'service offence' and 'civilian court' here have the same meanings as in the Armed Forces Act 2006.

(2) ...

(3)   Nothing in this Part of this Act shall prejudice any power of a court to exclude evidence (whether by preventing questions from being put or otherwise) at its discretion.

POLICE AND CRIMINAL EVIDENCE ACT 1984 (PACE) CODE A

REVISED CODE OF PRACTICE FOR THE EXERCISE BY: POLICE OFFICERS OF STATUTORY POWERS OF STOP AND SEARCH POLICE OFFICERS AND POLICE STAFF OF REQUIREMENTS TO RECORD PUBLIC ENCOUNTERS

Commencement – Transitional Arrangements

This code applies to any search by a police officer and the recording of public encounters taking place after midnight on 19 March 2015.

1.0.   General

1.01 This code of practice must be readily available at all police stations for consultation by police officers, police staff, detained persons and members of the public.

1.02 The notes for guidance included are not provisions of this code, but are guidance to police officers and others about its application and interpretation. Provisions in the annexes to the code are provisions of this code.

1.03 This code governs the exercise by police officers of statutory powers to search a person or a vehicle without first making an arrest. The main stop and search powers to which this code applies are set out in Annex A, but that list should not be regarded as definitive (see Note 1). In addition, it covers requirements on police officers and police staff to record encounters not governed by statutory powers (see paragraphs 2.11 and 4.12). This code does not apply to:

(a)   the powers of stop and search under:
   (i)   the Aviation Security Act 1982, section 27(2), and
   (ii) the Police and Criminal Evidence Act 1984 (PACE), section 6(1) (which relates specifically to powers of constables employed by statutory undertakers on the premises of the statutory undertakers);

(b)   searches carried out for the purposes of examination under Schedule 7 to the Terrorism Act 2000 and to which the Code of Practice issued under paragraph 6 of Schedule 14 to the Terrorism Act 2000 applies.

(c)   the powers to search persons and vehicles and to stop and search in specified locations to which the Code of Practice issued under section 47AB of the Terrorism Act 2000 applies

1.   Principles governing stop and search

1.1   Powers to stop and search must be used fairly, responsibly, with respect for people being searched and without unlawful discrimination. Under the Equality Act 2010, section 149, when police officers are carrying out their functions, they also have a duty to have due regard to the need to eliminate unlawful discrimination, harassment and victimisation, to advance equality of opportunity between people who have a relevant protected characteristic and people who do not share it, and to take steps to foster good relations between those persons. The Children Act 2004, section 11, also requires chief police officers and other specified persons and bodies to ensure that in the discharge of their functions they have regard to the need to safeguard and promote the welfare of all persons under the age of 18.

1.2   The intrusion on the liberty of the person stopped or searched must be brief and detention for the purposes of a search must take place at or near the location of the stop.

1.3   If these fundamental principles are not observed the use of powers to stop and search may be drawn into question. Failure to use the powers in the proper manner reduces their effectiveness. Stop and search can play an important role in the detection and prevention of crime, and using the powers fairly makes them more effective.

1.4   The primary purpose of stop and search powers is to enable officers to allay or confirm suspicions about individuals without exercising their power of arrest. Officers may be required to justify the use or authorisation of such powers, in relation both to individual searches and the overall pattern of their activity in this regard, to their supervisory officers or in court. Any misuse of the powers is likely to be harmful to policing and lead to mistrust of the police. Officers must also be able to explain their actions to the member of the public searched. The misuse of these powers can lead to disciplinary action.

1.5   An officer must not search a person, even with his or her consent, where no power to search is applicable. Even where a person is prepared to submit to a search voluntarily, the person must not be searched unless the necessary legal power exists, and the search must be in accordance with the relevant power and the provisions of this Code. The only exception, where an officer does not require a specific power, applies to searches of persons entering sports grounds or other premises carried out with their consent given as a condition of entry.

1.6   Evidence obtained from a search to which this Code applies may be open to challenge if the provisions of this Code are not observed.

2.   Explanation of powers to stop and search

2.1   This code applies to powers of stop and search as follows:
(a)   powers which require reasonable grounds for suspicion, before they may be exercised; that articles unlawfully obtained or possessed are being carried, or under Section 43 of the Terrorism Act 2000 that a person is a terrorist;
(b)   authorised under section 60 of the Criminal Justice and Public Order Act 1994, based upon a reasonable belief that incidents involving serious violence may take place or that people are carrying dangerous instruments or offensive weapons within any locality in the police area or that it is expedient to use the powers to find such instruments or weapons that have been used in incidents of serious violence;
(c)   *Not used.*
(d)   the powers in Schedule 5 to the Terrorism Prevention and Investigation Measures (TPIM) Act 2011 to search an individual who has not been arrested, conferred by:
(i)   paragraph 6(2)(a) at the time of serving a TPIM notice;
(ii)   paragraph 8(2)(a) under a search warrant for compliance purposes; and
(iii) paragraph 10 for public safety purposes. See paragraph 2.18A.
(e)   powers to search a person who has not been arrested in the exercise of a power to search premises (see Code B paragraph 2.4).

*(a) Stop and search powers requiring reasonable grounds for
suspicion – explanation
General*

2.2   Reasonable grounds for suspicion is the legal test which a police officer must satisfy before they can stop and detain individuals or vehicles to search them under powers such as section 1 of PACE (to find stolen or prohibited articles) and section 23 of the Misuse of Drugs Act 1971 (to find controlled drugs). This test must be applied to the particular circumstances in each case and is in two parts:
(i)   Firstly, the officer must have formed a genuine suspicion in their own mind that they will find the object for which the search power being exercised allows them to search (see Annex A, second column, for examples); and
(ii)   Secondly, the suspicion that the object will be found must be reasonable. This means that there must be an objective basis for that suspicion based on facts, information and/or intelligence which are relevant to the likelihood that the object in question will be found, so that a reasonable person would be entitled to reach the same conclusion based on the same facts and information and/or intelligence.
Officers must therefore be able to explain the basis for their suspicion by reference to intelligence or information about, or some specific behaviour by, the person concerned (see paragraphs 3.8(d), 4.6 and 5.5).

2.2A The exercise of these stop and search powers depends on the likelihood that the person searched is in possession of an item for which they may be searched; it does not depend on the person concerned being suspected of committing an offence in relation to the object of the search. A police officer who has reasonable grounds to suspect that a person is in innocent possession of a stolen or prohibited article, controlled drug or other item for which the officer is empowered to search, may stop and search the person even though there would be no power of arrest. This would apply when a child under the age of criminal responsibility (10 years) is suspected of carrying any such item, even if they knew they had it. (See Notes 1B and 1BA.)

Personal factors can never support reasonable grounds for suspicion

2.2B Reasonable suspicion can never be supported on the basis of personal factors. This means that unless the police have information or intelligence which provides a description of a person suspected of carrying an article for which there is a power to stop and search, the following cannot be used, alone or in combination with each other, or in combination with any other factor, as the reason for stopping and searching any individual, including any vehicle which they are driving or are being carried in:

(a)   A person's physical appearance with regard, for example, to any of the 'relevant protected characteristics' set out in the Equality Act 2010, section 149, which are age, disability, gender reassignment, pregnancy and maternity, race, religion or belief, sex and sexual orientation (see paragraph 1.1 and Note 1A), or the fact that the person is known to have a previous conviction; and

(b)   Generalisations or stereotypical images that certain groups or categories of people are more likely to be involved in criminal activity.

2.3 *Not used.*

Reasonable grounds for suspicion based on information and/or intelligence

2.4 Reasonable grounds for suspicion should normally be linked to accurate and current intelligence or information, relating to articles for which there is a power to stop and search, being carried by individuals or being in vehicles in any locality. This would include reports from members of the public or other officers describing:

• a person who has been seen carrying such an article or a vehicle in which such an article has been seen.

• crimes committed in relation to which such an article would constitute relevant evidence, for example, property stolen in a theft or burglary, an offensive weapon or bladed or sharply pointed article used to assault or threaten someone or an article used to cause criminal damage to property.

2.4A A Searches based on accurate and current intelligence or information are more likely to be effective. Targeting searches in a particular area at specified crime problems not only increases their effectiveness but also minimises inconvenience to law-abiding members of the public. It also helps in justifying the use of searches both to those who are searched and to the public. This does not, however, prevent stop and search powers being exercised in other locations where such powers may be exercised and reasonable suspicion exists.

2.5 *Not used.*

Reasonable grounds for suspicion and searching groups

2.6 Where there is reliable information or intelligence that members of a group or gang habitually carry knives unlawfully or weapons or controlled drugs, and wear a distinctive item of clothing or other means of identification in order to identify themselves as members of that group or gang, that distinctive item of clothing or other means of identification may provide reasonable grounds to stop and search any person believed to be a member of that group or gang. (See Note 9.)

2.6A A similar approach would apply to particular organised protest groups where there is reliable information or intelligence:

(a)   that the group in question arranges meetings and marches to which one or more members bring articles intended to be used to cause criminal damage and/or injury to others in support of the group's aims;

(b)   that at one or more previous meetings or marches arranged by that group, such articles have been used and resulted in damage and/or injury; and

(c)   that on the subsequent occasion in question, one or more members of the group have brought with them such articles with similar intentions

These circumstances may provide reasonable grounds to stop and search any members of the group to find such articles (see Note 9A). See also paragraphs 2.12 to 2.18, '*Searches authorised under section 60 of the Criminal Justice and Public Order Act 1994*', when serious violence is anticipated at meetings and marches.

Reasonable grounds for suspicion based on behaviour, time and location

2.6B Reasonable suspicion may also exist without specific information or intelligence and on the basis of the behaviour of a person. For example, if an officer encounters someone on the street at night who is obviously trying to hide something, the officer may (depending on the other surrounding circumstances) base such suspicion on the fact that this kind of behaviour is often linked to stolen or prohibited articles being carried. An officer who forms the opinion that a person is acting suspiciously or that they appear to be nervous must be able to explain, with reference to specific aspects of the person's behaviour or conduct which they have observed, why they formed that opinion (see paragraphs 3.8(d) and 5.5). A hunch or instinct which cannot be explained or justified to an objective observer can never amount to reasonable grounds.

2.7 *Not used.*

2.8 *Not used.*

Securing public confidence and promoting community relations

2.8A All police officers must recognise that searches are more likely to be effective, legitimate and secure public confidence when their reasonable grounds for suspicion are based on a range of objective factors. The overall use of these powers is more likely to be effective when up-to-date and accurate intelligence or information is communicated to officers and they are well-informed about local crime patterns. Local senior officers have a duty to ensure that those under their command who exercise stop and search powers have access to such information, and the officers exercising the powers have a duty to acquaint themselves with that information (see paragraphs 5.1 to 5.6).

Questioning to decide whether to carry out a search

2.9 An officer who has reasonable grounds for suspicion may detain the person concerned in order to carry out a search. Before carrying out the search the officer may ask questions about the person's behaviour or presence in circumstances which gave rise to the suspicion. As a result of questioning the detained person, the reasonable grounds for suspicion necessary to detain that person may be confirmed or, because of a satisfactory explanation, be dispelled. (See Notes 2 and 3.) Questioning may also reveal reasonable grounds to suspect the possession of a different kind of unlawful article from that originally suspected. Reasonable grounds for suspicion however cannot be provided retrospectively by such questioning during a person's detention or by refusal to answer any questions asked.

2.10 If, as a result of questioning before a search, or other circumstances which come to the attention of the officer, there cease to be reasonable grounds for suspecting that an article of a kind for which there is a power to stop and search is being carried, no search may take place. (See Note 3.) In the absence of any other lawful power to detain, the person is free to leave at will and must be so informed.

2.11 There is no power to stop or detain a person in order to find grounds for a search. Police officers have many encounters with members of the public which do not involve detaining people against their will and do not require any statutory power for an officer to speak to a person (see paragraph 4.12 and Note 1). However, if reasonable grounds for suspicion emerge during such an encounter, the officer may detain the person to A search them, even though no grounds existed when the encounter began. As soon as detention begins, and before searching, the officer must inform the person that they are being detained for the purpose of a search and take action in accordance with paragraphs 3.8 to 3.11 under '*Steps to be taken prior to a search*'.

(b) Searches authorised under section 60 of the
Criminal Justice and Public Order
Act 1994

2.12   Authority for a constable in uniform to stop and search under section 60 of the Criminal Justice and Public Order Act 1994 may be given if the authorising officer reasonably believes:

(a)   that incidents involving serious violence may take place in any locality in the officer's police area, and it is expedient to use these powers to prevent their occurrence;

(b)   that persons are carrying dangerous instruments or offensive weapons without good reason in any locality in the officer's police area or

(c)   that an incident involving serious violence has taken place in the officer's police area, a dangerous instrument or offensive weapon used in the incident is being carried by a person in any locality in that police area, and it is expedient to use these powers to find that instrument or weapon.

2.13   An authorisation under section 60 may only be given by an officer of the rank of inspector or above and in writing, or orally if paragraph 2.12(c) applies and it is not practicable to give the authorisation in writing. The authorisation (whether written or oral) must specify the grounds on which it was given, the locality in which the powers may be exercised and the period of time for which they are in force. The period authorised shall be no longer than appears reasonably necessary to prevent, or seek to prevent incidents of serious violence, or to deal with the problem of carrying dangerous instruments or offensive weapons or to find a dangerous instrument or offensive weapon that has been used. It may not exceed 24 hours. An oral authorisation given where paragraph 2.12(c) applies must be recorded in writing as soon as practicable. (See Notes 10–13.)

2.14   An inspector who gives an authorisation must, as soon as practicable, inform an officer of or above the rank of superintendent. This officer may direct that the authorisation shall be extended for a further 24 hours, if violence or the carrying of dangerous instruments or offensive weapons has occurred, or is suspected to have occurred, and the continued use of the powers is considered necessary to prevent or deal with further such activity or to find a dangerous instrument or offensive weapon used that has been used. That direction must be given in writing unless it is not practicable to do so, in which case it must be recorded in writing as soon as practicable afterwards. (See Note 12.)

2.14A The selection of persons and vehicles under section 60 to be stopped and, if appropriate, searched should reflect an objective assessment of the nature of the incident or weapon in question and the individuals and vehicles thought likely to be associated with that incident or those weapons (see Notes 10 and 11). The powers must not be used to stop and search persons and vehicles for reasons unconnected with the purpose of the authorisation. When selecting persons and vehicles to be stopped in response to a specific threat or incident, officers must take care not to discriminate unlawfully against anyone on the grounds of any of the protected characteristics set out in the Equality Act 2010 (see paragraph 1.1).

2.14B The driver of a vehicle which is stopped under section 60 and any person who is searched under section 60 are entitled to a written statement to that effect if they apply within twelve months from twelve months from the day the vehicle was stopped or the person was searched. This statement is a record which states that the vehicle was stopped or (as the case may be) that the person was searched under section 60 and it may form part of the search record or be supplied as a separate record.

Powers to require removal of face coverings

2.15   Section 60AA of the Criminal Justice and Public Order Act 1994 also provides a power to demand the removal of disguises. The officer exercising the power must reasonably believe that someone is wearing an item wholly or mainly for the purpose of concealing identity. There is also a power to seize such items where the officer believes that a person intends to wear them for this purpose. There is no power to stop and search for disguises. An officer may seize any such item which is discovered when exercising a power of search for something else, or which is being carried, and which the officer reasonably believes is intended to be used for concealing anyone's identity. This power can only be used if an authorisation given under section 60 or under section 60AA, is in force. (See Note 4.)

2.16 Authority under section 60AA for a constable in uniform to require the removal of disguises and to seize them may be given if the authorising officer reasonably believes that activities may take place in any locality in the officer's police area that are likely to involve the commission of offences and it is expedient to use these powers to prevent or control these activities.

2.17 An authorisation under section 60AA may only be given by an officer of the rank of inspector or above, in writing, specifying the grounds on which it was given, the locality in which the powers may be exercised and the period of time for which they are in force. The period authorised shall be no longer than appears reasonably necessary to prevent, or seek to prevent the commission of offences. It may not exceed 24 hours. (See Notes 10–13.)

2.18 An inspector who gives an authorisation must, as soon as practicable, inform an officer of or above the rank of superintendent. This officer may direct that the authorisation shall be extended for a further 24 hours, if crimes have been committed, or are suspected to have been committed, and the continued use of the powers is considered necessary to prevent or deal with further such activity. This direction must also be given in writing at the time or as soon as reasonably practicable afterwards. (See Note 12.)

(d) Searches under Schedule 5 to the Terrorism Prevention and Investigation Measures Act 2011

2.18A Paragraph 3 of Schedule 5 to the TPIM Act 2011 allows a constable to detain an individual to be searched under the following powers:
(i) paragraph 6(2)(a) when a TPIM notice is being, or has just been, served on the individual for the purpose of ascertaining whether there is anything on the individual that contravenes measures specified in the notice;
(ii) paragraph 8(2)(a) in accordance with a warrant to search the individual issued by a justice of the peace in England and Wales, a sheriff in Scotland or a lay magistrate in Northern Ireland who is satisfied that a search is necessary for the purpose of determining whether an individual in respect of whom a TPIM notice is in force is complying with measures specified in the notice (see paragraph 2.20); and
(iii) paragraph 10 to ascertain whether an individual in respect of whom a TPIM notice is in force is in possession of anything that could be used to threaten or harm any person.
See paragraph 2.1(e).

2.19 The exercise of the powers mentioned in paragraph 2.18A does not require the constable to have reasonable grounds to suspect that the individual:
(a) has been, or is, contravening any of the measures specified in the TPIM notice; or
(b) has on them anything which:
• in the case of the power in sub-paragraph (i), contravenes measures specified in the TPIM notice;
• in the case of the power in sub-paragraph (ii) is not complying with measures specified in the TPIM notice; or
• in the case of the power in sub-paragraph (iii), could be used to threaten or harm any person.

2.20 A search of an individual on warrant under the power mentioned in paragraph 2.18A(ii) must carried out within 28 days of the issue of the warrant and:
• the individual may be searched on one occasion only within that period;
• the search must take place at a reasonable hour unless it appears that this would frustrate the purposes of the search.

2.21 *Not used.*

2.22 *Not used.*

2.23 *Not used.*

2.24 *Not used.*

2.24A *Not used.*

2.25 *Not used.*

2.26 The powers under Schedule 5 allow a constable to conduct a search of an individual only for specified purposes relating to a TPIM notice as set out above. However, anything found may be seized and retained if there are reasonable grounds for believing that it is or it contains evidence of any offence for use at a trial for that offence or to prevent it being concealed, lost, damaged, altered, or destroyed. However, this would not prevent a search being carried out under other search powers if, in the course of exercising these powers, the officer formed reasonable grounds for suspicion.

(e) Powers to search in the exercise of a power to search premises

2.27 The following powers to search premises also authorise the search of a person, not under arrest, who is found on the premises during the course of the search:

(a)   section 139B of the Criminal Justice Act 1988 under which a constable may enter school premises and search the premises and any person on those premises for any bladed or pointed article or offensive weapon;

(b)   under a warrant issued under section 23(3) of the Misuse of Drugs Act 1971 to search premises for drugs or documents but only if the warrant specifically authorises the search of persons found on the premises; and

(c)   under a search warrant or order issued under paragraph 1, 3 or 11 of Schedule 5 to the Terrorism Act 2000 to search premises and any person found there for material likely to be of substantial value to a terrorist investigation.

2.28 Before the power under section 139B of the Criminal Justice Act 1988 may be exercised, the constable must have reasonable grounds to believe that an offence under section 139A of the Criminal Justice Act 1988 (having a bladed or pointed article or offensive weapon on school premises) has been or is being committed. A warrant to search premises and persons found therein may be issued under section 23(3) of the Misuse of Drugs Act 1971 if there are reasonable grounds to suspect that controlled drugs or certain documents are in the possession of a person on the premises.

2.29 The powers in paragraph 2.27 do not require prior specific grounds to suspect that the person to be searched is in possession of an item for which there is an existing power to search. However, it is still necessary to ensure that the selection and treatment of those searched under these powers is based upon objective factors connected with the search of the premises, and not upon personal prejudice.

3.   Conduct of searches

3.1 All stops and searches must be carried out with courtesy, consideration and respect for the person concerned. This has a significant impact on public confidence in the police. Every reasonable effort must be made to minimise the embarrassment that a person being searched may experience. (See Note 4.)

3.2 The co-operation of the person to be searched must be sought in every case, even if the person initially objects to the search. A forcible search may be made only if it has been established that the person is unwilling to co-operate or resists. Reasonable force may be used as a last resort if necessary to conduct a search or to detain a person or vehicle for the purposes of a search.

3.3 The length of time for which a person or vehicle may be detained must be reasonable and kept to a minimum. Where the exercise of the power requires reasonable suspicion, the thoroughness and extent of a search must depend on what is suspected of being carried, and by whom. If the suspicion relates to a particular article which is seen to be slipped into a person's pocket, then, in the absence of other grounds for suspicion or an opportunity for the article to be moved elsewhere, the search must be confined to that pocket. In the case of a small article which can readily be concealed, such as a drug, and which might be concealed anywhere on the person, a more extensive search may be necessary. In the case of searches mentioned in paragraph 2.1(b), (c), and (d), which do not require reasonable grounds for suspicion, officers may make any reasonable search to look for items for which they are empowered to search. (See Note 5.)

3.4 The search must be carried out at or near the place where the person or vehicle was first detained. (See Note 6.)

3.5 There is no power to require a person to remove any clothing in public other than an outer coat, jacket or gloves, except under section 60AA of the Criminal Justice and Public Order Act 1994 (which empowers a constable to require a person to remove any item worn to conceal identity). [See Notes 4 and 6] A search in public of a person's clothing which has not been removed must be restricted to superficial examination of outer garments. This does not, however, prevent an officer from placing his or her hand inside the pockets of the outer clothing, or feeling round the inside of collars, socks and shoes if this is reasonably necessary in the circumstances to look for the object of the search or to remove and examine any item reasonably suspected to be the object of the search. For the same reasons, subject to the restrictions on the removal of headgear, a person's hair may also be searched in public (see paragraphs 3.1 and 3.3).

3.6 Where on reasonable grounds it is considered necessary to conduct a more thorough search (e.g. by requiring a person to take off a T-shirt), this must be done out of public view, for example, in a police van unless paragraph 3.7 applies, or police station if there is one nearby. [See Note 6] Any search involving the removal of more than an outer coat, jacket, gloves, headgear or footwear, or any other item concealing identity, may only be made by an officer of the same sex as the person searched and may not be made in the presence of anyone of the opposite sex unless the person being searched specifically requests it. (See Annex F and Notes 4, 7 and 8.)

3.7 Searches involving exposure of intimate parts of the body must not be conducted as a routine extension of a less thorough search, simply because nothing is found in the course of the initial search. Searches involving exposure of intimate parts of the body may be carried out only at a nearby police station or other nearby location which is out of public view (but not a police vehicle). These searches must be conducted in accordance with paragraph 11 of Annex A to Code C except that an intimate search mentioned in paragraph 11(f) of Annex A to Code C may not be authorised or carried out under any stop and search powers. The other provisions of Code C do not apply to the conduct and recording of searches of persons detained at police stations in the exercise of stop and search powers. (See Note 7.)

Steps to be taken prior to a search

3.8 Before any search of a detained person or attended vehicle takes place the officer must take reasonable steps, if not in uniform (see paragraph 3.9), to show their warrant card to the person to be searched or in charge of the vehicle to be searched and whether or not in uniform, to give that person the following information:
(a) that they are being detained for the purposes of a search
(b) the officer's name (except in the case of enquiries linked to the investigation of terrorism, or otherwise where the officer reasonably believes that giving his or her name might put him or her in danger, in which case a warrant or other identification number shall be given) and the name of the police station to which the officer is attached;
(c) the legal search power which is being exercised; and
(d) a clear explanation of:
   (i) the object of the search in terms of the article or articles for which there is a power to search; and
   (ii) in the case of:
      • the power under section 60 of the Criminal Justice and Public Order Act 1994 (see paragraph 2.1(b)), the nature of the power, the authorisation and the fact that it has been given;
      • the powers under Schedule 5 to the Terrorism Prevention and Investigation Measures Act 2011 (see paragraph 2.1(e) and 2.18A):
         — the fact that a TPIM notice is in force or, (in the case of paragraph 6(2)(a)) that a TPIM notice is being served;
         — the nature of the power being exercised.
      For a search under paragraph 8 of Schedule 5, the warrant must be produced and the person provided with a copy of it.

- all other powers requiring reasonable suspicion (see paragraph 2.1(a)), the grounds for that suspicion. This means explaining the basis for the suspicion by reference to information and/or intelligence about, or some specific behaviour by, the person concerned (see paragraph 2.2).

(e)   that they are entitled to a copy of the record of the search if one is made (see section 4 below) if they ask within 3 months from the date of the search and:

   (i)   if they are not arrested and taken to a police station as a result of the search and it is practicable to make the record on the spot, that immediately after the search is completed they will be given, if they request, either:
   - a copy of the record, or
   - a receipt which explains how they can obtain a copy of the full record or access to an electronic copy of the record, or

   (ii)   if they are arrested and taken to a police station as a result of the search, that the record will be made at the station as part of their custody record and they will be given, if they request, a copy of their custody record which includes a record of the search as soon as practicable whilst they are at the station. (See Note 16.)

3.9 Stops and searches under the powers mentioned in paragraphs 2.1(b), and (c) may be undertaken only by a constable in uniform.

3.10 The person should also be given information about police powers to stop and search and the individual's rights in these circumstances.

3.11 If the person to be searched, or in charge of a vehicle to be searched, does not appear to understand what is being said, or there is any doubt about the person's ability to understand English, the officer must take reasonable steps to bring information regarding the person's rights and any relevant provisions of this Code to his or her attention. If the person is deaf or cannot understand English and is accompanied by someone, then the officer must try to establish whether that person can interpret or otherwise help the officer to give the required information.

4.   Recording requirements

(a) Searches which do not result in an arrest

4.1 When an officer carries out a search in the exercise of any power to which this Code applies and the search does not result in the person searched or person in charge of the vehicle searched being arrested and taken to a police station, a record must be made of it, electronically or on paper, unless there are exceptional circumstances which make this wholly impracticable (e.g. in situations involving public disorder or when the recording officer's presence is urgently required elsewhere). If a record is to be made, the officer carrying out the search must make the record on the spot unless this is not practicable, in which case, the officer must make the record as soon as practicable after the search is completed. (See Note 16.)

4.2 If the record is made at the time, the person who has been searched or who is in charge of the vehicle that has been searched must be asked if they want a copy and if they do, they must be given immediately, either:
- a copy of the record; or
- a receipt which explains how they can obtain a copy of the full record or access to an electronic copy of the record.

4.2A An officer is not required to provide a copy of the full record or a receipt at the time if they are called to an incident of higher priority. (See Note 21.)

(b) Searches which result in an arrest

4.2B If a search in the exercise of any power to which this Code applies results in a person being arrested and taken to a police station, the officer carrying out the search is responsible for ensuring that a record of the search is made as part of their custody record. The custody officer must then ensure that the person is asked if they want a copy of the record and, if they do, that they are given a copy as soon as practicable. (See Note 16.)

(c) Record of search

4.3   The record of a search must always include the following information:
(a)   A note of the self-defined ethnicity, and if different, the ethnicity as perceived by the officer making the search, of the person searched or of the person in charge of the vehicle searched (as the case may be) (see Note 18);
(b)   The date, time and place the person or vehicle was searched (see Note 6);
(c)   The object of the search in terms of the article or articles for which there is a power to search;
(d)   In the case of:
  • the power under section 60 of the Criminal Justice and Public Order Act 1994 (see paragraph 2.1(b)), the nature of the power, the authorisation and the fact that it has been given (see Note 17);
  • the powers under Schedule 5 to the Terrorism Prevention and Investigation Measures Act 2011 (see paragraphs 2.1(e) and 2.18A):
    —   the fact that a TPIM notice is in force or, (in the case of paragraph 6(2)(a)), that a TPIM notice is being served;
    —   the nature of the power, and
    —   for a search under paragraph 8, the date the search warrant was issued, the fact that the warrant was produced and a copy of it provided and the warrant must also be endorsed by the constable executing it to state whether anything was found and whether anything was seized, and
  • all other powers requiring reasonable suspicion (see paragraph 2.1(a)), the grounds for that suspicion.
(e)   subject to paragraph 3.8(b), the identity of the officer carrying out the search. (See Note 15.)

4.3A For the purposes of completing the search record, there is no requirement to record the name, address and date of birth of the person searched or the person in charge of a vehicle which is searched. The person is under no obligation to provide this information and they should not be asked to provide it for the purpose of completing the record.

4.4   Nothing in paragraph 4.3 requires the names of police officers to be shown on the search record or any other record required to be made under this Code in the case of enquiries linked to the investigation of terrorism or otherwise where an officer reasonably believes that recording names might endanger the officers. In such cases the record must show the officers' warrant or other identification number and duty station.

4.5   A record is required for each person and each vehicle searched. However, if a person is in a vehicle and both are searched, and the object and grounds of the search are the same, only one record need be completed. If more than one person in a vehicle is searched, separate records for each search of a person must be made. If only a vehicle is searched, the self-defined ethnic background of the person in charge of the vehicle must be recorded, unless the vehicle is unattended.

4.6   The record of the grounds for making a search must, briefly but informatively, explain
A the reason for suspecting the person concerned, by reference to information and/or intelligence about, or some specific behaviour by, the person concerned (see paragraph 2.2).

4.7   Where officers detain an individual with a view to performing a search, but the need to search is eliminated as a result of questioning the person detained, a search should not be carried out and a record is not required. (See paragraph 2.10 and Notes 3 and 22A.)

4.8   After searching an unattended vehicle, or anything in or on it, an officer must leave a notice in it (or on it, if things on it have been searched without opening it) recording the fact that it has been searched.

4.9   The notice must include the name of the police station to which the officer concerned is attached and state where a copy of the record of the search may be obtained and how (if applicable) an electronic copy may be accessed and where any application for compensation should be directed.

4.10   The vehicle must if practicable be left secure.

4.10A *Not used.*

4.10B *Not used.*

Recording of encounters not governed by statutory powers

4.11 *Not used.*

4.12 There is no national requirement for an officer who requests a person in a public place to account for themselves, i.e. their actions, behaviour, presence in an area or possession of anything, to make any record of the encounter or to give the person a receipt. (See paragraph 2.11 and Notes 22A and 22B.)

4.12A to 4.20 *Not used.*

5.   Monitoring and supervising the use of stop and search powers

General

5.1   Any misuse of stop and search powers is likely to be harmful to policing and lead to mistrust of the police by the local community and by the public in general. Supervising officers must monitor the use of stop and search powers and should consider in particular whether there is any evidence that they are being exercised on the basis of stereotyped images or inappropriate generalisations. Supervising officers must satisfy themselves that the practice of officers under their supervision in stopping, searching and recording is fully in accordance with this Code. Supervisors must also examine whether the records reveal any trends or patterns which give cause for concern and, if so, take appropriate action to address this. (See paragraph 2.8A.)

5.2   Senior officers with area or force-wide responsibilities must also monitor the broader use of stop and search powers and, where necessary, take action at the relevant level.

5.3   Supervision and monitoring must be supported by the compilation of comprehensive statistical records of stops and searches at force, area and local level. Any apparently disproportionate use of the powers by particular officers or groups of officers or in relation to specific sections of the community should be identified and investigated.

5.4   In order to promote public confidence in the use of the powers, forces, in consultation with police and crime commissioners, must make arrangements for the records to be scrutinised by representatives of the community, and to explain the use of the powers at a local level. (See Note 19.)

Suspected misuse of powers by individual officers

5.5   Police supervisors must monitor the use of stop and search powers by individual officers to ensure that they are being applied appropriately and lawfully. Monitoring takes many forms, such as direct supervision of the exercise of the powers, examining stop and search records (particularly examining the officer's documented reasonable grounds for suspicion) and asking the officer to account for the way in which they conducted and recorded particular searches or through complaints about a stop and search that an officer has carried out.

5.6   Where a supervisor identifies issues with the way that an officer has used a stop and search power, the facts of the case will determine whether the standards of professional behaviour as set out in the Code of Ethics (see www.app.college.police.uk) have been breached and which formal action is pursued. Improper use might be a result of poor performance or a conduct matter, which will require the supervisor to take appropriate action such as performance or misconduct procedures. It is imperative that supervisors take both timely and appropriate action to deal with all such cases that come to their notice.

Notes for Guidance

Officers exercising stop and search powers

1   This Code does not affect the ability of an officer to speak to or question a person in the ordinary course of the officer's duties without detaining the person or exercising any element of compulsion. It is not the purpose of the code to prohibit such encounters between the police and the community with the co-operation of the person concerned

A and neither does it affect the principle that all citizens have a duty to help police officers to prevent crime and discover offenders. This is a civic rather than a legal duty; but when a police officer is trying to discover whether, or by whom, an offence has been committed he or she may question any person from whom useful information might be obtained, subject to the restrictions imposed by Code C. A person's unwillingness to reply does not alter this entitlement, but in the absence of a power to arrest, or to detain in order to search, the person is free to leave at will and cannot be compelled to remain with the officer.

1A   In paragraphs 1.1 and 2.2B(a), the 'relevant protected characteristics' are: age, disability, gender reassignment, pregnancy and maternity, race, religion or belief, sex and sexual orientation.

1B   Innocent possession means that the person does [not] have the guilty knowledge that they are carrying an unlawful item which is required before an arrest on suspicion that the person has committed an offence in respect of the item sought (if arrest is necessary - see PACE Code G) and/or a criminal prosecution) can be considered. It is not uncommon for children under the age of criminal responsibility to be used by older children and adults to carry stolen property, drugs and weapons and, in some cases, firearms, for the criminal benefit of others, either:
- in the hope that police may not suspect they are being used for carrying the items; or
- knowing that if they are suspected of being couriers and are stopped and searched, they cannot be arrested or prosecuted for any criminal offence.

Stop and search powers therefore allow the police to intervene effectively to break up criminal gangs and groups that use young children to further their criminal activities.

1BA   Whenever a child under 10 is suspected of carrying unlawful items for someone else, or is found in circumstances which suggest that their welfare and safety may be at risk, the facts should be reported and actioned in accordance with established force safeguarding procedures. This will be in addition to treating them as a potentially vulnerable or intimidated witness in respect of their status as a witness to the serious criminal offence(s) committed by those using them as couriers. Safeguarding considerations will also apply to other persons aged under 18 who are stopped and searched under any of the powers to which this Code applies. See paragraph 1.1 with regard to the requirement under the Children Act 2004, section 11, for chief police officers and other specified persons and bodies, to ensure that in the discharge of their functions, they have regard to the need to safeguard and promote the welfare of all persons under the age of 18.

2   In some circumstances preparatory questioning may be unnecessary, but in general a brief conversation or exchange will be desirable not only as a means of avoiding unsuccessful searches, but to explain the grounds for the stop/search, to gain cooperation and reduce any tension there might be surrounding the stop/search.

3   Where a person is lawfully detained for the purpose of a search, but no search in the event takes place, the detention will not thereby have been rendered unlawful.

4   Many people customarily cover their heads or faces for religious reasons - for example, Muslim women, Sikh men, Sikh or Hindu women, or Rastafarian men or women. A police officer cannot order the removal of a head or face covering except where there is reason to believe that the item is being worn by the individual wholly or mainly for the purpose of disguising identity, not simply because it disguises identity. Where there may be religious sensitivities about ordering the removal of such an item, the officer should permit the item to be removed out of public view. Where practicable, the item should be removed in the presence of an officer of the same sex as the person and out of sight of anyone of the opposite sex (see Code C Annex L).

5   A search of a person in public should be completed as soon as possible.

6   A person may be detained under a stop and search power at a place other than where the person was first detained, only if that place, be it a police station or elsewhere, is nearby. Such a place should be located within a reasonable travelling distance using whatever mode of travel (on foot or by car) is appropriate. This applies to all searches under stop and search powers, whether or not they involve the removal of clothing or exposure of intimate parts of the body (see paragraphs 3.6 and 3.7) or take place in

or out of public view. It means, for example, that a search under the stop and search power in section 23 of the Misuse of Drugs Act 1971 which involves the compulsory removal of more than a person's outer coat, jacket or gloves cannot be carried out unless a place which is both nearby the place they were first detained and out of public view, is available. If a search involves exposure of intimate parts of the body and a police station is not nearby, particular care must be taken to ensure that the location is suitable in that it enables the search to be conducted in accordance with the requirements of paragraph 11 of Annex A to Code C.

7   A search in the street itself should be regarded as being in public7 A search in the street itself should be regarded as being in public for the purposes of paragraphs 3.6 and 3.7 above, even though it may be empty at the time a search begins. Although there is no power to require a person to do so, there is nothing to prevent an officer from asking a person voluntarily to remove more than an outer coat, jacket or gloves in public.

8   *Not used.*

9   Other means of identification might include jewellery, insignias, tattoos or other features which are known to identify members of the particular gang or group.

9A A decision to search individuals believed to be members of a particular group or gang must be judged on a case by case basis according to the circumstances applicable at the time of the proposed searches and in particular, having regard to:

(a)   the number of items suspected of being carried;

(b)   the nature of those items and the risk they pose; and

(c)   the number of individuals to be searched.

A group search will only be justified if it is a necessary and proportionate approach based on the facts and having regard to the nature of the suspicion in these cases. The extent and thoroughness of the searches must not be excessive.

The size of the group and the number of individuals it is proposed to search will be a key factor and steps should be taken to identify those who are to be searched to avoid unnecessary inconvenience to unconnected members of the public who are also present.

The onus is on the police to be satisfied and to demonstrate that their approach to the decision to search is in pursuit of a legitimate aim, necessary and proportionate.

Authorising officers

10 The powers under section 60 are separate from and additional to the normal stop and search powers which require reasonable grounds to suspect an individual of carrying an offensive weapon (or other article). Their overall purpose is to prevent serious violence and the widespread carrying of weapons which might lead to persons being seriously injured by disarming potential offenders or finding weapons that have been used in circumstances where other powers would not be sufficient. They should not therefore be used to replace or circumvent the normal powers for dealing with routine crime problems. A particular example might be an authorisation to prevent serious violence or the carrying of offensive weapons at a sports event by rival team supporters when the expected general appearance and age range of those likely to be responsible, alone, would not be sufficiently distinctive to support reasonable suspicion (see paragraph 2.6). The purpose of the powers under section 60AA is to prevent those involved in intimidatory or violent protests using face coverings to disguise identity.

11 Authorisations under section 60 require a reasonable belief on the part of the authorising officer. This must have an objective basis, for example: intelligence or relevant information such as a history of antagonism and violence between particular groups; previous incidents of violence at, or connected with, particular events or locations; a significant increase in knife-point robberies in a limited area; reports that individuals are regularly carrying weapons in a particular locality; information following an incident in which weapons were used about where the weapons might be found or in the case of section 60AA previous incidents of crimes being committed while wearing face coverings to conceal identity.

12   It is for the authorising officer to determine the period of time during which the powers mentioned in paragraph 2.1(b) may be exercised. The officer should set the minimum period he or she considers necessary to deal with the risk of violence, the carrying of knives or offensive weapons, or to find dangerous instruments or weapons that have been used. A direction to extend the period authorised under the powers mentioned in paragraph 2.1(b) may be given only once. Thereafter further use of the powers requires a new authorisation.

13   It is for the authorising officer to determine the geographical area in which the use of the powers is to be authorised. In doing so the officer may wish to take into account factors such as the nature and venue of the anticipated incident or the incident which has taken place, the number of people who may be in the immediate area of that incident, their access to surrounding areas and the anticipated or actual level of violence. The officer should not set a geographical area which is wider than that he or she believes necessary for the purpose of preventing anticipated violence, the carrying of knives or offensive weapons, or for finding a dangerous instrument or weapon that has been used or, in the case of section 60AA, the prevention of commission of offences. It is particularly important to ensure that constables exercising such powers are fully aware of the locality within which they may be used. The officer giving the authorisation should therefore specify either the streets which form the boundary of the locality or a divisional boundary if appropriate, within the force area. If the power is to be used in response to a threat or incident that straddles police force areas, an officer from each of the forces concerned will need to give an authorisation.

14   *Not used.*

Recording

15   Where a stop and search is conducted by more than one officer the identity of all the officers engaged in the search must be recorded on the record. Nothing prevents an officer who is present but not directly involved in searching from completing the record during the course of the encounter.

16   When the search results in the person searched or in charge of a vehicle which is searched being arrested, the requirement to make the record of the search as part of the person's custody record does not apply if the person is granted 'street bail' after arrest (see section 30A of PACE) to attend a police station and is not taken in custody to the police station An arrested person's entitlement to a copy of the search record which is made as part of their custody record does not affect their entitlement to a copy of their custody record or any other provisions of PACE Code C section 2 (Custody records).

17   It is important for monitoring purposes to specify when authority is given for exercising the stop and search power under section 60 of the Criminal Justice and Public Order Act 1994.

18   Officers should record the self-defined ethnicity of every person stopped according to the categories used in the 2001 census question listed in Annex B. The person should be asked to select one of the five main categories representing broad ethnic groups and then a more specific cultural background from within this group. The ethnic classification should be coded for recording purposes using the coding system in Annex B. An additional 'Not stated' box is available but should not be offered to respondents explicitly. Officers should be aware and explain to members of the public, especially where concerns are raised, that this information is required to obtain a true picture of stop and search activity and to help improve ethnic monitoring, tackle discriminatory practice, and promote effective use of the powers. If the person gives what appears to the officer to be an 'incorrect' answer (e.g. a person who appears to be white states that they are black), the officer should record the response that has been given and then record their own perception of the person's ethnic background by using the PNC classification system. If the 'Not stated' category is used the reason for this must be recorded on the form.

19   Arrangements for public scrutiny of records should take account of the right to confidentiality of those stopped and searched. Anonymised forms and/or statistics generated from records should be the focus of the examinations by members of the public. The groups that are consulted should always include children and young persons.

20 *Not used.*

21 In situations where it is not practicable to provide a written copy of the record or immediate access to an electronic copy of the record or a receipt of the search at the time (see paragraph 4.2A above), the officer should consider giving the person details of the station which they may attend for a copy of the record. A receipt may take the form of a simple business card which includes sufficient information to locate the record should the person ask for copy, for example, the date and place of the search, and a reference number or the name of the officer who carried out the search (unless paragraph 4.4 applies).

22 *Not used.*

22A Where there are concerns which make it necessary to monitor any local disproportionality, forces have discretion to direct officers to record the self-defined ethnicity of persons they request to account for themselves in a public place or who they detain with a view to searching but do not search. Guidance should be provided locally and efforts made to minimise the bureaucracy involved. Records should be closely monitored and supervised in line with paragraphs 5.1 to 5.6, and forces can suspend or re-instate recording of these encounters as appropriate.

22B A person who is asked to account for themselves should, if they request, be given information about how they can report their dissatisfaction about how they have been treated.

Definition of offensive weapon

23 'Offensive weapon' is defined as 'any article made or adapted for use for causing injury to the person, or intended by the person having it with him for such use by him or by someone else'. There are three categories of offensive weapons: those made for causing injury to the person; those adapted for such a purpose; and those not so made or adapted, but carried with the intention of causing injury to the person. A firearm, as defined by section 57 of the Firearms Act 1968, would fall within the definition of offensive weapon if any of the criteria above apply.

24 *Not used.*

25 *Not used.*

POLICE AND CRIMINAL EVIDENCE ACT 1984 (PACE) CODE B

REVISED

CODE OF PRACTICE FOR SEARCHES OF PREMISES BY POLICE OFFICERS AND THE SEIZURE OF PROPERTY FOUND BY POLICE OFFICERS ON PERSONS OR PREMISES

Commencement – Transitional Arrangements

This Code applies to applications for warrants made after 00.00 on 27 October 2013 and to searches and seizures taking place after 00.00 on 27 October 2013.

3. Search warrants and production orders

(a) Before making an application

3.1 When information appears to justify an application, the officer must take reasonable steps to check the information is accurate, recent and not provided maliciously or irresponsibly. An application may not be made on the basis of information from an anonymous source if corroboration has not been sought. (See Note 3A.)

3.2 The officer shall ascertain as specifically as possible the nature of the articles concerned and their location.

3.3 The officer shall make reasonable enquiries to:
(i)   establish if:
    • anything is known about the likely occupier of the premises and the nature of the premises themselves;
    • the premises have been searched previously and how recently;
(ii) obtain any other relevant information.

3.4 An application:

    (a)   to a justice of the peace for a search warrant or to a Circuit judge for a search warrant or production order under PACE, Schedule 1 must be supported by a signed written authority from an officer of inspector rank or above:

             Note: If the case is an urgent application to a justice of the peace and an inspector or above is not readily available, the next most senior officer on duty can give the written authority.

    (b)   to a circuit judge under the Terrorism Act 2000, Schedule 5 for:

- a production order;
- search warrant; or
- an order requiring an explanation of material seized or produced under such a warrant or production order;
- must be supported by a signed written authority from an officer of superintendent rank or above.

3.5 Except in a case of urgency, if there is reason to believe a search might have an adverse effect on relations between the police and the community, the officer in charge shall consult the local police/community liaison officer:

- before the search; or
- in urgent cases, as soon as practicable after the search.

(b) Making an application

3.6 A search warrant application must be supported in writing, specifying:

    (a)   the enactment under which the application is made (see Note 2A);

    (b)   (i)   whether the warrant is to authorise entry and search of:

- one set of premises; or
- if the application is under PACE section 8, or Schedule 1, paragraph 12, more than one set of specified premises or all premises occupied or controlled by a specified person, and

          (ii)   the premises to be searched;

    (c)   the object of the search (see Note 3B);

    (d)   the grounds for the application, including, when the purpose of the proposed search is to find evidence of an alleged offence, an indication of how the evidence relates to the investigation;

    (da)   Where the application is under PACE section 8, or Schedule 1, paragraph 12 for a single warrant to enter and search:

          (i)   more than one set of specified premises; the officer must specify each set of premises which it is desired to enter and search;

          (ii)   all premises occupied or controlled by a specified person; the officer must specify;

- as many sets of premises which it is desired to enter and search as it is reasonably practicable to specify;
- the person who is in occupation or control of those premises and any others which it is desired to search;
- why it is necessary to search more premises than those which can be specified; and
- why it is not reasonably practicable to specify all the premises which it is desired to enter and search;

    (db)   Whether an application under PACE section 8 is for a warrant authorising entry and search on more than one occasion, and if so, the officer must state the grounds for this and whether the desired number of entries authorised is unlimited or a specified maximum;

    (e)   That there are no reasonable grounds to believe the material to be sought, when making application to a:

          (i)   justice of the peace or a Circuit judge consists of or includes items subject to legal privilege;

          (ii)   justice of the peace, consists of or includes excluded material or special procedure material;

Note: this does not affect the additional powers of seizure in the Criminal Justice and Police Act 2001, Part 2 covered in paragraph 7.7 (see Note 3B).

(f) if applicable, a request for the warrant to authorise a person or persons to accompany the officer who executes the warrant. (See Note 3C.)

3.7 A search warrant application under PACE, Schedule 1, paragraph 12(a), shall if appropriate indicate why it is believed service of notice of an application for a production order may seriously prejudice the investigation. Applications for search warrants under the Terrorism Act 2000, Schedule 5, paragraph 11 must indicate why a production order would not be appropriate.

3.8 If a search warrant application is refused, a further application may not be made for those premises unless supported by additional grounds.

Notes for Guidance

3A The identity of an informant need not be disclosed when making an application, but the officer should be prepared to answer any questions the magistrate or judge may have about:
- the accuracy of previous information from that source, and
- any other related matters.

3B The information supporting a search warrant application should be as specific as possible, particularly in relation to the articles or persons being sought and where in the premises it is suspected they may be found. The meaning of 'items subject to legal privilege', 'excluded material' and 'special procedure material' are defined by PACE, sections 10, 11 and 14 respectively.

3C Under PACE, section 16(2), a search warrant may authorise persons other than police officers to accompany the constable who executes the warrant. This includes, e.g. any suitably qualified or skilled person or an expert in a particular field whose presence is needed to help accurately identify the material sought or to advise where certain evidence is most likely to be found and how it should be dealt with. It does not give them any right to force entry, but it gives them the right to be on the premises during the search and to search for or seize property without the occupier's permission.

4. Entry without warrant – particular powers

(a) Making an arrest etc

4.1 The conditions under which an officer may enter and search premises without a warrant are set out in PACE, section 17. It should be noted that this section does not create or confer any powers of arrest. See other powers in Note 2B(a).

(b) Search of premises where arrest takes place or the arrested person was immediately before arrest

4.2 When a person has been arrested for an indictable offence, a police officer has power under PACE, section 32 to search the premises where the person was arrested or where the person was immediately before being arrested.

(c) Search of premises occupied or controlled by the arrested person

4.3 The specific powers to search premises which are occupied or controlled by a person arrested for an indictable offence are set out in PACE, section 18. They may not be exercised, except if section 18(5) applies, unless an officer of inspector rank or above has given written authority. That authority should only be given when the authorising officer is satisfied that the premises are occupied or controlled by the arrested person and that the necessary grounds exist. If possible the authorising officer should record the authority on the Notice of Powers and Rights and, subject to paragraph 2.9, sign the Notice. The record of the grounds for the search and the nature of the evidence sought as required by section 18(7) of the Act should be made in:
- the custody record if there is one, otherwise
- the officer's pocket book, or
- the search record.

5.   Search with consent

5.1   Subject to paragraph 5.4, if it is proposed to search premises with the consent of a person entitled to grant entry the consent must, if practicable, be given in writing on the Notice of Powers and Rights before the search. The officer must make any necessary enquiries to be satisfied the person is in a position to give such consent. (See Notes 5A and 5B.)

5.2   Before seeking consent the officer in charge of the search shall state the purpose of the proposed search and its extent. This information must be as specific as possible, particularly regarding the articles or persons being sought and the parts of the premises to be searched. The person concerned must be clearly informed they are not obliged to consent, that any consent given can be withdrawn at any time, including before the search starts or while it is underway and anything seized may be produced in evidence. If at the time the person is not suspected of an offence, the officer shall say this when stating the purpose of the search.

5.3   An officer cannot enter and search or continue to search premises under paragraph 5.1 if consent is given under duress or withdrawn before the search is completed.

5.4   It is unnecessary to seek consent under paragraphs 5.1 and 5.2 if this would cause disproportionate inconvenience to the person concerned. (See Note 5C.)

Notes for Guidance

5A   In a lodging house, hostel or similar accommodation, every reasonable effort should be made to obtain the consent of the tenant, lodger or occupier. A search should not be made solely on the basis of the landlord's consent.

5B   If the intention is to search premises under the authority of a warrant or a power of entry and search without warrant, and the occupier of the premises co-operates in accordance with paragraph 6.4, there is no need to obtain written consent.

5C   Paragraph 5.4 is intended to apply when it is reasonable to assume innocent occupiers would agree to, and expect, police to take the proposed action, e.g. if:

- a suspect has fled the scene of a crime or to evade arrest and it is necessary quickly to check surrounding gardens and readily accessible places to see if the suspect is hiding, or
- police have arrested someone in the night after a pursuit and it is necessary to make a brief check of gardens along the pursuit route to see if stolen or incriminating articles have been discarded.

6.   Searching premises—general considerations

(a) Time of searches

6.1   Searches made under warrant must be made within three calendar months of the date the warrant is issued or within the period specified in the enactment under which the warrant is issued if this is shorter.

6.2   Searches must be made at a reasonable hour unless this might frustrate the purpose of the search.

6.3   When the extent or complexity of a search mean it is likely to take a long time, the officer in charge of the search may consider using the seize and sift powers referred to in section 7.

6.3A A warrant under PACE, section 8 may authorise entry to and search of premises on more than one occasion if, on the application, the justice of the peace is satisfied that it is necessary to authorise multiple entries in order to achieve the purpose for which the warrant is issued. No premises may be entered or searched on any subsequent occasions without the prior written authority of an officer of the rank of inspector who is not involved in the investigation. All other warrants authorise entry on one occasion only.

6.3B Where a warrant under PACE section 8, or Schedule 1, paragraph 12 authorises entry to and search of all premises occupied or controlled by a specified person, no premises which are not specified in the warrant may be entered and searched without the prior written authority of an officer of the rank of inspector who is not involved in the investigation.

(b) Entry other than with consent

6.4 The officer in charge of the search shall first try to communicate with the occupier, or any other person entitled to grant access to the premises, explain the authority under which entry is sought and ask the occupier to allow entry, unless:
    (i)   the search premises are unoccupied;
    (ii)   the occupier and any other person entitled to grant access are absent;
    (iii) there are reasonable grounds for believing that alerting the occupier or any other person entitled to grant access would frustrate the object of the search or endanger officers or other people.

6.5 Unless sub-paragraph 6.4(iii) applies, if the premises are occupied the officer, subject to paragraph 2.9, shall, before the search begins:
    (i)   identify him or herself, show their warrant card (if not in uniform) and state the purpose of, and grounds for, the search, and
    (ii)   identify and introduce any person accompanying the officer on the search (such persons should carry identification for production on request) and briefly describe that person's role in the process.

6.6 Reasonable and proportionate force may be used if necessary to enter premises if the officer in charge of the search is satisfied the premises are those specified in any warrant, or in exercise of the powers described in paragraphs 4.1 to 4.3, and if:
    (i)   the occupier or any other person entitled to grant access has refused entry;
    (ii)   it is impossible to communicate with the occupier or any other person entitled to grant access; or
    (iii) any of the provisions of paragraph 6.4 apply.

(c) Notice of Powers and Rights

6.7 If an officer conducts a search to which this Code applies the officer shall, unless it is impracticable to do so, provide the occupier with a copy of a Notice in a standard format:
    (i)   specifying if the search is made under warrant, with consent, or in the exercise of the powers described in paragraphs 4.1 to 4.3. Note: the notice format shall provide for authority or consent to be indicated (see paragraphs 4.3 and 5.1);
    (ii)   summarising the extent of the powers of search and seizure conferred by PACE and other relevant legislation as appropriate;
    (iii) explaining the rights of the occupier and the owner of the property seized;
    (iv) explaining compensation may be payable in appropriate cases for damages caused entering and searching premises, and giving the address to send a compensation application (see Note 6A), and
    (v)   stating this Code is available at any police station.

6.8 If the occupier is:
- present; copies of the Notice and warrant shall, if practicable, be given to them before the search begins, unless the officer in charge of the search reasonably believes this would frustrate the object of the search or endanger officers or other people;
- not present; copies of the Notice and warrant shall be left in a prominent place on the premises or appropriate part of the premises and endorsed, subject to paragraph 2.9 with the name of the officer in charge of the search, the date and time of the search.

The warrant shall be endorsed to show this has been done.

(d) Conduct of searches

6.9 Premises may be searched only to the extent necessary to achieve the purpose of the search, having regard to the size and nature of whatever is sought.

6.9A A search may not continue under:
- a warrant's authority once all the things specified in that warrant have been found;
- any other power once the object of that search has been achieved.

6.9B No search may continue once the officer in charge of the search is satisfied whatever is being sought is not on the premises (see Note 6B). This does not prevent a further search of the same premises if additional grounds come to light supporting a further application for a search warrant or exercise or further exercise of another power. For example, when, as a result of new information, it is believed articles previously not found or additional articles are on the premises.

6.10 Searches must be conducted with due consideration for the property and privacy of the occupier and with no more disturbance than necessary. Reasonable force may be used only when necessary and proportionate because the co-operation of the occupier cannot be obtained or is insufficient for the purpose. (See Note 6C.)

6.11 A friend, neighbour or other person must be allowed to witness the search if the occupier wishes unless the officer in charge of the search has reasonable grounds for believing the presence of the person asked for would seriously hinder the investigation or endanger officers or other people. A search need not be unreasonably delayed for this purpose. A record of the action taken should be made on the premises search record including the grounds for refusing the occupier's request.

6.12 A person is not required to be cautioned prior to being asked questions that are solely necessary for the purpose of furthering the proper and effective conduct of a search, see Code C, paragraph 10.1(c). For example, questions to discover the occupier of specified premises, to find a key to open a locked drawer or cupboard or to otherwise seek co-operation during the search or to determine if a particular item is liable to be seized.

6.12A If questioning goes beyond what is necessary for the purpose of the exemption in Code C, the exchange is likely to constitute an interview as defined by Code C, paragraph 11.1A and would require the associated safeguards included in Code C, section 10.

(e) Leaving premises

6.13 If premises have been entered by force, before leaving the officer in charge of the search must make sure they are secure by:
- arranging for the occupier or their agent to be present;
- any other appropriate means.

(f) Searches under PACE Schedule 1 or the Terrorism Act 2000, Schedule 5

6.14 An officer shall be appointed as the officer in charge of the search (see paragraph 2.10), in respect of any search made under a warrant issued under PACE Act 1984, Schedule 1 or the Terrorism Act 2000, Schedule 5. They are responsible for making sure the search is conducted with discretion and in a manner that causes the least possible disruption to any business or other activities carried out on the premises.

6.15 Once the officer in charge of the search is satisfied material may not be taken from the premises without their knowledge, they shall ask for the documents or other records concerned. The officer in charge of the search may also ask to see the index to files held on the premises, and the officers conducting the search may inspect any files which, according to the index, appear to contain the material sought. A more extensive search of the premises may be made only if:
- the person responsible for them refuses to:
  - produce the material sought, or
  - allow access to the index.
- it appears the index is:
  - inaccurate, or
  - incomplete.
- for any other reason the officer in charge of the search has reasonable grounds for believing such a search is necessary in order to find the material sought.

Notes for Guidance

6A Whether compensation is appropriate depends on the circumstances in each case. Compensation for damage caused when effecting entry is unlikely to be appropriate if the search was lawful, and the force used can be shown to be reasonable, proportionate and necessary to effect entry. If the wrong premises are searched by mistake everything possible should be done at the earliest opportunity to allay any sense of grievance and there should normally be a strong presumption in favour of paying compensation.

6B It is important that, when possible, all those involved in a search are fully briefed about any powers to be exercised and the extent and limits within which it should be conducted.

6C In all cases the number of officers and other persons involved in executing the warrant should be determined by what is reasonable and necessary according to the particular circumstances.

7. Seizure and retention of property

(a) Seizure

7.1 Subject to paragraph 7.2, an officer who is searching any person or premises under any statutory power or with the consent of the occupier may seize anything:

(a) covered by a warrant;

(b) the officer has reasonable grounds for believing is evidence of an offence or has been obtained in consequence of the commission of an offence but only if seizure is necessary to prevent the items being concealed, lost, disposed of, altered, damaged, destroyed or tampered with;

(c) covered by the powers in the Criminal Justice and Police Act 2001, Part 2 allowing an officer to seize property from persons or premises and retain it for sifting or examination elsewhere. (See Note 7B.)

7.2 No item may be seized which an officer has reasonable grounds for believing to be subject to legal privilege, as defined in PACE, section 10, other than under the Criminal Justice and Police Act 2001, Part 2.

7.3 Officers must be aware of the provisions in the Criminal Justice and Police Act 2001, section 59, allowing for applications to a judicial authority for the return of property seized and the subsequent duty to secure in section 60. (See paragraph 7.12(iii).)

7.4 An officer may decide it is not appropriate to seize property because of an explanation from the person holding it but may nevertheless have reasonable grounds for believing it was obtained in consequence of an offence by some person. In these circumstances, the officer should identify the property to the holder, inform the holder of their suspicions and explain the holder may be liable to civil or criminal proceedings if they dispose of, alter or destroy the property.

7.5 An officer may arrange to photograph, image or copy, any document or other article they have the power to seize in accordance with paragraph 7.1. This is subject to specific restrictions on the examination, imaging or copying of certain property seized under the Criminal Justice and Police Act 2001, Part 2. An officer must have regard to their statutory obligation to retain an original document or other article only when a photograph or copy is not sufficient.

7.6 If an officer considers information stored in any electronic form and accessible from the premises could be used in evidence, they may require the information to be produced in a form:

• which can be taken away and in which it is visible and legible, or

• from which it can readily be produced in a visible and legible form.

(b) Criminal Justice and Police Act 2001: Specific procedures for seize and sift powers

7.7 The Criminal Justice and Police Act 2001, Part 2 gives officers limited powers to seize property from premises or persons so they can sift or examine it elsewhere. Officers must be careful they only exercise these powers when it is essential and they do not remove any more material than necessary. The removal of large volumes of material, much of which may not ultimately be retainable, may have serious implications for the owners, particularly when they are involved in business or activities such as journalism or the provision of medical services. Officers must carefully consider if removing copies or images of relevant material or data would be a satisfactory alternative to removing originals. When originals are taken, officers must be prepared to facilitate the provision of copies or images for the owners when reasonably practicable. (See Note 7C.)

7.8 Property seized under the Criminal Justice and Police Act 2001, sections 50 or 51 must be kept securely and separately from any material seized under other powers. An examination under section 53 to determine which elements may be retained must be carried out at the earliest practicable time, having due regard to the desirability of allowing the person from whom the property was seized, or a person with an interest in the property, an opportunity of being present or represented at the examination.

7.8A All reasonable steps should be taken to accommodate an interested person's request to be present, provided the request is reasonable and subject to the need to prevent harm to, interference with, or unreasonable delay to the investigatory process. If an examination proceeds in the absence of an interested person who asked to attend or their representative, the officer who exercised the relevant seizure power must give that person a written notice of why the examination was carried out in those circumstances. If it is necessary for security reasons or to maintain confidentiality officers may exclude interested persons from decryption or other processes which facilitate the examination but do not form part of it. (See Note 7D.)

7.9 It is the responsibility of the officer in charge of the investigation to make sure property is returned in accordance with sections 53 to 55. Material which there is no power to retain must be:
- separated from the rest of the seized property, and
- returned as soon as reasonably practicable after examination of all the seized property.

7.9A Delay is only warranted if very clear and compelling reasons exist, for example:
- the unavailability of the person to whom the material is to be returned, or
- the need to agree a convenient time to return a large volume of material.

7.9B Legally privileged, excluded or special procedure material which cannot be retained must be returned:
- as soon as reasonably practicable, and
- without waiting for the whole examination.

7.9C As set out in section 58, material must be returned to the person from whom it was seized, except when it is clear some other person has a better right to it. (See Note 7E.)

7.10 When an officer involved in the investigation has reasonable grounds to believe a person with a relevant interest in property seized under section 50 or 51 intends to make an application under section 59 for the return of any legally privileged, special procedure or excluded material, the officer in charge of the investigation should be informed as soon as practicable and the material seized should be kept secure in accordance with section 61. (See Note 7C.)

7.11 The officer in charge of the investigation is responsible for making sure property is properly secured. Securing involves making sure the property is not examined, copied, imaged or put to any other use except at the request, or with the consent, of the applicant or in accordance with the directions of the appropriate judicial authority. Any request, consent or directions must be recorded in writing and signed by both the initiator and the officer in charge of the investigation. (See Notes 7F and 7G.)

7.12 When an officer exercises a power of seizure conferred by sections 50 or 51 they shall provide the occupier of the premises or the person from whom the property is being seized with a written notice:
(i) specifying what has been seized under the powers conferred by that section;
(ii) specifying the grounds for those powers;
(iii) setting out the effect of sections 59 to 61 covering the grounds for a person with a relevant interest in seized property to apply to a judicial authority for its return and the duty of officers to secure property in certain circumstances when an application is made, and
(iv) specifying the name and address of the person to whom:
- notice of an application to the appropriate judicial authority in respect of any of the seized property must be given;
- an application may be made to allow attendance at the initial examination of the property.

7.13 If the occupier is not present but there is someone in charge of the premises, the notice shall be given to them. If no suitable person is available, so the notice will easily be found it should either be:

- left in a prominent place on the premises, or
- attached to the exterior of the premises.

(c) Retention

7.14 Subject to paragraph 7.15, anything seized in accordance with the above provisions may be retained only for as long as is necessary. It may be retained, among other purposes:
  (i)   for use as evidence at a trial for an offence;
  (ii)   to facilitate the use in any investigation or proceedings of anything to which it is inextricably linked (see Note 7H);
  (iii) for forensic examination or other investigation in connection with an offence;
  (iv)   in order to establish its lawful owner when there are reasonable grounds for believing it has been stolen or obtained by the commission of an offence.
7.15 Property shall not be retained under paragraph 7.14(i), (ii) or (iii) if a copy or image would be sufficient.

(d) Rights of owners etc

7.16 If property is retained, the person who had custody or control of it immediately before seizure must, on request, be provided with a list or description of the property within a reasonable time.
7.17 That person or their representative must be allowed supervised access to the property to examine it or have it photographed or copied, or must be provided with a photograph or copy, in either case within a reasonable time of any request and at their own expense, unless the officer in charge of an investigation has reasonable grounds for believing this would:
  (i)   prejudice the investigation of any offence or criminal proceedings; or
  (ii)   lead to the commission of an offence by providing access to unlawful material such as pornography; A record of the grounds shall be made when access is denied.

Notes for Guidance

7A   Any person claiming property seized by the police may apply to a magistrates' court under the Police (Property) Act 1897 for its possession and should, if appropriate, be advised of this procedure.
7B   The powers of seizure conferred by PACE, sections 18(2) and 19(3) extend to the seizure of the whole premises when it is physically possible to seize and retain the premises in their totality and practical considerations make seizure desirable. For example, police may remove premises such as tents, vehicles or caravans to a police station for the purpose of preserving evidence.
7C   Officers should consider reaching agreement with owners and/or other interested parties on the procedures for examining a specific set of property, rather than awaiting the judicial authority's determination. Agreement can sometimes give a quicker and more satisfactory route for all concerned and minimise costs and legal complexities.
7D   What constitutes a relevant interest in specific material may depend on the nature of that material and the circumstances in which it is seized. Anyone with a reasonable claim to ownership of the material and anyone entrusted with its safe keeping by the owner should be considered.
7E   Requirements to secure and return property apply equally to all copies, images or other material created because of seizure of the original property.
7F   The mechanics of securing property vary according to the circumstances; 'bagging up', i.e. placing material in sealed bags or containers and strict subsequent control of access is the appropriate procedure in many cases.
7G   When material is seized under the powers of seizure conferred by PACE, the duty to retain it under the Code of Practice issued under the Criminal Procedure and Investigations Act 1996 is subject to the provisions on retention of seized material in PACE, section 22.
7H   Paragraph 7.14 (ii) applies if inextricably linked material is seized under the Criminal Justice and Police Act 2001, sections 50 or 51. Inextricably linked material is material it

is not reasonably practicable to separate from other linked material without prejudicing the use of that other material in any investigation or proceedings. For example, it may not be possible to separate items of data held on computer disk without damaging their evidential integrity. Inextricably linked material must not be examined, imaged, copied or used for any purpose other than for proving the source and/or integrity of the linked material.

8.   Action after searches

8.1   If premises are searched in circumstances where this Code applies, unless the exceptions in paragraph 2.3(a) apply, on arrival at a police station the officer in charge of the search shall make or have made a record of the search, to include:

(i)   the address of the searched premises;

(ii)   the date, time and duration of the search;

(iii)   the authority used for the search:
- if the search was made in exercise of a statutory power to search premises without warrant, the power which was used for the search:
- if the search was made under a warrant or with written consent;
  - a copy of the warrant and the written authority to apply for it, see paragraph 3.4; or
  - the written consent;

shall be appended to the record or the record shall show the location of the copy warrant or consent;

(iv)   subject to paragraph 2.9, the names of:
- the officer(s) in charge of the search;
- all other officers and authorised persons who conducted the search;

(v)   the names of any people on the premises if they are known;

(vi)   any grounds for refusing the occupier's request to have someone present during the search, see paragraph 6.11;

(vii)   a list of any articles seized or the location of a list and, if not covered by a warrant, the grounds for their seizure;

(viii) whether force was used, and the reason;

(ix)   details of any damage caused during the search, and the circumstances;

(x)   if applicable, the reason it was not practicable:
(a)   to give the occupier a copy of the Notice of Powers and Rights, see paragraph 6.7;
(b)   before the search to give the occupier a copy of the Notice, see paragraph 6.8;

(xi)   when the occupier was not present, the place where copies of the Notice of Powers and Rights and search warrant were left on the premises, see paragraph 6.8.

8.2   On each occasion when premises are searched under warrant, the warrant authorising the search on that occasion shall be endorsed to show:

(i)   if any articles specified in the warrant were found and the address where found;

(ii)   if any other articles were seized;

(iii)   the date and time it was executed and if present, the name of the occupier or if the occupier is not present the name of the person in charge of the premises;

(iv)   subject to paragraph 2.9, the names of the officers who executed it and any authorised persons who accompanied them, and

(v)   if a copy, together with a copy of the Notice of Powers and Rights was:
- handed to the occupier, or
- endorsed as required by paragraph 6.8; and left on the premises and where.

8.3   Any warrant shall be returned within three calendar months of its issue or sooner on completion of the search(es) authorised by that warrant, if it was issued by a:
- justice of the peace, to the designated officer for the local justice area in which the justice was acting when issuing the warrant; or
- judge, to the appropriate officer of the court concerned.

POLICE AND CRIMINAL EVIDENCE ACT 1984 (PACE) CODE C

REVISED

CODE OF PRACTICE FOR THE DETENTION, TREATMENT AND QUESTIONING OF PERSONS BY POLICE OFFICERS

Commencement – Transitional Arrangements

This Code applies to people in police detention after 00.00 on 31 July 2018, notwithstanding that their period of detention may have commenced before that time.

1.   General

1.0 The powers and procedures in this Code must be used fairly, responsibly, with respect for the people to whom they apply and without unlawful discrimination. Under the Equality Act 2010, section 149 (Public sector Equality Duty), police forces must, in carrying out their functions, have due regard to the need to eliminate unlawful discrimination, harassment, victimisation and any other conduct which is prohibited by that Act, to advance equality of opportunity between people who share a relevant protected characteristic and people who do not share it, and to foster good relations between those persons. The Equality Act also makes it unlawful for police officers to discriminate against, harass or victimise any person on the grounds of the 'protected characteristics' of age, disability, gender reassignment, race, religion or belief, sex and sexual orientation, marriage and civil partnership, pregnancy and maternity, when using their powers. See Notes 1A and 1AA.

1.1 All persons in custody must be dealt with expeditiously, and released as soon as the need for detention no longer applies.

1.1A A custody officer must perform the functions in this Code as soon as practicable. A custody officer will not be in breach of this Code if delay is justifiable and reasonable steps are taken to prevent unnecessary delay. The custody record shall show when a delay has occurred and the reason. See Note 1H.

1.2 This Code of Practice must be readily available at all police stations for consultation by:
- police officers;
- police staff;
- detained persons;
- members of the public.

1.3 The provisions of this Code:
- include the Annexes
- do not include the Notes for Guidance which form guidance to police officers and others about its application and interpretation.

1.4 If at any time an officer has any reason to suspect that a person of any age may be vulnerable (see paragraph 1.13(d)), in the absence of clear evidence to dispel that suspicion, that person shall be treated as such for the purposes of this Code and to establish whether any such reason may exist in relation to a person suspected of committing an offence (see paragraph 10.1 and Note 10A), the custody officer in the case of a detained person, or the officer investigating the offence in the case of a person who has not been arrested or detained, shall take, or cause to be taken, (see paragraph 3.5 and Note 3F) the following action:
   (a)   reasonable enquiries shall be made to ascertain what information is available that is relevant to any of the factors described in paragraph 1.13(d) as indicating that the person may be vulnerable might apply;
   (b)   a record shall be made describing whether any of those factors appear to apply and provide any reason to suspect that the person may be vulnerable or (as the case may be) may not be vulnerable; and
   (c)   the record mentioned in sub-paragraph (b) shall be made available to be taken into account by police officers, police staff and any others who, in accordance with the provisions of this or any other Code, are required or entitled to communicate

with the person in question. This would include any solicitor, appropriate adult and health care professional and is particularly relevant to communication by telephone or by means of a live link (see paragraphs 12.9A (interviews), 13.12 (interpretation), and 15.3C, 15.11A, 15.11B, 15.11C and 15.11D (reviews and extension of detention)).

See Notes 1G, 1GA, 1GB and 1GC.

1.5 Anyone who appears to be under 18, shall, in the absence of clear evidence that they are older, be treated as a juvenile for the purposes of this Code and any other Code. See Note 1L.

1.5A *Not used.*

1.6 If a person appears to be blind, seriously visually impaired, deaf, unable to read or speak or has difficulty orally because of a speech impediment, they shall be treated as such for the purposes of this Code in the absence of clear evidence to the contrary.

1.7 'The appropriate adult' means, in the case of a:

(a) juvenile:
 (i) the parent, guardian or, if the juvenile is in the care of a local authority or voluntary organisation, a person representing that authority or organisation (see Note 1B);
 (ii) a social worker of a local authority (see Note 1C);
 (iii) failing these, some other responsible adult aged 18 or over who is not:
  — a police officer;
  — employed by the police;
  — under the direction or control of the chief officer of a police force; or
  — a person who provides services under contractual arrangements (but without being employed by the chief officer of a police force), to assist that force in relation to the discharge of its chief officer's functions,
  whether or not they are on duty at the time.
 See Note 1F.

(b) a person who is vulnerable (see paragraph 1.4 and Note 1D):
 (i) a relative, guardian or other person responsible for their care or custody;
 (ii) someone experienced in dealing with vulnerable persons but who is not:
  — a police officer;
  — employed by the police;
  — under the direction or control of the chief officer of a police force;
  — a person who provides services under contractual arrangements (but without being employed by the chief officer of a police force), to assist that force in relation to the discharge of its chief officer's functions,
  whether or not they are on duty at the time.
 (iii) failing these, some other responsible adult aged 18 or over who is other than a person described in the bullet points in sub-paragraph (b)(ii) above.
 See Note 1F.

1.7A The role of the appropriate adult is to safeguard the rights, entitlements and welfare of juveniles and vulnerable persons (see paragraphs 1.4 and 1.5) to whom the provisions of this and any other Code of Practice apply. For this reason, the appropriate adult is expected, amongst other things, to:

- support, advise and assist them when, in accordance with this Code or any other Code of Practice, they are given or asked to provide information or participate in any procedure;
- observe whether the police are acting properly and fairly to respect their rights and entitlements, and inform an officer of the rank of inspector or above if they consider that they are not;
- assist them to communicate with the police whilst respecting their right to say nothing unless they want to as set out in the terms of the caution (see paragraphs 10.5 and 10.6);
- help them to understand their rights and ensure that those rights are protected and respected (see paragraphs 3.15, 3.17, 6.5A and 11.17).

1.8 If this Code requires a person be given certain information, they do not have to be given it if at the time they are incapable of understanding what is said, are violent or may become violent or in urgent need of medical attention, but they must be given it as soon as practicable.

1.9   References to a custody officer include any police officer who, for the time being, is performing the functions of a custody officer. 1.9A When this Code requires the prior authority or agreement of an officer of at least inspector or superintendent rank, that authority may be given by a sergeant or chief inspector authorised to perform the functions of the higher rank under the Police and Criminal Evidence Act 1984 (PACE), section 107.

1.9A When this Code requires the prior authority or agreement of an officer of at least inspector or superintendent rank, that authority may be given by a sergeant or chief inspector authorised to perform the functions of the higher rank under the Police and Criminal Evidence Act 1984 (PACE), section 107.

1.10 Subject to paragraph 1.12, this Code applies to people in custody at police stations in England and Wales, whether or not they have been arrested, and to those removed to a police station as a place of safety under the Mental Health Act 1983, sections 135 and 136, as amended by the Policing and Crime Act 2017 (see paragraph 3.16). Section 15 applies solely to people in police detention, e.g. those brought to a police station under arrest or arrested at a police station for an offence after going there voluntarily.

1.11 No part of this Code applies to a detained person:
(a)   to whom PACE Code H applies because:
   • they are detained following arrest under section 41 of the Terrorism Act 2000 (TACT) and not charged; or
   • an authorisation has been given under section 22 of the Counter-Terrorism Act 2008 (CTACT) (post-charge questioning of terrorist suspects) to interview them.
(b)   to whom the Code of Practice issued under paragraph 6 of Schedule 14 to TACT applies because they are detained for examination under Schedule 7 to TACT.

1.12 This Code does not apply to people in custody:
(i)   arrested by officers under the Criminal Justice and Public Order Act 1994, section 136(2) on warrants issued in Scotland, or arrested or detained without warrant under section 137(2) by officers from a police force in Scotland. In these cases, police powers and duties and the person's rights and entitlements whilst at a police station in England or Wales are the same as those in Scotland;
(ii)   arrested under the Immigration and Asylum Act 1999, section 142(3) in order to have their fingerprints taken;
(iii) whose detention has been authorised under Schedules 2 or 3 to the Immigration Act 1971 or section 62 of the Nationality, Immigration and Asylum Act 2002;
(iv)   who are convicted or remanded prisoners held in police cells on behalf of the Prison Service under the Imprisonment (Temporary Provisions) Act 1980;
(v)   *Not used.*
(vi)   detained for searches under stop and search powers except as required by Code A.
The provisions on conditions of detention and treatment in sections 8 and 9 must be considered as the minimum standards of treatment for such detainees.

1.13 In this Code:
(a)   'designated person' means a person other than a police officer, who has specified powers and duties conferred or imposed on them by designation under section 38 or 39 of the Police Reform Act 2002;
(b)   reference to a police officer includes a designated person acting in the exercise or performance of the powers and duties conferred or imposed on them by their designation;
(c)   where a search or other procedure to which this Code applies may only be carried out or observed by a person of the same sex as the detainee, the gender of the detainee and other parties present should be established and recorded in line with Annex L of this Code.
(d)   'vulnerable' applies to any person who, because of a mental health condition or mental disorder (see Notes 1G and 1GB):
   (i)   may have difficulty understanding or communicating effectively about the full implications for them of any procedures and processes connected with:

- their arrest and detention; or (as the case may be)
- their voluntary attendance at a police station or their presence elsewhere (see paragraph 3.21), for the purpose of a voluntary interview; and
- the exercise of their rights and entitlements.

(ii)   does not appear to understand the significance of what they are told, of questions they are asked or of their replies:

(iii)   appears to be particularly prone to:
- becoming confused and unclear about their position;
- providing unreliable, misleading or incriminating information without knowing or wishing to do so;
- accepting or acting on suggestions from others without consciously knowing or wishing to do so; or
- readily agreeing to suggestions or proposals without any protest or question.

(e)   'Live link' means:

(i)   for the purpose of paragraph 12.9A; an arrangement by means of which the interviewing officer who is not present at the police station where the detainee is held, is able to see and hear, and to be seen and heard by, the detainee concerned, the detainee's solicitor, appropriate adult and interpreter (as applicable) and the officer who has custody of that detainee (see Note 1N).

(ii)   for the purpose of paragraph 15.9A; an arrangement by means of which the review officer who is not present at the police station where the detainee is held, is able to see and hear, and to be seen and heard by, the detainee concerned, the detainee's solicitor, appropriate adult and interpreter (as applicable) (see Note 1N). The use of live link for decisions about detention under section 45A of PACE is subject to regulations made by the Secretary of State being in force.

(iii)   for the purpose of paragraph 15.11A; an arrangement by means of which the authorising officer who is not present at the police station where the detainee is held, is able to see and hear, and to be seen and heard by, the detainee concerned and the detainee's solicitor, appropriate adult and interpreter (as applicable) (see Note 1N).

(iv)   for the purpose of paragraph 15.11C; an arrangement by means of which the detainee when not present in the court where the hearing is being held, is able to see and hear, and to be seen and heard by, the court during the hearing (see Note 1N).

Note: Chief officers must be satisfied that live link used in their force area for the above purposes provides for accurate and secure communication between the detainee, the detainee's solicitor, appropriate adult and interpreter (as applicable). This includes ensuring that at any time during which the live link is being used: a person cannot see, hear or otherwise obtain access to any such communications unless so authorised or allowed by the custody officer or, in the case of an interview, the interviewer and that as applicable, the confidentiality of any private consultation between a suspect and their solicitor and appropriate adult is maintained.

1.14 Designated persons are entitled to use reasonable force as follows:

(a)   when exercising a power conferred on them which allows a police officer exercising that power to use reasonable force, a designated person has the same entitlement to use force; and

(b)   at other times when carrying out duties conferred or imposed on them that also entitle them to use reasonable force, for example:
- when at a police station carrying out the duty to keep detainees for whom they are responsible under control and to assist any police officer or designated person to keep any detainee under control and to prevent their escape;
- when securing, or assisting any police officer or designated person in securing, the detention of a person at a police station;
- when escorting, or assisting any police officer or designated person in escorting, a detainee within a police station;
- for the purpose of saving life or limb; or
- preventing serious damage to property.

1.15 Nothing in this Code prevents the custody officer, or other police officer or designated person (see paragraph 1.13(a)) given custody of the detainee by the custody officer, from allowing another person (see (a) and (b) below) to carry out individual procedures or tasks at the police station if the law allows. However, the officer or designated person given custody remains responsible for making sure the procedures and tasks are carried out correctly in accordance with the Codes of Practice (see paragraph 3.5 and Note 3F). The other person who is allowed to carry out the procedures or tasks must be someone *who at that time, is*:

(a)   under the direction and control of the chief officer of the force responsible for the police station in question; or

(b)   providing services under contractual arrangements (but without being employed by the chief officer the police force), to assist a police force in relation to the discharge of its chief officer's functions.

1.16 Designated persons and others mentioned in sub-paragraphs (a) and (b) of paragraph 1.15, must have regard to any relevant provisions of the Codes of Practice.

1.17 In any provision of this or any other Code which allows or requires police officers or police staff to make a record in their report book, the reference to report book shall include any official report book or electronic recording device issued to them that enables the record in question to be made and dealt with in accordance with that provision. References in this and any other Code to written records, forms and signatures include electronic records and forms and electronic confirmation that identifies the person making the record or completing the form. Chief officers must be satisfied as to the integrity and security of the devices, records and forms to which this paragraph applies and that use of those devices, records and forms satisfies relevant data protection legislation.

Notes for Guidance

1A   Although certain sections of this Code apply specifically to people in custody at police stations, a person who attends a police station or other location voluntarily to assist with an investigation should be treated with no less consideration, e.g. offered or allowed refreshments at appropriate times, and enjoy an absolute right to obtain legal advice or communicate with anyone outside the police station or other location (see paragraphs 3.21 and 3.22.

1AA In paragraph 1.0, under the Equality Act 2010, section 149, the 'relevant protected characteristics' are age, disability, gender reassignment, pregnancy and maternity, race, religion/belief and sex and sexual orientation …

1B   A person, including a parent or guardian, should not be an appropriate adult if they:
   • are:
      — suspected of involvement in the offence;
      — the victim;
      — a witness;
      — involved in the investigation.
   • received admissions prior to attending to act as the appropriate adult.
   Note: If a juvenile's parent is estranged from the juvenile, they should not be asked to act as the appropriate adult if the juvenile expressly and specifically objects to their presence.

1C   If a juvenile admits an offence to, or in the presence of, a social worker or member of a youth offending team other than during the time that person is acting as the juvenile's appropriate adult, another appropriate adult should be appointed in the interest of fairness.

1D   In the case of someone who is vulnerable, it may be more satisfactory if the appropriate adult is someone experienced or trained in their care rather than a relative lacking such qualifications. But if the person prefers a relative to a better qualified stranger or objects to a particular person their wishes should, if practicable, be respected.

1E   A detainee should always be given an opportunity, when an appropriate adult is called to the police station, to consult privately with a solicitor in the appropriate adult's absence if they want. An appropriate adult is not subject to legal privilege.

1F   An appropriate adult who is not a parent or guardian in the case of a juvenile, or a relative, guardian or carer in the case of a vulnerable person, must be independent of the police as their role is to safeguard the person's rights and entitlements. Additionally, a solicitor or independent custody visitor who is present at the police station and acting in that capacity, may not be the appropriate adult.

1G A person may be vulnerable as a result of a having a mental health condition or mental disorder. Similarly, simply because an individual does not have, or is not known to have, any such condition or disorder, does not mean that they are not vulnerable for the purposes of this Code. It is therefore important that the custody officer in the case of a detained person or the officer investigating the offence in the case of a person who has not been arrested or detained, as appropriate, considers on a case by case basis, whether any of the factors described in paragraph 1.13(d) might apply to the person in question. In doing so, the officer must take into account the particular circumstances of the individual and how the nature of the investigation might affect them and bear in mind that juveniles, by virtue of their age will always require an appropriate adult.

1GA For the purposes of paragraph 1.4(a), examples of relevant information that may be available include:
- the behaviour of the adult or juvenile;
- the mental health and capacity of the adult or juvenile;
- the mental health and capacity of the adult or juvenile;
- what the adult or juvenile says about themselves;
- information from relatives and friends of the adult or juvenile;
- information from police officers and staff and from police records;
- information from health and social care (including liaison and diversion services) and other professionals who know, or have had previous contact with, the individual and may be able to contribute to assessing their need for help and support from an appropriate adult. This includes contacts and assessments arranged by the police or at the request of the individual or (as applicable) their appropriate adult or solicitor.

1GB The Mental Health Act 1983 Code of Practice at page 26 describes the range of clinically recognised conditions which can fall with the meaning of mental disorder for the purpose of paragraph 1.13(d) … .

1GC When a person is under the influence of drink and/or drugs, it is not intended that they are to be treated as vulnerable and requiring an appropriate adult for the purpose of paragraph 1.4 unless other information indicates that any of the factors described in paragraph 1.13(d) may apply to that person. When the person has recovered from the effects of drink and/or drugs, they should be re-assessed in accordance with paragraph 1.4. See paragraph 15.4A for application to live link

1H Paragraph 1.1A is intended to cover delays which may occur in processing detainees e.g. if:
- a large number of suspects are brought into the station simultaneously to be placed in custody;
- interview rooms are all being used;
- there are difficulties contacting an appropriate adult, solicitor or interpreter.

1I The custody officer must remind the appropriate adult and detainee about the right to legal advice and record any reasons for waiving it in accordance with section 6.

1J *Not used.*

1K This Code does not affect the principle that all citizens have a duty to help police officers to prevent crime and discover offenders. This is a civic rather than a legal duty; but when police officers are trying to discover whether, or by whom, offences have been committed they are entitled to question any person from whom they think useful information can be obtained, subject to the restrictions imposed by this Code. A person's declaration that they are unwilling to reply does not alter this entitlement.

1L Paragraph 1.5 reflects the statutory definition of 'arrested juvenile' in section 37(15) of PACE. This section was amended by section 42 of the Criminal Justice and Courts Act 2015 with effect from 26 October 2015, and includes anyone who appears to be under the age of 18. This definition applies for the purposes of the detention and bail provisions in sections 34 to 51 of PACE. With effect from 3 April 2017, amendments made by the Policing and Crime Act 2017 require persons under the age of 18 to be treated as juveniles for the purposes of all other provisions of PACE and the Codes.

1M *Not used.*

1N For the purpose of the provisions of PACE that allow a live link to be used, any impairment of the detainee's eyesight or hearing is to be disregarded. This means that if a detainee's eyesight or hearing is impaired, the arrangements which would be needed to ensure effective communication if all parties were physically present in the same location, for example, using sign language, would apply to the live link arrangements.

2.   Custody records

2.1A When a person is brought to a police station:
- under arrest
- is arrested at the police station having attended there voluntarily or
- attends a police station to answer bail

they must be brought before the custody officer as soon as practicable after their arrival at the station or if applicable, following their arrest after attending the police station voluntarily. This applies to designated and non-designated police stations. A person is deemed to be 'at a police station' for these purposes if they are within the boundary of any building or enclosed yard which forms part of that police station.

2.1   A separate custody record must be opened as soon as practicable for each person brought to a police station under arrest or arrested at the station having gone there voluntarily or attending a police station in answer to street bail. All information recorded under this Code must be recorded as soon as practicable in the custody record unless otherwise specified. Any audio or video recording made in the custody area is not part of the custody record.

2.2   If any action requires the authority of an officer of a specified rank, subject to paragraph 2.6A, their name and rank must be noted in the custody record.

2.3   The custody officer is responsible for the custody record's accuracy and completeness and for making sure the record or copy of the record accompanies a detainee if they are transferred to another police station. The record shall show the:
- time and reason for transfer;
- time a person is released from detention.

2.3A If a person is arrested and taken to a police station as a result of a search in the exercise of any stop and search power to which PACE Code A (Stop and search) or the 'search powers code' issued under TACT applies, the officer carrying out the search is responsible for ensuring that the record of that stop and search, is made as part of the person's custody record. The custody officer must then ensure that the person is asked if they want a copy of the search record and if they do, that they are given a copy as soon as practicable. The person's entitlement to a copy of the search record which is made as part of their custody record is in addition to, and does not affect, their entitlement to a copy of their custody record or any other provisions of section 2 (Custody records) of this Code. (See Code A paragraph 4.2B and the TACT search powers code paragraph 5.3.5).

2.4   The detainee's solicitor and appropriate adult must be permitted to inspect the whole of the detainee's custody record as soon as practicable after their arrival at the station and at any other time on request, whilst the person is detained. This includes the following specific records relating to the reasons for the detainee's arrest and detention and the offence concerned to which paragraph 3.1(b) refers:
(a)   The information about the circumstances and reasons for the detainee's arrest as recorded in the custody record in accordance with paragraph 4.3 of Code G. This applies to any further offences for which the detainee is arrested whilst in custody;
(b)   The record of the grounds for each authorisation to keep the person in custody. The authorisations to which this applies are the same as those described at items (i)(a) to (d) in the table in paragraph 2 of Annex M of this Code.

Access to the records in sub-paragraphs (a) and (b) is in addition to the requirements in paragraphs 3.4(b), 11.1A, 15.0, 15,7A(c) and 16.7A to make certain documents and materials available and to provide information about the offence and the reasons for arrest and detention.

Access to the custody record for the purposes of this paragraph must be arranged and agreed with the custody officer and may not unreasonably interfere with the custody officer's duties. A record shall be made when access is allowed and whether it includes the records described in sub-paragraphs (a) and (b) above.

2.4A When a detainee leaves police detention or is taken before a court they, their legal representative or appropriate adult shall be given, on request, a copy of the custody record as soon as practicable. This entitlement lasts for 12 months after release.

2.5 The detainee, appropriate adult or legal representative shall be permitted to inspect the original custody record after the detainee has left police detention provided they give reasonable notice of their request. Any such inspection shall be noted in the custody record.

2.6 Subject to paragraph 2.6A, all entries in custody records must be timed and signed by the maker. Records entered on computer shall be timed and contain the operator's identification.

2.6A Nothing in this Code requires the identity of officers or other police staff to be recorded or disclosed:

(a) *Not used.*

(b) if the officer or police staff reasonably believe recording or disclosing their name might put them in danger.

In these cases, they shall use their warrant or other identification numbers and the name of their police station. See Note 2A.

2.7 The fact and time of any detainee's refusal to sign a custody record, when asked in accordance with this Code, must be recorded.

Note for Guidance

2A The purpose of paragraph 2.6A(b) is to protect those involved in serious organised crime investigations or arrests of particularly violent suspects when there is reliable information that those arrested or their associates may threaten or cause harm to those involved. In cases of doubt, an officer of inspector rank or above should be consulted.

3. Initial action
(a) Detained persons – normal procedure

3.1 When a person is brought to a police station under arrest or arrested at the station having gone there voluntarily, the custody officer must make sure the person is told clearly about:

(a) the following continuing rights, which may be exercised at any stage during the period in custody:

(i) their right to consult privately with a solicitor and that free independent legal advice is available as in section 6;

(ii) their right to have someone informed of their arrest as in section 5;

(iii) their right to consult the Codes of Practice (see Note 3D); and

(iv) if applicable, their right to interpretation and translation (see paragraph 3.12) and their right to communicate with their High Commission, Embassy or Consulate (see paragraph 3.12A).

(b) their right to be informed about the offence and (as the case may be) any further offences for which they are arrested whilst in custody and why they have been arrested and detained in accordance with paragraphs 2.4, 3.4(a) and 11.1A of this Code and paragraph 3.3 of Code G.

3.2 The detainee must also be given a written notice, which contains information:

(a) to allow them to exercise their rights by setting out:

(i) their rights under paragraph 3.1, paragraph 3.12 and 3.12A;

(ii) the arrangements for obtaining legal advice, see section 6;

(iii) their right to a copy of the custody record as in paragraph 2.4A;

(iv) their right to remain silent as set out in the caution in the terms prescribed in section 10;

(v) their right to have access to materials and documents which are essential to effectively challenging the lawfulness of their arrest and detention for any offence and (as the case may be) any further offences for which they are arrested whilst in custody, in accordance with paragraphs 3.4(b), 15.0, 15.7A(c) and 16.7A of this Code;

(vi) the maximum period for which they may be kept in police detention without being charged, when detention must be reviewed and when release is required;

(vii)   their right to medical assistance in accordance with section 9 of this Code;

(viii) their right, if they are prosecuted, to have access to the evidence in the case before their trial in accordance with the Criminal Procedure and Investigations Act 1996, the Attorney General's Guidelines on Disclosure, the common law and the Criminal Procedure Rules; and

(b)   briefly setting out their other entitlements while in custody, by:

    (i)   mentioning:

      — the provisions relating to the conduct of interviews;

      — the circumstances in which an appropriate adult should be available to assist the detainee and their statutory rights to make representations whenever the need for their detention is reviewed;

    (ii)   listing the entitlements in this Code, concerning;

      — reasonable standards of physical comfort;

      — adequate food and drink;

      — access to toilets and washing facilities, clothing, medical attention, and exercise when practicable.

(See Note 3A.)

3.2A The detainee must be given an opportunity to read the notice and shall be asked to sign the custody record to acknowledge receipt of the notice. Any refusal to sign must be recorded on the custody record.

3.3 *Not used.*

3.3A An 'easy read' illustrated version should also be provided if available (see Note 3A).

3.4 (a)   The custody officer shall:

- record the offence(s) that the detainee has been arrested for and the reason(s) for the arrest on the custody record. See paragraph 10.3 and Code G paragraphs 2.2 and 4.3;

- note on the custody record any comment the detainee makes in relation to the arresting officer's account but shall not invite comment. If the arresting officer is not physically present when the detainee is brought to a police station, the arresting officer's account must be made available to the custody officer remotely or by a third party on the arresting officer's behalf. If the custody officer authorises a person's detention, subject to paragraph 1.8, that officer must record the grounds for detention in the detainee's presence and at the same time, inform them of the grounds. The detainee must be informed of the grounds for their detention before they are questioned about any offence;

- note any comment the detainee makes in respect of the decision to detain them but shall not invite comment; not put specific questions to the detainee regarding their involvement in any offence, nor in respect of any comments they may make in response to the arresting officer's account or the decision to place them in detention. Such an exchange is likely to constitute an interview as in paragraph 11.1A and require the associated safeguards in section 11.

Note: This sub-paragraph also applies to any further offences and grounds for detention which come to light whilst the person is detained.

See paragraph 11.13 in respect of unsolicited comments.

(b)   Documents and materials which are essential to effectively challenging the lawfulness of the detainee's arrest and detention must be made available to the detainee or their solicitor. Documents and materials will be 'essential' for this purpose if they are capable of undermining the reasons and grounds which make the detainee's arrest and detention necessary. The decision about whether particular documents or materials must be made available for the purpose of this requirement therefore rests with the custody officer who determines whether detention is necessary, in consultation with the investigating officer who has the knowledge of the documents and materials in a particular case necessary to inform that decision. A note should be made in the detainee's custody record of the fact that documents or materials have been made available under this sub-paragraph and when. The investigating officer should make a separate note of what is made available and how it is made available in a particular case. This sub-paragraph also applies (with modifications) for the purposes of sections 15 (*Reviews and extensions of detention*) and 16 (*Charging detained persons*). See Note 3ZA and paragraphs 15.0 and 16.7A.

3.5   The custody officer or other custody staff as directed by the custody officer shall:
    (a)   ask the detainee whether at this time, they:
        (i)   would like legal advice, see paragraph 6.5;
        (ii)   want someone informed of their detention, see section 5;
    (b)   ask the detainee to sign the custody record to confirm their decisions in respect of (a);
    (c)   determine whether the detainee:
        (i)   is, or might be, in need of medical treatment or attention, see section 9;
        (ii)   requires:
- an appropriate adult (see paragraphs 1.4, 1.5, 1.5A and 3.15);
- help to check documentation (see paragraph 3.20);
- an interpreter (see paragraph 3.12 and Note 13B).

    (d)   record the decision in respect of (c).

Where any duties under this paragraph have been carried out by custody staff at the direction of the custody officer, the outcomes shall, as soon as practicable, be reported to the custody officer who retains overall responsibility for the detainee's care and treatment and ensuring that it complies with this Code. See Note 3F.

3.6   When the needs mentioned in paragraph 3.5(c) are being determined, the custody officer is responsible for initiating an assessment to consider whether the detainee is likely to present specific risks to custody staff, any individual who may have contact with detainee (e.g. legal advisers, medical staff) or themselves. This risk assessment must include the taking of reasonable steps to establish the detainee's identity and to obtain information about the detainee that is relevant to their safe custody, security and welfare and risks to others. Such assessments should therefore always include a check on the Police National Computer (PNC), to be carried out as soon as practicable, to identify any risks that have been highlighted in relation to the detainee. Although such assessments are primarily the custody officer's responsibility, it may be necessary for them to consult and involve others, e.g. the arresting officer or an appropriate healthcare professional, see paragraph 9.13. Other records held by or on behalf of the police and other UK law enforcement authorities that might provide information relevant to the detainee's safe custody, security and welfare and risk to others and to confirming their identity should also be checked. Reasons for delaying the initiation or completion of the assessment must be recorded.

3.7   Chief Officers should ensure that arrangements for proper and effective risk assessments required by paragraph 3.6 are implemented in respect of all detainees at police stations in their area.

3.8   Risk assessments must follow a structured process which clearly defines the categories of risk to be considered and the results must be incorporated in the detainee's custody record. The custody officer is responsible for making sure those responsible for the detainee's custody are appropriately briefed about the risks. If no specific risks are identified by the assessment, that should be noted in the custody record. See Note 3E and paragraph 9.14.

3.8A   The content of any risk assessment and any analysis of the level of risk relating to the person's detention is not required to be shown or provided to the detainee or any person acting on behalf of the detainee. But information should not be withheld from any person acting on the detainee's behalf, for example, an appropriate adult, solicitor or interpreter, if to do so might put that person at risk.

3.9   The custody officer is responsible for implementing the response to any specific risk assessment, e.g.:
- reducing opportunities for self harm;
- calling an appropriate healthcare professional;
- increasing levels of monitoring or observation;
- reducing the risk to those who come into contact with the detainee.

    (See Note 3E.)

3.10 Risk assessment is an ongoing process and assessments must always be subject to review if circumstances change.

3.11 If video cameras are installed in the custody area, notices shall be prominently displayed showing cameras are in use. Any request to have video cameras switched off shall be refused.

(b) Detained persons – special groups

3.12 If the detainee appears to be someone who does not speak or understand English or who has a hearing or speech impediment, the custody officer must ensure:

(a) that without delay, arrangements (see paragraph 13.1ZA) are made for the detainee to have the assistance of an interpreter in the action under paragraphs 3.1 to 3.5. If the person appears to have a hearing or speech impediment, the reference to 'interpreter' includes appropriate assistance necessary to comply with paragraphs 3.1 to 3.5. See paragraph 13.1C if the detainee is in Wales. See section 13 and Note 13B;

(b) that in addition to the continuing rights set out in paragraph 3.1(a)(i) to (iv), the detainee is told clearly about their right to interpretation and translation;

(c) that the written notice given to the detainee in accordance with paragraph 3.2 is in a language the detainee understands and includes the right to interpretation and translation together with information about the provisions in section 13 and Annex M, which explain how the right applies (see Note 3A); and

(d) that if the translation of the notice is not available, the information in the notice is given through an interpreter and a written translation provided without undue delay.

3.12A If the detainee is a citizen of an independent Commonwealth country or a national of a foreign country, including the Republic of Ireland, the custody officer must ensure that in addition to the continuing rights set out in paragraph 3.1(a)(i) to (iv), they are informed as soon as practicable about their rights of communication with their High Commission, Embassy or Consulate set out in section 7. This right must be included in the written notice given to the detainee in accordance with paragraph 3.2.

3.13 If the detainee is a juvenile, the custody officer must, if it is practicable, ascertain the identity of a person responsible for their welfare. That person:

- may be:
  - the parent or guardian;
  - if the juvenile is in local authority or voluntary organisation care, or is otherwise being looked after under the Children Act 1989, a person appointed by that authority or organisation to have responsibility for the juvenile's welfare;
  - any other person who has, for the time being, assumed responsibility for the juvenile's welfare.
- must be informed as soon as practicable that the juvenile has been arrested, why they have been arrested and where they are detained. This right is in addition to the juvenile's right in section 5 not to be held incommunicado. See Note 3C.

3.14 If a juvenile is known to be subject to a court order under which a person or organisation is given any degree of statutory responsibility to supervise or otherwise monitor them, reasonable steps must also be taken to notify that person or organisation (the 'responsible officer'). The responsible officer will normally be a member of a Youth Offending Team, except for a curfew order which involves electronic monitoring when the contractor providing the monitoring will normally be the responsible officer.

3.15 If the detainee is a juvenile or a vulnerable person, the custody officer must, as soon as practicable, ensure that:

- the detainee is informed of the decision that an appropriate adult is required and the reason for that decision (see paragraph 3.5(c)(ii) and;
- the detainee is advised:
  - of the duties of the appropriate adult as described in paragraph 1.7A; and
  - that they can consult privately with the appropriate adult at any time.
- the appropriate adult, who in the case of a juvenile may or may not be a person responsible for their welfare, as in paragraph 3.13, is informed of:
  - the grounds for their detention;
  - their whereabouts; and
- the attendance of the appropriate adult at the police station to see the detainee is secured.

3.16 It is imperative that a person detained under the Mental Health Act 1983, section 135 or 136, be assessed as soon as possible within the permitted period of detention specified in that Act. A police station may only be used as a place of safety in accordance with The Mental Health Act 1983 (Places of Safety) Regulations 2017.

If that assessment is to take place at the police station, an approved mental health professional and a registered medical practitioner shall be called to the station as soon as possible to carry it out. See Note 9D. The appropriate adult has no role in the assessment process and their presence is not required. Once the detainee has been assessed and suitable arrangements made for their treatment or care, they can no longer be detained under section 135 or 136. A detainee must be immediately discharged from detention if a registered medical practitioner, having examined them, concludes they are not mentally disordered within the meaning of the Act.

3.17 If the appropriate adult is:

- already at the police station, the provisions of paragraphs 3.1 to 3.5 must be complied with in the appropriate adult's presence;
- not at the station when these provisions are complied with, they must be complied with again in the presence of the appropriate adult when they arrive,
- and a copy of the notice given to the detainee in accordance with paragraph 3.2, shall also be given to the appropriate adult.

3.17A The custody officer must ensure that at the time the copy of the notice is given to the appropriate adult, or as soon as practicable thereafter, the appropriate adult is advised of the duties of the appropriate adult as described in paragraph 1.7A.

3.18 *Not used.*

3.19 If the detainee, or appropriate adult on the detainee's behalf, asks for a solicitor to be called to give legal advice, the provisions of section 6 apply (see paragraph 6.5A and Note 3H).

3.20 If the detainee is blind, seriously visually impaired or unable to read, the custody officer shall make sure their solicitor, relative, appropriate adult or some other person likely to take an interest in them and not involved in the investigation is available to help check any documentation. When this Code requires written consent or signing the person assisting may be asked to sign instead, if the detainee prefers. This paragraph does not require an appropriate adult to be called solely to assist in checking and signing documentation for a person who is not a juvenile, or is not vulnerable (see paragraph 3.15 and Note 13C).

3.20 A The Children and Young Persons Act 1933, section 31, requires that arrangements must be made for ensuring that a girl under the age of 18, while detained in a police station, is under the care of a woman. See Note 3G. It also requires that arrangements must be made for preventing any person under 18, while being detained in a police station, from associating with an adult charged with any offence, unless that adult is a relative or the adult is jointly charged with the same offence as the person under 18.

(c) Detained persons – Documentation

3.20B The grounds for a person's detention shall be recorded, in the person's presence if practicable. See paragraph 1.8.

3.20C Action taken under paragraphs 3.12 to 3.20A shall be recorded.

(d) Persons attending a police station or elsewhere voluntarily

3.21 Anybody attending a police station or other location (see paragraph 3.22 and Note 3I) voluntarily to assist police with the investigation of an offence may leave at will unless arrested. See Notes 1A and 1K. The person may only be prevented from leaving at will if their arrest on suspicion of committing the offence is necessary in accordance with Code G. See Code G Note 2G.

Action if arrest becomes necessary

(a) If during a person's voluntary attendance at a police station or other location it is decided for any reason that their arrest is necessary, they must:
- be informed at once that they are under arrest and of the grounds and reasons as required by Code G, and
- be brought before the custody officer at the police station where they are arrested or (as the case may be) at the police station to which they are taken after being arrested elsewhere. The custody officer is then responsible for making sure that a custody record is opened and that they are notified of their rights in the same way as other detainees as required by this Code.

Information to be given when arranging a voluntary interview:

(b) If the suspect's arrest is not necessary but they are cautioned as required in section 10, the person who, after describing the nature and circumstances of the suspected offence, gives the caution must at the same time, inform them that they are not under arrest and that they are not obliged to remain at the station or other location (see paragraph 3.22 and Note 3I). The rights, entitlements and safeguards that apply to the conduct and recording of interviews with suspects are not diminished simply because the interview is arranged on a voluntary basis. For the purpose of arranging a voluntary interview (see Code G Note 2F), the duty of the interviewer reflects that of the custody officer with regard to detained suspects. As a result:

(i)   the requirement in paragraph 3.5(c)(ii) to determine whether a detained suspect requires an appropriate adult, help to check documentation or an interpreter shall apply equally to a suspect who has not been arrested; and

(ii)   the suspect must not be asked to give their informed consent to be interviewed until after they have been informed of the rights, entitlements and safeguards that apply to voluntary interviews. These are set out in paragraph 3.21A and the interviewer is responsible for ensuring that the suspect is so informed and for explaining these rights, entitlements and safeguards.

3.21A The interviewer must inform the suspect that the purpose of the voluntary interview is to question them to obtain evidence about their involvement or suspected involvement in the offence(s) described when they were cautioned and told that they were not under arrest. The interviewer shall then inform the suspect that the following matters will apply if they agree to the voluntary interview proceeding:

(a)   Their right to information about the offence(s) in question by providing sufficient information to enable them to understand the nature of any such offence(s) and why they are suspected of committing it. This is in order to allow for the effective exercise of the rights of the defence as required by paragraph 11.1A. It applies whether or not they ask for legal advice and includes any further offences that come to light and are pointed out during the voluntary interview and for which they are cautioned.

(b)   Their right to free (see Note 3J) legal advice by:
(i)   explaining that they may obtain free and independent legal advice if they want it, and that this includes the right to speak with a solicitor on the telephone and to have the solicitor present during the interview;
(ii)   asking if they want legal advice and recording their reply; and
(iii)   if the person requests advice, securing its provision before the interview by contacting the Defence Solicitor Call Centre and explaining that the time and place of the interview will be arranged to enable them to obtain advice and that the interview will be delayed until they have received the advice unless, in accordance with paragraph 6.6(c) (Nominated solicitor not available and duty solicitor declined) or paragraph 6.6(d) (Change of mind), an officer of the rank of inspector or above agrees to the interview proceeding; or
(iv)   if the person declines to exercise the right, asking them why and recording any reasons given (see Note 6K).

Note: When explaining the right to legal advice and the arrangements, the interviewer must take care not to indicate, except to answer a direct question, that the time taken to arrange and complete the voluntary interview might be reduced if:
• the suspect does not ask for legal advice or does not want a solicitor present when they are interviewed; or
• the suspect asks for legal advice or (as the case may be) asks for a solicitor to be present when they are interviewed, but changes their mind and agrees to be interviewed without waiting for a solicitor.

(c)   Their right, if in accordance with paragraph 3.5(c)(ii) the interviewer determines:
(i)   that they are a juvenile or are vulnerable; or
(ii)   that they need help to check documentation (see paragraph 3.20),
(iii)   to have the appropriate adult present or (as the case may be) to have the necessary help to check documentation; and that the interview will be delayed until the presence of the appropriate adult or the necessary help, is secured.

(d)   If they are a juvenile or vulnerable and do not want legal advice, their appropriate adult has the right to ask for a solicitor to attend if this would be in their best interests and the appropriate adult must be so informed. In this case, action to secure the provision of advice if so requested by their appropriate adult will be taken without delay in the same way as if requested by the person (see sub-paragraph (b)(iii)). However, they cannot be forced to see the solicitor if they are adamant that they do not wish to do so (see paragraphs 3.19 and 6.5A).

(e)   Their right to an interpreter, if in accordance with, paragraphs 3.5(c)(ii) and 3.12, the interviewer determines that they require an interpreter and that if they require an interpreter, making the necessary arrangements in accordance with paragraph 13.1ZA and that the interview will be delayed to make the arrangements.

(f)   That interview will be arranged for a time and location (see paragraph 3.22 and Note 3I) that enables:

(i)   the suspect's rights described above to be fully respected; and

(ii)   the whole of the interview to be recorded using an authorised recording device in accordance with Code E (Code of Practice on Audio recording of interviews with suspects) or (as the case may be) Code F (Code of Practice on visual recording with sound of interviews with suspects); and

(g)   That their agreement to take part in the interview also signifies their agreement for that interview to be audio-recorded or (as the case may be) visually recorded with sound.

3.21B The provision by the interviewer of factual information described in paragraph 3.21A and, if asked by the suspect, further such information, does not constitute an interview for the purpose of this Code and when that information is provided:

(a)   the interviewer must remind the suspect about the caution as required in section 10 but must not invite comment about the offence or put specific questions to the suspect regarding their involvement in any offence, nor in respect of any comments they may make when given the information. Such an exchange is itself likely to constitute an interview as in paragraph 11.1A and require the associated interview safeguards in section 11.

(b)   Any comment the suspect makes when the information is given which might be relevant to the offence, must be recorded and dealt with in accordance with paragraph 11.13.

(c)   The suspect must be given a notice summarising the matters described in paragraph 3.21A and which includes the arrangements for obtaining legal advice. If a specific notice is not available, the notice given to detained suspects with references to detention-specific requirements and information redacted, may be used.

(d)   For juvenile and vulnerable suspects (see paragraphs 1.4 and 1.5):

(i)   the information must be provided or (as the case may be) provided again, together with the notice, in the presence of the appropriate adult;

(ii)   if cautioned in the absence of the appropriate adult, the caution must be repeated in the appropriate adult's presence (see paragraph 10.12);

(iii) the suspect must be informed of the decision that an appropriate is required and the reason (see paragraph 3.5(c)(ii);

(iv)   the suspect and the appropriate adult shall be advised:

• that the duties of the appropriate adult include giving advice and assistance in accordance with paragraphs 1.7A and 11.17; and

• that they can consult privately at any time. (v) their informed agreement to be interviewed voluntarily must be sought and given in the presence of the appropriate adult and for a juvenile, the agreement of a parent or guardian of the juvenile is also required.

3.22 If the other location mentioned in paragraph 3.21 is any place or premises for which the interviewer requires the informed consent of the suspect and/or occupier (if different) to remain, for example, the suspect's home (see Note 3I), then the references that the person is 'not obliged to remain' and that they 'may leave at will' mean that the suspect and/or occupier (if different) may also withdraw their consent and require the interviewer to leave.

Commencement of voluntary interview – general

3.22A Before asking the suspect any questions about their involvement in the offence they are suspected of committing, the interviewing officer must ask them to confirm that they agree to the interview proceeding. This confirmation shall be recorded in the interview record made in accordance with section 11 of this Code (written record) or Code E or Code F.

Documentation

3.22B Action taken under paragraphs 3.21A to 3.21B shall be recorded. The record shall include the date time and place the action was taken, who was present and anything said to or by the suspect and to or by those present.

3.23 *Not used.*

3.24 *Not used.*

(e) *Persons answering street bail*

3.25 When a person is answering street bail, the custody officer should link any documentation held in relation to arrest with the custody record. Any further action shall be recorded on the custody record in accordance with paragraphs 3.20B and 3.20C above.

(f) *Requirements for suspects to be informed of certain rights*

3.26 The provisions of this section identify the information which must be given to suspects who have been cautioned in accordance with section 10 of this Code according to whether or not they have been arrested and detained. It includes information required by EU Directive 2012/13 on the right to information in criminal proceedings. If a complaint is made by or on behalf of such a suspect that the information and (as the case may be) access to records and documents has not been provided as required, the matter shall be reported to an inspector to deal with as a complaint for the purposes of paragraph 9.2, or paragraph 12.9 if the challenge is made during an interview. This would include, for example:

(a) in the case of a detained suspect:
- not informing them of their rights (see paragraph 3.1);
- not giving them a copy of the Notice (see paragraph 3.2(a));
- not providing an opportunity to read the notice (see paragraph 3.2A);
- not providing the required information (see paragraphs 3.2(a), 3.12(b) and, 3.12A;
- not allowing access to the custody record (see paragraph 2.4);
- not providing a translation of the Notice (see paragraph 3.12(c) and (d)); and

(b) in the case of a suspect who is not detained:
- not informing them of their rights or providing the required information (see paragraphs 3.21(b) to 3.21B).

Notes for Guidance

3ZA *For the purposes of paragraphs 3.4(b) and 15.0*:

(a) Investigating officers are responsible for bringing to the attention of the officer who is responsible for authorising the suspect's detention or (as the case may be) continued detention (before or after charge), any documents and materials in their possession or control which appear to undermine the need to keep the suspect in custody. In accordance with Part IV of PACE, this officer will be either the custody officer, the officer reviewing the need for detention before or after charge (PACE, section 40), or the officer considering the need to extend detention without charge from 24 to 36 hours (PACE, section 42) who is then responsible for determining, which, if any, of those documents and materials are capable of undermining the need to detain the suspect and must therefore be made available to the suspect or their solicitor.

(b) the way in which documents and materials are 'made available', is a matter for the investigating officer to determine on a case by case basis and having regard to the nature and volume of the documents and materials involved. For example, they may be made available by supplying a copy or allowing supervised access to view. However, for view only access, it will be necessary to demonstrate that sufficient time is allowed for the suspect and solicitor to view and consider the documents and materials in question.

3A 3A For access to currently available notices, including 'easy-read' versions, see www.gov.uk/notice-of-rights-and-entitlements-a-persons-rights-in-police-detention

3B *Not used.*

3C If the juvenile is in local authority or voluntary organisation care but living with their parents or other adults responsible for their welfare, although there is no legal obligation to inform them, they should normally be contacted, as well as the authority or organisation unless they are suspected of involvement in the offence concerned. Even if the juvenile is not living with their parents, consideration should be given to informing them.

3D The right to consult the Codes of Practice does not entitle the person concerned to delay unreasonably any necessary investigative or administrative action whilst they do so. Examples of action which need not be delayed unreasonably include:
- procedures requiring the provision of breath, blood or urine specimens under the Road Traffic Act 1988 or the Transport and Works Act 1992;
- searching detainees at the police station;
- taking fingerprints, footwear impressions or non-intimate samples without consent for evidential purposes.

3E The Detention and Custody Authorised Professional Practice (APP) produced by the College of Policing (see www.app.college.police.uk) provides more detailed guidance on risk assessments and identifies key risk areas which should always be considered. See Home Office Circular 34/2007 (Safety of solicitors and probationary representatives at police station).

3F A custody officer or other officer who, in accordance with this Code, allows or directs the carrying out of any task or action relating to a detainee's care, treatment, rights and entitlements to another officer or any other person, must be satisfied that the officer or person concerned is suitable, trained and competent to carry out the task or action in question.

3G Guidance for police officers and police staff on the operational application of section 31 of the Children and Young Persons Act 1933 has been published by the College of Policing and is available at www.app.college.police.uk.

3H The purpose of the provisions at paragraphs 3.19 and 6.5A is to protect the rights of juvenile and vulnerable persons who may not understand the significance of what is said to them. They should always be given an opportunity, when an appropriate adult is called to the police station, to consult privately with a solicitor in the absence of the appropriate adult if they want.

3I An interviewer who is not sure, or has any doubt, about whether a place or location elsewhere than a police station is suitable for carrying out a voluntary interview, particularly in the case of a juvenile or vulnerable person, should consult an officer of the rank of sergeant or above for advice. Detailed guidance for police officers and staff concerning the conduct and recording of voluntary interviews is being developed by the College of Policing. It follows a review of operational issues arising when voluntary interviews need to be arranged. The aim is to ensure the effective implementation of the safeguards in paragraphs 3.21 to 3.22B particularly concerning the rights of suspects, the location for the interview and supervision.

3J For voluntary interviews conducted by non-police investigators, the provision of legal advice is set out by the Legal Aid Agency at paragraph 9.54 of the 2017 Standard Crime Contract Specification. This is published at ... and the rules mean that a non-police interviewer who does not have their own statutory power of arrest would have to inform the suspect that they have a right to seek legal advice if they wish, but payment would be a matter for them to arrange with the solicitor.

4. Detainee's property

(a) Action

4.1 The custody officer is responsible for:
- (a) ascertaining what property a detainee:
  - (i) has with them when they come to the police station, whether on:
    - arrest or re-detention on answering to bail;
    - commitment to prison custody on the order or sentence of a court;
    - lodgement at the police station with a view to their production in court from prison custody;
    - transfer from detention at another station or hospital;
    - detention under the Mental Health Act 1983, section 135 or 136;
    - remand into police custody on the authority of a court.

(ii)   might have acquired for an unlawful or harmful purpose while in custody;

(b)   the safekeeping of any property taken from a detainee which remains at the police station.

The custody officer may search the detainee or authorise their being searched to the extent they consider necessary, provided a search of intimate parts of the body or involving the removal of more than outer clothing is only made as in Annex A. A search may only be carried out by an officer of the same sex as the detainee. See Note 4A and Annex L.

4.2   Detainees may retain clothing and personal effects at their own risk unless the custody officer considers they may use them to cause harm to themselves or others, interfere with evidence, damage property, effect an escape or they are needed as evidence. In this event the custody officer may withhold such articles as they consider necessary and must tell the detainee why.

4.3   Personal effects are those items a detainee may lawfully need, use or refer to while in detention but do not include cash and other items of value.

(b)   Documentation

4.4   It is a matter for the custody officer to determine whether a record should be made of the property a detained person has with him or had taken from him on arrest. Any record made is not required to be kept as part of the custody record but the custody record should be noted as to where such a record exists. Whenever a record is made the detainee shall be allowed to check and sign the record of property as correct. Any refusal to sign shall be recorded.

4.5   If a detainee is not allowed to keep any article of clothing or personal effects, the reason must be recorded.

Notes for Guidance

4A   PACE, Section 54(1) and paragraph 4.1 require a detainee to be searched when it is clear the custody officer will have continuing duties in relation to that detainee or when that detainee's behaviour or offence makes an inventory appropriate. They do not require every detainee to be searched, e.g. if it is clear a person will only be detained for a short period and is not to be placed in a cell, the custody officer may decide not to search them. In such a case the custody record will be endorsed 'not searched', paragraph 4.4 will not apply, and the detainee will be invited to sign the entry. If the detainee refuses, the custody officer will be obliged to ascertain what property they have in accordance with paragraph 4.1.

4B   Paragraph 4.4 does not require the custody officer to record on the custody record property in the detainee's possession on arrest if, by virtue of its nature, quantity or size, it is not practicable to remove it to the police station.

4C   Paragraph 4.4 does not require items of clothing worn by the person be recorded unless withheld by the custody officer as in paragraph 4.2.

5.   Right not to be held incommunicado

(a)   Action

5.1   Subject to paragraph 5.7B, any person arrested and held in custody at a police station or other premises may, on request, have one person known to them or likely to take an interest in their welfare informed at public expense of their whereabouts as soon as practicable. If the person cannot be contacted the detainee may choose up to two alternatives. If they cannot be contacted, the person in charge of detention or the investigation has discretion to allow further attempts until the information has been conveyed. See Notes 5C and 5D.

5.2   The exercise of the above right in respect of each person nominated may be delayed only in accordance with Annex B.

5.3   The above right may be exercised each time a detainee is taken to another police station.

5.4   If the detainee agrees, they may at the custody officer's discretion, receive visits from friends, family or others likely to take an interest in their welfare, or in whose welfare the detainee has an interest. See Note 5B.

5.5   If a friend, relative or person with an interest in the detainee's welfare enquires about their whereabouts, this information shall be given if the suspect agrees and Annex B does not apply. See Note 5D.

5.6   The detainee shall be given writing materials, on request, and allowed to telephone one person for a reasonable time, see Notes 5A and 5E. Either or both these privileges may be denied or delayed if an officer of inspector rank or above considers sending a letter or making a telephone call may result in any of the consequences in:

(a)   Annex B paragraphs 1 and 2 and the person is detained in connection with an indictable offence;

(b)   *Not used.*

Nothing in this paragraph permits the restriction or denial of the rights in paragraphs 5.1 and 6.1.

5.7   Before any letter or message is sent, or telephone call made, the detainee shall be informed that what they say in any letter, call or message (other than in a communication to a solicitor) may be read or listened to and may be given in evidence. A telephone call may be terminated if it is being abused. The costs can be at public expense at the custody officer's discretion.

5.7A Any delay or denial of the rights in this section should be proportionate and should last no longer than necessary.

5.7B In the case of a person in police custody for specific purposes and periods in accordance with a direction under the Crime (Sentences) Act 1997, Schedule 1 (productions from prison etc), the exercise of the rights in this section shall be subject to any additional conditions specified in the direction for the purpose of regulating the detainee's contact and communication with others whilst in police custody. See Note 5F.

(b) Documentation

5.8   A record must be kept of any:

(a)   request made under this section and the action taken;

(b)   letters, messages or telephone calls made or received or visit received;

(c)   refusal by the detainee to have information about them given to an outside enquirer. The detainee must be asked to countersign the record accordingly and any refusal recorded.

Notes for Guidance

5A   A person may request an interpreter to interpret a telephone call or translate a letter.

5B   At the custody officer's discretion and subject to the detainee's consent, visits should be allowed when possible, subject to having sufficient personnel to supervise a visit and any possible hindrance to the investigation.

5C   If the detainee does not know anyone to contact for advice or support or cannot contact a friend or relative, the custody officer should bear in mind any local voluntary bodies or other organisations who might be able to help. Paragraph 6.1 applies if legal advice is required.

5D   In some circumstances it may not be appropriate to use the telephone to disclose information under paragraphs 5.1 and 5.5.

5E   The telephone call at paragraph 5.6 is in addition to any communication under paragraphs 5.1 and 6.1.

5F   Prison Service Instruction 26/2012 (Production of Prisoners at the Request of Warranted Law Enforcement Agencies) provides detailed guidance and instructions for police officers and Governors and Directors of Prisons regarding applications for prisoners to be transferred to police custody and their safe custody and treatment while in police custody.

6.   Right to legal advice

(a) Action

6.1   Unless Annex B applies, all detainees must be informed that they may at any time consult and communicate privately with a solicitor, whether in person, in writing or by telephone, and that free independent legal advice is available. (See paragraph 3.1, Notes 1I, 6B and 6J.)

6.2   *Not used.*

6.3   A poster advertising the right to legal advice must be prominently displayed in the charging area of every police station. See Note 6H.

6.4   No police officer should, at any time, do or say anything with the intention of dissuading any person who is entitled to legal advice in accordance with this Code, whether or not they have been arrested and are detained, from obtaining legal advice. (See Note 6ZA.)

6.5   The exercise of the right of access to legal advice may be delayed only as in Annex B. Whenever legal advice is requested, and unless Annex B applies, the custody officer must act without delay to secure the provision of such advice. If the detainee has the right to speak to a solicitor in person but declines to exercise the right the officer should point out that the right includes the right to speak with a solicitor on the telephone. If the detainee continues to waive this right, or a detainee whose right to free legal advice is limited to telephone advice from the Criminal Defence Service (CDS) Direct (see Note 6B) declines to exercise that right, the officer should ask them why and any reasons should be recorded on the custody record or the interview record as appropriate. Reminders of the right to legal advice must be given as in paragraphs 3.5, 11.2, 15.4,16.4, 2B of Annex A, 3 of Annex K and 16.5 of this Code and Code D, paragraphs 3.17(ii) and 6.3. Once it is clear a detainee does not want to speak to a solicitor in person or by telephone they should cease to be asked their reasons. (See Note 6K.)

6.5A   In the case of a person who is a juvenile or is vulnerable, an appropriate adult should consider whether legal advice from a solicitor is required. If such a detained person wants to exercise the right to legal advice, the appropriate action should be taken and should not be delayed until the appropriate adult arrives. If the person indicates that they do not want legal advice, the appropriate adult has the right to ask for a solicitor to attend if this would be in the best interests of the person and must be so informed. In this case, action to secure the provision of advice if so requested by the appropriate adult shall be taken without delay in the same way as when requested by the person. However, the person cannot be forced to see the solicitor if they are adamant that they do not wish to do so.

6.6   A detainee who wants legal advice may not be interviewed or continue to be interviewed until they have received such advice unless:

(a)   Annex B applies, when the restriction on drawing adverse inferences from silence in Annex C will apply because the detainee is not allowed an opportunity to consult a solicitor; or

(b)   an officer of superintendent rank or above has reasonable grounds for believing that:

    (i)   the consequent delay might:
- lead to interference with, or harm to, evidence connected with an offence;
- lead to interference with, or physical harm to, other people;
- lead to serious loss of, or damage to, property;
- lead to alerting other people suspected of having committed an offence but not yet arrested for it;
- hinder the recovery of property obtained in consequence of the commission of an offence.

    (See Note 6A.)

    (ii)   when a solicitor, including a duty solicitor, has been contacted and has agreed to attend, awaiting their arrival would cause unreasonable delay to the process of investigation.

Note: In these cases the restriction on drawing adverse inferences from silence in Annex C will apply because the detainee is not allowed an opportunity to consult a solicitor.

(c)   the solicitor the detainee has nominated or selected from a list:
    (i)   cannot be contacted;
    (ii)   has previously indicated they do not wish to be contacted; or
    (iii) having been contacted, has declined to attend; and
- the detainee has been advised of the Duty Solicitor Scheme but has declined to ask for the duty solicitor;
- in these circumstances the interview may be started or continued without further delay provided an officer of inspector rank or above has agreed to the interview proceeding.

Note: The restriction on drawing adverse inferences from silence in Annex C will not apply because the detainee is allowed an opportunity to consult the duty solicitor;

(d)   the detainee changes their mind about wanting legal advice or (as the case may be) about wanting a solicitor present at the interview and states that they no longer wish to speak to a solicitor. In these circumstances, the interview may be started or continued without delay provided that:

(i)   an officer of inspector rank or above:
- speaks to the detainee to enquire about the reasons for their change of mind (see Note 6K), and
- makes, or directs the making of, reasonable efforts to ascertain the solicitor's expected time of arrival and to inform the solicitor that the suspect has stated that they wish to change their mind and the reason (if given);

(ii)   the detainee's reason for their change of mind (if given) and the outcome of the action in (i) are recorded in the custody record;

(iii)   the detainee, after being informed of the outcome of the action in (i) above, confirms in writing that they want the interview to proceed without speaking or further speaking to a solicitor or (as the case may be) without a solicitor being present and do not wish to wait for a solicitor by signing an entry to this effect in the custody record;

(iv)   an officer of inspector rank or above is satisfied that it is proper for the interview to proceed in these circumstances and:
- gives authority in writing for the interview to proceed and if the authority is not recorded in the custody record, the officer must ensure that the custody record shows the date and time of the authority and where it is recorded, and
- takes or directs the taking of, reasonable steps to inform the solicitor that the authority has been given and the time when the interview is expected to commence, and records or causes to be recorded, the outcome of this action in the custody record.

(v)   When the interview starts and the interviewer reminds the suspect of their right to legal advice (see paragraph 11.2, Code E paragraph 4.5 and Code F paragraph 4.5), the interviewer shall then ensure that the following is recorded in the written interview record or the interview record made in accordance with Code E or F:
- confirmation that the detainee has changed their mind about wanting legal advice or (as the case may be) about wanting a solicitor present and the reasons for it if given;
- the fact that authority for the interview to proceed has been given and, subject to paragraph 2.6A, the name of the authorising officer;
- that if the solicitor arrives at the station before the interview is completed, the detainee will be so informed without delay and a break will be taken to allow them to speak to the solicitor if they wish, unless paragraph 6.6(a) applies, and
- that at any time during the interview, the detainee may again ask for legal advice and that if they do, a break will be taken to allow them to speak to the solicitor, unless paragraph 6.6(a), (b), or (c) applies.

Note: In these circumstances, the restriction on drawing adverse inferences from silence in Annex C will not apply because the detainee is allowed an opportunity to consult a solicitor if they wish.

6.7 If paragraph 6.6(a) applies, where the reason for authorising the delay ceases to apply, there may be no further delay in permitting the exercise of the right in the absence of a further authorisation unless paragraph 6.6(b), (c) or (d) applies. If paragraph 6.6(b)(i) applies, once sufficient information has been obtained to avert the risk, questioning must cease until the detainee has received legal advice unless paragraph 6.6(a), (b)(ii), (c) or (d) applies.

6.8 A detainee who has been permitted to consult a solicitor shall be entitled on request to have the solicitor present when they are interviewed unless one of the exceptions in paragraph 6.6 applies.

6.9 The solicitor may only be required to leave the interview if their conduct is such that the interviewer is unable properly to put questions to the suspect. (See Notes 6D and 6E.)

6.10 If the interviewer considers a solicitor is acting in such a way, they will stop the interview and consult an officer not below superintendent rank, if one is readily available, and otherwise an officer not below inspector rank not connected with the investigation. After speaking to the solicitor, the officer consulted will decide if the interview should continue in the presence of that solicitor. If they decide it should not, the suspect will be given the opportunity to consult another solicitor before the interview continues and that solicitor given an opportunity to be present at the interview. See Note 6E.

6.11 The removal of a solicitor from an interview is a serious step and, if it occurs, the officer of superintendent rank or above who took the decision will consider if the incident should be reported to the Solicitors Regulatory Authority. If the decision to remove the solicitor has been taken by an officer below superintendent rank, the facts must be reported to an officer of superintendent rank or above, who will similarly consider whether a report to the Solicitors Regulatory Authority would be appropriate. When the solicitor concerned is a duty solicitor, the report should be both to the Solicitors Regulatory Authority and to the Legal Aid Agency.

6.12 'Solicitor' in this Code means:
- a solicitor who holds a current practising certificate;
- an accredited or probationary representative included on the register of representatives maintained by the Legal Aid Agency.

6.12A An accredited or probationary representative sent to provide advice by, and on behalf of, a solicitor shall be admitted to the police station for this purpose unless an officer of inspector rank or above considers such a visit will hinder the investigation and directs otherwise. Hindering the investigation does not include giving proper legal advice to a detainee as in Note 6D. Once admitted to the police station, paragraphs 6.6 to 6.10 apply.

6.13 In exercising their discretion under paragraph 6.12A, the officer should take into account in particular:
- whether:
  - the identity and status of an accredited or probationary representative have been satisfactorily established;
  - they are of suitable character to provide legal advice, e.g. a person with a criminal record is unlikely to be suitable unless the conviction was for a minor offence and not recent.
- any other matters in any written letter of authorisation provided by the solicitor on whose behalf the person is attending the police station. See Note 6F.

6.14 If the inspector refuses access to an accredited or probationary representative or a decision is taken that such a person should not be permitted to remain at an interview, the inspector must notify the solicitor on whose behalf the representative was acting and give them an opportunity to make alternative arrangements. The detainee must be informed and the custody record noted.

6.15 If a solicitor arrives at the station to see a particular person, that person must, unless Annex B applies, be so informed whether or not they are being interviewed and asked if they would like to see the solicitor. This applies even if the detainee has declined legal advice or, having requested it, subsequently agreed to be interviewed without receiving advice. The solicitor's attendance and the detainee's decision must be noted in the custody record.

(b) Documentation

6.16 Any request for legal advice and the action taken shall be recorded.

6.17 A record shall be made in the interview record if a detainee asks for legal advice and an interview is begun either in the absence of a solicitor or their representative, or they have been required to leave an interview.

Notes for Guidance

6ZA No police officer or police staff shall indicate to any suspect, except to answer a direct question, that the period for which they are liable to be detained, or if not detained, the time taken to complete the interview, might be reduced:
- if they do not ask for legal advice or do not want a solicitor present when they are interviewed; or

- if they have asked for legal advice or (as the case may be) asked for a solicitor to be present when they are interviewed but change their mind and agree to be interviewed without waiting for a solicitor.

6A   In considering if paragraph 6.6(b) applies, the officer should, if practicable, ask the solicitor for an estimate of how long it will take to come to the station and relate this to the time detention is permitted, the time of day (i.e. whether the rest period under paragraph 12.2 is imminent) and the requirements of other investigations. If the solicitor is on their way or is to set off immediately, it will not normally be appropriate to begin an interview before they arrive. If it appears necessary to begin an interview before the solicitor's arrival, they should be given an indication of how long the police would be able to wait before 6.6(b) applies so there is an opportunity to make arrangements for someone else to provide legal advice.

6B   A detainee has a right to free legal advice and to be represented by a solicitor. This Note for Guidance explains the arrangements which enable detainees to obtain legal advice. An outline of these arrangements is also included in the Notice of Rights and Entitlements given to detainees in accordance with paragraph 3.2. The arrangements also apply, with appropriate modifications, to persons attending a police station or other location voluntarily who are cautioned prior to being interviewed. See paragraph 3.21. When a detainee asks for free legal advice, the Defence Solicitor Call Centre (DSCC) must be informed of the request.

Free legal advice will be limited to telephone advice provided by CDS Direct if a detainee is:

- detained for a non-imprisonable offence;
- arrested on a bench warrant for failing to appear and being held for production at court (except where the solicitor has clear documentary evidence available that would result in the client being released from custody);
- arrested for drink driving (driving/in charge with excess alcohol, failing to provide a specimen, driving/in charge whilst unfit through drink), or
- detained in relation to breach of police or court bail conditions unless one or more exceptions apply, in which case the DSCC should arrange for advice to be given by a solicitor at the police station, for example:
- the police want to interview the detainee or carry out an eye-witness identification procedure;
- the detainee needs an appropriate adult;
- the detainee is unable to communicate over the telephone;
- the detainee alleges serious misconduct by the police;
- the investigation includes another offence not included in the list,
- the solicitor to be assigned is already at the police station.

When free advice is not limited to telephone advice, a detainee can ask for free advice from a solicitor they know or if they do not know a solicitor or the solicitor they know cannot be contacted, from the duty solicitor.

To arrange free legal advice, the police should telephone the DSCC. The call centre will decide whether legal advice should be limited to telephone advice from CDS Direct, or whether a solicitor known to the detainee or the duty solicitor should speak to the detainee.

When a detainee wants to pay for legal advice themselves:

- the DSCC will contact a solicitor of their choice on their behalf;
- they may, when free advice is only available by telephone from CDS Direct, still speak to a solicitor of their choice on the telephone for advice, but the solicitor would not be paid by legal aid and may ask the person to pay for the advice;
- they should be given an opportunity to consult a specific solicitor or another solicitor from that solicitor's firm. If this solicitor is not available, they may choose up to two alternatives. If these alternatives are not available, the custody officer has discretion to allow further attempts until a solicitor has been contacted and agreed to provide advice;
- they are entitled to a private consultation with their chosen solicitor on the telephone or the solicitor may decide to come to the police station;
- If their chosen solicitor cannot be contacted, the DSCC may still be called to arrange free legal advice.

Apart from carrying out duties necessary to implement these arrangements, an officer must not advise the suspect about any particular firm of solicitors.

6B1 *Not used.*

6B2 *Not used.*

6C *Not used.*

6D The solicitor's only role in the police station is to protect and advance the legal rights of their client. On occasions this may require the solicitor to give advice which has the effect of the client avoiding giving evidence which strengthens a prosecution case. The solicitor may intervene in order to seek clarification, challenge an improper question to their client or the manner in which it is put, advise their client not to reply to particular questions, or if they wish to give their client further legal advice. Paragraph 6.9 only applies if the solicitor's approach or conduct prevents or unreasonably obstructs proper questions being put to the suspect or the suspect's response being recorded. Examples of unacceptable conduct include answering questions on a suspect's behalf or providing written replies for the suspect to quote.

6E An officer who takes the decision to exclude a solicitor must be in a position to satisfy the court the decision was properly made. In order to do this they may need to witness what is happening.

6F If an officer of at least inspector rank considers a particular solicitor or firm of solicitors is persistently sending probationary representatives who are unsuited to provide legal advice, they should inform an officer of at least superintendent rank, who may wish to take the matter up with the Solicitors Regulation Authority.

6G Subject to the constraints of Annex B, a solicitor may advise more than one client in an investigation if they wish. Any question of a conflict of interest is for the solicitor under their professional code of conduct. If, however, waiting for a solicitor to give advice to one client may lead to unreasonable delay to the interview with another, the provisions of paragraph 6.6(b) may apply.

6H In addition to a poster in English, a poster or posters containing translations into Welsh, the main minority ethnic languages and the principal European languages should be displayed wherever they are likely to be helpful and it is practicable to do so.

6I *Not used.*

6J Whenever a detainee exercises their right to legal advice by consulting or communicating with a solicitor, they must be allowed to do so in private. This right to consult or communicate in private is fundamental. If the requirement for privacy is compromised because what is said or written by the detainee or solicitor for the purpose of giving and receiving legal advice is overheard, listened to, or read by others without the informed consent of the detainee, the right will effectively have been denied. When a detainee speaks to a solicitor on the telephone, they should be allowed to do so in private unless this is impractical because of the design and layout of the custody area or the location of telephones. However, the normal expectation should be that facilities will be available, unless they are being used, at all police stations to enable detainees to speak in private to a solicitor either face to face or over the telephone.

6K A detainee is not obliged to give reasons for declining legal advice and should not be pressed to do so.

8. Conditions of detention

(a) Action

8.1 So far as it is practicable, not more than one detainee should be detained in each cell. (See Note 8C.)

8.2 Cells in use must be adequately heated, cleaned and ventilated. They must be adequately lit, subject to such dimming as is compatible with safety and security to allow people detained overnight to sleep. No additional restraints shall be used within a locked cell unless absolutely necessary and then only restraint equipment, approved for use in that force by the Chief Officer, which is reasonable and necessary in the circumstances having regard to the detainee's demeanour and with a view to ensuring their safety and the safety of others. If a detainee is deaf, mentally disordered or otherwise mentally vulnerable, particular care must be taken when deciding whether to use any form of approved restraints.

8.3 Blankets, mattresses, pillows and other bedding supplied shall be of a reasonable standard and in a clean and sanitary condition. (See Note 8A.)

8.4   Access to toilet and washing facilities must be provided.

8.5   If it is necessary to remove a detainee's clothes for the purposes of investigation, for hygiene, health reasons or cleaning, replacement clothing of a reasonable standard of comfort and cleanliness shall be provided. A detainee may not be interviewed unless adequate clothing has been offered.

8.6   At least two light meals and one main meal should be offered in any 24 hour period. See Note 8B. Drinks should be provided at meal times and upon reasonable request between meals. Whenever necessary, advice shall be sought from the appropriate healthcare professional, see Note 9A, on medical and dietary matters. As far as practicable, meals provided shall offer a varied diet and meet any specific dietary needs or religious beliefs the detainee may have. The detainee may, at the custody officer's discretion, have meals supplied by their family or friends at their expense. (See Note 8A.)

8.7   Brief outdoor exercise shall be offered daily if practicable.

8.8   A juvenile shall not be placed in a police cell unless no other secure accommodation is available and the custody officer considers it is not practicable to supervise them if they are not placed in a cell or that a cell provides more comfortable accommodation than other secure accommodation in the station. A juvenile may not be placed in a cell with a detained adult.

(b) Documentation

8.9   A record must be kept of replacement clothing and meals offered.

8.10 If a juvenile is placed in a cell, the reason must be recorded.

8.11 The use of any restraints on a detainee whilst in a cell, the reasons for it and, if appropriate, the arrangements for enhanced supervision of the detainee whilst so restrained, shall be recorded. (See paragraph 3.9.)

Notes for Guidance

8A   The provisions in paragraph 8.3 and 8.6 respectively are of particular importance in the case of a person likely to be detained for an extended period. In deciding whether to allow meals to be supplied by family or friends, the custody officer is entitled to take account of the risk of items being concealed in any food or package and the officer's duties and responsibilities under food handling legislation.

8B   Meals should, so far as practicable, be offered at recognised meal times, or at other times that take account of when the detainee last had a meal.

8C   The Detention and Custody Authorised Professional Practice (APP) produced by the College of Policing (see www.app.college.police.uk) provides more detailed guidance on matters concerning detainee healthcare and treatment and associated forensic issues which should be read in conjunction with sections 8 and 9 of this Code.

9.   Care and treatment of detained persons

(a) General

9.1   Nothing in this section prevents the police from calling an appropriate healthcare professional to examine a detainee for the purposes of obtaining evidence relating to any offence in which the detainee is suspected of being involved. (See Notes 9A and 8C.)

9.2   If a complaint is made by, or on behalf of, a detainee about their treatment since their arrest, or it comes to notice that a detainee may have been treated improperly, a report must be made as soon as practicable to an officer of inspector rank or above not connected with the investigation. If the matter concerns a possible assault or the possibility of the unnecessary or unreasonable use of force, an appropriate healthcare professional must also be called as soon as practicable.

9.3   Subject to paragraph 9.6 in the case of a person to whom The Mental Health Act 1983 (Places of Safety) Regulations 2017 apply, detainees should be visited at least every hour. If no reasonably foreseeable risk was identified in a risk assessment, see paragraphs 3.6 to 3.10, there is no need to wake a sleeping detainee. Those suspected of being under the influence of drink or drugs or both or of having swallowed drugs, see Note 9CA, or whose level of consciousness causes concern must, subject to any clinical directions given by the appropriate healthcare professional, see paragraph 9.13:
- be visited and roused at least every half hour;
- have their condition assessed as in Annex H;
- and clinical treatment arranged if appropriate.

See Notes 9B, 9C and 9H.

9.4 When arrangements are made to secure clinical attention for a detainee, the custody officer must make sure all relevant information which might assist in the treatment of the detainee's condition is made available to the responsible healthcare professional. This applies whether or not the healthcare professional asks for such information. Any officer or police staff with relevant information must inform the custody officer as soon as practicable.

(b) Clinical treatment and attention

9.5 The custody officer must make sure a detainee receives appropriate clinical attention as soon as reasonably practicable if the person:
   (a)   appears to be suffering from physical illness; or
   (b)   is injured; or
   (c)   appears to be suffering from a mental disorder; or
   (d)   appears to need clinical attention.

9.5A This applies even if the detainee makes no request for clinical attention and whether or not they have already received clinical attention elsewhere. If the need for attention appears urgent, e.g. when indicated as in Annex H, the nearest available healthcare professional or an ambulance must be called immediately.

9.5B The custody officer must also consider the need for clinical attention as set out in Note 9C in relation to those suffering the effects of alcohol or drugs.

9.6 Paragraph 9.5 is not meant to prevent or delay the transfer to a hospital if necessary of a person detained under the Mental Health Act 1983, sections 135 and 136, as amended by the Policing and Crime Act 2017. See Note 9D. When an assessment under that Act is to take place at a police station (see paragraph 3.16) the custody officer must also ensure that in accordance with The Mental Health Act 1983 (Places of Safety) Regulations 2017, a health professional is present and available to the person throughout the period they are detained at the police station and that at the welfare of the detainee is checked by the health professional at least once every thirty minutes and any appropriate action for the care and treatment of the detainee taken.

9.7 If it appears to the custody officer, or they are told, that a person brought to a station under arrest may be suffering from an infectious disease or condition, the custody officer must take reasonable steps to safeguard the health of the detainee and others at the station. In deciding what action to take, advice must be sought from an appropriate healthcare professional. See Note 9E. The custody officer has discretion to isolate the person and their property until clinical directions have been obtained.

9.8 If a detainee requests a clinical examination, an appropriate healthcare professional must be called as soon as practicable to assess the detainee's clinical needs. If a safe and appropriate care plan cannot be provided, the appropriate healthcare professional's advice must be sought. The detainee may also be examined by a medical practitioner of their choice at their expense.

9.9 If a detainee is required to take or apply any medication in compliance with clinical directions prescribed before their detention, the custody officer must consult the appropriate healthcare professional before the use of the medication. Subject to the restrictions in paragraph 9.10, the custody officer is responsible for the safekeeping of any medication and for making sure the detainee is given the opportunity to take or apply prescribed or approved medication. Any such consultation and its outcome shall be noted in the custody record.

9.10 No police officer may administer or supervise the self-administration of medically prescribed controlled drugs of the types and forms listed in the Misuse of Drugs Regulations 2001, Schedule 2 or 3. A detainee may only self-administer such drugs under the personal supervision of the registered medical practitioner authorising their use or other appropriate healthcare professional. The custody officer may supervise the self-administration of, or authorise other custody staff to supervise the self-administration of drugs listed in Schedule 4 or 5 if the officer has consulted the appropriate healthcare professional authorising their use and both are satisfied self-administration will not expose the detainee, police officers or anyone else to the risk of harm or injury.

9.11 When appropriate healthcare professionals administer drugs or authorise the use of other medications, supervise their self-administration or consult with the custody officer about allowing self administration of drugs listed in Schedule 4 or 5, it must be within current medicines legislation and the scope of practice as determined by their relevant statutory regulatory body.

9.12 If a detainee has in their possession, or claims to need, medication relating to a heart condition, diabetes, epilepsy or a condition of comparable potential seriousness then, even though paragraph 9.5 may not apply, the advice of the appropriate healthcare professional must be obtained.

9.13 Whenever the appropriate healthcare professional is called in accordance with this section to examine or treat a detainee, the custody officer shall ask for their opinion about:
- any risks or problems which police need to take into account when making decisions about the detainee's continued detention;
- when to carry out an interview if applicable; and
- the need for safeguards.

9.14 When clinical directions are given by the appropriate healthcare professional, whether orally or in writing, and the custody officer has any doubts or is in any way uncertain about any aspect of the directions, the custody officer shall ask for clarification. It is particularly important that directions concerning the frequency of visits are clear, precise and capable of being implemented. (See Note 9F.)

(c) Documentation

9.15 A record must be made in the custody record of:
- (a) the arrangements made for an examination by an appropriate healthcare professional under paragraph 9.2 and of any complaint reported under that paragraph together with any relevant remarks by the custody officer;
- (b) any arrangements made in accordance with paragraph 9.5;
- (c) any request for a clinical examination under paragraph 9.8 and any arrangements made in response;
- (d) the injury, ailment, condition or other reason which made it necessary to make the arrangements in (a) to (c); See Note 9G.
- (e) any clinical directions and advice, including any further clarifications, given to police by a healthcare professional concerning the care and treatment of the detainee in connection with any of the arrangements made in (a) to (c); See Notes 9E and 9F.
- (f) if applicable, the responses received when attempting to rouse a person using the procedure in Annex H. (See Note 9H.)

9.16 If a healthcare professional does not record their clinical findings in the custody record, the record must show where they are recorded. See Note 9G. However, information which is necessary to custody staff to ensure the effective ongoing care and well being of the detainee must be recorded openly in the custody record, see paragraph 3.8 and Annex G, paragraph 7.

9.17 Subject to the requirements of Section 4, the custody record shall include:
- a record of all medication a detainee has in their possession on arrival at the police station;
- a note of any such medication they claim to need but do not have with them.

Notes for Guidance

9A A 'healthcare professional' means a clinically qualified person working within the scope of practice as determined by their relevant statutory regulatory body. Whether a healthcare professional is 'appropriate' depends on the circumstances of the duties they carry out at the time.

9B Whenever possible juveniles and mentally vulnerable detainees should be visited more frequently.

9C A detainee who appears drunk or behaves abnormally may be suffering from illness, the effects of drugs or may have sustained injury, particularly a head injury which is not apparent. A detainee needing or dependent on certain drugs, including alcohol, may experience harmful effects within a short time of being deprived of their supply. In these circumstances, when there is any doubt, police should always act urgently to call an appropriate healthcare professional or an ambulance. Paragraph 9.5 does not apply to minor ailments or injuries which do not need attention. However, all such ailments or injuries must be recorded in the custody record and any doubt must be resolved in favour of calling the appropriate healthcare professional.

9CA Paragraph 9.3 would apply to a person in police custody by order of a magistrates' court under the Criminal Justice Act 1988, section 152 (as amended by the Drugs Act 2005, section 8) to facilitate the recovery of evidence after being charged with drug possession or drug trafficking and suspected of having swallowed drugs. In the case of the healthcare needs of a person who has swallowed drugs, the custody officer subject to any clinical directions, should consider the necessity for rousing every half hour. This does not negate the need for regular visiting of the suspect in the cell.

9D Except as allowed for under The Mental Health Act 1983 (Places of Safety) Regulations 2017, a police station must not be used as a place of safety for persons detained under section 135 or 136 of that Act. Chapter 16 of the Mental Health Act 1983 Code of Practice (as revised), provides more detailed guidance about arranging assessments under the Mental Health Act and transferring detainees from police stations to other places of safety. Additional guidance in relation to amendments made to the Mental Health Act in 2017 are published at … .

9E It is important to respect a person's right to privacy and information about their health must be kept confidential and only disclosed with their consent or in accordance with clinical advice when it is necessary to protect the detainee's health or that of others who come into contact with them.

9F The custody officer should always seek to clarify directions that the detainee requires constant observation or supervision and should ask the appropriate healthcare professional to explain precisely what action needs to be taken to implement such directions.

9G Paragraphs 9.15 and 9.16 do not require any information about the cause of any injury, ailment or condition to be recorded on the custody record if it appears capable of providing evidence of an offence.

9H The purpose of recording a person's responses when attempting to rouse them using the procedure in Annex H is to enable any change in the individual's consciousness level to be noted and clinical treatment arranged if appropriate.

10. Cautions

(a) When a caution must be given

10.1 A person whom there are grounds to suspect of an offence, see Note 10A, must be cautioned before any questions about an offence, or further questions if the answers provide the grounds for suspicion, are put to them if either the suspect's answers or silence, (i.e. failure or refusal to answer or answer satisfactorily) may be given in evidence to a court in a prosecution. A person need not be cautioned if questions are for other necessary purposes, e.g.:

(a)   solely to establish their identity or ownership of any vehicle;

(b)   to obtain information in accordance with any relevant statutory requirement, see paragraph 10.9;

(c)   in furtherance of the proper and effective conduct of a search, e.g. to determine the need to search in the exercise of powers of stop and search or to seek co-operation while carrying out a search;

(d)   to seek verification of a written record as in paragraph 11.13.

(e)   *Not used.*

10.2 Whenever a person not under arrest is initially cautioned, or reminded that they are under caution, that person must at the same time be told they are not under arrest and must be informed of the provisions of paragraphs 3.21 to 3.21B which explain that they need to agree to be interviewed, how they may obtain legal advice according to whether they are at a police station or elsewhere and the other rights and entitlements that apply to a voluntary interview. See Note 10C.

10.3 A person who is arrested, or further arrested, must be informed at the time if practicable, or if not, as soon as it becomes practicable thereafter, that they are under arrest and of the grounds and reasons for their arrest, see paragraph 3.4, Note 10B and Code G, paragraphs 2.2 and 4.3.

10.4 As required by Code G, section 3, a person who is arrested, or further arrested, must also be cautioned unless:

(a)   it is impracticable to do so by reason of their condition or behaviour at the time;

(b)   they have already been cautioned immediately prior to arrest as in paragraph 10.1.

(b) Terms of the cautions

10.5 The caution which must be given on:

(a)   arrest;

(b)   all other occasions before a person is charged or informed they may be prosecuted; see section 16,

should, unless the restriction on drawing adverse inferences from silence applies, see Annex C, be in the following terms:

> *'You do not have to say anything. But it may harm your defence if you do not mention when questioned something which you later rely on in Court. Anything you do say may be given in evidence.'*

Where the use of the Welsh Language is appropriate, a constable may provide the caution directly in Welsh in the following terms:

> *'Does dim rhaid i chi ddweud dim byd. Ond gall niweidio eich amddiffyniad os na fyddwch chi'n sôn, wrth gael eich holi, am rywbeth y byddwch chi'n dibynnu arno nes ymlaen yn y Llys. Gall unrhyw beth yr ydych yn ei ddweud gael ei roi fel tystiolaeth.'*

(See Note 10G.)

10.6 Annex C, paragraph 2 sets out the alternative terms of the caution to be used when the restriction on drawing adverse inferences from silence applies.

10.7 Minor deviations from the words of any caution given in accordance with this Code do not constitute a breach of this Code, provided the sense of the relevant caution is preserved. (See Note 10D.)

10.8 After any break in questioning under caution, the person being questioned must be made aware they remain under caution. If there is any doubt the relevant caution should be given again in full when the interview resumes. See Note 10E.

10.9 When, despite being cautioned, a person fails to co-operate or to answer particular questions which may affect their immediate treatment, the person should be informed of any relevant consequences and that those consequences are not affected by the caution. Examples are when a person's refusal to provide:

- their name and address when charged may make them liable to detention;
- particulars and information in accordance with a statutory requirement, e.g. under the Road Traffic Act 1988, may amount to an offence or may make the person liable to a further arrest.

(c) Special warnings under the Criminal Justice and Public Order Act 1994, sections 36 and 37

10.10 When a suspect interviewed at a police station or authorised place of detention after arrest fails or refuses to answer certain questions, or to answer satisfactorily, after due warning, see Note 10F, a court or jury may draw such inferences as appear proper under the Criminal Justice and Public Order Act 1994, sections 36 and 37. Such inferences may only be drawn when:

(a)   the restriction on drawing adverse inferences from silence, see Annex C, does not apply; and

(b)   the suspect is arrested by a constable and fails or refuses to account for any objects, marks or substances, or marks on such objects found:

- on their person;
- in or on their clothing or footwear;
- otherwise in their possession; or
- in the place they were arrested;

(c)   the arrested suspect was found by a constable at a place at or about the time the offence for which that officer has arrested them is alleged to have been committed, and the suspect fails or refuses to account for their presence there.

When the restriction on drawing adverse inferences from silence applies, the suspect may still be asked to account for any of the matters in (b) or (c) but the special warning described in paragraph 10.11 will not apply and must not be given.

10.11 For an inference to be drawn when a suspect fails or refuses to answer a question about one of these matters or to answer it satisfactorily, the suspect must first be told in ordinary language:

(a)   what offence is being investigated;

(b) what fact they are being asked to account for;

(c) this fact may be due to them taking part in the commission of the offence;

(d) a court may draw a proper inference if they fail or refuse to account for this fact;

(e) a record is being made of the interview and it may be given in evidence if they are brought to trial.

(d) Juveniles and vulnerable persons

10.11A The information required in paragraph 10.11 must not be given to a suspect who is a juvenile or a vulnerable person unless the appropriate adult is present.

10.12 If a juvenile or a vulnerable person is cautioned in the absence of the appropriate adult, the caution must be repeated in the appropriate adult's presence.

10.12A *Not used.*

(e) Documentation

10.13 A record shall be made when a caution is given under this section, either in the interviewer's report book or in the interview record.

Notes for Guidance

10A There must be some reasonable, objective grounds for the suspicion, based on known facts or information which are relevant to the likelihood the offence has been committed and the person to be questioned committed it.

10B An arrested person must be given sufficient information to enable them to understand that they have been deprived of their liberty and the reason they have been arrested, e.g. when a person is arrested on suspicion of committing an offence they must be informed of the suspected offence's nature, when and where it was committed. The suspect must also be informed of the reason or reasons why the arrest is considered necessary. Vague or technical language should be avoided.

10C The restriction on drawing inferences from silence, see Annex C, paragraph 1, does not apply to a person who has not been detained and who therefore cannot be prevented from seeking legal advice if they want, see paragraph 3.21.

10D If it appears a person does not understand the caution, the person giving it should explain it in their own words.

10E It may be necessary to show to the court that nothing occurred during an interview break or between interviews which influenced the suspect's recorded evidence. After a break in an interview or at the beginning of a subsequent interview, the interviewing officer should summarise the reason for the break and confirm this with the suspect.

10F The Criminal Justice and Public Order Act 1994, sections 36 and 37 apply only to suspects who have been arrested by a constable or an officer of Revenue and Customs and are given the relevant warning by the police or Revenue and Customs officer who made the arrest or who is investigating the offence. They do not apply to any interviews with suspects who have not been arrested.

10G Nothing in this Code requires a caution to be given or repeated when informing a person not under arrest they may be prosecuted for an offence. However, a court will not be able to draw any inferences under the Criminal Justice and Public Order Act 1994, section 34, if the person was not cautioned.

11. Interviews - general

(a) Action

11.1A An interview is the questioning of a person regarding their involvement or suspected involvement in a criminal offence or offences which, under paragraph 10.1, must be carried out under caution. Before a person is interviewed, they and, if they are represented, their solicitor must be given sufficient information to enable them to understand the nature of any such offence, and why they are suspected of committing it (see paragraphs 3.4(a) and 10.3), in order to allow for the effective exercise of the rights of the defence. However, whilst the information must always be sufficient for the person to understand the nature of any offence (see Note 11ZA), this does not require the disclosure of details at a time which might prejudice the criminal investigation. The decision about what needs to be disclosed for the purpose of this requirement therefore rests with the investigating officer who has sufficient knowledge of the case to make that decision. The officer who discloses the information shall make a record of the information disclosed and when it was disclosed. This record may be made in the interview record, in the officer's report book or other form provided for this purpose. Procedures under the Road Traffic Act 1988, section 7 or the Transport and Works Act 1992, section 31 do not constitute interviewing for the purpose of this Code.

11.1 Following a decision to arrest a suspect, they must not be interviewed about the relevant offence except at a police station or other authorised place of detention, unless the consequent delay would be likely to:

(a)   lead to:
  • interference with, or harm to, evidence connected with an offence;
  • interference with, or physical harm to, other people; or
  • serious loss of, or damage to, property;

(b)   lead to alerting other people suspected of committing an offence but not yet arrested for it; or

(c)   hinder the recovery of property obtained in consequence of the commission of an offence.

Interviewing in any of these circumstances shall cease once the relevant risk has been averted or the necessary questions have been put in order to attempt to avert that risk.

11.2 Immediately prior to the commencement or re-commencement of any interview at a police station or other authorised place of detention, the interviewer should remind the suspect of their entitlement to free legal advice and that the interview can be delayed for legal advice to be obtained, unless one of the exceptions in paragraph 6.6 applies. It is the interviewer's responsibility to make sure all reminders are recorded in the interview record.

11.3 *Not used.*

11.4 At the beginning of an interview the interviewer, after cautioning the suspect, see section 10, shall put to them any significant statement or silence which occurred in the presence and hearing of a police officer or other police staff before the start of the interview and which have not been put to the suspect in the course of a previous interview. See Note 11A. The interviewer shall ask the suspect whether they confirm or deny that earlier statement or silence and if they want to add anything.

11.4A A significant statement is one which appears capable of being used in evidence against the suspect, in particular a direct admission of guilt. A significant silence is a failure or refusal to answer a question or answer satisfactorily when under caution, which might, allowing for the restriction on drawing adverse inferences from silence, see Annex C, give rise to an inference under the Criminal Justice and Public Order Act 1994, Part III.

11.5 No interviewer may try to obtain answers or elicit a statement by the use of oppression. Except as in paragraph 10.9, no interviewer shall indicate, except to answer a direct question, what action will be taken by the police if the person being questioned answers questions, makes a statement or refuses to do either. If the person asks directly what action will be taken if they answer questions, make a statement or refuse to do either, the interviewer may inform them what action the police propose to take provided that action is itself proper and warranted.

11.6 The interview or further interview of a person about an offence with which that person has not been charged or for which they have not been informed they may be prosecuted, must cease when:

(a)   the officer in charge of the investigation is satisfied all the questions they consider relevant to obtaining accurate and reliable information about the offence have been put to the suspect, this includes allowing the suspect an opportunity to give an innocent explanation and asking questions to test if the explanation is accurate and reliable, e.g. to clear up ambiguities or clarify what the suspect said;

(b)   the officer in charge of the investigation has taken account of any other available evidence; and

(c)   the officer in charge of the investigation, or in the case of a detained suspect, the custody officer, see paragraph 16.1, reasonably believes there is sufficient evidence to provide a realistic prospect of conviction for that offence. See Note 11B.

This paragraph does not prevent officers in revenue cases or acting under the confiscation provisions of the Criminal Justice Act 1988 or the Drug Trafficking Act 1994 from inviting suspects to complete a formal question and answer record after the interview is concluded.

(b) Interview records

11.7 (a) An accurate record must be made of each interview, whether or not the interview takes place at a police station.

   (b) The record must state the place of interview, the time it begins and ends, any interview breaks and, subject to paragraph 2.6A, the names of all those present; and must be made on the forms provided for this purpose or in the interviewer's pocket book or in accordance with the Codes of Practice E or F.

   (c) Any written record must be made and completed during the interview, unless this would not be practicable or would interfere with the conduct of the interview, and must constitute either a verbatim record of what has been said or, failing this, an account of the interview which adequately and accurately summarises it.

11.8 If a written record is not made during the interview it must be made as soon as practicable after its completion.

11.9 Written interview records must be timed and signed by the maker.

11.10 If a written record is not completed during the interview the reason must be recorded in the interview record.

11.11 Unless it is impracticable, the person interviewed shall be given the opportunity to read the interview record and to sign it as correct or to indicate how they consider it inaccurate. If the person interviewed cannot read or refuses to read the record or sign it, the senior interviewer present shall read it to them and ask whether they would like to sign it as correct or make their mark or to indicate how they consider it inaccurate. The interviewer shall certify on the interview record itself what has occurred. See Note 11E.

11.12 If the appropriate adult or the person's solicitor is present during the interview, they should also be given an opportunity to read and sign the interview record or any written statement taken down during the interview.

11.13 A written record shall be made of any comments made by a suspect, including unsolicited comments, which are outside the context of an interview but which might be relevant to the offence. Any such record must be timed and signed by the maker. When practicable the suspect shall be given the opportunity to read that record and to sign it as correct or to indicate how they consider it inaccurate. (See Note 11E.)

11.14 Any refusal by a person to sign an interview record when asked in accordance with this Code must itself be recorded.

(c) Juveniles and vulnerable persons

11.15 A juvenile or vulnerable person must not be interviewed regarding their involvement or suspected involvement in a criminal offence or offences, or asked to provide or sign a written statement under caution or record of interview, in the absence of the appropriate adult unless paragraphs 11.1 or 11.18 to 11.20 apply. See Note 11C.

11.16 Juveniles may only be interviewed at their place of education in exceptional circumstances and only when the principal or their nominee agrees. Every effort should be made to notify the parent(s) or other person responsible for the juvenile's welfare and the appropriate adult, if this is a different person, that the police want to interview the juvenile and reasonable time should be allowed to enable the appropriate adult to be present at the interview. If awaiting the appropriate adult would cause unreasonable delay, and unless the juvenile is suspected of an offence against the educational establishment, the principal or their nominee can act as the appropriate adult for the purposes of the interview.

11.17 If an appropriate adult is present at an interview, they shall be informed:
- that they are not expected to act simply as an observer; and
- that the purpose of their presence is to:
  - advise the person being interviewed;
  - observe whether the interview is being conducted properly and fairly; and
  - facilitate communication with the person being interviewed.

   See paragraph 1.7A.

11.17A The appropriate adult may be required to leave the interview if their conduct is such that the interviewer is unable properly to put questions to the suspect. This will include situations where the appropriate adult's approach or conduct prevents or unreasonably obstructs proper questions being put to the suspect or the suspect's responses being recorded (see Note 11F). If the interviewer considers an appropriate adult is acting in such a way, they will stop the interview and consult an officer not below superintendent rank, if one is readily available, and otherwise an officer not below inspector rank not connected with the investigation. After speaking to the appropriate adult, the officer consulted must remind the adult that their role under paragraph 11.17 does not allow them to obstruct proper questioning and give the adult an opportunity to respond. The officer consulted will then decide if the interview should continue without the attendance of that appropriate adult. If they decide it should, another appropriate adult must be obtained before the interview continues, unless the provisions of paragraph 11.18 below apply.

(d)   Vulnerable suspects - urgent interviews at police stations

11.18 The following interviews may take place only if an officer of superintendent rank or above considers delaying the interview will lead to the consequences in paragraph 11.1(a) to (c), and is satisfied the interview would not significantly harm the person's physical or mental state (see Annex G):

(a)   an interview of a detained juvenile or vulnerable person without the appropriate adult being present (see Note 11C);

(b)   an interview of anyone detained other than in (a) who appears unable to:
  • appreciate the significance of questions and their answers; or
  • understand what is happening because of the effects of drink, drugs or any illness, ailment or condition;

(c)   an interview, without an interpreter having been arranged, of a detained person whom the custody officer has determined requires an interpreter (see paragraphs 3.5(c)(ii) and 3.12) which is carried out by an interviewer speaking the suspect's own language or (as the case may be) otherwise establishing effective communication which is sufficient to enable the necessary questions to be asked and answered in order to avert the consequences. See paragraphs 13.2 and 13.5.

11.19 These interviews may not continue once sufficient information has been obtained to avert the consequences in paragraph 11.1(a) to (c).

11.20 A record shall be made of the grounds for any decision to interview a person under paragraph 11.18.

(e)   Conduct and recording of Interviews at police stations - use of live link

11.21 When a suspect in police detention is interviewed using a live link by a police officer who is not at the police station where the detainee is held, the provisions of this section that govern the conduct and making a written record of that interview, shall be subject to paragraph 12.9B of this Code.

(f)   Witnesses

11.22 The provisions of this Code and Codes E and F which govern the conduct and recording of interviews do not apply to interviews with, or taking statements from, witnesses.

Notes for Guidance

11ZA The requirement in paragraph 11.1A for a suspect to be given sufficient information about the offence applies prior to the interview and whether or not they are legally represented. What is sufficient will depend on the circumstances of the case, but it should normally include, as a minimum, a description of the facts relating to the suspected offence that are known to the officer, including the time and place in question. This aims to avoid suspects being confused or unclear about what they are supposed to have done and to help an innocent suspect to clear the matter up more quickly.

11A Paragraph 11.4 does not prevent the interviewer from putting significant statements and silences to a suspect again at a later stage or a further interview.

11B The Criminal Procedure and Investigations Act 1996 Code of Practice, paragraph 3.5 states 'In conducting an investigation, the investigator should pursue all reasonable lines of enquiry, whether these point towards or away from the suspect. What is reasonable will depend on the particular circumstances.' Interviewers should keep this in mind when deciding what questions to ask in an interview.

11C Although juveniles or vulnerable persons are often capable of providing reliable evidence, they may, without knowing or wishing to do so, be particularly prone in certain circumstances to providing information that may be unreliable, misleading or self-incriminating. Special care should always be taken when questioning such a person, and the appropriate adult should be involved if there is any doubt about a person's age, mental state or capacity. Because of the risk of unreliable evidence it is also important to obtain corroboration of any facts admitted whenever possible. Because of the risks, which the presence of the appropriate adult is intended to minimise, officers of superintendent rank or above should exercise their discretion under paragraph 11.18(a) to authorise the commencement of an interview in the appropriate adult's absence only in exceptional cases, if it is necessary to avert one or more of the specified risks in paragraph 11.1.

11D Juveniles should not be arrested at their place of education unless this is unavoidable. When a juvenile is arrested at their place of education, the principal or their nominee must be informed.

11E Significant statements described in paragraph 11.4 will always be relevant to the offence and must be recorded. When a suspect agrees to read records of interviews and other comments and sign them as correct, they should be asked to endorse the record with, e.g. 'I agree that this is a correct record of what was said' and add their signature. If the suspect does not agree with the record, the interviewer should record the details of any disagreement and ask the suspect to read these details and sign them to the effect that they accurately reflect their disagreement. Any refusal to sign should be recorded.

11F The appropriate adult may intervene if they consider it is necessary to help the suspect understand any question asked and to help the suspect to answer any question. Paragraph 11.17A only applies if the appropriate adult's approach or conduct prevents or unreasonably obstructs proper questions being put to the suspect or the suspect's response being recorded. Examples of unacceptable conduct include answering questions on a suspect's behalf or providing written replies for the suspect to quote. An officer who takes the decision to exclude an appropriate adult must be in a position to satisfy the court the decision was properly made. In order to do this they may need to witness what is happening and give the suspect's solicitor (if they have one) who witnessed what happened, an opportunity to comment.

12. Interviews in police stations

(a) Action

When interviewer and suspect are present at the same police station

12.1 If a police officer wants to interview or conduct enquiries which require the presence of a detainee, the custody officer is responsible for deciding whether to deliver the detainee into the officer's custody. An investigating officer who is given custody of a detainee takes over responsibility for the detainee's care and safe custody for the purposes of this Code until they return the detainee to the custody officer when they must report the manner in which they complied with the Code whilst having custody of the detainee.

12.2 Except as below, in any period of 24 hours a detainee must be allowed a continuous period of at least 8 hours for rest, free from questioning, travel or any interruption in connection with the investigation concerned. This period should normally be at night or other appropriate time which takes account of when the detainee last slept or rested. If a detainee is arrested at a police station after going there voluntarily, the period of 24 hours runs from the time of their arrest and not the time of arrival at the police station. The period may not be interrupted or delayed, except:

    (a)   when there are reasonable grounds for believing not delaying or interrupting the period would:

        (i)   involve a risk of harm to people or serious loss of, or damage to, property;

        (ii)   delay unnecessarily the person's release from custody;

        (iii)   otherwise prejudice the outcome of the investigation;

    (b)   at the request of the detainee, their appropriate adult or legal representative;

    (c)   when a delay or interruption is necessary in order to:

        (i)   comply with the legal obligations and duties arising under section 15;

        (ii)   to take action required under section 9 or in accordance with medical advice.

If the period is interrupted in accordance with (a), a fresh period must be allowed. Interruptions under (b) and (c), do not require a fresh period to be allowed.

12.3 Before a detainee is interviewed the custody officer, in consultation with the officer in charge of the investigation and appropriate healthcare professionals as necessary, shall assess whether the detainee is fit enough to be interviewed. This means determining and considering the risks to the detainee's physical and mental state if the interview took place and determining what safeguards are needed to allow the interview to take place. See Annex G. The custody officer shall not allow a detainee to be interviewed if the custody officer considers it would cause significant harm to the detainee's physical or mental state. Vulnerable suspects listed at paragraph 11.18 shall be treated as always being at some risk during an interview and these persons may not be interviewed except in accordance with paragraphs 11.18 to 11.20.

12.4 As far as practicable interviews shall take place in interview rooms which are adequately heated, lit and ventilated.

12.5 A suspect whose detention without charge has been authorised under PACE, because the detention is necessary for an interview to obtain evidence of the offence for which they have been arrested, may choose not to answer questions but police do not require the suspect's consent or agreement to interview them for this purpose. If a suspect takes steps to prevent themselves being questioned or further questioned, e.g. by refusing to leave their cell to go to a suitable interview room or by trying to leave the interview room, they shall be advised their consent or agreement to interview is not required. The suspect shall be cautioned as in section 10, and informed if they fail or refuse to co-operate, the interview may take place in the cell and that their failure or refusal to co-operate may be given in evidence. The suspect shall then be invited to co-operate and go into the interview room.

12.6 People being questioned or making statements shall not be required to stand.

12.7 Before the interview commences each interviewer shall, subject to paragraph 2.6A, identify themselves and any other persons present to the interviewee.

12.8 Breaks from interviewing should be made at recognised meal times or at other times that take account of when an interviewee last had a meal. Short refreshment breaks shall be provided at approximately two hour intervals, subject to the interviewer's discretion to delay a break if there are reasonable grounds for believing it would:
(i)　　involve a:
- risk of harm to people;
- serious loss of, or damage to, property;
(i)　　unnecessarily delay the detainee's release;
(ii)　　otherwise prejudice the outcome of the investigation.
　　　　(See Note 12B.)

12.9 If during the interview a complaint is made by or on behalf of the interviewee concerning the provisions of any of the Codes, or it comes to the interviewer's notice that the interviewee may have been treated improperly, the interviewer should:
(i)　　record the matter in the interview record;
(ii)　　inform the custody officer, who is then responsible for dealing with it as in section 9.

Interviewer not present at the same station as the detainee – use of live link

12.9A Amendments to PACE, section 39, allow a person in police detention to be interviewed using a live link (see paragraph 1.13(e)(i)) by a police officer who is not at the police station where the detainee is held. Subject to sub-paragraphs (a) to (f) below, the custody officer is responsible for deciding on a case by case basis whether a detainee is fit to be interviewed (see paragraph 12.3) and should be delivered into the physical custody of an officer who is not involved in the investigation, for the purpose of enabling another officer who is investigating the offence for which the person is detained and who is not at the police station where the person is detained, to interview the detainee by means of a live link (see Note 12ZA).
(a)　　The custody officer must be satisfied that the live link to be used provides for accurate and secure communication with the suspect. The provisions of paragraph 13.13 shall apply to communications between the interviewing officer, the suspect and anyone else whose presence at the interview or, (as the case may be) whose access to any communications between the suspect and the interviewer, has been authorised by the custody officer or the interviewing officer.

(b)   Each decision must take account of the age, gender and vulnerability of the suspect, the nature and circumstances of the offence and the investigation and the impact on the suspect of carrying out the interview by means of a live link. For this reason, the custody officer must consider whether the ability of the particular suspect, to communicate confidently and effectively for the purpose of the interview is likely to be adversely affected or otherwise undermined or limited if the interviewing officer is not physically present and a live-link is used (see Note 12ZB). Although a suspect for whom an appropriate adult is required may be more likely to be adversely affected as described, it is important to note that a person who does not require an appropriate adult may also be adversely impacted if interviewed by means of a live link.

(c)   If the custody officer is satisfied that interviewing the detainee by means of a live link would not adversely affect or otherwise undermine or limit the suspect's ability to communicate confidently and effectively for the purpose of the interview, the officer must so inform the suspect, their solicitor and (if applicable) the appropriate adult. At the same time, the operation of the live-link must be explained and demonstrated to them (see Note 12ZC), they must be advised of the chief officer's obligations concerning the security of live-link communications under paragraph 13.13 and they must be asked if they wish to make representations that the live-link should not be used or if they require more information about the operation of the arrangements. They must also be told that at any time live-link is in use, they may make representations to the custody officer or the interviewer that its operation should cease and that the physical presence of the interviewer should be arranged.

When the authority of an inspector is required

(d)   If:
  (i)   representations are made that a live-link should not be used to carry out the interview, or that at any time it is in use, its operation should cease and the physical presence of the interviewer arranged; and
  (ii)   the custody officer in consultation with the interviewer is unable to allay the concerns raised;
         then live-link may not be used, or (as the case may be) continue to be used, unless authorised in writing by an officer of the rank of inspector or above in accordance with sub-paragraph (e).

(e)   Authority may be given if the officer is satisfied that interviewing the detainee by means of a live link is necessary and justified. In making this decision, the officer must have regard to:
  (i)   the circumstances of the suspect;
  (ii)   the nature and seriousness of the offence;
  (iii)   the requirements of the investigation, including its likely impact on both the suspect and any victim(s);
  (iv)   the representations made by the suspect, their solicitor and (if applicable) the appropriate adult that a live-link should not be used (see sub-paragraph (b));
  (v)   the impact on the investigation of making arrangements for the physical presence of the interviewer (see Note 12ZD); and
  (vi)   the risk if the interpreter is not physically present, evidence obtained using link interpretation might be excluded in subsequent criminal proceedings; and (vii) the likely impact on the suspect and the investigation of any consequential delay to arrange for the interpreter to be physically present with the suspect.

(f)   The officer given custody of the detainee and the interviewer take over responsibility for the detainee's care, treatment and safe custody for the purposes of this Code until the detainee is returned to the custody officer. On that return, both must report the manner in which they complied with the Code during period in question.

12.9B When a suspect detained at a police station is interviewed using a live link in accordance with paragraph 12.9A, the officer given custody of the detainee at the police station and the interviewer who is not present at the police station, take over responsibility for ensuring compliance with the provisions of sections 11 and 12 of this

Code, or Code E (Audio recording) or Code F (Audio visual recording) that govern the conduct and recording of that interview. In these circumstances:

(a)   the interviewer who is not at the police station where the detainee is held must direct the officer having physical custody of the suspect at the police station, to take the action required by those provisions and which the interviewer would be required to take if they were present at the police station.

(b)   the officer having physical custody of the suspect at the police station must take the action required by those provisions and which would otherwise be required to be taken by the interviewer if they were present at the police station. This applies whether or not the officer has been so directed by the interviewer but in such a case, the officer must inform the interviewer of the action taken.

(c)   during the course of the interview, the officers in (a) and (b) may consult each other as necessary to clarify any action to be taken and to avoid any misunderstanding. Such consultations must, if in the hearing of the suspect and any other person present with the suspect (for example, a solicitor, appropriate adult or interpreter) be recorded in the interview record.

(b) Documentation

12.10 A record must be made of the:

- time a detainee is not in the custody of the custody officer, and why
- reason for any refusal to deliver the detainee out of that custody.

12.11 A record shall be made of:

(a)   the reasons it was not practicable to use an interview room; and

(b)   any action taken as in paragraph 12.5.

The record shall be made on the custody record or in the interview record for action taken whilst an interview record is being kept, with a brief reference to this effect in the custody record.

12.12 Any decision to delay a break in an interview must be recorded, with reasons, in the interview record.

12.13 All written statements made at police stations under caution shall be written on forms provided for the purpose.

12.14 All written statements made under caution shall be taken in accordance with Annex D. Before a person makes a written statement under caution at a police station they shall be reminded about the right to legal advice. See Note 12A.

Notes for Guidance

12ZA 'Live link' means an arrangement by means of which the interviewing officer who is not at the police station is able to see and hear, and to be seen and heard by, the detainee concerned, the detainee's solicitor, any appropriate adult present and the officer who has custody of that detainee. See paragraphs 13.12 to 13.14 and Annex N for application to live-link interpretation.

12ZB In considering whether the use of the live link is appropriate in a particular case, the custody officer, in consultation with the interviewer, should make an assessment of the detainee's ability to understand and take part in the interviewing process and make a record of the outcome. If the suspect has asked for legal advice, their solicitor should be involved in the assessment and in the case of a juvenile or vulnerable person, the appropriate adult should be involved.

12ZC The explanation and demonstration of live-link interpretation is intended to help the suspect, solicitor and appropriate adult make an informed decision and to allay any concerns they may have.

12ZD Factors affecting the arrangements for the interviewer to be physically present will include the location of the police station where the interview would take place and the availability of an interviewer with sufficient knowledge of the investigation who can attend that station and carry out the interview.

12A It is not normally necessary to ask for a written statement if the interview was recorded in writing and the record signed in accordance with paragraph 11.11 or audibly or visually recorded in accordance with Code E or F. Statements under caution should normally be taken in these circumstances only at the person's express wish. A person may however be asked if they want to make such a statement.

12B Meal breaks should normally last at least 45 minutes and shorter breaks after two hours should last at least 15 minutes. If the interviewer delays a break in accordance with paragraph 12.8 and prolongs the interview, a longer break should be provided. If there is a short interview, and another short interview is contemplated, the length of the break may be reduced if there are reasonable grounds to believe this is necessary to avoid any of the consequences in paragraph 12.8(i) to (ii).

13. Interpreters

(a) General

13.1 Chief officers are responsible for making arrangements (see paragraph 13.1ZA) to provide appropriately qualified independent persons to act as interpreters and to provide translations of essential documents for:

(a)   detained suspects who, in accordance with paragraph 3.5(c)(ii), the custody officer has determined require an interpreter, and

(b)   suspects who are not under arrest but are cautioned as in section 10 who, in accordance with paragraph 3.21(b), the interviewer has determined require an interpreter. In these cases, the responsibilities of the custody officer are, if appropriate, assigned to the interviewer. An interviewer who has any doubts about whether and what arrangements for an interpreter must be made or about how the provisions of this section should be applied to a suspect who is not under arrest should seek advice from an officer of the rank of sergeant or above.

If the suspect has a hearing or speech impediment, references to 'interpreter' and 'interpretation' in this Code include arrangements for appropriate assistance necessary to establish effective communication with that person. See paragraph 13.1C below if the person is in Wales.

13.1ZA References in paragraph 13.1 above and elsewhere in this Code (see paragraphs 3.12(a), 13.2, 13.2A, 13.5, 13.6, 13.9, 13.10, 13.10A, 13.10D and 13.11 below and in any other Code, to making arrangements for an interpreter to assist a suspect, mean making arrangements for the interpreter to be physically present in the same location as the suspect unless the provisions in paragraph 13.12 below, and Part 1 of Annex N, allow live-link interpretation to be used.

13.1A The arrangements must comply with the minimum requirements set out in Directive 2010/64/EU of the European Parliament and of the Council of 20 October 2010 on the right to interpretation and translation in criminal proceedings (see Note 13A). The provisions of this Code implement the requirements for those to whom this Code applies. These requirements include the following:

- That the arrangements made and the quality of interpretation and translation provided shall be sufficient to 'safeguard the fairness of the proceedings, in particular by ensuring that suspected or accused persons have knowledge of the cases against them and are able to exercise their right of defence'. This term which is used by the Directive means that the suspect must be able to understand their position and be able to communicate effectively with police officers, interviewers, solicitors and appropriate adults as provided for by this and any other Code in the same way as a suspect who can speak and understand English and who does not have a hearing or speech impediment and who would therefore not require an interpreter. See paragraphs 13.12 to 13.14 and Annex N for application to live-link interpretation.
- The provision of a written translation of all documents considered essential for the person to exercise their right of defence and to 'safeguard the fairness of the proceedings' as described above. For the purposes of this Code, this includes any decision to authorise a person to be detained and details of any offence(s) with which the person has been charged or for which they have been told they may be prosecuted, see Annex M.
- Procedures to help determine:
  - whether a suspect can speak and understand English and needs the assistance of an interpreter, see paragraph 13.1 and Notes 13B and 13C; and
  - whether another interpreter should be arranged or another translation should be provided when a suspect complains about the quality of either or both, see paragraphs 13.10A and 13.10C.

13.1B All reasonable attempts should be made to make the suspect understand that interpretation and translation will be provided at public expense.

13.1C With regard to persons in Wales, nothing in this or any other Code affects the application of the Welsh Language Schemes produced by police and crime commissioners in Wales in accordance with the Welsh Language Act 1993. See paragraphs 3.12 and 13.1.

(b) Interviewing suspects - foreign languages

13.2 Unless paragraphs 11.1 or 11.18(c) apply, a suspect who for the purposes of this Code requires an interpreter because they do not appear to speak or understand English (see paragraphs 3.5(c)(ii) and 3.12) must not be interviewed unless arrangements are made for a person capable of interpreting to assist the suspect to understand and communicate.

13.2A If a person who is a juvenile or is mentally disordered or mentally vulnerable is interviewed and the person acting as the appropriate adult does not appear to speak or understand English, arrangements must be made for an interpreter to assist communication between the person, the appropriate adult and the interviewer, unless the interview is urgent and paragraphs 11.1 or 11.18(c) apply.

13.3 When a written record of the interview is made (see paragraph 11.7), the interviewer shall make sure the interpreter makes a note of the interview at the time in the person's language for use in the event of the interpreter being called to give evidence, and certifies its accuracy. The interviewer should allow sufficient time for the interpreter to note each question and answer after each is put, given and interpreted. The person should be allowed to read the record or have it read to them and sign it as correct or indicate the respects in which they consider it inaccurate. If an audio or visual record of the interview is made, the arrangements in Code E or F shall apply. See paragraphs 13.12 to 13.14 and Annex N for application to live-link interpretation.

13.4 In the case of a person making a statement under caution (see Annex D) to a police officer or other police staff in a language other than English:
  (a)   the interpreter shall record the statement in the language it is made;
  (b)   the person shall be invited to sign it;
  (c)   an official English translation shall be made in due course.
See paragraphs 13.12 to 13.14 and Annex N for application to live-link interpretation.

(c) Interviewing suspects who have a hearing or speech impediment.

13.5 Unless paragraphs 11.1 or 11.18(c) (urgent interviews) apply, a suspect who for the purposes of this Code requires an interpreter or other appropriate assistance to enable effective communication with them because they appear to have a hearing or speech impediment (see paragraphs 3.5(c)(ii) and 3.12) must not be interviewed without arrangements having been made to provide an independent person capable of interpreting or of providing other appropriate assistance.

13.6 An interpreter should also be arranged if a person who is a juvenile or who is mentally disordered or mentally vulnerable is interviewed and the person who is present as the appropriate adult, appears to have a hearing or speech impediment, unless the interview is urgent and paragraphs 11.1 or 11.18(c) apply.

13.7 If a written record of the interview is made, the interviewer shall make sure the interpreter is allowed to read the record and certify its accuracy in the event of the interpreter being called to give evidence. If an audio or visual recording is made, the arrangements in Code E or F apply.
See paragraphs 13.12 to 13.14 and Annex N for application to live-link interpretation.

(d) Additional rules for detained persons

13.8 *Not used.*

13.9 If paragraph 6.1 applies and the detainee cannot communicate with the solicitor because of language, hearing or speech difficulties, arrangements must be made for an interpreter to enable communication. A police officer or any other police staff may not be used for this purpose.

13.10 After the custody officer has determined that a detainee requires an interpreter (see paragraph 3.5(c)(ii)) and following the initial action in paragraphs 3.1 to 3.5, arrangements must also be made for an interpreter to:
- explain the grounds and reasons for any authorisation for their continued detention, before or after charge and any information about the authorisation given to them by the authorising officer and which is recorded in the custody record. See paragraphs 15.3, 15.4 and 15.16(a) and (b);
- to provide interpretation at the magistrates' court for the hearing of an application for a warrant of further detention or any extension or further extension of such warrant to explain any grounds and reasons for the application and any information about the authorisation of their further detention given to them by the court (see PACE, sections 43 and 44 and paragraphs 15.2 and 15.16(c)); and
- explain any offence with which the detainee is charged or for which they are informed they may be prosecuted and any other information about the offence given to them by or on behalf of the custody officer, see paragraphs 16.1 and 16.3.

13.10A If a detainee complains that they are not satisfied with the quality of interpretation, the custody officer or (as the case may be) the interviewer, is responsible for deciding whether to make arrangements for a different interpreter in accordance with the procedures set out in the arrangements made by the chief officer, see paragraph 13.1A.

(e) Translations of essential documents

13.10B Written translations, oral translations and oral summaries of essential documents in a language the detainee understands shall be provided in accordance with Annex M (Translations of documents and records).

13.10C If a detainee complains that they are not satisfied with the quality of the translation, the custody officer or (as the case may be) the interviewer, is responsible for deciding whether a further translation should be provided in accordance with the procedures set out in the arrangements made by the chief officer, see paragraph 13.1A.

(f) Decisions not to provide interpretation and translation.

13.10D If a suspect challenges a decision:
- made by the custody officer or (as the case may be) by the interviewer, in accordance with this Code (see paragraphs 3.5(c)(ii) and 3.21(b)) that they do not require an interpreter, or
- made in accordance with paragraphs 13.10A, 13.10B or 13.10C not to make arrangements to provide a different interpreter or another translation or not to translate a requested document,

the matter shall be reported to an inspector to deal with as a complaint for the purposes of paragraph 9.2 or paragraph 12.9 if the challenge is made during an interview.

(g) Documentation

13.11 The following must be recorded in the custody record or, as applicable, the interview record:
- (a) Action taken to arrange for an interpreter, including the live-link requirements in Annex N as applicable;
- (b) Action taken when a detainee is not satisfied about the standard of interpretation or translation provided, see paragraphs 13.10A and 13.10C;
- (c) When an urgent interview is carried out in accordance with paragraph 13.2 or 13.5 in the absence of an interpreter;
- (d) When a detainee has been assisted by an interpreter for the purpose of providing or being given information or being interviewed;
- (e) Action taken in accordance with Annex M when:
  - a written translation of an essential document is provided;
  - an oral translation or oral summary of an essential document is provided instead of a written translation and the authorising officer's reason(s) why this would not prejudice the fairness of the proceedings (see Annex M, paragraph 3);

- a suspect waives their right to a translation of an essential document (see Annex M, paragraph 4);
- when representations that a document which is not included in the table is essential and that a translation should be provided are refused and the reason for the refusal (see Annex M, paragraph 8).

(h) Live-link interpretation

13.12 In this section and in Annex N, 'live-link interpretation' means an arrangement to enable communication between the suspect and an interpreter who is not physically present with the suspect. The arrangement must ensure that anything said by any person in the suspect's presence and hearing can be interpreted in the same way as if the interpreter was physically present at that time. The communication must be by audio and visual means for the purpose of an interview, and for all other purposes it may be either; by audio and visual means, or by audio means only, as follows:

(a) Audio and visual communication

This applies for the purposes of an interview conducted and recorded in accordance with Code E (Audio recording) or Code F (Visual recording) and during that interview, live link interpretation must *enable*:

(i) the suspect, the interviewer, solicitor, appropriate adult and any other person physically present with the suspect at any time during the interview and an interpreter who is not physically present, to see and hear each other; and

(ii) the interview to be conducted and recorded in accordance with the provisions of Codes C, E and F, subject to the modifications in Part 2 of Annex N.

(b) Audio and visual or audio without visual communication.

This applies to communication for the purposes of any provision of this or any other Code except as described in (a), which requires or permits information to be given to, sought from, or provided by a suspect, whether orally or in writing, which would include communication between the suspect and their solicitor and/or appropriate adult, and for these cases, live link interpretation must:

(i) enable the suspect, the person giving or seeking that information, any other person physically present with the suspect at that time and an interpreter who is not so present, to either see and hear each other, or to hear without seeing each other (for example by using a telephone); and

(ii) enable that information to be given to, sought from, or provided by, the suspect in accordance with the provisions of this or any other Code that apply to that information, as modified for the purposes of the live-link, by Part 2 of Annex N.

13.12A The requirement in sub-paragraphs 13.12(a)(ii) and (b)(ii), that live-link interpretation must enable compliance with the relevant provisions of the Codes C, E and F, means that the arrangements must provide for any written or electronic record of what the suspect says in their own language which is made by the interpreter, to be securely transmitted without delay so that the suspect can be invited to read, check and if appropriate, sign or otherwise confirm that the record is correct or make corrections to the record.

13.13 Chief officers must be satisfied that live-link interpretation used in their force area for the purposes of paragraphs 13.12(a) and (b), provides for accurate and secure communication with the suspect. This includes ensuring that at any time during which live link interpretation is being used: a person cannot see, hear or otherwise obtain access to any communications between the suspect and interpreter or communicate with the suspect or interpreter unless so authorised or allowed by the custody officer or, in the case of an interview, the interviewer and that as applicable, the confidentiality of any private consultation between a suspect and their solicitor and appropriate adult (see paragraphs 13.2A, 13.6 and 13.9) is maintained. See Annex N paragraph 4.

Notes for Guidance

13A Chief officers have discretion when determining the individuals or organisations they use to provide interpretation and translation services for their forces provided that these are compatible with the requirements of the Directive. One example which chief officers may wish to consider is the Ministry of Justice commercial agreements for interpretation and translation services.

13B A procedure for determining whether a person needs an interpreter might involve a telephone interpreter service or using cue cards or similar visual aids which enable the detainee to indicate their ability to speak and understand English and their preferred language. This could be confirmed through an interpreter who could also assess the extent to which the person can speak and understand English.

13C There should also be a procedure for determining whether a suspect who requires an interpreter requires assistance in accordance with paragraph 3.20 to help them check and if applicable, sign any documentation.

14. Questioning—special restrictions

14.1 If a person is arrested by one police force on behalf of another and the lawful period of detention in respect of that offence has not yet commenced in accordance with PACE, section 41, no questions may be put to them about the offence while they are in transit between the forces except to clarify any voluntary statement they make.

14.2 If a person is in police detention at a hospital, they may not be questioned without the agreement of a responsible doctor. See Note 14A.

Note for Guidance

14A If questioning takes place at a hospital under paragraph 14.2, or on the way to or from a hospital, the period of questioning concerned counts towards the total period of detention permitted

15. Reviews and extensions of detention

(a) Persons detained under PACE

15.0 The requirement in paragraph 3.4(b) that documents and materials essential to challenging the lawfulness of the detainee's arrest and detention must be made available to the detainee or their solicitor, applies for the purposes of this section as follows:

(a)   The officer reviewing the need for detention without charge (PACE, section 40), or (as the case may be) the officer considering the need to extend detention without charge from 24 to 36 hours (PACE, section 42), is responsible, in consultation with the investigating officer, for deciding which documents and materials are essential and must be made available.

(b)   When paragraph 15.7A applies (application for a warrant of further detention or extension of such a warrant), the officer making the application is responsible for deciding which documents and materials are essential and must be made available before the hearing. See Note 3ZA.

15.1 The review officer is responsible under PACE, section 40 for periodically determining if a person's detention, before or after charge, continues to be necessary. This requirement continues throughout the detention period and except as in paragraph 15.10, the review officer must be present at the police station holding the detainee. See Notes 15A and 15B.

15.2 Under PACE, section 42, an officer of superintendent rank or above who is responsible for the station holding the detainee may give authority any time after the second review to extend the maximum period the person may be detained without charge by up to 12 hours. Further detention without charge may be authorised only by a magistrates' court in accordance with PACE, sections 43 and 44. See Notes 15C, 15D and 15E.

15.2A An authorisation under section 42(1) of PACE extends the maximum period of detention permitted before charge for indictable offences from 24 hours to 36 hours. Detaining a juvenile or mentally vulnerable person for longer than 24 hours will be dependent on the circumstances of the case and with regard to the person's:

(a)   special vulnerability;

(b)   the legal obligation to provide an opportunity for representations to be made prior to a decision about extending detention;

(c)   the need to consult and consider the views of any appropriate adult; and

(d)   any alternatives to police custody.

15.3 Before deciding whether to authorise continued detention the officer responsible under paragraph 15.1 or 15.2 shall give an opportunity to make representations about the detention to:

(a)   the detainee, unless in the case of a review as in paragraph 15.1, the detainee is asleep;

(b)   the detainee's solicitor if available at the time; and

(c)   the appropriate adult if available at the time.

(See Note 15CA.)

15.3A Other people having an interest in the detainee's welfare may also make representations at the authorising officer's discretion.

15.3B Subject to paragraph 15.10, the representations may be made orally in person or by telephone or in writing. The authorising officer may, however, refuse to hear oral representations from the detainee if the officer considers them unfit to make representations because of their condition or behaviour. (See Note 15C.)

15.3C The decision on whether the review takes place in person or by telephone or by live link (see paragraph 1.13(e)(ii)) is a matter for the review officer. In determining the form the review may take, the review officer must always take full account of the needs of the person in custody. The benefits of carrying out a review in person should always be considered, based on the individual circumstances of each case with specific additional consideration if the person is:

(a)   a juvenile (and the age of the juvenile); or

(b)   a vulnerable person; or

(c)   in need of medical attention for other than routine minor ailments; or

(d)   subject to presentational or community issues around their detention.

See paragraph 1.4(c).

15.4 Before conducting a review or determining whether to extend the maximum period of detention without charge, the officer responsible must make sure the detainee is reminded of their entitlement to free legal advice, see paragraph 6.5, unless in the case of a review the person is asleep. When determining whether to extend the maximum period of detention without charge, it should also be pointed out that for the purposes of paragraph 15.2, the superintendent or (as the case may be) the court, responsible for authorising any such extension, will not be able to use a live link unless the detainee has received legal advice on the use of the live link (see paragraphs 15.11A(ii) and 15.11C(ii)) and given consent to its use (see paragraphs 15.11A(iii) and 15.11C(iii). The detainee must also be given information about how the live link is used.

15.4A Following sections 45ZA and 45ZB of PACE, when the reminder and information concerning legal advice and about the use of the live link is given and the detainee's consent is sought, the presence of an appropriate adult is required if the detainee in question is a juvenile (see paragraph 1.5) or is a vulnerable adult by virtue of being a person aged 18 or over who, because of a mental disorder established in accordance paragraphs 1.4 and 1.13(d) or for any other reason (see paragraph 15.4B), may have difficulty understanding the purpose of:

(a)   an authorisation under section 42 of PACE or anything that occurs in connection with a decision whether to give it (see paragraphs 15.2 and 15.2A); or

(b)   a court hearing under section 43 or 44 of PACE or what occurs at the hearing it (see paragraphs 15.2 and 15.7A).

15.4B For the purpose of using a live link in accordance with sections 45ZA and 45ZB of PACE to authorise detention without charge (see paragraphs 15.11A and 15.11C), the reference to 'any other reason' would extend to difficulties in understanding the purposes mentioned in paragraph 15.4A that might arise if the person happened to be under the influence of drink or drugs at the time the live link is to be used. This does not however apply for the purposes of paragraphs 1.4 and 1.13(d) (see Note 1GC).

15.5 If, after considering any representations, the review officer under paragraph 15.1 decides to keep the detainee in detention or the superintendent under paragraph 15.2 extends the maximum period for which they may be detained without charge, then any comment made by the detainee shall be recorded. If applicable, the officer shall be informed of the comment as soon as practicable. See also paragraphs 11.4 and 11.13.

15.6 No officer shall put specific questions to the detainee:

• regarding their involvement in any offence; or

• in respect of any comments they may make:

— when given the opportunity to make representations; or

— in response to a decision to keep them in detention or extend the maximum period of detention.

Such an exchange could constitute an interview as in paragraph 11.1A and would be subject to the associated safeguards in section 11 and, in respect of a person who has been charged, paragraph 16.5. See also paragraph 11.13.

15.7 A detainee who is asleep at a review, see paragraph 15.1, and whose continued detention is authorised must be informed about the decision and reason as soon as practicable after waking.

15.7A When an application is made to a magistrates' court under PACE, section 43 for a warrant of further detention to extend detention without charge of a person arrested for an indictable offence, or under section 44, to extend or further extend that warrant, the detainee:

(a)   must, unless the court has given a live link direction as in paragraph 15.11C, be brought to court for the hearing of the application (see Note 15D);

(b)   is entitled to be legally represented if they wish, in which case, Annex B cannot apply; and

(c)   must be given a copy of the information which supports the application and states:

(i)   the nature of the offence for which the person to whom the application relates has been arrested;

(ii)   the general nature of the evidence on which the person was arrested;

(iii)   what inquiries about the offence have been made and what further inquiries are proposed;

(iv)   the reasons for believing continued detention is necessary for the purposes of the further inquiries;

Note: A warrant of further detention can only be issued or extended if the court has reasonable grounds for believing that the person's further detention is necessary for the purpose of obtaining evidence of an indictable offence for which the person has been arrested and that the investigation is being conducted diligently and expeditiously. See paragraph 15.0(b).

15.8 *Not used.*

(b)   *Review of detention by telephone or by using a live link (section 40A and 45A)*

15.9 PACE, section 40A provides that the officer responsible under section 40 for reviewing the detention of a person who has not been charged, need not attend the police station holding the detainee and may carry out the review by telephone.

15.9A PACE, section 45A(2) provides that the officer responsible under section 40 for reviewing the detention of a person who has not been charged, need not attend the police station holding the detainee and may carry out the review using a live link. See paragraph 1.13(e)(ii).

15.9B A telephone review is not permitted where facilities for review using a live link exist and it is practicable to use them.

15.9C The review officer can decide at any stage that a telephone review or review by live link should be terminated and that the review will be conducted in person. The reasons for doing so should be noted in the custody record. See Note 15F.

15.10 When a review is carried out by telephone or by using a live link, an officer at the station holding the detainee shall be required by the review officer to fulfil that officer's obligations under PACE, section 40 and this Code by:

(a)   making any record connected with the review in the detainee's custody record;

(b)   if applicable, making the record in (a) in the presence of the detainee; and

(c)   for a review by telephone, giving the detainee information about the review.

15.11 When a review is carried out by telephone or by using a live link, or the requirement in paragraph 15.3 will be satisfied:

(a)   if facilities exist for the immediate transmission of written representations to the review officer, e.g. fax or email message, by allowing those who are given the opportunity to make representations, to make their representations:

(i)   orally by telephone or (as the case may be) by means of the live link; or

(ii)   in writing using the facilities for the immediate transmission of written representations; and

(b)   in all other cases, by allowing those who are given the opportunity to make representations, to make their representations orally by telephone or by means of the live link.

(c) Authorisation to extend detention using live link (sections 45ZA and 45ZB)

15.11A For the purpose of paragraphs 15.2 and 15.2A, a superintendent who is not present at the police station where the detainee is being held but who has access to the use of a live link (see paragraph 1.13(e)(iii)) may, using that live link, give authority to extend the maximum period of detention permitted before charge, if, and only if, the following conditions are satisfied:

(i)   the custody officer considers that the use of the live link is appropriate (see Note 15H);

(ii)   the detainee in question has requested and received legal advice on the use of the live link (see paragraph 15.4).

(iii) the detainee has given their consent to the live link being used (see paragraph 15.11D

15.11B When a live link is used:

(a)   the authorising superintendent shall, with regard to any record connected with the authorisation which PACE, section 42 and this Code require to be made by the authorising officer, require an officer at the station holding the detainee to make that record in the detainee's custody record;

(b)   the requirement in paragraph 15.3 (allowing opportunity to make representations) will be satisfied:

(i)   if facilities exist for the immediate transmission of written representations to the authorising officer, e.g. fax or email message, by allowing those who are given the opportunity to make representations, to make their representations:

• in writing by means of those facilities or
• orally by means of the live link; or

(ii)   in all other cases, by allowing those who are given the opportunity to make representations, to make their representations orally by means of the live link.

(c)   The authorising officer can decide at any stage to terminate the live link and attend the police station where the detainee is held to carry out the procedure in person. The reasons for doing so should be noted in the custody record.

15.11C For the purpose of paragraph 15.7A and the hearing of an application to a magistrates' court under PACE, section 43 for a warrant of further detention to extend detention without charge of a person arrested for an indictable offence, or under PACE, section 44, to extend or further extend that warrant, the magistrates' court may give a direction that a live link (see paragraph 1.13(e)(iv)) be used for the purposes of the hearing if, and only if, the following conditions are satisfied:

(i)   the custody officer considers that the use of the live link for the purpose of the hearing is appropriate (see Note 15H);

(ii)   the detainee in question has requested and received legal advice on the use of the live link (see paragraph 15.4);

(iii) the detainee has given their consent to the live link being used (see paragraph 15.11D); and

(iv)   it is not contrary to the interests of justice to give the direction.

15.11D References in paragraphs 15.11A(iii) and 15.11C(iii) to the consent of the detainee mean:

(a)   if detainee is aged 18 or over, the consent of that detainee;

(b)   if the detainee is aged 14 and under 18, the consent of the detainee and their parent or guardian; and

(c)   if the detainee is aged under 14, the consent of their parent or guardian.

15.11E The consent described in paragraph 15.11D will only be valid if:

(i)   in the case of a detainee aged 18 or over who is a vulnerable adult as described in paragraph 15.4A), information about how the live link is used and the reminder about their right to legal advice mentioned in paragraph 15.4 and their consent, are given in the presence of the appropriate adult; and

(ii)   in the case of a juvenile:
- if information about how the live link is used and the reminder about their right to legal advice mentioned in paragraph 15.4 are given in the presence of the appropriate adult (who may or may not be their parent or guardian); and
- if the juvenile is aged 14 or over, their consent is given in the presence of the appropriate adult (who may or may not be their parent or guardian).

Note: If the juvenile is aged under 14, the consent of their parent or guardian is sufficient in its own right (see Note 15I).

(d) *Documentation*

15.12 It is the officer's responsibility to make sure all reminders given under paragraph 15.4 are noted in the custody record.

15.13 The grounds for, and extent of, any delay in conducting a review shall be recorded.

15.14 When a review is carried out by telephone or video conferencing facilities, a record shall be made of:

(a)   the reason the review officer did not attend the station holding the detainee;

(b)   the place the review officer was;

(c)   the method representations, oral or written, were made to the review officer, see paragraph 15.11.

15.15 Any written representations shall be retained.

15.16 A record shall be made as soon as practicable of:

(a)   the outcome of each review of detention before or after charge, and if paragraph 15.7 applies, of when the person was informed and by whom;

(b)   the outcome of any determination under PACE, section 42 by a superintendent whether to extend the maximum period of detention without charge beyond 24 hours from the relevant time. If an authorisation is given, the record shall state the number of hours and minutes by which the detention period is extended or further extended.

(c)   the outcome of each application under PACE, section 43, for a warrant of further detention or under section 44, for an extension or further extension of that warrant. If a warrant for further detention is granted under section 43 or extended or further extended under 44, the record shall state the detention period authorised by the warrant and the date and time it was granted or (as the case may be) the period by which the warrant is extended or further extended.

Note: Any period during which a person is released on bail does not count towards the maximum period of detention without charge allowed under PACE, sections 41 to 44.

Notes for Guidance

15A Review officer for the purposes of:
- PACE, sections 40, 40A and 45A means, in the case of a person arrested but not charged, an officer of at least inspector rank not directly involved in the investigation and, if a person has been arrested and charged, the custody officer.

15B The detention of persons in police custody not subject to the statutory review requirement in paragraph 15.1 should still be reviewed periodically as a matter of good practice. Such reviews can be carried out by an officer of the rank of sergeant or above. The purpose of such reviews is to check the particular power under which a detainee is held continues to apply, any associated conditions are complied with and to make sure appropriate action is taken to deal with any changes. This includes the detainee's prompt release when the power no longer applies, or their transfer if the power requires the detainee be taken elsewhere as soon as the necessary arrangements are made. Examples include persons:

(a)   arrested on warrant because they failed to answer bail to appear at court;

(b)   arrested under the Bail Act 1976, section 7(3) for breaching a condition of bail granted after charge;

(c)   in police custody for specific purposes and periods under the Crime (Sentences) Act 1997, Schedule 1;

(d)   convicted, or remand prisoners, held in police stations on behalf of the Prison Service under the Imprisonment (Temporary Provisions) Act 1980, section 6;

(e)   being detained to prevent them causing a breach of the peace;

(f)   detained at police stations on behalf of the Immigration Service;

(g)   detained by order of a magistrates' court under the Criminal Justice Act 1988, section 152 (as amended by the Drugs Act 2005, section 8) to facilitate the recovery of evidence after being charged with drug possession or drug trafficking and suspected of having swallowed drugs.

The detention of persons remanded into police detention by order of a court under the Magistrates' Courts Act 1980, section 128 is subject to a statutory requirement to review that detention. This is to make sure the detainee is taken back to court no later than the end of the period authorised by the court or when the need for their detention by police ceases, whichever is the sooner.

15C In the case of a review of detention, but not an extension, the detainee need not be woken for the review. However, if the detainee is likely to be asleep, e.g. during a period of rest allowed as in paragraph 12.2, at the latest time a review or authorisation to extend detention may take place, the officer should, if the legal obligations and time constraints permit, bring forward the procedure to allow the detainee to make representations. A detainee not asleep during the review must be present when the grounds for their continued detention are recorded and must at the same time be informed of those grounds unless the review officer considers the person is incapable of understanding what is said, violent or likely to become violent or in urgent need of medical attention.

15CA In paragraph 15.3(b) and (c), 'available' includes being contactable in time to enable them to make representations remotely by telephone or other electronic means or in person by attending the station. Reasonable efforts should therefore be made to give the solicitor and appropriate adult sufficient notice of the time the decision is expected to be made so that they can make themselves available.

15D An application to a Magistrates' Court under PACE, sections 43 or 44 for a warrant of further detention or its extension should be made between 10am and 9pm, and if possible during normal court hours. It will not usually be practicable to arrange for a court to sit specially outside the hours of 10am to 9pm. If it appears a special sitting may be needed

outside normal court hours but between 10am and 9pm, the clerk to the justices should be given notice and informed of this possibility, while the court is sitting if possible.

15E In paragraph 15.2, the officer responsible for the station holding the detainee includes a superintendent or above who, in accordance with their force operational policy or police regulations, is given that responsibility on a temporary basis whilst the appointed long-term holder is off duty or otherwise unavailable.

15F The provisions of PACE, section 40A allowing telephone reviews do not apply to reviews of detention after charge by the custody officer. When video conferencing is not required, they allow the use of a telephone to carry out a review of detention before charge. The procedure under PACE, section 42 must be done in person.

15G *Not used.*

15H In considering whether the use of the live link is appropriate in the case of a juvenile or vulnerable person, the custody officer and the superintendent should have regard to the detainee's ability to understand the purpose of the authorisation or (as the case may be) the court hearing, and be satisfied that the suspect is able to take part effectively in the process (see paragraphs 1.4(c)). The appropriate adult should always be involved.

15I For the purpose of paragraphs 15.11D and 15.11E, the consent required from a parent or guardian may, for a juvenile in the care of a local authority or voluntary organisation, be given by that authority or organisation. In the case of a juvenile, nothing in paragraphs 15.11D and 15.11E require the parent, guardian or representative of a local authority or voluntary organisation to be present with the juvenile to give their consent, unless they are acting as the appropriate adult. However, it is important that the parent, guardian or representative of a local authority or voluntary organisation who is not present is fully informed before being asked to consent. They must be given the same information as that given to the juvenile and the appropriate adult in accordance with paragraph 15.11E. They must also be allowed to speak to the juvenile and the appropriate adult if they wish. Provided the consent is fully informed and is not withdrawn, it may be obtained at any time before the live link is used.

16. Charging detained persons

(a) Action

16.1 When the officer in charge of the investigation reasonably believes there is sufficient evidence to provide a realistic prospect of conviction for the offence (see paragraph 11.6), they shall without delay, and subject to the following qualification, inform the custody officer who will be responsible for considering whether the detainee should be charged. See Notes 11B and 16A. When a person is detained in respect of more than one offence it is permissible to delay informing the custody officer until the above conditions are satisfied in respect of all the offences, but see paragraph 11.6. If the detainee is a juvenile or a vulnerable person, any resulting action shall be taken in the presence of the appropriate adult if they are present at the time.
See Notes 16B and 16C.

16.1A Where guidance issued by the Director of Public Prosecutions under PACE, section 37A is in force the custody officer must comply with that Guidance in deciding how to act in dealing with the detainee. See Notes 16AA and 16AB.

16.1B Where in compliance with the DPP's Guidance the custody officer decides that the case should be immediately referred to the CPS to make the charging decision, consultation should take place with a Crown Prosecutor as soon as is reasonably practicable. Where the Crown Prosecutor is unable to make the charging decision on the information available at that time, the detainee may be released without charge and on bail (with conditions if necessary) under section 37(7)(a). In such circumstances, the detainee should be informed that they are being released to enable the Director of Public Prosecutions to make a decision under section 37B.

16.2 When a detainee is charged with or informed they may be prosecuted for an offence, see Note 16B, they shall, unless the restriction on drawing adverse inferences from silence applies, see Annex C, be cautioned as follows:

> 'You do not have to say anything. But it may harm your defence if you do not mention now something which you later rely on in court. Anything you do say may be given in evidence.'

Where the use of the Welsh Language is appropriate, a constable may provide the caution directly in Welsh in the following terms:

> 'Does dim rhaid i chi ddweud dim byd. Ond gall niweidio eich amddiffyniad os na fyddwch chi'n sôn, yn awr, am rywbeth y byddwch chi'n dibynnu arno nes ymlaen yn y llys. Gall unrhyw beth yr ydych yn ei ddweud gael ei roi fel tystiolaeth.'

Annex C, paragraph 2 sets out the alternative terms of the caution to be used when the restriction on drawing adverse inferences from silence applies.

16.3 When a detainee is charged they shall be given a written notice showing particulars of the offence and, subject to paragraph 2.6A, the officer's name and the case reference number. As far as possible the particulars of the charge shall be stated in simple terms, but they shall also show the precise offence in law with which the detainee is charged. The notice shall begin:

> 'You are charged with the offence(s) shown below.' Followed by the caution.

If the detainee is a juvenile, mentally disordered or otherwise mentally vulnerable, a copy of the notice should also be given to the appropriate adult.

16.4 If, after a detainee has been charged with or informed they may be prosecuted for an offence, an officer wants to tell them about any written statement or interview with another person relating to such an offence, the detainee shall either be handed a true copy of the written statement or the content of the interview record brought to their attention. Nothing shall be done to invite any reply or comment except to:

(a) caution the detainee, 'You do not have to say anything, but anything you do say may be given in evidence.';
Where the use of the Welsh Language is appropriate, caution the detainee in the following terms:

> 'Does dim rhaid i chi ddweud dim byd, ond gall unrhyw beth yr ydych yn ei ddweud gael ei roi fel tystiolaeth.'

and

(b) remind the detainee about their right to legal advice.

16.4A If the detainee:

- cannot read, the document may be read to them

- is a juvenile, mentally disordered or otherwise mentally vulnerable, the appropriate adult shall also be given a copy, or the interview record shall be brought to their attention

16.5 A detainee may not be interviewed about an offence after they have been charged with, or informed they may be prosecuted for it, unless the interview is necessary:

- to prevent or minimise harm or loss to some other person, or the public
- to clear up an ambiguity in a previous answer or statement
- in the interests of justice for the detainee to have put to them, and have an opportunity to comment on, information concerning the offence which has come to light since they were charged or informed they might be prosecuted

Before any such interview, the interviewer shall:

(a)   caution the detainee, *'You do not have to say anything, but anything you do say may be given in evidence.'*

Where the use of the Welsh Language is appropriate, the interviewer shall caution the detainee:

'Does dim rhaid i chi ddweud dim byd, ond gall unrhyw beth yr ydych yn ei ddweud gael ei roi fel tystiolaeth.'

(b)   remind the detainee about their right to legal advice.

(See Note 16B.)

16.6 The provisions of paragraphs 16.2 to 16.5 must be complied with in the appropriate adult's presence if they are already at the police station. If they are not at the police station then these provisions must be complied with again in their presence when they arrive unless the detainee has been released. See Note 16C.

16.7 When a juvenile is charged with an offence and the custody officer authorises their continued detention after charge, the custody officer must make arrangements for the juvenile to be taken into the care of a local authority to be detained pending appearance in court unless the custody officer certifies in accordance with PACE, section 38(6), that:

(a)   for any juvenile; it is impracticable to do so and the reasons why it is impracticable must be set out in the certificate that must be produced to the court; or,

(b)   in the case of a juvenile of at least 12 years old, no secure accommodation is available and other accommodation would not be adequate to protect the public from serious harm from that juvenile. See Note 16D.

Note: Chief officers should ensure that the operation of these provisions at police stations in their areas is subject to supervision and monitoring by an officer of the rank of inspector or above.

See Note 16E.

16.7A The requirement in paragraph 3.4(b) that documents and materials essential to effectively challenging the lawfulness of the detainee's arrest and detention must be made available to the detainee and, if they are represented, their solicitor, applies for the purposes of this section and a person's detention after charge. This means that the custody officer making the bail decision (PACE, section 38) or reviewing the need for detention after charge (PACE, section 40), is responsible for determining what, if any, documents or materials are essential and must be made available to the detainee or their solicitor. See Note 3ZA.

(b)   *Documentation*

16.8 A record shall be made of anything a detainee says when charged.

16.9 Any questions put in an interview after charge and answers given relating to the offence shall be recorded in full during the interview on forms for that purpose and the record signed by the detainee or, if they refuse, by the interviewer and any third parties present. If the questions are audibly recorded or visually recorded the arrangements in Code E or F apply.

16.10 If arrangements for a juvenile's transfer into local authority care as in paragraph 16.7 are not made, the custody officer must record the reasons in a certificate which must be produced before the court with the juvenile. (See Note 16D.)

Notes for Guidance

16A The custody officer must take into account alternatives to prosecution under the Crime and Disorder Act 1998, reprimands and warnings applicable to persons under 18, and in national guidance on the cautioning of offenders, for persons aged 18 and over.

16AA When a person is arrested under the provisions of the Criminal Justice Act 2003 which allow a person to be re-tried after being acquitted of a serious offence which is a qualifying offence specified in Schedule 5 to that Act and not precluded from further prosecution by virtue of section 75(3) of that Act the detention provisions of PACE are modified and make an officer of the rank of superintendent or above who has not been directly involved in the investigation responsible for determining whether the evidence is sufficient to charge.

16AB Where Guidance issued by the Director of Public Prosecutions under section 37B is in force, a custody officer who determines in accordance with that Guidance that there is sufficient evidence to charge the detainee, may detain that person for no longer than is reasonably necessary to decide how that person is to be dealt with under PACE, section 37(7)(a) to (d), including, where appropriate, consultation with the Duty Prosecutor. The period is subject to the maximum period of detention before charge determined by PACE, sections 41 to 44. Where in accordance with the Guidance the case is referred to the CPS for decision, the custody officer should ensure that an officer involved in the investigation sends to the CPS such information as is specified in the Guidance.

16B The giving of a warning or the service of the Notice of Intended Prosecution required by the Road Traffic Offenders Act 1988, section 1 does not amount to informing a detainee they may be prosecuted for an offence and so does not preclude further questioning in relation to that offence.

16C There is no power under PACE to detain a person and delay action under paragraphs 16.2 to 16.5 solely to await the arrival of the appropriate adult. Reasonable efforts should therefore be made to give the appropriate adult sufficient notice of the time the decision (charge etc) is to be implemented so that they can be present. If the appropriate adult is not, or cannot be, present at that time, the detainee should be released on bail to return for the decision to be implemented when the adult is present, unless the custody officer determines that the absence of the appropriate adult makes the detainee unsuitable for bail for this purpose. After charge, bail cannot be refused, or release on bail delayed, simply because an appropriate adult is not available, unless the absence of that adult provides the custody officer with the necessary grounds to authorise detention after charge under PACE, section 38.

16D Except as in paragraph 16.7, neither a juvenile's behaviour nor the nature of the offence provides grounds for the custody officer to decide it is impracticable to arrange the juvenile's transfer to local authority care. Impracticability concerns the transport and travel requirements and the lack of secure accommodation which is provided for the purposes of restricting liberty does not make it impracticable to transfer the juvenile. The availability of secure accommodation is only a factor in relation to a juvenile aged 12 or over when other local authority accommodation would not be adequate to protect the public from serious harm from them. The obligation to transfer a juvenile to local authority accommodation applies as much to a juvenile charged during the daytime as to a juvenile to be held overnight, subject to a requirement to bring the juvenile before a court under PACE, section 46.

16E The Concordat on Children in Custody published by the Home Office in 2017 provides detailed guidance with the aim of preventing the detention of children in police stations following charge. It is available here …:

POLICE AND CRIMINAL EVIDENCE ACT 1984 (PACE) CODE D

CODE OF PRACTICE FOR THE IDENTIFICATION OF PERSONS BY POLICE OFFICERS

Commencement – Transitional Arrangements

This code has effect in relation to any identification procedure carried out after midnight on 23 February 2017.

1.   Introduction

1.1 This Code of Practice concerns the principal methods used by police to identify people in connection with the investigation of offences and the keeping of accurate and reliable criminal records. The powers and procedures in this code must be used fairly, responsibly, with respect for the people to whom they apply and without unlawful discrimination. Under the Equality Act 2010, section 149 (Public sector Equality Duty), police forces must, in carrying out their functions, have due regard to the need to eliminate unlawful discrimination, harassment, victimisation and any other conduct which is prohibited by that Act, to advance equality of opportunity between people who share a relevant protected characteristic and people who do not share it, and to foster good relations between those persons. The Equality Act also makes it unlawful for police officers to discriminate against, harass or victimise any person on the grounds of the 'protected characteristics' of age, disability, gender reassignment, race, religion or belief, sex and sexual orientation, marriage and civil partnership, pregnancy and maternity when using their powers. See Note 1A.

1.2 In this code, identification by an eye-witness arises when a witness who has seen the offender committing the crime and is given an opportunity to identify a person suspected of involvement in the offence in a video identification, identification parade or similar procedure. These eye-witness identification procedures (see Part A of section 3 below) are designed to:
- test the witness' ability to identify the suspect as the person they saw on a previous occasion
- provide safeguards against mistaken identification.

While this Code concentrates on visual identification procedures, it does not preclude the police making use of aural identification procedures such as a 'voice identification parade', where they judge that appropriate.

1.2A In this code, separate provisions in Part B of section 3 below apply when any person, including a police officer, is asked if they recognise anyone they see in an image as being someone they know and to test their claim that they recognise that person as someone who is known to them. Except where stated, these separate provisions are not subject to the eye-witnesses identification procedures described in paragraph 1.2.

1.3 Identification by fingerprints applies when a person's fingerprints are taken to:
- compare with fingerprints found at the scene of a crime
- check and prove convictions
- help to ascertain a person's identity.

1.3A Identification using footwear impressions applies when a person's footwear impressions are taken to compare with impressions found at the scene of a crime.

1.4 Identification by body samples and impressions includes taking samples such as blood or hair to generate a DNA profile for comparison with material obtained from the scene of a crime, or a victim.

1.5 Taking photographs of arrested people applies to recording and checking identity and locating and tracing persons who:
- are wanted for offences
- fail to answer their bail.

1.6 Another method of identification involves searching and examining detained suspects to find, e.g., marks such as tattoos or scars which may help establish their identity or whether they have been involved in committing an offence.

1.7 The provisions of the Police and Criminal Evidence Act 1984 (PACE) and this Code are designed to make sure fingerprints, samples, impressions and photographs are taken, used and retained, and identification procedures carried out, only when justified and necessary for preventing, detecting or investigating crime. If these provisions are not observed, the application of the relevant procedures in particular cases may be open to question.

1.8 The provisions of this Code do not authorise, or otherwise permit, fingerprints or samples to be taken from a person detained solely for the purposes of assessment under section 136 of the Mental Health Act 1983.

Note for Guidance

1A In paragraph 1.1, under the Equality Act 1949, section 149, the 'relevant protected characteristics' are: age, disability, gender reassignment, pregnancy and maternity, race, religion/belief, sex and sexual orientation. For further detailed guidance and advice on the Equality Act, (see www.gov.uk/guidance/equality-act-2010-guidance).

1B See Home Office Circular 57/2003 'Advice on the use of voice identification parades'.

2.   **General**

2.1   This Code must be readily available at all police stations for consultation by:
      * police officers and police staff
      * detained persons
      * members of the public

2.2   The provisions of this Code:
      * include the Annexes
      * do not include the Notes for guidance.

2.3   Code C, paragraph 1.4, regarding a person who may be mentally disordered or otherwise mentally vulnerable and the Notes for guidance applicable to those provisions apply to this Code.

2.4   Code C, paragraph 1.5, regarding a person who appears to be under the age of 17 applies to this Code.

2.5   Code C, paragraph 1.6, regarding a person who appears to be blind, seriously visually impaired, deaf, unable to read or speak or has difficulty communicating orally because of a speech impediment applies to this Code.

2.6   In this Code:
      * 'appropriate adult' means the same as in Code C, paragraph 1.7
      * 'solicitor' means the same as in Code C, paragraph 6.12
      and the Notes for guidance applicable to those provisions apply to this Code.
      * where a search or other procedure under this code may only be carried out or observed by a person of the same sex as the person to whom the search or procedure applies, the gender of the detainee and other persons present should be established and recorded in line with Annex F of Code A.

2.7   References to custody officers include those performing the functions of custody officer, see paragraph 1.9 of Code C.

2.8   When a record of any action requiring the authority of an officer of a specified rank is made under this Code, subject to paragraph 2.18, the officer's name and rank must be recorded.

2.9   When this Code requires the prior authority or agreement of an officer of at least inspector or superintendent rank, that authority may be given by a sergeant or chief inspector who has been authorised to perform the functions of the higher rank under PACE, section 107.

2.10 Subject to paragraph 2.18, all records must be timed and signed by the maker.

2.11 Records must be made in the custody record, unless otherwise specified. References to 'pocket book' include any official report book issued to police officers or police staff.

2.12 If any procedure in this Code requires a person's consent, the consent of a:
      * mentally disordered or otherwise mentally vulnerable person is only valid if given in the presence of the appropriate adult
      * juvenile is only valid if their parent's or guardian's consent is also obtained unless the juvenile is under 14, when their parent's or guardian's consent is sufficient in its own right. If the only obstacle to an identification procedure in section 3 is that a juvenile's parent or guardian refuses consent or reasonable efforts to obtain it have failed, the identification officer may apply the provisions of paragraph 3.21. See Note 2A

2.13 If a person is blind, seriously visually impaired or unable to read, the custody officer or identification officer shall make sure their solicitor, relative, appropriate adult or some other person likely to take an interest in them and not involved in the investigation is available to help check any documentation. When this Code requires written consent or signing, the person assisting may be asked to sign instead, if the detainee prefers. This paragraph does not require an appropriate adult to be called solely to assist in checking and signing documentation for a person who is not a juvenile, or mentally disordered or otherwise mentally vulnerable (see Note 2B and Code C paragraph 3.15).

2.14 If any procedure in this Code requires information to be given to or sought from a suspect, it must be given or sought in the appropriate adult's presence if the suspect is mentally disordered, otherwise mentally vulnerable or a juvenile. If the appropriate adult is not present when the information is first given or sought, the procedure must be repeated in the presence of the appropriate adult when they arrive. If the suspect appears deaf or there is doubt about their hearing or speaking ability or ability to understand English, and effective communication cannot be established, the information must be given or sought through an interpreter.

2.15 Any procedure in this Code involving the participation of a suspect who is mentally disordered, otherwise mentally vulnerable or a juvenile must take place in the presence of the appropriate adult. See Code C paragraph 1.4.

2.15A Any procedure in this Code involving the participation of a witness who is or appears to be mentally disordered, otherwise mentally vulnerable or a juvenile should take place in the presence of a pre-trial support person unless the witness states that they do not want a support person to be present. A support person must not be allowed to prompt any identification of a suspect by a witness. See Note 2AB.

2.16 References to:
- 'taking a photograph', include the use of any process to produce a single, still or moving, visual image
- 'photographing a person', should be construed accordingly
- 'photographs', 'films', 'negatives' and 'copies' include relevant visual images recorded, stored, or reproduced through any medium
- 'destruction' includes the deletion of computer data relating to such images or making access to that data impossible

2.17 Except as described, nothing in this Code affects the powers and procedures:
(i)   for requiring and taking samples of breath, blood and urine in relation to driving offences, etc, when under the influence of drink, drugs or excess alcohol under the:
- Road Traffic Act 1988, sections 4 to 11
- Road Traffic Offenders Act 1988, sections 15 and 16
- Transport and Works Act 1992, sections 26 to 38;
(ii)   under the Immigration Act 1971, Schedule 2, paragraph 18, for taking photographs and fingerprints from persons detained under that Act, Schedule 2, paragraph 16 (Administrative Controls as to Control on Entry etc); for taking fingerprints in accordance with the Immigration and Asylum Act 1999; sections 141 and 142(3), or other methods for collecting information about a person's external physical characteristics provided for by regulations made under that Act, section 144;
(iii)   under the Terrorism Act 2000, Schedule 8, for taking photographs, fingerprints, skin impressions, body samples or impressions from people:
- arrested under that Act, section 41,
- detained for the purposes of examination under that Act, Schedule 7, and to whom the Code of Practice issued under that Act, Schedule 14, paragraph 6, applies ('the terrorism provisions')
See Note 2C;
(iv)   for taking photographs, fingerprints, skin impressions, body samples or impressions from people who have been:
- arrested on warrants issued in Scotland, by officers exercising powers under the Criminal Justice and Public Order Act 1994, section 136(2)
- arrested or detained without warrant by officers from a police force in Scotland exercising their powers of arrest or detention under the Criminal Justice and Public Order Act 1994, section 137(2), (Cross Border powers of arrest etc).

Note: In these cases, police powers and duties and the person's rights and entitlements whilst at a police station in England and Wales are the same as if the person had been arrested in Scotland by a Scottish police officer.

2.18 Nothing in this Code requires the identity of officers or police staff to be recorded or disclosed:
(a)   in the case of enquiries linked to the investigation of terrorism;
(b)   if the officers or police staff reasonably believe recording or disclosing their names might put them in danger.

In these cases, they shall use warrant or other identification numbers and the name of their police station. (See Note 2D.)

2.19 In this Code:
(a)   'designated person' means a person other than a police officer, designated under the Police Reform Act 2002, Part 4, who has specified powers and duties of police officers conferred or imposed on them;

(b)   any reference to a police officer includes a designated person acting in the exercise or performance of the powers and duties conferred or imposed on them by their designation.

2.20 If a power conferred on a designated person:

(a)   allows reasonable force to be used when exercised by a police officer, a designated person exercising that power has the same entitlement to use force;

(b)   includes power to use force to enter any premises, that power is not exercisable by that designated person except:

(i)   in the company, and under the supervision, of a police officer; or

(ii)   for the purpose of:

- saving life or limb; or
- preventing serious damage to property.

2.21 In the case of a detained person, nothing in this Code prevents the custody officer, or other police officer or designated person given custody of the detainee by the custody officer for the purposes of the investigation of an offence for which the person is detained, from allowing another person (see (a) and (b) below) to carry out individual procedures or tasks at the police station if the law allows. However, the officer or designated person given custody remains responsible for making sure the procedures and tasks are carried out correctly in accordance with the Codes of Practice. The other person who is allowed to carry out the procedures or tasks must be someone who at that time is:

(a)   under the direction and control of the chief officer of the force responsible for the police station in question; or;

(b)   providing services under contractual arrangements (but without being employed by the chief officer the police force), to assist a police force in relation to the discharge of its chief officer's functions.

2.22 Designated persons and other police staff must have regard to any relevant provisions of the Codes of Practice.

Notes for Guidance

2A   For the purposes of paragraph 2.12, the consent required from a parent or guardian may, for a juvenile in the care of a local authority or voluntary organisation, be given by that authority or organisation. In the case of a juvenile, nothing in paragraph 2.12 requires the parent, guardian or representative of a local authority or voluntary organisation to be present to give their consent, unless they are acting as the appropriate adult under paragraphs 2.14 or 2.15. However, it is important that a parent or guardian not present is fully informed before being asked to consent. They must be given the same information about the procedure and the juvenile's suspected involvement in the offence as the juvenile and appropriate adult. The parent or guardian must also be allowed to speak to the juvenile and the appropriate adult if they wish. Provided the consent is fully informed and is not withdrawn, it may be obtained at any time before the procedure takes place.

2AB   The Youth Justice and Criminal Evidence Act 1999 guidance 'Achieving Best Evidence in Criminal Proceedings' indicates that a pre-trial support person should accompany a vulnerable witness during any identification procedure unless the witness states that they do not want a support person to be present. It states that this support person should not be (or not be likely to be) a witness in the investigation.

2B   People who are seriously visually impaired or unable to read may be unwilling to sign police documents. The alternative, i.e. their representative signing on their behalf, seeks to protect the interests of both police and suspects.

2C   Photographs, fingerprints, samples and impressions may be taken from a person detained under the terrorism provisions to help determine whether they are, or have been, involved in terrorism, as well as when there are reasonable grounds for suspecting their involvement in a particular offence.

2D   The purpose of paragraph 2.18(b) is to protect those involved in serious organised crime investigations or arrests of particularly violent suspects when there is reliable information that those arrested or their associates may threaten or cause harm to the officers. In cases of doubt, an officer of inspector rank or above should be consulted.

3.   Identification and recognition of suspects

Part (A)   identification of a suspect by an eye-witness

3.0 This part applies when an eye-witness has seen the offender committing the crime or in any other circumstances which tend to prove or disprove the involvement of the person they saw in the crime, for example, close to the scene of the crime, immediately before or immediately after it was committed. It sets out the procedures to be used to test the ability of that eye-witness to identify a person suspected of involvement in the offence as the person they saw on the previous occasion. Except where stated, this part does not apply to the procedures described in Part B and Note 3AA.

3.1 A record shall be made of the suspect's description as first given by a potential witness. This record must:

(a)   be made and kept in a form which enables details of that description to be accurately produced from it, in a visible and legible form, which can be given to the suspect or the suspect's solicitor in accordance with this Code; and

(b)   unless otherwise specified, be made before the witness takes part in any identification procedures under paragraphs 3.5 to 3.10, 3.21 or 3.23.

A copy of the record shall where practicable, be given to the suspect or their solicitor before any procedures under paragraphs 3.5 to 3.10, 3.21 or 3.23 are carried out. (See Note 3E.)

3.1A References in this Part:

(a)   to the identity of the suspect being 'known' mean that there is sufficient information known to the police to establish, in accordance with Code G (Arrest), that there are reasonable grounds to suspect a particular person of involvement in the offence;

(b)   to the suspect being 'available' mean that the suspect is immediately available, or will be available within a reasonably short time, in order that they can be invited to take part in at least one of the eye-witness identification procedures under paragraphs 3.5 to 3.10 and it is practicable to arrange an effective procedure under paragraphs 3.5 to 3.10; and

(c)   to the eye-witness identification procedures under paragraphs 3.5 to 3.10 mean:
  • Video identification (paragraphs 3.5 and 3.6);
  • Identification parade (paragraphs 3.7 and 3.8); and
  • Group identification (paragraphs 3.9 and 3.10).

(a) Cases when the suspect's identity is not known

3.2 In cases when the suspect's identity is not known, a witness may be taken to a particular neighbourhood or place to see whether they can identify the person they saw on a previous occasion. Although the number, age, sex, race, general description and style of clothing of other people present at the location and the way in which any identification is made cannot be controlled, the principles applicable to the formal procedures under paragraphs 3.5 to 3.10 shall be followed as far as practicable. For example:

(a)   where it is practicable to do so, a record should be made of the witness' description of the suspect, as in paragraph 3.1 (a), before asking the witness to make an identification;

(b)   care must be taken not to direct the witness' attention to any individual unless, taking into account all the circumstances, this cannot be avoided. However, this does not prevent a witness being asked to look carefully at the people around at the time or to look towards a group or in a particular direction, if this appears necessary to make sure that the witness does not overlook a possible suspect simply because the witness is looking in the opposite direction and also to enable the witness to make comparisons between any suspect and others who are in the area; See Note 3F

(c)   where there is more than one witness, every effort should be made to keep them separate and witnesses should be taken to see whether they can identify a person independently;

(d)   once there is sufficient information to justify the arrest of a particular individual for suspected involvement in the offence, e.g., after a witness makes a positive identification, the provisions set out from paragraph 3.4 onwards shall apply for any other witnesses in relation to that individual.;

(e) the officer or police staff accompanying the eye-witness must record, in their report book, the action taken as soon as practicable and in as much detail, as possible. The record should include:

(i) the date, time and place of the relevant occasion when the eye-witness claims to have previously seen the person committing the offence in question or in any other circumstances which tend to prove or disprove the involvement of the person they saw in a crime (see paragraph 3.0); and

(ii) where any identification was made:

how it was made and the conditions at the time (e.g., the distance the eyewitness was from the suspect, the weather and light);

if the eye-witness's attention was drawn to the suspect; the reason for this; and anything said by the eye-witness or the suspect about the identification or the conduct of the procedure.

(See Note 3F.)

3.3 An eye-witness must not be shown photographs, computerised or artist's composite likenesses or similar likenesses or pictures (including 'E-fit' images) if in accordance with paragraph 3.1A, the identity of the suspect is known and they are available to take part in one of the procedures under paragraphs 3.5 to 3.10. If the suspect's identity is not known, the showing of any such images to an eye-witness to see if they can identify a person whose image they are shown as the person they saw on a previous occasion must be done in accordance with Annex E.

(b) *Cases when the suspect is known and available*

3.4 If the suspect's identity is known to the police and they are available, the identification procedures set out in paragraphs 3.5 to 3.10 may be used. References in this section to a suspect being 'known' mean there is sufficient information known to the police to justify the arrest of a particular person for suspected involvement in the offence. A suspect being 'available' means they are immediately available or will be within a reasonably short time and willing to take an effective part in at least one of the following which it is practicable to arrange:

- video identification;
- identification parade; or
- group identification.

(i) Video identification

3.5 A 'video identification' is when the eye-witness is shown images of a known suspect, together with similar images of others who resemble the suspect. Moving images must be used unless the conditions in sub-paragraph (a) or (b) below apply:

(a) this sub-paragraph applies if:

(i) the identification officer, in consultation with the officer in charge of the investigation, is satisfied that because of aging, or other physical changes or differences, the appearance of the suspect has significantly changed since the previous occasion when the eye-witness claims to have seen the suspect (see paragraph 3.0 and Note 3ZA);

(ii) an image (moving or still) is available which the identification officer and the officer in charge of the investigation reasonably believe shows the appearance of the suspect as it was at the time the suspect was seen by the eye-witness; and

(iii) having regard to the extent of change and the purpose of eye-witness identification procedures (see paragraph 3.0), the identification officer believes that that such an image should be shown to the eye-witness.

In such a case, the identification officer may arrange a video identification procedure using the image described in (ii). In accordance with the 'Notice to suspect' (see paragraph 3.17(vi)), the suspect must first be given an opportunity to provide their own image(s) for use in the procedure but it is for the identification officer and officer in charge of the investigation to decide whether, following (ii) and (iii), any image(s) provided by the suspect should be used.

A video identification using an image described above may, at the discretion of the identification officer be arranged in addition to, or as an alternative to, a video identification using moving images taken after the suspect has been given the information and notice described in paragraphs 3.17 and 3.18.

See paragraph 3.21 and Note 3D in any case where the suspect deliberately takes steps to frustrate the eye-witness identification arrangements and procedures.

(b)   this sub-paragraph applies if, in accordance with paragraph 2A of Annex A of this Code, the identification officer does not consider that replication of a physical feature or concealment of the location of the feature can be achieved using a moving image. In these cases, still images may be used.

3.6 Video identifications must be carried out in accordance with Annex A.

(ii) Identification parade

3.7 An 'identification parade' is when the witness sees the suspect in a line of others who resemble the suspect.

3.8 identification parades must be carried out in accordance with Annex B.

(iii) Group identification

3.9 A 'group identification' is when the witness sees the suspect in an informal group of people.

3.10 Group identifications must be carried out in accordance with Annex C.

Arranging eye-witness identification procedures – duties of identification officer

3.11 Except as provided for in paragraph 3.19, the arrangements for, and conduct of, the eyewitness identification procedures in paragraphs 3.5 to 3.10 and circumstances in which any such identification procedure must be held shall be the responsibility of an officer not below inspector rank who is not involved with the investigation ('the identification officer'). The identification officer may direct another officer or police staff, see paragraph 2.21, to make arrangements for, and to conduct, any of these identification procedures and except as provided for in paragraph 7 of Annex A, any reference in this section to the identification officer includes the officer or police staff to whom the arrangements for, and/or conduct of, any of these procedure has been delegated. In delegating these arrangements and procedures, the identification officer must be able to supervise effectively and either intervene or be contacted for advice. Where any action referred to in this paragraph is taken by another officer or police staff at the direction of the identification officer, the outcome shall, as soon as practicable, be reported to the identification officer. For the purpose of these procedures, the identification officer retains overall responsibility for ensuring that the procedure complies with this Code and in addition, in the case of detained suspect, their care and treatment until returned to the custody officer. Except as permitted by this Code, no officer or any other person involved with the investigation of the case against the suspect may take any part in these procedures or act as the identification officer.

This paragraph does not prevent the identification officer from consulting the officer in charge of the investigation to determine which procedure to use. When an identification procedure is required, in the interest of fairness to suspects and eye-witnesses, it must be held as soon as practicable.

Circumstances in which an eye-witness identification procedure must be held

3.12 If, before any identification procedure set out in paragraphs 3.5 to 3.10 has been held

(a)   an eye-witness has identified a suspect or purported to have identified them; or

(b)   there is an eye-witness available who expresses an ability to identify the suspect; or

(c)   there is a reasonable chance of an eye-witness being able to identify the suspect and the eye-witness in (a) to (c) has not been given an opportunity to identify the suspect in any of the procedures set out in paragraphs 3.5 to 3.10, then an identification procedure shall be held if the suspect disputes being the person the eye-witness claims to have seen on a previous occasion (see paragraph 3.0), unless:

(i)   it is not practicable to hold any such procedure; or

(ii)   any such procedure would serve no useful purpose in proving or disproving whether the suspect was involved in committing the offence, for example

• where the suspect admits being at the scene of the crime and gives an account of what took place and the eye-witness does not see anything which contradicts that; or

• when it is not disputed that the suspect is already known to the eye-witness who claims to have recognised them when seeing them commit the crime.

3.13 An eye-witness identification procedure may also be held if the officer in charge of the investigation considers it would be useful.

Selecting an eye-witness identification procedure

3.14 If, because of paragraph 3.12, an identification procedure is to be held, the suspect shall initially be offered a video identification unless:

(a)   a video identification is not practicable; or

(b)   an identification parade is both practicable and more suitable than a video identification; or

(c)   paragraph 3.16 applies.

The identification officer and the officer in charge of the investigation shall consult each other to determine which option is to be offered. An identification parade may not be practicable because of factors relating to the witnesses, such as their number, state of health, availability and travelling requirements. A video identification would normally be more suitable if it could be arranged and completed sooner than an identification parade. Before an option is offered the suspect must also be reminded of their entitlement to have free legal advice, see Code C, paragraph 6.5.

3.15 A suspect who refuses the identification procedure first offered shall be asked to state their reason for refusing and may get advice from their solicitor and/or if present, their appropriate adult. The suspect, solicitor and/or appropriate adult shall be allowed to make representations about why another procedure should be used. A record should be made of the reasons for refusal and any representations made. After considering any reasons given, and representations made, the identification officer shall, if appropriate, arrange for the suspect to be offered an alternative which the officer considers suitable and practicable. If the officer decides it is not suitable and practicable to offer an alternative identification procedure, the reasons for that decision shall be recorded.

3.16 A group identification may initially be offered if the officer in charge of the investigation considers it is more suitable than a video identification or an identification parade and the identification officer considers it practicable to arrange.

Notice to suspect

3.17 Unless paragraph 3.20 applies, before a video identification, an identification parade or group identification is arranged, the following shall be explained to the suspect:

(i)   the purposes of the video identification, identification parade or group identification;

(ii)   their entitlement to free legal advice; see Code C, paragraph 6.5;

(iii)   the procedures for holding it, including their right to have a solicitor or friend present;

(iv)   that they do not have to consent to or co-operate in a video identification, identification parade or group identification;

(v)   that if they do not consent to, and co-operate in, a video identification, identification parade or group identification, their refusal may be given in evidence in any subsequent trial and police may proceed covertly without their consent or make other arrangements to test whether a witness can identify them, see paragraph 3.21;

(vi)   whether, for the purposes of a video identification procedure, images of them have previously been obtained either:

• in accordance with paragraph 3.20, and if so, that they may co-operate in providing further, suitable images to be used instead; or

• in accordance with paragraph 3.5(a), and if so, that they may provide their own images for the identification officer to consider using.

(vii)   if appropriate, the special arrangements for juveniles;

(viii)   if appropriate, the special arrangements for mentally disordered or otherwise mentally vulnerable people;

(ix)   that if they significantly alter their appearance between being offered an identification procedure and any attempt to hold an identification procedure, this may be given in evidence if the case comes to trial, and the identification officer may then consider other forms of identification, see paragraph 3.21 and Note 3C;

(x)   that a moving image or photograph may be taken of them when they attend for any identification procedure;

(xi)   whether, before their identity became known, the witness was shown photographs, a computerised or artist's composite likeness or similar likeness or image by the police, see Note 3B;

(xii)   that if they change their appearance before an identification parade, it may not be practicable to arrange one on the day or subsequently and, because of the appearance change, the identification officer may consider alternative methods of identification, see Note 3C;

(xiii) that they or their solicitor will be provided with details of the description of the suspect as first given by any witnesses who are to attend the video identification, identification parade, group identification or confrontation, see paragraph 3.1.

3.18 This information must also be recorded in a written notice handed to the suspect. The suspect must be given a reasonable opportunity to read the notice, after which, they should be asked to sign a second copy to indicate if they are willing to co-operate with the making of a video or take part in the identification parade or group identification. The signed copy shall be retained by the identification officer.

3.19 The duties of the identification officer under paragraphs 3.17 and 3.18 may be performed by the custody officer or other officer not involved in the investigation if:

(a)   it is proposed to release the suspect in order that an identification procedure can be arranged and carried out and an inspector is not available to act as the identification officer, see paragraph 3.11, before the suspect leaves the station; or

(b)   it is proposed to keep the suspect in police detention whilst the procedure is arranged and carried out and waiting for an inspector to act as the identification officer, see paragraph 3.11, would cause unreasonable delay to the investigation.

The officer concerned shall inform the identification officer of the action taken and give them the signed copy of the notice. (See Note 3C.)

3.20 If the identification officer and officer in charge of the investigation suspect, on reasonable grounds that if the suspect was given the information and notice as in paragraphs 3.17 and 3.18, they would then take steps to avoid being seen by a witness in any identification procedure, the identification officer may arrange for images of the suspect suitable for use in a video identification procedure to be obtained before giving the information and notice. If suspect's images are obtained in these circumstances, the suspect may, for the purposes of a video identification procedure, co-operate in providing new images which if suitable, would be used instead, see paragraph 3.17(vi).

(c)   Cases when the suspect is known but not available

3.21 When a known suspect is not available or has ceased to be available, see paragraph 3.4, the identification officer may make arrangements for a video identification (see Annex A). If necessary, the identification officer may follow the video identification procedures but using still images. Any suitable moving or still images may be used and these may be obtained covertly if necessary. Alternatively, the identification officer may make arrangements for a group identification. See Note 3D. These provisions may also be applied to juveniles where the consent of their parent or guardian is either refused or reasonable efforts to obtain that consent have failed. (see paragraph 2.12).

3.22 Any covert activity should be strictly limited to that necessary to test the ability of the witness to identify the suspect.

3.23 The identification officer may arrange for the suspect to be confronted by the witness if none of the options referred to in paragraphs 3.5 to 3.10 or 3.21 are practicable. A 'confrontation' is when the suspect is directly confronted by the witness. A confrontation does not require the suspect's consent. Confrontations must be carried out in accordance with Annex D.

3.24 Requirements for information to be given to, or sought from, a suspect or for the suspect to be given an opportunity to view images before they are shown to a witness, do not apply if the suspect's lack of co-operation prevents the necessary action.

(d)   Documentation

3.25 A record shall be made of the video identification, identification parade, group identification or confrontation on forms provided for the purpose.

3.26 If the identification officer considers it is not practicable to hold a video identification or identification parade requested by the suspect, the reasons shall be recorded and explained to the suspect.

3.27 A record shall be made of a person's failure or refusal to co-operate in a video identification, identification parade or group identification and, if applicable, of the grounds for obtaining images in accordance with paragraph 3.20.

(e) Not used.

3.28 *Not used.*

3.29 *Not used.*

(f) Destruction and retention of photographs taken or used in eye-witness identification procedures

3.30 PACE, section 64A, see paragraph 5.12, provides powers to take photographs of suspects and allows these photographs to be used or disclosed only for purposes related to the prevention or detection of crime, the investigation of offences or the conduct of prosecutions by, or on behalf of, police or other law enforcement and prosecuting authorities inside and outside the United Kingdom or the enforcement of a sentence. After being so used or disclosed, they may be retained but can only be used or disclosed for the same purposes.

3.31 Subject to paragraph 3.33, the photographs (and all negatives and copies), of suspects not taken in accordance with the provisions in paragraph 5.12 which are taken for the purposes of, or in connection with, the identification procedures in paragraphs 3.5 to 3.10, 3.21 or 3.23 must be destroyed unless the suspect:

(a)   is charged with, or informed they may be prosecuted for, a recordable offence;

(b)   is prosecuted for a recordable offence;

(c)   is cautioned for a recordable offence or given a warning or reprimand in accordance with the Crime and Disorder Act 1998 for a recordable offence; or

(d)   gives informed consent, in writing, for the photograph or images to be retained for purposes described in paragraph 3.30.

3.32 When paragraph 3.31 requires the destruction of any photograph, the person must be given an opportunity to witness the destruction or to have a certificate confirming the destruction if they request one within five days of being informed that the destruction is required.

3.33 Nothing in paragraph 3.31 affects any separate requirement under the Criminal Procedure and Investigations Act 1996 to retain material in connection with criminal investigations.

Part (B) Recognition by controlled showing of films, photographs and images

3.34 This Part of this section applies when, for the purposes of obtaining evidence of recognition, arrangements are made for a person, including a police officer, who is not an eye-witness (see Note 3AA):

(a)   to view a film, photograph or any other visual medium; and

(b)   on the occasion of the viewing, to be asked whether they recognise anyone whose image is shown in the material as someone who is known to them.

The arrangements for such viewings may be made by the officer in charge of the relevant investigation. Although there is no requirement for the identification officer to make the arrangements or to be consulted about the arrangements, nothing prevents this. (See Notes 3AA and 3G.)

3.35 To provide safeguards against mistaken recognition and to avoid any possibility of collusion, on the occasion of the viewing, the arrangements should ensure:

(a)   that the films, photographs and other images are shown on an individual basis;

(b)   that any person who views the material;

(i)   is unable to communicate with any other individual to whom the material has been, or is to be, shown;

(ii)   is not reminded of any photograph or description of any individual whose image is shown or given any other indication as to the identity of any such individual;

(iii)   is not to be told whether a previous witness has recognised any one;

(c)   that immediately before a person views the material, they are told that:

(i)   an individual who is known to them may, or may not, appear in the material they are shown and that if they do not recognise anyone, they should say so;

(ii)   at any point, they may ask to see a particular part of the material frozen for them to study and there is no limit on how many times they can view the whole or any part or parts of the material; and

(d)   that the person who views the material is not asked to make any decision as to whether they recognise anyone whose image they have seen as someone known to them until they have seen the whole of the material at least twice, unless the officer in charge of the viewing decides that because of the number of images the person has been invited to view, it would not be reasonable to ask them to view the whole of the material for a second time. A record of this decision must be included in the record that is made in accordance with paragraph 3.36.

(See Note 3G.)

3.36 A record of the circumstances and conditions under which the person is given an opportunity to recognise the individual must be made and the record must include:

(a)   Whether the person knew or was given information concerning the name or identity of any suspect.

(b)   What the person has been told before the viewing about the offence, the person(s) depicted in the images or the offender and by whom.

(c)   How and by whom the witness was asked to view the image or look at the individual.

(d)   Whether the viewing was alone or with others and if with others, the reason for it.

(e)   The arrangements under which the person viewed the film or saw the individual and by whom those arrangements were made.

(f)   Whether the viewing of any images was arranged as part of a mass circulation to police and the public or for selected persons.

(g)   The date time and place images were viewed or further viewed or the individual was seen.

(h)   The times between which the images were viewed or the individual was seen.

(i)   How the viewing of images or sighting of the individual was controlled and by whom.

(j)   Whether the person was familiar with the location shown in any images or the place where they saw the individual and if so, why.

(k)   Whether or not on this occasion, the person claims to recognise any image shown, or any individual seen, as being someone known to them, and if they do:

(i)   the reason

(ii)   the words of recognition

(iii)   any expressions of doubt

(iv)   what features of the image or the individual triggered the recognition.

3.37 The record required under paragraph 3.36 may be made by the person who views the image or sees the individual and makes the recognition; and if applicable, by the officer or police staff in charge of showing the images to that person or in charge of the conditions under which that person sees the individual. The person must be asked to read and check the completed record and as applicable, confirm that it is correctly and accurately reflects the part they played in the viewing (see Note 3H).

Part (C) Recognition by uncontrolled viewing of films, photographs and images

3.38 This Part applies when, for the purpose of identifying and tracing suspects, films and photographs of incidents or other images are:

(a)   shown to the public (which may include police officers and police staff as well as members of the public) through the national or local media or any social media networking site; or

(b)   circulated through local or national police communication systems for viewing by police officers and police staff; and

the viewing is not formally controlled and supervised as set out in Part B.

3.39 A copy of the relevant material released to the national or local media for showing as described in sub-paragraph 3.38(a), shall be kept. The suspect or their solicitor shall be allowed to view such material before any eye-witness identification procedure under paragraphs 3.5 to 3.10, 3.21 or 3.23 of Part A are carried out, provided it is practicable and would not unreasonably delay the investigation. This paragraph does not affect any separate requirement under the Criminal Procedure and Investigations Act 1996 to retain material in connection with criminal investigations that might apply to sub-paragraphs 3.38(a) and (b).

3.40 Each eye-witness involved in any eye-witness identification procedure under paragraphs 3.5 to 3.10, 3.21 or 3.23 shall be asked, after they have taken part, whether they have seen any film, photograph or image relating to the offence or any description of the suspect which has been broadcast or published as described in paragraph 3.38(a) and their reply recorded. If they have, they should be asked to give details of the circumstances and subject to the eye-witness's recollection, the record described in paragraph 3.41 should be completed.

3.41 As soon as practicable after an individual (member of the public, police officer or police staff) indicates in response to a viewing that they may have information relating to the identity and whereabouts of anyone they have seen in that viewing, arrangements should be made to ensure that they are asked to give details of the circumstances and, subject to the individual's recollection, a record of the circumstances and conditions under which the viewing took place is made. This record shall be made in accordance with the provisions of paragraph 3.36 insofar as they can be applied to the viewing in question (see Note 3H).

Notes for Guidance

3AA The eye-witness identification procedures in Part A should not be used to test whether a witness can recognise a person as someone they know and would be able to give evidence of recognition along the lines that 'On (describe date, time location) I saw an image of an individual who I recognised as AB.' In these cases, the procedures in Part B shall apply.

3ZA In paragraph 3.5(a)(i), examples of physical changes or differences that the identification officer may wish to consider include hair style and colour, weight, facial hair, wearing or removal of spectacles and tinted contact lenses, facial injuries, tattoos and makeup.

3A Except for the provisions of Annex E, paragraph 1, a police officer who is a witness for the purposes of this part of the Code is subject to the same principles and procedures as a civilian witness.

3B When a witness attending an identification procedure has previously been shown photographs, or been shown or provided with computerised or artist's composite likenesses, or similar likenesses or pictures, it is the officer in charge of the investigation's responsibility to make the identification officer aware of this.

3C The purpose of paragraph 3.19 is to avoid or reduce delay in arranging identification procedures by enabling the required information and warnings, see sub-paragraphs 3.17(ix) and 3.17(xii), to be given at the earliest opportunity.

3D Paragraph 3.21 would apply when a known suspect deliberately makes themselves 'unavailable' in order to delay or frustrate arrangements for obtaining identification evidence. It also applies when a suspect refuses or fails to take part in a video identification, an identification parade or a group identification, or refuses or fails to take part in the only practicable options from that list. It enables any suitable images of the suspect, moving or still, which are available or can be obtained, to be used in an identification procedure. Examples include images from custody and other CCTV systems and from visually recorded interview records, see Code F Note for Guidance 2D.

3E When it is proposed to show photographs to a witness in accordance with Annex E, it is the responsibility of the officer in charge of the investigation to confirm to the officer responsible for supervising and directing the showing, that the first description of the suspect given by that witness has been recorded. If this description has not been recorded, the procedure under Annex E must be postponed. See Annex E paragraph 2

3F The admissibility and value of identification evidence obtained when carrying out the procedure under paragraph 3.2 may be compromised if: .
(a) before a person is identified, the witness' attention is specifically drawn to that person; or
(b) the suspect's identity becomes known before the procedure.

3G The admissibility and value of evidence of recognition obtained when carrying out the procedures in Part B may be compromised if before the person is recognised, the witness who has claimed to know them is given or is made, or becomes aware of, information about the person which was not previously known to them personally but which they have purported to rely on to support their claim that the person is in fact known to them.

3H   It is important that the record referred to in paragraphs 3.36 and 3.41 is made as soon as practicable after the viewing and whilst it is fresh in the mind of the individual who makes the recognition.

4.   Identification by fingerprints and footwear impressions

(A)   *Taking fingerprints in connection with a criminal investigation*

(a)   *General*

4.1   References to 'fingerprints' means any record, produced by any method, of the skin pattern and other physical characteristics or features of a person's:

(i)   fingers; or

(ii)   palms.

(b)   *Action*

4.2   A person's fingerprints may be taken in connection with the investigation of an offence only with their consent or if paragraph 4.3 applies. If the person is at a police station consent must be in writing.

4.3   PACE, section 61, provides powers to take fingerprints without consent from any person over the age of ten years:

(a)   under section 61(3), from a person detained at a police station in consequence of being arrested for a recordable offence, see Note 4A, if they have not had their fingerprints taken in the course of the investigation of the offence unless those previously taken fingerprints are not a complete set or some or all of those fingerprints are not of sufficient quality to allow satisfactory analysis, comparison or matching.

(b)   under section 61(4), from a person detained at a police station who has been charged with a recordable offence, see Note 4A, or informed they will be reported for such an offence if they have not had their fingerprints taken in the course of the investigation of the offence unless those previously taken fingerprints are not a complete set or some or all of those fingerprints are not of sufficient quality to allow satisfactory analysis, comparison or matching.

(c)   under section 61(4A), from a person who has been bailed to appear at a court or police station if the person:

(i)   has answered to bail for a person whose fingerprints were taken previously and there are reasonable grounds for believing they are not the same person; or

(ii)   who has answered to bail claims to be a different person from a person whose fingerprints were previously taken;

and in either case, the court or an officer of inspector rank or above, authorises the fingerprints to be taken at the court or police station (an inspector's authority may be given in writing or orally and confirmed in writing, as soon as practicable);

(ca)   under section 61(5A) from a person who has been arrested for a recordable offence and released if the person:

(i)   is on bail and has not had their fingerprints taken in the course of the investigation of the offence, or;

(ii)   has had their fingerprints taken in the course of the investigation of the offence, but they do not constitute a complete set or some, or all, of the fingerprints are not of sufficient quality to allow satisfactory analysis, comparison or matching.

(cb)   under section 61(5B) from a person not detained at a police station who has been charged with a recordable offence or informed they will be reported for such an offence if they have not had their fingerprints taken in the course of the investigation or their fingerprints have been taken in the course of the investigation of the offence, but they do not constitute a complete set or some, or all, of the fingerprints are not of sufficient quality to allow satisfactory analysis, comparison or matching.

(d)   under section 61(6), from a person who has been:

(i)   convicted of a recordable offence;

(ii)   given a caution in respect of a recordable offence which, at the time of the caution, the person admitted; or

(iii)   warned or reprimanded under the Crime and Disorder Act 1998, section 65, for a recordable offence, if, since their conviction, caution, warning or reprimand their fingerprints have not been taken or their fingerprints which have been taken since then do not constitute a complete set or some, or all, of the fingerprints are not of sufficient quality to allow satisfactory analysis, comparison or matching, and in either case, an officer of inspector rank or above, is satisfied that taking the fingerprints is necessary to assist in the prevention or detection of crime and authorises the taking;

(e) under section 61(6A) from a person a constable reasonably suspects is committing or attempting to commit, or has committed or attempted to commit, any offence if either:

- the person's name is unknown and cannot be readily ascertained by the constable; or
- the constable has reasonable grounds for doubting whether a name given by the person is their real name.

Note: fingerprints taken under this power are not regarded as having been taken in the course of the investigation of an offence.
(See Note 4C.)

(f) under section 61(6D) from a person who has been convicted outside England and Wales of an offence which if committed in England and Wales would be a qualifying offence as defined by PACE, section 65A (see Note 4AB) if:

(i) the person's fingerprints have not been taken previously under this power or their fingerprints have been so taken on a previous occasion but they do not constitute a complete set or some, or all, of the fingerprints are not of sufficient quality to allow satisfactory analysis, comparison or matching; and

(ii) a police officer of inspector rank or above is satisfied that taking fingerprints is necessary to assist in the prevention or detection of crime and authorises them to be taken.

4.4 PACE, section 63A(4) and Schedule 2A provide powers to:

(a) make a requirement (in accordance with Annex G) for a person to attend a police station to have their fingerprints taken in the exercise of certain powers in paragraph 4.3 above when that power applies at the time the fingerprints would be taken in accordance with the requirement. Those powers are:

(i) section 61(5A) – Persons arrested for a recordable offence and released, see paragraph 4.3(ca): The requirement may not be made more than six months from the day the investigating officer was informed that the fingerprints previously taken were incomplete or below standard.

(ii) section 61(5B) – Persons charged etc with a recordable offence, see paragraph 4.3(cb): The requirement may not be made more than six months from:

- the day the person was charged or reported if fingerprints have not been taken since then; or
- the day the investigating officer was informed that the fingerprints previously taken were incomplete or below standard.

(iii) section 61(6) – Person convicted, cautioned, warned or reprimanded for a recordable offence in England and Wales, see paragraph 4.3(d): Where the offence for which the person was convicted etc is also a qualifying offence (see Note 4AB), there is no time limit for the exercise of this power. Where the conviction etc. is for a recordable offence which is not a qualifying offence, the requirement may not be made more than two years from:

- the day the person was convicted, cautioned, warned or reprimanded, or the day Schedule 2A comes into force (if later), if fingerprints have not been taken since then; or
- the day an officer from the force investigating the offence was informed that the fingerprints previously taken were incomplete or below standard or the day Schedule 2A comes into force (if later).

(iv) section 61(6D) – A person who has been convicted of a qualifying offence (see Note 4AB) outside England and Wales, see paragraph 4.3(g): There is no time limit for making the requirement.

Note: A person who has had their fingerprints taken under any of the powers in section 61 mentioned in paragraph 4.3 on two occasions in relation to any offence may not be required under Schedule 2A to attend a police station for their fingerprints to be taken again under section 61 in relation to that offence, unless authorised by an officer of inspector rank or above. The fact of the authorisation and the reasons for giving it must be recorded as soon as practicable.

(b)   arrest, without warrant, a person who fails to comply with the requirement.

4.5 A person's fingerprints may be taken, as above, electronically.

4.6 Reasonable force may be used, if necessary, to take a person's fingerprints without their consent under the powers as in paragraphs 4.3 and 4.4.

4.7 Before any fingerprints are taken:

(a)   without consent under any power mentioned in paragraphs 4.3 and 4.4 above, the person must be informed of:

(i)   the reason their fingerprints are to be taken;

(ii)   the power under which they are to be taken; and

(iii)   the fact that the relevant authority has been given if any power mentioned in paragraph 4.3(c), (d) or (f) applies

(b)   with or without consent at a police station or elsewhere, the person must be informed:

(i)   that their fingerprints may be subject of a speculative search against other fingerprints, see Note 4B; and

(ii)   that their fingerprints may be retained in accordance with Annex F, Part (a) unless they were taken under the power mentioned in paragraph 4.3(e) when they must be destroyed after they have being checked. (See Note 4C.)

(c) Documentation

4.8A A record must be made as soon as practicable after the fingerprints are taken, of:

• the matters in paragraph 4.7(a)(i) to (iii) and the fact that the person has been informed of those matters; and

• the fact that the person has been informed of the matters in paragraph 4.7(b) (i) and (ii).

The record must be made in the person's custody record if they are detained at a police station when the fingerprints are taken.

4.8 If force is used, a record shall be made of the circumstances and those present.

4.9 *Not used.*

(B) Not used.

4.10 *Not used.*

4.11 *Not used.*

4.12 *Not used.*

4.13 *Not used.*

4.14 *Not used.*

4.15 *Not used.*

(C) Taking footwear impressions in connection with a criminal investigation

(a) Action

4.16 Impressions of a person's footwear may be taken in connection with the investigation of an offence only with their consent or if paragraph 4.17 applies. If the person is at a police station consent must be in writing.

4.17 PACE, section 61A, provides power for a police officer to take footwear impressions without consent from any person over the age of ten years who is detained at a police station:

(a)   in consequence of being arrested for a recordable offence, see Note 4A; or if the detainee has been charged with a recordable offence, or informed they will be reported for such an offence; and

(b)   the detainee has not had an impression of their footwear taken in the course of the investigation of the offence unless the previously taken impression is not complete or is not of sufficient quality to allow satisfactory analysis, comparison or matching (whether in the case in question or generally).

4.18 Reasonable force may be used, if necessary, to take a footwear impression from a detainee without consent under the power in paragraph 4.17.

4.19 Before any footwear impression is taken with, or without, consent as above, the person must be informed:

(a)   of the reason the impression is to be taken;

(b)   that the impression may be retained and may be subject of a speculative search against other impressions, see Note 4B, unless destruction of the impression is required in accordance with Annex F, Part (a).

(b) Documentation

4.20 A record must be made as soon as possible, of the reason for taking a person's footwear impressions without consent. If force is used, a record shall be made of the circumstances and those present.

4.21 A record shall be made when a person has been informed under the terms of paragraph 4.19(b), of the possibility that their footwear impressions may be subject of a speculative search.

Notes for Guidance

4A   References to 'recordable offences' in this Code relate to those offences for which convictions, cautions, reprimands and warnings may be recorded in national police records. See PACE, section 27(4).

4AB A qualifying offence is one of the offences specified in PACE, section 65A.

4B   Fingerprints, footwear impressions or a DNA sample (and the information derived from it) taken from a person arrested on suspicion of being involved in a recordable offence, or charged with such an offence, or informed they will be reported for such an offence, may be subject of a speculative search. This means the fingerprints, footwear impressions or DNA sample may be checked against other fingerprints, footwear impressions and DNA records held by, or on behalf of, the police and other law enforcement authorities in, or outside, the UK, or held in connection with, or as a result of, an investigation of an offence inside or outside the UK.

4C   The power under section 61(6A) of PACE described in paragraph 4.3(e) allows fingerprints of a suspect who has not been arrested to be taken in connection with any offence (whether recordable or not) using a mobile device and then checked on the street against the database containing the national fingerprint collection. Fingerprints taken under this power cannot be retained after they have been checked. The results may make an arrest for the suspected offence based on the name condition unnecessary (See Code G paragraph 2.9(a)) and enable the offence to be disposed of without arrest, for example, by summons/charging by post, penalty notice or words of advice. If arrest for a non-recordable offence is necessary for any other reasons, this power may also be exercised at the station. Before the power is exercised, the officer should:

•   inform the person of the nature of the suspected offence and why they are suspected of committing it.

•   give them a reasonable opportunity to establish their real name before deciding that their name is unknown and cannot be readily ascertained or that there are reasonable grounds to doubt that a name they have given is their real name.

•   as applicable, inform the person of the reason why their name is not known and cannot be readily ascertained or of the grounds for doubting that a name they have given is their real name, including, for example, the reason why a particular document the person has produced to verify their real name, is not sufficient.

4D   *Not used.*

5.   Examinations to establish identity and the taking of photographs

(A) Detainees at police stations

(a) Searching or examination of detainees at police stations

5.1   PACE, section 54A(1), allows a detainee at a police station to be searched or examined or both, to establish:

(a)   whether they have any marks, features or injuries that would tend to identify them as a person involved in the commission of an offence and to photograph any identifying marks, see paragraph 5.5; or

(b)   their identity, see Note 5A.

A person detained at a police station to be searched under a stop and search power, see Code A, is not a detainee for the purposes of these powers.

5.2 A search and/or examination to find marks under section 54A (1) (a) may be carried out without the detainee's consent, see paragraph 2.12, only if authorised by an officer of at least inspector rank when consent has been withheld or it is not practicable to obtain consent, see Note 5D.

5.3 A search or examination to establish a suspect's identity under section 54A (1) (b) may be carried out without the detainee's consent, see paragraph 2.12, only if authorised by an officer of at least inspector rank when the detainee has refused to identify themselves or the authorising officer has reasonable grounds for suspecting the person is not who they claim to be.

5.4 Any marks that assist in establishing the detainee's identity, or their identification as a person involved in the commission of an offence, are identifying marks. Such marks may be photographed with the detainee's consent, see paragraph 2.12; or without their consent if it is withheld or it is not practicable to obtain it, see Note 5D.

5.5 A detainee may only be searched, examined and photographed under section 54A, by a police officer of the same sex.

5.6 Any photographs of identifying marks, taken under section 54A, may be used or disclosed only for purposes related to the prevention or detection of crime, the investigation of offences or the conduct of prosecutions by, or on behalf of, police or other law enforcement and prosecuting authorities inside, and outside, the UK. After being so used or disclosed, the photograph may be retained but must not be used or disclosed except for these purposes, see Note 5B.

5.7 The powers, as in paragraph 5.1, do not affect any separate requirement under the Criminal Procedure and Investigations Act 1996 to retain material in connection with criminal investigations.

5.8 Authority for the search and/or examination for the purposes of paragraphs 5.2 and 5.3 may be given orally or in writing. If given orally, the authorising officer must confirm it in writing as soon as practicable. A separate authority is required for each purpose which applies.

5.9 If it is established a person is unwilling to co-operate sufficiently to enable a search and/ or examination to take place or a suitable photograph to be taken, an officer may use reasonable force to:

(a)　　search and/or examine a detainee without their consent; and

(b)　　photograph any identifying marks without their consent.

5.10 The thoroughness and extent of any search or examination carried out in accordance with the powers in section 54A must be no more than the officer considers necessary to achieve the required purpose. Any search or examination which involves the removal of more than the person's outer clothing shall be conducted in accordance with Code C, Annex A, paragraph 11.

5.11 An intimate search may not be carried out under the powers in section 54A.

(b) **Photographing detainees at police stations and other persons elsewhere than at a police station**

5.12 Under PACE, section 64A, an officer may photograph:

(a)　　any person whilst they are detained at a police station; and

(b)　　any person who is elsewhere than at a police station and who has been:

(i)　　arrested by a constable for an offence;

(ii)　　taken into custody by a constable after being arrested for an offence by a person other than a constable;

(iii)　　made subject to a requirement to wait with a community support officer under paragraph 2(3) or (3B) of Schedule 4 to the Police Reform Act 2002;

(iiia)　　given a direction by a constable under section 27 of the Violent Crime Reduction Act 2006.

(iv)　　given a penalty notice by a constable in uniform under Chapter 1 of Part 1 of the Criminal Justice and Police Act 2001, a penalty notice by a constable under section 444A of the Education Act 1996, or a fixed penalty notice by a constable in uniform under section 54 of the Road Traffic Offenders Act 1988;

(v)　　given a notice in relation to a relevant fixed penalty offence (within the meaning of paragraph 1 of Schedule 4 to the Police Reform Act 2002) by a community support officer by virtue of a designation applying that paragraph to him;

(vi)   given a notice in relation to a relevant fixed penalty offence (within the meaning of paragraph 1 of Schedule 5 to the Police Reform Act 2002) by an accredited person by virtue of accreditation specifying that that paragraph applies to him; or

(vii)   given a direction to leave and not return to a specified location for up to 48 hours by a police constable (under section 27 of the Violent Crime Reduction Act 2006).

5.12A Photographs taken under PACE, section 64A:

(a)   may be taken with the person's consent, or without their consent if consent is withheld or it is not practicable to obtain their consent, see Note 5E; and

(b)   may be used or disclosed only for purposes related to the prevention or detection of crime, the investigation of offences or the conduct of prosecutions by, or on behalf of, police or other law enforcement and prosecuting authorities inside and outside the United Kingdom or the enforcement of any sentence or order made by a court when dealing with an offence. After being so used or disclosed, they may be retained but can only be used or disclosed for the same purposes. See Note 5B.

5.13 The officer proposing to take a detainee's photograph may, for this purpose, require the person to remove any item or substance worn on, or over, all, or any part of, their head or face. If they do not comply with such a requirement, the officer may remove the item or substance.

5.14 If it is established the detainee is unwilling to co-operate sufficiently to enable a suitable photograph to be taken and it is not reasonably practicable to take the photograph covertly, an officer may use reasonable force, see Note 5F.

(a)   to take their photograph without their consent; and

(b)   for the purpose of taking the photograph, remove any item or substance worn on, or over, all, or any part of, the person's head or face which they have failed to remove when asked.

5.15 For the purposes of this Code, a photograph may be obtained without the person's consent by making a copy of an image of them taken at any time on a camera system installed anywhere in the police station.

(c) *Information to be given*

5.16 When a person is searched, examined or photographed under the provisions as in paragraph 5.1 and 5.12, or their photograph obtained as in paragraph 5.15, they must be informed of the:

(a)   purpose of the search, examination or photograph;

(b)   grounds on which the relevant authority, if applicable, has been given; and

(c)   purposes for which the photograph may be used, disclosed or retained.

This information must be given before the search or examination commences or the photograph is taken, except if the photograph is:

(i)   to be taken covertly;

(ii)   obtained as in paragraph 5.15, in which case the person must be informed as soon as practicable after the photograph is taken or obtained.

(d) *Documentation*

5.17 A record must be made when a detainee is searched, examined, or a photograph of the person, or any identifying marks found on them, are taken. The record must include the:

(a)   identity, subject to paragraph 2.18, of the officer carrying out the search, examination or taking the photograph;

(b)   purpose of the search, examination or photograph and the outcome;

(c)   detainee's consent to the search, examination or photograph, or the reason the person was searched, examined or photographed without consent;

(d)   giving of any authority as in paragraphs 5.2 and 5.3, the grounds for giving it and the authorising officer.

5.18 If force is used when searching, examining or taking a photograph in accordance with this section, a record shall be made of the circumstances and those present.

(B) *Persons at police stations not detained*

5.19 When there are reasonable grounds for suspecting the involvement of a person in a criminal offence, but that person is at a police station voluntarily and not detained, the provisions of paragraphs 5.1 to 5.18 should apply, subject to the modifications in the following paragraphs.

5.20 References to the 'person being detained' and to the powers mentioned in paragraph 5.1 which apply only to detainees at police stations shall be omitted.

5.21 Force may not be used to:
  (a)   search and/or examine the person to:
    (i)   discover whether they have any marks that would tend to identify them as a person involved in the commission of an offence; or
    (ii)   establish their identity, see Note 5A;
  (b)   take photographs of any identifying marks, see paragraph 5.4; or
  (c)   take a photograph of the person.

5.22 Subject to paragraph 5.24, the photographs of persons or of their identifying marks which are not taken in accordance with the provisions mentioned in paragraphs 5.1 or 5.12, must be destroyed (together with any negatives and copies) unless the person:
  (a)   is charged with, or informed they may be prosecuted for, a recordable offence;
  (b)   is prosecuted for a recordable offence;
  (c)   is cautioned for a recordable offence or given a warning or reprimand in accordance with the Crime and Disorder Act 1998 for a recordable offence; or
  (d)   gives informed consent, in writing, for the photograph or image to be retained as in paragraph 5.6.

5.23 When paragraph 5.22 requires the destruction of any photograph, the person must be given an opportunity to witness the destruction or to have a certificate confirming the destruction provided they so request the certificate within five days of being informed the destruction is required.

5.24 Nothing in paragraph 5.22 affects any separate requirement under the Criminal Procedure and Investigations Act 1996 to retain material in connection with criminal investigations.

Notes for Guidance

5A   The conditions under which fingerprints may be taken to assist in establishing a person's identity, are described in Section 4.

5B   Examples of purposes related to the prevention or detection of crime, the investigation of offences or the conduct of prosecutions include:
  (a)   checking the photograph against other photographs held in records or in connection with, or as a result of, an investigation of an offence to establish whether the person is liable to arrest for other offences;
  (b)   when the person is arrested at the same time as other people, or at a time when it is likely that other people will be arrested, using the photograph to help establish who was arrested, at what time and where;
  (c)   when the real identity of the person is not known and cannot be readily ascertained or there are reasonable grounds for doubting a name and other personal details given by the person, are their real name and personal details. In these circumstances, using or disclosing the photograph to help to establish or verify their real identity or determine whether they are liable to arrest for some other offence, e.g. by checking it against other photographs held in records or in connection with, or as a result of, an investigation of an offence;
  (d)   when it appears any identification procedure in section 3 may need to be arranged for which the person's photograph would assist;
  (e)   when the person's release without charge may be required, and if the release is:
    (i)   on bail to appear at a police station, using the photograph to help verify the person's identity when they answer their bail and if the person does not answer their bail, to assist in arresting them; or
    (ii)   without bail, using the photograph to help verify their identity or assist in locating them for the purposes of serving them with a summons to appear at court in criminal proceedings;
  (f)   when the person has answered to bail at a police station and there are reasonable grounds for doubting they are the person who was previously granted bail, using the photograph to help establish or verify their identity;

(g) when the person arrested on a warrant claims to be a different person from the person named on the warrant and a photograph would help to confirm or disprove their claim;

(h) when the person has been charged with, reported for, or convicted of, a recordable offence and their photograph is not already on record as a result of (a) to (f) or their photograph is on record but their appearance has changed since it was taken and the person has not yet been released or brought before a court.

5C There is no power to arrest a person convicted of a recordable offence solely to take their photograph. The power to take photographs in this section applies only where the person is in custody as a result of the exercise of another power, e.g. arrest for fingerprinting under PACE, section 27.

5D Examples of when it would not be practicable to obtain a detainee's consent, see paragraph 2.12, to a search, examination or the taking of a photograph of an identifying mark include:

(a) when the person is drunk or otherwise unfit to give consent;

(b) when there are reasonable grounds to suspect that if the person became aware a search or examination was to take place or an identifying mark was to be photographed, they would take steps to prevent this happening, e.g. by violently resisting, covering or concealing the mark etc and it would not otherwise be possible to carry out the search or examination or to photograph any identifying mark;

(c) in the case of a juvenile, if the parent or guardian cannot be contacted in sufficient time to allow the search or examination to be carried out or the photograph to be taken.

5E Examples of when it would not be practicable to obtain the person's consent, see paragraph 2.12, to a photograph being taken include:

(a) when the person is drunk or otherwise unfit to give consent;

(b) when there are reasonable grounds to suspect that if the person became aware a photograph, suitable to be used or disclosed for the use and disclosure described in paragraph 5.6, was to be taken, they would take steps to prevent it being taken, e.g. by violently resisting, covering or distorting their face etc, and it would not otherwise be possible to take a suitable photograph;

(c) when, in order to obtain a suitable photograph, it is necessary to take it covertly; and

(d) in the case of a juvenile, if the parent or guardian cannot be contacted in sufficient time to allow the photograph to be taken.

5F The use of reasonable force to take the photograph of a suspect elsewhere than at a police station must be carefully considered. In order to obtain a suspect's consent and co-operation to remove an item of religious headwear to take their photograph, a constable should consider whether in the circumstances of the situation the removal of the headwear and the taking of the photograph should be by an officer of the same sex as the person. It would be appropriate for these actions to be conducted out of public view.

6. Identification by body samples and impressions

(A) General

6.1 References to:

(a) an 'intimate sample' mean a dental impression or sample of blood, semen or any other tissue fluid, urine, or pubic hair, or a swab taken from any part of a person's genitals or from a person's body orifice other than the mouth;

(b) a 'non-intimate sample' means:

(i) a sample of hair, other than pubic hair, which includes hair plucked with the root, see Note 6A;

(ii) a sample taken from a nail or from under a nail;

(iii) a swab taken from any part of a person's body other than a part from which a swab taken would be an intimate sample;

(iv) saliva;

(v) a skin impression which means any record, other than a fingerprint, which is a record, in any form and produced by any method, of the skin pattern and other physical characteristics or features of the whole, or any part of, a person's foot or of any other part of their body.

(B) Action

(a) Intimate samples

6.2 PACE, section 62, provides that intimate samples may be taken under:

    (a)   section 62(1), from a person in police detention only:

        (i)   if a police officer of inspector rank or above has reasonable grounds to believe such an impression or sample will tend to confirm or disprove the suspect's involvement in a recordable offence, see Note 4A, and gives authorisation for a sample to be taken; and

        (ii)   with the suspect's written consent;

    (b)   section 62(1A), from a person not in police detention but from whom two or more non-intimate samples have been taken in the course of an investigation of an offence and the samples, though suitable, have proved insufficient if:

        (i)   a police officer of inspector rank or above authorises it to be taken; and

        (ii)   the person concerned gives their written consent. See Notes 6B and 6C

    (c)   section 62(2A), from a person convicted outside England and Wales of an offence which if committed in England and Wales would be qualifying offence as defined by PACE, section 65A (see Note 4AB) from whom two or more non-intimate samples taken under section 63(3E) (see paragraph 6.6(h)) have proved insufficient if:

        (i)   a police officer of inspector rank or above is satisfied that taking the sample is necessary to assist in the prevention or detection of crime and authorises it to be taken; and

        (ii)   the person concerned gives their written consent.

6.2A PACE, section 63A(4) and Schedule 2A provide powers to:

    (a)   make a requirement (in accordance with Annex G) for a person to attend a police station to have an intimate sample taken in the exercise of one of the following powers in paragraph 6.2 when that power applies at the time the sample is to be taken in accordance with the requirement or after the person's arrest if they fail to comply with the requirement:

        (i)   section 62(1A) – Persons from whom two or more non-intimate samples have been taken and proved to be insufficient, see paragraph 6.2(b): There is no time limit for making the requirement.

        (ii)   section 62(2A) – Persons convicted outside England and Wales from whom two or more non-intimate samples taken under section 63(3E) (see paragraph 6.6(h)) have proved insufficient, see paragraph 6.2(c): There is no time limit for making the requirement.

6.3 Before a suspect is asked to provide an intimate sample, they must be:

    (a)   informed:

        (i)   of the reason, including the nature of the suspected offence (except if taken under paragraph 6.2(c) from a person convicted outside England and Wales.

        (ii)   that authorisation has been given and the provisions under which given;

        (iii)   that a sample taken at a police station may be subject of a speculative search;

    (b)   warned that if they refuse without good cause their refusal may harm their case if it comes to trial, see Note 6D. If the suspect is in police detention and not legally represented, they must also be reminded of their entitlement to have free legal advice, see Code C, paragraph 6.5, and the reminder noted in the custody record. If paragraph 6.2(b) applies and the person is attending a station voluntarily, their entitlement to free legal advice as in Code C, paragraph 3.21 shall be explained to them.

6.4 Dental impressions may only be taken by a registered dentist. Other intimate samples, except for samples of urine, may only be taken by a registered medical practitioner or registered nurse or registered paramedic.

(b) Non-intimate samples

6.5 A non-intimate sample may be taken from a detainee only with their written consent or if paragraph 6.6 applies.

6.6 a non-intimate sample may be taken from a person without the appropriate consent in the following circumstances:

(a) under section 63(2A) from a person who is in police detention as a consequence of being arrested for a recordable offence and who has not had a non-intimate sample of the same type and from the same part of the body taken in the course of the investigation of the offence by the police or they have had such a sample taken but it proved insufficient.

(b) Under section 63(3) from a person who is being held in custody by the police on the authority of a court if an officer of at least the rank of inspector authorises it to be taken. An authorisation may be given:

 (i) if the authorising officer has reasonable grounds for suspecting the person of involvement in a recordable offence and for believing that the sample will tend to confirm or disprove that involvement, and

 (ii) in writing or orally and confirmed in writing, as soon as practicable;

 but an authorisation may not be given to take from the same part of the body a further non-intimate sample consisting of a skin impression unless the previously taken impression proved insufficient

(c) under section 63(3ZA) from a person who has been arrested for a recordable offence and released if the person:

 (i) is on bail and has not had a sample of the same type and from the same part of the body taken in the course of the investigation of the offence, or;

 (ii) has had such a sample taken in the course of the investigation of the offence, but it proved unsuitable or insufficient.

(d) under section 63(3A), from a person (whether or not in police detention or held in custody by the police on the authority of a court) who has been charged with a recordable offence or informed they will be reported for such an offence if the person:

 (i) has not had a non-intimate sample taken from them in the course of the investigation of the offence;

 (ii) has had a sample so taken, but it proved unsuitable or insufficient, see Note 6B; or

 (iii) has had a sample taken in the course of the investigation of the offence and the sample has been destroyed and in proceedings relating to that offence there is a dispute as to whether a DNA profile relevant to the proceedings was derived from the destroyed sample.

(e) under section 63(3B), from a person who has been:

 (i) convicted of a recordable offence;

 (ii) given a caution in respect of a recordable offence which, at the time of the caution, the person admitted; or

 (iii) warned or reprimanded under the Crime and Disorder Act 1998, section 65, for a recordable offence,

 if, since their conviction, caution, warning or reprimand a non-intimate sample has not been taken from them or a sample which has been taken since then has proved to be unsuitable or insufficient and in either case, an officer of inspector rank or above, is satisfied that taking the fingerprints is necessary to assist in the prevention or detection of crime and authorises the taking;

(f) under section 63(3C) from a person to whom section 2 of the Criminal Evidence (Amendment) Act 1997 applies (persons detained following acquittal on grounds of insanity or finding of unfitness to plead).

(g) under section 63(3E) from a person who has been convicted outside England and Wales of an offence which if committed in England and Wales would be a qualifying offence as defined by PACE, section 65A (see Note 4AB) if:

 (i) a non-intimate sample has not been taken previously under this power or unless a sample was so taken but was unsuitable or insufficient; and

 (ii) a police officer of inspector rank or above is satisfied that taking a sample is necessary to assist in the prevention or detection of crime and authorises it to be taken.

6.6A PACE, section 63A(4) and Schedule 2A provide powers to:

(a)   make a requirement (in accordance with Annex G) for a person to attend a police station to have a non-intimate sample taken in the exercise of one of the following powers in paragraph 6.6 when that power applies at the time the sample would be taken in accordance with the requirement:

   (i)   section 63(3ZA) – Persons arrested for a recordable offence and released, see paragraph 6.6(c): The requirement may not be made more than six months from the day the investigating officer was informed that the sample previously taken was unsuitable or insufficient.

   (ii)   section 63(3A) – Persons charged etc with a recordable offence, see paragraph 6.6(d): The requirement may not be made more than six months from:

   • the day the person was charged or reported if a sample has not been taken since then; or

   • the day the investigating officer was informed that the sample previously taken was unsuitable or insufficient.

   (iii) section 63(3B) – Person convicted, cautioned, warned or reprimanded for a recordable offence in England and Wales, see paragraph 6.6(e): Where the offence for which the person was convicted etc is also a qualifying offence (see Note 4AB), there is no time limit for the exercise of this power. Where the conviction etc was for a recordable offence that is not a qualifying offence, the requirement may not be made more than two years from:

   • the day the person was convicted, cautioned, warned or reprimanded, or the day Schedule 2A comes into force (if later), if a samples has not been taken since then; or

   • the day an officer from the force investigating the offence was informed that the sample previously taken was unsuitable or insufficient or the day Schedule 2A comes into force (if later).

   (iv)   section 63(3E) – A person who has been convicted of qualifying offence (see Note 4AB) outside England and Wales, see paragraph 6.6(h): There is no time limit for making the requirement.

   Note: A person who has had a non-intimate sample taken under any of the powers in section 63 mentioned in paragraph 6.6 on two occasions in relation to any offence may not be required under Schedule 2A to attend a police station for a sample to be taken again under section 63 in relation to that offence, unless authorised by an officer of inspector rank or above. The fact of the authorisation and the reasons for giving it must be recorded as soon as practicable.

(b)   arrest, without warrant, a person who fails to comply with the requirement.

6.7   Reasonable force may be used, if necessary, to take a non-intimate sample from a person without their consent under the powers mentioned in paragraph 6.6.

6.8   Before any non-intimate sample is taken:

(a)   without consent under any power mentioned in paragraphs 6.6 and 6.6A, the person must be informed of:

   (i)   the reason for taking the sample;

   (ii)   the power under which the sample is to be taken;

   (iii) the fact that the relevant authority has been given if any power mentioned in paragraph 6.6(b), (e) or (h) applies;

(b)   with or without consent at a police station or elsewhere, the person must be informed:

   (i)   that their sample or information derived from it may be subject of a speculative search against other samples and information derived from them, see Note 6E and

   (ii)   that their sample and the information derived from it may be retained in accordance with Annex F, Part (a).

(c)   *Removal of clothing*

6.9   When clothing needs to be removed in circumstances likely to cause embarrassment to the person, no person of the opposite sex who is not a registered medical practitioner or registered health care professional shall be present, (unless in the case of a juvenile, mentally disordered or mentally vulnerable person, that person specifically requests the presence of an appropriate adult of the opposite sex who is readily available) nor shall anyone whose presence is unnecessary. However, in the case of a juvenile, this is subject to the overriding proviso that such a removal of clothing may take place in the absence of the appropriate adult only if the juvenile signifies in their presence, that they prefer the adult's absence and they agree.

(d) Documentation

6.10 A record must be made as soon as practicable after the sample is taken of:

- The matters in paragraph 6.8(a)(i) to (iii) and the fact that the person has been informed of those matters; and
- The fact that the person has been informed of the matters in paragraph 6.8(b) (i) and (ii).

6.10A If force is used, a record shall be made of the circumstances and those present.

6.11 A record must be made of a warning given as required by paragraph 6.3.

6.12 *Not used.*

Notes for Guidance

6A When hair samples are taken for the purpose of DNA analysis (rather than for other purposes such as making a visual match), the suspect should be permitted a reasonable choice as to what part of the body the hairs are taken from. When hairs are plucked, they should be plucked individually, unless the suspect prefers otherwise and no more should be plucked than the person taking them reasonably considers necessary for a sufficient sample.

6B (a) An insufficient sample is one which is not sufficient either in quantity or quality to provide information for a particular form of analysis, such as DNA analysis. A sample may also be insufficient if enough information cannot be obtained from it by analysis because of loss, destruction, damage or contamination of the sample or as a result of an earlier, unsuccessful attempt at analysis.

    (b) An unsuitable sample is one which, by its nature, is not suitable for a particular form of analysis.

6C Nothing in paragraph 6.2 prevents intimate samples being taken for elimination purposes with the consent of the person concerned but the provisions of paragraph 2.12 relating to the role of the appropriate adult, should be applied. Paragraph 6.2(b) does not, however, apply where the non-intimate samples were previously taken under the Terrorism Act 2000, Schedule 8, paragraph 10.

6D In warning a person who is asked to provide an intimate sample as in paragraph 6.3, the following form of words may be used:

'You do not have to provide this sample/allow this swab or impression to be taken, but I must warn you that if you refuse without good cause, your refusal may harm your case if it comes to trial.'

6E Fingerprints or a DNA sample and the information derived from it taken from a person arrested on suspicion of being involved in a recordable offence, or charged with such an offence, or informed they will be reported for such an offence, may be subject of a speculative search. This means they may be checked against other fingerprints and DNA records held by, or on behalf of, the police and other law enforcement authorities in or outside the UK or held in connection with, or as a result of, an investigation of an offence inside or outside the UK.

See Annex F regarding the retention and use of fingerprints and samples taken with consent for elimination purposes.

6F Samples of urine and non-intimate samples taken in accordance with sections 63B and 63C of PACE may not be used for identification purposes in accordance with this Code. See Code C note for guidance 17D.

Annex A – Video identification

(a) General

1. The arrangements for obtaining and ensuring the availability of a suitable set of images to be used in a video identification must be the responsibility of an identification officer, who has no direct involvement with the case.

2. The set of images must include the suspect and at least eight other people who, so far as possible, resemble the suspect in age, general appearance and position in life. Only one suspect shall appear in any set unless there are two suspects of roughly similar appearance, in which case they may be shown together with at least twelve other people.

2A If the suspect has an unusual physical feature, e.g., a facial scar, tattoo or distinctive hairstyle or hair colour which does not appear on the images of the other people that are available to be used, steps may be taken to:

(a) conceal the location of the feature on the images of the suspect and the other people; or

(b) replicate that feature on the images of the other people.

For these purposes, the feature may be concealed or replicated electronically or by any other method which it is practicable to use to ensure that the images of the suspect and other people resemble each other. The identification officer has discretion to choose whether to conceal or replicate the feature and the method to be used. If an unusual physical feature has been described by the witness, the identification officer should, if practicable, have that feature replicated. If it has not been described, concealment may be more appropriate.

2B If the identification officer decides that a feature should be concealed or replicated, the reason for the decision and whether the feature was concealed or replicated in the images shown to any witness shall be recorded.

2C If the witness requests to view an image where an unusual physical feature has been concealed or replicated without the feature being concealed or replicated, the witness may be allowed to do so.

3. The images used to conduct a video identification shall, as far as possible, show the suspect and other people in the same positions or carrying out the same sequence of movements. They shall also show the suspect and other people under identical conditions unless the identification officer reasonably believes:

(a) because of the suspect's failure or refusal to co-operate or other reasons, it is not practicable for the conditions to be identical; and

(b) any difference in the conditions would not direct a witness' attention to any individual image.

4. The reasons identical conditions are not practicable shall be recorded on forms provided for the purpose.

5. Provision must be made for each person shown to be identified by number.

6. If police officers are shown, any numerals or other identifying badges must be concealed. If a prison inmate is shown, either as a suspect or not, then either all, or none of, the people shown should be in prison clothing.

7. The suspect or their solicitor, friend, or appropriate adult must be given a reasonable opportunity to see the complete set of images before it is shown to any witness. If the suspect has a reasonable objection to the set of images or any of the participants, the suspect shall be asked to state the reasons for the objection. Steps shall, if practicable, be taken to remove the grounds for objection. If this is not practicable, the suspect and/or their representative shall be told why their objections cannot be met and the objection, the reason given for it and why it cannot be met shall be recorded on forms provided for the purpose.

8. Before the images are shown in accordance with paragraph 7, the suspect or their solicitor shall be provided with details of the first description of the suspect by any witnesses who are to attend the video identification. When a broadcast or publication is made, as in paragraph 3.28, the suspect or their solicitor must also be allowed to view any material released to the media by the police for the purpose of recognising or tracing the suspect, provided it is practicable and would not unreasonably delay the investigation.

9. No unauthorised people may be present when the video identification is conducted. The suspect's solicitor, if practicable, shall be given reasonable notification of the time and place the video identification is to be conducted. The suspect's solicitor may only be present at the video identification on request and with the prior agreement of the identification officer, if the officer is satisfied that the solicitor's presence will not deter or distract any eye-witness from viewing the images and making an identification. If the identification officer is not satisfied and does not agree to the request, the reason must be recorded. The solicitor must be informed of the decision and the reason for it. and that they may then make

representations about why they should be allowed to be present. The representations may be made orally or in writing, in person or remotely by electronic communication and must be recorded. These representations must be considered by an officer of at least the rank of inspector who is not involved with the investigation and responsibility for this may not be delegated under paragraph 3.11. If, after considering the representations, the officer is satisfied that the solicitor's presence will deter or distract the eye-witness, the officer shall inform the solicitor of the decision and reason for it and ensure that any response by the solicitor is also recorded. If allowed to be present, the solicitor is not entitled to communicate in any way with an eye-witness during the procedure but this does not prevent the solicitor from communicating with the identification officer. The suspect may not be present when the images are shown to any eye-witness and is not entitled to be informed of the time and place the video identification procedure is to be conducted. The video identification procedure itself shall be recorded on video with sound. The recording must show all persons present within the sight or hearing of the eye-witness whilst the images are being viewed and must include what the eye-witness says and what is said to them by the identification officer and by any other person present at the video identification procedure. A supervised viewing of the recording of the video identification procedure by the suspect and/or their solicitor may be arranged on request, at the discretion of the investigating officer. Where the recording of the video identification procedure is to be shown to the suspect and/or their solicitor, the investigating officer may arrange for anything in the recording that might allow the eye-witness to be identified to be concealed if the investigating officer considers that this is justified (see Note A2). In accordance with paragraph 2.18, the investigating officer may also arrange for anything in that recording that might allow any police officers or police staff to be identified to be concealed.

(b)   ***Conducting the video identification***
10.   The identification officer is responsible for making the appropriate arrangements to make sure, before they see the set of images, witnesses are not able to communicate with each other about the case, see any of the images which are to be shown, see, or be reminded of, any photograph or description of the suspect or be given any other indication as to the suspect's identity, or overhear a witness who has already seen the material. There must be no discussion with the witness about the composition of the set of images and they must not be told whether a previous witness has made any identification.

11.   Only one witness may see the set of images at a time. Immediately before the images are shown, the witness shall be told that the person they saw on a specified earlier occasion may, or may not, appear in the images they are shown and that if they cannot make a positive identification, they should say so. The witness shall be advised that at any point, they may ask to see a particular part of the set of images or to have a particular image frozen for them to study. Furthermore, it should be pointed out to the witness that there is no limit on how many times they can view the whole set of images or any part of them. However, they should be asked not to make any decision as to whether the person they saw is on the set of images until they have seen the whole set at least twice.

12.   Once the witness has seen the whole set of images at least twice and has indicated that they do not want to view the images, or any part of them, again, the witness shall be asked to say whether the individual they saw in person on a specified earlier occasion has been shown and, if so, to identify them by number of the image. The witness will then be shown that image to confirm the identification, see paragraph 17.

13.   Care must be taken not to direct the witness' attention to any one individual image or give any indication of the suspect's identity. Where a witness has previously made an identification by photographs, or a computerised or artist's composite or similar likeness, the witness must not be reminded of such a photograph or composite likeness once a suspect is available for identification by other means in accordance with this Code. Nor must the witness be reminded of any description of the suspect.

13A.   If after the video identification procedure has ended, the eye-witness informs any police officer or police staff involved in the post-viewing arrangements that they wish to change their decision about their identification, or they have not made an identification when in fact they could have made one, an accurate record of the words used by the eye-witness and of the circumstances immediately after the procedure ended, shall be made. If the eyewitness has not had an opportunity to communicate with other people about the procedure, the identification officer has the discretion to allow the eye-witness a second opportunity to make an identification by repeating the video identification procedure using the same images but in different positions.

14.   After the procedure, action required in accordance with paragraph 3.40 applies.

(c)   ***Image security and destruction***

15.   Arrangements shall be made for all relevant material containing sets of images used for specific identification procedures to be kept securely and their movements accounted for. In particular, no-one involved in the investigation shall be permitted to view the material prior to it being shown to any witness.

16.   As appropriate, paragraph 3.30 or 3.31 applies to the destruction or retention of relevant sets of images.

(d)   ***Documentation***

17.   A record must be made of all those participating in, or seeing, the set of images whose names are known to the police.

18.   A record of the conduct of the video identification must be made on forms provided for the purpose. This shall include anything said by the witness about any identifications or the conduct of the procedure and any reasons it was not practicable to comply with any of the provisions of this Code governing the conduct of video identifications.

Annex B – identification parades

(a)   ***General***

1.   A suspect must be given a reasonable opportunity to have a solicitor or friend present, and the suspect shall be asked to indicate on a second copy of the notice whether or not they wish to do so.

2.   An identification parade may take place either in a normal room or one equipped with a screen permitting witnesses to see members of the identification parade without being seen. The procedures for the composition and conduct of the identification parade are the same in both cases, subject to paragraph 8 (except that an identification parade involving a screen may take place only when the suspect's solicitor, friend or appropriate adult is present or the identification parade is recorded on video).

3.   Before the identification parade takes place, the suspect or their solicitor shall be provided with details of the first description of the suspect by any witnesses who are attending the identification parade. When a broadcast or publication is made as in paragraph 3.28, the suspect or their solicitor should also be allowed to view any material released to the media by the police for the purpose of recognising or tracing the suspect, provided it is practicable to do so and would not unreasonably delay the investigation.

(b)   ***Identification parades involving prison inmates***

4.   If a prison inmate is required for identification, and there are no security problems about the person leaving the establishment, they may be asked to participate in an identification parade or video identification.

5.   An identification parade may be held in a Prison Department establishment but shall be conducted, as far as practicable under normal identification parade rules. Members of the public shall make up the identification parade unless there are serious security, or control, objections to their admission to the establishment. In such cases, or if a group or video identification is arranged within the establishment, other inmates may participate. If an inmate is the suspect, they are not required to wear prison clothing for the identification parade unless the other people taking part are other inmates in similar clothing, or are members of the public who are prepared to wear prison clothing for the occasion.

(c)   ***Conduct of the identification parade***

6.   Immediately before the identification parade, the suspect must be reminded of the procedures governing its conduct and cautioned in the terms of Code C, paragraphs 10.5 or 10.6, as appropriate.

7.   All unauthorised people must be excluded from the place where the identification parade is held.

8.   Once the identification parade has been formed, everything afterwards, in respect of it, shall take place in the presence and hearing of the suspect and any interpreter, solicitor, friend or appropriate adult who is present (unless the identification parade involves a screen, in which case everything said to, or by, any witness at the place where the identification parade is held, must be said in the hearing and presence of the suspect's solicitor, friend or appropriate adult or be recorded on video).

9. The identification parade shall consist of at least eight people (in addition to the suspect) who, so far as possible, resemble the suspect in age, height, general appearance and position in life. Only one suspect shall be included in an identification parade unless there are two suspects of roughly similar appearance, in which case they may be paraded together with at least twelve other people. In no circumstances shall more than two suspects be included in one identification parade and where there are separate identification parades, they shall be made up of different people.

10. If the suspect has an unusual physical feature, e.g., a facial scar, tattoo or distinctive hairstyle or hair colour which cannot be replicated on other members of the identification parade, steps may be taken to conceal the location of that feature on the suspect and the other members of the identification parade if the suspect and their solicitor, or appropriate adult, agree. For example, by use of a plaster or a hat, so that all members of the identification parade resemble each other in general appearance.

11. When all members of a similar group are possible suspects, separate identification parades shall be held for each unless there are two suspects of similar appearance when they may appear on the same identification parade with at least twelve other members of the group who are not suspects. When police officers in uniform form an identification parade any numerals or other identifying badges shall be concealed.

12. When the suspect is brought to the place where the identification parade is to be held, they shall be asked if they have any objection to the arrangements for the identification parade or to any of the other participants in it and to state the reasons for the objection. The suspect may obtain advice from their solicitor or friend, if present, before the identification parade proceeds. If the suspect has a reasonable objection to the arrangements or any of the participants, steps shall, if practicable, be taken to remove the grounds for objection. When it is not practicable to do so, the suspect shall be told why their objections cannot be met and the objection, the reason given for it and why it cannot be met, shall be recorded on forms provided for the purpose.

13. The suspect may select their own position in the line, but may not otherwise interfere with the order of the people forming the line. When there is more than one witness, the suspect must be told, after each witness has left the room, that they can, if they wish, change position in the line. Each position in the line must be clearly numbered, whether by means of a number laid on the floor in front of each identification parade member or by other means.

14. Appropriate arrangements must be made to make sure, before witnesses attend the identification parade, they are not able to:
    (i) communicate with each other about the case or overhear a witness who has already seen the identification parade;
    (ii) see any member of the identification parade;
    (iii) see, or be reminded of, any photograph or description of the suspect or be given any other indication as to the suspect's identity; or
    (iv) see the suspect before or after the identification parade.

15. The person conducting a witness to an identification parade must not discuss with them the composition of the identification parade and, in particular, must not disclose whether a previous witness has made any identification.

16. Witnesses shall be brought in one at a time. Immediately before the witness inspects the identification parade, they shall be told the person they saw on a specified earlier occasion may, or may not, be present and if they cannot make a positive identification, they should say so. The witness must also be told they should not make any decision about whether the person they saw is on the identification parade until they have looked at each member at least twice.

17. When the officer or police staff (see paragraph 3.11) conducting the identification procedure is satisfied the witness has properly looked at each member of the identification parade, they shall ask the witness whether the person they saw on a specified earlier occasion is on the identification parade and, if so, to indicate the number of the person concerned, see paragraph 28.

18. If the witness wishes to hear any identification parade member speak, adopt any specified posture or move, they shall first be asked whether they can identify any person(s) on the identification parade on the basis of appearance only. When the request is to hear members of the identification parade speak, the witness shall be reminded that the participants in the

identification parade have been chosen on the basis of physical appearance only. Members of the identification parade may then be asked to comply with the witness' request to hear them speak, see them move or adopt any specified posture.

19.   If the witness requests that the person they have indicated remove anything used for the purposes of paragraph 10 to conceal the location of an unusual physical feature, that person may be asked to remove it.

20.   If the witness makes an identification after the identification parade has ended, the suspect and, if present, their solicitor, interpreter or friend shall be informed. When this occurs, consideration should be given to allowing the witness a second opportunity to identify the suspect.

21.   After the procedure, action required in accordance with paragraph 3.40 applies.

22.   When the last witness has left, the suspect shall be asked whether they wish to make any comments on the conduct of the identification parade.

(d)   Documentation

23.   A video recording must normally be taken of the identification parade. If that is impracticable, a colour photograph must be taken. A copy of the video recording or photograph shall be supplied, on request, to the suspect or their solicitor within a reasonable time.

24.   As appropriate, paragraph 3.30 or 3.31, should apply to any photograph or video taken as in paragraph 23.

25.   If any person is asked to leave an identification parade because they are interfering with its conduct, the circumstances shall be recorded.

26.   A record must be made of all those present at an identification parade whose names are known to the police.

27.   If prison inmates make up an identification parade, the circumstances must be recorded.

28.   A record of the conduct of any identification parade must be made on forms provided for the purpose. This shall include anything said by the witness or the suspect about any identifications or the conduct of the procedure, and any reasons it was not practicable to comply with any of this Code's provisions.

Annex C – Group identification

(a)   General

1.   The purpose of this Annex is to make sure, as far as possible, group identifications follow the principles and procedures for identification parades so the conditions are fair to the suspect in the way they test the witness' ability to make an identification.

2.   Group identifications may take place either with the suspect's consent and cooperation or covertly without their consent.

3.   The location of the group identification is a matter for the identification officer, although the officer may take into account any representations made by the suspect, appropriate adult, their solicitor or friend.

4.   The place where the group identification is held should be one where other people are either passing by or waiting around informally, in groups such that the suspect is able to join them and be capable of being seen by the witness at the same time as others in the group. For example people leaving an escalator, pedestrians walking through a shopping centre, passengers on railway and bus stations, waiting in queues or groups or where people are standing or sitting in groups in other public places.

5.   If the group identification is to be held covertly, the choice of locations will be limited by the places where the suspect can be found and the number of other people present at that time. In these cases, suitable locations might be along regular routes travelled by the suspect, including buses or trains or public places frequented by the suspect.

6.   Although the number, age, sex, race and general description and style of clothing of other people present at the location cannot be controlled by the identification officer, in selecting the location the officer must consider the general appearance and numbers of people likely to be present. In particular, the officer must reasonably expect that over the period the witness observes the group, they will be able to see, from time to time, a number of others whose appearance is broadly similar to that of the suspect.

7.   A group identification need not be held if the identification officer believes, because of the unusual appearance of the suspect, none of the locations it would be practicable to use, satisfy the requirements of paragraph 6 necessary to make the identification fair.

8.   Immediately after a group identification procedure has taken place (with or without the suspect's consent), a colour photograph or video should be taken of the general scene, if

practicable, to give a general impression of the scene and the number of people present. Alternatively, if it is practicable, the group identification may be video recorded.

9. If it is not practicable to take the photograph or video in accordance with paragraph 8, a photograph or film of the scene should be taken later at a time determined by the identification officer if the officer considers it practicable to do so.

10. An identification carried out in accordance with this Code remains a group identification even though, at the time of being seen by the witness, the suspect was on their own rather than in a group.

11. Before the group identification takes place, the suspect or their solicitor shall be provided with details of the first description of the suspect by any witnesses who are to attend the identification. When a broadcast or publication is made, as in paragraph 3.28, the suspect or their solicitor should also be allowed to view any material released by the police to the media for the purposes of recognising or tracing the suspect, provided that it is practicable and would not unreasonably delay the investigation.

12. After the procedure, action required in accordance with paragraph 3.40 applies.

(b) ***Identification with the consent of the suspect***

13. A suspect must be given a reasonable opportunity to have a solicitor or friend present. They shall be asked to indicate on a second copy of the notice whether or not they wish to do so.

14. The witness, the person carrying out the procedure and the suspect's solicitor, appropriate adult, friend or any interpreter for the witness, may be concealed from the sight of the individuals in the group they are observing, if the person carrying out the procedure considers this assists the conduct of the identification.

15. The person conducting a witness to a group identification must not discuss with them the forthcoming group identification and, in particular, must not disclose whether a previous witness has made any identification.

16. Anything said to, or by, the witness during the procedure about the identification should be said in the presence and hearing of those present at the procedure.

17. Appropriate arrangements must be made to make sure, before witnesses attend the group identification, they are not able to:
    (i)   communicate with each other about the case or overhear a witness who has already been given an opportunity to see the suspect in the group;
    (ii) see the suspect; or
    (iii) see, or be reminded of, any photographs or description of the suspect or be given any other indication of the suspect's identity.

18. Witnesses shall be brought one at a time to the place where they are to observe the group. Immediately before the witness is asked to look at the group, the person conducting the procedure shall tell them that the person they saw may, or may not, be in the group and that if they cannot make a positive identification, they should say so. The witness shall be asked to observe the group in which the suspect is to appear. The way in which the witness should do this will depend on whether the group is moving or stationary.

Moving group

19. When the group in which the suspect is to appear is moving, e.g. leaving an escalator, the provisions of paragraphs 20 to 24 should be followed.

20. If two or more suspects consent to a group identification, each should be the subject of separate identification procedures. These may be conducted consecutively on the same occasion.

21. The person conducting the procedure shall tell the witness to observe the group and ask them to point out any person they think they saw on the specified earlier occasion.

22. Once the witness has been informed as in paragraph 21 the suspect should be allowed to take whatever position in the group they wish.

23. When the witness points out a person as in paragraph 21 they shall, if practicable, be asked to take a closer look at the person to confirm the identification. If this is not practicable, or they cannot confirm the identification, they shall be asked how sure they are that the person they have indicated is the relevant person.

24. The witness should continue to observe the group for the period which the person conducting the procedure reasonably believes is necessary in the circumstances for them to be able to make comparisons between the suspect and other individuals of broadly similar appearance to the suspect as in paragraph 6.

Stationary groups

25.   When the group in which the suspect is to appear is stationary, e.g. people waiting in a queue, the provisions of paragraphs 26 to 29 should be followed.

26.   If two or more suspects consent to a group identification, each should be subject to separate identification procedures unless they are of broadly similar appearance when they may appear in the same group. When separate group identifications are held, the groups must be made up of different people.

27.   The suspect may take whatever position in the group they wish. If there is more than one witness, the suspect must be told, out of the sight and hearing of any witness, that they can, if they wish, change their position in the group.

28.   The witness shall be asked to pass along, or amongst, the group and to look at each person in the group at least twice, taking as much care and time as possible according to the circumstances, before making an identification. Once the witness has done this, they shall be asked whether the person they saw on the specified earlier occasion is in the group and to indicate any such person by whatever means the person conducting the procedure considers appropriate in the circumstances. If this is not practicable, the witness shall be asked to point out any person they think they saw on the earlier occasion.

29.   When the witness makes an indication as in paragraph 28, arrangements shall be made, if practicable, for the witness to take a closer look at the person to confirm the identification. If this is not practicable, or the witness is unable to confirm the identification, they shall be asked how sure they are that the person they have indicated is the relevant person.

All cases

30.   If the suspect unreasonably delays joining the group, or having joined the group, deliberately conceals themselves from the sight of the witness, this may be treated as a refusal to co-operate in a group identification.

31.   If the witness identifies a person other than the suspect, that person should be informed what has happened and asked if they are prepared to give their name and address. There is no obligation upon any member of the public to give these details. There shall be no duty to record any details of any other member of the public present in the group or at the place where the procedure is conducted.

32.   When the group identification has been completed, the suspect shall be asked whether they wish to make any comments on the conduct of the procedure.

33.   If the suspect has not been previously informed, they shall be told of any identifications made by the witnesses.

(c)   *Identification without the suspect's consent*

34.   Group identifications held covertly without the suspect's consent should, as far as practicable, follow the rules for conduct of group identification by consent.

35.   A suspect has no right to have a solicitor, appropriate adult or friend present as the identification will take place without the knowledge of the suspect.

36.   Any number of suspects may be identified at the same time.

(d)   *Identifications in police stations*

37.   Group identifications should only take place in police stations for reasons of safety, security or because it is not practicable to hold them elsewhere.

38.   The group identification may take place either in a room equipped with a screen permitting witnesses to see members of the group without being seen, or anywhere else in the police station that the identification officer considers appropriate.

39.   Any of the additional safeguards applicable to identification parades should be followed if the identification officer considers it is practicable to do so in the circumstances.

(e)   *Identifications involving prison inmates*

40.   A group identification involving a prison inmate may only be arranged in the prison or at a police station.

41.   When a group identification takes place involving a prison inmate, whether in a prison or in a police station, the arrangements should follow those in paragraphs 37 to 39. If a group identification takes place within a prison, other inmates may participate. If an inmate is the suspect, they do not have to wear prison clothing for the group identification unless the other participants are wearing the same clothing.

(f)   *Documentation*

42.   When a photograph or video is taken as in paragraph 8 or 9, a copy of the photograph or video shall be supplied on request to the suspect or their solicitor within a reasonable time.

43.   Paragraph 3.30 or 3.31, as appropriate, shall apply when the photograph or film taken in accordance with paragraph 8 or 9 includes the suspect.

44.   A record of the conduct of any group identification must be made on forms provided for the purpose. This shall include anything said by the witness or suspect about any identifications or the conduct of the procedure and any reasons why it was not practicable to comply with any of the provisions of this Code governing the conduct of group identifications.

Annex D – Confrontation by an eye-witness

1.   Before the confrontation takes place, the witness must be told that the person they saw may, or may not, be the person they are to confront and that if they are not that person, then the witness should say so.

2.   Before the confrontation takes place the suspect or their solicitor shall be provided with details of the first description of the suspect given by any witness who is to attend. When a broadcast or publication is made, as in paragraph 3.28, the suspect or their solicitor should also be allowed to view any material released to the media for the purposes of recognising or tracing the suspect, provided it is practicable to do so and would not unreasonably delay the investigation.

3.   Force may not be used to make the suspect's face visible to the witness.

4.   Confrontation must take place in the presence of the suspect's solicitor, interpreter or friend unless this would cause unreasonable delay.

5.   The suspect shall be confronted independently by each witness, who shall be asked 'Is this the person?'. If the witness identifies the person but is unable to confirm the identification, they shall be asked how sure they are that the person is the one they saw on the earlier occasion.

6.   The confrontation should normally take place in the police station, either in a normal room or one equipped with a screen permitting a witness to see the suspect without being seen. In both cases, the procedures are the same except that a room equipped with a screen may be used only when the suspect's solicitor, friend or appropriate adult is present or the confrontation is recorded on video.

7.   After the procedure, action required in accordance with paragraph 3.40 applies.

Annex E – Showing photographs

(a)   Action

1.   An officer of sergeant rank or above shall be responsible for supervising and directing the showing of photographs. The actual showing may be done by another officer or police staff, see paragraph 3.11.

2.   The supervising officer must confirm the first description of the suspect given by the witness has been recorded before they are shown the photographs. If the supervising officer is unable to confirm the description has been recorded they shall postpone showing the photographs.

3.   Only one witness shall be shown photographs at any one time. Each witness shall be given as much privacy as practicable and shall not be allowed to communicate with any other witness in the case.

4.   The witness shall be shown not less than twelve photographs at a time, which shall, as far as possible, all be of a similar type.

5.   When the witness is shown the photographs, they shall be told the photograph of the person they saw may, or may not, be amongst them and if they cannot make a positive identification, they should say so. The witness shall also be told they should not make a decision until they have viewed at least twelve photographs. The witness shall not be prompted or guided in any way but shall be left to make any selection without help.

6.   If a witness makes a positive identification from photographs, unless the person identified is otherwise eliminated from enquiries or is not available, other witnesses shall not be shown photographs. But both they, and the witness who has made the identification, shall be asked to attend a video identification, an identification parade or group identification unless there is no dispute about the suspect's identification.

7.   If the witness makes a selection but is unable to confirm the identification, the person showing the photographs shall ask them how sure they are that the photograph they have indicated is the person they saw on the specified earlier occasion.

8.   When the use of a computerised or artist's composite or similar likeness has led to there being a known suspect who can be asked to participate in a video identification, appear on an identification parade or participate in a group identification, that likeness shall not be shown to other potential witnesses.

9. When a witness attending a video identification, an identification parade or group identification has previously been shown photographs or computerised or artist's composite or similar likeness (and it is the responsibility of the officer in charge of the investigation to make the identification officer aware that this is the case), the suspect and their solicitor must be informed of this fact before the identification procedure takes place.

10. None of the photographs shown shall be destroyed, whether or not an identification is made, since they may be required for production in court. The photographs shall be numbered and a separate photograph taken of the frame or part of the album from which the witness made an identification as an aid to reconstituting it.

(b) Documentation

11. Whether or not an identification is made, a record shall be kept of the showing of photographs on forms provided for the purpose. This shall include anything said by the witness about any identification or the conduct of the procedure, any reasons it was not practicable to comply with any of the provisions of this Code governing the showing of photographs and the name and rank of the supervising officer.

12. The supervising officer shall inspect and sign the record as soon as practicable.

Annex F – Fingerprints, footwear impressions and samples – destruction and speculative searches

Part A: Fingerprints and samples

DNA samples

1. A DNA sample is an individual's biological material, containing all of their genetic information. The Act requires all DNA samples to be destroyed within 6 months of being taken. This allows sufficient time for the sample to be analysed and a DNA profile to be produced for use on the database.

2. The only exception to this is if the sample is or may be required for disclosure as evidence, in which case it may be retained for as long as this need exists under the Criminal Procedure and Investigations Act 1996.

DNA profiles and fingerprints

3. A DNA profile consists of a string of 16 pairs of numbers and 2 letters (XX for women, XY for men) to indicate gender. This number string is stored on the National DNA Database (NDNAD). It allows the person to be identified if they leave their DNA at a crime scene.

4. Fingerprints are usually scanned electronically from the individual in custody and the images stored on IDENT1, the national fingerprint database.

Retention Periods: Fingerprints and DNA profiles

5. The retention period depends on the outcome of the investigation of the recordable offence in connection with which the fingerprints and DNA samples was taken, the age of the person at the time the offence was committed and whether the recordable offence is a qualifying offence and whether it is an excluded offence ...

Part B: Footwear impressions

13. Footwear impressions taken in accordance with section 61A of PACE (see paragraphs 4.16 to 4.21) may be retained for as long as is necessary for purposes related to the prevention or detection of crime, the investigation of an offence or the conduct of a prosecution.

Part C: Fingerprints, samples and footwear impressions taken in connection with a criminal investigation from a person not suspected of committing the offence under investigation for elimination purposes.

14. When fingerprints, footwear impressions or DNA samples are taken from a person in connection with an investigation and the person is not suspected of having committed the offence, see Note F1, they must be destroyed as soon as they have fulfilled the purpose for which they were taken unless:

   (a) they were taken for the purposes of an investigation of an offence for which a person has been convicted; and

   (b) fingerprints, footwear impressions or samples were also taken from the convicted person for the purposes of that investigation.

   However, subject to paragraph 14, the fingerprints, footwear impressions and samples, and the information derived from samples, may not be used in the investigation of any offence or in evidence against the person who is, or would be, entitled to the destruction of the fingerprints, footwear impressions and samples, see Note F2.

15. The requirement to destroy fingerprints, footwear impressions and DNA samples, and information derived from samples and restrictions on their retention and use in paragraph 14 do not apply if the person gives their written consent for their fingerprints, footwear

impressions or sample to be retained and used after they have fulfilled the purpose for which they were taken, see Note F1. This consent can be withdrawn at any time.

16. When a person's fingerprints, footwear impressions or sample are to be destroyed:

(a) any copies of the fingerprints and footwear impressions must also be destroyed; and

(b) neither the fingerprints, footwear impressions, the sample, or any information derived from the sample, may be used in the investigation of any offence or in evidence against the person who is, or would be, entitled to its destruction.

Annex G - Requirement for a person to attend a police station for fingerprints and samples.

1. A requirement under Schedule 2A for a person to attend a police station to have fingerprints or samples taken:

(a) must give the person a period of at least seven days within which to attend the police station; and

(b) may direct them to attend at a specified time of day or between specified times of day.

2. When specifying the period and times of attendance, the officer making the requirements must consider whether the fingerprints or samples could reasonably be taken at a time when the person is required to attend the police station for any other reason. See Note G1.

3. An officer of the rank of inspector or above may authorise a period shorter than 7 days if there is an urgent need for person's fingerprints or sample for the purposes of the investigation of an offence. The fact of the authorisation and the reasons for giving it must be recorded as soon as practicable.

4. The constable making a requirement and the person to whom it applies may agree to vary it so as to specify any period within which, or date or time at which, the person is to attend. However, variation shall not have effect for the purposes of enforcement, unless it is confirmed by the constable in writing.

Notes for Guidance

G1 The specified period within which the person is to attend need not fall within the period allowed (if applicable) for making the requirement.

G2 To justify the arrest without warrant of a person who fails to comply with a requirement, (see paragraph 4.4(b) above), the officer making the requirement, or confirming a variation, should be prepared to explain how, when and where the requirement was made or the variation was confirmed and what steps were taken to ensure the person understood what to do and the consequences of not complying with the requirement.

POLICE AND CRIMINAL EVIDENCE ACT 1984 (PACE) CODE E

CODE OF PRACTICE ON AUDIO RECORDING INTERVIEWS WITH SUSPECTS

Commencement – Transitional Arrangements

This Code applies to interviews carried out after 00.00 on 31 July 2018, notwithstanding that the interview may have commenced before that time.

...

2. Interviews and other matters to be audio recorded under this Code

(a) Requirement to use authorised audio-recording device when available.

2.1 Subject to paragraph 2.3, if an authorised recording device (see paragraph 1.6(a)) in working order and an interview room or other location (see Note 1A) suitable for that device to be used, are available, then that device shall be used to record the following matters:

(a) any interview with a person cautioned in accordance with Code C, section 10 in respect of any summary offence or any indictable offence, which includes any offence triable either way, when:

(i) that person (the suspect) is questioned about their involvement or suspected involvement in that offence and they have not been charged or informed they may be prosecuted for that offence; and

(ii)   exceptionally, further questions are put to a person about any offence after they have been charged with, or told they may be prosecuted for, that offence (see Code C, paragraph 16.5 and Note 2C).

(b)   when a person who has been charged with, or informed they may be prosecuted for, any offence, is told about any written statement or interview with another person and they are handed a true copy of the written statement or the content of the interview record is brought to their attention in accordance with Code C, paragraph 16.4 and Note 2D.

See Note 2A

2.2   The whole of each of the matters described in paragraph 2.1 shall be audio-recorded, including the taking and reading back of any statement as applicable.

2.3   A written record of the matters described in paragraph 2.1(a) and (b) shall be made in accordance with Code C, section 11, only if,

(a)   an authorised recording device (see paragraph 1.6(a)) in working order is not available; or

(b)   such a device is available but a location suitable for using that device to make the audio recording of the matter in question is not available; and

(c)   the 'relevant officer' described in paragraph 2.4 considers on reasonable grounds, that the proposed interview or (as the case may be) continuation of the interview or other action, should not be delayed until an authorised recording device in working order and a suitable interview room or other location become available (see Note 2E) and decides that a written record shall be made;

(d)   if in accordance with paragraph 3.9, the suspect or the appropriate adult on their behalf, objects to the interview being audibly recorded and the 'relevant officer' described in paragraph 2.4, after having regard to the nature and circumstances of the objections (see Note 2F), decides that a written record shall be made;

(e)   in the case of a detainee who refuses to go into or remain in a suitable interview room and in accordance with Code C paragraphs 12.5 and 12.11, the custody officer directs that interview be conducted in a cell and considers that an authorised recording device cannot be safely used in the cell.

Note: When the suspect appears to have a hearing impediment, this paragraph does not affect the separate requirement in paragraphs 3.7 and 4.4 for the interviewer to make a written note of the interview at the same time as the audio recording'.

(b)   Meaning of 'relevant officer'

2.4   In paragraph 2.3(c):

(a)   if the person to be interviewed is arrested elsewhere than at a police station for an offence and before they arrive at a police station, an urgent interview in accordance with Code C paragraph 11.1 is necessary to avert one or more of the risks mentioned in sub-paragraphs (a) to (c) of that paragraph, the 'relevant officer' means the interviewer, who may or may not be the arresting officer, who must have regard to the time, place and urgency of the proposed interview.

(b)   if the person in question has been taken to a police station after being arrested elsewhere for an offence or is arrested for an offence whilst at a police station after attending voluntarily and is detained at that police station or elsewhere in the charge of a constable, the 'relevant officer' means the custody officer at the station where the person's detention was last authorised. The custody officer must have regard to the nature of the investigation and in accordance with Code C paragraph 1.1, ensure that the detainee is dealt with expeditiously, and released as soon as the need for their detention no longer applies.

(c)   In the case of a voluntary interview (see Code C paragraph 3.21 to 3.22) which takes place:

(i)   at a police station and the offence in question is an indictable offence, the 'relevant officer' means an officer of the rank of sergeant or above, in consultation with the investigating officer;

(ii)   at a police station and the offence in question is a summary offence, the 'relevant officer' means the interviewer in consultation with the investigating officer if different,

(iii)   elsewhere than at a police station and the offence is one of the four indictable offence types which satisfy the conditions in Part 1 of the Annex to this Code, the 'relevant officer' means the interviewer in consultation with the investigating officer, if different.

(iv) elsewhere than at a police station and the offence in question is an indictable offence which is not one of the four indictable offence types which satisfy the conditions in Part 1 of the Annex to this Code, the 'relevant officer' means an officer of the rank of sergeant or above, in consultation with the investigating officer.

(v) elsewhere than at a police station and the offence in question is a summary only offence, the 'relevant officer' means the interviewer in consultation with the investigating officer, if different.

(c) Duties of the 'relevant officer' and the interviewer

2.5 When, in accordance with paragraph 2.3, a written record is made:

(a) the relevant officer must:

    (i) record the reasons for not making an audio recording and the date and time the decision in paragraph 2.3(c) or (as applicable) paragraph 2.3(d) was made; and

    (ii) ensure that the suspect is informed that a written record will be made;

(b) the interviewer must ensure that the written record includes:

    (i) the date and time the decision in paragraph 2.3(c) or (as applicable) paragraph 2.3(d) was made, who made it and where the decision is recorded, and

    (ii) the fact that the suspect was informed.

(c) the written record shall be made in accordance with Code C, section 11;

See Note 2B

(d) Remote monitoring of interviews

2.6 If the interview room or other location where the interview takes place is equipped with facilities that enable audio recorded interviews to be remotely monitored as they take place, the interviewer must ensure that suspects, their legal representatives and any appropriate adults are fully aware of what this means and that there is no possibility of privileged conversations being listened to. With this in mind, the following safeguards should be applied:

(a) The remote monitoring system should only be able to operate when the audio recording device has been turned on.

(b) The equipment should incorporate a light, clearly visible to all in the interview room, which is automatically illuminated as soon as remote monitoring is activated.

(c) Interview rooms and other locations fitted with remote monitoring equipment must contain a notice, prominently displayed, referring to the capacity for remote monitoring and to the fact that the warning light will illuminate whenever monitoring is taking place.

(d) At the beginning of the interview, the interviewer must explain the contents of the notice to the suspect and if present, to the solicitor and appropriate adult and that explanation should itself be audio recorded.

(e) The fact that an interview, or part of an interview, was remotely monitored should be recorded in the suspect's custody record or, if the suspect is not in detention, the interviewer's pocket book. That record should include the names of the officers doing the monitoring and the purpose of the monitoring (e.g. for training, to assist with the investigation, etc.)

(e) Use of live link – Interviewer not present at the same station as the detainee

2.7 Code C paragraphs 12.9A and 12.9B set out the conditions which, if satisfied allow a suspect in police detention to be interviewed using a live link by a police officer who is not present at the police station where the detainee is held. These provisions also set out the duties and responsibilities of the custody officer, the officer having physical custody of the suspect and the interviewer and the modifications that apply to ensure that any such interview is conducted and audio recorded in accordance with this Code or (as the case may be) visually recorded in accordance with Code F.

Notes for Guidance

2A Nothing in this Code is intended to preclude audio-recording at police discretion at police stations or elsewhere when persons are charged with, or told they may be prosecuted for, an offence or they respond after being so charged or informed.

2B   A decision made in accordance with paragraph 2.3 not to audio-record an interview for any reason may be the subject of comment in court. The 'relevant officer' responsible should be prepared to justify that decision.

2C   Code C sets out the circumstances in which a suspect may be questioned about an offence after being charged with it.

2D   Code C sets out the procedures to be followed when a person's attention is drawn after charge, to a statement made by another person. One method of bringing the content of an interview with another person to the notice of a suspect may be to play them a recording of that interview. The person may not be questioned about the statement or interview record unless this is allowed in accordance with paragraph 16.5 of Code C.

2E   A voluntary interview should be arranged for a time and place when it can be audio recorded and enable the safeguards and requirements set out in Code C paragraphs 3.21 to 3.22B to be implemented. It would normally be reasonable to delay the interview to enable audio recording unless the delay to do so would be likely to compromise the outcome of the interview or investigation, for example if there are grounds to suspect that the suspect would use the delay to fabricate an innocent explanation, influence witnesses or tamper with other material evidence.

2F   Objections for the purpose of paragraphs 2.3(d) and 3.9 are meant to apply to objections based on the suspect's genuine and honestly held beliefs and to allow officers to exercise their discretion to decide that a written interview record is to be made according to the circumstances surrounding the suspect and the investigation. Objections that appear to be frivolous with the intentions of frustrating or delaying the investigation would not be relevant.

3.   Interview recording using removable recording media device

(a) *Recording and sealing master recordings – general*

3.1   When using an authorised removable recording media device (see paragraph 1.6(a)(i)), one recording, the master recording, will be sealed in the suspect's presence. A second recording will be used as a working copy. The master recording is any of the recordings made by a multi-deck/drive machine or the only recording made by a single deck/drive machine. The working copy is one of the other recordings made by a multi-deck/drive machine or a copy of the master recording made by a single deck/drive machine.

3.2   The purpose of sealing the master recording before it leaves the suspect's presence is to establish their confidence that the integrity of the recording is preserved. If a single deck/drive machine is used the working copy of the master recording must be made in the suspect's presence and without the master recording leaving their sight. The working copy shall be used for making further copies if needed.

(b) *Commencement of interviews*

3.3   When the suspect is brought into the interview room or arrives at the location where the interview is to take place, the interviewer shall, without delay but in the suspect's sight, unwrap or open the new recording media, load the recording device with new recording media and set it to record.

3.4   The interviewer must point out the sign or indicator which shows that the recording equipment is activated and is recording (see paragraph 1.6(a)(i)) and shall then:

    (a)   tell the suspect that the interview is being audibly recorded using an authorised removable recording media device and outline the recording process (see Note 3A);

    (b)   subject to paragraph 1.13, give their name and rank and that of any other interviewer present;

    (c)   ask the suspect and any other party present, e.g. the appropriate adult, a solicitor or interpreter, to identify themselves (see Note 3A);

    (d)   state the date, time of commencement and place of the interview;

    (e)   tell the suspect that:

        • they will be given a copy of the recording of the interview in the event that they are charged or informed that they will be prosecuted but if they are not charged or informed that they will be prosecuted they will only be given a copy as agreed with the police or on the order of a court; and

- they will be given a written notice at the end of the interview setting out their right to a copy of the recording and what will happen to the recording and;

(f)   if equipment for remote monitoring of interviews as described in paragraph 2.6 is installed, explain the contents of the notice to the suspect, solicitor and appropriate adult as required by paragraph 2.6(d) and point out the light that illuminates automatically as soon as remote monitoring is activated.

3.5 Any person entering the interview room after the interview has commenced shall be invited by the interviewer to identify themselves for the purpose of the audio recording and state the reason why they have entered the interview room.

3.6 The interviewer shall:
- caution the suspect, see Code C section 10; and
- if they are detained, remind them of their entitlement to free legal advice, see Code C, paragraph 11.2; or
- if they are not detained under arrest, explain this and their entitlement to free legal advice (see Code C, paragraph 3.21) and ask the suspect to confirm that they agree to the voluntary interview proceeding (see Code C paragraph 3.22A).

3.7 The interviewer shall put to the suspect any significant statement or silence, see Code C, paragraph 11.4.

(c)   Interviews with suspects who appear to have a hearing impediment

3.8 If the suspect appears to have a hearing impediment, the interviewer shall make a written note of the interview in accordance with Code C, at the same time as audio recording it in accordance with this Code. (See Notes 3B and 3C.)

(d)   Objections and complaints by the suspect

3.9 If the suspect or an appropriate adult on their behalf, objects to the interview being audibly recorded either at the outset, during the interview or during a break, the interviewer shall explain that the interview is being audibly recorded and that this Code requires the objections to be recorded on the audio recording. When any objections have been audibly recorded or the suspect or appropriate adult have refused to have their objections recorded, the relevant officer shall decide in accordance with paragraph 2.3(d) (which requires the officer to have regard to the nature and circumstances of the objections) whether a written record of the interview or its continuation, is to be made and that audio recording should be turned off. Following a decision that a written record is to be made, the interviewer shall say they are turning off the recorder and shall then make a written record of the interview as in Code C, section 11. If, however, following a decision that a written record is not to be made, the interviewer may proceed to question the suspect with the audio recording still on. This procedure also applies in cases where the suspect has previously objected to the interview being visually recorded, see Code F paragraph 2.7, and the investigating officer has decided to audibly record the interview. (See Notes 2F and 3D.)

3.10 If in the course of an interview a complaint is made by or on behalf of the person being questioned concerning the provisions of this or any other Codes, or it comes to the interviewer's notice that the person may have been treated improperly, the interviewer shall act as in Code C, paragraph 12.9. (See Notes 3E and 3F.)

3.11 If the suspect indicates they want to tell the interviewer about matters not directly connected with the offence of which they are suspected and they are unwilling for these matters to be audio recorded, the suspect should be given the opportunity to tell the interviewer about these matters after the conclusion of the formal interview.

(e)   Changing recording media

3.12 When the recorder shows the recording media only has a short time left to run, the interviewer shall so inform the person being interviewed and round off that part of the interview. If the interviewer leaves the room for a second set of recording media, the suspect shall not be left unattended. The interviewer will remove the recording media from the recorder and insert the new recording media which shall be unwrapped or opened in the suspect's presence. The recorder should be set to record on the new media. To avoid confusion between the recording media, the interviewer shall mark the media with an identification number immediately after it is removed from the recorder.

(f)   Taking a break during interview

3.13 When a break is taken, the fact that a break is to be taken, the reason for it and the time shall be recorded on the audio recording.

3.14 When the break is taken and the interview room vacated by the suspect, the recording media shall be removed from the recorder and the procedures for the conclusion of an interview followed, see paragraph 3.19.

3.15 When a break is a short one and both the suspect and an interviewer remain in the interview room, the recording may be stopped. There is no need to remove the recording media and when the interview recommences the recording should continue on the same recording media. The time the interview recommences shall be recorded on the audio recording.

3.16 After any break in the interview the interviewer must, before resuming the interview, remind the person being questioned of their right to legal advice if they have not exercised it and that they remain under caution or, if there is any doubt, give the caution in full again. (See Note 3G).

(g) Failure of recording equipment

3.17 If there is an equipment failure which can be rectified quickly, e.g. by inserting new recording media, the interviewer shall follow the appropriate procedures as in paragraph 3.12. When the recording is resumed the interviewer shall explain what happened and record the time the interview recommences. However, if it is not possible to continue recording using the same recording device or by using a replacement device , the interview should be audio-recorded using a secure digital recording network device as in paragraph 4.1, if the necessary equipment is available. If it is not available, the interview may continue and be recorded in writing in accordance with paragraph 2.3 as directed by the relevant officer'. (See Note 3H.)

(h) Removing recording media from the recorder

3.18 Recording media which is removed from the recorder during the interview shall be retained and the procedures in paragraph 3.12 followed.

(i) Conclusion of interview

3.19 At the conclusion of the interview, the suspect shall be offered the opportunity to clarify anything they have said and asked if there is anything they want to add.

3.20 At the conclusion of the interview, including the taking and reading back of any written statement, the time shall be recorded and the recording shall be stopped. The interviewer shall seal the master recording with a master recording label and treat it as an exhibit in accordance with force standing orders. The interviewer shall sign the label and ask the suspect and any third party present during the interview to sign it. If the suspect or third party refuse to sign the label an officer of at least the rank of inspector, or if not available the custody officer, or if the suspect has not been arrested, a sergeant, shall be called into the interview room and asked, subject to paragraph 1.13, to sign it.

3.21 The suspect shall be handed a notice which explains:
- how the audio recording will be used;
- the arrangements for access to it;
- that if they are charged or informed they will be prosecuted, a copy of the audio recording will be supplied as soon as practicable or as otherwise agreed between the suspect and the police or on the order of a court.

(j) After the interview

3.22 The interviewer shall make a note in their pocket book that the interview has taken place and that it was audibly recorded, the time it commenced, its duration and date and identification number of the master recording (see Note 3I).

3.23 If no proceedings follow in respect of the person whose interview was recorded, the recording media must be kept securely as in paragraph 3.22 and Note 3J

(k) Master Recording security

(i) General

3.24 The officer in charge of each police station at which interviews with suspects are recorded or as the case may be, where recordings of interviews carried out elsewhere than at a police station are held, shall make arrangements for master recordings to be kept securely and their movements accounted for on the same basis as material which may be used for evidential purposes, in accordance with force standing orders. (See Note 3J.)

...

Notes for guidance

Commencement of interviews (paragraph 3.3)

3A   When outlining the recording process, the interviewer should refer to paragraph 1.6(a)(ii) and (iii) and briefly describe how the recording device being used is operated and how recordings are made. For the purpose of voice identification the interviewer should ask the suspect and any other people present to identify themselves

Interviews with suspects who appear to have a hearing impediment (paragraph 3.8)

3B   This provision is to give a person who is deaf or has impaired hearing equivalent rights of access to the full interview record as far as this is possible using audio recording.

3C   The provisions of Code C on interpreters for suspects who do not appear to speak or understand English or who appear to have a hearing or speech impediment, continue to apply.

Objections and complaints by the suspect (paragraph 3.9)

3D   The relevant officer should be aware that a decision to continue recording against the wishes of the suspect may be the subject of comment in court.

3E   If the custody officer, or in the case of a person who has not been arrested, a sergeant, is called to deal with the complaint, the recorder should, if possible, be left on until the officer has entered the room and spoken to the person being interviewed. Continuation or termination of the interview should be at the interviewer's discretion pending action by an inspector under Code C, paragraph 9.2.

3F   If the complaint is about a matter not connected with this Code or Code C, the decision to continue is at the interviewer's discretion. When the interviewer decides to continue the interview, they shall tell the suspect that at the conclusion of the interview, the complaint will be brought to the attention of the custody officer, or in the case of a person who has not been arrested, a sergeant. When the interview is concluded the interviewer must, as soon as practicable, inform the custody officer or, as the case may be, the sergeant, about the existence and nature of the complaint made.

3G   In considering whether to caution again after a break, the interviewer should bear in mind that they may have to satisfy a court that the person understood that they were still under caution when the interview resumed. The interviewer should also remember that it may be necessary to show to the court that nothing occurred during a break or between interviews which influenced the suspect's recorded evidence. After a break or at the beginning of a subsequent interview, the interviewer should consider summarising on the record the reason for the break and confirming this with the suspect. Failure of recording equipment (paragraph 3.17)

3H   Where the interview is being recorded and the media or the recording equipment fails the interviewer should stop the interview immediately. Where part of the interview is unaffected by the error and is still accessible on the media, that part shall be copied and sealed in the suspect's presence as a master copy and the interview recommenced using new equipment/media as required. Where the content of the interview has been lost in its entirety, the media should be sealed in the suspect's presence and the interview begun again. If the recording equipment cannot be fixed and no replacement is immediately available, subject to paragraph 2.3, the interview should be recorded in accordance with Code C, section 11.

3I   Any written record of an audio recorded interview should be made in accordance with current national guidelines for police officers, police staff and CPS prosecutors concerned with the preparation, processing and submission of prosecution files. Master Recording security (paragraphs 3.24 to 3.30)

3J   This section is concerned with the security of the master recording sealed at the conclusion of the interview. Care must be taken of working copy recordings because their loss or destruction may lead unnecessarily to the need to access master recordings.

4.   Interview recording using secure digital recording network device

(a) General

4.1   An authorised secure digital recording network device (see paragraph 1.6(a)(iii) does not use removable media and this section specifies the provisions which will apply when such a device is used. For ease of reference, it repeats in full some of the provisions of section 3 that apply to both types of recording device.

(b) Commencement of interviews

4.2   When the suspect is brought into the interview room or arrives at the location where the interview is to take place, the interviewer shall without delay and in the sight of the suspect, switch on the recording equipment and in accordance with the manufacturer's instructions start recording.

4.3   The interviewer must point out the sign or indicator which shows that the recording equipment is activated and is recording (see paragraph 1.6(a)(iii)) and shall then:

    (a)   tell the suspect that the interview is being audibly recorded using an authorised secure digital recording network device and outline the recording process (see Note 3A);

    (b)   subject to paragraph 1.13, give their name and rank and that of any other interviewer present;

    (c)   ask the suspect and any other party present, e.g. the appropriate adult, a solicitor or interpreter, to identify themselves (see Note 3A);

    (d)   state the date, time of commencement and place of the interview; and

    (e)   inform the person that:

        • they will be given access to the recording of the interview in the event that they are charged or informed that they will be prosecuted but if they are not charged or informed that they will be prosecuted they will only be given access as agreed with the police or on the order of a court; and

        • they will be given a written notice at the end of the interview setting out their rights to access the recording and what will happen to the recording.

    (f)   If equipment for remote monitoring of interviews as described in paragraph 2.6 is installed, explain the contents of the notice to the suspect, solicitor and appropriate adult as required by paragraph 2.6(d) and point out the light that illuminates automatically as soon as remote monitoring is activated.

4.4A Paragraphs 3.5 to 3.7 apply.

(c) Interviews with suspects who appear to have a hearing impediment

4.5   Paragraph 3.8 applies.

(d) Objections and complaints by the suspect

4.6   Paragraphs 3.9, 3.10 and 3.11 apply.

(e) Taking a break during interview

4.7   When a break is taken, the fact that a break is to be taken, the reason for it and the time shall be recorded on the audio recording. The recording shall be stopped and the procedures in paragraphs 4.11 and 4.12 for the conclusion of interview followed.

4.8   When the interview recommences the procedures in paragraphs 4.2 to 4.3 for commencing an interview shall be followed to create a new file to record the continuation of the interview. The time the interview recommences shall be recorded on the audio recording.

4.9   After any break in the interview the interviewer must, before resuming the interview, remind the person being questioned of their right to legal advice if they have not exercised it and that they remain under caution or, if there is any doubt, give the caution in full again (see Note 3G). (F) Failure of recording equipment

4.10 If there is an equipment failure which can be rectified quickly, e.g. by commencing a new secure digital network recording using the same device or a replacement device, the interviewer shall follow the appropriate procedures as in paragraphs 4.7 to 4.9 (Taking a break during interview). When the recording is resumed, the interviewer shall explain what happened and record the time the interview recommences. However, if it is not possible to continue recording on the same device or by using a replacement device, the interview should be audio-recorded on removable media as in paragraph 3.3, if the necessary equipment is available. If it is not available, the interview may continue and be recorded in writing in accordance with paragraph 2.3 as directed by the 'relevant officer'. (See Note 3H.)

(g) Conclusion of interview

4.11 At the conclusion of the interview, the suspect shall be offered the opportunity to clarify anything he or she has said and asked if there is anything they want to add.

4.12 At the conclusion of the interview, including the taking and reading back of any written statement:

(a) the time shall be orally recorded.

(b) the suspect shall be handed a notice (see Note 4A) which explains
  - how the audio recording will be used
  - the arrangements for access to it
  - that if they are charged or informed that they will be prosecuted, they will be given access to the recording of the interview either electronically or by being given a copy on removable recording media, but if they are not charged or informed that they will prosecuted, they will only be given access as agreed with the police or on the order of a court.

(c) the suspect must be asked to confirm that he or she has received a copy of the notice at subparagraph (b) above. If the suspect fails to accept or to acknowledge receipt of the notice, the interviewer will state for the recording that a copy of the notice has been provided to the suspect and that he or she has refused to take a copy of the notice or has refused to acknowledge receipt.

(d) the time shall be recorded and the interviewer shall ensure that the interview record is saved to the device in the presence of the suspect and any third party present during the interview and notify them accordingly. The interviewer must then explain that the record will be transferred securely to the remote secure network file server (see paragraph 4.15). If the equipment is available to enable the record to be transferred there and then in the suspect's presence, then it should be so transferred. If it is transferred at a later time, the time and place of the transfer must be recorded. The suspect should then be informed that the interview is terminated.

(h) After the interview

4.13 The interviewer shall make a note in their pocket book that the interview has taken place and that it was audibly recorded, time it commenced, its duration and date and the identification number, filename or other reference for the recording (see Note 3I).

4.14 If no proceedings follow in respect of the person whose interview was recorded, the recordings must be kept securely as in paragraphs 4.14 and 4.15.

(i) Security of secure digital network interview records

4.15 The recordings are first saved locally on the device before being transferred to the remote network file server system (see paragraph 1.6(a)(iii)). The recording remains on the local device until the transfer is complete. If for any reason the network connection fails, the recording will be transferred when the network connection is restored (see paragraph 4.12(d)). The interview record files are stored in read only form on non-removable storage devices, for example, hard disk drives, to ensure their integrity.

4.16 Access to interview recordings, including copying to removable media, must be strictly controlled and monitored to ensure that access is restricted to those who have been given specific permission to access for specified purposes when this is necessary. For example, police officers and CPS lawyers involved in the preparation of any prosecution case, persons interviewed if they have been charged or informed they may be prosecuted and their legal representatives.

Note for Guidance

4A The notice at paragraph 4.12(b) above should provide a brief explanation of the secure digital network and how access to the recording is strictly limited. The notice should also explain the access rights of the suspect, their legal representative, the police and the prosecutor to the recording of the interview. Space should be provided on the form to insert the date, the identification number, filename or other reference for the interview recording.

ANNEX: PARAGRAPH 2.4(c)(iii) – FOUR INDICTABLE OFFENCE TYPES FOR WHICH THE INTERVIEWER MAY DECIDE TO MAKE A WRITTEN RECORD OF A VOLUNTARY INTERVIEW ELSEWHERE THAN AT A POLICE STATION WHEN AN AUTHORISED AUDIO RECORDING DEVICE CANNOT BE USED.

See Notes 2 and 3.

Part 1: Four specified indictable offence types – two conditions

1.   The first condition is that the indictable offence in respect of which the person has been cautioned is one of the following:

 (a)   Possession of a controlled drug contrary to section 5(2) of the Misuse of Drugs Act 1971 if the drug is cannabis as defined by that Act and in a form commonly known as herbal cannabis or cannabis resin (see Note 5);

 (b)   Possession of a controlled drug contrary to section 5(2) of the Misuse of Drugs Act 1971 if the drug is khat as defined by that Act (see Note 5);

 (c)   Retail theft (shoplifting) contrary to section 1 of the Theft Act 1968 (see Note 6); and

 (d)   Criminal damage to property contrary to section 1(1) of the Criminal Damage Act 1971 (see Note 6),

 and in this paragraph, the reference to each of the above offences applies to an attempt to commit that offence as defined by section 1 of the Criminal Attempts Act 1981.

2.   The second condition is that:

 (a)   where the person has been cautioned in respect of an offence described in paragraph 1(a) (Possession of herbal cannabis or cannabis resin) or paragraph 1(b) (Possession of khat), the requirements of paragraphs 3 and 4 are satisfied; or

 (b)   where the person has been cautioned in respect of an offence described in paragraph 1(c) (Retail theft), the requirements of paragraphs 3 and 5 are satisfied; or

 (c)   where the person has been cautioned in respect of an offence described in paragraph 1(d) (criminal damage), the requirements of paragraphs 3 and 6 are satisfied.

3.   The requirements of this paragraph that apply to all four offences described in paragraph 1 are that:

 (i)   with regard to the person suspected of committing the offence:

 • they appear to be aged 18 or over;

 • there is no reason to suspect that they are a vulnerable person for whom an appropriate adult is required (see paragraph 1.5 of this Code);

 • they do not appear to be unable to understand what is happening because of the effects of drink, drugs or illness, ailment or condition;

 • they do not require an interpreter in accordance with Code C section 13; and

 • in accordance with Code G (Arrest), their arrest is not necessary in order to investigate the offence;

 (ii)   it appears that the commission of the offence:

 • has not resulted in any injury to any person;

 • has not involved any realistic threat or risk of injury to any person; and

 • has not caused any substantial financial or material loss to the private property of any individual; and

 (iii)   the person is not being interviewed about any other offence.

 See Notes 3 and 8.

4.   The requirements of this paragraph that apply to the offences described in paragraph 1(a) (possession of herbal cannabis or cannabis resin) and paragraph 1(b) (possession of khat) are that a police officer who is experienced in the recognition of the physical appearance, texture and smell of herbal cannabis, cannabis resin or (as the case may be) khat, is able to say that the substance which has been found in the suspect's possession by that officer or, as the case may be, by any other officer not so experienced and trained:

 (i)   is a controlled drug being either herbal cannabis, cannabis resin or khat; and

      (ii)   the quantity of the substance found is consistent with personal use by the suspect and does not provide any grounds to suspect an intention to supply others.
      See Note 5.

5.   The requirements of this paragraph that apply to the offence described in paragraph 1(c) (retail theft), are that it appears to the officer:
      (i)   that the value of the property stolen does not exceed £100 inclusive of VAT;
      (ii)   that the stolen property has been recovered and remains fit for sale unless the items stolen comprised drink or food and have been consumed; and
      (iii)   that the person suspected of stealing the property is not employed (whether paid or not) by the person, company or organisation to which the property belongs.
      See Note 3.

6.   The requirements of this paragraph that apply to the offence described in paragraph 1(d) (Criminal damage), are that it appears to the officer:
      (i)   that the value of the criminal damage does not exceed £300; and
      (ii)   that the person suspected of damaging the property is not employed (whether paid or not) by the person, company or organisation to which the property belongs.
      See Note 3.

Part 2: Other provisions applicable to all interviews to which this Annex applies

7.   Paragraphs 3.21 to 3.22B of Code C set out the responsibilities of the interviewing officer for ensuring compliance with the provisions of Code C that apply to the conduct and recording of voluntary interviews to which this Annex applies.
      See Note 7.

8.   If it appears to the interviewing officer that before the conclusion of an interview, any of the requirements in paragraphs 3 to 6 of Part 1 that apply to the offence in question described in paragraph 1 of Part 1 have ceased to apply; this Annex shall cease to apply. The person being interviewed must be so informed and a break in the interview must be taken. The reason must be recorded in the written interview record and the continuation of the interview shall be audio recorded in accordance with section 2 of this Code. For the purpose of the continuation, the provisions of paragraphs 3.3 and 4.2 (Commencement of interviews) shall apply. See Note 8.

Notes for Guidance

1   *Not used.*

2   The purpose of allowing the interviewer to decide that a written record is to be made is to support the policy which gives police in England and Wales options for dealing with low level offences quickly and non-bureaucratically in a proportionate manner
     ...

3   A decision in relation to a particular indictable offence that the conditions and requirements in this Annex are satisfied is an operational matter for the interviewing officer according to all the particular circumstances of the case. These circumstances include the outcome of the officer's investigation at that time and any other matters that are relevant to the officer's consideration as to how to deal with the matter.

4   *Not used.*

5   Under the Misuse of Drugs Act 1971 as at the date this Code comes into force: (a) cannabis includes any part of the cannabis plant but not mature stalks and seeds separated from the plant, cannabis resin and cannabis oil, but paragraph 1(a) applies only to the possession of herbal cannabis and cannabis resin; and (b) khat includes the leaves, stems and shoots of the plant.

6   The power to issue a Penalty Notice for Disorder (PND) for an offence contrary to section 1 of the Theft Act 1968 applies when the value of the goods stolen does not exceed £100 inclusive of VAT. The power to issue a PND for an offence contrary to section 1(1) of the Criminal Damage Act 1971 applies when the value of the damage does not exceed £300.

7   The provisions of Code C that apply to the conduct and recording of voluntary interviews to which this Annex applies are described in paragraphs 3.21 to 3.22B

of Code C. They include the suspect's right to free legal advice, the provision of information about the offence before the interview (see Code C paragraph 11.1A) and the right to interpretation and translation (see Code C section 13). These and other rights and entitlements are summarised in the notice that must be given to the suspect.

8   The requirements in paragraph 3 of Part 1 will cease to apply if, for example during the course of an interview, as a result of what the suspect says or other information which comes to the interviewing officer's notice:
- it appears that the suspect:
    - is aged under 18;
    - does require an appropriate adult;
    - is unable to appreciate the significance of questions and their answers;
    - is unable to understand what is happening because of the effects of drink, drugs or illness, ailment or condition; or
    - requires an interpreter; or
- the police officer decides that the suspect's arrest is now necessary (see Code G).

5.   After the interview

5.1   The interviewer shall make a note in their pocket book that the interview has taken place and that it was audibly recorded, the time it commenced, its duration and date and identification number of the master recording.

5.2   If no proceedings follow in respect of the person whose interview was recorded, the recording media must be kept securely as in paragraph 6.1 and Note 6A.
[This section (paragraphs 5.1, 5.2 and Note 5A) does not apply to interviews recorded using a secure digital network, see paragraphs 7.4 and 7.14 to 7.15.]

Note for Guidance

5A   Any written record of an audio recorded interview should be made in accordance with current national guidelines for police officers, police staff and CPS prosecutors concerned with the preparation, processing and submission of prosecution files.

6.   Master Recording security

(a) General

6.1   The officer in charge of each police station at which interviews with suspects are recorded or as the case may be, where recordings of interviews carried out elsewhere than at a police station are held, shall make arrangements for master recordings to be kept securely and their movements accounted for on the same basis as material which may be used for evidential purposes, in accordance with force standing orders. (See Note 6A.)

(b) Breaking master recording seal for criminal proceedings

6.2   A police officer has no authority to break the seal on a master recording which is required for criminal trial or appeal proceedings. If it is necessary to gain access to the master recording, the police officer shall arrange for its seal to be broken in the presence of a representative of the Crown Prosecution Service. The defendant or their legal adviser should be informed and given a reasonable opportunity to be present. If the defendant or their legal representative is present they shall be invited to re-seal and sign the master recording. If either refuses or neither is present this should be done by the representative of the Crown Prosecution Service. (See Notes 6B and 6C.)

(c) Breaking master recording seal: other cases

6.3   The chief officer of police is responsible for establishing arrangements for breaking the seal of the master copy where no criminal proceedings result, or the criminal proceedings to which the interview relates, have been concluded and it becomes necessary to break the seal. These arrangements should be those which the chief officer considers are reasonably necessary to demonstrate to the person interviewed and any other party who may wish to use or refer to the interview record that the master copy has not been tampered with and that the interview record remains accurate. (See Note 6D.)

6.3A Subject to paragraph 6.3C, a representative of each party must be given a reasonable opportunity to be present when the seal is broken and the master recording copied and resealed.

6.3B If one or more of the parties is not present when the master copy seal is broken because they cannot be contacted or refuse to attend or paragraph 6.3C applies, arrangements should be made for an independent person such as a custody visitor, to be present. Alternatively, or as an additional safeguard, arrangements should be made for a film or photographs to be taken of the procedure.

6.3C Paragraph 6.3A does not require a person to be given an opportunity to be present when;

(a) it is necessary to break the master copy seal for the proper and effective further investigation of the original offence or the investigation of some other offence; and

(b) the officer in charge of the investigation has reasonable grounds to suspect that allowing an opportunity might prejudice any such an investigation or criminal proceedings which may be brought as a result or endanger any person. (See Note 6E.)

(d) Documentation

6.4 When the master recording seal is broken, a record must be made of the procedure followed, including the date, time, place and persons present.
[This section (paragraphs 6.1 to 6.4 and Notes 6A to 6E) does not apply to interviews recorded using a secure digital network, see paragraphs 7.4 and 7.14 to 7.15.]

Notes for Guidance

6A This section is concerned with the security of the master recording sealed at the conclusion of the interview. Care must be taken of working recordings because their loss or destruction may lead unnecessarily to the need to access master recordings.

6B If the master recording has been delivered to the crown court for their keeping after committal for trial the crown prosecutor will apply to the chief clerk of the crown court centre for the release of the recording for unsealing by the crown prosecutor.

6C Reference to the Crown Prosecution Service or to the crown prosecutor in this part of the Code should be taken to include any other body or person with a statutory responsibility for the proceedings for which the police recorded interview is required.

6D The most common reasons for needing access to master copies that are not required for criminal proceedings arise from civil actions and complaints against police and civil actions between individuals arising out of allegations of crime investigated by police.

6E Paragraph 6.3C could apply, for example, when one or more of the outcomes or likely outcomes of the investigation might be;

(i) the prosecution of one or more of the original suspects;

(ii) the prosecution of someone previously not suspected, including someone who was originally a witness, and

(iii) any original suspect being treated as a prosecution witness and when premature disclosure of any police action, particularly through contact with any parties involved, could lead to a real risk of compromising the investigation and endangering witnesses.

7. Recording of Interviews by Secure Digital Network

7.1 A secure digital network does not use removable media and this section specifies the provisions which will apply when a secure digital network is used.

7.2 Not used.

7.3 The following requirements are solely applicable to the use of a secure digital network for the recording of interviews.

(a) Application of sections 1 to 6 of Code E

7.4 Sections 1 to 6 of Code E above apply except for the following paragraphs:
- Paragraph 2.2 under 'Recording and sealing of master recordings'
- Paragraph 4.3 under '(b) Commencement of interviews'
- Paragraph 4.4(e) under '(b) Commencement of interviews'
- Paragraphs 4.11 to 4.19 under '(e) Changing recording media', '(f) Taking a break during interview', '(g) Failure of recording equipment', '(h) Removing recording media from the recorder' and '(i) Conclusion of interview'
- Paragraphs 6.1 to 6.4 and Notes 6A to 6E under 'Media security'

(b) Commencement of Interviews

7.5 When the suspect is brought into the interview room, the interviewer shall without delay and in the sight of the suspect, switch on the recording equipment and enter the information necessary to log on to the secure network and start recording.

7.6 The interviewer must then inform the suspect that the interview is being recorded using a secure digital network and that recording has commenced.

7.7 In addition to the requirements of paragraph 4.4(a) to (d) above, the interviewer must inform the person that:

- they will be given access to the recording of the interview in the event that they are charged or informed that they will be prosecuted but if they are not charged or informed that they will be prosecuted they will only be given access as agreed with the police or on the order of a court; and
- they will be given a written notice at the end of the interview setting out their rights to access the recording and what will happen to the recording.

(c) Taking a break during interview

7.8 When a break is taken, the fact that a break is to be taken, the reason for it and the time shall be recorded on the audio recording. The recording shall be stopped and the procedures in paragraphs 7.12 and 7.13 for the conclusion of an interview followed.

7.9 When the interview recommences the procedures in paragraphs 7.5 to 7.7 for commencing an interview shall be followed to create a new file to record the continuation of the interview. The time the interview recommences shall be recorded on the audio recording.

7.10 After any break in the interview the interviewer must, before resuming the interview, remind the person being questioned that they remain under caution or, if there is any doubt, give the caution in full again. (See Note 4G.)

(d) Failure of recording equipment

7.11 If there is an equipment failure which can be rectified quickly, e.g. by commencing a new secure digital network recording, the interviewer shall follow the appropriate procedures as in paragraphs 7.8 to 7.10. When the recording is resumed the interviewer shall explain what happened and record the time the interview recommences. If, however, it is not possible to continue recording on the secure digital network the interview should be recorded on removable media as in paragraph 4.3 unless the necessary equipment is not available. If this happens the interview may continue without being audibly recorded and the interviewer shall seek the authority of the custody officer authority or a sergeant as in paragraph 3.3(a) or (b). (See Note 4H.)

(e) Conclusion of interview

7.12 At the conclusion of the interview, the suspect shall be offered the opportunity to clarify anything he or she has said and asked if there is anything they want to add.

7.13 At the conclusion of the interview, including the taking and reading back of any written statement:

(a) the time shall be orally recorded.

(b) the suspect shall be handed a notice (see Note 7A) which explains:
- how the audio recording will be used
- the arrangements for access to it
- that if they are charged or informed that they will be prosecuted, they will be given access to the recording of the interview either electronically or by being given a copy on removable recording media, but if they are not charged or informed that they will prosecuted, they will only be given access as agreed with the police or on the order of a court.

(c) the suspect must be asked to confirm that he or she has received a copy of the notice at sub-paragraph (b) above. If the suspect fails to accept or to acknowledge receipt of the notice, the interviewer will state for the recording that a copy of the notice has been provided to the suspect and that he or she has refused to take a copy of the notice or has refused to acknowledge receipt.

(d)   the time shall be recorded and the interviewer shall notify the suspect that the recording is being saved to the secure network. The interviewer must save the recording in the presence of the suspect. The suspect should then be informed that the interview is terminated.

(f) After the interview

7.14 The interviewer shall make a note in their pocket book that the interview has taken place and that it was audibly recorded, time it commenced, its duration and date and the identification number of the original recording.

7.15 If no proceedings follow in respect of the person whose interview was recorded, the recordings must be kept securely as in paragraphs 7.16 and 7.17. (See Note 5A.)

(g) Security of secure digital network interview records

7.16 Interview record files are stored in read only format on non-removable storage devices, for example, hard disk drives, to ensure their integrity. The recordings are first saved locally to a secure non-removable device before being transferred to the remote network device. If for any reason the network connection fails, the recording remains on the local device and will be transferred when the network connections are restored.

7.17 Access to interview recordings, including copying to removable media, must be strictly controlled and monitored to ensure that access is restricted to those who have been given specific permission to access for specified purposes when this is necessary. For example, police officers and CPS lawyers involved in the preparation of any prosecution case, persons interviewed if they have been charged or informed they may be prosecuted and their legal representatives.

Note for Guidance

7A   The notice at paragraph 7.13 above should provide a brief explanation of the secure digital network and how access to the recording is strictly limited. The notice should also explain the access rights of the suspect, his or her legal representative, the police and the prosecutor to the recording of the interview. Space should be provided on the form to insert the date and the file reference number for the interview.

POLICE AND CRIMINAL EVIDENCE ACT (PACE) CODE F

REVISED

CODE OF PRACTICE ON VISUAL RECORDING WITH SOUND OF INTERVIEWS WITH SUSPECTS

Commencement – Transitional Arrangements

This contents of this Code should be considered if an interviewer proposes to make a visual recording with sound of an interview with a suspect after 00.00 on 31 July 2018.

There is no statutory requirement under PACE to visually record interviews.

...

2.   When interviews and matters to which Code F applies may be visually recorded with sound and provisions for their conduct and recording.

(a) General

2.1 For the purpose of this Code, a visual recording with sound means an audio recording of an interview or other matter made in accordance with the requirement in paragraph 2.1 of the Code of Practice on audio recording interviews with suspects (Code E) (see Note 2A) during which a simultaneous visual recording is made which shows the suspect, the interviewer and those in whose presence and hearing the audio recording was made.

2.2 There is no statutory requirement to make a visual recording, however, the provisions of this Code shall be followed on any occasion that the 'relevant officer' described in Code E paragraph 2.4 considers that a visual recording of any matters mentioned in paragraph 2.1 should be made. Having regard to the safeguards described in paragraph 1.5A, examples of occasions when the relevant officer is likely to consider that a visual recording should be made include when:

(a) the suspect (whether or not detained) requires an appropriate adult;

(b) the suspect or their solicitor or appropriate adult requests that the interview be recorded visually;

(c) the suspect or other person whose presence is necessary is deaf or deaf/blind or speech impaired and uses sign language to communicate;

(d) the interviewer anticipates that when asking the suspect about their involvement in the offence concerned, they will invite the suspect to demonstrate their actions or behaviour at the time or to examine a particular item or object which is handed to them;

(e) the officer in charge of the investigation believes that a visual recording with sound will assist in the conduct of the investigation, for example, when briefing other officers about the suspect or matters coming to light during the course of the interview; and

(f) the authorised recording device that would be used in accordance with paragraph 2.1 of Code E incorporates a camera and creates a combined audio and visual recording and does not allow the visual recording function to operate independently of the audio recording function.

2.3 For the purpose of making such a visual recording, the provisions of Code E and the relevant Notes for Guidance shall apply equally to visual recordings with sound as they do to audio-only recordings, subject to the additional provisions in paragraphs 2.5 to 2.12 below which apply exclusively to visual recordings. (See Note 2E.)

2.4 This Code does not apply to the conduct and recording in England and Wales, of:

(a) interviews of persons detained under section 41 of, or Schedule 7 to, the Terrorism Act 2000, and

(b) post-charge questioning of persons authorised under section 22 of the Counter Terrorism Act 2008.

These must be video recorded with sound in accordance with the provisions of the separate Code of Practice issued under paragraph 3 of Schedule 8 to the Terrorism Act 2000 and under section 25 of the Counter-Terrorism Act 2008. If, during the course of an interview or questioning being visually recorded under this Code, it becomes apparent that the interview or questioning should be conducted under that separate Code, the interview should only continue in accordance with that Code (see Code E paragraph 1.4).

(B)   Application of Code E – additional provisions that apply to visual recording with sound.

(i) General

2.5 Before visual recording commences, the interviewer must inform the suspect that in accordance with paragraph 2.2, a visual recording is being made and explain the visual and audio recording arrangements. If the suspect is a juvenile or a vulnerable person (see Code C, paragraphs 1.4, 1.5 and 1.13(d)), the information and explanation must be provided or (as the case may be) provided again, in the presence of the appropriate adult.

2.6 The device used to make the visual recording at the same time as the audio recording (see paragraph 2.1) must ensure coverage of as much of the room or location where the interview takes place as it is practically possible to achieve whilst the interview takes place (see Note 2B).

2.7 In cases to which paragraph 1.13 of Code E (disclosure of identity of officers or police staff conducting interviews) applies: (a) the officers and staff may have their backs to the visual recording device; and (b) when in accordance with Code E paragraph 3.21 or 4.12 as they apply to this Code, arrangements are made for the suspect to have access to the visual recording, the investigating officer may arrange for anything in the recording that might allow the officers or police staff to be identified to be concealed.

2.8 Following a decision made by the relevant officer in accordance with paragraph 2.2 that an interview or other matter mentioned in paragraph 2.1 above should be visually recorded, the relevant officer may decide that the interview is not to be visually recorded if it no longer appears that a visual recording should be made or because of a fault in the recording device. However, a decision not to make a visual recording does not detract in any way from the requirement for the interview to be audio recorded in accordance with paragraph 2.1 of Code E. (See Note 2C.)

2.9 The provisions in Code E paragraph 2.6 for remote monitoring of interviews shall apply to visually recorded interviews.

(ii) Objections and complaints by the suspect about visual recording

2.10 If the suspect or an appropriate adult on their behalf objects to the interview being visually recorded either at the outset or during the interview or during a break in the interview, the interviewer shall explain that the visual recording is being made in accordance with paragraph 2.2 and that this Code requires the objections to be recorded on the visual recording. When any objections have been recorded or the suspect or the appropriate adult have refused to have their objections recorded visually, the relevant officer shall decide in accordance with paragraph 2.8 and having regard to the nature and circumstances of the objections, whether visual recording should be turned off (see Note 2D). Following a decision that visual recording should be turned off, the interviewer shall say that they are turning off the visual recording. The audio recording required to be maintained in accordance with Code E shall continue and the interviewer shall ask the person to record their objections to the interview being visually recorded on the audiorecording. If the relevant officer considers that visual recording should not be turned off, the interviewer may proceed to question the suspect with the visual recording still on. If the suspect also objects to the interview being audio recorded, paragraph 3.9 of Code E will apply if a removable recording media device (see Code E paragraph 1.6(a)(ii)) is being used) and paragraph 4.6 of Code E will apply if a secure digital recording device (see Code E paragraph 1.6(a)(iii)) is being used.

2.11 If the suspect indicates that they wish to tell the interviewer about matters not directly connected with the offence of which they are suspected and that they are unwilling for these matters to be visually recorded, the suspect should be given the opportunity to tell the interviewer about these matters after the conclusion of the formal interview. (ii) Failure of visual recording device

2.12 If there is a failure of equipment and it is not possible to continue visual recording using the same type of recording device (i.e. a removable recording media device as in Code E paragraph 1.6(a)(ii) or a secure digital recording network device as in Code E paragraph 1.6(a)(iii)) or by using a replacement device of either type, the relevant officer may decide that the interview is to continue without being visually recorded. In these circumstances, the continuation of the interview must be conducted and recorded in accordance with the provisions of Code E. (See Note 2F.)

Notes for Guidance

2A Paragraph 2.1 of Code E describes the requirement that authorised audio-recording devices are to be used for recording interviews and other matters.

2B Interviewers will wish to arrange that, as far as possible, visual recording arrangements are unobtrusive. It must be clear to the suspect, however, that there is no opportunity to interfere with the recording equipment or the recording media.

2C A decision made in accordance with paragraph 2.8 not to record an interview visually for any reason may be the subject of comment in court. The 'relevant officer' responsible should therefore be prepared to justify that decision.

2D Objections for the purpose of paragraph 2.10 are meant to apply to objections based on the suspect's genuine and honestly held beliefs and to allow officers to exercise their discretion to decide whether a visual recording is to be made according to the circumstances surrounding the suspect and the investigation. Objections that appear to be frivolous with the intentions of frustrating or delaying the investigation would not be relevant.

2E The visual recording made in accordance with this Code may be used for eye-witness identification procedures to which paragraph 3.21 and Annex E of Code D apply.

2F Where the interview is being visually recorded and the media or the recording device fails, the interviewer should stop the interview immediately. Where part of the interview is unaffected by the error and is still accessible on the media or on the network device, that part shall be copied and sealed in the suspect's presence as a master copy or saved as a new secure digital network recording as appropriate. The interview should then be recommenced using a functioning recording device and new recording media as appropriate. Where the media content of the interview has been lost in its entirety, the media should be sealed in the suspect's presence and the interview begun again. If the visual recording equipment cannot be fixed and a replacement device is not immediately available, the interview should be audio recorded in accordance with Code E.

2G The relevant officer should be aware that a decision to continue visual recording against the wishes of the suspect may be the subject of comment in court.

3. Interviews to be visually recorded

3.1 Subject to paragraph 3.2 below, when an interviewer is deciding whether to make a visual recording, these are the areas where it might be appropriate:

(a) with a suspect in respect of an indictable offence (including an offence triable either way) (see Notes 3A and 3B);

(b) which takes place as a result of an interviewer exceptionally putting further questions to a suspect about an offence described in sub-paragraph (a) above after they have been charged with, or informed they may be prosecuted for, that offence (see Note 3C);

(c) in which an interviewer wishes to bring to the notice of a person, after that person has been charged with, or informed they may be prosecuted for an offence described in sub-paragraph (a) above, any written statement made by another person, or the content of an interview with another person (see Note 3D);

(d) with, or in the presence of, a deaf or deaf/blind or speech impaired person who uses sign language to communicate;

(e) with, or in the presence of anyone who requires an appropriate adult, or

(f) in any case where the suspect or their representative requests that the interview be recorded visually.

3.2 The Terrorism Act 2000 and the Counter-Terrorism Act 2008 make separate provisions for a Code of Practice for the video recording with sound of:

- interviews of persons detained under section 41 of, or Schedule 7 to, the 2000 Act; and
- post-charge questioning of persons authorised under section 22 or 23 of the 2008 Act.

The provisions of this code do not therefore apply to such interviews. (See Note 3E.)

3.3 Following a decision by an interviewer to visually record any interview mentioned in paragraph 3.1 above, the custody officer in the case of a detained person, or a sergeant in the case of a suspect who has not been arrested, may authorise the interviewer not to make a visual record and for the purpose of this Code (F), the provisions of Code E paragraphs 3.1, 3.2, 3.3, 3.3A and 3.4 shall apply as appropriate. However, authority not to make a visual recording does not detract in any way from the requirement for audio recording. This would require a further authorisation not to make in accordance with Code E. (See Note 3F.)

3.4 *Not used.*

3.5 The whole of each interview shall be recorded visually, including the taking and reading back of any statement.

3.6 A sign or indicator which is visible to the suspect must show when the visual recording equipment is recording.

Notes for Guidance

3A Nothing in the code is intended to preclude visual recording at police discretion of interviews at police stations or elsewhere with people cautioned in respect of offences not covered by paragraph 3.1, or responses made by persons after they have been charged with, or informed they may be prosecuted for, an offence, provided that this code is complied with.

3B   Attention is drawn to the provisions set out in Code C about the matters to be considered when deciding whether a detained person is fit to be interviewed.

3C   Code C sets out the circumstances in which a suspect may be questioned about an offence after being charged with it.

3D   Code C sets out the procedures to be followed when a person's attention is drawn after charge, to a statement made by another person. One method of bringing the content of an interview with another person to the notice of a suspect may be to play them a recording of that interview.

3E   If, during the course of an interview under this Code, it becomes apparent that the interview should be conducted under the terrorism code for the video recording with sound of interviews, the interview should only continue in accordance with that code.

3F   A decision not to record an interview visually for any reason may be the subject of comment in court. The authorising officer should therefore be prepared to justify their decision in each case.

4.   The Interview

(a) General

4.1   The provisions of Code C in relation to cautions and interviews and the Notes for Guidance applicable to those provisions shall apply to the conduct of interviews to which this Code applies.

4.2   Particular attention is drawn to those parts of Code C that describe the restrictions on drawing adverse inferences from an arrested suspect's failure or refusal to say anything about their involvement in the offence when interviewed, or after being charged or informed they may be prosecuted and how those restrictions affect the terms of the caution and determine whether a special warning under Sections 36 and 37 of the Criminal Justice and Public Order Act 1994 can be given.

(b) Commencement of interviews

4.3   When the suspect is brought into the interview room the interviewer shall without delay, but in sight of the suspect, load the recording equipment and set it to record. The recording media must be unwrapped or otherwise opened in the presence of the suspect. (See Note 4A.)

4.4   The interviewer shall then tell the suspect formally about the visual recording and point out the sign or indicator which shows that the recording equipment is activated and recording (see paragraph 3.6). The interviewer shall:

(a)   explain that the interview is being visually recorded;

(b)   subject to paragraph 2.5, give their name and rank, and that of any other interviewer present;

(c)   ask the suspect and any other party present (e.g. the appropriate adult, a solicitor or interpreter) to identify themselves;

(d)   state the date, time of commencement and place of the interview, and

(e)   state that the suspect will be given a notice about what will happen to the recording. (See Note 4AA.)

4.4 A Any person entering the interview room after the interview has commenced shall be invited by the interviewer to identify themselves for the purpose of the recording and state the reason why they have entered the interview room.

4.5   The interviewer shall then caution the suspect, see Code C, section 10 and:

- if they are detained, remind them of their entitlement to free legal advice, see Code C paragraph 11.2, or
- if they are not detained under arrest, explain this and their entitlement to free legal advice, see Code C paragraph 3.21.

4.6   The interviewer shall then put to the suspect any significant statement or silence, see Code C, paragraph 11.4.

(c) Interviews with suspects who appear to require an interpreter.

4.7   The provisions of Code C on interpreters for suspects who do not appear to speak or understand English, or who appear to have a hearing or speech impediment, continue to apply.

(d) Objections and complaints by the suspect

4.8 If the suspect or an appropriate adult on their behalf, objects to the interview being visually recorded either at the outset or during the interview or during a break in the interview, the interviewer shall explain that the interview is being visually recorded and that this Code requires that the objections to be recorded on the visual recording. When any objections have been recorded or the suspect or the appropriate adult have refused to have their objections recorded, the interviewer shall say that they are turning off the visual recording, give their reasons and turn it off. If a separate audio recording is being maintained, the interviewer shall ask the person to record the reasons for refusing to agree to the interview being visually recorded. Paragraph 4.8 of Code E will apply if the person also objects to the interview being audio recorded. If the interviewer reasonably considers they may proceed to question the suspect with the visual recording still on, the interviewer may do so. (See Note 4G.)

4.9 If in the course of an interview a complaint is made by the person being questioned, or on their behalf, concerning the provisions of this or any other Code, or it comes to the interviewer's notice that the person may have been treated improperly, then the interviewer shall act as in Code C, paragraph 12.9. (See Notes 4B and 4C.)

4.10 If the suspect indicates that they wish to tell the interviewer about matters not directly connected with the offence of which they are suspected and that they are unwilling for these matters to be visually recorded, the suspect should be given the opportunity to tell the interviewer about these matters after the conclusion of the formal interview.

(e) Changing the recording media

4.11 In instances where the recording medium is not of sufficient length to record all of the interview with the suspect, further certified recording medium will be used. When the recording equipment indicates that the recording medium has only a short time left to run, the interviewer shall advise the suspect and round off that part of the interview. If the interviewer wishes to continue the interview but does not already have further certified recording media with him, they shall obtain a set. The suspect should not be left unattended in the interview room. The interviewer will remove the recording media from the recording equipment and insert the new ones which have been unwrapped or otherwise opened in the suspect's presence. The recording equipment shall then be set to record. Care must be taken, particularly when a number of sets of recording media have been used, to ensure that there is no confusion between them. This could be achieved by marking the sets of recording media with consecutive identification numbers.

(f) Taking a break during the interview

4.12 When a break is taken, the fact that a break is to be taken, the reason for it and the time shall be recorded on the visual record.

4.12A When the break is taken and the interview room vacated by the suspect, the recording media shall be removed from the recorder and the procedures for the conclusion of an interview followed. (See paragraph 4.18.)

4.13 When a break is a short one and both the suspect and an interviewer remain in the interview room, the recording may be stopped. There is no need to remove the recording media and when the interview recommences the recording should continue on the same recording media. The time at which the interview recommences shall be recorded.

4.14 After any break in the interview the interviewer must, before resuming the interview, remind the person being questioned of their right to legal advice if they have not exercised it and that they remain under caution or, if there is any doubt, give the caution in full again. (See Notes 4D and 4E.)

(g) Failure of recording equipment

4.15 If there is a failure of equipment which can be rectified quickly, the appropriate procedures set out in paragraph 4.12 shall be followed. When the recording is resumed the interviewer shall explain what has happened and record the time the interview recommences. If, however, it is not possible to continue recording on that particular recorder and no alternative equipment is readily available, the interview may continue without being recorded visually. In such circumstances, the procedures set out in paragraph 3.3 of this code for seeking the authority of the custody officer or a sergeant will be followed. (See Note 4F.)

(h) Removing used recording media from recording equipment

4.16 Where used recording media are removed from the recording equipment during the course of an interview, they shall be retained and the procedures set out in paragraph 4.18 below followed.

(i) Conclusion of interview

4.17 Before the conclusion of the interview, the suspect shall be offered the opportunity to clarify anything he or she has said and asked if there is anything that they wish to add.

4.18 At the conclusion of the interview, including the taking and reading back of any written statement, the time shall be recorded and the recording equipment switched off. The master recording shall be removed from the recording equipment, sealed with a master recording label and treated as an exhibit in accordance with the force standing orders. The interviewer shall sign the label and also ask the suspect and any third party present during the interview to sign it. If the suspect or third party refuses to sign the label, an officer of at least the rank of inspector, or if one is not available, the custody officer or, if the suspect has not been arrested, a sergeant, shall be called into the interview room and asked, subject to paragraph 2.5, to sign it.

4.19 The suspect shall be handed a notice which explains the use which will be made of the recording and the arrangements for access to it. The notice will also advise the suspect that a copy of the tape shall be supplied as soon as practicable if the person is charged or informed that he will be prosecuted.

Notes for Guidance

4AA For the purpose of voice identification the interviewer should ask the suspect and any other people present to identify themselves.

4A The interviewer should attempt to estimate the likely length of the interview and ensure that an appropriate quantity of certified recording media and labels with which to seal the master copies are available in the interview room.

4B Where the custody officer, or in the case of a person who has not been arrested, a sergeant, is called to deal with the complaint, wherever possible the recorder should be left to run until the officer has entered the interview room and spoken to the person being interviewed. Continuation or termination of the interview should be at the discretion of the interviewer pending action by an inspector under Code C paragraph 9.2.

4C Where the complaint is about a matter not connected with this Code or Code C, the decision to continue with the interview is at the interviewer's discretion. Where the interviewer decides to continue with the interview, the person being interviewed shall be told that at the conclusion of the interview, the complaint will be brought to the attention of the custody officer, or in the case of a person who has not been arrested, a sergeant. When the interview is concluded, the interviewer must, as soon as practicable, inform the custody officer or the sergeant of the existence and nature of the complaint made.

4D In considering whether to caution again after a break, the interviewer should bear in mind that they may have to satisfy a court that the person understood that they were still under caution when the interview resumed.

4E The officer should bear in mind that it may be necessary to satisfy the court that nothing occurred during a break in an interview or between interviews which influenced the suspect's recorded evidence. On the re-commencement of an interview, the interviewer should consider summarising on the record the reason for the break and confirming this with the suspect.

4F Where the interview is being recorded and the media or the recording equipment fails, the interviewer should stop the interview immediately. Where part of the interview is unaffected by the error and is still accessible on the media, that part shall be copied and sealed in the suspect's presence as a master copy and the interview recommenced using new equipment/media as required. Where the content of the interview has been lost in its entirety, the media should be sealed in the suspect's presence and the interview begun again. If the recording equipment cannot be fixed or no replacement is immediately available, the interview should be audio recorded in accordance with Code E.

4G The interviewer should be aware that a decision to continue recording against the wishes of the suspect may be the subject of comment in court.

5. After the Interview

5.1 The interviewer shall make a note in his or her pocket book of the fact that the interview has taken place and has been recorded, its time, duration and date and the identification number of the master copy of the recording media.

5.2 Where no proceedings follow in respect of the person whose interview was recorded, the recording media must nevertheless be kept securely in accordance with paragraph 6.1 and Note 6A.

Note for Guidance

5A Any written record of a recorded interview shall be made in accordance with current national guidelines for police officers, police staff and CPS prosecutors concerned with the preparation, processing and submission of files.

6. Master Recording Security

(a) General

6.1 The officer in charge of the police station at which interviews with suspects are recorded or as the case may be, where recordings of interviews carried out elsewhere than at a police station are held, shall make arrangements for the master copies to be kept securely and their movements accounted for on the same basis as other material which may be used for evidential purposes, in accordance with force standing orders. (See Note 6A.)

(b) Breaking master recording seal for criminal proceedings

6.2 A police officer has no authority to break the seal on a master copy which is required for criminal trial or appeal proceedings. If it is necessary to gain access to the master copy, the police officer shall arrange for its seal to be broken in the presence of a representative of the Crown Prosecution Service. The defendant or their legal adviser shall be informed and given a reasonable opportunity to be present. If the defendant or their legal representative is present they shall be invited to reseal and sign the master copy. If either refuses or neither is present, this shall be done by the representative of the Crown Prosecution Service. (See Notes 6B and 6C.)

(c) Breaking master recording seal: other cases

6.3 The chief officer of police is responsible for establishing arrangements for breaking the seal of the master copy where no criminal proceedings result, or the criminal proceedings to which the interview relates, have been concluded and it becomes necessary to break the seal. These arrangements should be those which the chief officer considers are reasonably necessary to demonstrate to the person interviewed and any other party who may wish to use or refer to the interview record that the master copy has not been tampered with and that the interview record remains accurate. (See Note 6D.)

6.4 Subject to paragraph 6.6, a representative of each party must be given a reasonable opportunity to be present when the seal is broken and the master recording copied and re-sealed.

6.5 If one or more of the parties is not present when the master copy seal is broken because they cannot be contacted or refuse to attend or paragraph 6.6 applies, arrangements should be made for an independent person such as a custody visitor, to be present. Alternatively, or as an additional safeguard, arrangement should be made for a film or photographs to be taken of the procedure.

6.6 Paragraph 6.4 does not require a person to be given an opportunity to be present when:

(a)   it is necessary to break the master copy seal for the proper and effective further investigation of the original offence or the investigation of some other offence; and

(b)   the officer in charge of the investigation has reasonable grounds to suspect that allowing an opportunity might prejudice any such an investigation or criminal proceedings which may be brought as a result or endanger any person. (See Note 6E.)

(d) Documentation

6.7 When the master copy seal is broken, copied and re-sealed, a record must be made of the procedure followed, including the date time and place and persons present.

Notes for Guidance

6A   This section is concerned with the security of the master recordings which will have been sealed at the conclusion of the interview. Care should, however, be taken of working recordings since their loss or destruction may lead unnecessarily to the need to have access to master copies.

6B   If the master recording has been delivered to the Crown Court for their keeping after committal for trial, the Crown Prosecutor will apply to the Chief Clerk of the Crown Court Centre for its release for unsealing by the Crown Prosecutor.

6C   Reference to the Crown Prosecution Service or to the Crown Prosecutor in this part of the code shall be taken to include any other body or person with a statutory responsibility for prosecution for whom the police conduct any recorded interviews.

6D   The most common reasons for needing access to master recordings that are not required for criminal proceedings arise from civil actions and complaints against police and civil actions between individuals arising out of allegations of crime investigated by police.

6E   Paragraph 6.6 could apply, for example, when one or more of the outcomes or likely outcomes of the investigation might be:

(i)   the prosecution of one or more of the original suspects;

(ii)   the prosecution of someone previously not suspected, including someone who was originally a witness; and

(iii)   any original suspect being treated as a prosecution witness and when premature disclosure of any police action, particularly through contact with any parties involved, could lead to a real risk of compromising the investigation and endangering witnesses.

POLICE AND CRIMINAL EVIDENCE ACT 1984 (PACE) CODE G

REVISED
CODE OF PRACTICE FOR THE STATUTORY
POWER OF ARREST BY POLICE OFFICERS

Commencement – Transitional Arrangements

This Code applies to any arrest made by a police officer after 00:00 on
12 November 2012

1.   Introduction

1.1 This Code of Practice deals with the statutory power of police to arrest a person who is involved, or suspected of being involved, in a criminal offence. The power of arrest must be used fairly, responsibly, with respect for people suspected of committing offences and without unlawful discrimination. The Equality Act 2010 makes it unlawful for police officers to discriminate against, harass or victimise any person on the grounds of the 'protected characteristics' of age, disability, gender reassignment, race, religion or belief, sex and sexual orientation, marriage and civil partnership, pregnancy and maternity when using their powers. When police forces are carrying out their functions they also have a duty to have regard to the need to eliminate unlawful discrimination, harassment and victimisation and to take steps to foster good relations.

1.2 The exercise of the power of arrest represents an obvious and significant interference with the Right to Liberty and Security under Article 5 of the European Convention on Human Rights set out in Part I of Schedule 1 to the Human Rights Act 1998.

1.3 The use of the power must be fully justified and officers exercising the power should consider if the necessary objectives can be met by other, less intrusive means. Absence of justification for exercising the power of arrest may lead to challenges should the case proceed to court. It could also lead to civil claims against police for unlawful arrest and false imprisonment. When the power of arrest is exercised it is essential that it is exercised in a non-discriminatory and proportionate manner which is compatible with the Right to Liberty under Article 5. See Note 1B.

1.4 Section 24 of the Police and Criminal Evidence Act 1984 (as substituted by section 110 of the Serious Organised Crime and Police Act 2005) provides the statutory power for a constable to arrest without warrant for all offences. If the provisions of the Act and this Code are not observed, both the arrest and the conduct of any subsequent investigation may be open to question.

1.5 This Code of Practice must be readily available at all police stations for consultation by police officers and police staff, detained persons and members of the public.

1.6 The Notes for Guidance are not provisions of this code.

2. Elements of Arrest under section 24 PACE

2.1 A lawful arrest requires two elements:
A person's involvement or suspected involvement or attempted involvement in the commission of a criminal offence;
AND
Reasonable grounds for believing that the person's arrest is necessary.
- both elements must be satisfied, and
- it can never be necessary to arrest a person unless there are reasonable grounds to suspect them of committing an offence.

2.2 The arrested person must be informed that they have been arrested, even if this fact is obvious, and of the relevant circumstances of the arrest in relation to both the above elements. The custody officer must be informed of these matters on arrival at the police station. See paragraphs 2.9, 3.3 and Note 3 and Code C paragraph 3.4.

(a) 'Involvement in the commission of an offence'

2.3 A constable may arrest without warrant in relation to any offence (see Notes 1 and 1A) anyone:
- who is about to commit an offence or is in the act of committing an offence;
- whom the officer has reasonable grounds for suspecting is about to commit an offence or to be committing an offence;
- whom the officer has reasonable grounds to suspect of being guilty of an offence which he or she has reasonable grounds for suspecting has been committed;
- anyone who is guilty of an offence which has been committed or anyone whom the officer has reasonable grounds for suspecting to be guilty of that offence.

2.3A There must be some reasonable, objective grounds for the suspicion, based on known facts and information which are relevant to the likelihood the offence has been committed and the person liable to arrest committed it. See Notes 2 and 2A.

(b) Necessity criteria

2.4 The power of arrest is only exercisable if the constable has reasonable grounds for believing that it is necessary to arrest the person. The statutory criteria for what may constitute necessity are set out in paragraph 2.9 and it remains an operational decision at the discretion of the constable to decide:
- which one or more of the necessity criteria (if any) applies to the individual; and
- if any of the criteria do apply, whether to arrest, grant street bail after arrest, report for summons or for charging by post, issue a penalty notice or take any other action that is open to the officer.

2.5　In applying the criteria, the arresting officer has to be satisfied that at least one of the reasons supporting the need for arrest is satisfied.

2.6　Extending the power of arrest to all offences provides a constable with the ability to use that power to deal with any situation. However applying the necessity criteria requires the constable to examine and justify the reason or reasons why a person needs to be arrested or (as the case may be) further arrested, for an offence for the custody officer to decide whether to authorise their detention for that offence. See Note 2C

2.7　The criteria in paragraph 2.9 below which are set out in section 24 of PACE as substituted by section 110 of the Serious Organised Crime and Police Act 2005 are exhaustive. However, the circumstances that may satisfy those criteria remain a matter for the operational discretion of individual officers. Some examples are given to illustrate what those circumstances might be and what officers might consider when deciding whether arrest is necessary.

2.8　In considering the individual circumstances, the constable must take into account the situation of the victim, the nature of the offence, the circumstances of the suspect and the needs of the investigative process.

2.9　When it is practicable to tell a person why their arrest is necessary (as required by paragraphs 2.2, 3.3 and Note 3), the constable should outline the facts, information and other circumstances which provide the grounds for believing that their arrest is necessary and which the officer considers satisfy one or more of the statutory criteria in sub-paragraphs (a) to (f), namely:

(a)　to enable the name of the person in question to be ascertained (in the case where the constable does not know, and cannot readily ascertain, the person's name, or has reasonable grounds for doubting whether a name given by the person as his name is his real name):

An officer might decide that a person's name cannot be readily ascertained if they fail or refuse to give it when asked, particularly after being warned that failure or refusal is likely to make their arrest necessary (see Note 2D). Grounds to doubt a name given may arise if the person appears reluctant or hesitant when asked to give their name or to verify the name they have given.

Where mobile fingerprinting is available and the suspect's name cannot be ascertained or is doubted, the officer should consider using the power under section 61(6A) of PACE (see Code D paragraph 4.3(e)) to take and check the fingerprints of a suspect as this may avoid the need to arrest solely to enable their name to be ascertained.

(b)　correspondingly as regards the person's address:

An officer might decide that a person's address cannot be readily ascertained if they fail or refuse to give it when asked, particularly after being warned that such a failure or refusal is likely to make their arrest necessary. See Note 2D. Grounds to doubt an address given may arise if the person appears reluctant or hesitant when asked to give their address or is unable to provide verifiable details of the locality they claim to live in.

When considering reporting to consider summons or charging by post as alternatives to arrest, an address would be satisfactory if the person will be at it for a sufficiently long period for it to be possible to serve them with the summons or requisition and charge; or, that some other person at that address specified by the person will accept service on their behalf. When considering issuing a penalty notice, the address should be one where the person will be in the event of enforcement action if the person does not pay the penalty or is convicted and fined after a court hearing.

(c)　to prevent the person in question:

(i)　causing physical injury to himself or any other person;

This might apply where the suspect has already used or threatened violence against others and it is thought likely that they may assault others if they are not arrested. (See Note 2D.)

(ii)　suffering physical injury;

This might apply where the suspect's behaviour and actions are believed likely to provoke, or have provoked, others to want to assault the suspect unless the suspect is arrested for their own protection. (See Note 2D.)

    (iii)   causing loss or damage to property;
        This might apply where the suspect is a known persistent offender with a history of serial offending against property (theft and criminal damage) and it is thought likely that they may continue offending if they are not arrested.

    (iv)   committing an offence against public decency (only applies where members of the public going about their normal business cannot reasonably be expected to avoid the person in question);
        This might apply when an offence against public decency is being committed in a place to which the public have access and is likely to be repeated in that or some other public place at a time when the public are likely to encounter the suspect. (See Note 2D.)

    (v)   causing an unlawful obstruction of the highway;
        This might apply to any offence where its commission causes an unlawful obstruction which it is believed may continue or be repeated if the person is not arrested, particularly if the person has been warned that they are causing an obstruction. (See Note 2D.)

(d)   to protect a child or other vulnerable person from the person in question.
    This might apply when the health (physical or mental) or welfare of a child or vulnerable person is likely to be harmed or is at risk of being harmed, if the person is not arrested in cases where it is not practicable and appropriate to make alternative arrangements to prevent the suspect from having any harmful or potentially harmful contact with the child or vulnerable person.

(e)   to allow the prompt and effective investigation of the offence or of the conduct of the person in question. (See Note 2E.)
    This may arise when it is thought likely that unless the person is arrested and then either taken in custody to the police station or granted 'street bail' to attend the station later, see Note 2J, further action considered necessary to properly investigate their involvement in the offence would be frustrated, unreasonably delayed or otherwise hindered and therefore be impracticable. Examples of such actions include:

    (i)   interviewing the suspect on occasions when the person's voluntary attendance is not considered to be a practicable alternative to arrest, because for example:
- it is thought unlikely that the person would attend the police station voluntarily to be interviewed.
- it is necessary to interview the suspect about the outcome of other investigative action for which their arrest is necessary, see (ii) to (v) below.
- arrest would enable the special warning to be given in accordance with Code C paragraphs 10.10 and 10.11 when the suspect is found:
  - in possession of incriminating objects, or at a place where such objects are found;
  - at or near the scene of the crime at or about the time it was committed.
- the person has made false statements and/or presented false evidence;
- it is thought likely that the person:
  - may steal or destroy evidence;
  - may collude or make contact with, co-suspects or conspirators;
  - may intimidate or threaten or make contact with, witnesses.

        (See Notes 2F and 2G.)

    (ii)   when considering arrest in connection with the investigation of an indictable offence (see Note 6), there is a need:
- to enter and search without a search warrant any premises occupied or controlled by the arrested person or where the person was when arrested or immediately before arrest;
- to prevent the arrested person from having contact with others;
- to detain the arrested person for more than 24 hours before charge.

    (iii)   when considering arrest in connection with any recordable offence and it is necessary to secure or preserve evidence of that offence by taking fingerprints, footwear impressions or samples from the suspect for evidential comparison or matching with other material relating to that offence, for example, from the crime scene. See Note 2H

(iv) when considering arrest in connection with any offence and it is necessary to search, examine or photograph the person to obtain evidence. (See Note 2H.)

(v) when considering arrest in connection with an offence to which the statutory Class A drug testing requirements in Code C section 17 apply, to enable testing when it is thought that drug misuse might have caused or contributed to the offence. (See Note 2I.)

(f) to prevent any prosecution for the offence from being hindered by the disappearance of the person in question.

This may arise when it is thought that:

- if the person is not arrested they are unlikely to attend court if they are prosecuted;
- the address given is not a satisfactory address for service of a summons or a written charge and requisition to appear at court because the person will not be at it for a sufficiently long period for the summons or charge and requisition to be served and no other person at that specified address will accept service on their behalf.

3. Information to be given on Arrest

(a) Cautions - when a caution must be given

3.1 Code C paragraphs 10.1 and 10.2 set out the requirement for a person whom there are grounds to suspect of an offence (see Note 2) to be cautioned before being questioned or further questioned about an offence.

3.2 *Not used.*

3.3 A person who is arrested, or further arrested, must be informed at the time if practicable, or if not, as soon as it becomes practicable thereafter, that they are under arrest and of the grounds and reasons for their arrest, see paragraphs 2.2 and Note 3.

3.4 A person who is arrested, or further arrested, must be cautioned unless:

(a) it is impracticable to do so by reason of their condition or behaviour at the time;
(b) they have already been cautioned immediately prior to arrest as in paragraph 3.1.

(b) Terms of the caution (Taken from Code C section 10)

3.5 The caution, which must be given on arrest, should be in the following terms:

'You do not have to say anything. But it may harm your defence if you do not mention when questioned something which you later rely on in Court. Anything you do say may be given in evidence.'

Where the use of the Welsh Language is appropriate, a constable may provide the caution directly in Welsh in the following terms:

'Does dim rhaid i chi ddweud dim byd. Ond gall niweidio eich amddiffyniad os na fyddwch chi'n sôn, wrth gael eich holi, am rywbeth y byddwch chi'n dibynnu arno nes ymlaen yn y Llys. Gall unrhyw beth yr ydych yn ei ddweud gael ei roi fel tystiolaeth.'

(See Note 4.)

3.6 Minor deviations from the words of any caution given in accordance with this Code do not constitute a breach of this Code, provided the sense of the relevant caution is preserved. (See Note 5.)

3.7 *Not used.*

4. Records of Arrest

(a) General

4.1 The arresting officer is required to record in his pocket book or by other methods used for recording information:

- the nature and circumstances of the offence leading to the arrest;
- the reason or reasons why arrest was necessary;
- the giving of the caution; and
- anything said by the person at the time of arrest.

4.2 Such a record should be made at the time of the arrest unless impracticable to do. If not made at that time, the record should then be completed as soon as possible thereafter.

4.3 On arrival at the police station or after being first arrested at the police station, the arrested person must be brought before the custody officer as soon as practicable and a custody record must be opened in accordance with section 2 of Code C. The information given by the arresting officer on the circumstances and reason or reasons for arrest shall be recorded as part of the custody record. Alternatively, a copy of the record made by the officer in accordance with paragraph 4.1 above shall be attached as part of the custody record. See paragraph 2.2 and Code C paragraphs 3.4 and 10.3.

4.4 The custody record will serve as a record of the arrest. Copies of the custody record will be provided in accordance with paragraphs 2.4 and 2.4A of Code C and access for inspection of the original record in accordance with paragraph 2.5 of Code C.

(b) **Interviews and arrests**

4.5 Records of interview, significant statements or silences will be treated in the same way as set out in sections 10 and 11 of Code C and in Codes E and F (audio and visual recording of interviews).

Notes for Guidance

1 For the purposes of this Code, 'offence' means any statutory or common law offence for which a person may be tried by a magistrates' court or the Crown court and punished if convicted. Statutory offences include assault, rape, criminal damage, theft, robbery, burglary, fraud, possession of controlled drugs and offences under road traffic, liquor licensing, gambling and immigration legislation and local government byelaws. Common law offences include murder, manslaughter, kidnapping, false imprisonment, perverting the course of justice and escape from lawful custody.

1A This code does not apply to powers of arrest conferred on constables under any arrest warrant, for example, a warrant issued under the Magistrates' Courts Act 1980, sections 1 or 13, or the Bail Act 1976, section 7(1), or to the powers of constables to arrest without warrant other than under section 24 of PACE for an offence. These other powers to arrest without warrant do not depend on the arrested person committing any specific offence and include:

- PACE, section 46A, arrest of person who fails to answer police bail to attend police station or is suspected of breaching any condition of that bail for the custody officer to decide whether they should be kept in police detention which applies whether or not the person commits an offence under section 6 of the Bail Act 1976 (e.g. failing without reasonable cause to surrender to custody);
- Bail Act 1976, section 7(3), arrest of person bailed to attend court who is suspected of breaching, or is believed likely to breach, any condition of bail to take them to court for bail to be re-considered;
- Children & Young Persons Act 1969, section 32(1A) (absconding) - arrest to return the person to the place where they are required to reside;
- Immigration Act 1971, Schedule 2 to arrest a person liable to examination to determine their right to remain in the UK;
- Mental Health Act 1983, section 136 to remove person suffering from mental disorder to place of safety for assessment;
- Prison Act 1952, section 49, arrest to return person unlawfully at large to the prison etc where they are liable to be detained;
- Road Traffic Act 1988, section 6D arrest of driver following the outcome of a preliminary roadside test requirement to enable the driver to be required to provide an evidential sample;
- Common law power to stop or prevent a Breach of the Peace - after arrest a person aged 18 or over may be brought before a justice of the peace court to show cause why they should not be bound over to keep the peace - not criminal proceedings.

1B Juveniles should not be arrested at their place of education unless this is unavoidable. When a juvenile is arrested at their place of education, the principal or their nominee must be informed. (From Code C Note 11D.)

2 Facts and information relevant to a person's suspected involvement in an offence should not be confined to those which tend to indicate the person has committed or attempted to commit the offence. Before making a decision to arrest, a constable

should take account of any facts and information that are available, including claims of innocence made by the person, that might dispel the suspicion.

2A Particular examples of facts and information which might point to a person's innocence and may tend to dispel suspicion include those which relate to the statutory defence provided by the Criminal Law Act 1967, section 3(1) which allows the use of reasonable force in the prevention of crime or making an arrest and the common law of self-defence. This may be relevant when a person appears, or claims, to have been acting reasonably in defence of themselves or others or to prevent their property or the property of others from being stolen, destroyed or damaged, particularly if the offence alleged is based on the use of unlawful force, e.g. a criminal assault. When investigating allegations involving the use of force by school staff, the power given to all school staff under the Education and Inspections Act 2006, section 93, to use reasonable force to prevent their pupils from committing any offence, injuring persons, damaging property or prejudicing the maintenance of good order and discipline may be similarly relevant. The Association of Chief Police Officers and the Crown Prosecution Service have published joint guidance to help the public understand the meaning of reasonable force and what to expect from the police and CPS in cases which involve claims of self-defence. Separate advice for school staff on their powers to use reasonable force is available from the Department for Education

2B If a constable who is dealing with an allegation of crime and considering the need to arrest becomes an investigator for the purposes of the Code of Practice under the Criminal Procedure and Investigations Act 1996, the officer should, in accordance with paragraph 3.5 of that Code, 'pursue all reasonable lines of inquiry, whether these point towards or away from the suspect. What is reasonable in each case will depend on the particular circumstances.'

2C For a constable to have reasonable grounds for believing it necessary to arrest, he or she is not required to be satisfied that there is no viable alternative to arrest. However, it does mean that in all cases, the officer should consider that arrest is the practical, sensible and proportionate option in all the circumstances at the time the decision is made. This applies equally to a person in police detention after being arrested for an offence who is suspected of involvement in a further offence and the necessity to arrest them for that further offence is being considered.

2D Although a warning is not expressly required, officers should if practicable, consider whether a warning which points out their offending behaviour, and explains why, if they do not stop, the resulting consequences may make their arrest necessary. Such a warning might:
  • if heeded, avoid the need to arrest, or
  • if it is ignored, support the need to arrest and also help prove the mental element of certain offences, for example, the person's intent or awareness, or help to rebut a defence that they were acting reasonably.
  A person who is warned that they may be liable to arrest if their real name and address cannot be ascertained, should be given a reasonable opportunity to establish their real name and address before deciding that either or both are unknown and cannot be readily ascertained or that there are reasonable grounds to doubt that a name and address they have given is their real name and address. They should be told why their name is not known and cannot be readily ascertained and (as the case may be) of the grounds for doubting that a name and address they have given is their real name and address, including, for example, the reason why a particular document the person has produced to verify their real name and/or address, is not sufficient.

2E The meaning of 'prompt' should be considered on a case by case basis taking account of all the circumstances. It indicates that the progress of the investigation should not be delayed to the extent that it would adversely affect the effectiveness of the investigation. The arresting officer also has discretion to release the arrested person on 'street bail' as an alternative to taking the person directly to the station. (See Note 2J.)

2F An officer who believes that it is necessary to interview the person suspected of committing the offence must then consider whether their arrest is necessary in order to carry out the interview. The officer is not required to interrogate the suspect to determine whether they will attend a police station voluntarily to be interviewed but they must consider whether the suspect's voluntary attendance is a practicable alternative for carrying out the interview. If it is, then arrest would not be necessary. Conversely, an officer who considers this option but is not satisfied that it is a practicable alternative, may have reasonable grounds for deciding that the arrest is necessary at the outset 'on the street'. Without such considerations, the officer would not be able to establish that arrest was necessary in order to interview.

Circumstances which suggest that a person's arrest 'on the street' would not be necessary to interview them might be where the officer:

- is satisfied as to their identity and address and that they will attend the police station voluntarily to be interviewed, either immediately or by arrangement at a future date and time; and
- is not aware of any other circumstances which indicate that voluntary attendance would not be a practicable alternative. See paragraph 2.9(e)(i) to (v).

When making arrangements for the person's voluntary attendance, the officer should tell the person:

- that to properly investigate their suspected involvement in the offence they must be interviewed under caution at the police station, but in the circumstances their arrest for this purpose will not be necessary if they attend the police station voluntarily to be interviewed;
- that if they attend voluntarily, they will be entitled to free legal advice before, and to have a solicitor present at, the interview;
- that the date and time of the interview will take account of their circumstances and the needs of the investigation; and
- that if they do not agree to attend voluntarily at a time which meets the needs of the investigation, or having so agreed, fail to attend, or having attended, fail to remain for the interview to be completed, their arrest will be necessary to enable them to be interviewed.

2G   When the person attends the police station voluntarily for interview by arrangement as in Note 2F above, their arrest on arrival at the station prior to interview would only be justified if:

- new information coming to light after the arrangements were made indicates that from that time, voluntary attendance ceased to be a practicable alternative and the person's arrest became necessary; and
- it was not reasonably practicable for the person to be arrested before they attended the station.

If a person who attends the police station voluntarily to be interviewed decides to leave before the interview is complete, the police would at that point be entitled to consider whether their arrest was necessary to carry out the interview. The possibility that the person might decide to leave during the interview is therefore not a valid reason for arresting them before the interview has commenced. See Code C paragraph 3.21.

2H   The necessity criteria do not permit arrest solely to enable the routine taking, checking (speculative searching) and retention of fingerprints, samples, footwear impressions and photographs when there are no prior grounds to believe that checking and comparing the fingerprints etc or taking a photograph would provide relevant evidence of the person's involvement in the offence concerned or would help to ascertain or verify their real identity.

2I   The necessity criteria do not permit arrest for an offence solely because it happens to be one of the statutory drug testing 'trigger offences' (see Code C Note 17E) when there is no suspicion that Class A drug misuse might have caused or contributed to the offence.

2J   Having determined that the necessity criteria have been met and having made the arrest, the officer can then consider the use of street bail on the basis of the effective and efficient progress of the investigation of the offence in question. It gives the officer discretion to compel the person to attend a police station at a date/time that best suits the overall needs of the particular investigation. Its use is not confined to dealing with child care issues or allowing officers to attend to more urgent operational duties and granting street bail does not retrospectively negate the need to arrest.

3   An arrested person must be given sufficient information to enable them to understand they have been deprived of their liberty and the reason they have been arrested, as soon as practicable after the arrest, e.g. when a person is arrested on suspicion of committing

an offence they must be informed of the nature of the suspected offence and when and where it was committed. The suspect must also be informed of the reason or reasons why arrest is considered necessary. Vague or technical language should be avoided. When explaining why one or more of the arrest criteria apply, it is not necessary to disclose any specific details that might undermine or otherwise adversely affect any investigative processes. An example might be the conduct of a formal interview when prior disclosure of such details might give the suspect an opportunity to fabricate an innocent explanation or to otherwise conceal lies from the interviewer.

4   Nothing in this Code requires a caution to be given or repeated when informing a person not under arrest they may be prosecuted for an offence. However, a court will not be able to draw any inferences under the Criminal Justice and Public Order Act 1994, section 34, if the person was not cautioned.

5   If it appears a person does not understand the caution, the person giving it should explain it in their own words.

6   Certain powers available as the result of an arrest - for example, entry and search of premises, detention without charge beyond 24 hours, holding a person incommunicado and delaying access to legal advice - only apply in respect of indictable offences and are subject to the specific requirements on authorisation as set out in PACE and the relevant Code of Practice.

POLICE REFORM ACT 2002
(2002, c. 30)

9.   The Independent Office for Police Conduct

(1)   The body corporate previously known as the Independent Police Complaints Commission—
   (a)   is to continue to exist, and
   (b)   is to be known instead as the Independent Office for Police Conduct.

(2)   The Office is to consist of—
   (a)   a Director General appointed by Her Majesty, and
   (b)   at least six other members.

(2A) The other members must consist of—
   (a)   persons appointed as non-executive members (see paragraph 1A of Schedule 2), and
   (b)   persons appointed as employee members (see paragraph 1B of that Schedule), but the powers of appointment under those paragraphs must be exercised so as to secure that a majority of members of the Office (including the Director General) are non-executive members.

   ...

10.   General functions of the Director General

(1)   The functions of the Director General shall be—
   (a)   to secure the maintenance by the Director General, and by local policing bodies and chief officers, of suitable arrangements with respect to the matters mentioned in subsection (2);
   (b)   to keep under review all arrangements maintained with respect to those matters;
   (c)   to secure that arrangements maintained with respect to those matters comply with the requirements of the following provisions of this Part, are efficient and effective and contain and manifest an appropriate degree of independence;
   (d)   to secure that public confidence is established and maintained in the existence of suitable arrangements with respect to those matters and with the operation of the arrangements that are in fact maintained with respect to those matters;
   (e)   to make such recommendations, and to give such advice, for the modification of the arrangements maintained with respect to those matters, and also of police practice in relation to other matters, as appear, from the carrying out by the Director General of the Director General's other functions, to be necessary or desirable;

(f)   to such extent as the Director General may be required to do so by regulations made by the Secretary of State, to carry out functions in relation to bodies of constables maintained otherwise than by local policing bodies which broadly correspond to those conferred on the Director General in relation to police forces by the preceding paragraphs of this subsection; and

(g)   to carry out functions in relation to the National Crime Agency which correspond to those conferred on the Director General in relation to police forces by paragraph (e) of this subsection.

(ga)   to carry out such corresponding functions in relation to officers of the Gangmasters and Labour Abuse Authority in their capacity as labour abuse prevention officers (see section 114B of the Police and Criminal Evidence Act 1984 (PACE powers for labour abuse prevention officers)).

(2)   Those matters are—

(a)   the handling of complaints made about the conduct of persons serving with the police;

(b)   the recording of matters from which it appears that there may have been conduct by such persons which constitutes or involves the commission of a criminal offence or behaviour justifying disciplinary proceedings;

(ba)   the recording of matters from which it appears that a person has died or suffered serious injury during, or following, contact with a person serving with the police;

(c)   the manner in which any such complaints or any such matters as are mentioned in paragraph (b) are investigated or otherwise handled and dealt with.

(3)   The Director General shall also have the functions which are conferred on the Director General by—

(b)   any agreement or order under section 26 of this Act (other bodies of constables);

(bc)   any regulations under section 26C of this Act (the National Crime Agency);

(bd)   any regulations under section 26D of this Act (labour abuse prevention officers);

(c)   any regulations under section 39 of this Act (police powers for contracted-out staff); or

(d)   any regulations or arrangements relating to disciplinary or similar proceedings against persons serving with the police, or against members of any body of constables maintained otherwise than by a local policing body.

(4)   It shall be the duty of the Director General—

(a)   to exercise the powers and perform the duties conferred on the Director General by the following provisions of this Part in the manner that the Director General considers best calculated for the purpose of securing the proper carrying out of the Director General's functions under subsections (1) and (3); and

(b)   to secure that arrangements exist which are conducive to, and facilitate, the reporting of misconduct by persons in relation to whose conduct the Director General has functions.

(5)   It shall also be the duty of the Director General—

(a)   to enter into arrangements with the chief inspector of constabulary for the purpose of securing co-operation, in the carrying out of their respective functions, between the Director General and the inspectors of constabulary; and

(b)   to provide those inspectors with all such assistance and co-operation as may be required by those arrangements, or as otherwise appears to the Director General to be appropriate, for facilitating the carrying out by those inspectors of their functions.

(5A) In carrying out functions the Director General must have regard to any advice provided to the Director General by the Office (see section 10A(1)(c)).

(6)   Subject to the other provisions of this Part, the Director General may do anything which appears to the Director General to be calculated to facilitate, or is incidental or conducive to, the carrying out of the Director General's functions.

(7)   The Office may, in connection with the making of any recommendation or the giving of any advice to any person for the purpose of carrying out—

(a)   the Director General's function under subsection (1)(e),

(b)   any corresponding function conferred on the Director General by virtue of subsection (1)(f), or

(c)   the Director General's function under subsection (1)(g) or (h), impose any such charge on that person for anything done by the Director General for the purposes of, or in connection with, the carrying out of that function as the Director General thinks fit.

POWERS OF CRIMINAL COURTS (SENTENCING) ACT 2000
(2000, c. 6)

1. Deferment of sentence

(1) The Crown Court or a magistrates' court may defer passing sentence on an offender for the purpose of enabling the court, or any other court to which it falls to deal with him, to have regard in dealing with him to—

   (a) his conduct after conviction (including, where appropriate, the making by him of reparation for his offence); or

   (b) any change in his circumstances;

but this is subject to subsections (3) and (4) below.

(2) Without prejudice to the generality of subsection (1) above, the matters to which the court to which it falls to deal with the offender may have regard by virtue of paragraph (a) of that subsection include the extent to which the offender has complied with any requirements imposed under subsection (3)(b) below.

(3) The power conferred by subsection (1) above shall be exercisable only if—

   (a) the offender consents;

   (b) the offender undertakes to comply with any requirements as to his conduct during the period of the deferment that the court considers it appropriate to impose; and

   (c) the court is satisfied, having regard to the nature of the offence and the character and circumstances of the offender, that it would be in the interests of justice to exercise the power.

(4) Any deferment under this section shall be until such date as may be specified by the court, not being more than six months after the date on which the deferment is announced by the court; and, subject to section 1D(3) below, where the passing of sentence has been deferred under this section it shall not be further so deferred.

(5) Where a court has under this section deferred passing sentence on an offender, it shall forthwith give a copy of the order deferring the passing of sentence and setting out any requirements imposed under subsection (3)(b) above—

   (a) to the offender,

   (b) where an officer of a local probation board has been appointed to act as a supervisor in relation to him, to that board,

   (ba) where an officer of a provider of probation services has been appointed to act as a supervisor in relation to him, to that provider, and

   (c) where a person has been appointed under section 1A(2)(b) below to act as a supervisor in relation to him, to that person.

(6) Notwithstanding any enactment, a court which under this section defers passing sentence on an offender shall not on the same occasion remand him.

(7) Where—

   (a) a court which under this section has deferred passing sentence on an offender proposes to deal with him on the date originally specified by the court, or

   (b) the offender does not appear on the day so specified,

the court may issue a summons requiring him to appear before the court at a time and place specified in the summons, or may issue a warrant to arrest him and bring him before the court at a time and place specified in the warrant.

(8) Nothing in this section or sections 1ZA to 1D below shall affect—

   (a) the power of the Crown Court to bind over an offender to come up for judgment when called upon; or

   (b) the power of any court to defer passing sentence for any purpose for which it may lawfully do so apart from this section.

1ZA.   Undertakings to participate in restorative justice activities

(1)   Without prejudice to the generality of paragraph (b) of section 1(3), the requirements that may be imposed under that paragraph include restorative justice requirements.

(2)   Any reference in this section to a restorative justice requirement is to a requirement to participate in an activity—

    (a)   where the participants consist of, or include, the offender and one or more of the victims,

    (b)   which aims to maximise the offender's awareness of the impact of the offending concerned on the victims, and

    (c)   which gives an opportunity to a victim or victims to talk about, or by other means express experience of, the offending and its impact.

(3)   Imposition under section 1(3)(b) of a restorative justice requirement requires, in addition to the offender's consent and undertaking under section 1(3), the consent of every other person who would be a participant in the activity concerned.

(4)   For the purposes of subsection (3), a supervisor appointed under section 1A(2) does not count as a proposed participant.

(5)   Where a restorative justice requirement is imposed under section 1(3)(b), the duty under section 1(5) (to give copies of order) extends to every person who would be a participant in the activity concerned.

(6)   In a case where there is such a restorative justice requirement, a person running the activity concerned must in doing that have regard to any guidance that is issued, with a view to encouraging good practice in connection with such an activity, by the Secretary of State.

(7)   In this section 'victim' means a victim of, or other person affected by, the offending concerned.

1A.   Further provision about undertakings

(1)   Without prejudice to the generality of paragraph (b) of section 1(3) above, the requirements that may be imposed by virtue of that paragraph include requirements as to the residence of the offender during the whole or any part of the period of deferment.

(2)   Where an offender has undertaken to comply with any requirements imposed under section 1(3)(b) above the court may appoint—

    (a)   an officer of a local probation board or an officer of a provider of probation services, or

    (b)   any other person whom the court thinks appropriate,

to act as a supervisor in relation to him.

(3)   A person shall not be appointed under subsection (2)(b) above without his consent.

(4)   It shall be the duty of a supervisor appointed under subsection (2) above—

    (a)   to monitor the offender's compliance with the requirements; and

    (b)   to provide the court to which it falls to deal with the offender in respect of the offence in question with such information as the court may require relating to the offender's compliance with the requirements.

1B.   Breach of undertakings

(1)   A court which under section 1 above has deferred passing sentence on an offender may deal with him before the end of the period of deferment if—

    (a)   he appears or is brought before the court under subsection (3) below; and

    (b)   the court is satisfied that he has failed to comply with one or more requirements imposed under section 1(3)(b) above in connection with the deferment.

(2)   Subsection (3) below applies where—

    (a)   a court has under section 1 above deferred passing sentence on an offender;

    (b)   the offender undertook to comply with one or more requirements imposed under section 1(3)(b) above in connection with the deferment; and

    (c)   a person appointed under section 1A(2) above to act as a supervisor in relation to the offender has reported to the court that the offender has failed to comply with one or more of those requirements.

(3)   Where this subsection applies, the court may issue—

    (a)   a summons requiring the offender to appear before the court at a time and place specified in the summons; or

(b)   a warrant to arrest him and bring him before the court at a time and place specified in the warrant.

1C.   Conviction of offence during period of deferment

(1)   A court which under section 1 above has deferred passing sentence on an offender may deal with him before the end of the period of deferment if during that period he is convicted in Great Britain of any offence.

(2)   Subsection (3) below applies where a court has under section 1 above deferred passing sentence on an offender in respect of one or more offences and during the period of deferment the offender is convicted in England and Wales of any offence ('the later offence').

(3)   Where this subsection applies, then (without prejudice to subsection (1) above and whether or not the offender is sentenced for the later offence during the period of deferment), the court which passes sentence on him for the later offence may also, if this has not already been done, deal with him for the offence or offences for which passing of sentence has been deferred, except that—

(a)   the power conferred by this subsection shall not be exercised by a magistrates' court if the court which deferred passing sentence was the Crown Court; and

(b)   the Crown Court, in exercising that power in a case in which the court which deferred passing sentence was a magistrates' court, shall not pass any sentence which could not have been passed by a magistrates' court in exercising that power.

(4)   Where a court which under section 1 above has deferred passing sentence on an offender proposes to deal with him by virtue of subsection (1) above before the end of the period of deferment, the court may issue—

(a)   a summons requiring him to appear before the court at a time and place specified in the summons; or

(b)   a warrant to arrest him and bring him before the court at a time and place specified in the warrant.

1D.   Deferment of sentence: supplementary

(1)   In deferring the passing of sentence under section 1 above a magistrates' court shall be regarded as exercising the power of adjourning the trial conferred by section 10(1) of the Magistrates' Courts Act 1980, and accordingly sections 11(1) and 13(1) to (3A) and (5) of that Act (non-appearance of the accused) apply (without prejudice to section 1(7) above) if the offender does not appear on the date specified under section 1(4) above.

(2)   Where the passing of sentence on an offender has been deferred by a court ('the original court') under section 1 above, the power of that court under that section to deal with the offender at the end of the period of deferment and any power of that court under section 1B(1) or 1C(1) above, or of any court under section 1C(3) above, to deal with the offender—

(a)   is power to deal with him, in respect of the offence for which passing of sentence has been deferred, in any way in which the original court could have dealt with him if it had not deferred passing sentence; and

(b)   without prejudice to the generality of paragraph (a) above, in the case of a magistrates' court, includes the power conferred by section 3 below to commit him to the Crown Court for sentence.

(3)   Where—

(a)   the passing of sentence on an offender in respect of one or more offences has been deferred under section 1 above, and

(b)   a magistrates' court deals with him in respect of the offence or any of the offences by committing him to the Crown Court under section 3 below,

the power of the Crown Court to deal with him includes the same power to defer passing sentence on him as if he had just been convicted of the offence or offences on indictment before the court.

(4)   Subsection (5) below applies where—

    (a)   the passing of sentence on an offender in respect of one or more offences has been deferred under section 1 above;

    (b)   it falls to a magistrates' court to determine a relevant matter; and

    (c)   a justice of the peace is satisfied—

        (i)   that a person appointed under section 1A(2)(b) above to act as a supervisor in relation to the offender is likely to be able to give evidence that may assist the court in determining that matter; and

        (ii)   that that person will not voluntarily attend as a witness.

(5)   The justice may issue a summons directed to that person requiring him to attend before the court at the time and place appointed in the summons to give evidence.

(6)   For the purposes of subsection (4) above a court determines a relevant matter if it—

    (a)   deals with the offender in respect of the offence, or any of the offences, for which the passing of sentence has been deferred; or

    (b)   determines, for the purposes of section 1B(1)(b) above, whether the offender has failed to comply with any requirements imposed under section 1(3)(b) above.

3.   Committal for sentence on summary trial of offence triable either way

(1)   Subject to subsection (4) below, this section applies where on the summary trial of an offence triable either way a person aged 18 or over is convicted of the offence.

(2)   If the court is of the opinion—

    (a)   that the offence or the combination of the offence and one or more offences associated with it was so serious that the Crown Court should, in the court's opinion, have the power to deal with the offender in any way it could deal with him if he had been convicted on indictment,

    (b)   ...

    the court may commit the offender in custody or on bail to the Crown Court for sentence in accordance with section 5(1) below.

(3)   Where the court commits a person under subsection (2) above, section 6 below (which enables a magistrates' court, where it commits a person under this section in respect of an offence, also to commit him to the Crown Court to be dealt with in respect of certain other offences) shall apply accordingly.

(4)   This section does not apply in relation to an offence as regards which this section is excluded by section 17D or 33 of the Magistrates' Courts Act 1980 (certain offences where value involved is small).

(5)   The preceding provisions of this section shall apply in relation to a corporation as if—

    (a)   the corporation were an individual aged 18 or over; and

    (b)   in subsection (2) above, the words 'in custody or on bail' were omitted.

3A.   Committal for sentence of dangerous adult offenders

(1)   This section applies where on the summary trial of a specified offence triable either way a person aged 18 or over is convicted of the offence.

(2)   If, in relation to the offence, it appears to the court that the criteria for the imposition of a sentence under section 226A of the Criminal Justice Act 2003 would be met, the court must commit the offender in custody or on bail to the Crown Court for sentence in accordance with section 5(1) below.

    ...

3B.   Committal for sentence of young offenders on summary trial of certain serious offences

(1)   This section applies where on the summary trial of an offence mentioned in section 91(1) of this Act a person aged under 18 is convicted of the offence.

(2)   If the court is of the opinion that—

    (a)   the offence; or

    (b)   the combination of the offence and one or more offences associated with it,

    was such that the Crown Court should, in the court's opinion, have power to deal with the offender as if the provisions of section 91(3) below applied, the court may commit him in custody or on bail to the Crown Court for sentence in accordance with section 5A(1) below.

(3) Where the court commits a person under subsection (2) above, section 6 below (which enables a magistrates' court, where it commits a person under this section in respect of an offence, also to commit him to the Crown Court to be dealt with in respect of certain other offences) shall apply accordingly.

3C. Committal for sentence of dangerous young offenders

(1) This section applies where on the summary trial of a specified offence a person aged under 18 is convicted of the offence.

(2) If, in relation to the offence, it appears to the court that the criteria for the imposition of a sentence under section 226B of the Criminal Justice Act 2003 would be met, the court must commit the offender in custody or on bail to the Crown Court for sentence in accordance with section 5A(1) below.

4. Committal for sentence on indication of guilty plea to offence triable either way

(1) This section applies where—

    (a) a person aged 18 or over appears or is brought before a magistrates' court ('the court') on an information charging him with an offence triable either way ('the offence');

    (b) he or his representative indicates under section 17A, 17B or 20(7) of the Magistrates' Courts Act 1980 that he would plead guilty if the offence were to proceed to trial; and

    (c) proceeding as if section 9(1) of the Magistrates' Courts Act 1980 were complied with and he pleaded guilty under it, the court convicts him of the offence.

(1A) But this section does not apply to an offence as regards which this section is excluded by section 17D of that Act (certain offences where value involved is small).

(2) If the court has sent the offender to the Crown Court for trial for one or more related offences, that is to say, one or more offences which, in its opinion, are related to the offence, it may commit him in custody or on bail to the Crown Court to be dealt with in respect of the offence in accordance with section 5(1) below.

(3) If the power conferred by subsection (2) is not exercisable but the court is still to determine to, or determine whether to, send the offender to the Crown Court for trial under section 51 or 51A of the Crime and Disorder Act 1998 for one or more related offences—

    (a) it shall adjourn the proceedings relating to the offence until after it has made those determinations; and

    (b) if it sends the offender to the Crown Court for trial for one or more related offences, it may then exercise that power.

(4) Where the court—

    (a) under subsection (2) above commits the offender to the Crown Court to be dealt with in respect of the offence, and

    (b) does not state that, in its opinion, it also has power so to commit him under section 3(2) or, as the case may be, section 3A(2) above,

section 5(1) below shall not apply unless he is convicted before the Crown Court of one or more of the related offences.

(5) Where section 5(1) below does not apply, the Crown Court may deal with the offender in respect of the offence in any way in which the magistrates' court could deal with him if it had just convicted him of the offence.

(6) Where the court commits a person under subsection (2) above, section 6 below (which enables a magistrates' court, where it commits a person under this section in respect of an offence, also to commit him to the Crown Court to be dealt with in respect of certain other offences) shall apply accordingly.

(7) For the purposes of this section one offence is related to another if, were they both to be prosecuted on indictment, the charges for them could be joined in the same indictment.

(8) In reaching any decision under or taking any step contemplated by this section—

(a)   the court shall not be bound by any indication of sentence given in respect of the offence under section 20 of the Magistrates Courts Act 1980 (procedure where summary trial appears more suitable); and

(b)   nothing the court does under this section may be challenged or be the subject of any appeal in any court on the ground that it is not consistent with an indication of sentence.

5.   Power of Crown Court on committal for sentence under sections 3, 3A and 4

(1)   Where an offender is committed by a magistrates' court for sentence under section 3, 3A or 4 above, the Crown Court shall inquire into the circumstances of the case and may deal with the offender in any way in which it could deal with him if he had just been convicted of the offence on indictment before the court.

...

6.   Committal for sentence in certain cases where offender committed in respect of another offence

(1)   This section applies where a magistrates' court ('the committing court') commits a person in custody or on bail to the Crown Court under any enactment mentioned in subsection (4) below to be sentenced or otherwise dealt with in respect of an offence ('the relevant offence').

(2)   Where this section applies and the relevant offence is an indictable offence, the committing court may also commit the offender, in custody or on bail as the case may require, to the Crown Court to be dealt with in respect of any other offence whatsoever in respect of which the committing court has power to deal with him (being an offence of which he has been convicted by that or any other court).

(3)   Where this section applies and the relevant offence is a summary offence, the committing court may commit the offender, in custody or on bail as the case may require, to the Crown Court to be dealt with in respect of—

(a)   any other offence of which the committing court has convicted him, being either—

(i)   an offence punishable with imprisonment; or

(ii)   an offence in respect of which the committing court has a power or duty to order him to be disqualified under section 34, 35 or 36 of the Road Traffic Offenders Act 1988 (disqualification for certain motoring offences); or

(b)   any suspended sentence in respect of which the committing court has under paragraph 11(1) of Schedule 12 to the Criminal Justice Act 2003 power to deal with him.

(4)   The enactments referred to in subsection (1) above are—

(a)   ...

(b)   sections 3 to 4A above (committal for sentence for offences triable either way);

(c)   section 13(5) below (conditionally discharged person convicted of further offence); and

(d)   ...

(e)   paragraph 11(2) of Schedule 12 to the Criminal Justice Act 2003 (committal to Crown Court where offender convicted during operational period of suspended sentence).

7.   Power of Crown Court on committal for sentence under section 6

(1)   Where under section 6 above a magistrates' court commits a person to be dealt with by the Crown Court in respect of an offence, the Crown Court may after inquiring into the circumstances of the case deal with him in any way in which the magistrates' court could deal with him if it had just convicted him of the offence.

(2)   Subsection (1) above does not apply where under section 6 above a magistrates' court commits a person to be dealt with by the Crown Court in respect of a suspended sentence, but in such a case the powers under paragraphs 8 and 9 of Schedule 12 to the Criminal Justice Act 2003 (power of court to deal with suspended sentence) shall be exercisable by the Crown Court.

(3)   Without prejudice to subsections (1) and (2) above, where under section 6 above or any enactment mentioned in subsection (4) of that section a magistrates' court commits a person to be dealt with by the Crown Court, any duty or power which, apart from this subsection, would fall to be discharged or exercised by the magistrates' court shall not be discharged or exercised by that court but shall instead be discharged or may instead be exercised by the Crown Court.

(4)   Where under section 6 above a magistrates' court commits a person to be dealt with by the Crown Court in respect of an offence triable only on indictment in the case of an adult (being an offence which was tried summarily because of the offender's being under 18 years of age), the Crown Court's powers under subsection (1) above in respect of the offender after he attains the age of 18 shall be powers to do either or both of the following—

(a)   to impose a fine not exceeding £5,000;

(b)   to deal with the offender in respect of the offence in any way in which the magistrates' court could deal with him if it had just convicted him of an offence punishable with imprisonment for a term not exceeding six months.

8.   Power and duty to remit young offenders to youth courts for sentence

(1)   Subsection (2) below applies where a child or young person (that is to say, any person aged under 18) is convicted by or before any court of an offence other than homicide.

(2)   The court may and, if it is not a youth court, shall unless satisfied that it would be undesirable to do so, remit the case—

(a)   if the offender was sent to the Crown Court for trial under section 51 or 51A of the Crime and Disorder Act 1998, to a youth court acting for the place where he was sent to the Crown Court for trial;

(b)   in any other case, to a youth court acting either for the same place as the remitting court or for the place where the offender habitually resides;

...

...

12.   Absolute and conditional discharge

(1)   Where a court by or before which a person is convicted of an offence (not being an offence the sentence for which is fixed by law or falls to be imposed under a provision mentioned in subsection (1A)) is of the opinion, having regard to the circumstances including the nature of the offence and the character of the offender, that it is inexpedient to inflict punishment, the court may make an order either—

(a)   discharging him absolutely; or

(b)   if the court thinks fit, discharging him subject to the condition that he commits no offence during such period, not exceeding three years from the date of the order, as may be specified in the order.

(1A)   The provisions referred to in subsection (1) are—

(a)   section 1(2B) or 1A(5) of the Prevention of Crime Act 1953;

(b)   section 51A(2) of the Firearms Act 1968;

(c)   section 139(6B), 139A(5B) or 139AA(7) of the Criminal Justice Act 1988;

(d)   section 110(2) or 111(2) of this Act;

(e)   section 224A, 225(2) or 226(2) of the Criminal Justice Act 2003;

(f)   section 29(4) or (6) of the Violent Crime Reduction Act 2006.

(2)   Subsection (1)(b) above has effect subject to section 66ZB(6) of the Crime and Disorder Act 1998 (youth cautions).

(3)   An order discharging a person subject to such a condition as is mentioned in subsection (1)(b) above is in this Act referred to as an 'order for conditional discharge'; and the period specified in any such order is in this Act referred to as 'the period of conditional discharge'.

...

(5)   If (by virtue of section 13 below) a person conditionally discharged under this section is sentenced for the offence in respect of which the order for conditional discharge was made, that order shall cease to have effect.

(6)   On making an order for conditional discharge, the court may, if it thinks it expedient for the purpose of the offender's reformation, allow any person who consents to do so to give security for the good behaviour of the offender.

(7) Nothing in this section shall be construed as preventing a court, on discharging an offender absolutely or conditionally in respect of any offence, from imposing any disqualification on him or from making in respect of the offence an order under section 130, 143 or 148 below (compensation orders, deprivation orders and restitution orders) or from making in respect of the offence an unlawful profit order under section 4 of the Prevention of Social Housing Fraud Act 2013.

(8) Nothing in this section shall be construed as preventing a court, on discharging an offender absolutely or conditionally in respect of an offence, from—

(a) making an order under section 21A of the Prosecution of Offences Act 1985 (criminal courts charge), or

(b) making an order for costs against the offender.

13. Commission of further offence by person conditionally discharged

(1) If it appears to the Crown Court, where that court has jurisdiction in accordance with subsection (2) below, or to a justice of the peace having jurisdiction in accordance with that subsection, that a person in whose case an order for conditional discharge has been made—

(a) has been convicted by a court in Great Britain of an offence committed during the period of conditional discharge, and

(b) has been dealt with in respect of that offence, that court or justice may, subject to subsection (3) below, issue a summons requiring that person to appear at the place and time specified in it or a warrant for his arrest.

(2) Jurisdiction for the purposes of subsection (1) above may be exercised—

(a) if the order for conditional discharge was made by the Crown Court, by that court;

(b) if the order was made by a magistrates' court, by a justice of the peace.

(3) A justice of the peace shall not issue a summons under this section except on information and shall not issue a warrant under this section except on information in writing and on oath.

(4) A summons or warrant issued under this section shall direct the person to whom it relates to appear or to be brought before the court by which the order for conditional discharge was made.

(5) If a person in whose case an order for conditional discharge has been made by the Crown Court is convicted by a magistrates' court of an offence committed during the period of conditional discharge, the magistrates' court—

(a) may commit him to custody or release him on bail until he can be brought or appear before the Crown Court; and

(b) if it does so, shall send to the Crown Court a copy of the minute or memorandum of the conviction entered in the register, signed by the designated officer by whom the register is kept.

(6) Where it is proved to the satisfaction of the court by which an order for conditional discharge was made that the person in whose case the order was made has been convicted of an offence committed during the period of conditional discharge, the court may deal with him, for the offence for which the order was made, in any way in which it could deal with him if he had just been convicted by or before that court of that offence.

(7) If a person in whose case an order for conditional discharge has been made by a magistrates' court—

(a) is convicted before the Crown Court of an offence committed during the period of conditional discharge, or

(b) is dealt with by the Crown Court for any such offence in respect of which he was committed for sentence to the Crown Court,

the Crown Court may deal with him, for the offence for which the order was made, in any way in which the magistrates' court could deal with him if it had just convicted him of that offence.

(8) If a person in whose case an order for conditional discharge has been made by a magistrates' court is convicted by another magistrates' court of any offence committed during the period of conditional discharge, that other court may, with the consent of the court which made the order, deal with him, for the offence for which the order was made, in any way in which the court could deal with him if it had just convicted him of that offence.

(9)   Where an order for conditional discharge has been made by a magistrates' court in the case of an offender under 18 years of age in respect of an offence triable only on indictment in the case of an adult, any powers exercisable under subsection (6), (7) or (8) above by that or any other court in respect of the offender after he attains the age of 18 shall be powers to do either or both of the following—

    (a)   to impose a fine not exceeding £5,000 for the offence in respect of which the order was made;

    (b)   to deal with the offender for that offence in any way in which a magistrates' court could deal with him if it had just convicted him of an offence punishable with imprisonment for a term not exceeding six months.

(10) The reference in subsection (6) above to a person's having been convicted of an offence committed during the period of conditional discharge is a reference to his having been so convicted by a court in Great Britain.

14.   Effect of discharge

(1)   Subject to subsection (2) below, a conviction of an offence for which an order is made under section 12 above discharging the offender absolutely or conditionally shall be deemed not to be a conviction for any purpose other than the purposes of the proceedings in which the order is made and of any subsequent proceedings which may be taken against the offender under section 13 above.

(2)   Where the offender was aged 18 or over at the time of his conviction of the offence in question and is subsequently sentenced (under section 13 above) for that offence, subsection (1) above shall cease to apply to the conviction.

(3)   Without prejudice to subsections (1) and (2) above, the conviction of an offender who is discharged absolutely or conditionally under section 12 above shall in any event be disregarded for the purposes of any enactment or instrument which—

    (a)   imposes any disqualification or disability upon convicted persons; or

    (b)   authorises or requires the imposition of any such disqualification or disability.

(4)   Subsections (1) to (3) above shall not affect—

    (a)   any right of an offender discharged absolutely or conditionally under section 12 above to rely on his conviction in bar of any subsequent proceedings for the same offence;

    (b)   the restoration of any property in consequence of the conviction of any such offender; or

    (c)   the operation, in relation to any such offender, of any enactment or instrument in force on 1st July 1974 which is expressed to extend to persons dealt with under section 1(1) of the Probation of Offenders Act 1907 as well as to convicted persons.

    ...

(6)   Subsection (1) above has effect subject to section 50(1A) of the Criminal Appeal Act 1968 and section 108(1A) of the Magistrates' Courts Act 1980 (rights of appeal); and this subsection shall not be taken to prejudice any other enactment that excludes the effect of subsection (1) or (3) above for particular purposes.

(7)   Without prejudice to paragraph 1(3) of Schedule 11 to this Act (references to provisions of this Act to be construed as including references to corresponding old enactments), in this section—

    (a)   any reference to an order made under section 12 above discharging an offender absolutely or conditionally includes a reference to an order which was made under any provision of Part I of the Powers of Criminal Courts Act 1973 (whether or not reproduced in this Act) discharging the offender absolutely or conditionally;

    (b)   any reference to an offender who is discharged absolutely or conditionally under section 12 includes a reference to an offender who was discharged absolutely or conditionally under any such provision.

16.   Duty and power to refer certain young offenders to youth offender panels

(1)   This section applies where a youth court or other magistrates' court is dealing with a person aged under 18 for an offence and—

    (a)   neither the offence nor any connected offence is one for which the sentence is fixed by law;

    (b)   the court is not, in respect of the offence or any connected offence, proposing to impose a custodial sentence on the offender or make a hospital order (within the meaning of the Mental Health Act 1983) in his case; and

    (c)   the court is not proposing to discharge him, whether absolutely or conditionally, in respect of the offence.

(2)   If—

    (a)   the compulsory referral conditions are satisfied in accordance with section 17 below, and

    (b)   referral is available to the court,

the court shall sentence the offender for the offence by ordering him to be referred to a youth offender panel.

(3)   If—

    (a)   the discretionary referral conditions are satisfied in accordance with section 17 below, and

    (b)   referral is available to the court,

the court may sentence the offender for the offence by ordering him to be referred to a youth offender panel.

(4)   For the purposes of this Part an offence is connected with another if the offender falls to be dealt with for it at the same time as he is dealt with for the other offence (whether or not he is convicted of the offences at the same time or by or before the same court).

(5)   For the purposes of this section referral is available to a court if—

    (a)   the court has been notified by the Secretary of State that arrangements for the implementation of referral orders are available in the area in which it appears to the court that the offender resides or will reside; and

    (b)   the notice has not been withdrawn.

(6)   An order under subsection (2) or (3) above is in this Act referred to as a 'referral order'.

17.   The referral conditions

(1)   For the purposes of section 16(2) above and subsection (2) below the compulsory referral conditions are satisfied in relation to an offence if the offence is an offence punishable with imprisonment and the offender—

    (a)   pleaded guilty to the offence and to any connected offence; and

    (b)   has never been—

        (i)   convicted by or before a court in the United Kingdom of any offence other than the offence and any connected offence, or

        (ii)   convicted by or before a court in another member State of any offence.

(2)   For the purposes of section 16(3) above, the discretionary referral conditions are satisfied in relation to an offence if—

    (a)   the compulsory referral conditions are not satisfied in relation to the offence; and

    (b)   the offender pleaded guilty—

        (i)   to the offence; or

        (ii)   if the offender is being dealt with by the court for the offence and any connected offence, to at least one of those offences.

73.   Reparation orders

(1)   Where a child or young person (that is to say, any person aged under 18) is convicted of an offence other than one for which the sentence is fixed by law, the court by or before which he is convicted may make an order requiring him to make reparation specified in the order—

    (a)   to a person or persons so specified; or

    (b)   to the community at large;

and any person so specified must be a person identified by the court as a victim of the offence or a person otherwise affected by it.

(2)   An order under subsection (1) above is in this Act referred to as a 'reparation order'.

(3)   In this section and section 74 below 'make reparation', in relation to an offender, means make reparation for the offence otherwise than by the payment of compensation; and the requirements that may be specified in a reparation order are subject to section 74(1) to (3).

(4)   The court shall not make a reparation order in respect of the offender if it proposes—
    (a)   to pass on him a custodial sentence; or
    (b)   to make in respect of him a youth rehabilitation order or a referral order.

(4A) The court shall not make a reparation order in respect of the offender at a time when a youth rehabilitation order is in force in respect of him unless when it makes the reparation order it revokes the youth rehabilitation order.

(4B) When a youth rehabilitation order is revoked under subsection (4A), paragraph 24 of schedule 2 to the Criminal Justice and Immigration Act 2008 (breach, revocation and amendment of youth rehabilitation orders) applies to the revocation.

(5)   Before making a reparation order, a court shall obtain and consider a written report by an officer of a local probation board, an officer of a provider of probation services, a social worker of a local authority or a member of a youth offending team indicating—
    (a)   the type of work that is suitable for the offender; and
    (b)   the attitude of the victim or victims to the requirements proposed to be included in the order.

(6)   The court shall not make a reparation order unless it has been notified by the Secretary of State that arrangements for implementing such orders are available in the area proposed to be named in the order under section 74(4) below and the notice has not been withdrawn.

(7)   ...

(8)   The court shall give reasons if it does not make a reparation order in a case where it has power to do so.

74.   Requirements and provisions of reparation order, and obligations of person subject to it

(1)   A reparation order shall not require the offender—
    (a)   to work for more than 24 hours in aggregate; or
    (b)   to make reparation to any person without the consent of that person.

(2)   Subject to subsection (1) above, requirements specified in a reparation order shall be such as in the opinion of the court are commensurate with the seriousness of the offence, or the combination of the offence and one or more offences associated with it.

(3)   Requirements so specified shall, as far as practicable, be such as to avoid—
    (a)   any conflict with the offender's religious beliefs or with the requirements of any youth community order to which he may be subject ...; and
    (b)   any interference with the times, if any, at which he normally works or attends school or any other educational establishment.

(4)   A reparation order shall name the local justice area in which it appears to the court making the order (or to the court amending under Schedule 8 to this Act any provision included in the order in pursuance of this subsection) that the offender resides or will reside.

(5)   In this Act 'responsible officer', in relation to an offender subject to a reparation order, means one of the following who is specified in the order, namely—
    (a)   an officer of a local probation board or an officer of a provider of probation services (as the case may be);
    (b)   a social worker of a local authority;
    (c)   a member of a youth offending team.

(6)   Where a reparation order specifies an officer of a local probation board under subsection (5) above, the officer specified must be an officer appointed for or assigned to the local justice area named in the order.

(6A) Where a reparation order specifies an officer of a provider of probation services under subsection (5) above, the officer specified must be an officer acting in the local justice area named in the order.

(7)   Where a reparation order specifies under that subsection—
    (a)   a social worker of a local authority, or
    (b)   a member of a youth offending team,

the social worker or member specified must be a social worker of, or a member of a youth offending team established by, the local authority within whose area it appears to the court that the offender resides or will reside.

(8)　Any reparation required by a reparation order—
    (a)　shall be made under the supervision of the responsible officer; and
    (b)　shall be made within a period of three months from the date of the making of the order.

76.　Meaning of 'custodial sentence'

(1)　In this Act 'custodial sentence' means—
    (a)　a sentence of imprisonment (as to which, see section 89(1)(a) below);
    (b)　a sentence of detention under section 90 or 91 below;
    (bb)　a sentence of detention for public protection under section 226 of the Criminal Justice Act 2003;
    (bc)　a sentence of detention under section 226B or 228 of that Act;
    (c)　a sentence of custody for life under section 93 or 94 below;
    (d)　a sentence of detention in a young offender institution (under section 96 below or otherwise); or
    (e)　a detention and training order (under section 100 below).
(2)　In subsection (1) above 'sentence of imprisonment' does not include a committal for contempt of court or any kindred offence.

77.　Liability to imprisonment on conviction on indictment

Where a person is convicted on indictment of an offence against any enactment and is for that offence liable to be sentenced to imprisonment, but the sentence is not by any enactment either limited to a specified term or expressed to extend to imprisonment for life, the person so convicted shall be liable to imprisonment for not more than two years.

78.　General limit on magistrates' court's power to impose imprisonment or detention in a young offender institution

(1)　A magistrates' court shall not have power to impose imprisonment, or detention in a young offender institution, for more than six months in respect of any one offence.
(2)　Unless expressly excluded, subsection (1) above shall apply even if the offence in question is one for which a person would otherwise be liable on summary conviction to imprisonment or detention in a young offender institution for more than six months.
(3)　Subsection (1) above is without prejudice to section 133 of the Magistrates' Courts Act 1980 (consecutive terms of imprisonment).
(4)　Any power of a magistrates' court to impose a term of imprisonment for non-payment of a fine, or for want of sufficient goods to satisfy a fine, shall not be limited by virtue of subsection (1) above.

82A.　Determination of tariffs

(1)　This section applies if a court passes a life sentence in circumstances where the sentence is not fixed by law.
(2)　The court shall, unless it makes an order under subsection (4) below, order that the provisions of section 28(5) to (8) of the Crime (Sentences) Act 1997 (referred to in this section as the 'early release provisions') shall apply to the offender as soon as he has served the part of his sentence which is specified in the order.
(3)　The part of his sentence shall be such as the court considers appropriate taking into account—
    (a)　the seriousness of the offence, or of the combination of the offence and one or more offences associated with it;
    (b)　the effect that the following would have if the court had sentenced the offender to a term of imprisonment—
        (i)　section 240ZA of the Criminal Justice Act 2003 (crediting periods of remand in custody);
        (ii)　section 246 of the Armed Forces Act 2006 (equivalent provision for service courts);

        (iii)   any direction which the court would have given under section 240A of the Criminal Justice Act 2003 (crediting periods of remand on bail subject to certain types of condition);

    (c)   the early release provisions as compared with section 244(1) of the Criminal Justice Act 2003.

(4)   If the offender was aged 21 or over when he committed the offence and the court is of the opinion that, because of the seriousness of the offence or of the combination of the offence and one or more offences associated with it, no order should be made under subsection (2) above, the court shall order that ... the early release provisions shall not apply to the offender.

    ...

83. Restriction on imposing custodial sentences on persons not legally represented

(1)   A magistrates' court on summary conviction, or the Crown Court on committal for sentence or on conviction on indictment, shall not pass a sentence of imprisonment on a person who—

    (a)   is not legally represented in that court, and

    (b)   has not been previously sentenced to that punishment by a court in any part of the United Kingdom,

    unless he is a person to whom subsection (3) below applies.

(2)   A magistrates' court on summary conviction, or the Crown Court on committal for sentence or on conviction on indictment, shall not—

    (a)   pass a sentence of detention under section 90 or 91 below,

    (b)   pass a sentence of custody for life under section 93 or 94 below,

    (c)   pass a sentence of detention in a young offender institution, or

    (d)   make a detention and training order,

    on or in respect of a person who is not legally represented in that court unless he is a person to whom subsection (3) below applies.

(3)   This subsection applies to a person if either—

    (a)   representation was made available to him for the purposes of the proceedings under Part 1 of the Legal Aid, Sentencing and Punishment of Offenders Act 2012 but was withdrawn because of his conduct or because it appeared that his financial resources were such that he was not eligible for such representation;

    (aa)   he applied for such representation and the application was refused because it appeared that his financial resources were such that he was not eligible for such representation; or

    (b)   having been informed of his right to apply for such representation and having had the opportunity to do so, he refused or failed to apply.

(4)   For the purposes of this section a person is to be treated as legally represented in a court if, but only if, he has the assistance of counsel or a solicitor to represent him in the proceedings in that court at some time after he is found guilty and before he is sentenced.

(5)   For the purposes of subsection (1)(b) above a previous sentence of imprisonment which has been suspended and which has not taken effect under section 119 below ... shall be disregarded.

(6)   In this section 'sentence of imprisonment' does not include a committal for contempt of court or any kindred offence.

89. Restriction on imposing imprisonment on persons under 21

(1)   Subject to subsection (2) below, no court shall—

    (a)   pass a sentence of imprisonment on a person for an offence if he is aged under 21 when convicted of the offence; or

    (b)   commit a person aged under 21 to prison for any reason.

(2)   Nothing in subsection (1) above shall prevent the committal to prison of a person aged under 21 who is—

    (a)   remanded in custody;

    (b)   committed in custody for ... sentence; or

     (c)   sent in custody for trial under section 51 or 51A of the Crime and Disorder Act 1998.

90.   Offenders who commit murder when under 18: duty to detain at Her Majesty's pleasure

Where a person convicted of murder or any other offence the sentence for which is fixed by law as life imprisonment appears to the court to have been aged under 18 at the time the offence was committed, the court shall (notwithstanding anything in this or any other Act) sentence him to be detained during Her Majesty's pleasure.

91.   Offenders under 18 convicted of certain serious offences: power to detain for specified period

(1)   Subsection (3) below applies where a person aged under 18 is convicted on indictment of—

    (a)   an offence punishable in the case of a person aged 21 or over with imprisonment for 14 years or more, not being an offence the sentence for which is fixed by law; or

    (b)   an offence under section 3 of the Sexual Offences Act 2003 (in this section, 'the 2003 Act') (sexual assault); or

    (c)   an offence under section 13 of the 2003 Act (child sex offences committed by children or young persons): or

    (d)   an offence under section 25 of the 2003 Act (sexual activity with a child family member); or

    (e)   an offence under section 26 of the 2003 Act (inciting a child family member to engage in sexual activity).

(1A) Subsection (3) below also applies where—

    (a)   a person aged under 18 is convicted on indictment of an offence—

        (i)   under subsection (1)(a), (ab), (aba), (ac), (ad), (ae), (af) or (c) of section 5 of the Firearms Act 1968 (prohibited weapons), or

        (ii)   under subsection (1A)(a) of that section,

    (b)   the offence was committed after the commencement of section 51A of that Act and for the purposes of subsection (3) of that section at a time when he was aged 16 or over, and

    (c)   the court is of the opinion mentioned in section 51A(2) of that Act (exceptional circumstances which justify its not imposing required custodial sentence).

(1B) Subsection (3) below also applies where—

    (a)   a person aged under 18 is convicted on indictment of an offence under the Firearms Act 1968 that is listed in section 51A(1A)(b), or (f) of that Act and was committed in respect of a firearm or ammunition specified in section 5(1)(a), (b), (ab), (aba), (ac), (ad), (ae), (af) or (c) or section 5(1A(a) of that Act.

    (b)   The offence was committed after the commencement of section 30 of the Violent Crime Reduction Act 2006 and for the purposes of section 51A(3) of the Firearms Act 1968 at a time when he was aged 16 or over; and

    (c)   The court is of the opinion mentioned in section 51A(2) of the Firearms Act 1968.

(1C) Subsection (3) below also applies where—

    (a)   a person aged under 18 is convicted of an offence under section 28 of the Violent Crime Reduction Act 2006 (using someone to mind a weapon);

    (b)   section 29(3) of that Act applies (minimum sentences in certain cases); and

    (c)   the court is of the opinion mentioned in section 29(6) of that Act (exceptional circumstances which justify not imposing the minimum sentence).

    ...

(3)   If the court is of the opinion that neither a youth rehabilitation order nor a detention and training order is suitable, the court may sentence the offender to be detained for such period, not exceeding the maximum term of imprisonment with which the offence is punishable in the case of a person aged 21 or over, as may be specified in the sentence.

(4) Subsection (3) above is subject to (in particular) section 152 and 153 of the Criminal Justice Act 2003.

(5) Where—

  (a) subsection (2) of section 51A of the Firearms Act 1968, or

  (b) subsection (6) of section 29 of the Violent Crime Reduction Act 2006

  requires the imposition of a sentence of detention under this section for a term of at least the term provided for in that section, the court shall sentence the offender to be detained for such period, of at least the term so provided for but not exceeding the maximum term of imprisonment with which the offence is punishable in the case of a person aged 18 or over, as may be specified in the sentence.

93. Duty to impose custody for life in certain cases where offender under 21

Where a person aged under 21 is convicted of murder or any other offence the sentence for which is fixed by law as imprisonment for life, the court shall sentence him to custody for life unless he is liable to be detained under section 90 above.

94. Power to impose custody for life in certain other cases where offender at least 18 but under 21

(1) Where a person aged at least 18 but under 21 is convicted of an offence—

  (a) for which the sentence is not fixed by law, but

  (b) for which a person aged 21 or over would be liable to imprisonment for life,

  the court shall, if it considers that a sentence for life would be appropriate, sentence him to custody for life.

(2) Subsection (1) above is subject to (in particular) sections 79 and 80 above, but this subsection does not apply in relation to a sentence which falls to be imposed under section 109(2) below.

96. Detention in a young offender institution for other cases where offender at least 18 but under 21

Subject to sections 90, 93 and 94 above, where—

  (a) a person aged at least 18 but under 21 is convicted of an offence which is punishable with imprisonment in the case of a person aged 21 or over, and

  (b) the court is of the opinion that either or both of paragraphs (a) and (b) of section 79(2) above apply or the case falls within section 79(3),

  the sentence that the court is to pass is a sentence of detention in a young offender institution.

97. Term of detention in a young offender institution, and consecutive sentences

(1) The maximum term of detention in a young offender institution that a court may impose for an offence is the same as the maximum term of imprisonment that it may impose for that offence.

(2) A court shall not pass a sentence for an offender's detention in a young offender institution for less than 21 days.

(3) ...

(4) Where—

  (a) an offender is convicted of more than one offence for which he is liable to a sentence of detention in a young offender institution, or

  (b) an offender who is serving a sentence of detention in a young offender institution is convicted of one or more further offences for which he is liable to such a sentence,

  the court shall have the same power to pass consecutive sentences of detention in a young offender institution as if they were sentences of imprisonment.

(5) Subject to section 84 above (restriction on consecutive sentences for released prisoners), where an offender who—

  (a) is serving a sentence of detention in a young offender institution, and

  (b) is aged 21 or over,

is convicted of one or more further offences for which he is liable to imprisonment, the court shall have the power to pass one or more sentences of imprisonment to run consecutively upon the sentence of detention in a young offender institution.

100. Offenders under 18: detention and training orders

(1) Subject to sections 90 and 91 above, sections 226 and 226B of the Criminal Justice Act 2003, and subsection (2) below, where—

    (a) a child or young person (that is to say, any person aged under 18) is convicted of an offence which is punishable with imprisonment in the case of a person aged 21 or over, and

    (b) the court is of the opinion that subsection (2) of section 152 of the Criminal Justice Act 2003 applies or the case falls within subsection (3) of that section,

the sentence that the court is to pass is a detention and training order.

(1A) Subsection (1) applies with the omission of paragraph (b) in the case of an offence the sentence for which falls to be imposed under these provisions—

    (a) section 1(2B) or 1A(5) of the Prevention of Crime Act 1953 (minimum sentence for certain offences involving offensive weapons);

    (b) section 139(6B), 139A(5B) or 139AA(7) of the Criminal Justice Act 1988 (minimum sentence for certain offences involving article with blade or point or offensive weapon).

(2) A court shall not make a detention and training order—

    (a) in the case of an offender under the age of 15 at the time of the conviction, unless it is of the opinion that he is a persistent offender;

    (b) in the case of an offender under the age of 12 at that time, unless—

        (i) it is of the opinion that only a custodial sentence would be adequate to protect the public from further offending by him; and

        (ii) the offence was committed on or after such date as the Secretary of State may by order appoint.

(3) A detention and training order is an order that the offender in respect of whom it is made shall be subject, for the term specified in the order, to a period of detention and training followed by a period of supervision.

101. Term of order, consecutive terms and taking account of remands

(1) Subject to subsection (2) below, the term of a detention and training order made in respect of an offence (whether by a magistrates' court or otherwise) shall be 4, 6, 8, 10, 12, 18 or 24 months.

(2) The term of a detention and training order may not exceed the maximum term of imprisonment that the Crown Court could (in the case of an offender aged 21 or over) impose for the offence.

(3) Subject to subsections (4) and (6) below, a court making a detention and training order may order that its term shall commence on the expiry of the term of any other detention and training order made by that or any other court.

(4) A court shall not make in respect of an offender a detention and training order the effect of which would be that he would be subject to detention and training orders for a term which exceeds 24 months.

(5) Where the term of the detention and training orders to which an offender would otherwise be subject exceeds 24 months, the excess shall be treated as remitted.

(6) A court making a detention and training order shall not order that its term shall commence on the expiry of the term of a detention and training order under which the period of supervision has already begun (under section 103(1) below).

(7) Where a detention and training order ('the new order') is made in respect of an offender who is subject to a detention and training order under which the period of supervision has begun ('the old order'), the old order shall be disregarded in determining—

    (a) for the purposes of subsection (4) above whether the effect of the new order would be that the offender would be subject to detention and training orders for a term which exceeds 24 months; and

(b)   for the purposes of subsection (5) above whether the term of the detention and training orders to which the offender would (apart from that subsection) be subject exceeds 24 months.

(8)   In determining the term of a detention and training order for an offence, the court shall take account of any period for which the offender has been remanded—

   (a)   in custody, or

   (b)   on bail subject to a qualifying curfew and an electronic monitoring condition (within the meaning of section 240A of the Criminal Justice Act 2003)

   in connection with the offence, or any other offence the charge for which was founded on the same facts or evidence.

(9)   Where a court proposes to make detention and training orders in respect of an offender for two or more offences—

   (a)   subsection (8) above shall not apply; but

   (b)   in determining the total term of the detention and training orders it proposes to make in respect of the offender, the court shall take account of the total period (if any) for which he has been remanded as mentioned in that subsection in connection with any of those offences, or any other offence the charge for which was founded on the same facts or evidence.

(10) Once a period of remand has, under subsection (8) or (9) above, been taken account of in relation to a detention and training order made in respect of an offender for any offence or offences, it shall not subsequently be taken account of (under either of those subsections) in relation to such an order made in respect of the offender for any other offence or offences.

(11) Any reference in subsection (8) or (9) above to an offender's being remanded in custody is a reference to his being—

   (a)   held in police detention;

   (b)   remanded in or committed to custody by an order of a court;

   (c)   remanded to youth detention accommodation under section 91(4) of the Legal Aid, Sentencing and Punishment of Offenders Act 2012; or

   (d)   remanded, admitted or removed to hospital under section 35, 36, 38 or 48 of the Mental Health Act 1983.

(12) A person is in police detention for the purposes of subsection (11) above—

   (a)   at any time when he is in police detention for the purposes of the Police and Criminal Evidence Act 1984; and

   (b)   at any time when he is detained under section 41 of the Terrorism Act 2000;

   ...

(12A) Section 243 of the Criminal Justice Act (persons extradited to the United Kingdom) applies in relation to a person sentenced to a detention and training order as it applies to in relation to a fixed-term prisoner, with the reference in subsection (2A) of that section to section 240ZA being read as a reference to subsection (8) above.

(13) For the purpose of any reference in sections 102 to 105 below to the term of a detention and training order, consecutive terms of such orders and terms of such orders which are wholly or partly concurrent shall be treated as a single term if—

   (a)   the orders were made on the same occasion; or

   (b)   where they were made on different occasions, the offender has not been released (by virtue of subsection (2), (3), (4) or (5) of section 102 below) at any time during the period beginning with the first and ending with the last of those occasions.

102.   The period of detention and training

(1)   An offender shall serve the period of detention and training under a detention and training order in such secure accommodation as may be determined by the Secretary of State.

(2)   Subject to subsections (3) to (5) below, the period of detention and training under a detention and training order shall be one-half of the term of the order.

(3)   The Secretary of State may at any time release the offender if he is satisfied that exceptional circumstances exist which justify the offender's release on compassionate grounds.

(4) The Secretary of State may release the offender—

    (a) in the case of an order for a term of 8 months or more but less than 18 months, at any time during the period of one month ending with the half-way point of the term of the order; and

    (b) in the case of an order for a term of 18 months or more, at any time during the period of two months ending with that point.

(5) If a youth court so orders on an application made by the Secretary of State for the purpose, the Secretary of State shall release the offender—

    (a) in the case of an order for a term of 8 months or more but less than 18 months, one month after the half-way point of the term of the order; and

    (b) in the case of an order for a term of 18 months or more, one month or two months after that point.

(6) An offender detained in pursuance of a detention and training order shall be deemed to be in legal custody.

103. The period of supervision

(1) The period of supervision of an offender who is subject to a detention and training order—

    (a) shall begin with the offender's release, whether at the half-way point of the term of the order or otherwise; and

    (b) subject to subsection (2) below, shall end when the term of the order ends.

(2) Subject to subsection (2A) the Secretary of State may by order provide that the period of supervision shall end at such point during the term of a detention and training order as may be specified in the order under this subsection.

(2A) An order under subsection (2) may not include provision about cases in which—

    (a) the offender is aged 18 or over at the half-way point of the term of the detention and training order, and

    (b) the order was imposed in respect of an offence committed on or after the day on which section 6(4) of the Offender Rehabilitation Act 2014 came into force.

(3) During the period of supervision, the offender shall be under the supervision of—

    (a) an officer of a local probation board or an officer of a provider of probation services;

    (b) ...

    (c) a member of a youth offending team;

and the category of person to supervise the offender shall be determined from time to time by the Secretary of State.

...

(6) The offender shall be given a notice from the Secretary of State specifying—

    (a) the category of person for the time being responsible for his supervision; and

    (b) any requirements with which he must for the time being comply.

...

104. Breach of supervision requirements

(1) Where a detention and training order is in force in respect of an offender and it appears on information to a justice of the peace that the offender has failed to comply with requirements under section 103(6)(b) above, the justice—

    (a) may issue a summons requiring the offender to appear at the place and time specified in the summons ...; or

    (b) if the information is in writing and on oath, may issue a warrant for the offender's arrest ... .

...

(3) If it is proved to the satisfaction of the youth court before which the offender appears or is brought under this section that he has failed to comply with requirements under section 103(6)(b) above, that court may—

    (a) order the offender to be detained, in such youth detention accommodation as the Secretary of State may determine, for such period, not exceeding the maximum period found under subsection (3A) below as the court may specify; or (aa)   order the offender to be subject to such period of supervision, not exceeding the maximum period found under subsection (3A) below, as the court may specify; or

(b)   impose on the offender a fine not exceeding level 3 on the standard scale.

(3A) The maximum period referred to in subsection (3)(a) and (aa) above is the shorter of—

(a)   three months, and

(b)   the period beginning with the date of the offender's failure and ending with the last day of the term of the detention and training order.

(3B) For the purposes of subsection (3A) above a failure that is found to have occurred over two or more days is to be taken to have occurred on the first of those days.

(3C) A court may order a period of detention or supervision, or impose a fine, under subsection (3) above before or after the end of the term of the detention and training order.

(3D) A period of detention or supervision ordered under subsection (3) above—

(a)   begins on the date the order is made, and

(b)   may overlap to any extent with the period of supervision under the detention and training order.

(4)   An offender detained in pursuance of an order under subsection (3)(a) above shall be deemed to be in legal custody.

...

(6)   An offender may appeal to the Crown Court against any order made under subsection (3)(a), (aa), or (b) above.

105.   Offences during currency of order

(1)   This section applies to a person subject to a detention and training order if—

(a)   after his release and before the date on which the term of the order ends, he commits an offence punishable with imprisonment in the case of a person aged 21 or over ('the new offence'); and

(b)   whether before or after that date, he is convicted of the new offence.

(2)   Subject to section 8(6) above (duty of adult magistrates' court to remit young offenders to youth court for sentence), the court by or before which a person to whom this section applies is convicted of the new offence may, whether or not it passes any other sentence on him, order him to be detained in such youth detention accommodation as the Secretary of State may determine for the whole or any part of the period which—

(a)   begins with the date of the court's order; and

(b)   is equal in length to the period between the date on which the new offence was committed and the date mentioned in subsection (1) above.

(3)   The period for which a person to whom this section applies is ordered under subsection (2) above to be detained in youth detention accommodation—

(a)   shall, as the court may direct, either be served before and be followed by, or be served concurrently with, any sentence imposed for the new offence; and

(b)   in either case, shall be disregarded in determining the appropriate length of that sentence.

(4)   Where the new offence is found to have been committed over a period of two or more days, or at some time during a period of two or more days, it shall be taken for the purposes of this section to have been committed on the last of those days.

(5)   A person detained in pursuance of an order under subsection (2) above shall be deemed to be in legal custody.

106.   Interaction with sentences of detention in a young offender institution

(1)   Where a court passes a sentence of detention in a young offender institution in the case of an offender who is subject to a detention and training order, the sentence shall take effect as follows—

(a)   if the offender has been released by virtue of subsection (2), (3), (4) or (5) of section 102 above, at the beginning of the day on which it is passed;

(b)   if not, either as mentioned in paragraph (a) above or, if the court so orders, at the time when the offender would otherwise be released by virtue of subsection (2), (3), (4) or (5) of section 102.

(2), (3) ...

(4) Subject to subsection (5) below, where at any time an offender is subject concurrently—
    (a) to a detention and training order, and
    (b) to a sentence of detention in a young offender institution,
he shall be treated for the purposes of sections 102 to 105 above and of section 98 above (place of detention), Chapter IV of this Part (return to detention) and Part II of the Criminal Justice Act 1991 (early release) as if he were subject only to the one of them that was imposed on the later occasion.

(5) Nothing in subsection (4) above shall require the offender to be released in respect of either the order or the sentence unless and until he is required to be released in respect of each of them.

(6) Where, by virtue of any enactment giving a court power to deal with a person in a way in which a court on a previous occasion could have dealt with him, a detention and training order for any term is made in the case of a person who has attained the age of 18, the person shall be treated as if he had been sentenced to detention in a young offender institution for the same term.

106A. Interaction with sentences of detention

(1) In this section—
'the 2003 Act' means the Criminal Justice Act 2003;
'sentence of detention' means—
    (a) a sentence of detention under section 91 above, or
    (b) a sentence of detention under section 226B or 228 of the 2003 Act (extended sentence for certain violent, sexual or terrorism offences: persons under 18).

(2) Where a court passes a sentence of detention in the case of an offender who is subject to a detention and training order, the sentence shall take effect as follows—
    (a) if the offender has at any time been released by virtue of subsection (2), (3), (4) or of section 102 above, at the beginning of the day on which the sentence is passed, and
    (b) if not, either as mentioned in paragraph (a) above or, if the court so orders, at the time when the offender would otherwise be released by virtue of subsection (2), (3), or (5) of section 102.

(3) Where a court makes a detention and training order in the case of an offender who is subject to a sentence of detention, the order shall take effect as follows—
    (a) if the offender has at any time been released under Chapter 6 of Part 12 of the 2003 Act (release on licence of fixed-term prisoners), at the beginning of the day on which the order is made, and
    (b) if not, either as mentioned in paragraph (a) above or, if the court so orders, at the time when the offender would otherwise be released under that Chapter.

108. Detention of persons aged at least 18 but under 21 for default or contempt

(1) In any case where, but for section 89(1) above, a court would have power—
    (a) to commit a person aged at least 18 but under 21 to prison for default in payment of a fine or any other sum of money, or
    (b) to make an order fixing a term of imprisonment in the event of such a default by such a person, or
    (c) to commit such a person to prison for contempt of court or any kindred offence,
the court shall have power, subject to subsection (3) below, to commit him to be detained under this section or, as the case may be, to make an order fixing a term of detention under this section in the event of default, for a term not exceeding the term of imprisonment.
...

(3) No court shall commit a person to be detained under this section unless it is of the opinion that no other method of dealing with him is appropriate; and in forming any such opinion, the court—
    (a) shall take into account all such information about the circumstances of the default or contempt (including any aggravating or mitigating factors) as is available to it; and
    (b) may take into account any information about that person which is before it.

(4)   Where a magistrates' court commits a person to be detained under this section, it shall—

    (a)   state in open court the reason for its opinion that no other method of dealing with him is appropriate; and

    (b)   cause that reason to be specified in the warrant of commitment and to be entered in the register.

    ...

110. Minimum of seven years for third class A drug trafficking offence

(1)   This section applies where—

    (a)   a person is convicted of a class A drug trafficking offence committed after 30th September 1997;

    (b)   at the time when that offence was committed, he was 18 or over and had two relevant drug convictions; and

    (c)   one of those other offences was committed after he had been convicted of the other.

(2)   The court shall impose an appropriate custodial sentence for a term of at least seven years except where the court is of the opinion that there are particular circumstances which—

    (a)   relate to any of the offences or to the offender; and

    (b)   would make it unjust to do so in all the circumstances.

(2A)   For the purposes of subsection (1)—

    (a)   a 'relevant drug conviction' means—

        (i)   a conviction in any part of the United Kingdom of a class A drug trafficking offence, or

        (ii)   a conviction in another member State of an offence which was committed after the relevant date and would, if done in the United Kingdom at the time of the conviction, have constituted a class A drug trafficking offence; and

    (b)   'the relevant date' means the date on which this subsection comes into force.

    ...

(4)   Where—

    (a)   a person is charged with a class A drug trafficking offence (which, apart from this subsection, would be triable either way), and

    (b)   the circumstances are such that, if he were convicted of the offence, he could be sentenced for it under subsection (2) above,

    the offence shall be triable only on indictment.

(5)   In this section 'class A drug trafficking offence' means a drug trafficking offence committed in respect of a class A drug; and for this purpose—

    'class A drug' has the same meaning as in the Misuse of Drugs Act 1971;

    'drug trafficking offence' means any offence which is specified in—

    (a)   paragraph 1 of Schedule 2 to the Proceeds of Crime Act 2002 (drug trafficking offences), or

    (b)   so far as it relates to that paragraph, paragraph 10 of that Schedule.

(6)   In this section 'an appropriate custodial sentence' means—

    (a)   in relation to a person who is 21 or over when convicted of the offence mentioned in subsection (1)(a) above, a sentence of imprisonment;

    (b)   in relation to a person who is under 21 at that time, a sentence of detention in a young offender institution.

111. Minimum of three years for third domestic burglary

(1)   This section applies where—

    (a)   a person is convicted of a domestic burglary committed after 30th November 1999;

    (b)   at the time when that burglary was committed, he was 18 or over and had two relevant domestic burglary convictions; and

    (c)   one of those other burglaries was committed after he had been convicted of the other, and both of them were committed after the relevant date.

(2)   The court shall impose an appropriate custodial sentence for a term of at least three years except where the court is of the opinion that there are particular circumstances which—
    (a)   relate to any of the offences or to the offender; and
    (b)   would make it unjust to do so in all the circumstances.
(2A) For the purposes of subsection (1)—
    (a)   a 'relevant domestic burglary conviction' means—
        (i)   a conviction in England and Wales of a domestic burglary, or
        (ii)   a conviction in any other part of the United Kingdom or any other member State of an offence which would, if done in England and Wales at the time of the conviction, have constituted domestic burglary;
    (b)   'the relevant date' in relation to a relevant domestic burglary conviction means—
        (i)   in respect of a conviction in England and Wales, 30 November 1999, and
        (ii)   in any other case, the day on which this subsection comes into force.
    ...
(4)   Where—
    (a)   a person is charged with a domestic burglary which, apart from this subsection, would be triable either way, and
    (b)   the circumstances are such that, if he were convicted of the burglary, he could be sentenced for it under subsection (2) above,
    the burglary shall be triable only on indictment.
(5)   In this section 'domestic burglary' means a burglary committed in respect of a building or part of a building which is a dwelling.
(6)   In this section 'an appropriate custodial sentence' means—
    (a)   in relation to a person who is 21 or over when convicted of the offence mentioned in subsection (1)(a) above, a sentence of imprisonment;
    (b)   in relation to a person who is under 21 at that time, a sentence of detention in a young offender institution.

130. Compensation orders against convicted persons

(1)   A court by or before which a person is convicted of an offence, instead of or in addition to dealing with him in any other way, may, on application or otherwise, make an order (in this Act referred to as a 'compensation order') requiring him—
    (a)   to pay compensation for any personal injury, loss or damage resulting from that offence or any other offence which is taken into consideration by the court in determining sentence; or
    (b)   to make payments for funeral expenses or bereavement in respect of a death resulting from any such offence, other than a death due to an accident arising out of the presence of a motor vehicle on a road;
    but this is subject to the following provisions of this section and to section 131 below.
(2)   Where the person is convicted of an offence the sentence for which is fixed by law or falls to be imposed under a provision mentioned in subsection (2ZA) subsection (1) above shall have effect as if the words 'instead of or' were omitted.
(2ZA) The provisions referred to in subsection (2) are—
    (a)   section 1(2B) or 1A(5) of the Prevention of Crime Act 1953;
    (b)   section 51A(2) of the Firearms Act 1968;
    (c)   section 139(6B), 139A(5B) or 139AA(7) of the Criminal Justice Act 1988;
    (d)   section 110(2) or 111(2) of this Act;
    (e)   section 224A, 225(2) or 226(2) of the Criminal Justice Act 2003;
    (f)   section 29(4) or (6) of the Violent Crime Reduction Act 2006.
(2A) A court must consider making a compensation order in any case where this section empowers it to do so.
(3)   A court shall give reasons, on passing sentence, if it does not make a compensation order in a case where this section empowers it to do so.
(4)   Compensation under subsection (1) above shall be of such amount as the court considers appropriate, having regard to any evidence and to any representations that are made by or on behalf of the accused or the prosecutor.
(5)   In the case of an offence under the Theft Act 1968 or Fraud Act 2006, where the property in question is recovered, any damage to the property occurring while it was

out of the owner's possession shall be treated for the purposes of subsection (1) above as having resulted from the offence, however and by whomever the damage was caused.

(6) A compensation order may only be made in respect of injury, loss or damage (other than loss suffered by a person's dependants in consequence of his death) which was due to an accident arising out of the presence of a motor vehicle on a road, if—

    (a) it is in respect of damage which is treated by subsection (5) above as resulting from an offence under the Theft Act 1968 or Fraud Act 2006; or

    (b) it is in respect of injury, loss or damage as respects which—

        (i) the offender is uninsured in relation to the use of the vehicle; and

        (ii) compensation is not payable under any arrangements to which the Secretary of State is a party.

(7) Where a compensation order is made in respect of injury, loss or damage due to an accident arising out of the presence of a motor vehicle on a road, the amount to be paid may include an amount representing the whole or part of any loss of or reduction in preferential rates of insurance attributable to the accident.

(8) A vehicle the use of which is exempted from insurance by section 144 of the Road Traffic Act 1988 is not uninsured for the purposes of subsection (6) above.

(9) A compensation order in respect of funeral expenses may be made for the benefit of anyone who incurred the expenses.

(10) A compensation order in respect of bereavement may be made only for the benefit of a person for whose benefit a claim for damages for bereavement could be made under section 1A of the Fatal Accidents Act 1976; and the amount of compensation in respect of bereavement shall not exceed the amount for the time being specified in section 1A(3) of that Act.

(11) In determining the amount to be paid by any person under such an order, the court shall have regard to his means so far as they appear or are known to the court.

(12) Where the court considers—

    (a) that it would be appropriate both to impose a fine and to make a compensation order, but

    (b) that the offender has insufficient means to pay both an appropriate fine and appropriate compensation,

the court shall give preference to compensation (though it may impose a fine as well).

131. Limit on amount payable under compensation order of magistrates' court in case of young offender

(A1) This section applies if (but only if) a magistrates' court has convicted a person aged under 18 (the offender) of an offence or offences.

(1) The compensation to be paid under a compensation order made by the court in respect of the offence, or any one of the offences shall not exceed £5,000.

(2) The compensation or total compensation to be paid under a compensation order or compensation orders made by the court in respect of any offence or offences taken into consideration in determining sentence shall not exceed the difference (if any) between—

    (a) the amount or total amount which under subsection (1) above is the maximum for the offence or offences of which the offender has been convicted; and

    (b) the amount or total amounts (if any) which are in fact ordered to be paid in respect of that offence or those offences.

135. Limit on fines imposed by magistrates' courts in respect of young offenders

(1) Where a person aged under 18 is found guilty by a magistrates' court of an offence for which, apart from this section, the court would have power to impose a fine of an amount exceeding £1,000, the amount of any fine imposed by the court shall not exceed £1,000.

(2) In relation to a person aged under 14, subsection (1) above shall have effect as if for '£1,000', in both places where it occurs, there were substituted '£250'.

137. Power to order parent or guardian to pay fine, costs, compensation or surcharge

(1) Where—

    (a) a child or young person (that is to say, any person aged under 18) is convicted of any offence for the commission of which a fine or costs may be imposed or a compensation order may be made, and

    (b) the court is of the opinion that the case would best be met by the imposition of a fine or costs or the making of such an order, whether with or without any other punishment,

the court shall order that the fine, compensation or costs awarded be paid by the parent or guardian of the child or young person instead of by the child or young person himself, unless the court is satisfied—

    (i) that the parent or guardian cannot be found; or

    (ii) that it would be unreasonable to make an order for payment, having regard to the circumstances of the case.

(1A) Where but for this subsection court would order a child or young person to pay a surcharge under section 161A of the Criminal Justice Act 2003, the court shall order that the surcharge be paid by the parent or guardian of the child or young person instead of by the child or young person himself, unless the court is satisfied—

    (a) that the parent or guardian cannot be found; or

    (b) that it would be unreasonable to make an order for payment, having regard to the circumstances of the case.

(2) Where but for this subsection a court would impose a fine on a child or young person under—

    (za) paragraph 6(2)(a) or 8(2)(a) of Schedule 2 to the Criminal Justice and Immigration Act 2008 (breach of youth rehabilitation order),

    (a) ...

    (b) para 2(1)(a) of Schedule 5 to this Act (breach of attendance centre order or attendance centre rules),

    (c) ...

    (d) paragraph 2(2)(a) of Schedule 3 to this Act (breach of reparation order),

    (e) section 104(3)(b) above (breach of requirements of supervision under a detention and training order), or

    (f) section 4(3)(b) of the Criminal Justice and Public Order Act 1994 (breach of requirements of supervision under a secure training order),

the court shall order that the fine be paid by the parent or guardian of the child or young person instead of by the child or young person himself, unless the court is satisfied—

    (i) that the parent or guardian cannot be found; or

    (ii) that it would be unreasonable to make an order for payment, having regard to the circumstances of the case.

(3) In the case of a young person aged 16 or over, subsections (1) and (2) above shall have effect as if, instead of imposing a duty, they conferred a power to make such an order as is mentioned in those subsections.

(4) Subject to subsection (5) below, no order shall be made under this section without giving the parent or guardian an opportunity of being heard.

(5) An order under this section may be made against a parent or guardian who, having been required to attend, has failed to do so.

(6) A parent or guardian may appeal to the Crown Court against an order under this section made by a magistrates' court.

(7) A parent or guardian may appeal to the Court of Appeal against an order under this section made by the Crown Court, as if he had been convicted on indictment and the order were a sentence passed on his conviction.

(8) In relation to a child or young person for whom a local authority have parental responsibility and who—

    (a) is in their care, or

    (b) is provided with accommodation by them in the exercise of social services functions,

references in this section to his parent or guardian shall be construed as references to that authority.

(8A) In subsection (8) social services functions are—

    (a)   any functions (in particular those under the Children Act 1989) which are social services functions within the meaning of the Local Authority Social Services Act 1970, or

    (b)   any functions (in particular those under Part 6 of the Social Services and Well-being (Wales) Act 2014) which are social services functions for the purposes of that Act.

(9)   In subsection (8) above 'local authority' and 'parental responsibility' have the same meanings as in the Children Act 1989.

143. Powers to deprive offender of property used etc for purposes of crime

(1)   Where a person is convicted of an offence and the court by or before which he is convicted is satisfied that any property which has been lawfully seized from him, or which was in his possession or under his control at the time when he was apprehended for the offence or when a summons in respect of it was issued—

    (a)   has been used for the purpose of committing, or facilitating the commission of, any offence, or

    (b)   as intended by him to be used for that purpose,

the court may (subject to subsection (5) below) make an order under this section in respect of that property.

(2)   Where a person is convicted of an offence and the offence, or an offence which the court has taken into consideration in determining his sentence, consists of unlawful possession of property which—

    (a)   has been lawfully seized from him, or

    (b)   was in his possession or under his control at the time when he was apprehended for the offence of which he has been convicted or when a summons in respect of that offence was issued,

the court may (subject to subsection (5) below) make an order under this section in respect of that property.

(3)   An order under this section shall operate to deprive the offender of his rights, if any, in the property to which it relates, and the property shall (if not already in their possession) be taken into the possession of the police.

(4)   Any power conferred on a court by subsection (1) or (2) above may be exercised—

    (a)   whether or not the court also deals with the offender in any other way in respect of the offence of which he has been convicted; and

    (b)   without regard to any restrictions on forfeiture in any enactment contained in an Act passed before 29th July 1988.

(5)   In considering whether to make an order under this section in respect of any property, a court shall have regard—

    (a)   to the value of the property; and

    (b)   to the likely financial and other effects on the offender of the making of the order (taken together with any other order that the court contemplates making).

...

146. Driving disqualification for any offence

(1)   The court by or before which a person is convicted of an offence committed after 31st December 1997 may, instead of or in addition to dealing with him in any other way, order him to be disqualified, for such period as it thinks fit, for holding or obtaining a driving licence.

(2)   Where the person is convicted of an offence the sentence for which is fixed by law or falls to be imposed under a provision mentioned in subsection (2A) , subsection (1) above shall have effect as if the words 'instead of or' were omitted.

(2A) The provisions referred to in subsection (2) are—

    (a)   section 1(2B) or 1A(5) of the Prevention of Crime Act 1953;

    (b)   section 51A(2) of the Firearms Act 1968;

    (c)   section 139(6B), 139A(5B) or 139AA(7) of the Criminal Justice Act 1988;

    (d)   section 110(2) or 111(2) of this Act;

    (e)   section 224A, 225(2) or 226(2) of the Criminal Justice Act 2003;

    (f)   section 29(4) or (6) of the Violent Crime Reduction Act 2006.

...

147. Driving disqualification where vehicle used for purposes of crime

(1)   This section applies where a person—

    (a)   is convicted before the Crown Court of an offence punishable on indictment with imprisonment for a term of two years or more; or

    (b)   having been convicted by a magistrates' court of such an offence, is committed under section 3 above to the Crown Court for sentence.

(2)   This section also applies where a person is convicted by or before any court of common assault or of any other offence involving an assault (including an offence of aiding, abetting, counselling or procuring, or inciting to the commission of, an offence).

(3)   If, in a case to which this section applies by virtue of subsection (1) above, the Crown Court is satisfied that a motor vehicle was used (by the person convicted or by anyone else) for the purpose of committing, or facilitating the commission of, the offence in question, the court may order the person convicted to be disqualified, for such period as the court thinks fit, for holding or obtaining a driving licence.

...

147A. Extension of disqualification where custodial sentence also imposed

(1)   This section applies where a person is convicted of an offence for which the court—

    (a)   imposes a custodial sentence, and

    (b)   orders the person to be disqualified under section 146 or 147 for holding or obtaining a driving licence.

(2)   The order under section 146 or 147 must provide for the person to be disqualified for the appropriate extension period, in addition to the discretionary disqualification period.

(3)   The discretionary disqualification period is the period for which, in the absence of this section, the court would have disqualified the person under section 146 or 147.

(4)   The appropriate extension period is—

    (a)   where an order under section 82A of this Act (determination of tariffs) is made in relation to the custodial sentence, a period equal to the part of the sentence specified in that order;

    (b)   in the case of a detention and training order undersection 100 of this Act (offenders under 18: detention and training orders), a period equal to half the term of that order;

    (c), (d) ...

    (e)   where section 226A of the Criminal Justice Act 2003 (extended sentence for certain violent, sexual or terrorism offences: persons 18 or over) applies in relation to the custodial sentence, a period equal to two-thirds of the term imposed pursuant to section 226A(5) of that Act;

    (f)   where section 226B of that Act (extended sentence for certain violent, sexual or terrorism offences: persons under 18) applies in relation to the custodial sentence, a period equal to two-thirds of the term imposed pursuant to section 226B(3)(a) of that Act;

    (fa)   in the case of a sentence under section 236A of that Act (special custodial sentence for certain offenders of particular concern), a period equal to half of the term imposed pursuant to section 236A(2)(a) of that Act;

    (g)   where an order under section 269(2) of that Act (determination of minimum term in relation to mandatory life sentence: early release) is made in relation to the custodial sentence, a period equal to the part of the sentence specified in that order;

    (h)   in any other case, a period equal to half the custodial sentence imposed.

(5)   If a period determined under subsection (4) includes a fraction of a day, that period is to be rounded up to the nearest number of whole days.

(7)   This section does not apply where—

    (a)   the custodial sentence was a suspended sentence,

    (b)   the court has made an order under section 269(4) of the Criminal Justice Act 2003 (determination of minimum term in relation to mandatory life sentence: no early release) in relation to the custodial sentence, or

    (c)   the court has made an order under section 82A(4) of this Act (determination of minimum term in relation to discretionary life sentence: no early release) in relation to the custodial sentence.

147B. Effect of custodial sentence in other cases

(1) This section applies where a person is convicted of an offence for which a court proposes to order the person to be disqualified under section 146or 147 for holding or obtaining a driving licence and—

(a) the court proposes to impose on the person a custodial sentence (other than a suspended sentence) for another offence, or

(b) at the time of sentencing for the offence, a custodial sentence imposed on the person on an earlier occasion has not expired.

(2) In determining the period for which the person is to be disqualified under section 146 or 147, the court must have regard to the consideration in subsection (3) if and to the extent that it is appropriate to do so.

(3) The consideration is the diminished effect of disqualification as a distinct punishment if the person who is disqualified is also detained in pursuance of a custodial sentence.

(4) If the court proposes to order the person to be disqualified under section 146 or 147 and to impose a custodial sentence for the same offence, the court may not in relation to that disqualification take that custodial sentence into account for the purposes of subsection (2).

(5) In this section 'suspended sentence' has the same meaning as in section 147A.

148. Restitution orders

(1) This section applies where goods have been stolen, and either—

(a) a person is convicted of any offence with reference to the theft (whether or not the stealing is the gist of his offence); or

(b) a person is convicted of any other offence, but such an offence as is mentioned in paragraph (a) above is taken into consideration in determining his sentence.

(2) Where this section applies, the court by or before which the offender is convicted may on the conviction (whether or not the passing of sentence is in other respects deferred) exercise any of the following powers—

(a) the court may order anyone having possession or control of the stolen goods to restore them to any person entitled to recover them from him; or

(b) on the application of a person entitled to recover from the person convicted any other goods directly or indirectly representing the stolen goods (as being the proceeds of any disposal or realisation of the whole or part of them or of goods so representing them), the court may order those other goods to be delivered or transferred to the applicant; or

(c) the court may order that a sum not exceeding the value of the stolen goods shall be paid, out of any money of the person convicted which was taken out of his possession on his apprehension, to any person who, if those goods were in the possession of the person convicted, would be entitled to recover them from him;

and in this subsection 'the stolen goods' means the goods referred to in subsection (1) above.

(3) Where the court has power on a person's conviction to make an order against him both under paragraph (b) and under paragraph (c) of subsection (2) above with reference to the stealing of the same goods, the court may make orders under both paragraphs provided that the person in whose favour the orders are made does not thereby recover more than the value of those goods.

(4) Where the court on a person's conviction makes an order under subsection (2)(a) above for the restoration of any goods, and it appears to the court that the person convicted—

(a) has sold the goods to a person acting in good faith, or

(b) has borrowed money on the security of them from a person so acting,

the court may order that there shall be paid to the purchaser or lender, out of any money of the person convicted which was taken out of his possession on his apprehension, a sum not exceeding the amount paid for the purchase by the purchaser or, as the case may be, the amount owed to the lender in respect of the loan.

(5) The court shall not exercise the powers conferred by this section unless in the opinion of the court the relevant facts sufficiently appear from evidence given at the trial or the available documents, together with admissions made by or on behalf of any person in connection with any proposed exercise of the powers.

(6)   In subsection (5) above 'the available documents' means—
   (a)   any written statements or admissions which were made for use, and would have been admissible, as evidence at the trial; and
   (b)   such documents as were served on the offender in pursuance of regulations made under paragraph 1 of Schedule 3 to the Crime and Disorder Act 1998.
(7)   Any order under this section shall be treated as an order for the restitution of property within the meaning of section 30 of the M1Criminal Appeal Act 1968 (which relates to the effect on such orders of appeals).
(8)   Subject to subsection (9) below, references in this section to stealing shall be construed in accordance with section 1(1) of the M2Theft Act 1968 (read with the provisions of that Act relating to the construction of section 1(1)).
(9)   Subsections (1) and (4) of section 24 of that Act (interpretation of certain provisions) shall also apply in relation to this section as they apply in relation to the provisions of that Act relating to goods which have been stolen.
(10)   In this section and section 149 below, 'goods', except in so far as the context otherwise requires, includes money and every other description of property (within the meaning of the Theft Act 1968) except land, and includes things severed from the land by stealing.
(11)   An order may be made under this section in respect of money owed by the Crown.

149.   Restitution orders: supplementary

(1)   The following provisions of this section shall have effect with respect to section 148 above.
(2)   The powers conferred by subsections (2)(c) and (4) of that section shall be exercisable without any application being made in that behalf or on the application of any person appearing to the court to be interested in the property concerned.
(3)   Where an order is made under that section against any person in respect of an offence taken into consideration in determining his sentence—
   (a)   the order shall cease to have effect if he successfully appeals against his conviction of the offence or, if more than one, all the offences, of which he was convicted in the proceedings in which the order was made;
   (b)   he may appeal against the order as if it were part of the sentence imposed in respect of the offence or, if more than one, any of the offences, of which he was so convicted.
(4)   Any order under that section made by a magistrates' court shall be suspended—
   (a)   in any case until the end of the period for the time being prescribed by law for the giving of notice of appeal against a decision of a magistrates' court;
   (b)   where notice of appeal is given within the period so prescribed, until the determination of the appeal;
   but this subsection shall not apply where the order is made under section 148(2)(a) or (b) and the court so directs, being of the opinion that the title to the goods to be restored or, as the case may be, delivered or transferred under the order is not in dispute.

150.   Binding over of parent or guardian

(1)   Where a child or young person (that is to say, any person aged under 18) is convicted of an offence, the powers conferred by this section shall be exercisable by the court by which he is sentenced for that offence, and where the offender is aged under 16 when sentenced it shall be the duty of that court—
   (a)   to exercise those powers if it is satisfied, having regard to the circumstances of the case, that their exercise would be desirable in the interests of preventing the commission by him of further offences; and
   (b)   if it does not exercise them, to state in open court that it is not satisfied as mentioned in paragraph (a) above and why it is not so satisfied;
   but this subsection has effect subject to section 19(5) above and paragraph 13(5) of Schedule 1 to this Act (cases where referral orders made or extended).
(2)   The powers conferred by this section are as follows—
   (a)   with the consent of the offender's parent or guardian, to order the parent or guardian to enter into a recognizance to take proper care of him and exercise proper control over him; and

(b)   if the parent or guardian refuses consent and the court considers the refusal unreasonable, to order the parent or guardian to pay a fine not exceeding £1,000; and where the court has passed a community sentence on the offender, it may include in the recognizance a provision that the offender's parent or guardian ensure that the offender complies with the requirements of that sentence.

(3)   An order under this section shall not require the parent or guardian to enter into a recognizance for an amount exceeding £1,000.

(4)   An order under this section shall not require the parent or guardian to enter into a recognizance—
    (a)   for a period exceeding three years; or
    (b)   where the offender will attain the age of 18 in a period shorter than three years, for a period exceeding that shorter period.

(5)   Section 120 of the Magistrates' Courts Act 1980 (forfeiture of recognizances) shall apply in relation to a recognizance entered into in pursuance of an order under this section as it applies in relation to a recognizance to keep the peace.

(6)   A fine imposed under subsection (2)(b) above shall be deemed, for the purposes of any enactment, to be a sum adjudged to be paid by a conviction.

(7)   In fixing the amount of a recognizance under this section, the court shall take into account among other things the means of the parent or guardian so far as they appear or are known to the court; and this subsection applies whether taking into account the means of the parent or guardian has the effect of increasing or reducing the amount of the recognizance.

(8)   A parent or guardian may appeal to the Crown Court against an order under this section made by a magistrates' court.

(9)   A parent or guardian may appeal to the Court of Appeal against an order under this section made by the Crown Court, as if he had been convicted on indictment and the order were a sentence passed on his conviction.

(10)   A court may vary or revoke an order made by it under this section if, on the application of the parent or guardian, it appears to the court, having regard to any change in the circumstances since the order was made, to be in the interests of justice to do so.

(11)   For the purposes of this section, taking 'care' of a person includes giving him protection and guidance and 'control' includes discipline.

154.   Commencement of Crown Court sentence

(1)   A sentence imposed, or other order made, by the Crown Court when dealing with an offender shall take effect from the beginning of the day on which it is imposed, unless the court otherwise directs.

(2)   The power to give a direction under subsection (1) above has effect subject to section 265 of the Criminal Justice Act 2003 (restriction on consecutive sentences for released prisoners).

(3)   In this section 'sentence' and 'order' shall be construed in accordance with section 155(8) below.

155.   Alteration of Crown Court sentence

(1)   Subject to the following provisions of this section, a sentence imposed, or other order made, by the Crown Court when dealing with an offender may be varied or rescinded by the Crown Court within the period of 56 days beginning with the day on which the sentence or other order was imposed or made.

(1A)   The power conferred by subsection (1) may not be exercised in relation to any sentence or order if an appeal, or an application for leave to appeal, against that sentence or order has been determined.

(2), (3) ...

(4)   A sentence or other order shall not be varied or rescinded under this section except by the court constituted as it was when the sentence or other order was imposed or made, or, where that court comprised one or more justices of the peace, a court so constituted except for the omission of any one or more of those justices.

(5)   Subject to subsection (6) below, where a sentence or other order is varied under this section the sentence or other order, as so varied, shall take effect from the beginning of the day on which it was originally imposed or made, unless the court otherwise directs.

(8)   In this section—
'sentence' includes a recommendation for deportation made when dealing with an offender;
'order' does not include an order relating to a requirement to make a payment under regulations under section 23 or 24 of the Legal Aid, Sentencing and Punishment of Offenders Act 2012.

PREVENTION OF CRIME ACT 1953
(1953, c. 14)

1.   Prohibition of the carrying of offensive weapons without lawful authority or reasonable excuse

(1)   Any person who without lawful authority or reasonable excuse, the proof whereof shall lie on him, has with him in any public place any offensive weapon shall be guilty of an offence, and shall be liable—
   (a)   on summary conviction, to imprisonment for a term not exceeding six months or a fine not exceeding the prescribed sum, or both;
   (b)   on conviction on indictment, to imprisonment for a term not exceeding four years or a fine, or both.
(2)   Where any person is convicted of an offence under subsection (1) of this section the court may make an order for the forfeiture or disposal of any weapon in respect of which the offence was committed.
(2A)   Subsection (2B) applies where—
   (a)   a person is convicted of an offence under subsection (1) committed after this subsection is commenced, and
   (b)   when the offence was committed, the person was aged 16 or over and had at least one relevant conviction (see section 1ZA).
(2B)   Where this subsection applies, the court must impose an appropriate custodial sentence (with or without a fine) unless the court is of the opinion that there are particular circumstances which—
   (a)   relate to the offence, to the previous offence or to the offender, and
   (b)   would make it unjust to do so in all the circumstances.
(2C)   In this section 'appropriate custodial sentence' means—
   (a)   in the case of a person who is aged 18 or over when convicted, a sentence of imprisonment for a term of at least 6 months;
   (b)   in the case of a person who is aged at least 16 but under 18 when convicted, a detention and training order of at least 4 months.
(2D)   In considering whether it is of the opinion mentioned in subsection (2B) in the case of a person aged 16 or 17, the court must have regard to its duty under section 44 of the Children and Young Persons Act (general considerations).

1ZA.   Offence under section 1: previous relevant convictions

(1)   For the purposes of section 1, 'relevant conviction' means—
   (a)   a conviction for an offence under—
      (i)   section 1 or 1A of this Act, or
      (ii)   section 139, 139A or 139AA of the Criminal Justice Act 1988,
      (a 'relevant offence'), whenever committed,
   (b)   a conviction in Scotland, Northern Ireland or a member State other than the United Kingdom for a civilian offence, whenever committed, which would have constituted a relevant offence if committed in England and Wales at the time of that conviction …

1A.   Offence of threatening with offensive weapon in public

(1)   A person is guilty of an offence if that person—
   (a)   has an offensive weapon with him or her in a public place,
   (b)   unlawfully and intentionally threatens another person with the weapon, and

     (c)   does so in such a way that there is an immediate risk of serious physical harm to that other person.

(2)   For the purposes of this section physical harm is serious if it amounts to grievous bodily harm for the purposes of the Offences against the Person Act 1981.

    ...

(4)   A person guilty of an offence under this section is liable—
    (a)   on summary conviction, to imprisonment for a term not exceeding 12 months or to a fine not exceeding the statutory maximum, or to both;
    (b)   on conviction on indictment, to imprisonment for a term not exceeding 4 years or to a fine, or to both.

(5)   Where a person is aged 16 or over is convicted of an offence under this section, the court must impose an appropriate custodial sentence (with or without a fine) unless the court is of the opinion that there are particular circumstances which—
    (a)   relate to the offence or to the offender, and
    (b)   would make it unjust to do so in all the circumstances.

(6)   In this section 'appropriate custodial sentence' means—
    (a)   in the case of a person who is aged 18 and over when convicted, a sentence of imprisonment for a term of at least 6 months;
    (b)   in the case of a person who is aged at least 16 but under 18 when convicted, a detention and training order of at least 4 months.

(7)   In considering whether it is of the opinion mentioned in subsection (5) in the case of a person aged under 18, the court must have regard to its duty under section 44 of the Children and Young Persons Act 1933.

    ...

PROCEEDS OF CRIME ACT 2002
(2002, c. 29)

6.   **Making of order**

(1)   The Crown Court must proceed under this section if the following two conditions are satisfied.

(2)   The first condition is that a defendant falls within any of the following paragraphs—
    (a)   he is convicted of an offence or offences in proceedings before the Crown Court;
    (b)   he is committed to the Crown Court for sentence in respect of an offence or offences under section 3, 3A, 3B, 3C, 4, 4A or 6 of the Sentencing Act;
    (c)   he is committed to the Crown Court in respect of an offence or offences under section 70 below (committal with a view to a confiscation order being considered).

(3)   The second condition is that—
    (a)   the prosecutor asks the court to proceed under this section, or
    (b)   the court believes it is appropriate for it to do so.

(4)   The court must proceed as follows—
    (a)   it must decide whether the defendant has a criminal lifestyle;
    (b)   if it decides that he has a criminal lifestyle it must decide whether he has benefited from his general criminal conduct;
    (c)   if it decides that he does not have a criminal lifestyle it must decide whether he has benefited from his particular criminal conduct.

(5)   If the court decides under subsection (4)(b) or (c) that the defendant has benefited from the conduct referred to it must—
    (a)   decide the recoverable amount, and
    (b)   make an order (a confiscation order) requiring him to pay that amount. Paragraph (b) applies only if, or to the extent that, it would not be disproportionate to require the defendant to pay the recoverable amount.

(6)   But the court must treat the duty in subsection (5) as a power if it believes that any victim of the conduct has at any time started or intends to start proceedings against the defendant in respect of loss, injury or damage sustained in connection with the conduct.

(6A) The court must also treat the duty in subsection (5) as a power if—

    (a) an order has been made, or it believes an order may be made, against the defendant under section 4 (criminal unlawful profit orders) of the Prevention of Social Housing Fraud Act 2013 in respect of profit made by the defendant in connection with the conduct, or

    (b) it believes that a person has at any time started or intends to start proceedings against the defendant under section 5 (civil unlawful profit orders) of that Act in respect of such profit.

(7) The court must decide any question arising under subsection (4) or (5) on a balance of probabilities.

(8) The first condition is not satisfied if the defendant absconds (but section 27 may apply).

(9) References in this Part to the offence (or offences) concerned are to the offence (or offences) mentioned in subsection (2).

7.   Recoverable amount

(1) The recoverable amount for the purposes of section 6 is an amount equal to the defendant's benefit from the conduct concerned.

(2) But if the defendant shows that the available amount is less than that benefit the recoverable amount is—

    (a) the available amount, or

    (b) a nominal amount, if the available amount is nil.

(3) But if section 6(6) or (6A) applies the recoverable amount is such amount as—

    (a) the court believes is just, but

    (b) does not exceed the amount found under subsection (1) or (2) (as the case may be).

(4) In calculating the defendant's benefit from the conduct concerned for the purposes of subsection (1), the following must be ignored—

    (a) any property in respect of which a recovery order is in force under section 266,

    (b) any property which has been forfeited in pursuance of a forfeiture notice under section 297A or an account forfeiture notice under section 303Z9,

    (c) any property in respect of which a forfeiture order is in place under section 298(2), 303O(3), 303R(3) or 303Z14(4); and

    (d) any property which is the forfeitable property in relation to an order under section 303Q(1).

(5) If the court decides the available amount, it must include in the confiscation order a statement of its findings as to the matters relevant for deciding that amount.

8.   Defendant's benefit

(1) If the court is proceeding under section 6 this section applies for the purpose of—

    (a) deciding whether the defendant has benefited from conduct, and

    (b) deciding his benefit from the conduct.

(2) The court must—

    (a) take account of conduct occurring up to the time it makes its decision;

    (b) take account of property obtained up to that time.

(3) Subsection (4) applies if—

    (a) the conduct concerned is general criminal conduct,

    (b) a confiscation order mentioned in subsection (5) has at an earlier time been made against the defendant, and

    (c) his benefit for the purposes of that order was benefit from his general criminal conduct.

(4) His benefit found at the time the last confiscation order mentioned in subsection (3)(c) was made against him must be taken for the purposes of this section to be his benefit from his general criminal conduct at that time.

(5) If the conduct concerned is general criminal conduct the court must deduct the aggregate of the following amounts—

    (a) the amount ordered to be paid under each confiscation order previously made against the defendant;

    (b) the amount ordered to be paid under each confiscation order previously made against him under any of the provisions listed in subsection (7).

(6) But subsection (5) does not apply to an amount which has been taken into account for the purposes of a deduction under that subsection on any earlier occasion.

(7) These are the provisions—

    (a) the Drug Trafficking Offences Act 1986;

    (b) Part 1 of the Criminal Justice (Scotland) Act 1987;

    (c) Part 6 of the Criminal Justice Act 1988;

    (d) the Criminal Justice (Confiscation) (Northern Ireland) Order 1990;

    (e) Part 1 of the Drug Trafficking Act 1994;

    (f) Part 1 of the Proceeds of Crime (Scotland) Act 1995;

    (g) the Proceeds of Crime (Northern Ireland) Order 1996;

    (h) Part 3 or 4 of this Act.

(8) The reference to general criminal conduct in the case of a confiscation order made under any of the provisions listed in subsection (7) is a reference to conduct in respect of which a court is required or entitled to make one or more assumptions for the purpose of assessing a person's benefit from the conduct.

9. Available amount

(1) For the purposes of deciding the recoverable amount, the available amount is the aggregate of—

    (a) the total of the values (at the time the confiscation order is made) of all the free property then held by the defendant minus the total amount payable in pursuance of obligations which then have priority, and

    (b) the total of the values (at that time) of all tainted gifts.

(2) An obligation has priority if it is an obligation of the defendant—

    (a) to pay an amount due in respect of a fine or other order of a court which was imposed or made on conviction of an offence and at any time before the time the confiscation order is made, or

    (b) to pay a sum which would be included among the preferential debts if the defendant's bankruptcy had commenced on the date of the confiscation order or his winding up had been ordered on that date.

(3) 'Preferential debts' has the meaning given by section 386 of the Insolvency Act 1986.

10. Assumptions to be made in case of criminal lifestyle

(1) If the court decides under section 6 that the defendant has a criminal lifestyle it must make the following four assumptions for the purpose of—

    (a) deciding whether he has benefited from his general criminal conduct, and

    (b) deciding his benefit from the conduct.

(2) The first assumption is that any property transferred to the defendant at any time after the relevant day was obtained by him—

    (a) as a result of his general criminal conduct, and

    (b) at the earliest time he appears to have held it.

(3) The second assumption is that any property held by the defendant at any time after the date of conviction was obtained by him—

    (a) as a result of his general criminal conduct, and

    (b) at the earliest time he appears to have held it.

(4) The third assumption is that any expenditure incurred by the defendant at any time after the relevant day was met from property obtained by him as a result of his general criminal conduct.

(5) The fourth assumption is that, for the purpose of valuing any property obtained (or assumed to have been obtained) by the defendant, he obtained it free of any other interests in it.

(6) But the court must not make a required assumption in relation to particular property or expenditure if—

    (a) the assumption is shown to be incorrect, or

    (b) there would be a serious risk of injustice if the assumption were made.

(7) If the court does not make one or more of the required assumptions it must state its reasons.

(8) The relevant day is the first day of the period of six years ending with—

    (a) the day when proceedings for the offence concerned were started against the defendant, or

(b)   if there are two or more offences and proceedings for them were started on different days, the earliest of those days.

(9)   But if a confiscation order mentioned in section 8(3)(c) has been made against the defendant at any time during the period mentioned in subsection (8)—

(a)   the relevant day is the day when the defendant's benefit was calculated for the purposes of the last such confiscation order;

(b)   the second assumption does not apply to any property which was held by him on or before the relevant day.

(10)   The date of conviction is—

(a)   the date on which the defendant was convicted of the offence concerned, or

(b)   if there are two or more offences and the convictions were on different dates, the date of the latest.

10A.   Determination of extent of defendant's interest in property

(1)   Where it appears to a court making a confiscation order that—

(a)   there is property held by the defendant that is likely to be realised or otherwise used to satisfy the order, and

(b)   a person other than the defendant holds, or may hold, an interest in the property, the court may, if it thinks it appropriate to do so, determine the extent (at the time the confiscation order is made) of the defendant's interest in the property.

(2)   The court must not exercise the power conferred by subsection (1) unless it gives to anyone who the court thinks is or may be a person holding an interest in the property a reasonable opportunity to make representations to it.

(3)   A determination under this section is conclusive in relation to any question as to the extent of the defendant's interest in the property that arises in connection with—

(a)   the realisation of the property, or the transfer of an interest in the property, with a view to satisfying the confiscation order, or

(b)   any action or proceedings taken for the purposes of any such realisation or transfer.

(4)   Subsection (3)—

(a)   is subject to section 51(8B), and

(b)   does not apply in relation to a question that arises in proceedings before the Court of Appeal or the Supreme Court.

(5)   In this Part, the 'extent' of the defendant's interest in property means the proportion that the value of the defendant's interest in it bears to the value of the property itself.

11.   Time for payment

(1)   The amount ordered to be paid under a confiscation order must be paid on the making of the order; but this is subject to the following provisions of this section.

(2)   If the defendant shows that he needs time to pay the amount ordered to be paid, the court making the confiscation order may make an order allowing payment to be made in a specified period.

(3)   The specified period—

(a)   must start with the day on which the confiscation order is made, and

(b)   must not exceed three months.

(4)   If—

(a)   within any specified period the defendant applies to the Crown Court for that period to be extended, and

(b)   the court is satisfied that, despite having made all reasonable efforts, the defendant is unable to pay the amount to which the specified period relates within that period,

the court may make an order extending the period (for all or any part or parts of the amount in question).

(5)   The extended period—

(a)   must start with the day on which the confiscation order is made, and

(b)   must not exceed six months.

(6)   An order under subsection (4)—

(a)   may be made after the end of the specified period, but

(b)   must not be made after the end of the period of six months starting with the day on which the confiscation order is made.

(7)   Periods specified or extended under this section must be such that, where the court believes that a defendant will by a particular day be able—

   (a)   to pay the amount remaining to be paid, or

   (b)   to pay an amount towards what remains to be paid,

that amount is required to be paid no later than that day.

(8)   The court must not make an order under subsection (2) or (4) unless it gives the prosecutor an opportunity to make representations.

12. Interest on unpaid sums

(1)   If the amount required to be paid by a person under a confiscation order is not paid when it is required to be paid, he must pay interest on the amount for the period for which it remains unpaid.

(2)   The rate of interest is the same rate as that for the time being specified in section 17 of the Judgments Act 1838 (interest on civil judgment debts).

(3)   If—

   (a)   an application has been made under section 11(4) for a specified period to be extended,

   (b)   the application has not been determined by the court, and

   (c)   the period of six months starting with the day on which the confiscation order was made has not ended,

the amount on which interest is payable under this section does not include the amount to which the specified period relates.

(4)   In applying this Part the amount of the interest must be treated as part of the amount to be paid under the confiscation order.

13. Effect of order on court's other powers

(1)   If the court makes a confiscation order it must proceed as mentioned in subsections (2) and (4) in respect of the offence or offences concerned.

(2)   The court must take account of the confiscation order before—

   (a)   it imposes a fine on the defendant, or

   (b)   it makes an order falling within subsection (3).

(3)   These orders fall within this subsection—

   (a)   an order involving payment by the defendant, other than an order under section 21A of the Prosecution of Offences Act 1985 (criminal courts charge) or a priority order;

   (b)   an order under section 27 of the Misuse of Drugs Act 1971 (forfeiture orders);

   (c)   an order under section 143 of the Sentencing Act (deprivation orders);

   (d)   an order under section 23 or 23A of the Terrorism Act 2000 (forfeiture orders).

(3A) In this section 'priority order' means any of the following—

   (a)   a compensation order under section 130 of the Sentencing Act;

   (b)   an order requiring payment of a surcharge under section 161A of the Criminal Justice Act 2003;

   (c)   an unlawful profit order under section 4 of the Prevention of Social Housing Fraud Act 2013;

   (d)   a slavery and trafficking reparation order under section 8 of the Modern Slavery Act 2015.

(4)   Subject to subsection (2), the court must leave the confiscation order out of account in deciding the appropriate sentence for the defendant.

(5)   Subsection (6) applies if—

   (a)   the Crown Court makes both a confiscation order and an order for the payment of compensation under section 130 of the Sentencing Act against the same person in the same proceedings, and

   (b)   the court believes he will not have sufficient means to satisfy both the orders in full.

(6)   In such a case the court must direct that so much of the amount payable under the priority order (or orders) as it specifies is to be paid out of any sums recovered under the confiscation order; and the amount it specifies must be the amount it believes will not be recoverable because of the insufficiency of the person's means.

13A. Orders for securing compliance with confiscation order

(1) This section applies where the court makes a confiscation order.

(2) The court may make such order as it believes is appropriate for the purpose of ensuring that the confiscation order is effective (a 'compliance order').

(3) The court must consider whether to make a compliance order—

    (a) on the making of the confiscation order, and

    (b) if it does not make a compliance order then, at any later time (while the confiscation order is still in effect) on the application of the prosecutor.

(4) In considering whether to make a compliance order, the court must, in particular, consider whether any restriction or prohibition on the defendant's travel outside the United Kingdom ought to be imposed for the purpose mentioned in subsection (2).

(5) The court may discharge or vary a compliance order on an application made by—

    (a) the prosecutor;

    (b) any person affected by the order.

14. Postponement

(1) The court may—

    (a) proceed under section 6 before it sentences the defendant for the offence (or any of the offences) concerned, or

    (b) postpone proceedings under section 6 for a specified period.

(2) A period of postponement may be extended.

(3) A period of postponement (including one as extended) must not end after the permitted period ends.

(4) But subsection (3) does not apply if there are exceptional circumstances.

(5) The permitted period is the period of two years starting with the date of conviction.

(6) But if—

    (a) the defendant appeals against his conviction for the offence (or any of the offences) concerned, and

    (b) the period of three months (starting with the day when the appeal is determined or otherwise disposed of) ends after the period found under subsection (5),

    the permitted period is that period of three months.

(7) A postponement or extension may be made—

    (a) on application by the defendant;

    (b) on application by the prosecutor;

    (c) by the court of its own motion.

(8) If—

    (a) proceedings are postponed for a period, and

    (b) an application to extend the period is made before it ends, the application may be granted even after the period ends.

(9) The date of conviction is—

    (a) the date on which the defendant was convicted of the offence concerned, or

    (b) if there are two or more offences and the convictions were on different dates, the date of the latest.

(10) References to appealing include references to applying under section 111 of the Magistrates' Courts Act 1980 (statement of case).

(11) A confiscation order must not be quashed only on the ground that there was a defect or omission in the procedure connected with the application for or the granting of a postponement.

(12) But subsection (11) does not apply if before it made the confiscation order the court—

    (a) imposed a fine on the defendant;

    (b) made an order falling within section 13(3);

    (c) made an order under section 130 of the Sentencing Act (compensation orders).

    (ca) made an order under section 161A of the Criminal Justice Act 2003 (orders requiring payment of surcharge);

    (d) made an order under section 4 of the Prevention of Social Housing Fraud Act 2013 (unlawful profit orders).

15.   Effect of postponement

(1)   If the court postpones proceedings under section 6 it may proceed to sentence the defendant for the offence (or any of the offences) concerned.

(2)   In sentencing the defendant for the offence (or any of the offences) concerned in the postponement period the court must not—

    (a)   impose a fine on him,

    (b)   make an order falling within section 13(3), or

    (c)   make an order for the payment of compensation under section 130 of the Sentencing Act,

    (ca)   make an order for the payment of a surcharge under section 161A of the Criminal Justice Act 2003, or

    (d)   make an unlawful profit order under section 4 of the Prevention of Social Housing Fraud Act 2013.

(3)   If the court sentences the defendant for the offence (or any of the offences) concerned in the postponement period, after that period ends it may vary the sentence by—

    (a)   imposing a fine on him,

    (b)   making an order falling within section 13(3), or

    (c)   making an order for the payment of compensation under section 130 of the Sentencing Act.

    (ca)   making an order for the payment of a surcharge under section 161A of the Criminal Justice Act 2003, or

    (d)   making an unlawful profit order under section 4 of the Prevention of Social Housing Fraud Act 2013.

(4)   But the court may proceed under subsection (3) only within the period of 28 days which starts with the last day of the postponement period.

(5)   For the purposes of—

    (a)   section 18(2) of the Criminal Appeal Act 1968 (time limit for notice of appeal or of application for leave to appeal), and

    (b)   paragraph 1 of Schedule 3 to the Criminal Justice Act 1988 (time limit for notice of application for leave to refer a case under section 36 of that Act),

the sentence must be regarded as imposed or made on the day on which it is varied under subsection (3).

(6)   If the court proceeds to sentence the defendant under subsection (1), section 6 has effect as if the defendant's particular criminal conduct included conduct which constitutes offences which the court has taken into consideration in deciding his sentence for the offence or offences concerned.

(7)   The postponement period is the period for which proceedings under section 6 are postponed.

16.   Statement of information

(1)   If the court is proceeding under section 6 in a case where section 6(3)(a) applies, the prosecutor must give the court a statement of information within the period the court orders.

(2)   If the court is proceeding under section 6 in a case where section 6(3)(b) applies and it orders the prosecutor to give it a statement of information, the prosecutor must give it such a statement within the period the court orders.

(3)   If the prosecutor believes the defendant has a criminal lifestyle the statement of information is a statement of matters the prosecutor believes are relevant in connection with deciding these issues—

    (a)   whether the defendant has a criminal lifestyle;

    (b)   whether he has benefited from his general criminal conduct;

    (c)   his benefit from the conduct.

(4)   A statement under subsection (3) must include information the prosecutor believes is relevant—

    (a)   in connection with the making by the court of a required assumption under section 10;

    (b)   for the purpose of enabling the court to decide if the circumstances are such that it must not make such an assumption.

(5)   If the prosecutor does not believe the defendant has a criminal lifestyle the statement of information is a statement of matters the prosecutor believes are relevant in connection with deciding these issues—

     (a)   whether the defendant has benefited from his particular criminal conduct;

     (b)   his benefit from the conduct.

(6)   If the prosecutor gives the court a statement of information—

     (a)   he may at any time give the court a further statement of information;

     (b)   he must give the court a further statement of information if it orders him to do so, and he must give it within the period the court orders.

(6A)   A statement of information (other than one to which subsection (6B) applies) must include any information known to the prosecutor which the prosecutor believes is or would be relevant for the purpose of enabling the court to decide—

     (a)   whether to make a determination under section 10A, or

     (b)   what determination to make (if the court decides to make one).

(6B)   If the court has decided to make a determination under section 10A, a further statement of information under subsection (6)(b) must, if the court so orders, include specified information that is relevant to the determination.

(7)   If the court makes an order under this section it may at any time vary it by making another one.

17.   Defendant's response to statement of information

(1)   If the prosecutor gives the court a statement of information and a copy is served on the defendant, the court may order the defendant—

     (a)   to indicate (within the period it orders) the extent to which he accepts each allegation in the statement, and

     (b)   so far as he does not accept such an allegation, to give particulars of any matters he proposes to rely on.

(2)   If the defendant accepts to any extent an allegation in a statement of information the court may treat his acceptance as conclusive of the matters to which it relates for the purpose of deciding the issues referred to in section 16(3) or (5) (as the case may be).

(3)   If the defendant fails in any respect to comply with an order under subsection (1) he may be treated for the purposes of subsection (2) as accepting every allegation in the statement of information apart from—

     (a)   any allegation in respect of which he has complied with the requirement;

     (b)   any allegation that he has benefited from his general or particular criminal conduct.

(4)   For the purposes of this section an allegation may be accepted or particulars may be given in a manner ordered by the court.

(5)   If the court makes an order under this section it may at any time vary it by making another one.

(6)   No acceptance under this section that the defendant has benefited from conduct is admissible in evidence in proceedings for an offence.

18.   Provision of information by defendant

(1)   This section applies if—

     (a)   the court is proceeding under section 6 in a case where section 6(3)(a) applies, or

     (b)   it is proceeding under section 6 in a case where section 6(3)(b) applies or it is considering whether to proceed.

(2)   For the purpose of obtaining information to help it in carrying out its functions (including functions under section 10A) the court may at any time order the defendant to give it information specified in the order.

(3)   An order under this section may require all or a specified part of the information to be given in a specified manner and before a specified date.

(4)   If the defendant fails without reasonable excuse to comply with an order under this section the court may draw such inference as it believes is appropriate.

(5)   Subsection (4) does not affect any power of the court to deal with the defendant in respect of a failure to comply with an order under this section.

(6)   If the prosecutor accepts to any extent an allegation made by the defendant—

(a)   in giving information required by an order under this section, or

(b)   in any other statement given to the court in relation to any matter relevant to deciding—

    (i)   the available amount under section 9, or

    (ii)   whether to make a determination under section 10A, or what determination to make (if the court decides to make one),

the court may treat the acceptance as conclusive of the matters to which it relates.

(7)   For the purposes of this section an allegation may be accepted in a manner ordered by the court.

(8)   If the court makes an order under this section it may at any time vary it by making another one.

(9)   No information given under this section which amounts to an admission by the defendant that he has benefited from criminal conduct is admissible in evidence in proceedings for an offence.

18A. Provision of information as to defendant's interest in property

(1)   This section applies if the court—

(a)   is considering whether to make a determination under section 10A of the extent of the defendant's interest in any property, or

(b)   is deciding what determination to make (if the court has decided to make a determination under that section).

In this section 'interested person' means a person (other than the defendant) who the court thinks is or may be a person holding an interest in the property.

(2)   For the purpose of obtaining information to help it in carrying out its functions under section 10A the court may at any time order an interested person to give it information specified in the order.

(3)   An order under this section may require all or a specified part of the information to be given in a specified manner and before a specified date.

(4)   If an interested person fails without reasonable excuse to comply with an order under this section the court may draw such inference as it believes is appropriate.

(5)   Subsection (4) does not affect any power of the court to deal with the person in respect of a failure to comply with an order under this section.

(6)   If the prosecutor accepts to any extent an allegation made by an interested person—

(a)   in giving information required by an order under this section, or

(b)   in any other statement given to the court in relation to any matter relevant to a determination under section 10A,

the court may treat the acceptance as conclusive of the matters to which it relates.

(7)   For the purposes of this section an allegation may be accepted in a manner ordered by the court.

(8)   If the court makes an order under this section it may at any time vary it by making another one.

(9)   No information given by a person under this section is admissible in evidence in proceedings against that person for an offence.

19. No order made: reconsideration of case

(1)   This section applies if—

(a)   the first condition in section 6 is satisfied but no court has proceeded under that section,

(b)   there is evidence which was not available to the prosecutor on the relevant date,

(c)   before the end of the period of six years starting with the date of conviction the prosecutor applies to the Crown Court to consider the evidence, and

(d)   after considering the evidence the court believes it is appropriate for it to proceed under section 6.

(2)   If this section applies the court must proceed under section 6, and when it does so subsections (3) to (8) below apply.

(3)   If the court has already sentenced the defendant for the offence (or any of the offences) concerned, section 6 has effect as if his particular criminal conduct included conduct which constitutes offences which the court has taken into consideration in deciding his sentence for the offence or offences concerned.

(4)   Section 8(2) does not apply, and the rules applying instead are that the court must—
    (a)   take account of conduct occurring before the relevant date;
    (b)   take account of property obtained before that date;
    (c)   take account of property obtained on or after that date if it was obtained as a result of or in connection with conduct occurring before that date.

(5)   In section 10—
    (a)   the first and second assumptions do not apply with regard to property first held by the defendant on or after the relevant date;
    (b)   the third assumption does not apply with regard to expenditure incurred by him on or after that date;
    (c)   the fourth assumption does not apply with regard to property obtained (or assumed to have been obtained) by him on or after that date.

(6)   The recoverable amount for the purposes of section 6 is such amount as—
    (a)   the court believes is just, but
    (b)   does not exceed the amount found under section 7.

(7)   In arriving at the just amount the court must have regard in particular to—
    (a)   the amount found under section 7;
    (b)   any fine imposed on the defendant in respect of the offence (or any of the offences) concerned;
    (c)   any order which falls within section 13(3) and has been made against him in respect of the offence (or any of the offences) concerned and has not already been taken into account by the court in deciding what is the free property held by him for the purposes of section 9;
    (d)   any order which has been made against him in respect of the offence (or any of the offences) concerned under section 130 of the Sentencing Act (compensation orders).
    (da)   any order which has been made against the defendant in respect of the offence (or any of the offences) concerned under section 161A of the Criminal Justice Act 2003 (orders requiring payment of surcharge);
    (e)   any order which has been made against the defendant in respect of the offence (or any of the offences) concerned under section 4 of the Prevention of Social Housing Fraud Act 2013 (unlawful profit orders).

(8)   If an order for the payment of compensation under section 130 of the Sentencing Act, a surcharge under section 161A of the Criminal Justice Act 2003 or an unlawful profit order under section 4 of the Prevention of Social Housing Fraud Act 2013 has been made against the defendant in respect of the offence or offences concerned, section 13(5) and (6) above do not apply in relation to it.

(9)   The relevant date is—
    (a)   if the court made a decision not to proceed under section 6, the date of the decision;
    (b)   if the court did not make such a decision, the date of conviction.

(10)   The date of conviction is—
    (a)   the date on which the defendant was convicted of the offence concerned, or
    (b)   if there are two or more offences and the convictions were on different dates, the date of the latest.

20.   No order made: reconsideration of benefit

(1)   This section applies if the following two conditions are satisfied.

(2)   The first condition is that in proceeding under section 6 the court has decided that—
    (a)   the defendant has a criminal lifestyle but has not benefited from his general criminal conduct, or
    (b)   the defendant does not have a criminal lifestyle and has not benefited from his particular criminal conduct.

(3)   ...

(4)   The second condition is that—
    (a)   there is evidence which was not available to the prosecutor when the court decided that the defendant had not benefited from his general or particular criminal conduct,
    (b)   before the end of the period of six years starting with the date of conviction the prosecutor applies to the Crown Court to consider the evidence, and

(c)   after considering the evidence the court concludes that it would have decided that the defendant had benefited from his general or particular criminal conduct (as the case may be) if the evidence had been available to it.

(5)   If this section applies the court—

    (a)   must make a fresh decision under section 6(4)(b) or (c) whether the defendant has benefited from his general or particular criminal conduct (as the case may be);

    (b)   may make a confiscation order under that section.

(6)   Subsections (7) to (12) below apply if the court proceeds under section 6 in pursuance of this section.

(7)   If the court has already sentenced the defendant for the offence (or any of the offences) concerned, section 6 has effect as if his particular criminal conduct included conduct which constitutes offences which the court has taken into consideration in deciding his sentence for the offence or offences concerned.

(8)   Section 8(2) does not apply, and the rules applying instead are that the court must—

    (a)   take account of conduct occurring before the date of the original decision that the defendant had not benefited from his general or particular criminal conduct;

    (b)   take account of property obtained before that date;

    (c)   take account of property obtained on or after that date if it was obtained as a result of or in connection with conduct occurring before that date.

(9)   In section 10—

    (a)   the first and second assumptions do not apply with regard to property first held by the defendant on or after the date of the original decision that the defendant had not benefited from his general or particular criminal conduct;

    (b)   the third assumption does not apply with regard to expenditure incurred by him on or after that date;

    (c)   the fourth assumption does not apply with regard to property obtained (or assumed to have been obtained) by him on or after that date.

(10)   The recoverable amount for the purposes of section 6 is such amount as—

    (a)   the court believes is just, but

    (b)   does not exceed the amount found under section 7.

(11)   In arriving at the just amount the court must have regard in particular to—

    (a)   the amount found under section 7;

    (b)   any fine imposed on the defendant in respect of the offence (or any of the offences) concerned;

    (c)   any order which falls within section 13(3) and has been made against him in respect of the offence (or any of the offences) concerned and has not already been taken into account by the court in deciding what is the free property held by him for the purposes of section 9;

    (d)   any order which has been made against him in respect of the offence (or any of the offences) concerned under section 130 of the Sentencing Act (compensation orders);

    (da)   any order which has been made against the defendant in respect of the offence (or any of the offences) concerned under section 161A of the Criminal Justice Act 2003 (orders requiring payment of surcharge);

    (e)   any order which has been made against the defendant in respect of the offence (or any of the offences) concerned under section 4 of the Prevention of Social Housing Fraud Act 2013 (unlawful profit orders).

(12)   If an order for the payment of compensation under section 130 of the Sentencing Act, a surcharge under section 161A of the Criminal Justice Act 2003 or an unlawful profit order under section 4 of the Prevention of Social Housing Fraud Act 2013 has been made against the defendant in respect of the offence or offences concerned, section 13(5) and (6) above do not apply in relation to it.

(13)   The date of conviction is the date found by applying section 19(10).

21.   Order made: reconsideration of benefit

(1)   This section applies if—

    (a)   a court has made a confiscation order,

    (b)   there is evidence which was not available to the prosecutor or the Director at the relevant time,

    (c)   the prosecutor believes that if the court were to find the amount of the defendant's benefit in pursuance of this section it would exceed the relevant amount,

    (d)   before the end of the period of six years starting with the date of conviction the prosecutor applies to the Crown Court to consider the evidence, and

    (e)   after considering the evidence the court believes it is appropriate for it to proceed under this section.

(2)   The court must make a new calculation of the defendant's benefit from the conduct concerned, and when it does so subsections (3) to (6) below apply.

(3)   If a court has already sentenced the defendant for the offence (or any of the offences) concerned section 6 has effect as if his particular criminal conduct included conduct which constitutes offences which the court has taken into consideration in deciding his sentence for the offence or offences concerned.

(4)   Section 8(2) does not apply, and the rules applying instead are that the court must—

    (a)   take account of conduct occurring up to the time it decided the defendant's benefit for the purposes of the confiscation order;

    (b)   take account of property obtained up to that time;

    (c)   take account of property obtained after that time if it was obtained as a result of or in connection with conduct occurring before that time.

(5)   In applying section 8(5) the confiscation order must be ignored.

(6)   In section 10—

    (a)   the first and second assumptions do not apply with regard to property first held by the defendant after the time the court decided his benefit for the purposes of the confiscation order;

    (b)   the third assumption does not apply with regard to expenditure incurred by him after that time;

    (c)   the fourth assumption does not apply with regard to property obtained (or assumed to have been obtained) by him after that time.

(7)   If the amount found under the new calculation of the defendant's benefit exceeds the relevant amount the court—

    (a)   must make a new calculation of the recoverable amount for the purposes of section 6, and

    (b)   if it exceeds the amount required to be paid under the confiscation order, may vary the order by substituting for the amount required to be paid such amount as it believes is just.

(8)   In applying subsection (7)(a) the court must—

    (a)   take the new calculation of the defendant's benefit;

    (b)   apply section 9 as if references to the time the confiscation order is made were to the time of the new calculation of the recoverable amount and as if references to the date of the confiscation order were to the date of that new calculation.

(9)   In applying subsection (7)(b) the court must have regard in particular to—

    (a)   any fine imposed on the defendant for the offence (or any of the offences) concerned;

    (b)   any order which falls within section 13(3) and has been made against him in respect of the offence (or any of the offences) concerned and has not already been taken into account by the court in deciding what is the free property held by him for the purposes of section 9;

    (c)   any order which has been made against him in respect of the offence (or any of the offences) concerned under section 130 of the Sentencing Act (compensation orders);

    (ca)   any order which has been made against the defendant in respect of the offence (or any of the offences) concerned under section 161A of the Criminal Justice Act 2003 (orders requiring payment of surcharge);

    (d)   any order which has been made against the defendant in respect of the offence (or any of the offences) concerned under section 4 of the Prevention of Social Housing Fraud Act 2013 (unlawful profit orders).

(10)   But in applying subsection (7)(b) the court must not have regard to an order falling within subsection (9)(c), (ca) or (d) if a court has made a direction under section 13(6).

(11)   In deciding under this section whether one amount exceeds another the court must take account of any change in the value of money.

(12) The relevant time is—
- (a) when the court calculated the defendant's benefit for the purposes of the confiscation order, if this section has not applied previously;
- (b) when the court last calculated the defendant's benefit in pursuance of this section, if this section has applied previously.

(13) The relevant amount is—
- (a) the amount found as the defendant's benefit for the purposes of the confiscation order, if this section has not applied previously;
- (b) the amount last found as the defendant's benefit in pursuance of this section, if this section has applied previously.

(14) The date of conviction is the date found by applying section 19(10).

22. Order made: reconsideration of available amount

(1) This section applies if—
- (a) a court has made a confiscation order,
- (b) the amount required to be paid was the amount found under section 7(2), and
- (c) an applicant falling within subsection (2) applies to the Crown Court to make a new calculation of the available amount.

(2) These applicants fall within this subsection—
- (a) the prosecutor;
- (b) ...
- (c) a receiver appointed under section 50.

(3) In a case where this section applies the court must make the new calculation, and in doing so it must apply section 9 as if references to the time the confiscation order is made were to the time of the new calculation and as if references to the date of the confiscation order were to the date of the new calculation.

(4) If the amount found under the new calculation exceeds the relevant amount the court may vary the order by substituting for the amount required to be paid such amount as—
- (a) it believes is just, but
- (b) does not exceed the amount found as the defendant's benefit from the conduct concerned.

(5) In deciding what is just the court must have regard in particular to—
- (a) any fine imposed on the defendant for the offence (or any of the offences) concerned;
- (b) any order which falls within section 13(3) and has been made against him in respect of the offence (or any of the offences) concerned and has not already been taken into account by the court in deciding what is the free property held by him for the purposes of section 9;
- (c) any order which has been made against him in respect of the offence (or any of the offences) concerned under section 130 of the Sentencing Act (compensation orders);
- (d) any order which has been made against the defendant in respect of the offence (or any of the offences) concerned under section 161A of the Criminal Justice Act 2003 (orders requiring payment of surcharge).

(6) But in deciding what is just the court must not have regard to an order falling within subsection (5)(c) or (d) if a court has made a direction under section 13(6).

(7) In deciding under this section whether one amount exceeds another the court must take account of any change in the value of money.

(8) The relevant amount is—
- (a) the amount found as the available amount for the purposes of the confiscation order, if this section has not applied previously;
- (b) the amount last found as the available amount in pursuance of this section, if this section has applied previously.

(9) The amount found as the defendant's benefit from the conduct concerned is—
- (a) the amount so found when the confiscation order was made, or
- (b) if one or more new calculations of the defendant's benefit have been made under section 21 the amount found on the occasion of the last such calculation.

23.   Inadequacy of available amount: variation of order

(1)   This section applies if—

     (a)   a court has made a confiscation order, and

     (b)   the defendant, or the prosecutor or a receiver appointed under section 50, applies to the Crown Court to vary the order under this section.

(2)   In such a case the court must calculate the available amount, and in doing so it must apply section 9 as if references to the time the confiscation order is made were to the time of the calculation and as if references to the date of the confiscation order were to the date of the calculation.

(3)   If the court finds that the available amount (as so calculated) is inadequate for the payment of any amount remaining to be paid under the confiscation order it may vary the order by substituting for the amount required to be paid such smaller amount as the court believes is just.

(4)   If a person has been made bankrupt or his estate has been sequestrated, or if an order for the winding up of a company has been made, the court must take into account the extent to which realisable property held by that person or that company may be distributed among creditors.

(5)   The court may disregard any inadequacy which it believes is attributable (wholly or partly) to anything done by the defendant for the purpose of preserving property held by the recipient of a tainted gift from any risk of realisation under this Part.

(6)   In subsection (4) 'company' means any company which may be wound up under the Insolvency Act 1986 or the Insolvency (Northern Ireland) Order 1989.

24.   Inadequacy of available amount: discharge of order

(1)   This section applies if—

     (a)   a court has made a confiscation order,

     (b)   the designated officer for a magistrates' court applies to the Crown Court for the discharge of the order, and

     (c)   the amount remaining to be paid under the order is less than £1,000.

(2)   In such a case the court must calculate the available amount, and in doing so it must apply section 9 as if references to the time the confiscation order is made were to the time of the calculation and as if references to the date of the confiscation order were to the date of the calculation.

(3)   If the court—

     (a)   finds that the available amount (as so calculated) is inadequate to meet the amount remaining to be paid, and

     (b)   is satisfied that the inadequacy is due wholly to a specified reason or a combination of specified reasons,

     it may discharge the confiscation order.

(4)   The specified reasons are—

     (a)   in a case where any of the realisable property consists of money in a currency other than sterling, that fluctuations in currency exchange rates have occurred;

     (b)   any reason specified by the Secretary of State by order.

(5)   The Secretary of State may by order vary the amount for the time being specified in subsection (1)(c).

(6)   The discharge of a confiscation order under this section does not prevent the making of an application in respect of the order under section 21(1)(d) or 22(1)(c).

(7)   Where on such an application the court determines that the order should be varied under section 21(7) or (as the case may be) 22(4), the court may provide that its discharge under this section is revoked.

25.   Small amount outstanding: discharge of order

(1)   This section applies if—

     (a)   a court has made a confiscation order,

     (b)   the designated officer for a magistrates' court applies to the Crown Court for the discharge of the order, and

     (c)   the amount remaining to be paid under the order is £50 or less.

(2)   In such a case the court may discharge the order.

(3)   The Secretary of State may by order vary the amount for the time being specified in subsection (1)(c).

(4)   The discharge of a confiscation order under this section does not prevent the making of an application in respect of the order under section 21(1)(d) or 22(1)(c).

(5)   Where on such an application the court determines that the order should be varied under section 21(7) or (as the case may be) 22(4), the court may provide that its discharge under this section is revoked.

25A. Recovery from estate of deceased defendant impractical: discharge of order

(1)   This section applies if—

    (a)   a court has made a confiscation order,

    (b)   the defendant dies while the order is not satisfied, and

    (c)   the designated officer for a magistrates' court applies to the Crown Court for the discharge of the order.

(2)   The court may discharge the order if it appears to the court that—

    (a)   it is not possible to recover anything from the estate of the deceased for the purpose of satisfying the order to any extent, or

    (b)   it would not be reasonable to make any attempt, or further attempt, to recover anything from the estate of the deceased for that purpose.

26. Information

(1)   This section applies if—

    (a)   the court proceeds under section 6 in pursuance of section 19 or 20, or

    (b)   the prosecutor applies under section 21.

(2)   In such a case—

    (a)   the prosecutor must give the court a statement of information within the period the court orders;

    (b)   section 16 applies accordingly (with appropriate modifications where the prosecutor applies under section 21);

    (c)   section 17 applies accordingly;

    (d)   section 18 applies as it applies in the circumstances mentioned in section 18(1).

31. Appeal by prosecutor

(1)   If the Crown Court makes a confiscation order the prosecutor may appeal to the Court of Appeal in respect of the order.

(2)   If the Crown Court decides not to make a confiscation order the prosecutor may appeal to the Court of Appeal against the decision.

(3)   Subsections (1) and (2) do not apply to an order or decision made by virtue of section 10A, 19, 20, 27 or 28.

(4)   An appeal lies to the Court of Appeal against a determination, under section 10A, of the extent of the defendant's interest in property.

(5)   An appeal under subsection (4) lies at the instance of—

    (a)   the prosecutor;

    (b)   a person who the Court of Appeal thinks is or may be a person holding an interest in the property, if subsection (6) or (7) applies.

(6)   This subsection applies if the person was not given a reasonable opportunity to make representations when the determination was made.

(7)   This subsection applies if it appears to the Court of Appeal to be arguable that giving effect to the determination would result in a serious risk of injustice to the person.

(8)   An appeal does not lie under subsection (4) where—

    (a)   the Court of Appeal believes that an application under section 50 is to be made by the prosecutor for the appointment of a receiver,

    (b)   such an application has been made but has not yet been determined, or

    (c)   a receiver has been appointed under section 50.

32. Court's powers on appeal

(1) On an appeal under section 31(1) the Court of Appeal may confirm, quash or vary the confiscation order.

(2) On an appeal under section 31(2) the Court of Appeal may confirm the decision, or if it believes the decision was wrong it may—

    (a) itself proceed under section 6 (ignoring subsections (1) to (3)), or

    (b) direct the Crown Court to proceed afresh under section 6.

(2A) On an appeal under section 31(4) the Court of Appeal may—

    (a) confirm the determination, or

    (b) make such order as it believes is appropriate.

(3) In proceeding afresh in pursuance of this section the Crown Court must comply with any directions the Court of Appeal may make.

(4) If a court makes or varies a confiscation order under this section or in pursuance of a direction under this section it must—

    (a) have regard to any fine imposed on the defendant in respect of the offence (or any of the offences) concerned;

    (b) have regard to any order which falls within section 13(3) and has been made against him in respect of the offence (or any of the offences) concerned, unless the order has already been taken into account by a court in deciding what is the free property held by the defendant for the purposes of section 9.

(5) If the Court of Appeal proceeds under section 6 or the Crown Court proceeds afresh under that section in pursuance of a direction under this section subsections (6) to (10) apply.

(6) If a court has already sentenced the defendant for the offence (or any of the offences) concerned, section 6 has effect as if his particular criminal conduct included conduct which constitutes offences which the court has taken into consideration in deciding his sentence for the offence or offences concerned.

(7) If an order has been made against the defendant in respect of the offence (or any of the offences) concerned under section 130 of the Sentencing Act (compensation orders), section 161A of the Criminal Justice Act 2003 (orders requiring payment of surcharge) or section 4 of the Prevention of Social Housing Fraud Act (unlawful profit orders)—

    (a) the court must have regard to it, and

    (b) section 13(5) and (6) above do not apply in relation to it .

(8) Section 8(2) does not apply, and the rules applying instead are that the court must—

    (a) take account of conduct occurring before the relevant date;

    (b) take account of property obtained before that date;

    (c) take account of property obtained on or after that date if it was obtained as a result of or in connection with conduct occurring before that date.

(9) In section 10—

    (a) the first and second assumptions do not apply with regard to property first held by the defendant on or after the relevant date;

    (b) the third assumption does not apply with regard to expenditure incurred by him on or after that date;

    (c) the fourth assumption does not apply with regard to property obtained (or assumed to have been obtained) by him on or after that date.

(10) Section 26 applies as it applies in the circumstances mentioned in subsection (1) of that section.

(11) The relevant date is the date on which the Crown Court decided not to make a confiscation order.

33. Appeal to Supreme Court

(1) An appeal lies to the Supreme Court from a decision of the Court of Appeal on an appeal under section 31.

(2) An appeal under this section lies at the instance of—

    (a) the defendant or the prosecutor (except where paragraph (b) applies);

    (b) if the proceedings in the Court of Appeal were proceedings on an appeal under section 31(4), any person who was a party to those proceedings.

(3) On an appeal from a decision of the Court of Appeal to confirm, vary or make a confiscation order the Supreme Court may confirm, quash or vary the order.

(3A) On an appeal under this section from a decision under section 32(2A) the Supreme Court may—
    (a)   confirm the decision of the Court of Appeal, or
    (b)   make such order as it believes is appropriate.

(4) On an appeal from a decision of the Court of Appeal to confirm the decision of the Crown Court not to make a confiscation order or from a decision of the Court of Appeal to quash a confiscation order the Supreme Court may—
    (a)   confirm the decision, or
    (b)   direct the Crown Court to proceed afresh under section 6 if it believes the decision was wrong.

(5) In proceeding afresh in pursuance of this section the Crown Court must comply with any directions the Supreme Court may make.

(6) If a court varies a confiscation order under this section or makes a confiscation order in pursuance of a direction under this section it must—
    (a)   have regard to any fine imposed on the defendant in respect of the offence (or any of the offences) concerned;
    (b)   have regard to any order which falls within section 13(3) and has been made against him in respect of the offence (or any of the offences) concerned, unless the order has already been taken into account by a court in deciding what is the free property held by the defendant for the purposes of section 9.

(7) If the Crown Court proceeds afresh under section 6 in pursuance of a direction under this section subsections (8) to (12) apply.

(8) If a court has already sentenced the defendant for the offence (or any of the offences) concerned, section 6 has effect as if his particular criminal conduct included conduct which constitutes offences which the court has taken into consideration in deciding his sentence for the offence or offences concerned.

(9) If an order has been made against the defendant in respect of the offence (or any of the offences) concerned under section 130 of the Sentencing Act (compensation orders), section 161A of the Criminal Justice Act 2003 (orders requiring payment of surcharge) or section 4 of the Prevention of Social Housing Fraud Act 2013 (unlawful profit orders)—
    (a)   the Crown Court must have regard to it, and
    (b)   sections 13(5) and (6) above do not apply in relation to it.

(10) Section 8(2) does not apply, and the rules applying instead are that the Crown Court must—
    (a)   take account of conduct occurring before the relevant date;
    (b)   take account of property obtained before that date;
    (c)   take account of property obtained on or after that date if it was obtained as a result of or in connection with conduct occurring before that date.

(11) In section 10—
    (a)   the first and second assumptions do not apply with regard to property first held by the defendant on or after the relevant date;
    (b)   the third assumption does not apply with regard to expenditure incurred by him on or after that date;
    (c)   the fourth assumption does not apply with regard to property obtained (or assumed to have been obtained) by him on or after that date.

(12) Section 26 applies as it applies in the circumstances mentioned in subsection (1) of that section.

(13) The relevant date is—
    (a)   in a case where the Crown Court made a confiscation order which was quashed by the Court of Appeal, the date on which the Crown Court made the order;
    (b)   in any other case, the date on which the Crown Court decided not to make a confiscation order.

362A. Unexplained wealth orders

(1) The High Court may, on an application made by an enforcement authority, make an unexplained wealth order in respect of any property if the court is satisfied that each of the requirements for the making of the order is fulfilled.

(2)   An application for an order must—
    (a)   specify or describe the property in respect of which the order is sought, and
    (b)   specify the person whom the enforcement authority thinks holds the property ('the respondent') (and the person specified may include a person outside the United Kingdom).

(3)   An unexplained wealth order is an order requiring the respondent to provide a statement—
    (a)   setting out the nature and extent of the respondent's interest in the property in respect of which the order is made,
    (b)   explaining how the respondent obtained the property (including, in particular, how any costs incurred in obtaining it were met),
    (c)   where the property is held by the trustees of a settlement, setting out such details of the settlement as may be specified in the order, and
    (d)   setting out such other information in connection with the property as may be so specified.

(4)   The order must specify—
    (a)   the form and manner in which the statement is to be given,
    (b)   the person to whom it is to be given, and
    (c)   the place at which it is to be given or, if it is to be given in writing, the address to which it is to be sent.

(5)   The order may, in connection with requiring the respondent to provide the statement mentioned in subsection (3), also require the respondent to produce documents of a kind specified or described in the order.

(6)   The respondent must comply with the requirements imposed by an unexplained wealth order within whatever period the court may specify (and different periods may be specified in relation to different requirements).

(7) In this Chapter '*enforcement authority*' means—
    (a)   the National Crime Agency,
    (b)   Her Majesty's Revenue and Customs,
    (c)   the Financial Conduct Authority,
    (d)   the Director of the Serious Fraud Office, or
    (e)   the Director of Public Prosecutions (in relation to England and Wales) or the Director of Public Prosecutions for Northern Ireland (in relation to Northern Ireland).

362B. Requirements for making of unexplained wealth order

(1)   These are the requirements for the making of an unexplained wealth order in respect of any property.

(2)   The High Court must be satisfied that there is reasonable cause to believe that—
    (a)   the respondent holds the property, and
    (b)   the value of the property is greater than £50,000.

(3)   The High Court must be satisfied that there are reasonable grounds for suspecting that the known sources of the respondent's lawfully obtained income would have been insufficient for the purposes of enabling the respondent to obtain the property.

(4)   The High Court must be satisfied that—
    (a)   the respondent is a politically exposed person, or
    (a)   there are reasonable grounds for suspecting that—
       (i)   the respondent is, or has been, involved in serious crime (whether in a part of the United Kingdom or elsewhere), or
       (ii)   a person connected with the respondent is, or has been, so involved.

(5)   It does not matter for the purposes of subsection (2)(a)—
    (a)   whether or not there are other persons who also hold the property;
    (b)   whether the property was obtained by the respondent before or after the coming into force of this section.

(6)   For the purposes of subsection (3)—
    (a)   regard is to be had to any mortgage, charge or other kind of security that it is reasonable to assume was or may have been available to the respondent for the purposes of obtaining the property;
    (b)   it is to be assumed that the respondent obtained the property for a price equivalent to its market value;

    (c)   income is 'lawfully obtained' if it is obtained lawfully under the laws of the country from where the income arises;

    (d)   'known' sources of the respondent's income are the sources of income (whether arising from employment, assets or otherwise) that are reasonably ascertainable from available information at the time of the making of the application for the order;

    (e)   where the property is an interest in other property comprised in a settlement, the reference to the respondent obtaining the property is to be taken as if it were a reference to the respondent obtaining direct ownership of such share in the settled property as relates to, or is fairly represented by, that interest.

(7)   In subsection (4)(a), *politically exposed person* means a person who is—

    (a)   an individual who is, or has been, entrusted with prominent public functions by an international organisation or by a State other than the United Kingdom or another EEA State,

    (b)   a family member of a person within paragraph (a),

    (c)   known to be a close associate of a person within that paragraph, or

    (d)   otherwise connected with a person within that paragraph.

(8)   Article 3 of Directive 2015/849/EU of the European Parliament and of the Council of 20 May 2015 applies for the purposes of determining—

    (a)   whether a person has been entrusted with prominent public functions (see point (9) of that Article),

    (b)   whether a person is a family member (see point (10) of that Article), and

    (c)   whether a person is known to be a close associate of another (see point (11) of that Article).

(9)   For the purposes of this section—

    (a)   a person is involved in serious crime in a part of the United Kingdom or elsewhere if the person would be so involved for the purposes of Part 1 of the Serious Crime Act 2007 (see in particular sections 2, 2A and 3 of that Act);

    (b)   section 1122 of the Corporation Tax Act 2010 ('connected' persons) applies in determining whether a person is connected with another.

(10)   Where the property in respect of which the order is sought comprises more than one item of property, the reference in subsection (2)(b) to the value of the property is to the total value of those items.

362E. Offence

(1)   A person commits an offence if, in purported compliance with a requirement imposed by an unexplained wealth order, the person—

    (a)   makes a statement that the person knows to be false or misleading in a material particular, or

    (b)   recklessly makes a statement that is false or misleading in a material particular.

(2)   A person guilty of an offence under this section is liable—

    (a)   on conviction on indictment, to imprisonment for a term not exceeding 2 years, or to a fine, or to both;

    (b)   on summary conviction in England and Wales, to imprisonment for a term not exceeding 12 months, or to a fine, or to both.

PROSECUTION OF OFFENCES ACT 1985
(1985, c. 23)

1.   The Crown Prosecution Service

(1)   There shall be a prosecuting service for England and Wales (to be known as the 'Crown Prosecution Service') consisting of—

    (a)   the Director of Public Prosecutions, who shall be head of the Service;

    (b)   the Chief Crown Prosecutors, designated under subsection (4) below, each of whom shall be the member of the Service responsible to the Director for supervising the operation of the Service in his area; and

    (c)   the other staff appointed by the Director under this section.

...

(3)   The Director may designate any member of the Service who has a general qualification (within the meaning of section 71 of the Courts and Legal Services Act 1990) for the purposes of this subsection, and any person so designated shall be known as a Crown Prosecutor.

...

(6)   Without prejudice to any functions which may have been assigned to him in his capacity as a member of the Service, every Crown Prosecutor shall have all the powers of the Director as to the institution and conduct of proceedings but shall exercise those powers under the direction of the Director.

(7)   Where any enactment (whenever passed)—

    (a)   prevents any step from being taken without the consent of the Director or without his consent or the consent of another; or

    (b)   requires any step to be taken by or in relation to the Director;

any consent given by or, as the case may be, taken by or in relation to, a Crown Prosecutor shall be treated, for the purposes of that enactment, as given by or, as the case may be, taken by or in relation to the Director.

3.   Functions of the Director

(1)   The Director shall discharge his functions under this or any other enactment under the superintendence of the Attorney General.

(2)   It shall be the duty of the Director, subject to any provisions contained in the Criminal Justice Act 1987—

    (a)   to take over the conduct of all criminal proceedings, other than specified proceedings, instituted on behalf of a police force (whether by a member of that force or by any other person);

    (aa) to take over the conduct of any criminal proceedings instituted by an immigration officer (as defined for the purposes of the Immigration Act 1971) acting in his capacity as such an officer;

    (ab) to take over the conduct of any criminal proceedings instituted in England and Wales by the Revenue and Customs;

    (ac) to take over the conduct of any criminal proceedings instituted on behalf of the National Crime Agency;

    (b)   to institute and have the conduct of criminal proceedings in any case where it appears to him that—

        (i)   the importance or difficulty of the case makes it appropriate that proceedings should be instituted by him; or

        (ii)   it is otherwise appropriate for proceedings to be instituted by him;

    (ba) to institute and have the conduct of any criminal proceedings in any case where the proceedings relate to the subject-matter of a report a copy of which has been sent to him under paragraph 23 or 24 of Schedule 3 to the Police Reform Act 2002 (reports on investigations into conduct of persons serving with the police);

    (bb) where it appears to him appropriate to do so, to institute and have the conduct of any criminal proceedings in England and Wales relating to a criminal investigation by the Revenue and Customs;

    (bc) where it appears to him appropriate to do so, to institute and have the conduct of any criminal proceedings relating to a criminal investigation by the National Crime Agency;

    (c)   to take over the conduct of all binding over proceedings instituted on behalf of a police force (whether by a member of that force or by any other person);

    (d)   to take over the conduct of all proceedings begun by summons issued under section 3 of the Obscene Publications Act 1959 (forfeiture of obscene articles);

    (e)   to give, to such extent as he considers appropriate, advice to police forces on all matters relating to criminal offences;

    (ea) to have the conduct of any extradition proceedings;

    (eb) to give, to such extent as he considers appropriate, and to such persons as he considers appropriate, advice on any matters relating to extradition proceedings or proposed extradition proceedings;

(ec) to give, to such extent as he considers appropriate, advice to immigration officers on matters relating to criminal offences;

(ed) to give advice, to such extent as he considers appropriate and to such person as he considers appropriate, in relation to—
    (i)   criminal investigations by the National Crime Agency, or
    (ii)   criminal proceedings arising out of such investigations;

(ee) to give, to such extent as he considers appropriate, and to such persons as he considers appropriate, advice on matters relating to—
    (i)   a criminal investigation by the Revenue and Customs; or
    (ii)   criminal proceedings instituted in England and Wales relating to a criminal investigation by the Revenue and Customs;

(f) to appear for the prosecution, when directed by the court to do so, on any appeal under—
    (i)   section 1 of the Administration of Justice Act 1960 (appeal from the High Court in criminal cases);
    (ii)   Part I or Part II of the Criminal Appeal Act 1968 (appeals from the Crown Court to the criminal division of the Court of Appeal and thence to the Supreme Court); or
    (iii) section 108 of the Magistrates' Courts Act 1980 (right of appeal to Crown Court) as it applies, by virtue of subsection (5) of section 12 of the Contempt of Court Act 1981, to orders made under section 12 (contempt of magistrates' courts); ...

(fa) to have the conduct of applications for orders under section 1C of the Crime and Disorder Act 1998 (orders made on conviction of certain offences) and section 14A of the Football Spectators Act 1989 (banning orders made on conviction of certain offences);

(faa) where it appears to him appropriate to do so, to have the conduct of applications made by him for orders under section 14B of the Football Spectators Act 1989 (banning orders made on complaint);

(fb) where it appears to him appropriate to do so, to have the conduct of applications under section 1CA(3) of the Crime and Disorder Act 1998 for the variation or discharge of orders made under section 1C of that Act;

(fc) where it appears to him appropriate to do so, to appear on any application under section 1CA of that Act made by a person subject to an order under section 1C of that Act for the variation or discharge of the order;

(fd), (fe) ...

(ff) to discharge such duties as are conferred on him by, or in relation to, Part 5 or Part 8 of the Proceeds of Crime Act 2002 (civil recovery of the proceeds etc of unlawful conduct, civil recovery investigations and disclosure orders in relation to confiscation investigations);

(g) to discharge such other functions as may from time to time be assigned to him by the Attorney General in pursuance of this paragraph.

...

PROTECTION FROM HARASSMENT ACT 1997
(1997, c. 40)

5.   Restraining orders on conviction

(1) A court sentencing or otherwise dealing with a person ('the defendant') convicted of an offence may (as well as sentencing him or dealing with him in any other way) make an order under this section.

(2) The order may, for the purpose of protecting the victim or victims of the offence, or any other person mentioned in the order, from ... conduct which—
    (a)   amounts to harassment, or
    (b)   will cause a fear of violence,
prohibit the defendant from doing anything described in the order.

(3) The order may have effect for a specified period or until further order.

(3A) In proceedings under this section both the prosecution and the defence may lead, as further evidence, any evidence that would be admissible in proceedings for an injunction under section 3.

(4)   The prosecutor, the defendant or any other person mentioned in the order may apply to the court which made the order for it to be varied or discharged by a further order.

(4A) Any person mentioned in the order is entitled to be heard on the hearing of an application under subsection (4).

(5)   If without reasonable excuse the defendant does anything which he is prohibited from doing by an order under this section, he is guilty of an offence.

(6)   A person guilty of an offence under this section is liable—
   (a)   on conviction on indictment, to imprisonment for a term not exceeding five years, or a fine, or both, or
   (b)   on summary conviction, to imprisonment for a term not exceeding six months, or a fine not exceeding the statutory maximum, or both.

(7)   A court dealing with a person for an offence under this section may vary or discharge the order in question by a further order.

5A.   Restraining orders on acquittal

(1)   A court before which a person ('the defendant') is acquitted of an offence may, if it considers it necessary to do so to protect a person from harassment by the defendant, make an order prohibiting the defendant from doing anything described in the order.

(2)   Subsections (3) to (7) of section 5 apply to an order under this section as they apply to an order under that one.

(3)   Where the Court of Appeal allows an appeal against conviction it may remit the case to the Crown Court to consider whether to proceed under this section.

(4)   Where—
   (a)   the Crown Court allows an appeal against conviction, or
   (b)   a case is remitted to the Crown Court under subsection (3),
the reference in subsection (1) to a court before which a person is acquitted of an offence is to be read as referring to that court.

(5)   A person made subject to an order under this section has the same right of appeal against the order as if—
   (a)   he had been convicted of the offence before the court which made the order, and
   (b)   the order had been made under section 5.

PSYCHOACTIVE SUBSTANCES ACT 2016
(2016, c. 2)

1.   Overview

(1)   This Act contains provision about psychoactive substances.

(2)   Section 2 defines what is meant by a 'psychoactive substance'.

(3)   Sections 4 to 10 contain provision about offences relating to psychoactive substances.

(4)   Section 11 provides for exceptions to those offences.

(5)   Sections 12 to 35 contain powers for dealing with prohibited activities in respect of psychoactive substances, in particular powers to give prohibition notices and make prohibition orders.

(6)   Sections 36 to 54 contain enforcement powers.

2.   Meaning of 'psychoactive substance' etc

(1)   In this Act 'psychoactive substance' means any substance which—
   (a)   is capable of producing a psychoactive effect in a person who consumes it, and
   (b)   is not an exempted substance.

(2)   For the purposes of this Act a substance produces a psychoactive effect in a person if, by stimulating or depressing the person's central nervous system, it affects the person's mental functioning or emotional state; and references to a substance's psychoactive effects are to be read accordingly.

(3) For the purposes of this Act a person consumes a substance if the person causes or allows the substance, or fumes given off by the substance, to enter the person's body in any way.

ROAD TRAFFIC OFFENDERS ACT 1988
(1988, c. 53)

34. Disqualification for certain offences

(1) Where a person is convicted of an offence involving obligatory disqualification, the court must order him to be disqualified for such period not less than twelve months as the court thinks fit unless the court for special reasons thinks fit to order him to be disqualified for a shorter period or not to order him to be disqualified.

(1A) Where a person is convicted of an offence under section 12A of the Theft Act 1968 (aggravated vehicle-taking), the fact that he did not drive the vehicle in question at any particular time or at all shall not be regarded as a special reason for the purposes of subsection (1) above.

(2) Where a person is convicted of an offence involving discretionary disqualification, and either—

    (a) the penalty points to be taken into account on that occasion number fewer than twelve, or

    (b) the offence is not one involving obligatory endorsement,

the court may order him to be disqualified for such period as the court thinks fit.

(3) Where a person convicted of an offence under any of the following provisions of the Road Traffic Act 1988, that is—

    (aa) section 3A (causing death by careless driving when under the influence of drink or drugs),

    (a) section 4(1) (driving or attempting to drive while unfit),

    (b) section 5(1)(a) (driving or attempting to drive with excess alcohol), ...

    (ba) section 5A(1)(a) and (2) (driving or attempting to drive with concentration of specified controlled drug above specified limit),

    (c) section 7(6) (failing to provide a specimen) where that is an offence involving obligatory disqualification,

    (d) section 7A(6) (failing to allow a specimen to be subjected to laboratory test) where that is an offence involving obligatory disqualification;

has within the ten years immediately preceding the commission of the offence been convicted of any such offence, subsection (1) above shall apply in relation to him as if the reference to twelve months were a reference to three years.

(4) Subject to subsection (3) above, subsection (1) above shall apply as if the reference to twelve months were a reference to two years—

    (a) in relation to a person convicted of—

        (i)   manslaughter, or in Scotland culpable homicide, or

        (ii) an offence under section 1 of the Road Traffic Act 1988 (causing death by dangerous driving), or

        (iia) an offence under section 1A of that Act (causing serious injury by dangerous driving), or

        (iib) an offence under section 3ZC of that Act (causing death by driving: disqualified drivers), or

        (iic) an offence under section 3ZD of that Act (causing serious injury by driving: disqualified drivers), or

        (iii) an offence under section 3A of that Act (causing death by careless driving while under the influence of drink or drugs), and

    (b) in relation to a person on whom more than one disqualification for a fixed period of 56 days or more has been imposed within the three years immediately preceding the commission of the offence.

(4A) For the purposes of subsection (4)(b) above there shall be disregarded any disqualification imposed under section 26 of this Act or section 147 of the Powers of

Criminal Courts (Sentencing) Act 2000 ... (offences committed by using vehicles) and any disqualification imposed in respect of an offence of stealing a motor vehicle, an offence under section 12 or 25 of the Theft Act 1968, an offence under section 178 of the Road Traffic Act 1988, or an attempt to commit such an offence.

(4B) Where a person convicted of an offence under section 40A of the Road Traffic Act 1988 (using a vehicle in a dangerous condition etc) has within the three years immediately preceding the commission of the offence been convicted of any such offence, subsection (1) above shall apply in relation to him as if the reference to twelve months were a reference to six months.

(5) The preceding provisions of this section shall apply in relation to a conviction of an offence committed by aiding, abetting, counselling or procuring, or inciting to the commission of, an offence involving obligatory disqualification as if the offence were an offence involving discretionary disqualification.

(6) This section is subject to section 48 of this Act.

34A. Reduced disqualification for attendance on courses

(1) This section applies where—
   (a) a person is convicted of a relevant drink offence or a specified offence by or before a court, and
   (b) the court makes an order under section 34 of this Act disqualifying him for a period of not less than twelve months (disregarding any extension period added pursuant to section 35A or 35C).

(2) In this section 'relevant drink offence' means—
   (a) an offence under paragraph (a) of subsection (1) of section 3A of the Road Traffic Act 1988 (causing death by careless driving when unfit to drive through drink) committed when unfit to drive through drink,
   (b) an offence under paragraph (b) of that subsection (causing death by careless driving with excess alcohol),
   (c) an offence under paragraph (c) of that subsection (failing to provide a specimen) where the specimen is required in connection with drink or consumption of alcohol,
   (d) an offence under section 4 of that Act (driving or being in charge when under influence of drink) committed by reason of unfitness through drink,
   (e) an offence under section 5(1) of that Act (driving or being in charge with excess alcohol),
   (f) an offence under section 7(6) of that Act (failing to provide a specimen) committed in the course of an investigation into an offence within any of the preceding paragraphs, or
   (g) an offence under section 7A(6) of that Act (failing to allow a specimen to be subjected to a laboratory test) in the course of an investigation into an offence within any of the preceding paragraphs.

(3) In this section 'specified offence' means—
   (a) an offence under section 3 of the Road Traffic Act (careless, and inconsiderate, driving),
   (b) an offence under section 36 of that Act (failing to comply with traffic signs),
   (c) an offence under section 17(4) of the Road Traffic Regulation Act 1984 (use of special road contrary to scheme or regulations), or
   (d) an offence under section 89(1) of that Act (exceeding speed limit).

(3A) 'The reduced period' is the period of disqualification imposed under section 34 of this Act (disregarding any extension period added pursuant to section 35A or 35C) as reduced by an order under this section.

(4) But the Secretary of State may by regulations amend subsection (3) above by adding other offences or removing offences.

(5) Where this section applies, the court may make an order that the period of disqualification imposed under section 34 of this Act ('the unreduced period') shall be reduced if, by the relevant date, the offender satisfactorily completes an approved course specified in the order but including any extension period added pursuant to section 35A or 35C.

(6) In subsection (5) above—

'an approved course' means a course approved by the appropriate national authority for the purposes of this section in relation to the description of offence of which the offender is convicted, and

'the relevant date' means such date, at least two months before the last day of the period of disqualification as reduced by the order, as is specified in the order.

(7) The reduction made in a period of disqualification by an order under this section is a period specified in the order of—

    (a)   not less than three months, and

    (b)   not more than one quarter of the unreduced period,

(and, accordingly, where the unreduced period is twelve months, the reduced period is nine months).

(8) A court shall not make an order under this section in the case of an offender convicted of a specified offence if—

    (a)   the offender has, during the period of three years ending with the date on which the offence was committed, committed a specified offence and successfully completed an approved course pursuant to an order made under this section or section 30A of this Act on conviction of that offence, or

    (b)   the specified offence was committed during his probationary period.

(9) A court shall not make an order under this section in the case of an offender unless—

    (a)   the court is satisfied that a place on the course specified in the order will be available for the offender,

    (b)   the offender appears to the court to be of or over the age of 17,

    (c)   the court has informed the offender (orally or in writing and in ordinary language) of the effect of the order and of the amount of the fees which he is required to pay for the course and when he must pay them, and

    (d)   the offender has agreed that the order should be made.

35. Disqualification for repeated offences

(1) Where—

    (a)   a person is convicted of an offence to which this subsection applies, and

    (b)   the penalty points to be taken into account on that occasion number twelve or more,

the court must order him to be disqualified for not less than the minimum period unless the court is satisfied, having regard to all the circumstances, that there are grounds for mitigating the normal consequences of the conviction and thinks fit to order him to be disqualified for a shorter period or not to order him to be disqualified.

(1A) Subsection (1) above applies to—

    (a)   an offence involving discretionary disqualification and obligatory endorsement, and

    (b)   an offence involving obligatory disqualification in respect of which no order is made under section 34 of this Act.

(2) The minimum period referred to in subsection (1) above is—

    (a)   six months if no previous disqualification imposed on the offender is to be taken into account, and

    (b)   one year if one, and two years if more than one, such disqualification is to be taken into account;

and a previous disqualification imposed on an offender is to be taken into account if it was for a fixed period of 56 days or more and was imposed within the three years immediately preceding the commission of the latest offence in respect of which penalty points are taken into account under section 29 of this Act.

(3) Where an offender is convicted on the same occasion of more than one offence to which subsection (1) above applies—

    (a)   not more than one disqualification shall be imposed on him under subsection (1) above,

    (b)   in determining the period of the disqualification the court must take into account all the offences, and

    (c)   for the purposes of any appeal any disqualification imposed under subsection (1) above shall be treated as an order made on the conviction of each of the offences.

(4)   No account is to be taken under subsection (1) above of any of the following circumstances—

(a)   any circumstances that are alleged to make the offence or any of the offences not a serious one,

(b)   hardship, other than exceptional hardship, or

(c)   any circumstances which, within the three years immediately preceding the conviction, have been taken into account under that subsection in ordering the offender to be disqualified for a shorter period or not ordering him to be disqualified.

(5)   References in this section to disqualification do not include a disqualification imposed under section 26 of this Act or section 147 of the Powers of Criminal Courts (Sentencing) Act 2000 ... (offences committed by using vehicles) or a disqualification imposed in respect of an offence of stealing a motor vehicle, an offence under section 12 or 25 of the Theft Act 1968, an offence under section 178 of the Road Traffic Act 1988, or an attempt to commit such an offence.

(5A) The preceding provisions of this section shall apply in relation to a conviction of an offence committed by aiding, abetting, counselling, procuring, or inciting to the commission of, an offence involving obligatory disqualification as if the offence were an offence involving discretionary disqualification.

...

(7)   This section is subject to section 48 of this Act.

35A.   Extension of disqualification where custodial sentence also imposed

(1)   This section applies where a person is convicted in England and Wales of an offence for which the court—

(a)   imposes a custodial sentence, and

(b)   orders the person to be disqualified under section 34 or 35.

(2)   The order under section 34 or 35 must provide for the person to be disqualified for the appropriate extension period, in addition to the discretionary disqualification period.

(3)   The discretionary disqualification period is the period for which, in the absence of this section, the court would have disqualified the person under section 34 or 35.

(4)   The appropriate extension period is—

(a)   where an order under section 82A(2) of the Powers of Criminal Courts (Sentencing) Act 2000 (life sentence: determination of tariffs) is made in relation to the custodial sentence, a period equal to the part of the sentence specified in that order;

(b)   in the case of a detention and training order under section 100 of that Act (offenders under 18: detention and training orders), a period equal to half the term of that order;

(c), (d) ...

(e)   where section 226A of that Act (extended sentence for certain violent, sexual or terrorism offenders: persons aged 18 or over) applies in relation to the custodial sentence, a period equal to two thirds of the term imposed pursuant to section 226A(5)(a) of that Act calculated after that term has been reduced by any relevant discount;

(f)   where section 226B of that Act (extended sentence for certain violent, sexual or terrorism offenders: persons under 18) applies in relation to the custodial sentence, a period equal to two thirds of the term imposed pursuant to section 226B(3)(a) of that Act calculated after that term has been reduced by any relevant discount;

(fa) in the case of a sentence under section 236A of that Act (special custodial sentence for certain offenders of particular concern), a period equal to half of the term imposed pursuant to section 236A(2)(a) of that Act;

(g)   where an order under section 269(2) of this Act (determination of minimum term in relation to mandatory life sentence: early release) is made in relation to the custodial sentence, a period equal to the part of the sentence specified in the order;

(h)   in any other case, a period equal to half the custodial sentence imposed calculated after that sentence has been reduced by any relevant discount.

(5)   If a period determined under subsection (4) includes a fraction of a day, that period is to be rounded up to the nearest number of whole days.

(6) The 'relevant discount' is the total number of days to count as time served by virtue of—

    (a)   section 240ZA of the Criminal Justice Act 2003 (crediting periods of remand in custody), or

    (b)   a direction under section 240A of that Act (crediting periods of remand on bail).

(7) This section does not apply where—

    (a)   the custodial sentence was a suspended sentence,

    (b)   the court has made an order under section 269(4) of the Criminal Justice Act 2003 (determination of minimum term in relation to mandatory life sentence: no early release) in relation to the custodial sentence, or

    (c)   the court has made an order under section 82A(4) of the Powers of Criminal Courts (Sentencing) Act 2000 (determination of minimum term in relation to discretionary life sentence: no early release) in relation to the custodial sentence.

...

35B. Effect of custodial sentence in other cases

(1) This section applies where a person is convicted in England and Wales of an offence for which a court proposes to order the person to be disqualified under section 34 or 35 and—

    (a)   the court proposes to impose on the person a custodial sentence (other than a suspended sentence) for another offence, or

    (b)   at the time of sentencing for the offence, a custodial sentence imposed on the person on an earlier occasion has not expired.

(2) In determining the period for which the person is to be disqualified under section 34 or 35, the court must have regard to the consideration in subsection (3) if and to the extent that it is appropriate to do so.

(3) The consideration is the diminished effect of disqualification as a distinct punishment if the person who is disqualified is also detained in pursuance of a custodial sentence.

(4) If the court proposes to order the person to be disqualified under section 34 or 35 and to impose a custodial sentence for the same offence, the court may not in relation to that disqualification take that custodial sentence into account for the purposes of subsection (2).

(5) In this section 'custodial sentence' and 'suspended sentence' have the same meaning as in section 35A.

36. Disqualification until test is passed

(1) Where this subsection applies to a person the court must order him to be disqualified until he passes the appropriate driving test.

(2) Subsection (1) above applies to a person who is disqualified under section 34 of this Act on conviction of—

    (a)   manslaughter, or in Scotland culpable homicide, by the driver of a motor vehicle,

    (b)   an offence under section 1 (causing death by dangerous driving),

    (c)   an offence under section 1A of that Act (causing serious injury by dangerous driving),

    (d)   an offence under section 2 of that Act (dangerous driving),

    (e)   an offence under section 3ZC of that Act (causing death by driving: disqualified drivers), or

    (f)   an offence under section 3ZD of that Act (causing serious injury by driving: disqualified drivers).

(3) Subsection (1) above also applies—

    (a)   to a person who is disqualified under section 34 or 35 of this Act in such circumstances or for such period as the Secretary of State may by order prescribe, or

    (b)   to such other persons convicted of such offences involving obligatory endorsement as may be so prescribed.

(4) Where a person to whom subsection (1) above does not apply is convicted of an offence involving obligatory endorsement, the court may order him to be disqualified until he passes the appropriate driving test (whether or not he has previously passed any test).

(5)   In this section—
'appropriate driving test' means—
(a)   an extended driving test, where a person is convicted of an offence involving obligatory disqualification or is disqualified under section 35 of this Act,
(b)   a test of competence to drive, other than an extended driving test, in any other case,
'extended driving test' means a test of competence to drive prescribed for the purposes of this section, and
'test of competence to drive' means a test prescribed by virtue of section 89(3) of the Road Traffic Act 1988.
(6)   In determining whether to make an order under subsection (4) above, the court shall have regard to the safety of road users.
(7)   Where a person is disqualified until he passes the extended driving test—
(a)   any earlier order under this section shall cease to have effect, and
(b)   a court shall not make a further order under this section while he is so disqualified.
...

37.   Effect of order of disqualification

(1)   Where the holder of a licence is disqualified by an order of a court, the licence shall be treated as being revoked with effect from the beginning of the period of disqualification.
(1A)   Where—
(a)   the disqualification is for a fixed period shorter than 56 days in respect of an offence involving obligatory endorsement, or
(b)   the order is made under section 26 of this Act,
subsection (1) above shall not prevent the licence from again having effect at the end of the period of disqualification.
...

SENIOR COURTS ACT 1981
(1981, c. 54)

28.   Appeals from Crown Court and inferior courts

(1)   Subject to subsection (2), any order, judgment or other decision of the Crown Court may be questioned by any party to the proceedings, on the ground that it is wrong in law or is in excess of jurisdiction, by applying to the Crown Court to have a case stated by that court for the opinion of the High Court.
(2)   Subsection (1) shall not apply to—
(a)   a judgment or other decision of the Crown Court relating to trial on indictment; or
(b)   any decision of that court under the Local Government (Miscellaneous Provisions) Act 1982 which, by any provision of any of those Acts, is to be final.
...
(3)   Subject to the provisions of this Act and to rules of court, the High Court shall, in accordance with section 19(2), have jurisdiction to hear and determine—
(a)   any application, or any appeal (whether by way of case stated or otherwise), which it has power to hear and determine under or by virtue of this or any other Act; and
(b)   all such other appeals as it had jurisdiction to hear and determine immediately before the commencement of this Act.
(4)   In subsection (2)(a) the reference to a decision of the Crown Court relating to trial on indictment does not include a decision relating to an order under section 23 or 24 of the Legal Aid, Sentencing and Punishment of Offenders Act 2012.

28A.   Proceedings on case stated by magistrates' court or Crown Court

(1)   This section applies where a case is stated for the opinion of the High Court—
(a)   by a magistrates' court under section 111 of the Magistrates' Courts Act 1980; or
(b)   by the Crown Court under section 28(1) of this Act.

(2)   The High Court may, if it thinks fit, cause the case to be sent back for amendment and, where it does so, the case shall be amended accordingly.

(3)   The High Court shall hear and determine the question arising on the case (or the case as amended) and shall—

    (a)   reverse, affirm or amend the determination in respect of which the case has been stated; or

    (b)   remit the matter to the magistrates' court, or the Crown Court, with the opinion of the High Court,

and may make such other order in relation to the matter (including as to costs) as it thinks fit.

(4)   Except as provided by the Administration of Justice Act 1960 (right of appeal to Supreme Court in criminal cases), a decision of the High Court under this section is final.

...

43.   Power of High Court to vary sentence on application for quashing order

(1)   Where a person who has been sentenced for an offence—

    (a)   by a magistrates' court; or

    (b)   by the Crown Court after being convicted of the offence by a magistrates' court and committed to the Crown Court for sentence; or

    (c)   by the Crown Court on appeal against conviction or sentence,

applies to the High Court in accordance with section 31 for a quashing order to remove the proceedings of the magistrates' court or the Crown Court into the High Court, then, if the High Court determines that the magistrates' court or the Crown Court had no power to pass the sentence, the High Court may, instead of quashing the conviction, amend it by substituting for the sentence passed any sentence which the magistrates' court or, in a case within paragraph (b), the Crown Court had power to impose.

(2)   Any sentence passed by the High Court by virtue of this section in substitution for the sentence passed in the proceedings of the magistrates' court or the Crown Court shall, unless the High Court otherwise directs, begin to run from the time when it would have begun to run if passed in those proceedings; but in computing the term of the sentence, any time during which the offender was released on bail in pursuance of section 37(1)(d) of the Criminal Justice Act 1948 shall be disregarded.

(3)   Subsections (1) and (2) shall, with the necessary modifications, apply in relation to any order of a magistrates' court or the Crown Court which is made on, but does not form part of, the conviction of an offender as they apply in relation to a conviction and sentence.

48.   Appeals to Crown Court

(1)   The Crown Court may, in the course of hearing any appeal, correct any error or mistake in the order or judgment incorporating the decision which is the subject of the appeal.

(2)   On the termination of the hearing of an appeal the Crown Court—

    (a)   may confirm, reverse or vary any part of the decision appealed against, including a determination not to impose a separate penalty in respect of an offence; or

    (b)   may remit the matter with its opinion thereon to the authority whose decision is appealed against; or

    (c)   may make such other order in the matter as the court thinks just, and by such order exercise any power which the said authority might have exercised.

(3)   Subsection (2) has effect subject to any enactment relating to any such appeal which expressly limits or restricts the powers of the court on the appeal.

(4)   Subject to section 11(6) of the Criminal Appeal Act 1995, if the appeal is against a conviction or a sentence, the preceding provisions of this section shall be construed as including power to award any punishment, whether more or less severe than that awarded by the magistrates' court whose decision is appealed against, if that is a punishment which that magistrates' court might have awarded.

(5)   This section applies whether or not the appeal is against the whole of the decision.

(6) In this section 'sentence' includes any order made by a court when dealing with an offender including

    (a) a hospital order under Part III of the Mental Health Act 1983, with or without a restriction order, and an interim hospital order under that Act, and

    (b) a recommendation for deportation made when dealing with an offender. Subsections (7) and (8) are omitted.

...

SERIOUS CRIME ACT 2007
(2007, c. 27)

6. Any individual must be 18 or over

An individual under the age of 18 may not be the subject of a serious crime prevention order.

8. Limited class of applicants for making of orders

A serious crime prevention order may be made only on an application by—

    (a) in the case of an order in England and Wales—

        (i) the Director of Public Prosecutions;

        (ii) ...

        (iii) the Director of the Serious Fraud Office; and

    (aa) in the case of an order in Scotland, the Lord Advocate;

    (b) in the case of an order in Northern Ireland, the Director of Public Prosecutions for Northern Ireland.

9. Right of third parties to make representations

...

(4) The Crown Court must, on an application by a person, give the person an opportunity to make representations in proceedings before it arising by virtue of section 19, 20, 21 or 22E if it considers that the making or variation of the serious crime prevention order concerned (or a decision not to vary it) would be likely to have a significant adverse effect on that person.

(5) A court which is considering an appeal in relation to a serious crime prevention order must, on an application by a person, give the person an opportunity to make representations in the proceedings if that person was given an opportunity to make representations in the proceedings which are the subject of the appeal.

16. Duration of orders

(1) A serious crime prevention order must specify when it is to come into force and when it is to cease to be in force.

(2) An order is not to be in force for more than 5 years beginning with the coming into force of the order.

(3) An order can specify different times for the coming into force, or ceasing to be in force, of different provisions of the order.

(4) Where it specifies different times in accordance with subsection (3), the order—

    (a) must specify when each provision is to come into force and cease to be in force; and

    (b) is not to be in force for more than 5 years beginning with the coming into force of the first provision of the order to come into force.

(5) The fact that an order, or any provision of an order, ceases to be in force does not prevent the court from making a new order to the same or similar effect.

(6) A new order may be made in anticipation of an earlier order or provision ceasing to be in force.

(7) Subsections (2) and (4)(b) have effect subject to section 22E.

19.   Orders by Crown Court on conviction

(1)   Subsection (2) applies where the Crown Court in England and Wales is dealing with a person who—

    (a)   has been convicted by or before a magistrates' court of having committed a serious offence in England and Wales and has been committed to the Crown Court to be dealt with; or

    (b)   has been convicted by or before the Crown Court of having committed a serious offence in England and Wales.

(2)   The Crown Court may, in addition to dealing with the person in relation to the offence, make an order if it has reasonable grounds to believe that the order would protect the public by preventing, restricting or disrupting involvement by the person in serious crime in England and Wales.

...

(5)   An order under this section may contain—

    (a)   such prohibitions, restrictions or requirements; and

    (b)   such other terms;

as the court considers appropriate for the purpose of protecting the public by preventing, restricting or disrupting involvement by the person concerned in serious crime in England and Wales or (as the case may be) Northern Ireland.

(6)   The powers of the court in respect of an order under this section are subject to sections 6 to 15 (safeguards).

(7)   An order must not be made under this section except—

    (a)   in addition to a sentence imposed in respect of the offence concerned; or

    (b)   in addition to an order discharging the person conditionally.

(8)   An order under this section is also called a serious crime prevention order.

22E.   Extension of orders pending outcome of criminal proceedings

(1)   This section applies where a person subject to a serious crime prevention order is charged with—

    (a)   a serious offence, or

    (b)   an offence under section 25 of failing to comply with the serious crime prevention order.

(2)   The relevant applicant authority may make an application under this section to—

    (a)   the Crown Court in England and Wales, in the case of a serious crime prevention order in England and Wales;

    (b)   the High Court of Justiciary or the sheriff, in the case of a serious crime prevention order in Scotland;

    (c)   the Crown Court in Northern Ireland, in the case of a serious crime prevention order in Northern Ireland.

(3)   On an application under this section, the court or sheriff may vary the serious crime prevention order so that it continues in effect until one of the events listed in subsection (4) occurs (if the order would otherwise cease to have effect before then).

(4)   The events are—

    (a)   following the person's conviction of the offence mentioned in subsection (1)—

        (i)   the order is varied under section 21 or 21, or under section 22B or 22C, by reference to the offence,

        (ii)   a new serious crime prevention order is made under section 19 or 21, or under section 22A or 22C, by reference to the offence, or

        (iii)   the court or sheriff deals with the person for the offence without varying the order or making a new one;

    (b)   the person is acquitted of the offence;

    (c)   the charge is withdrawn;

    (d)   in the case of a serious crime prevention order in England and Wales or Northern Ireland—

        (i)   proceedings in respect of the charge are discontinued, or

        (ii)   an order is made for the charge to lie on the file;

(e)   in the case of a serious crime prevention order in Scotland—

    (i)   proceedings against the person are deserted *simpliciter*,

    (ii)   proceedings against the person are deserted *pro loco et tempore* and no trial diet is appointed,

    (iii) the indictment or complaint relating to the person falls or for any other reason does not proceed to trial, or

    (iv)   the diet not having been continued, adjourned or postponed, no further proceedings are in contemplation in relation to the person.

(5)   An order may be made under this section only if—

    (a)   the serious crime prevention order is still in force, and

    (b)   the court or sheriff has reasonable grounds for believing that the order would protect the public by preventing, restricting or disrupting involvement by the person in serious crime.

(6)   In subsection (5)(b) 'serious crime' means—

    (a)   serious crime in England and Wales, in the case of a serious crime prevention order in England and Wales;

    (b)   serious crime in Scotland, in the case of a serious crime prevention order in Scotland;

    (c)   serious crime in Northern Ireland, in the case of a serious crime prevention order in Northern Ireland.

24.   Appeals from Crown Court

(1)   An appeal against a decision of the Crown Court in relation to a serious crime prevention order may be made to the Court of Appeal by—

    (a)   the person who is the subject of the order; or

    (b)   the relevant applicant authority.

(2)   In addition, an appeal may be made to the Court of Appeal in relation to a decision of the Crown Court—

    (a)   to make a serious crime prevention order; or

    (b)   to vary, or not to vary, such an order;

by any person who was given an opportunity to make representations in the proceedings concerned by virtue of section 9(4).

(3)   Subject to subsection (4), an appeal under subsection (1) or (2) lies only with the leave of the Court of Appeal.

(4)   An appeal under subsection (1) or (2) lies without the leave of the Court of Appeal if the judge who made the decision grants a certificate that the decision is fit for appeal under this section.

...

SERIOUS ORGANISED CRIME AND POLICE ACT 2005
(2005, c. 15)

73.   Assistance by defendant: reduction in sentence

(1)   This section applies if a defendant—

    (a)   following a plea of guilty is either convicted of an offence in proceedings in the Crown Court or is committed to the Crown Court for sentence, and

    (b)   has, pursuant to a written agreement made with a specified prosecutor, assisted or offered to assist the investigator or prosecutor in relation to that or any other offence.

(2)   In determining what sentence to pass on the defendant the court may take into account the extent and nature of the assistance given or offered.

(3)   If the court passes a sentence which is less than it would have passed but for the assistance given or offered, it must state in open court—

    (a)   that it has passed a lesser sentence than it would otherwise have passed, and

    (b)   what the greater sentence would have been.

(4)   Subsection (3) does not apply if the court thinks that it would not be in the public interest to disclose that the sentence has been discounted; but in such a case the

court must give written notice of the matters specified in paragraphs (a) and (b) of subsection (3) to both the prosecutor and the defendant.

(5) Nothing in any enactment which—

   (a) requires that a minimum sentence is passed in respect of any offence or an offence of any description or by reference to the circumstances of any offender (whether or not the enactment also permits the court to pass a lesser sentence in particular circumstances), or

   (b) in the case of a sentence which is fixed by law, requires the court to take into account certain matters for the purposes of making an order which determines or has the effect of determining the minimum period of imprisonment which the offender must serve (whether or not the enactment also permits the court to fix a lesser period in particular circumstances),

affects the power of a court to act under subsection (2).

(6) If, in determining what sentence to pass on the defendant, the court takes into account the extent and nature of the assistance given or offered as mentioned in subsection (2), that does not prevent the court from also taking account of any other matter which it is entitled by virtue of any other enactment to take account of for the purposes of determining—

   (a) the sentence, or

   (b) in the case of a sentence which is fixed by law, any minimum period of imprisonment which an offender must serve.

(7) If subsection (3) above does not apply by virtue of subsection (4) above, sections 174(1)(a) and 270 of the Criminal Justice Act 2003 (requirement to explain reasons for sentence or other order) do not apply to the extent that the explanation will disclose that a sentence has been discounted in pursuance of this section.

(8) In this section—

   (a) a reference to a sentence includes, in the case of a sentence which is fixed by law, a reference to the minimum period an offender is required to serve, and a reference to a lesser sentence must be construed accordingly;

   (b) a reference to imprisonment includes a reference to any other custodial sentence within the meaning of section 76 of the Powers of Criminal Courts (Sentencing) Act 2000 or Article 2 of the Criminal Justice (Northern Ireland) Order 1996.

(9) An agreement with a specified prosecutor may provide for assistance to be given to that prosecutor or to any other prosecutor.

(10) References to a specified prosecutor must be construed in accordance with section 71.

74. Assistance by defendant: review of sentence

(1) This section applies if—

   (a) the Crown Court has passed a sentence on a person in respect of an offence, and

   (b) the person falls within subsection (2).

(2) A person falls within this subsection if—

   (a) he receives a discounted sentence in consequence of his having offered in pursuance of a written agreement to give assistance to the prosecutor or investigator of an offence but he knowingly fails to any extent to give assistance in accordance with the agreement;

   (b) he receives a discounted sentence in consequence of his having offered in pursuance of a written agreement to give assistance to the prosecutor or investigator of an offence and, having given the assistance in accordance with the agreement, in pursuance of another written agreement gives or offers to give further assistance;

   (c) he receives a sentence which is not discounted but in pursuance of a written agreement he subsequently gives or offers to give assistance to the prosecutor or investigator of an offence.

(3) A specified prosecutor may at any time refer the case back to the court by which the sentence was passed if—

   (a) the person is still serving his sentence, and

   (b) the specified prosecutor thinks it is in the interests of justice to do so.

(4)   A case so referred must, if possible, be heard by the judge who passed the sentence to which the referral relates.

(5)   If the court is satisfied that a person who falls within subsection (2)(a) knowingly failed to give the assistance it may substitute for the sentence to which the referral relates such greater sentence (not exceeding that which it would have passed but for the agreement to give assistance) as it thinks appropriate.

(6)   In a case of a person who falls within subsection (2)(b) or (c) the court may—

     (a)   take into account the extent and nature of the assistance given or offered;

     (b)   substitute for the sentence to which the referral relates such lesser sentence as it thinks appropriate.

(7)   Any part of the sentence to which the referral relates which the person has already served must be taken into account in determining when a greater or lesser sentence imposed by subsection (5) or (6) has been served.

(8)   A person in respect of whom a reference is made under this section and the specified prosecutor may with the leave of the Court of Appeal appeal to the Court of Appeal against the decision of the Crown Court.

(9)   Section 33(3) of the Criminal Appeal Act 1968 (limitation on appeal from the criminal division of the Court of Appeal) does not prevent an appeal to the Supreme Court under this section.

(10)   A discounted sentence is a sentence passed in pursuance of section 73 or subsection (6) above.

(11)   References—

     (a)   to a written agreement are to an agreement made in writing with a specified prosecutor;

     (b)   to a specified prosecutor must be construed in accordance with section 71.

(12)   In relation to any proceedings under this section—

     (a)   the Secretary of State may, in relation to proceedings in England and Wales, make an order containing provision corresponding to any provision in the Criminal Appeal Act 1968 (subject to any specified modifications);

     (b)   ...

Subsections (13) to (15) are omitted.

75.   Proceedings under section 74: exclusion of public

(1)   This section applies to—

     (a)   any proceedings relating to a reference made under section 74(3), and

     (b)   any other proceedings arising in consequence of such proceedings.

(2)   The court in which the proceedings will be or are being heard may make such order as it thinks appropriate—

     (a)   to exclude from the proceedings any person who does not fall within subsection (4);

     (b)   to give such directions as it thinks appropriate prohibiting the publication of any matter relating to the proceedings (including the fact that the reference has been made).

(3)   An order under subsection (2) may be made only to the extent that the court thinks—

     (a)   that it is necessary to do so to protect the safety of any person, and

     (b)   that it is in the interests of justice.

(4)   The following persons fall within this subsection—

     (a)   a member or officer of the court;

     (b)   a party to the proceedings;

     (c)   counsel or a solicitor for a party to the proceedings;

     (d)   a person otherwise directly concerned with the proceedings.

(5)   This section does not affect any other power which the court has by virtue of any rule of law or other enactment—

     (a)   to exclude any person from proceedings, or

     (b)   to restrict the publication of any matter relating to proceedings.

112.   Power to direct a person to leave a place

(1)   A constable may direct a person to leave a place if he believes, on reasonable grounds, that the person is in the place at a time when he would be prohibited from entering it by virtue of—

(a)   an order to which subsection (2) applies, or

(b)   a condition to which subsection (3) applies.

(2)   This subsection applies to an order which—

(a)   was made, by virtue of any enactment, following the person's conviction of an offence, and

(b)   prohibits the person from entering the place or from doing so during a period specified in the order.

(3)   This subsection applies to a condition which—

(a)   was imposed, by virtue of any enactment, as a condition of the person's release from a prison in which he was serving a sentence of imprisonment following his conviction of an offence, and

(b)   prohibits the person from entering the place or from doing so during a period specified in the condition.

(4)   A direction under this section may be given orally.

(5)   Any person who knowingly contravenes a direction given to him under this section is guilty of an offence and liable on summary conviction to imprisonment for a term not exceeding 51 weeks or to a fine not exceeding level 4 on the standard scale, or to both.

SEXUAL OFFENCES ACT 2003
(2003, c. 42)

103A. Sexual harm prevention orders: applications and grounds

(1)   A court may make an order under this section (a 'sexual harm prevention order') in respect of a person ('the defendant') where subsection (2) or (3) applies to the defendant.

(2)   This subsection applies to the defendant where—

(a)   the court deals with the defendant in respect of—

(i)   an offence listed in Schedule 3 or 5, or

(ii)   a finding that the defendant is not guilty of an offence listed in Schedule 3 or 5 by reason of insanity, or

(iii)   a finding that the defendant is under a disability and has done the act charged against the defendant in respect of an offence listed in Schedule 3 or 5,

and

(b)   the court is satisfied that it is necessary to make a sexual harm prevention order, for the purpose of—

(i)   protecting the public or any particular members of the public from sexual harm from the defendant, or

(ii)   protecting children or vulnerable adults generally, or any particular children or vulnerable adults, from sexual harm from the defendant outside the United Kingdom.

(3)   This subsection applies to the defendant where—

(a)   an application under subsection (4) has been made in respect of the defendant and it is proved on the application that the defendant is a qualifying offender, and

(b)   the court is satisfied that the defendant's behaviour since the appropriate date makes it necessary to make a sexual harm prevention order, for the purpose of—

(i)   protecting the public or any particular members of the public from sexual harm from the defendant, or

(ii)   protecting children or vulnerable adults generally, or any particular children or vulnerable adults, from sexual harm from the defendant outside the United Kingdom.

(4)   A chief officer of police or the Director General of the National Crime Agency ('the Director General') may by complaint to a magistrates' court apply for a sexual harm prevention order in respect of a person if it appears to the chief officer or the Director General that—

(a)   the person is a qualifying offender, and

   (b)   the person has since the appropriate date acted in such a way as to give reasonable cause to believe that it is necessary for such an order to be made.

(5)   A chief officer of police may make an application under subsection (4) only in respect of a person—

   (a)   who resides in the chief officer's police area, or

   (b)   who the chief officer believes is in that area or is intending to come to it.

(6)   An application under subsection (4) may be made to any magistrates' court acting for a local justice area that includes—

   (a)   any part of a relevant police area, or

   (b)   any place where it is alleged that the person acted in a way mentioned in subsection (4)(b).

(7)   The Director General must as soon as practicable notify the chief officer of police for a relevant police area of any application that the Director has made under subsection (4).

(8)   Where the defendant is a child, a reference in this section to a magistrates' court is to be taken as referring to a youth court (subject to any rules of court made under section 103K(1)).

(9)   In this section 'relevant police area' means—

   (a)   where the applicant is a chief officer of police, the officer's police area;

   (b)   where the applicant is the Director General—

      (i)   the police area where the person in question resides, or

      (ii)   a police area which the Director General believes the person is in or is intending to come to.

103B. Section 103A: supplemental

(1)   In section 103A—

'appropriate date', in relation to a qualifying offender, means the date or (as the case may be) the first date on which the offender was convicted, found or cautioned as mentioned in subsection (2) or (3) below;

'child' means a person under 18;

'the public' means the public in the United Kingdom;

'sexual harm' from a person means physical or psychological harm caused—

   (a)   by the person committing one or more offences listed in Schedule 3, or

   (b)   (in the context of harm outside the United Kingdom) by the person doing, outside the United Kingdom, anything which would constitute an offence listed in Schedule 3 if done in any part of the United Kingdom;

'qualifying offender' means a person within subsection (2) or (3) below;

'vulnerable adult' means a person aged 18 or over whose ability to protect himself or herself from physical or psychological harm is significantly impaired through physical or mental disability or illness, through old age or otherwise.

(2)   A person is within this subsection if, whether before or after the commencement of this Part, the person—

   (a)   has been convicted of an offence listed in Schedule 3 (other than at paragraph 60) or in Schedule 5,

   (b)   has been found not guilty of such an offence by reason of insanity,

   (c)   has been found to be under a disability and to have done the act charged against him in respect of such an offence, or

   (d)   has been cautioned in respect of such an offence.

(3)   A person is within this subsection if, under the law in force in a country outside the United Kingdom and whether before or after the commencement of this Part—

   (a)   the person has been convicted of a relevant offence (whether or not the person has been punished for it),

   (b)   a court exercising jurisdiction under that law has made in respect of a relevant offence a finding equivalent to a finding that the person is not guilty by reason of insanity,

   (c)   such a court has made in respect of a relevant offence a finding equivalent to a finding that the person is under a disability and did the act charged against the person in respect of the offence, or

   (d)   the person has been cautioned in respect of a relevant offence.

(4)   In subsection (3), 'relevant offence' means an act which—
   (a)   constituted an offence under the law in force in the country concerned, and
   (b)   would have constituted an offence listed in Schedule 3 (other than at paragraph 60) or in Schedule 5 if it had been done in any part of the United Kingdom.
   For this purpose an act punishable under the law in force in a country outside the United Kingdom constitutes an offence under that law, however it is described in that law.
(5)   For the purposes of section 103A, acts, behaviour, convictions and findings include those occurring before the commencement of this Part.
(6)   Subject to subsection (7), on an application under section 103A(4) the condition in subsection (4)(b) above (where relevant) is to be taken as met unless, not later than rules of court may provide, the defendant serves on the applicant a notice—
   (a)   stating that, on the facts as alleged with respect to the act concerned, the condition is not in the defendant's opinion met,
   (b)   showing the grounds for that opinion, and
   (c)   requiring the applicant to prove that the condition is met.
(7)   The court, if it thinks fit, may permit the defendant to require the applicant to prove that the condition is met without service of a notice under subsection (6).
(8)   Subsection (9) applies for the purposes of section 103A and this section.
(9)   In construing any reference to an offence listed in Schedule 3, any condition subject to which an offence is so listed that relates—
   (a)   to the way in which the defendant is dealt with in respect of an offence so listed or a relevant finding (as defined by section 132(9)), or
   (b)   to the age of any person,
   is to be disregarded.

103C. SHPOs: effect

(1)   A sexual harm prevention order prohibits the defendant from doing anything described in the order.
(2)   Subject to section 103D(1), a prohibition contained in a sexual harm prevention order has effect—
   (a)   for a fixed period, specified in the order, of at least 5 years, or
   (b)   until further order.
(3)   A sexual harm prevention order—
   (a)   may specify that some of its prohibitions have effect until further order and some for a fixed period;
   (b)   may specify different periods for different prohibitions.
(4)   The only prohibitions that may be included in a sexual harm prevention order are those necessary for the purpose of—
   (a)   protecting the public or any particular members of the public from sexual harm from the defendant, or
   (b)   protecting children or vulnerable adults generally, or any particular children or vulnerable adults, from sexual harm from the defendant outside the United Kingdom.
(5)   In subsection (4) 'the public', 'sexual harm', 'child' and 'vulnerable adult' each has the meaning given in section 103B(1).
(6)   Where a court makes a sexual harm prevention order in relation to a person who is already subject to such an order (whether made by that court or another), the earlier order ceases to have effect.

103D. SHPOs: prohibitions on foreign travel

(1)   A prohibition on foreign travel contained in a sexual harm prevention order must be for a fixed period of not more than 5 years.
   ...

103E. SHPOs: variations, renewals and discharges

(1)   A person within subsection (2) may apply to the appropriate court for an order varying, renewing or discharging a sexual harm prevention order.

(2) The persons are—
  (a) the defendant;
  (b) the chief officer of police for the area in which the defendant resides;
  (c) a chief officer of police who believes that the defendant is in, or is intending to come to, that officer's police area;
  (d) where the order was made on an application by a chief officer of police under section 103A(4), that officer.
(3) An application under subsection (1) may be made—
  (a) where the appropriate court is the Crown Court, in accordance with rules of court;
  (b) in any other case, by complaint.
  ...

TERRORISM ACT 2000
(2000, c. 11)

41.   Arrest without warrant
(1) A constable may arrest without a warrant a person whom he reasonably suspects to be a terrorist.
(2) Where a person is arrested under this section the provisions of Schedule 8 (detention: treatment, review and extension) shall apply.
(3) Subject to subsections (4) to (7), a person detained under this section shall (unless detained under any other power) be released not later than the end of the period of 48 hours beginning—
  (a) with the time of his arrest under this section, or
  (b) if he was being detained under Schedule 7 or under Part I of Schedule 3 to the Counter-Terrorism and Border Security Act 2019 when he was arrested under this section, with the time when his examination under that Schedule began.
(4) If on a review of a person's detention under Part II of Schedule 8 the review officer does not authorise continued detention, the person shall (unless detained in accordance with subsection (5) or (6) or under any other power) be released.
(5) Where a police officer intends to make an application for a warrant under paragraph 29 of Schedule 8 extending a person's detention, the person may be detained pending the making of the application.
(6) Where an application has been made under paragraph 29 or 36 of Schedule 8 in respect of a person's detention, he may be detained pending the conclusion of proceedings on the application.
(7) Where an application under paragraph 29 or 36 of Schedule 8 is granted in respect of a person's detention, he may be detained, subject to paragraph 37 of that Schedule, during the period specified in the warrant.
(8) The refusal of an application in respect of a person's detention under paragraph 29 or 36 of Schedule 8 shall not prevent his continued detention in accordance with this section.
(9) A person who has the powers of a constable in one Part of the United Kingdom may exercise the power under subsection (1) in any Part of the United Kingdom.

42.   Search of premises
(1) A justice of the peace may on the application of a constable issue a warrant in relation to specified premises if he is satisfied that there are reasonable grounds for suspecting that a person whom the constable reasonably suspects to be a person falling within section 40(1)(b) is to be found there.
(2) A warrant under this section shall authorise any constable to enter and search the specified premises for the purpose of arresting the person referred to in subsection (1) under section 41.
  ...

43. Search of persons

(1) A constable may stop and search a person whom he reasonably suspects to be a terrorist to discover whether he has in his possession anything which may constitute evidence that he is a terrorist.

(2) A constable may search a person arrested under section 41 to discover whether he has in his possession anything which may constitute evidence that he is a terrorist.

(3) ...

(4) A constable may seize and retain anything which he discovers in the course of a search of a person under subsection (1) or (2) and which he reasonably suspects may constitute evidence that the person is a terrorist.

(4A) Subsection (4B) applies if a constable, in exercising the power under subsection (1) to stop a person whom the constable reasonably suspects to be a terrorist, stops a vehicle (see section 116(2)).

(4B) The constable—

    (a) may search the vehicle and anything in or on it to discover whether there is anything which may constitute evidence that the person concerned is a terrorist, and

    (b) may seize and retain anything which the constable—

        (i) discovers in the course of such a search, and

        (ii) reasonably suspects may constitute evidence that the person is a terrorist.

(4C) Nothing in subsection (4B) confers a power to search any person but the power to search in that subsection is in addition to the power in subsection (1) to search a person whom the constable reasonably suspects to be a terrorist.

(5) A person who has the powers of a constable in one Part of the United Kingdom may exercise a power under this section in any Part of the United Kingdom.

43A. Search of vehicles

(1) Subsection (2) applies if a constable reasonably suspects that a vehicle is being used for the purposes of terrorism.

(2) The constable may stop and search—

    (a) the vehicle;

    (b) the driver of the vehicle;

    (c) a passenger in the vehicle;

    (d) anything in or on the vehicle or carried by the driver or a passenger;

to discover whether there is anything which may constitute evidence that the vehicle is being used for the purposes of terrorism.

(3) A constable may seize and retain anything which the constable—

    (a) discovers in the course of a search under this section, and

    (b) reasonably suspects may constitute evidence that the vehicle is being used for the purposes of terrorism.

(4) A person who has the powers of a constable in one Part of the United Kingdom may exercise a power under this section in any Part of the United Kingdom.

(5) In this section 'driver', in relation to an aircraft, hovercraft or vessel, means the captain, pilot or other person with control of the aircraft, hovercraft or vessel or any member of its crew and, in relation to a train, includes any member of its crew.

47A. Searches in specified areas or places

(1) A senior police officer may give an authorisation under subsection (2) or (3) in relation to a specified area or place if the officer—

    (a) reasonably suspects that an act of terrorism will take place; and

    (b) reasonably considers that—

        (i) the authorisation is necessary to prevent such an act;

        (ii) the specified area or place is no greater than is necessary to prevent such an act; and

        (iii) the duration of the authorisation is no longer than is necessary to prevent such an act.

(2) An authorisation under this subsection authorises any constable in uniform to stop a vehicle in the specified area or place and to search—

    (a) the vehicle;

(b)   the driver of the vehicle;
(c)   a passenger in the vehicle;
(d)   anything in or on the vehicle or carried by the driver or a passenger.

(3)   An authorisation under this subsection authorises any constable in uniform to stop a pedestrian in the specified area or place and to search—
(a)   the pedestrian;
(b)   anything carried by the pedestrian.

(4)   A constable in uniform may exercise the power conferred by an authorisation under subsection (2) or (3) only for the purpose of discovering whether there is anything which may constitute evidence that the vehicle concerned is being used for the purposes of terrorism or (as the case may be) that the person concerned is a person falling within section 40(1)(b).

(5)   But the power conferred by such an authorisation may be exercised whether or not the constable reasonably suspects that there is such evidence.

(6)   A constable may seize and retain anything which the constable—
(a)   discovers in the course of a search under such an authorisation; and
(b)   reasonably suspects may constitute evidence that the vehicle concerned is being used for the purposes of terrorism or (as the case may be) that the person concerned is a person falling within section 40(1)(b).

(7)   Schedule 6B (which makes supplementary provision about authorisations under this section) has effect.

(8)   In this section—
- 'driver' has the meaning given by section 43A(5);
- 'senior police officer' has the same meaning as in Schedule 6B (see paragraph 14(1) and (2) of that Schedule);
- 'specified' means specified in an authorisation.

UK BORDERS ACT 2007
(2007, c. 30)

32.   Automatic deportation

(1)   In this section 'foreign criminal' means a person—
(a)   who is not a British citizen,
(b)   who is convicted in the United Kingdom of an offence, and
(c)   to whom Condition 1 or 2 applies.

(2)   Condition 1 is that the person is sentenced to a period of imprisonment of at least 12 months.

(3)   Condition 2 is that—
(a)   the offence is specified by order of the Secretary of State under section 72(4)(a) of the Nationality, Immigration and Asylum Act 2002 (serious criminal), and
(b)   the person is sentenced to a period of imprisonment.

...

38.   Interpretation

(1)   In section 32(2) the reference to a person who is sentenced to a period of imprisonment of at least 12 months—
(a)   does not include a reference to a person who receives a suspended sentence (unless a court subsequently orders that the sentence or any part of it (of whatever length) is to take effect),
(b)   does not include a reference to a person who is sentenced to a period of imprisonment of at least 12 months only by virtue of being sentenced to consecutive sentences amounting in aggregate to more than 12 months,
(c)   includes a reference to a person who is sentenced to detention, or ordered or directed to be detained, in an institution other than a prison (including, in particular, a hospital or an institution for young offenders) for at least 12 months, and

(d)   includes a reference to a person who is sentenced to imprisonment or detention, or ordered or directed to be detained, for an indeterminate period (provided that it may last for 12 months).

...

VIOLENT CRIME REDUCTION ACT 2006
(2006, c. 38)

28.   Using someone to mind a weapon

(1)   A person is guilty of an offence if—

    (a)   he uses another to look after, hide or transport a dangerous weapon for him; and

    (b)   he does so under arrangements or in circumstances that facilitate, or are intended to facilitate, the weapon's being available to him for an unlawful purpose.

(2)   For the purposes of this section the cases in which a dangerous weapon is to be regarded as available to a person for an unlawful purpose include any case where—

    (a)   the weapon is available for him to take possession of it at a time and place; and

    (b)   his possession of the weapon at that time and place would constitute, or be likely to involve or to lead to, the commission by him of an offence.

(3)   In this section 'dangerous weapon' means—

    (a)   a firearm other than an air weapon or a component part of, or accessory to, an air weapon; or

    (b)   a weapon to which section 141 or 141A of the Criminal Justice Act 1988 applies (specified offensive weapons, knives and bladed weapons).

...

29.   Penalties etc for offence under s 28

(1)   This section applies where a person ('the offender') is guilty of an offence under section 28.

(2)   Where the dangerous weapon in respect of which the offence was committed is a weapon to which section 141 or 141A of the Criminal Justice Act 1988 (specified offensive weapons, knives and bladed weapons) applies, the offender shall be liable, on conviction on indictment, to imprisonment for a term not exceeding 4 years or to a fine, or to both.

(3)   Where—

    (a)   at the time of the offence, the offender was aged 16 or over, and

    (b)   the dangerous weapon in respect of which the offence was committed was a firearm mentioned in section 5(1)(a) to (af) or (c) or section 5(1A)(a) of the 1968 Act (firearms possession of which attracts a minimum sentence),

the offender shall be liable, on conviction on indictment, to imprisonment for a term not exceeding 10 years or to a fine, or to both.

(4)   On a conviction in England and Wales, where—

    (a)   subsection (3) applies, and

    (b)   the offender is aged 18 or over at the time of conviction,

the court must impose (with or without a fine) a term of imprisonment of not less than 5 years, unless it is of the opinion that there are exceptional circumstances relating to the offence or to the offender which justify its not doing so.

(5)   In relation to times before the commencement of paragraph 180 of Schedule 7 to the Criminal Justice and Court Services Act 2000, the reference in subsection (4) to a sentence of imprisonment, in relation to an offender aged under 21 at the time of conviction, is to be read as a reference to a sentence of detention in a young offender institution.

(6)   On a conviction in England and Wales, where—

    (a)   subsection (3) applies, and

    (b)   the offender is aged under 18 at the time of conviction,

the court must impose (with or without a fine) a term of detention under section 91 of the Powers of Criminal Courts (Sentencing) Act 2000 of not less than 3 years, unless it is of the opinion that there are exceptional circumstances relating to the offence or to the offender which justify its not doing so.

...

(10) In any case not mentioned in subsection (2) or (3), the offender shall be liable, on conviction on indictment, to imprisonment for a term not exceeding 5 years or to a fine, or to both.

(11) Where—

    (a)   a court is considering for the purposes of sentencing the seriousness of an offence under section 28, and

    (b)   at the time of the offence the offender was aged 18 or over and the person used to look after, hide or transport the weapon was not,

the court must treat the fact that that person was under the age of 18 at that time as an aggravating factor (that is to say, a factor increasing the seriousness of the offence).

(12) Where a court treats a person's age as an aggravating factor in accordance with subsection (11), it must state in open court that the offence was aggravated as mentioned in that subsection.

...

YOUTH JUSTICE AND CRIMINAL EVIDENCE ACT 1999
(1999, c. 23)

16.   **Witnesses eligible for assistance on grounds of age or incapacity**

(1) For the purposes of this Chapter a witness in criminal proceedings (other than the accused) is eligible for assistance by virtue of this section—

    (a)   if under the age of 18 at the time of the hearing; or

    (b)   if the court considers that the quality of evidence given by the witness is likely to be diminished by reason of any circumstances falling within subsection (2).

(2) The circumstances falling within this subsection are—

    (a)   that the witness—

        (i)   suffers from mental disorder within the meaning of the Mental Health Act 1983, or

        (ii)   otherwise has a significant impairment of intelligence and social functioning;

    (b)   that the witness has a physical disability or is suffering from a physical disorder.

(3) In subsection (1)(a) 'the time of the hearing', in relation to a witness, means the time when it falls to the court to make a determination for the purposes of section 19(2) in relation to the witness.

(4) In determining whether a witness falls within subsection (1)(b) the court must consider any views expressed by the witness.

(5) In this Chapter references to the quality of a witness's evidence are to its quality in terms of completeness, coherence and accuracy; and for this purpose 'coherence' refers to a witness's ability in giving evidence to give answers which address the questions put to the witness and can be understood both individually and collectively.

17.   **Witnesses eligible for assistance on grounds of fear or distress about testifying**

(1) For the purposes of this Chapter a witness in criminal proceedings (other than the accused) is eligible for assistance by virtue of this subsection if the court is satisfied that the quality of evidence given by the witness is likely to be diminished by reason of fear or distress on the part of the witness in connection with testifying in the proceedings.

(2) In determining whether a witness falls within subsection (1) the court must take into account, in particular—

    (a)   the nature and alleged circumstances of the offence to which the proceedings relate;

    (b)   the age of the witness;

    (c)   such of the following matters as appear to the court to be relevant, namely—
        (i)   the social and cultural background and ethnic origins of the witness,
        (ii)   the domestic and employment circumstances of the witness, and
        (iii)   any religious beliefs or political opinions of the witness;
    (d)   any behaviour towards the witness on the part of—
        (i)   the accused,
        (ii)   members of the family or associates of the accused, or
        (iii)   any other person who is likely to be an accused or a witness in the proceedings.

(3)   In determining that question the court must in addition consider any views expressed by the witness.

(4)   Where the complainant in respect of a sexual offence or an offence under section 1 or 2 of the Modern Slavery Act 2015 is a witness in proceedings relating to that offence (or to that offence and any other offences), the witness is eligible for assistance in relation to those proceedings by virtue of this subsection unless the witness has informed the court of the witness' wish not to be so eligible by virtue of this subsection.

(5)   A witness in proceedings relating to a relevant offence (or to a relevant offence and any other offences) is eligible for assistance in relation to those proceedings by virtue of this subsection unless the witness has informed the court of the witness's wish not to be so eligible by virtue of this subsection.

(6)   For the purposes of subsection (5) an offence is a relevant offence if it is an offence described in Schedule 1A.

(7)   The Secretary of State may by order amend Schedule 1A.

23.   Screening witness from accused

(1)   A special measures direction may provide for the witness, while giving testimony or being sworn in court, to be prevented by means of a screen or other arrangement from seeing the accused.

(2)   But the screen or other arrangement must not prevent the witness from being able to see, and to be seen by—
    (a)   the judge or justices (or both) and the jury (if there is one);
    (b)   legal representatives acting in the proceedings; and
    (c)   any interpreter or other person appointed (in pursuance of the direction or otherwise) to assist the witness.

(3)   Where two or more legal representatives are acting for a party to the proceedings, subsection (2)(b) is to be regarded as satisfied in relation to those representatives if the witness is able at all material times to see and be seen by at least one of them.

24.   Evidence by live link

(1)   A special measures direction may provide for the witness to give evidence by means of a live link.

(1A)   Such a direction may also provide for a specified person to accompany the witness while the witness is giving evidence by live link.

(1B)   In determining who may accompany the witness, the court must have regard to the wishes of the witness.

(2)   Where a direction provides for the witness to give evidence by means of a live link, the witness may not give evidence in any other way without the permission of the court.

(3)   The court may give permission for the purposes of subsection (2) if it appears to the court to be in the interests of justice to do so, and may do so either—
    (a)   on an application by a party to the proceedings, if there has been a material change of circumstances since the relevant time, or
    (b)   of its own motion.

(4)   In subsection (3) 'the relevant time' means—
    (a)   the time when the direction was given, or
    (b)   if a previous application has been made under that subsection, the time when the application (or last application) was made.

...

(8)   In this Chapter 'live link' means a live television link or other arrangement whereby a witness, while absent from the courtroom or other place where the proceedings are being held, is able to see and hear a person there and to be seen and heard by the persons specified in section 23(2)(a) to (c).

26.   Removal of wigs and gowns

A special measures direction may provide for the wearing of wigs or gowns to be dispensed with during the giving of the witness's evidence.

27.   Video recorded evidence in chief

(1)   A special measures direction may provide for a video recording of an interview of the witness to be admitted as evidence in chief of the witness.

(2)   A special measures direction may, however, not provide for a video recording, or a part of such a recording, to be admitted under this section if the court is of the opinion, having regard to all the circumstances of the case, that in the interests of justice the recording, or that part of it, should not be so admitted.

(3)   In considering for the purposes of subsection (2) whether any part of a recording should not be admitted under this section, the court must consider whether any prejudice to the accused which might result from that part being so admitted is outweighed by the desirability of showing the whole, or substantially the whole, of the recorded interview.

(4)   Where a special measures direction provides for a recording to be admitted under this section, the court may nevertheless subsequently direct that it is not to be so admitted if—

    (a)   it appears to the court that—

        (i)   the witness will not be available for cross-examination (whether conducted in the ordinary way or in accordance with any such direction), and

        (ii)   the parties to the proceedings have not agreed that there is no need for the witness to be so available; or

    (b)   any Criminal Procedure Rules requiring disclosure of the circumstances in which the recording was made have not been complied with to the satisfaction of the court.

(5)   Where a recording is admitted under this section—

    (a)   the witness must be called by the party tendering it in evidence, unless—

        (i)   a special measures direction provides for the witness's evidence on cross-examination to be given in any recording admissible under section 28, or

        (ii)   the parties to the proceedings have agreed as mentioned in subsection (4)(a)(ii); and

    (b)   the witness may not without the permission of the court give evidence in chief otherwise than by means of the recording as to any matter which, in the opinion of the court, is dealt with in the witness's recorded testimony.

(6)   Where in accordance with subsection (2) a special measures direction provides for part only of a recording to be admitted under this section, references in subsections (4) and (5) to the recording or to the witness's recorded testimony are references to the part of the recording or testimony which is to be so admitted.

(7)   The court may give permission for the purposes of subsection (5)(b) if it appears to the court to be in the interests of justice to do so, and may do so either—

    (a)   on an application by a party to the proceedings, or

    (b)   of its own motion.

...

(9)   The court may, in giving permission for the purposes of subsection (5)(b), direct that the evidence in question is to be given by the witness by means of a live link.

(9A) If the court directs under subsection (9) that evidence is to be given by live link, it may also make such provision in that direction as it could make under section 24(1A) in a special measures direction.

...

(11) Nothing in this section affects the admissibility of any video recording which would be admissible apart from this section.

28. Video recorded cross-examination or re-examination

(1) Where a special measures direction provides for a video recording to be admitted under section 27 as evidence in chief of the witness, the direction may also provide—

    (a) for any cross-examination of the witness, and any re-examination, to be recorded by means of a video recording; and

    (b) for such a recording to be admitted, so far as it relates to any such cross-examination or re-examination, as evidence of the witness under cross-examination or on re-examination, as the case may be.

(2) Such a recording must be made in the presence of such persons as Criminal Procedure Rules or the direction may provide and in the absence of the accused, but in circumstances in which—

    (a) the judge or justices (or both) and legal representatives acting in the proceedings are able to see and hear the examination of the witness and to communicate with the persons in whose presence the recording is being made, and

    (b) the accused is able to see and hear any such examination and to communicate with any legal representative acting for him.

(3) Where two or more legal representatives are acting for a party to the proceedings, subsection (2)(a) and (b) are to be regarded as satisfied in relation to those representatives if at all material times they are satisfied in relation to at least one of them.

(4) Where a special measures direction provides for a recording to be admitted under this section, the court may nevertheless subsequently direct that it is not to be so admitted if any requirement of subsection (2) or Criminal Procedure Rules or the direction has not been complied with to the satisfaction of the court.

(5) Where in pursuance of subsection (1) a recording has been made of any examination of the witness, the witness may not be subsequently cross-examined or re-examined in respect of any evidence given by the witness in the proceedings (whether in any recording admissible under section 27 or this section or otherwise than in such a recording) unless the court gives a further special measures direction making such provision as is mentioned in subsection (1)(a) and (b) in relation to any subsequent cross-examination, and re-examination, of the witness.

(6) The court may only give such a further direction if it appears to the court—

    (a) that the proposed cross-examination is sought by a party to the proceedings as a result of that party having become aware, since the time when the original recording was made in pursuance of subsection (1), of a matter which that party could not with reasonable diligence have ascertained by then, or

    (b) that for any other reason it is in the interests of justice to give the further direction.

(7) Nothing in this section shall be read as applying in relation to any cross-examination of the witness by the accused in person (in a case where the accused is to be able to conduct any such cross-examination).

29. Examination of witness through intermediary

(1) A special measures direction may provide for any examination of the witness (however and wherever conducted) to be conducted through an interpreter or other person approved by the court for the purposes of this section ('an intermediary').

(2) The function of an intermediary is to communicate—

    (a) to the witness, questions put to the witness, and

    (b) to any person asking such questions, the answers given by the witness in reply to them,

and to explain such questions or answers so far as necessary to enable them to be understood by the witness or person in question.

(3) Any examination of the witness in pursuance of subsection (1) must take place in the presence of such persons as Criminal Procedure Rules or the direction may provide, but in circumstances in which—

    (a) the judge or justices (or both) and legal representatives acting in the proceedings are able to see and hear the examination of the witness and to communicate with the intermediary, and

    (b)   (except in the case of a video recorded examination) the jury (if there is one) are able to see and hear the examination of the witness.

(4)   Where two or more legal representatives are acting for a party to the proceedings, subsection (3)(a) is to be regarded as satisfied in relation to those representatives if at all material times it is satisfied in relation to at least one of them.

(5)   A person may not act as an intermediary in a particular case except after making a declaration, in such form as may be prescribed by Criminal Procedure Rules, that he will faithfully perform his function as intermediary.

(6)   Subsection (1) does not apply to an interview of the witness which is recorded by means of a video recording with a view to its admission as evidence in chief of the witness; but a special measures direction may provide for such a recording to be admitted under section 27 if the interview was conducted through an intermediary and—

    (a)   that person complied with subsection (5) before the interview began, and

    (b)   the court's approval for the purposes of this section is given before the direction is given.

(7)   Section 1 of the Perjury Act 1911 (perjury) shall apply in relation to a person acting as an intermediary as it applies in relation to a person lawfully sworn as an interpreter in a judicial proceeding; and for this purpose, where a person acts as an intermediary in any proceeding which is not a judicial proceeding for the purposes of that section, that proceeding shall be taken to be part of the judicial proceeding in which the witness's evidence is given.

30.   Aids to communication

A special measures direction may provide for the witness, while giving evidence (whether by testimony in court or otherwise), to be provided with such device as the court considers appropriate with a view to enabling questions or answers to be communicated to or by the witness despite any disability or disorder or other impairment which the witness has or suffers from.

INDEX